In His Name: Comparative Studies in the Quest for the Historical Jesus
Life of Jesus Research in Germany and America

European University Studies

Europäische Hochschulschriften
Publications Universitaires Européennes

Series XXIII

Theology

Reihe XXIII Série XXIII

Theologie
Théologie

Vol./Bd. 367

PETER LANG
Frankfurt am Main · Bern · New York · Paris

Elisabeth Hurth

In His Name: Comparative Studies in the Quest for the Historical Jesus

Life of Jesus Research in Germany and America

PETER LANG
Frankfurt am Main · Bern · New York · Paris

CIP-Titelaufnahme der Deutschen Bibliothek

Hurth, Elisabeth:

In His name: Comparative studies in the quest for the historical Jesus : life of Jesus research in Germany and America / Elisabeth Hurth. - Frankfurt am Main ; Bern ; New York ; Paris : Lang, 1989

(Europäische Hochschulschriften : Reihe 23, Theologie ; Bd. 367)

Zugl.: Boston, Univ., Diss., 1988

ISBN 3-631-41955-4

NE: Europäische Hochschulschriften / 23

ISSN 0721-3409

ISBN 3-631-41955-4

Printed in Germany

To Home

Acknowledgements

The present study grew out of a dissertation submitted to the American Studies Program at Boston University in 1988. Thanks are due to each of the dissertation committee members and dissertation readers, David Hall, Norman Pettit, Millicent Bell, Dana Robert, William Vance and Carter Lindberg, for their contributions to the present study.

Special thanks are also due to the librarians and staff members of the research libraries at the Harvard Divinity School, the Andover Newton Theological Seminary, the Boston Public Library, the Houghton Library, the Massachusetts Historical Society, and the Harvard University Archives.

Preface

When in 1778 the Hamburg dramatist, literary critic and amateur theologian Gotthold Ephraim Lessing published the last of seven fragments of Hermann Samuel Reimarus entitled The Aims of Jesus and His Disciples, critics were confronted head-on with the concept of "the historical Jesus" as well as with the scientific research on the life of Jesus, the so-called quest for the historical Jesus. This research revolved around the dual question of how Christianity was grounded in historical contingency and of whether and how the historical Jesus could be invoked as the authentic basis and content of Christian faith. On this 'historical' front, the life of Jesus research, so far as it presented an attempt to peel away centuries of accretions and embellishments and to discover the first-century Jesus, bore the stamp of the perennial problem of faith and history. The quest could not proceed without dealing with the problem which Enlightenment philosophy referred to, in the terms of Lessing, as the "ugly broad ditch" between "accidental truths of history" and "necessary truths of reason."(1) The historical character of revelation, Lessing's metaphor of disjunction asserted, is not capable of conveying the necessary, unchanging core of transcendent truth. Historically mediated rational truth is accordingly a contradiction in terms, a contradiction sharpened by the fact that even the reconstruction of historical truth is "accidental" and that therefore a distinction must be drawn between immediate revelation and the historical report of it.

This important conceptual opposition did not lead the early Jesus of history movement to historical scepticism. In focusing on Jesus as a historical character rather than on his influence in history or his work as the "exalted Christ," the life of Jesus research flowed from the assumption that the historical Jesus could be a link across "the ugly broad ditch." The premise that this link was to be reached by empirical means provided the epistemic foundation for Reimarus' insistence that the Jesus of history should be placed in opposition to the Christ of faith. Reimarus' here proceeded on a central tenet, made in the final published fragment and in remarkable fashion anticipatory of the themes of the future life of Jesus research, namely that a pronounced dichotomy existed between the historical figure of Jesus and the interpretation imposed upon this figure by the apostolic church. Jesus, the spiritual Messiah of church teaching and the Gospels was quite clearly not identical with the historical and, according to Reimarus, expressly political Messiah behind the Gospels.(2)

Reimarus' focus on a historical Jesus opposed to church dogma and isolated from apostolic preaching was of relatively recent origin. From the time of Tatian, the older Catholic and Confessional Christianity had been confident that the Gospels as canonical Scripture were historically substantial. Paraphrases and harmonies of the Gospels were produced on the assumption that the historical Jesus was identical with the ecclesiastical image of Christ. Elements of concern to source criticism of a later day, such as the relatively late dates of the Gospel narratives and the divergences between the synoptic records did not lead to elaborate considerations of the technical problem of the historical Jesus but rather to harmonizations of substantial inconsistencies into unilateral accounts. For Reimarus, however, the historical Jesus became a problem, one that spurred critical reflection on the Gospels as historical documents and triggered off a vigorous debate over the authentic purpose and teaching of Jesus. This debate found its most pronounced treatment in the

Leben-Jesu-Forschung, a movement held together by the reduction of the biblical Christ to the dimensions of a historical person to whom the same laws of historical causation and psychological development applied as to any other person. Under the slogan "back to Jesus, the man from Nazareth," the Leben-Jesu-Forschung retold the history of Jesus in a multitude of "lives" setting out to penetrate beneath the accretions of dogmatic overlay and to discover the authentic picture of the historical Jesus. Both biblical critics and historians sought in their "lives" to disentangle the residual 'religion of Jesus' from its enclosure in the 'religion about Jesus' by separating Jesus' public ministry and teaching from the theological interpretations imposed on the life of Jesus by the apologetic interests of the apostolic age. With this separation, "liberal-positive" questers like Theodor Keim and Daniel Schenkel were convinced, Jesus' history could be established as a series of events objectively available for scientific analysis.

If the "liberal-positive" "lives" seemed to put the historical Jesus within the reach of critical research, Albert Schweitzer was to formulate an indictment of the quest which exposed the Jesus emerging from the psychologized and imaginative "lives" as a phantom. Schweitzer's Geschichte der Leben-Jesu-Forschung, the seminal account of the life of Jesus literature from the eighteenth to the twentieth century, viewed the history of the life of Jesus genre as a unique attempt to substitute the historical Jesus quest for traditional christological dogma. This attempt, Schweitzer judged, "did not take its rise from a purely historical interest;" rather, "it turned to the Jesus of history as an ally in the struggle against the tyranny of dogma."(3) The Christ of dogma presented an abstract entity to contemplate, not a living personality to follow, and the life of Jesus movement here emerged as a liberating ally of critical natural reason, freeing Christians from what was perceived to be an outmoded supernaturalism.

But in recording the many attempts made between 1778 and 1901 - "from Reimarus to Wrede" - to apply the methodology of a critical historiography to the historical personage of Jesus, Schweitzer demonstrated the complete collapse of the Leben-Jesu-Forschung. Schweitzer's history of the quest for the historical Jesus charged that the century and a half of persistent efforts to provide a biography of Jesus was in vain. The portrait of the historical Jesus which the Leben-Jesu-Forschung actually developed was not drawn from the historical sources but rather distorted by the presuppositions of authors who "rediscovered (their) own ideas in Jesus." "It was not only each epoch that found its reflection in Jesus," Schweitzer observed, "each individual created him in accordance with his own true character."(4) The quest's reconstructed historical Jesus therefore inevitably fell short of the Jesus of Nazareth and strikingly resembled a nineteenth century idealist wearing first-century Galilean clothes. The attempt of the quest to recover a historical Jesus freed from churchly dogma and isolated from apostolic preaching thus gave way to historicism and the illusory belief in the objective restitution of facts. Most authors of the "lives" merely produced a truncated history without the "kerygma," without the "proclamation" of the early Christian community about Jesus Christ, and presented instead "a half-historical, half-modern Jesus" who failed to fulfill the theological expectations which had led to his construction.(5)

Schweitzer's history of 1906 erected a barrier against the quest which came close to suspending the quest altogether. After Schweitzer had penned his verdict to the quest for the historical Jesus, the conviction grew that the advocates of the Leben-Jesu-Forschung had looked down the deep well of human history only to see their own faces reflected at the bottom.(6) But while Schweitzer used this insight to terminate the search for the historically reconstructed Jesus, the present study contends that the course of the quest and the theological literature built around it does not completely follow the assumptions of Schweitzer's verdict. This contention is derived from a corpus of material which reveals that the quest was not confined to the biblical and theological protagonists of the Leben-Jesu-Forschung whose "lives" constitute the primary sources for Schweitzer's history. Parallel to the enterprise chronicled by Schweitzer from 1778 to 1901, nineteenth century American biblical and historical scholarship witnessed the rise of yet another form of inquiry into the life of Jesus. This inquiry, the primary point of departure for the present study, took shape and was rendered self-conscious during the first half of the nineteenth century among representatives of the Unitarian-Transcendentalist communities. The outlines of this American quest for the historical Jesus were indistinct: Its beginning coalesced with the rise of Boston Unitarianism and encompassed the reception of the Leben-Jesu-Forschung in the works of Joseph Buckminster, William Ellery Channing and Andrews Norton; its growth was obvious in the "lives" of William Henry Furness and Francis Greenwood Peabody; its continuation was evidenced in the uninterrupted flow of lives of Jesus produced by the Social Gospel movement.(7)

This form of the original quest grew under the stimulus of two formidable forces, first, the historico-critical approach to Scripture, the higher criticism, and second, the impact of the sceptical, deistic critique of religion with its accompanying denial of the historicity of Jesus, an influence evidenced in the continuing popularity of Bayle, Volney and Voltaire. The first line of influence crucial to the development of the American quest, the higher criticism, which studied the Bible as a collection of literary documents presenting the same problems as any other ancient writing, surfaced in Unitarian and Trinitarian thought at the Harvard Divinity School and Andover Seminary where biblical studies followed the path established by Moses Stuart, Joseph Stevens Buckminster, William Ellery Channing and Andrews Norton.(8) Initially, Lockean empiricism and common-sense philosophy dominated the reception of the historico-critical method and contributed to the use of the new principles as an exegetical helpmate in the debates with orthodox Calvinism. The interest in the higher critical procedures was thus primarily "apologetical or sectarian."(9) The Unitarian party generally used the exegetical methods pioneered by the Leben-Jesu-Forschung to buttress the traditional theology of "evidences." The orthodox were quick to follow suit and undertook to establish Andover Seminary as an American center for the "lower criticism" of the Bible. In the hands of Moses Stuart, Andover's premier biblical critic, "lower criticism" set out to establish the exact wording of the original text of the biblical narratives and took as its starting point a meticulous grammatico-historical analysis which stopped well short of questioning the authenticity of Scripture.

It was in the course of responding to the higher criticism that representatives of both sides of the camp were increasingly forced to confront a crucial theological issue, the question of the relation between the Jesus of history and what was variously referred to as the Christ of theology, faith, dogma or religion. The resulting literature was complex and, in terms of its genre affiliation, unfocused and shifting. A "life" might appear under the aegis of an epistolary novel, as in Joseph Holt Ingraham's The Prince of the House of David, or in the context of historical romances, as in William Ware's Julian; or Scenes in Judea. A life of Jesus could originate in a critique of a foreign "life," such as Andrew P. Peabody's refutation of Ernest Renan's life of Jesus in his Christianity and Science. A "life" might also make its appearance in the context of a sermon, as in George Ripley's "Jesus Christ, the Same Yesterday, Today and Forever," or among lecture material as in James Freeman Clarke's "Christ and Christianity."(10)

Pamphlet, lecture, sermon or novel - the topic of the life of Jesus knew no fixed affiliations and labels. The adaptability of the life of Jesus 'genre' was striking and cut across the territory of historians, theologians and social critics. In the course of the American life of Jesus research, questers of all types could be observed to explore the "Leben Jesu." The Unitarian historian William Henry Furness with his Thoughts on the Life and Character of Jesus of Nazareth, the Unitarian minister Henry Ware Jr. with his History of Jesus, the Social Gospelist Francis G. Peabody with his Jesus Christ and the Social Question and the Free Religionist O. B. Frothingham with his The Cradle of the Christ all came together in their effort to reconstruct the data of the Jesus of Nazareth.

Most of these studies were derivative, modelled after European originals and heavily indebted to the reviews of foreign "lives" produced by theological periodicals like the Christian Examiner, the Christian Disciple, the Bibliotheca Sacra and the Scriptural Interpreter. Until the end of the first decade of the nineteenth century, studies of this kind were virtually unknown in the American, and above all the New England theological scene. New England divinity then was in most quarters unaware of the exegetical principles of the quest, or once exposed to the new methods, inclined to discredit them. During this period conservative Protestants formed a strong phalanx of opposition against studies undercutting the factual veracity of the biblical text. It was not until the second dècade of the century, when Harvard students were sent to the universities of Göttingen and Berlin and exposed to the new advances in historical criticism as well as the flourishing literature of the quest that biblical critics and historians became interested in life of Jesus research.

In the first decade of the century the theological periodicals of New England divinity still hesitated to take on European works of the quest. Johann Jakob Hess, F. V. Reinhard und J. G. Herder went untranslated and virtually unnoticed. In the course of the next decade, the General Repository and Review, the Christian Disciple and the North American Review began to open their pages to the quest in "critical notices" of the literature of the quest.(11) With the return of the first students from abroad, the phalanx of hostility and discredit concerning the quest further begañ to break up. Translations, lectures and reviews were now steadily opening foreign "lives" to American readers and raised highly significant questions as to the reliability of biblical data, their basis of authority, and the nature of inspiration. It was also at this time that Harvard began to collect works relating to the quest on a larger scale. In May of 1817, the North American Review had reported of new substantial additions "for the use of gentlemen of the goverment, and recent graduates in divinity."(12) Turning to the 1830 Harvard catalogue, one finds the quest represented by the names of Eichhorn, Herder and Schleiermacher. The 1834 catalogue shows a marked increase, now including the names of Jacobi and Lessing.

By the mid-thirties, then, the materials for the study of the "Leben Jesu" were available in New England, and they continued to yield substantial literary results in major translations. In 1836, Theodore Parker began to work on his translation of De Wette, who had already received wide publicity in 1819 through Moses Stuart's letters to Dr. Channing. Between 1835 und 1837, Ripley's articles on Herder in the Christian Examiner helped to propagate the work of one of the early practitioners of the quest. In the winter of 1836-1837, Margaret Fuller followed suit translating together with William Ellery Channing Herder and De Wette. Translations from the "Athenaeum of modern times" reached their peak around 1840 with the production of four important translations of De Wette's works: the novel Theodore or the Sceptic's Conversion translated by James Freeman Clarke for Ripley's "Specimens of Foreign Standard Literature," Human Life, translated by Samuel Osgood; the Introduction to the Old Testament translated by Theodore Parker, and the Introduction to the Canonical Books of the New Testament, translated from the fifth edition by Frederick Frothingham.(13)

From 1846 onwards the shape of the American quest also hinged on the ready access to the British market. After 1835, English religious periodicals began to take note of the controversy triggered by Strauss' Leben Jesu. But it was not until the translation of the fourth edition of Strauss' work by George Eliot in 1846 that the Leben Jesu began to play a part in contributing to the growth of scepticism and served to stimulate the production of British "lives" such as Stephen Thomas' Gospel History of our Lord and Saviour Jesus Christ, George Rogers' Footprints of Jesus and above all John Robert Seeley's Ecce Homo.(14) After 1860, the influence of these "lives" on the American market was also supplemented by the impact of Ernest Renan, who with his pioneering literary approach to the life of Jesus contributed significantly to American thinking on the quest.(15)

The fact that the quest was not fully taken up in America until the mid-1840s reveals a striking time lag between the quest recapitulated by Schweitzer and its American counterpart. Examining the "causes of the decline of interest in critical theology," George R. Noyes in 1847 urged his Unitarian colleagues to produce an independent refutation of Strauss, a demand which found its perhaps most impressive fulfillment in the "lives" produced by William Henry Furness.(16) Furness' History of Jesus, his Thoughts on the Life and Character of Jesus of Nazareth and his The Veil Party Lifted and Jesus Becoming Visible make clear that the relationship between the Leben-Jesu-Forschung and the American inquiry into the "Leben Jesu" cannot be pressed to the point of identity. In the latter form of inquiry the connections between theology and biblical studies delayed the shift to a critical view of the life of Jesus narratives and caused much more difficulties for the continuation of critical exegesis along the lines of the Leben-Jesu-Forschung. While the Transcendentalist ministers frequently bypassed the issues of biblical criticsm too quickly with an intuitionist approach which did not allow a tradition of critical exegesis to build and develop, their Unitarian brethren also did not fall in line with the tangled world of literary, textual, lexicographical and grammatical findings uncovered by the Leben Jesu researchers. An exegesis applying the conclusions of historical-critical analysis to Scripture thus did not fully take root in the ante-bellum period. The main sources on which American practitioners of the quest drew were still those representing an evidentialist tradition which flanked the attack made by rationalistic criticism on the historical foundations of Christianity.

The pervasiveness of evidentialist apologetics was perhaps most apparent in the general confidence about the availability of the historical Jesus and in the frank emphasis on the factual veracity of the biblical life of Jesus narratives. Most American protagonists of the quest who assimilated their reconstructions to evidentialist patterns as a principal bastion against historical scepticism were not hampered by serious obstructions to the knowability of Jesus and rested secure in the conviction that historical analyses of the biblical narratives as authentic documents for the life of Jesus were sufficient for the quest of the historical Jesus. The intent and direction of this quest cannot be identified with a formative system of theological and philosophical principles. But what stands out for the American reviews of the quest and the original lives of Jesus is that they yield insights and arguments not uncovered by Schweitzer's survey of the life of Jesus movement. To recount the rise and development of the American quest for the historical Jesus against the background of the Leben-Jesu-Forschung is therefore also to correct Schweitzer's narrative of the quest at several key points.

Schweitzer's critical review of the Leben-Jesu-Forschung contributed significantly to scepticism concerning the possibility of a historically reliable picture of Jesus. Yet Schweitzer himself stayed within the essentially positivistic orientation of the older "lives" and remained convinced "that the two oldest Synoptics transmit real history."(17) This positivistic stance showed perhaps most clearly in Schweitzer's portrait of the Straussian life of Jesus research which expressly stressed the "historically positive" elements over and against skepticism about the historicity of Jesus. American reviewers of Strauss' life of Jesus judged differently. To the conservative Unitarian camp around Andrews Norton, Strauss' essental error was that he questioned the historicity of Jesus and reduced the significance of personality and history for the spiritual life. According to this testimony, the enterprise of the "lives" included a sustained tendency to dissolve the historical Christ event. Thus, what Schweitzer regarded as one of the central reasons for the quest's demise, the positivistic attempt to bridge Lessing's "ugly broad ditch," appears to have actually been carried to the opposite extreme by the quest, namely to the near dissolution of historical positivity. And in this context the impossibility of reconstructing the historical Jesus emerged as a calculated option within the course of the quest.

The question about the knowability of the historical Jesus posed not only an epistemological problem but also a historico-critical issue slighted by Schweitzer. The hermeneutical locus of the quest was a shift in biblical interpretation undermining the factuality and unity of Scripture. The quest participated in a seminal transition in the interpretation and application of Scripture which drew on the breakdown of the precritical scholary consensus about the harmony of the literal sense with the historical reference of the biblical narratives. Behind this breakdown lay the factors that shaped the historico-critical exegesis of the quest: the emphasis on the literal-grammatical sense of the scriptural accounts, the reliance upon the internal evidence of the text as the basis for determining documentary integrity and authorship, and the refusal to acknowledge traditional interpretations or appeals to divine origin as valid.(18)

In presenting the history of the life of Jesus research as an evolving opposition between historical criticism and dogma, Schweitzer slighted yet another issue of concern to the contemporary American reviewers of the quest. To Schweitzer, the replacement of dogma and creed by the Jesus quest constituted primarily a historical, not a christological issue, one that Schweitzer viewed as original and unique with the quest. Yet when the authors of the "lives" substituted the historical Jesus quest for traditional christological dogma, they did adopt a particular christological option in asserting that christology commenced with the historical life of Jesus and then worked back to the question of his pre-existence and incarnation.(19) This particular emphasis placed the quest against the main line of christological development leading from the early Fathers to the Reformers and into post-Reformation scholastics, a line which cohered in the assumption that in the Word incarnate there was both full humanity and full divinity in a single person. This consensus, primarily associated in early christological creedal development with the Chalcedonian formula, was seriously challenged in the eighteenth century when the dualsided christology broke down in a revival of subordinationism and Ebionitism. It was with the dissolution of the two-nature dogma that the quest evolved. It was also here that the quest made its decisive contributions. The quest tended towards Ebionitism; it began and ended with the "historical Jesus" and delivered christology from affiliations with the abstract categories of ancient metaphysics.(20) And in this context the quest revealed itself not as a unique and original "bolt from the blue," as Schweitzer had claimed, but rather as deeply entrenched in reinterpretations and critiques of early christological doctrines.

In the resurgence of interest in the historical Jesus in the "new quest" launched from the early 1950s onwards, the focus of the Leben-Jesu-Forschung on a christology "from below," on the figure of Jesus as a truly human subject, shifted to a pronounced emphasis on the "kerygma." In contrast to the "biographical" approach of the Leben-Jesu-Forschung, this shift enlarged the historico-critical reconstruction of what Jesus "did" to an existential interpretation of what Jesus "meant" and "means" today. The convergence of these two lines of emphasis defined the point of departure for the "new quest:" No longer the research program of the historical-critical reconstruction of Jesus but rather the understanding of existence essential to Jesus' person was now regarded as constitutive of the quest's aims.(21) Within the American quest, in contrast, the most notable feature of the theological scene has been the persistence of the research effort to recover the "original" Jesus of Nazareth. An echo of this uninterrupted effort was to be heard repeatedly in the devaluation of the "new quest" as a "generalization," a "reduction" and an "abstraction" dehistoricizing the kerygma.(22) Historically, this critique emerged as a legacy of the nineteenth century American quest and its confidence in the availability of the Jesus of history. It appeared here that the futility of the traditional historical Jesus quest uncovered by Schweitzer and the new questers still could leave open the possibility and legitimacy of the original quest.

TABLE OF CONTENTS

	Acknowledgements	VII
	Preface	IX
	Table of Contents	1
	Introduction	3
Part I	THE LEBEN-JESU-FORSCHUNG	
1	In Quest of the Historical Jesus	16
2	From Harmonies to Lives	39
3	The Kernel and the Husk	62
4	The Jesus of History and the Christ of Faith: Strauss and After	79
Part II	AN AMERICAN QUEST	
5	Towards the Quest	97
6	Anxieties of Influence	119
7	"Signs and Wonders:" The Fortress of Miracles	142
8	The "Uses" of the <u>Leben Jesu</u>	159
Part III	THE QUEST CONTINUED	
9	"Footsteps of the Master:" From History to Fiction	180
10	"The Historic and the Ideal Christ"	200
11	"The Aim and Hope of Jesus"	222
12	Rediscovering the Historical Jesus	236
	Abbreviations	263
	Notes	265
	Bibliography	323

Introduction

According to Schweitzer, the first "great alternative which the study of the life of Jesus had to meet ... was laid down by Strauss: either purely historical or purely supernatural."(1) From 1835 onwards this "alternative" was worked out in particular in "liberal-positive" "lives" like Daniel Schenkel's Das Charakterbild Jesu, Theodor Keim's Die Geschichte Jesu von Nazara and Karl Hase's Geschichte Jesu. The basic presupposition underlying these "lives" was that of a sharp tension between the Jesus of history and the Christ of faith, the intention here being to supply through the instrumentality of a scientific historical reconstruction a Jesus of history who would be a corrective to the Christ of "dogma" described by the professional or popular theology of the church. In this emphasis on the discontinuity between the Jesus of history and the Christ of faith, the notion of 'the historical Jesus' carried an anti-dogmatic, anti-theological ring which showed in the quest's attempts to set the "original" Jesus "over against the dogmatic Christ" and to get behind the christological doctrines of the church back to the rabbi from Galilee.(2) The historical Jesus of the Leben-Jesu-Forschung was accordingly no longer confined to the original Jesus of patristic christology, a figure both human and divine complying with the 'two natures in one person' doctrine, but rather focused on the "earthly Jesus" as a historical phenomenon. While the orthodox Christ of faith was available through dogma and creed, the category of the historical Jesus designated Jesus in so far as he was available as an object of methodical, critical, historical research.(3) The historical Jesus here was aligned with the appearance of a historical source criticism and the application of its methodology to the Gospel narratives, first in a pre-critical, rationalistic form, later in a more self-conscious, historico-critical manner which flowed from the new conviction that it was methodologically possible to penetrate the embellishments of creed and tradition and to recover the original Jesus of Nazareth.

The Leben-Jesu-Forschung

From the perspective of nineteenth century historico-critical research, it was assumed that the reconstruction of Jesus' biography by means of objective historical method coincided with the "real Jesus as he actually existed."(4) From the perspective of twentieth century form criticism represented by Martin Dibelius and Rudolf Bultmann this was no longer valid. Form criticism largely left behind the movement described by the phrase 'Jesus of history' and treated the Gospels as testimonies to the faith of the early churches. The Gospel records, form critics asserted, were "kerygmatic," not biographical, in nature and ruled out a historico-critical evaluation of the biblical narratives as source documents chronologizing the history of Jesus. The pendulum thus swung in the opposite direction: The quest for the historical Jesus now was to be discarded not only because the Gospels failed to yield the picture of Jesus on which the Leben-Jesu-Forschung based its theology but also because the Jesus of history was theologically irrelevant. The synoptic accounts, form critics claimed, are not intent on a historiographic purpose; they are not primarily concerned with the Jesus of history but rather with the Christ who is present in proclamation and liturgy.(5)

It was in particular the existentialist kerygma theology of Bultmann which further undercut the revelance of the historical Jesus to faith. According to Bultmann, Jesus confronts the believer only in the kerygma, "and nowhere else."(6) Essential to this confrontation is the existential demand to which Christian preaching summons the individual. Thus faith is concerned only with the kerygma and can settle for the mere fact of the historical appearance of Jesus, with no regard for its manner and content. Any attempt to go back behind the kerygma and to demonstrate its historical basis in the person and proclamation of Jesus, any attempt at a historical proof of the identity between the historical Jesus and the proclaimed Christ was, Bultmann argued, an illegitimate theological procedure.(7) The historical factuality of the life of Jesus belonged for Bultmann to the confines of historical probability only and was irrelevant to faith in the Christ event.

On this very point the category of the historical Jesus closely corresponded to Martin Kähler's distinction between "the so-called historical Jesus" and "the historic, biblical Christ."(8) For Kähler, it was the Christ of faith who was central, while "the so-called historical Jesus" represented an outgrowth of "Jesiolatry" and a reconstruction subject to the uncertainties of historico-critical research. The intention of the Gospels, however, was simply to be the church's witness to its faith and to proclaim the Christ of faith in the garb of the historical Jesus. "The reminiscences of the Jesus of history were preserved, shaped and interpreted within the framework of the proclamation of the risen one, and this interpretation," Kähler insisted, "is the right and legitimate one for the Christian faith." In this emphasis on the early Christian proclamation of Jesus Christ as Lord, history was asserted to have survived only as kerygma. The term 'historical Jesus' accordingly raised the question of faith and not the problematic question of historical research. Thus, while the watchword of the Leben-Jesu-Forschung used to be 'the original Jesus of history', it was henceforward "the Christ who is preached."(9)

In the post World War II period the pendulum swung again and now pointed in yet another direction, one pushing forward the "new quest" of the historical Jesus. To new questers like Ernst Fuchs and Gerhard Ebeling the form critical canon ran the risk of affirming a docetic view of Jesus and of eliminating the historical anchorage of Christian thought and discourse.(10) Against both the form critical devaluation of the historical Jesus and the old quest's reliance on positivistic historiography, the "new quest" avoided putting a one-sided emphasis on either the Jesus of history or the kerygma and emphasized instead the continuity between the message of Jesus and the post-Easter christology of the earliest churches, an emphasis which served as a corrective to Bultmann's reduction of the significance of Jesus for the Christian kerygma to the terms of factuality.(11)

In the classical Leben-Jesu-Forschung, the "old quest," this insistence on the continuity between the Jesus of history and the early Christian kerygma was not acknowledged and submerged in historistic premises. The life of Jesus theology was confident that the "personality" of Jesus embedded in his teaching, inner development and influence could be reconstructed through undistorted historical analysis and would yield an historically unassailable basis for faith distinguished "by its completely unmetaphysical nature."(12) Within certain limits, the liberal Leben-Jesu-Forschung here proceeded on the assumption of the synoptic Gospels' historical trustworthiness and judged that in particular Mark's biographical outline contained an authentic portrait of Jesus' personality.

Under this premise the "liberal-positive" quest was propagated as an express rejection of the christological dogma of the church. This rejection cut across divergent theological camps, the supernaturalist, the rationalist, the idealist and the liberal alike and encompassed a theological spectrum harboring a striking variety of Jesus portraits. Thus, with regard to methodology, the quest led from H. E. G. Paulus' thorough-going application of the historico-critical method to Strauss' bypassing of the considerations of historical criticism, and with regard to source materials, from Hase's dependence on the Fourth Gospel to Christian Hermann Weisse's and Christian G. Wilke's reliance on the Markan account and the Q-collection of Jesus' sayings as source materials for a life of Jesus.

With regard to the reconstructions themselves, the Leben-Jesu-Forschung produced an equally remarkable shift of fronts in theology. Reimarus' life of Jesus research was conceived in terms of the question about Jesus' aims. Five decades later the question was taken up again by rationalist theologians who sought to divest the figure of Jesus of supernatural categories and viewed the historical Jesus as an exemplary teacher stimulating men to the highest form of moral religion. In the hands of Schleiermacher's theology of "feeling" the antisupernatural interpretation of Jesus took the form of presenting Jesus as a man who personified the highest God-consciousness. Under the increased influence of Hegelianism with its "substitution" of the "ideal Christ" for the "dogmatic Christ" this position was displaced by Strauss' pronounced scepticism against the historicity of the Gospel tradition.(13) The key to christology, Strauss argued, was the "idea" of God-manhood which found no realisation in the objective-historical Jesus. Yet the life of Jesus research after Strauss was reluctant to settle for the apparent impossibility of reconstructing the Jesus of history and focused on "restoring (the) credibility (of the Gospel tradition) in its main outlines."(14) Virtually all the questing of the "liberal-positive" "lives" after Strauss was in pursuit of a figure who was held to be amenable to the epistemic apparatus of an ordinary historic individual within the limiting categories of a normal 'birth to death' lifespan. The concrete, the empirical, the rational now were the watchwords of the Leben Jesu theology which presented the "simple Jesus," a "pioneer," "leader," "hero," and "example."(15)

The narrative shape of this quest had many strands three of which are explored throughout the first part of the study. The first concerns the relationship of 'contingent' history to Christian faith, a relationship revolving around the crucial problem Lessing formulated at the beginning of the Leben-Jesu-Forschung with his assertion of the disjunction between "accidental historical truths" and "necessary rational truths." The post-Straussian "lives" ran expressly counter to this sceptical insistence on the "ugly broad ditch" of history. They were thoroughly convinced that the historical Jesus could bridge "the ugly broad ditch" and form a basis for revelation. The "liberal-positive" "lives" accordingly sought to make contact with the humanity of Jesus as the Christ in historical rather than metaphysical categories. While the Christ of dogma and ecclesiastical language seemed abstract and lifeless, the quest constituted an attempt to fix Jesus in time and place on the basis of a science of history and to present him as "life-like and graphic in his words and deeds."(16)

This was a remarkable, yet constricted undertaking which subjected revelation to critical historical inquiry and proceeded on the alignment of the methods used in the reconstruction of the historical Jesus with a critical historiography. On this count, the advocates of the quest were moved less by a concern to establish the sovereignty and autonomy of history than by the desire to establish its place within the spreading movement of natural science. With the elevation of natural religion at the expense of revelation through history in the late seventeenth and early eighteenth centuries, this tendency had been accentuated and now fed into the quest's conviction that the Christ of faith did not ally with the picture of the Jesus of history derived from a critical study of the scriptural and extra-scriptural sources.

In its first and most obvious sense, the quest's notion of history was here under the influence of the natural science paradigm. The 'historical' designated past facticity; the historical Jesus of Nazareth was accordingly reduced to the historical "facts" of Jesus' life as established by a court of positivistic historiography subject to the Rankean premise of presenting the past "as it actually happened" - "wie es eigentlich gewesen."(17) The 'historical' was in this context opposed to the fictitious, the legendary or the mythical, yet the quest also knew the option of non-historicity, first represented at the end of the eighteenth century by the French "philosophes," Charles F. Dupuis and Constantin F. Volney, and continued in the attacks on Jesus' historicity by Bruno Bauer, Albert Kalthoff and Arthur Drews.(18) Correlative to the skepticism about the "that" of the historical Jesus were the uncertainties cast on the "what" of Jesus' life by the questioning of the credibility of the Gospel accounts in Strauss' opposition between the Synoptics and the Fourth Gospel as sources and William Wrede's discovery of Mark's unhistorical, editorial creation of the "messianic secret."(19)

For yet another usage of the term 'historical' these challenges to Jesus' historicity and the credibility of the Gospel tradition were secondary and emerged as belonging to a limited, factual "Historie." In the version of the quest represented by Martin Kähler the 'historical Jesus,' as opposed to the conjectural reconstruction of critical research, was not subject to the positivistic historical-critical method but rather designated Jesus in terms of the 'effectiveness,' the lasting influence he had on his disciples, an influence determinative for the Gospel portrait of Jesus as the Christ. Kähler himself regarded this 'effectiveness" of the traditional Christ as proof for the conviction that "the risen Lord is not the historical Jesus behind the Gospels, but the Christ of the apostolic preaching, of the whole New Testament."(20) This assertion of the 'effectiveness' of the traditional Christ involved a corresponding distinction between two modes of historicity, the objective-historical - "historisch" - and the existential-historical - "geschichtlich" - type. The latter distinction played in turn on the difference between two modes of knowledge: The Jesus of "Historie" was approached through the element of facticity, by means of positivistic historico-critical research; the Christ of "Geschichte" was known through personal encounter and had an existential significance for the present.(21) Only the first mode of knowledge was primary for nineteenth century Leben Jesu researchers. For the classical Leben-Jesu-Forschung the sense of past facticity prevailed over "Geschichtlichkeit" as the central feature of history. Therefore, when Strauss dared to call the historicity of the Gospel tradition into question, the "liberal-positive" "lives" of Daniel Schenkel and Theodor Keim rushed to defend the Jesus of history according to the terms of historical factuality.

A second recurrent theme in the narrative of the life of Jesus movement also took its impetus from this conception of history: the redefinition and re-evaluation of christology inherent in the quest's emancipation from traditional christological dogma. On this point, the life of Jesus theology participated in the broad nineteenth-century movement towards a christology "von unten nach oben" and further corroborated the premise that all assertions about Christ's person and work flowed from his historical life. The most tangible consequence of this premise was the spawning of countless lives of Jesus which rejected the metaphysical christologies of orthodoxy. The express intention of the "lives" was to force a way through all christology and to reformulate the Chalcedonian formula of the two natures of Christ and the medieval and Calvinist doctrines of substitutionary atonement and vicarious satisfaction. The conviction underlying this revolt against the classical system of christology was that beneath the edifice of christological dogma there stood the historical Jesus, a person whose "nature" was not to be distorted by the intrusion of ontological attributes.

At precisely this juncture the Leben-Jesu-Forschung made the decisive turn to the new attempt to construct a christology "from below" grounding all doctrines concerning the nature of Christ in his humanly historical existence. The humanity of Jesus here emerged as the pivot of the quest's reconstructions and emphasized the notion of "personality" as being dependent on self-consciousness rather than on the traditional language of "persona" and "substantia" of christological dogma. Jesus' humanity was affirmed, no longer by maintaining that there was in him a fully human nature coexisting with a divine nature, but by urging that the unity of Jesus' person constituted a oneness of consciousness in which "the empirical ego (was) also the absolute" and in which Jesus' humanity was "archetypal" rather than substantial.(22) The christological result of this emphasis was frequently some form of Arianism or Ebionitism which pictured Jesus as semi-divine or reduced him to an example of humanity and thereby relinquished the belief in the doctrine of the preexistence of Christ as well as the classical formulations of the doctrine of the trinity and the logos.

In these christological emphases a third theme was predominant - the problem of biblical authority and the credibility of the scriptural portrait of Jesus. There was not a single phase in the quest's course where the force of the close interrelationship between Gospel criticism and the historical search for Jesus was not felt acutely. The life of Jesus movement took as its point of departure an emphatic denial of the validity of all christological speculation which depended for its justification on the supernatural authority of Scripture. Underlying this point was the presupposition that the Gospel narratives contained material concerning Jesus which warranted correction in the light of historico-critical thought. The quest emerged in this context as the testing ground for the broader issues of the nature of inspiration, the reliability of biblical data and the terms of scriptural authority. These issues, commonly associated with the higher criticism, drew on the use of critical historiography in the interpretation of biblical texts practiced among outcast thinkers like Hobbes, Spinoza and Richard Simon and grew in the hands of the deist and the rationalist French mythographers. The quest coupled this historico-critical program with the premise that the Gospels were authentic historical documents of the original historical Jesus - a premise which drove the quest forward to the "liberal-positive" "lives'" reconstruction of the historical Jesus in terms of the "character" development and historical "personality" alleged to be documented in the Markan account.

An American Quest

On all three counts - historical criticism, christology and biblical criticism - Schweitzer judged that the effort of the nineteenth century questers had ended in bankruptcy. Surveying the course of the movement at the end of his account, Schweitzer reiterated that the quest's attempt to disentangle the historical Jesus from dogma and creed was hopeless. In this verdict of demise Schweitzer relied on the rush of "lives" produced by the theological tradition from Reimarus to Wrede; he was only partially concerned with the quest going on in French and British scholarship for which similar verdicts of failure have been pronounced.(23) Yet another corpus of material, however, the nineteenth century American inquiry into the life of Jesus, which is not covered by Schweitzer and is of major concern to the second part of the present study, suggests a different verdict. In the American version, the quest was marked by a pronounced confidence in the knowability of Jesus which persisted well beyond the period that witnessed according to Schweitzer's narrative the demise of the Leben-Jesu-Forschung.

One of the important directions into which a study of this version of the life of Jesus research leads is a re-evaluation of the assumptions and methodologies of traditional criticism on the Unitarian-Transcendentalist communities under consideration in the second section of the present study. A central premise for this argument is that the quest's significance resides not only in its direct historical influence or theological import, but also in the critical corrective it provides on issues crucial to the religious and intellectual history of the Unitarian-Transcendentalist tradition. Thus, the present study will not rehearse position that Transcendentalism constituted a philosophical rebellion against the Lockean epistemology of Unitarianism, a view which ignores the shared consensus of supernatural rationalism that surfaced in the response to the Leben-Jesu-Forschung and aligned the Transcendentalist ministers with their Unitarian forebears.(24) Nor will the present study rehearse the view that the Unitarian-Transcendentalist tradition represented a nativist movement, a position which slights the international connections that rendered this tradition as much a foreign import as a native development.(25) Nor, finally, will the present study go to the opposite extreme and assume that the influences of contemporary European philosophy created the Transcendentalist movement, a view which ignores in the case of the quest that the life of Jesus research served as a catalyst for theological traditions already deeply engrained in New England divinity.(26)

With regard to the latter issues of "influence," this study establishes that the emergence of the problem of the historical Jesus did not represent a sudden focusing of religious concern on the question of faith and history. The avalanche of American commentary dealing with the life of Jesus in the late 1830s and early 1840s reveals that the causes for the focus on the life of Jesus were not wholly indigenous. Although principles of cultural immanentism and autonomy flowed especially from Unitarian "self-culture" and Emersonian "self-reliance," the American quest grew under a dual stimulus, one provided by the Leben-Jesu-Forschung, the other by the Anglo-American axis of the quest. In the absence of an independent historico-critical tradition, the American quest was thus bound up with transatlantic, international contexts and presented a peculiar compound of native critical developments, British influences and German importations, a compound issuing in complex and extensive debts that formed an inextricable part of the cultural matrix from which the Unitarian-Transcendentalist communities emerged.

How New England divinity first greeted the "lives" with animosity, branded them as heretical and still grew to regard them as "constructive" rather than "negative or polemic" and then refashioned the quest into a dogmatic or apologetic tool is another striking theme to emerge from the material.(27) Here is also a neat example of peculiar "anxieties of influence:" Unitarian and Transcendentalist representatives reviewed German, French, and English "lives;" they appropriated or imitated them and yet contrived to claim the autonomy of "self-culture" and an express independence from European models according to the Gospel of "self-reliance."

The broad scope and the complexity of the quest's influence issued in particular modes of transmission. With regard to the philosophical background of relevance to New England divinity, the mode and nature of European influences on the Unitarian and Transcendentalist communities constitute well-covered critical ground. The consensus is that "New Englanders wanted ... not so much an itinerary as a passport," a passport corroborating a world view which refuted scepticism and materialism.(28) On the epistemological count, the most obvious manifestation of this pattern of corroboration was the Transcendentalist appropriation of Kantian idealism. The Kantian "reason"-"understanding" distinction provided Transcendentalism with a welcome reinforcement of an intuitional idealism combining an idealistic-pantheistic metaphysics with an intuitionist theory of knowledge. Within this combination, the external world was the object of the lower mental function, the "understanding," whereas "reason" formed its ideas according to an a priori intuitionism, "resting only on the original and instinctive principles of (man's) nature, independent of all experience...."(29)

Yet in using the Kantian canon to cut themselves off from a dependence on Lockean empiricism, the Transcendentalist ministers appropriated Kant in a distorted fashion and made no sustained use of the Kantian table of categories for an analysis of the grounds of knowledge and the sources of man's phenomenal perceptions. Kant had put forward definite limits to the arena within which "pure reason" operated and had argued that "pure reason," while providing the "categories" of understanding could not be applied practically to the "field of possible experience" because it concerned itself only with "concepts" and not with objects of experience.(30) Disregarding this boundary, the Transcendentalist reviewers of Kant quickly moved on to identify "reason" with "whatever belongs to the class of intuitive thought."(31) Man has a power beyond "pure reason," the Transcendentalists insisted, to know a realm of reality independent of the categories and laws which operate in the sensible world. In aligning this direct intuiting of the supersensible with "reason," the 'Transcendentalists' stepped outside the boundaries of Kantian "pure reason," equating the term 'transcendental' with concepts Kant had designated as 'transcendent.'(32) Moreover, in this very equation of Kant's "Transcendental Ideas" with "affirmations (which) ... transcend the Understanding and its perceptions," the 'Transcendentalist' "new school" obscured the fact that Kant had shifted the focus from an epistemological issue pertaining to the external cause of man's knowledge to a metyphysical one dealing with the nature of phenomenal perceptions.(33)

The flawed assimilation of the epistemological consequences of Kantian idealism was of one piece with the quest's influence on Unitarian-Transcendentalist shores. The Unitarian-Transcendentalist tradition had no definite theological system to deal with the quest in systematic fashion and failed to appropriate the life of Jesus movement intact. Thus, the conservative Unitarian camp treated the historical Jesus quest as a source of "pantheism" which subverted the evidentialist basis of Christianity, while the Transcendentalist party misconstrued the quest along intuitionist lines, thereby ignoring the definite limits which the rationalist and "positive" "lives" had set to the dispensability of the historical Jesus. On first sight, both camps here seemed to follow the pattern of intellectual corroboration and reassurance characteristic of the impact of Kantian idealism and European philosophy of religion on New England divinity. Thus the course of the quest on Unitarian-Transcendentalist shores was in effect not so much that of its acceptance and assimilation as of its transformation into forms confirming assumptions New Englanders brought to it. Throughout the first decades of the century, for instance, it was mainly the questers from the supernaturalist and "mediating" camp whom Unitarian practitioners appropriated. They depended on Hengstenberg, Tholuck, Olshausen and Neander and used the exegetical methods of the quest to buttress the arguments for Christianity in the rational tradition of William Paley and Samuel Clarke.(34)

The quest was thus consciously put to the cause of reassurance, enabling American practitioners to embrace the findings of the new historical criticism without sacrificing the framework of supernatural rationalism. In this apologetic strand of appropriation the "speculative" advocates of the quest "had a bad name." With men like Andrews Norton, O. B. Frothingham's history of the Unitarian tradition judged, Schleiermacher was a "'veilmaker,' Strauss a 'man of straw'" who relinquished all claims to the "genuineness" and historical factuality of the Gospel tradition.(35) The immediate influence of the quest's assumptions was accordingly slight. Despite the presence of a formidable body of Leben Jesu studies on American soil, the life of Jesus works used and produced during the opening decades of the nineteenth century marked no significant departure from the classic evidentialist pattern. Nor did American productions lead to a consistent body of criticism on the interpretation of life of Jesus narratives. American pracitioners remained too much focused on the issue of "genuineness" to allow a sustained interest in this type of criticism to develop.

Yet over against this pattern of corroboration and reassurance, the quest emerged in the peculiar context of the Unitarian-Transcendentalist debates also as a double-edged phenomenon capable of both synthesizing divergent theological camps and of provoking a sharp breach between evangelical orthodoxy on the one hand and proponents of the historico-critical method on the other. The presuppositions of the life of Jesus theology harbored flexible and ambivalent traditions, including destructive tendencies which carried the force of the quest against orthodox intent. Thus, in the hands of Moses Stuart and Andrews Norton the exegetical tools of the quest fit the apologetic demands of both orthodox Trinitarians and conservative Unitarians. But in the hands of 'liberal' Unitarians like Edward Everett, George Ticknor and George Bancroft, the quest worked by contrast as a destructive force, undermining the foundations of the post-Lockean "theology of evidences" and sowing the seeds of subversion within Unitarian ranks.(36)

Again, however, the quest cut two ways. The quest figured prominently as a backdrop to the miracles controversy and here played into the formation of those Concord Transcendentalists whose express rejection of "historical Christianity" moved them "to distinguish between the transient and permanent in religion" and to denounce the Unitarian camp as "too hard," "too cold, too lifeless."(37) The quest put this critique truly to test. In Schleiermacher, the Transcendentalist party claimed to find a pronounced impatience with evidentialist presuppositions as well as a devaluation of the institutional basis of religion. In Strauss, the Transcendentalist camp saw a conception of Jesus as the Christ "myth," a poetic symbol validating the "new school's" premise that "not Jesus alone, but every spirit in human form is divine." The quest in this way fully accorded with the terms of a movement whose "mission" was "to spiritualize the too hard and literal Christianity that is common and make the religion of Jesus a true and more sanctifying principle to many souls."(38)

In the context of the Unitarian-Transcendentalist debates, then, the quest contributed significantly to the intellectual and theological flux that gave rise to Transcendentalism and fed into the very rhetoric of a generation of men who sought release from Unitarian dogma. And yet - despite these affinities, the Leben-Jesu-Forschung and its American counterpart travelled separate paths. In the case of conservative Unitarians led by Andrews Norton, the new techniques and approaches of the quest were associated with a learned heresy that cut against the grain of the traditional canon of rational supernaturalism. On this count, however, the decisive European influences proved to be not those of the Leben-Jesu-Forschung but those of British evidentialism and Scottish common sense realism. And the exposure to these sources here created a striking common alliance, in particular with the British quest where a similar phalanx of opposition emerged against the inroads of Strauss' life of Jesus research. Hesitant to follow the Leben Jesu researchers to the purely historico-critical interpretation rampant within the quest since Strauss, both American and British questers long preferred to take their stand with the evidentialist school represented by such leaders as Samuel Clarke and William Paley.(39)

Significantly, the strong phalanx of defense around the doctrines of traditional christology and the evidential nature of revelation not only cut across the denominational lines of orthodox Trinitarianism and conservative Unitarianism, but extended also to the Transcendentalist camp. The Transcendentalists were not unanimously prepared to align the premises of the quest with the extreme position of Emersonian intuitionism and self-reliance. At the opposite end of the Transcendentalist continuum, Convers Francis, James Freeman Clarke and Frederick Henry Hedge presented notable examples of Transcendentalists who shifted back to a conservative stance that preserved the objective, historical pole of God's self-disclosure in the person of Jesus. The "new school's" critical response to the philosophical underpinnings of the quest had no place for the Hegelian substructure of Strauss' interpretation of the life of Jesus and preferred to rest its case philosophically with the amalgam of Scottish realism and Kantian idealism propounded by the French eclectics Victor Cousin and Theodore Jouffrey, and theologically with the "reconcilers of all antagonism, such as Jacobi, De Wette, Schleiermacher, Neander," who did not impugn the necessity of a "historical manifestation" of the "idea" of the God-man.(40) And consonant with the "old school's" persistent reiteration of the "genuineness" of the history of Jesus, the Transcendentalist "new school" was in no way prepared to participate in the recurrent attempts of Leben Jesu researchers after Strauss to deny the historicity of the Christ-event. The scope of the responses to the quest may have been broad enough to harbor the 'transhistorical' intuitionism of Emerson and Parker, yet the consensus was throughout that "without some history of Christ, there could have been no belief in Christ, and no proper Christianity."(41)

This consensus may be taken as a clue to something larger; it reveals a conservative strain in a movement commonly identified with anti-historical, intuitional idealism. The evidence of the lives of Jesus strikingly counteracts the allegedly anti-historical bias of the Transcendentalist movement. Beneath the Transcendentalist response to the quest and its literary outpourings lay the continuing influence of the tradition of supernatural rationalism which led the majority of Transcendentalist practitioners to draw back from Strauss' questioning of the historicity of the Gospel accounts. The premises embodied in the work of American advocates of the quest thus did not entail a substantial reordering of theological discourse and religious experience comparable to the studies of Strauss or Hegel. This sort of 'reconstruction' was present in particular in Emerson and Parker, and here, too, not able to persist and grow into a stable position. The problem of faith and history was still defined quite differently than it had been in the Leben-Jesu-Forschung of the Straussian variety, and the pervasiveness of rational supernaturalism was still too strong to be completely discarded.

It is at this juncture that the quest plays into and contributes to another broader issue, namely the assessment of the relationship between the Unitarian and Transcendentalist camps. The existing critical view still pays tribute to the argument advanced by Henry Gray, H. C. Goddard, August Pochmann, Perry Miller, and George Hochfield that Transcendentalism stood on both epistemological and religious grounds in stark opposition to the Unitarian camp.(42) For the literature of the historical Jesus quest this does not quite hold true. The Transcendentalist statements on the quest were still very much consistent with evidentialism and revealed a common ground between the Transcendental gospel and Unitarian Christianity. On the issue of the historicity of the Gospel narratives, no gulf of epistemology or religious polemics separated the Transcendentalist, Unitarian and for that matter also Trinitarian camps. Given the presence of a broad-ranged consensus pertaining to the historical value of the Gospel tradition and its Jesus portrait, the Transcendentalists could not be credited with a clear-cut rejection of the 'orthodoxy' of their Unitarian forebears. Both parties came together in their adherence to the objective nature of revelation and appreciated the allegedly antimaterialist sentiments of the quest much more than its theological and historico-critical premises. Both camps were in their response to the quest primarily "spiritual and practical rather than metyphysical" and in this respect fulfilled The Dial's 1841 prediction regarding "The Unitarian movement in New England" that members of New England divinity "will be known in church history, not so much as reformers in theology, as in the character of champions for the rights of the soul...."(43)

The Quest Continued

With the American quest, the interest in the historical Jesus was not an exclusive property of doctrinal and biographical "lives" but rather also extended into the realm of fiction and social theology on the basis of a strong confidence in the possibility of reconstructing the historical Jesus. In this extension, of concern to the third part of the present study, the lessons of Schweitzer's verdict of demise were lost. For the novelistic "lives" contemporaneous with the "liberal-positive" "lives" of the Leben-Jesu-Forschung and the "lives" produced by the Social Gospel from the 1880s onwards it was neither illegitimate nor impossible to attempt a reconstruction of the historical Jeus under the premise of a harmony between faith and historical criticism.

The application of the quest's themes to a more aesthetic sphere was precipitated by Unitarian ministers who introduced fictional techniques into the pulpit's canon. Ministers like F. W. P. Greenwood joined the move to biblical embellishment by retelling biblical scenes of the life of Jesus. "Imagine the scene for a moment," Greenwood addressed his audience in a sermon on Luke 18, 16, "the disciples are standing aside, abashed, and subdued; the gratified feelings of mothers and fathers are flowing forth in tears; and the multitude looks on, ... while he who commanded the wind and sea, and they obeyed him, receives with outstretched arms the children who are brought to him."(44) With this shift of the techniques of preaching towards a more creative rendition of the life of Jesus narratives the path was broken for fictional adaptations of the historical Jesus. The practitioners of these adaptations, authors like Joseph Holt Ingraham, Charles M. Sheldon, Florence Morse Kingsley and William T. Stead, broadened the scope of the American quest beyond the Unitarian-Transcendentalist tradition and worked within a diverse array of genres represented by William Ware's historical romance Julian: Or Scenes in Judea, Ingraham's epistolary novel The Prince of the House of David and Kingsley's martyr novel Titus, a Comrade of the Cross.

The extension of the theories and practices of the quest into the realm of fiction and social theology was frequently tied up with the task of establishing the traditional Christ, a task deliberately counteracted by the major representatives of the Transcendentalist movement. Emerson's essay on "The Poet" of 1844 proclaimed that "the universe has three children, which reappear under different names in every system of thought, ... the Father, the Spirit, and the Son, but which (Emerson preferred to) call here the Knower, the Doer, and the Sayer." (CW, III, 6). For Emerson, Christ was the poet whose task was to be "sayer" and "namer." Like Christ, the poet is "representative" and "stands among partial men for the complete man." The "office" of both is "to show ... that God is not was; that He speaketh, not spake." Otherwise, "the true Christianity - a faith like Christ's in the infinitude of men - is lost." (CW, III, 5)

In this position, the poetic conception of the person of Jesus went hand in hand with a denial of the historic faith of Unitarianism. On the ground of biblical fiction, however, the fictional adaptation of the historical Jesus served more as a means of reassurance and as a propagation of "the arguments and proofs of the divinity of Christ" which would "convince the infidel Gentile that He is the very Son of the Lord and Saviour of the world...."(45) Fiction here did not represent "a random form of literature, a mere vehicle of amusement," but rather one of the most effective "vehicles" for the perpetuation of evidentialist apologetics, a perpetuation in which the fictional pretense of authenticity and verisimilitude was of one piece with the doctrinal reassertion of the historical reliability of the life of Jesus narratives.(46) In a literary context "the character of the Saviour himself (was thus) everywhere allowed to stand out in its original simple truth (and) majesty...."(47)

The transformation of the quest's issues into entertaining fiction brought in its wake a subversion of critical exegesis and a shift away from complex theological doctrines. In the fictional "lives" of Harriet Beecher Stowe, Elizabeth Stuart Phelps and Joseph Holt Ingraham, the exegetical techniques were clearly subordinated to the requirements of narrative effect and dramatic force. Through the displacement of theological doctrine by the secularizations of the religious bestseller, the literary adaptations of the life of Jesus offered a Christ whom readers "could understand without simultaneously accepting stories which they could no longer understand."(48) This marked a new stage in the link between history and religion, one in which the reconstruction of the life of Jesus was increasingly done along non-supernaturalist lines.

Non-supernaturalist emphases were also a prerequisite for the application of the quest to the social theology propagated by Social Gospel advocates. The Social Gospel revealed that the appropriation of the quest's themes spanned a spectrum broad enough to include socio-economic concerns which found expression in a rich literature extending from Walter Rauschenbusch's pamphlet Das Leben Jesu to Lyman Abbott's textbook for Sunday school classes entitled Christianity and Social Problems. These works focused on the teaching of Jesus rather than on his "person" or christology. Throughout, there was no pronounced concern with a critical exegesis of the "social program" of the historical Jesus. What prevailed instead, as in the case of biblical fiction, was once again the confidence in the easy harmony of faith and history which no attack on the historicity of Jesus produced by the Leben-Jesu-Forschung seemed to be able to undermine.

By the time Walter Rauschenbusch and Shailer Mathews used the historico-critical reconstruction of the figure of Jesus for their social theologies, the "liberal-positive" Leben-Jesu-Forschung had in 1892 expressly been rejected by Martin Kähler as a truncated historicism and psychologism. Kähler's critique of the quest established a difference between the historicity of divine revelation and the historicity of the biblical reports. In the first context, historicity depended on the immediate certainty of faith; in the second context historicity was an index of the probability derived from historical criticism. To confuse the two contexts and to attempt to establish faith by demonstrating that the facts of Jesus' life reconstructed by historical research demand belief in him as the Christ, Kähler deemed destructive of faith.(49) Moreover, even within the realm of historico-critical reconstruction Kähler perceived important limitations. Reading the Gospel accounts as the testimonies and confessions of believers in Christ, Kähler judged that it was impossible to bypass the primitive Christian testimony about Christ and recover the Jesus of history. The Gospel tradition represented faith's witness to kerygmatic history and not historical faith as such.

Kähler's argument conformed to the scriptural testimony that the New Testament is a record of the "signs" "Jesus did ... in the presence of the disciples; ... but these are written that you may believe that Jesus is the Christ, the Son of God, and that believing you may have life in his name." (Joh 20, 30-31) In the context of the Leben-Jesu-Forschung after Kähler, the axis upon which this text turned was the insight that the Jesus of history could never have the solid grounding in historical "signs" alone. Faith is not based on the evidence of the senses or on miracles, the Marburg quester Wilhelm Herrmann asserted, but on an individual experience of the power of the risen life. The believer no longer sees in Jesus "a historical problem" and is not concerned with historical verifiability.(50) The New Testament record in this respect constitutes the response of the believing community to the mission and ministry of Jesus the Christ. In contrast to the premises of the Leben-Jesu-Forschung, this asked for neither a quest for a historical Jesus behind the kerygma nor a dehistoricized version of the kerygma, but rather for the affirmation of the biblical picture of Jesus as the Christ which the New Testament witnesses present as the basis of life "in his name." In the classical Leben-Jesu-Forschung, however, a different aim prevailed. The Leben Jesu researchers who followed the historical Jesu "in his name" also looked for "names ... which ... expressed their recognition of Him...." The questers in this way confronted the object of their research with the question, "Tell us Thy name in our speech and for our day!"(51)

Part I The Leben-Jesu-Forschung

1. In Quest of the Historical Jesus

The Jesus of the Leben-Jesu-Forschung, Martin Kähler observed in his The So-called Historical Jesus and the Historic Biblical Christ of 1892, which presents a convenient "terminus ad quem" of the life of Jesus theology, is "merely a modern example of human creativity, and not an iota better than the notorius dogmatic Christ of Byzantine Christology. One is as far removed from the real Christ as is the other."(1) In what has been poetically described as the "quest for the historical Jesus" Martin Kähler's sceptical judgement had no place. The nineteenth-century 'liberal Protestant' reconstruction of Jesus produced by the Leben-Jesu-Forschung entertained no doubts about the validity of the "Jesus of history" or the "historical Jesus" who was said to have been rescued from the debris of church dogma and christological creed. The advocates of the quest brought the Christ of traditional dogmatic theology to the bar of a method which focused solely on the scientific examination of historical materials and rejected the edifice of doctrine regarding the metaphysical Christ of the Chalcedonian formula. Students of the life of Jesus drew diverse portraits, presenting Jesus as an eschatological fanatic, an Essene propagandist, an exemplary teacher or a sentimental moralist, but they all agreed that they treated an empirical figure, subject to the demands of positivity and the canons of secular historical criticism.

The representatives of the quest were "simply concerned," Heinrich Julius Holtzmann asserted in 1863 in a classic formulation of the movement's aims, "with the question, whether it is now still possible to describe the historical figure of the one from whom Christianity derives its very name and existence, in such a way as to satisfy all just claims of a scrupulous historical-critical investigation."(2) In this historico-critical emphasis the question of the relation of New Testament kerygma to historical reality was not of primary interest. The practitioners of the quest were preoccupied instead with the considerable diffences between traditional christological dogma and the "Jesus of the history." The aim of the quest was to divest the New Testament Jesus of the apostolic and ecclesiastical dogmatic edifice which had been superimposed on him by the faith of the earliest congregation and to return to the 'Jesus of Nazareth who actually lived in first-century Palestine.' Under the aegis of this antidogmatic thrust, the practitioners of the quest produced countless lives of Jesus all united by the interest in the personality of Jesus and by the concern "to picture Him as truly and purely human, to strip from Him the robes of splendour with which He had been apparelled and clothe Him once more with the coarse garments in which He had walked in Galilee."(3) In trying to recapture the historical figure of Jesus from the traditions of church and creed, the quest thus moved from the biblical Christ to the historical Jesus. The resultant "Jesusbild" was that of a Jesus freed from dogma and reduced to scaled-down, ethical terms, a Jesus geared to a theology divested of the "Mysterium Christi."

Form critics of the first half of the twentieth-century discarded the quest because they regarded the Gospel materials as essentially kerygmatic and defiant of every attempt to treat the Gospel narratives as biographical records of the life of Jesus. This sceptical position, primarily associated in European New Testament scholarship with the "no quest" attitude of Rudolf Bultmann, went on to dismiss the quest as hermeneutically naive insofar as its advocates produced "presentistic" modernizations designed to fulfill the demands of the modern rationalist, idealist, socialist, or romanticist. "The research into the life of Jesus of the liberal theologians of the last century," Emil Brunner observed in a restatement of this critique of the quest, "unconsciously confused the rational-ethical and religious humanitarianism of their own ideal of religion with the thought and purpose of Jesus, the result was that this school of thought succeeded in representing Jesus as a teacher of general ethical and religious truths, a man who was distinguished from others by the fact that in his own life he exemplified these general and religion truths in an unusual way. ... This Jesus never existed."(4)

In retrospect, Brunner's critique of the quest appears as a renewed obituary to a movement which four decades earlier had already been terminated by Albert Schweitzer's epoch-making history of the Leben-Jesu-Forschung. Schweitzer's seminal account of the quest demonstrated that the lives of Jesus had set before themselves an impossible goal. From the start, the quest was marred not only by the inadequacy of the available sources but also by the incomprehensible nature of its subject. "In the very moment," Schweitzer declared, "when we are coming nearer to the historical Jesus than men had ever come before, and were already stretching out our hands to draw Him into our own time, we have been obliged to give up the attempt and awknowledge our failure...."(5)

Most students of the life of Jesus in the opening decade of the twentieth century acknowledged that Schweitzer's verdict dealt "the real death blow" to the quest: "When once his views had become known to ... students ... the conviction rapidly gained ground that things could never be the same again."(6) Contemporary reviewers greeted Schweitzer's work as a welcome antidote to the imaginative lives of Jesus which nineteenth century liberal Protestantism had produced and focused on Schweitzer's own theological solution to the Jesus quest, his quasi-mystical idea of "the real immovable historical foundation which is independent of any historical confirmation or justification," whereby Jesus "means something to our world because a mighty spiritual force streams forth from Him and flows through our time also."(7)

Schweitzer proposed his solution in the context of three preliminary theses: the recognition of the failure of the quest for a Jesus recaptured from the traditions of church and creed, the theory of "thoroughgoing" or "consistent eschatology," and the conception of the structure of the life of Jesus movement as an attempt to substitute the historical quest of Jesus for traditional christological dogma. In the development of these theses Schweitzer treated the Jesus quest from Reimarus to Wrede as a self-enclosed unit and an independent historical problem. Schweitzer's study in this respect marked a significant departure from previous histories of the life of Jesus. Karl Hase had started his history of the life-of-Jesus movement with the early harmonies, most notably with Tatian's <u>Diatessaron</u>. F. Nippold's <u>Handbuch der neuesten Kirchengeschichte</u> had let the quest begin with Strauss' life of Jesus. Martin Kähler and Strauss further added to the problem of chronology that of thematic classification. Kähler subjected the quest to christological issues, while Strauss located the origins of the quest in the early debates between typological and allegorical modes of exegesis.(8)

Schweitzer's history, by contrast, placed the origins of the Leben-Jesu-Forschung in antidogmatism as documented in particular by H. S. Reimarus. Schweitzer rendered the antidogmatic thrust of the quest in the observation that most "lives" were written "out of hate ... not so much hate directed against the person of Jesus as against the supernatural nimbus with which he had come to be surrounded." "The dogma had first to be shattered before man could once more go in quest of the historical Jesus...."(9) Most of the protagonists of the quest were antagonistic to the orthodox dogmatic teaching about Christ. More extreme questers were hostile to the development of doctrine even within the bounds of the New Testament and rejected the apostolic proclamation of the Christ underlying that dogma. This more extreme form of anti-dogmatism came sharply to light in the breach that was developed between the historical figures of Jesus and Paul. Here the reconstructed picture of Jesus was set over and against that of Paul as the founder of Christianity who distorted the simple teaching of Jesus. "Free from Paul" - "Los von Paul" - now was the slogan of "lives" setting out to make their way back to the rabbi from Galilee.(10)

In recounting the quest's antidogmatic stance, Schweitzer eventually was to reject the antidogmatic portraits of the "lives" as illegitimate modernizations, but Schweitzer did so not without offering his own version of the life of Jesus. Schweitzer's attempt to add to the long gallery of Jesus portraits one of his own marked a new stage in the Leben-Jesu-Forschung. For while the quest in previous studies had been in pursuit of a figure who could be neatly classified, be it as a liberal humanist in the Ritschlian mold, a social reformer in Kalthoff's cast or a sublime idealist in the Hegelian framework, Schweitzer expressly undercut the incessant historical inquiry by which his predecessors hoped to make Jesus relevant and revealed Jesus instead in all his distance from modern thought: "the historical Jesus will be to our time a stranger and enigma;" he is an "unknown" who "does not stay," "passes by our time and returns to His own...."(11) Significantly, however, Schweitzer himself, even though he erected a bulwark against a psychological modernizing of Jesus, could not escape the dilemma that his predecessors in the Leben-Jesu-Forschung had faced and relapsed in part to the nineteenth century "liberal-positive" quest.

From the Biblical Christ to the Jesus of History

The premises of the movement Schweitzer judged doomed had been long in the making. They traced back at least as far as to the sixteenth century when Socinian critics and sectarians like Michael Servetus and Kaspar Schwenkfeld demonstrated that a distinction existed between the intentions of Jesus and the creedal interpretation of Jesus. To these critics, the traditions of church and creed falsely highlighted the divinity of Jesus and misrepresented his role as an ethical and religious teacher.(11) Through the rise of modern historical method with its techniques of source analysis, the quest was able to pursue this position in a new way and inaugurate a new era in christological reflection. What was advanced by the quest was a methodological shift, a christology whose starting point was "from below," wholly grounded in the historical career of Jesus. All varieties of this form of christology agreed that first and foremost Jesus should be studied as a historic person, in terms of the environment in which he had lived.

The premises envisaged in the reorientation of christology to the quest's anthropocentric religious consciousness emancipated the "Jesusbild" from intrusions of traditional ontological interpretations of Christ. From the historical presuppositions for research into the life of Jesus flowed a pronounced objection to all outlines of patristic christological creeds which obliterated or partialized the history of Jesus. To the quest, the historical life of Jesus did not exist prior to the union with the divine, nor did it present a mere external garment that the logos put on. The quest pushed rather for an ebionite Christ, deprived of the old definitions of the hypostatic union and trinity and the traditional distinctions between substance and person. In this anti-metaphysical bent, the "humanity" of the man Jesus was asserted not in terms of consubstantiality but with reference to the historical being and person of Jesus as a psychological unity subject to historico-critical reconstruction.(12)

The quest's critique of traditional ontological terminology was scarcely a new one. Controversies about the implications of the terms "substantia," "hypostasis" and "ousia" had been one of the persistent motifs of patristic christology.(13) The structure of these controversies hinged on two distinct developments. During a first period culminating in the Niceno-Constantinopolitan creed, the christological debates of the ancient church focused on the repudiation of ebionite and docetic views by asserting the divinity of Jesus in terms of his consubstantiality with the Father and by maintaining the integrity and completeness of Jesus' divine and human natures. Against the heretical christologies of docetists, who maintained that Christ was human in appearance only, and against the adoptionism of the Ebionites who denied to Jesus an essential divinity, the christological debates were heavily weighted on the side of the divine rather than on the human problems in the doctrine of the incarnation. After Nicaea, the emphasis shifted towards the axiom that Christ was the divine logos made flesh, existing that is, in a human way or united to humanity.(14) Explorations of this problem gave birth to a variety of solutions extending from the concern to align the person of Jesus with the praeexistent Son of God to the focus on the integrity of the praeexistent logos and the humanity of Jesus. These solutions were assimilated into the Chalcedonian creed and codified in the formula of the 'two natures in one person' which was to persist in the patristic theologians, the medieval schoolmen, and the Reformers and their scholastic interpreters.

The main line of these two phases of patristic christology led to two conflicting interpretive traditions, the Alexandrian logos-sarx christology and the Antiochean logos-anthropos christology.(15) The Antiochene school, represented by Malchion, Lukian and Theodor, worked within Aristotelian premises and emphasized on the basis of the full co-presence of two simultaneous natures, Godhead and manhood, that the divine Word was shown with and through the human Jesus and not apart from him. Typically, then, this christology was concerned to acknowledge the full and complete integrity of Jesus' humanity and viewed the two "natures" as conjoined but continually divided. In Antiochene usage, the divine Word and the human Jesus, could come together, and the two natures could thus appropriate a new form, a "prosopon," the person of Christ.(16)

In contrast, the logos-sarx christology represented by Clemens and Origen, emphasized the idea of the priesthood and hegemony of the logos. As a Platonic christology it led to a removal of the soul or 'hegemonic principle' in Jesus' humanity and posited the logos as the ground of unity in keeping with the biblical classical of the logos-sarx christology, the Prologue to the Fourth Gospel. In its extreme form, the logos-sarx christology opened the door to the Arian heresy according to which the logos who took flesh in Christ presented the instrument of creation. Consonant with the Arian cosmological orientation, Christ the logos was accordingly asserted to be not of the same substance as the Father. Unlike the Father, he was changeable, or alterable and presented at best a kind of demigod subordinated to the Father.(17) With this conception, Arianism belonged within the process leading to the emphasis on the humanity of Jesus. Yet while the conception of the logos as finite and creaturely, as subject to all the limitations of an ordinary human being initially reversed the emphasis of docetism by playing down the divinity of Jesus in favor of his humanity, the subsequent reaction against Arianism was substantially responsible for the exaltation of the divine Jesus.

The christology of the quest expressly departed from the Alexandrian and Antiochean tradition. The questers focused on the historical Jesus with far greater emphasis on the earthly Jesus in his humanity than patristic creeds. To "liberal-positive" questers, the Christ of traditional christologies appeared as a figure remote from the Jesus of the Gospels and from the life of ordinary men. The quest accordingly drew attention to the psychological dimensions of the person of Christ, describing his consciousness and growth. It was no longer possible for the quest, in the Antiochene style, to dismiss this psychological dimension as a characteristic of the human nature alone. Nor was it possible for liberal questers to regard the logos as the immediate subject of the incarnate experience without confronting the charge of a heretical denigration of Jesus' essential divinity.(18) The Alexandrian school of thought on the other hand, questers argued, tended to connect the human and the divine in Christ so closely that the human element was fully relinquished. In the Alexandrian framework, the logos was the ultimate subject even of the incarnate experience of Christ. The Word here was supplanted or, in case of Apollinaris, simply displaced the operating center of Jesus' humanity. In insisting that the human element in Christ was completely governed by the logos, the Alexandrians were in the questers' opinion thus unable to discern an authentic human psychology in Christ. The Alexandrian Christ only seemed to be logos and sarx.(19)

Against the patristic background of the logos-sarx and logos-anthropos traditions the quest appeared as a hybrid form of inquiry. Like the Alexandrines, questers insisted on the necessity of Jesus' personal unity. And like the Antiochenes, the questers took as their starting point the person of Jesus, the historical figure of the Gospel rather than the eternal Word. But what the patristic exegetes referred to as the "manhood" and "humanity" of Jesus was very different from the "historical Jesus" of interest to the questers. The quest turned essentially on the notion of "personality" as being equivalent to consciousness. The "personality" of a historic figure, however, the quest maintained, was not defined by the omnipotence and omnipresence determinative for the divine logos.(20) In the context of the antidogmatism of rationalist questers and the antimetaphysical bent of Ritschlian questers, the equation of the personality of Jesus with ontological categories came close to rendering the historical Jesus an abstract entity. An abstract entity, however, was in the questers' view not something one dared to imitate and follow. Moreover, an abstract entity bore no relationship to the "soul" and "consciousness" of Jesus which revealed for the questers the "supreme value" of Jesus' "personality."(21)

This positition carried the quest against another palladium of orthodoxy - Nicaea. The immediate problem before Nicaea was the repudiation of the subordinationism of Arius, but more broadly, the Council also set out to reject any attempt that preserved the reality of Jesus' human nature by "scaling down," as it were, the divinity of Jesus so as to allow for his humanity. At this juncture a philosophical term was inserted into the creed which set patristic christology on the path eventually leading to Chalcedon - "homoousios," the expression of the identity of the substance of the Son and the Father. In a new and more acute way, this term stressed the closest unity between Father and Son and uncovered the inadequacy of the Arian position through the complementary affirmation that the Son was co-equal, consubstantial with the Father.(22) From the quest's perspective, however, Nicaea emphasized the true divinity of Jesus at the expense of losing sight of Jesus' humanity. Nicaea, questers reiterated, regarded Jesus by an abstract formula; it left the historical Jesus very much a philosophical abstraction, subject to an ontological framework revolving around the unity and distinction of divine and human natures. For the questers, the issues raised by the historical life of Jesus were far deeper than Nicaea's ontological formula could grasp. Traditional christological dogma therefore constituted merely the "heap of rubbish" through which real Christianity was obscured.(23)

To patristic theologians themselves, the Nicene insistence on a unity of subject in the sense of a christology "from above" also appeared incomplete. The Nicene Creed affirmed unequivocally the divinity of Jesus Christ as "homoousios" with the Father; furthermore, it stressed in opposition to Gnostic docetism the humanity of Jesus Christ. But Nicaea did not clarify how the divine and human were united in one person. The post-Nicene period witnessed as a result a marked shift in christological controversy which culminated in the premise that God-made man involved some form of omission from humanity to make room for the Godhead, a premise leading in its applications yet another step away from the quest. The shift was initiated when Apollinarius of Laodicea, himself a faithful defender of the anti-Arian position at the Council of Nicaea, subjected the trinitarian results of Nicaea to a christological interpretation which threatened the genuine humanity of Jesus.(24) Apollinarius' christological position affirmed the Nicene solution as to the divinity of Jesus. But Apollinarius was not prepared to acknowledge on that count that in a unified nature there could be two perfect and complete natures. To Apollinarius, the union of the divine Son with a complete human being would necessitate two minds, two selves and hence two Sons. The only way to conceive this union was, Apollinarius held, by arguing that the immutable logos became the integrating core of a human soul in Christ. The logos "contributes a special energy" to Christ's "composite nature" because it has replaced the soul's cognitive part - the "nous" or intellect.(25)

Apollinarius' christology came closer than any other of the patristic period to the concerns of the nineteenth century quest. Like the life of Jesus researchers, Apollinarius acknowledged that the reality of Jesus' human life could not be approached by identifying some elements as part of the human nature and others of the divine. Yet Apollinarius, questers charged, in insisting on the displacement of the reasoning mind by the divine logos, fell victim to docetism and rendered the humanity of Jesus incomplete. Deprived of its reasoning mind, the "nous," the human nature of Christ could with Apollinarius not be a genuine human nature.(26) The logos completely took the place of a normal human psychology in Christ.

Apollinarius thus in effect set the stage for a reductionist view of Jesus' human nature of which no psychological account was possible.

Patristic christology witnessed a diverse reaction to Apollinariansm which was fought out in the struggle between two theologians of the Alexandrian and Antiochian variety, Cyril, bishop of Alexandria and Nestorius, bishop of Constantinopel. Nestorius' position flowed from a persistent criticism brought up against Antiochene christology, namely its insufficient account of the unity of Christ and the resultant doctrine of the two subjects in Christ. All through the fifth century Nestorius' critique determined the insistence on the fully human reality of Jesus. The extreme form of this insistence went so far as to regard Christ's human nature as an "assumed man" practically distinct from his divine nature.(27) With this version of the "logos-anthropos" christology, Nestorius made two propositions central. First, the humanity of Christ was asserted to be full and complete and to include the possession of a rational soul or intellect. Second, in their union in Christ, both the humanity and the divinity were granted all of their essential characteristics. The only possible level at which the union could take place was that of "prosopon" which harbored two natures and two "ousiai."(28)

To Cyril, the rival bishop from Alexandria whose christology was to prevail at Ephesus, the term "prosopon," used in Antioch to describe the union of the two natures in Christ, was insufficient; it made the union of the two natures in Christ merely operational, not substantial. While Nestorius contended tenaciously for the unity of the two natures, Cyril therefore focused on that of the "person," a union embedded in the christological technique of the "communicatio idiomatum" as the exchange of attributes between human and divine. The "manhood" and "Godhead" of Christ were thus conceived as indistinguishable after the hypostatic union. The logos actually became man and did not, as the Antiochians asserted, merely assume manhood. Cyril's decisive contribution in this context lay in his description of the union of the logos with flesh as a hypostatic and 'natural' union. In Jesus Christ, Cyril reiterated, there was "a coming together of things and hypostases," a "composition" of Godhead and manhood, "a concurrence into union of unequal and unlike natures."(29)

The questers espoused aims akin to both great rival advocates of patristic christology. Nestorius' effort to protect Jesus' humanity by describing the two 'natures' as conjoined but continually divided was congenial to questers. Nestorius' theological vocabulary, however, did not have at its disposal adequate terms to describe the modern concept of "person" as opposed to nature. This applied in a similar way to Cyril. Cyril's importance for the quest consisted in the proclamation of a positive and theologically creative concept: that of a christic humanity wholly human, wholly "appropriated" by the logos, and constituting the principle of the deification prefigured in the work and person of Christ. Here was once again an important principle congenial to the quest. The quest devalued the insistence on a fully human nature coexisting with a divine nature and stressed the archetypal relevance of Jesus' humanity for all those who were "in Christ."(30) In the Cyrillian version, however, this emphasis shut the door against a critical study of the historic life of Jesus and gave sanction and perpetuity to the doctrine that the "hypostasis" of the logos formed the bond of unity. To questers, this idea of the joining of the human nature to the "hypostasis" or "persona" inevitably entailed the impersonality of Christ. With Cyril, the divine person of Christ assumed a human nature that was without its own "person."

The logos here remained the essential subject since Jesus took on human nature without assuming human personality. The reality of the human nature of Jesus was thus in constant danger of being submerged.(31)

This danger was further accentuated when Chalcedon codified patristic christology in terms of the doctrine of the two natures and one person. The Chalcedonian creed sought to advance the solution to two disputed problems that had arisen in previous christological controversies: Jesus' relation to the Father and the relation of divinity and humanity in the figure of Jesus. The overriding concern throughout was to express both the distinction and the completeness of Godhead and manhood. To this end, Chalcedon recalled the controversial term "homoousios" to be used of both Godhead and the manhood and confessed "one and the same Christ ... in two natures without confusion, without change, without division, without separation, the difference of the natures having been in no wise taken away by reason of the union but rather the properties of each being preserved and both concurring into one person and one hypostasis."(32) The definition carried the marks of the christological model of "perichoresis," of a logic of copenetration and mutual permeation. It asserted the unity of the person of Christ and the distinction of the two natures in such a way that the uniqueness of the natures was preserved and the unity of person confirmed.(33)

The immediate purpose of this framework was to maintain, as against Monophysitism, the "duality" of the two natures in Christ and to affirm, as against the Arian and Apollinarian denial of the completeness of Christ's human nature, the "one Christ" as "true God and true man, perfect in Godhead, perfect in manhood." Doctrinally, the Chalcedonian settlement was a logical consequence of the earlier Trinitarian doctrine. Chalcedon took up the Nicene concern and reaffirmed its faith in Jesus Christ as consubstantial with the Father, but it also extended the use of the technical term "homoousios" to include Jesus' humanness. From this basis Chalcedon was able to reconcile the opposing Alexandrian und Antiochene christologies and asserted that there was no conversion of the divine, nor adoption of the human. It was to a human nature, an "ousia" rather than a person, a "hypostasis" or "prosopon" that the logos was joined, with each nature retaining the functions determinative to it after union.(34)

Divine and human, Godhead and manhood - this conjunction was the crux for the quest. To the questers, the doctrine of God-manhood was the point where the deficiencies of the Chalcedonian creed came to sharpest focus. Chalcedon, questers reiterated, put forward two abstractions instead of one reality. In response, the Leben-Jesu-Forschung advocated the concept of the 'Jesus of history' to distinguish the figure reconstructed by higher criticism and cleansed from the intrusion of incompatible attributes devised by traditional Christian dogmatics. It was to this anti-dogmatic thrust and to a view of revelation as centered in the historical Jesus that the "lives" of Jesus gave vogue. Thus Harnack's shift of emphasis from christology to the Divine Fatherhood was motivated by the aim of setting Jesus free from the shackles of christological dogma. In a similar vein, Ritschlian questers rejected the Chalcedonian formula as an intrusion of Hellenistic metaphysics into the pure, original Gospel of Jesus.(35) From this perspective, the traditional christological dogma constituted merely an encrustation which obscured the authentic Christan message.

In the context of a christology "from below," the Chalcedonian formula was insufficient in yet another way. The questers charged Chalcedon with selling the Gospel to the docetist implication that the humanity was no more than an 'external garment' which clothed the logos without really affecting him. Moreover, the Chalcedonian formula sanctioned the view of a double life within Christ's person and thus excluded all intelligible study of Jesus' life as a historical figure and psychologized subject. The Chalcedonian doctrine of person had been expressed in ontological terms and did not in any way consider the psychological dimensions of the person but rather imported into the life of Christ a thoroughgoing dualism. With this, Chalcedon counteracted once more the quest's focus on Jesus' unique personality and its insistence on consciousness and growth. To agree with Chalcedon that the historical Christ was "in two natures," amounted to admitting the existence of two separate beings in Christ.(36) Drawing on a christology "from below" allied to the new interest in psychology and anthropology, the quest, in contrast, approached the person of Christ in terms of _one_ nature, human in a pristine way and in this respect divine.

From the Dual-Natured Christ to the Historical "Person" of Jesus

The pervasiveness of christological issues in the questers' "lives" counteracts Schweitzer's central thesis of the structure of the quest as an evolving opposition between historical criticism and christological dogma. Schweitzer's interpretation of the quest as an attempt to substitute the historical question about Jesus for traditional christological dogma held firm to the principle that the figure of Jesus must be demonstrated to have a referent within the categories of historical research rather than christological doctrine. The christological emphasis of the life of Jesus productions, however, suggests that the historical question about Jesus was part of the Christ question and belonged in the context of the long history of christological debates.(37)

The critique of patristic dogma was not unique with the Leben-Jesu-Forschung. A similar critique had been advanced by the Arians, the Abelardians and the Socinians of the Reformation period with their Unitarianism and subordinationism. A principal shift, however, and this constituted one of the movement's chief accomplishments, came with the development of the quest. Thus Schleiermacher no longer approached the divine and human in Christ in terms of "being" and "nature" and restated the doctrine of Christ in terms of "consciousness" and "personality."(38) The Chalcedonian creed, Schleiermacher charged, left unexplored the precise relationship between the natures. The definition identified the area within which the relationship between Christ's "natures" was to be found - without confusion, change, division or separation - but did not address the question what the mechanics of that relationship were. Moreover, to Schleiermacher, the Chalcedonian formula of "persona" and "hypostasis" seemed incompatible with the newly emerging conception of personhood or personality. The Chalcedonian doctrine of person, Schleiermacher argued, was conceived in ontological terms and ignored the psychological dimension of personhood centering in self-consciousness.(39)

The quest here took issue with a central assertion of historic christology codified in the Chalcedonian creed and developed in opposition to the Arian heresy. Chalcedon acknowledged the two natures, "physeis," of Christ as coming together to form one person, "prosopon" or subsistence. This terminology of "one person in two natures" was expressly dialectical; it affirmed the presence, within the person of Christ, of the natures of God and man, and at the same time insisted on the integrity and completeness of each of them. Confronted with the Alexandrian insistence on "mia physis" and the Antiochenes' "duo physeis," Chalcedon persisted in its affirmation of a permanent duality in Christ: Christ is one and the same Son, Lord, only-begotten, but "in two natures" and not "from two natures." The natures remain "without confusion" and "without division;" they interpenetrate one another based upon a "sharing of attributes;" the "communicatio idiomatum," yet they do not become unlike themselves.(40)

In the quest's christology this systematization of the relations of the two natures in hypostatic union had no place. The quest sought to make visual the union of the divine and the human in Jesus without relying on the classical two natures conception. It was impossible, Schleiermacher judged, to bring "divine and human ... together under any single conception, as if they could both be more exact determinations, co-ordinated to each other, of one and the same universal."(41) This conception purchased the divinity of Christ at the cost of reducing his humanity to a mere appearance. It was inconceivable that "the unity of life (could) coexist with the duality of natures, unless the one gives way to the other, ... or unless they melt into each other...."(42) Above all, the term "nature" in its contemporary usage designated for the quest this-worldly reality only and allowed for no return to religious self-consciouness as the locus of the self-actualization of the Christian principle.

For the questers around Schleiermacher, the uniqueness and value of Christ resided in the union of "finite and infinite, human and divine." The patristic christological tradition, however, questers charged tended "to vacillate between the opposite errors of ... either neglecting the unity of the person in order to separate the two natures more distinctly, or, in order to keep hold of the unity of the person, disturbing the necessary balance, and making one nature less important than the other...."(43) This no doubt applied to patristic christological debates, yet the express purpose of these "errors" was to locate the origin of Jesus' human reality not in itself but in the trinity. By means of the formula of the "enhypostasis" Jesus was asserted to have the ground of his existence, his hypostasis, not in himself as man but "in the eternal logos," in the second person. The quest's basic reorientation consisted in the attempt to locate genuine human reality in itself. While to patristic christology the human nature of Christ was enhypostatic, for the questers the human nature of Christ was self-sufficient; it existed independent of the divine hypostasis of the logos and outside the traditional conception of the incarnation. In this disruption of the internal relations of the trinity, the incarnation constituted merely an instance of inspiration. The overriding thrust was to a Sabellian direction, the logos being no more than a mode in which God had appeared, a divine 'energy' rather than a 'person.'(44)

This tendency to dissolve the objective categories of the historical Christ-event flowed from a "dogmatic" christological motivation. Thus, however divergent the "lives" after Strauss, their authors came together in the desire to re-affirm the validity of the "vere homo" against the dissolution of the Christ of faith into Strauss' and Bruno Bauer's speculative "idea" and Arthur Drews' "Christusmythe." At issue here was not the substitution of christological dogma, as Schweitzer had claimed, but rather its historical interpretation. A distinctive form of this interpretation was the "kenotic" theology in which the openness of the mediating position to a re-affirmation of classical christological options was most pronounced. Typically, the kenotic christology endeavored to corroborate the intent of the classical two-natures christology against Strauss' exclusion of traditional christological formulas from the interpretation of Jesus' significance. The questers caught up in the movement, like the Erlangen theologians J. C. K. Hofmann and G. Thomasius, saw in the "kenosis" motif a means of integrating the quest's new focus on the "personality" and self-consciousness of Jesus into the traditional understanding of Jesus' divinity.(45) This conservative christological option was developed parallel to the Leben-Jesu-Forschung after Strauss and countered the charge that the orthodox view of Christ did not do justice to his human attributes by developing the doctrine of "kenosis" as the laying aside or "self-divesting" of the aspects of omnipotence, omniscience and omnipresence in the historical life of Jesus. The kenotic christology, starting "from below," assumed both a limitation and a continuity of the divine consciousness in the figure of Jesus. "The second person of the deity" 'depotentiated' himself and gave himself over "into the form of human limitation, and thereby to the limits of a spatio-temporal existence, under the conditions of a human development, in the bounds of an historical concrete being, in order to live in and through our nature the life of our race in the fullest sense of the word without on that account ceasing to be God."(46)

This was a reshuffling of traditional doctrinal elements - of the emphasis on Christ's exaltation and humiliation in becoming man characteristic of Calvinistic doctrine and the formula of the 'interchange of properties' characteristic of Lutheran theology. To the kenotic questers, it was Lutheran christology which came closest to their own ground by asserting that the divine and human natures were not only joined in the unity of one "hypostasis" or "persona" but also actually imparted to each other. According to the doctrine of the "communicatio idiomatum," both natures were in effect so intimately related that the attributes of the one were predicated of the other. This extension of the idea of the hypostatic union postulated the surrender of the use of the divine attributes and further implied that the subject of the art of "self-divesting" was the incarnate word. The kenotic theologians were as committed to the "communicatio idiomatum" as had been their Lutheran forebears, yet they interpreted the 'interchange of properties' not as the transfer of qualities from the divine to the human but rather in reverse. The logos himself, kenotic theologians asserted, in the act of incarnation, underwent a self-limitation, divesting himself of those aspects of divinity that were incompatible with a genuinely human existence.(47)

Kenoticists in this way succeeded in approaching the humanity of Jesus with a new depth and direction which marked a significant advance in the quest's response to Strauss' dissolution of the historical Jesus. With the kenotic model, the Jesus of history could be assigned a fully human self-consciousness because the logos was asserted to have reduced himself to human limitations and to human nature in the incarnation. In the transition from existence "in the form of God" to a fully human existence "in the form of a servant," the humanity did not simply represent the garment by which the divine could appear as being human. Kenotic christology expressly precluded docetism and affirmed the full humanity of Jesus as subject to finitude and limitations like any other expression of humanness. "The eternal Son of God gave up the form of eternity and in free self-limitation assumed the existence form of a human life-center, a human soul; he had, as it were, reduced himself to a human soul."(48)

Historically, this interpretative principle served as a bridge between traditional christology and the inroads of Strauss' Leben Jesu. Doctrinally, this model resolved the tension between the "archetypal," "ideal" Christ and the Jesus of history and demonstrated that the two-natured Christ of faith could be approached as the historical Jesus. With regard to the principle of "mediation" between the "archetypal" and the historical, the kenotic model found a common front of approval; but with regard to the interpretation of the two-natures christology as a dynamic process debasement and exaltation, the consensus promised by the kenotic motif quickly broke down. From I. A. Dorner came a cogent critique of Thomasius' work which uncovered the "anthropopathic" tendencies inherent in kenotic christology and charged that the notion of a self-divesting of the logos not only disrupted the internal relations of the trinity but also surrendered the concept of immutability. One point, however, did emerge from the arguments of both sides. For Dorner as for the kenoticists, the overriding intent remained the same - to validate, contra Strauss, the empirical and objective status of the figure of Jesus and the Gospel events. And for both sides, the scientific verifiability of their conception of Christ here hinged on the belief in Christ as the one "in whom the perfect personal union of the divine and human appeared historically." "Neither a merely historical nor a merely ideal and metyphysical significance," it was assumed, "belongs to Christ, but rather ... both are absolutely one in His perfect Person."(49)

From Redeemer to "Example"

Correlative to Schweitzer's reductive treatment of the christological themes of the quest was his tendency to slight the fact that a movement claiming to free the historical Jesus from orthodox christology also downplayed, if not bypassed the issue of soteriology. On this count Martin Kähler had fourteen years before Schweitzer already rejected the entire life of Jesus movement as a "blind alley."(50) According to Kähler, the quest had no sources for a biography of Jesus of Nazareth which met the standards of contemporary historical science. In addition to the difficulties resulting from the inadequate, unreliable nature of the sources available to the Leben-Jesu-Forschung, the quest was for Kähler also marred by a deficient christology which exalted merely the "personality" of Jesus. The quest, Kähler judged, replaced christology with a Jesuanism; its piety was a case of hero-worship and failed to perceive that the Chalcedonian definition of Christ's person, far from being 'speculative' in character, was not limited to assertions about the person of Christ but also included His saving activity.(51) With regard to this latter issue, Kähler, unlike Schweitzer, realized that the quest's 'Jesus of history' lacked the soteriological significance of the 'Christ of faith.' Its soteriologically evacuated "historischer Jesus" could not justify sinners, awaken faith or give assurance of salvation. Soteriologically, the "lives" thus appeared reductionist, unjustly restricting the biblical Christ to the dimensions of a factual person who could not truly save.

In the Chalcedonian formula the person and work of Christ co-inhered; its christology was linked with a soteriological interest in salvation "pro nos." The special character of Jesus' work emerged against the idea of "substitution:" "the death of Jesus was regarded, now as a ransom paid by him to the devil for the liberation of mankind, who had fallen into the power of the evil through one sin; now as a means devised by God for removing guilt, and enabling him to remit the punishment threatened to the sins of man, without detriment to his truthfulness, Christ having taken that punishment on himself."(52) In the quest, these variations of the idea of substitution lost much of their significance. The quest devalued the terms of satisfaction of a divine requirement or substitution of the life of Jesus for penalty to be paid by sinful man. For the quest, it was the "Christ in us" rather than the "Christ for us" that was at stake.

This view departed from both the "legal" view of the atonement according to which Christ was substituted as an expiatory victim in the place of humanity for the debt legally incurred by man's sins, and the "governmental" theory of the atonement in which Christ's sacrifice served to maintain the integrity of the divine moral order.(53) In the quest, forensic and judicial terms retreated behind an "illustrative" emphasis, and supernatural 'arbitrariness" behind "the attempt ... to represent the Atonement as a transaction in which God is reconciled to man, as well as man reconciled to God."(54) The quest in this way achieved a major recasting of the traditional "schema" of the three-fold office of Christ, the "munus triplex." In place of the traditional office of Christ as a "prophet" proclaiming God's will, as a "king" reigning over God's people, and as a "priest" offering the sacrifice of his death, the quest substituted the emphasis on the work of Christ as a promotion of human perfection, of a "supremely excellent and complete morality."(55)

Within the course of the quest, this shift from a judicial and "substitutionary" to an "inspirational" and "illustrative" conception of the work of Christ was brought to its highest point in Schleiermacher's insistence on Jesus' religious consciousness as the redemptive element. For Schleiermacher, the work of Christ was not identical with the supernatural idea of redemption in the traditional and orthodox theology but rather flowed from the terms of God-consciousness. "The Redeemer assumes believers into the power of God-consciousness, and this is His redemptive activity."(56) Under this influence one acquired the "God-consciousness" that found its supreme realization in the filial consciousness of Jesus. Accordingly, "the evil condition can not only consist in an obstruction or arrest of the vitality of the higher self-consciousness."(57) Sin does not constitute an offense against God for which satisfaction is required; rather, sin is essentially the disturbance of the human God-consciousness, a failure to place "God consciousness" over other impulses. In contrast to Anselm's notion of debt incurred by sin and Calvin's and Luther's notion of bondage under the Law, Schleiermacher thus highlighted the transformation of present religious experience to the exclusion of any general scheme of "salvation."

In a soteriology which approached sin in terms of self-consciousness it was consistent that no sufficient place was made for the penal suffering of Christ as satisfaction for sin. Jesus' suffering was according to Schleiermacher's programme vicarious, but this vicariousness was not satisfactory. In the classical formulations of substitutionary atonement the import of the work of Christ rested upon his satisfying the offended honor and justice of God by suffering the punishment man could never bear. In Schleiermacher's objection to orthodox doctrine, by contrast, the older doctrine of the atonement shifted to one of "example," to a doctrine determined by the idea of "representative" rather than substitutionary sacrifice. Schleiermacher in this way replaced the theory of Christ's vicarious satisfaction with the theory of satisfactory vicariousness which divested Christ's priestly work of all sacrificial and penal functions.(58) Jesus did not die "in our place;" his work was not to be viewed under the legal categories of merit and satisfaction. Rather, Jesus represents man's "satisfying representative" "in the sense, first, that in virtue of His ideal dignity He so represents, in His redemptive activity, the perfecting of human nature, ... and, second, that His sympathy with sin ... serves to make complete and perfect our imperfect consciousness sin."(59)

The chief virtue of this position was that it sought to include the historical Jesus in such a way that the figure of Jesus could be approached in human terms without surrendering the "archetypal." According to Schleiermacher's overriding premise, both sides, the historical and the archetypal, were reconciled in the figure of Jesus. In this reconciliation the terms of Schweitzer's opposition between historical criticism and the Christ question did not apply. Schleiermacher defined "God-consciousness" as that which was historically manifested in Jesus of Nazareth. The historical aspects of christology and soteriology essentially here coalesced in a "Christ-idea" or principle and did not entail an affirmation of the belief in the literal resurrection and ascension of Christ. The historico-critical validation of "what is presented in experience and history regarding the personal existence of Christ" mattered little to Schleiermacher when he "(regarded) the beginning of the life of Jesus as the completed creation of human nature."(60)

From "Prophet" to "Reformer"

One of the chief contributions of Schweitzer's understanding of Jesus was that he put Jesus back in the first century world of Jewish apocalyptic and presented him as a remote and "alien" character, thus standing the "liberal-positive" modernization of Jesus on its head. Schweitzer's position flowed from the introduction of an element into the Leben-Jesu-Forschung which since the days of H. S. Reimarus had for the most part been overlooked. Systematic theology did not assimilate Reimarus' recognition of the all-commanding eschatological dimension of the New Testament and moved instead towards the Ritschlian view of the kingdom of God in the message of Jesus as a this-worldly goal and supreme ethical ideal. With regard to eschatology, the entire nineteenth century quest for the historical Jesus appeared therefore to Schweitzer to be retrograde after Reimarus. While Reimarus had highlighted the significance of the eschatological elements in the Gospels, the Ritschlian system viewed the eschatological ideas of the Gospels merely as accomodations to an ancient local and temporal milieu which expected the imminent coming of the kingdom. What Jesus actually envisioned, according to the Ritschlian canon, was a progressive coming of the kingdom, realizable by human plan and ethical endeavor. In a similar vein, Harnack's <u>What is Christianity</u> regarded the eschatological perspective of the Gospels as completely peripheral and unessential. The eschatological and otherworldly language of Jesus, Harnack maintained, constituted the "shell" of Jesus' teaching concealing his true historical being and had no place in those Gospel narratives in which the "kingdom" was described as something "inward" which was already present.(61)

Over and against Harnack's immanentist, individualistic position and the Ritschlian view of the Kingdom as a hoped-for, this-worldly goal,

Schweitzer presented the eschatological element as the decisive key to unlocking the history of Jesus. The portrait of Jesus which emerged from Schweitzer's Quest was that of an unworldly, apocalyptic figure who shared the imminent eschatological expectations of late Judaism. Within this context of late Jewish eschatological thought, Schweitzer held that Jesus did not idealize the current Messianic expectation by projecting it into a distant and indeterminate future vaguely classified as "spiritual;" rather, Jesus' life history, Schweitzer argued, was molded by His expectation of the imminent dawning of the Kingdom of God. Jesus was convinced that God had chosen Him to be revealed at the Kingdom's arrival as the supernatural Messiah, and He set out to hasten that climatic moment. But whereas the older prophets had expected the Messianic Kingdom within the course of human history, for Schweitzer's Jesus it was to arrive as a cosmic catastrophe which would terminate human history and would lead, in fullfillment of the apocalyptic prophecy of David, to Jesus' manifestation as the "Son of Man," the emissary of a new aeon.(62)

This eschatological conception had been in the field of New Testament exegesis since its elaborate investigation in Johannes Weiss' monograph 1892 on the preaching of Jesus. Cutting himself loose from Ritschl, Johannes Weiss demonstrated that "the idea of the Kingdom of God in Ritschl's theology and in the preaching of Jesus are two very different things." The Kingdom was not, as the Ritschlians mistakenly supposed, "an innerworldly ethical idea, ... a vestige of a Kantian ideal. ... The Kingdom of God, as Jesus thought of it, is never something subjective, inward or spiritual, but always the objective messianic Kingdom, which is usually portrayed as a territory into which one enters, ... or a treasure which comes down from heaven." Ritschl's view of Jesus as the teacher of a Kingdom whose innerworldly terms were immediately applicable and could be actualized by human initiative seemed thus questionable. "The actualization of the Kingdom of God," Weiss reiterated, "is not a matter for human initiative, but entirely a matter of God's initiative. The only thing man can do about it is to preform the conditions required by God."(63)

This argument was slow to penetrate into New Testament exegesis until it received the powerful support of Schweitzer's Quest.(64) In Schweitzer's opinion, however, the "Eschatological School" represented by "Johannes Weiss und his followers" had not gone far enough. "They related eschatology only to Jesus' preaching ... rather than clarifying, in terms of the newly-won insight, the whole public ministry, the events' connections and lack of connections...." It was "quite inexplicable" to Schweitzer that the eschatological school," with its clear perception of the eschatological element in the preaching of the Kingdom of God, did not also hit the thought of the 'dogmatic' element in the history of Jesus."(65) Schweitzer undertook to reveal this "dogmatic" element as the actual historical element. The "chaotic confusion" of the Gospel narratives was for Schweitzer not caused by the faulty transmission of the tradition but rather indicative of the "volcanic force of an incalculable personality."(66) Schweitzer accordingly was not led to doubt the reliability of the sources on which his eschatological theory relied. On the contrary, Schweitzer acknowledged as authentic the Gospel record that Jesus preached his own messianic parousia.

But what Schweitzer affirmed with one hand, he undermined with the other. Schweitzer conceded to his audience the historicity of the eschatological Jesus and the authenticity of the relevant narratives, but he undercut much of the questers' ground for turning Jesus into an exemplary moral teacher or liberal humanist. Schweitzer's Jesus, a thoroughgoing eschatologist, driven by His belief in the imminent end of the world and in His own messianic parousia, came close to being a deluded visionary; His history was the history of a faith that was disappointed by the unsuccessfull effort to bring all ordinary history to a close. For this reading, Matthew 10,23 was the crucial text which Schweitzer regarded as an authentic saying from a time when Jesus sent out his disciples to proclaim the imminence of the Kingdom: "When they persecute you in one town, flee to the next; for truly, I say to you, you will not have gone through all the towns of Israel, before the Son of man comes." Until this point in his ministry Jesus had, in keeping with traditional Jewish apocalyptic speculations, expected the suffering of the disciples to precede the Kingdom. Hence his prophecies of sufferings and persecutions the disciples are to face in the mission speech of Matthew 10. Jesus "does not expect to see them back in the present age. The Parousia of the Son of Man, which is logically and temporally identical with the dawn of the Kingdom, will take place before they shall have completed a hasty journey through the cities of Israel to announce it."(67)

But the disciples did come back to Jesus. The Kingdom of God and the Son of Man had not arrived. In response, Jesus altered the course of His entire ministry and shifted the suffering to his own experience. His own trial and suffering will initiate the final tribulation, a conviction Jesus shares with his disciples near Caesarea Philippi. "In the secret of the passion," Schweitzer explains, "which Jesus reveals to the disciples at Caesarea Philippi the pre-Messianic tribulation is for others set aside, abolished, concentrated on Himself alone, and that in the form that they are fullfilled in His own passion and death at Jerusalem."(68) This identification of Jesus' own sufferings with the expected apocalyptic tribulations of the end-time constituted, according to Schweitzer, a unique contribution to eschatology. In contrast to the purely artificial characters of Jewish apocalypticism, "there now enter into the field of eschatology men, living acting men, ... the only time ... that ever happened in Jewish eschatology."(69) Moreover, in contrast to the contemporary view that throughout the greater part of his life Jesus did not think of his passion until the idea was imposed on him by the hostility of the scribes, Schweitzer lifted the secret of the passion into the center of Jesus' messianic mission: Jesus would take on the "messianic woes;" he would suffer like the suffering Servant of Isaiah in order to compel the Kingdom's arrival. But Jesus' own sufferings, Schweitzer's narrative uncovers, did not usher in the tribulation of the last days. The historical, eschatological Jesus had been deluded - again.

Schweitzer described his interpretation as one of "thoroughgoing" or "consistent" eschatology, one which applied "the term eschatology ... only when reference (was) made to the end of the world as expected in the immediate future, and the events, hopes, and fears connected therewith."(70) Schweitzer here did not distinguish between eschatology and apocalypticism. Equating eschatology with apocalypticism, Schweitzer argued that the event of the cross certified the de-eschatologizing process of the New Testament according to the construction of a 'proleptic' messianic consciousness. But Schweitzer's resultant de-eschatologizing thesis presupposed on the basis of a futuristic eschatology a linear eschatology of the prolonged time axis. This linear eschatology "charged the idea of the Kingdom of God with ethical forces - an "interim ethics" detached from apocalypticism and designed to prepare for the coming of the Kingdom.(71)

Schweitzer's "interim ethics" did not entail a meticulous observation of the minute details of the law, nor did it inculcate timeless absolutes as guides to moral life. Nor could the ethic of the Kingdom be used as a helpmate in the transformation or amelioration of the socio-economic order. "With political expectations," Schweitzer claimed, "this Kingdom has nothing whatever to do." Jesus preached "only an ethic which in this world makes men free from the world and prepared to enter unimpeded into the Kingdom."(72)

Schweitzer's position was of one piece with his proposition of a system of ethics strictly adapted to the interim before the immanent coming of the Kingdom. Schweitzer's theory of "thoroughgoing eschatology," however, failed to recognize the political and socio-critical efficacy of the life of Jesus question and slighted the quest's contribution and place in social history. The pioneering life of Jesus by H. S. Reimarus made clear from the start that the issue of Jesus' "aims" was not to be separated from an eschatological-political ideology. Reimarus' "life" presented a wordly deliverer whom the disciples later exalted to the status of a spiritual ruler. Basic to Reimarus' reconstruction of a political historical Jesus and his rejection of the erroneous "dogmatic" interpretation of Jesus as the Christ was the assertion that Jesus stood wholly within the orbit of ordinary Jewish thought. Reimarus' Jesus did not introduce "articles of faith and mysteries" into the Jewish religion, nor did he set out to found a new religion; rather, he preserved the ceremonial law.(73) At the most, Reimarus would hold that Jesus strove for the moral elevation of mankind and "intended to improve man inwardly" through the cultivation of "purely moral duties."(74) On this count, Reimarus' Jesus remained firmly embedded in Jewish thought and practice which constituted the "first systema," the system of Jesus as the moral enlightener. But Reimarus also recognized as a crucial aspect of this "system" Jesus' eschatological-political ideology. Jesus shared during his life time with his disciples the aim of setting up in the immediate future a theocratic kingdom centered on himself as the "wordly king." "It was clearly then," Reimarus insisted, "not the intention or the object of Jesus to suffer or to die, but to build up a worldly kingdom, and to deliver the Israelites from bondage. It was in this that God had forsaken him, it was in this that his hopes that been frustrated."(75)

Focusing on the essential distinction between the teaching of Jesus, the first "systema," and the teaching of the apostles, the second "systema" Reimarus' account reiterated that Jesus preached the coming of a messianic kingdom in an earthly, secular and political sense. From Reimarus' descriptions of Jesus' entry into Jerusalem, Jesus' "interruption of order in the Temple," and his "seditious speeches to the people against the high council" emerged a "herald" well aware of the political implications of a messianic pronouncement and firmly rooted in the belligerent Jewish tradition.(76) Jesus went, Reimarus reiterated, to the core of Jewish particularism, consciously drawing on the Jewish hope of a Davidic Messiah who would establish a temporal, this-worldly kingdom over Israel. The Gospel accounts, however, belie this portrait, they present "the new system of a suffering spiritual savior, which no one had ever known or thought before."(77) While Jesus in Reimarus' account actually deserved his condemnation - "nach allen Rechten und politischen Regeln" - the disciples fabricated the "new system" of Jesus' sacrificial suffering and death and were goaded by the inglorius downfall of their leader into using the fraudulent inventions of the resurrection message and of Christ's second coming.(78)

Reimarus had proposed the distinction between the eschatological-political Jesus of history and the Christ of faith for dogmatic reasons, in an effort to undermine the orthodox portrait of Christ. Yet in the aftermath of the publication of the Wolfenbüttel Fragments two corollary premises of Reimarus' thesis emerged in which the validity of the socio-political interpretation of Jesus' preaching received no sustained treatment: First, from the antidogmatic bias of the movement grew the conviction of the "lives" that over against "abstract dogmatism" the person and religion of Jesus himself were to be decisive.(79) Second, corroborated by the historico-critical bias of the quest, the conviction intensified that it was methodologically possible and theologically imperative to secure an historically impregnable position for faith and free Christianity from what was perceived to be a false dogmatic overlay of interpretation.(80)

According to the first premise, the proper key to understanding Jesus was not speculation about his ontological status. The basis of historical truth upon which Christian faith resided was not ontological or supernatural, but rather grounded in the personality of Jesus, independent of embellishments to the Gospel narratives as well as of anachronistic dogmatic formulations of a later age. While the Christ of faith belonged to the realms of "theology" and "speculation," the Jesus of history was assigned to the realms of "religion" and "piety." And it was readily assumed here that the historico-critical procedure would arrive at a "firmly drawn and life-like portrait, which, with a few bold strokes, would bring out clearly and originally the force, the personality of Jesus."(81)

In this anti-christological focus on the "personality" of Jesus, however, the question of the social principles of the historical Jesus did not fully come into play and was instead more aligned with the second premise entailed in Reimarus' distinction between the Jesus of history and the Christ of faith. The Jesus quest took as its point of departure an express rejection of the conception of sacred history as a valuable source of knowledge grounded in divine revelation and to be accepted uncritically. Aligned with historico-critical analysis, the quest treated the Gospel narratives as historical sources like any others, placed them in the historical context of related contemporary documents, and thus sought to recover the original teachings and aims of Jesus. Within a broad spectrum of reconstructions, the underlying premise here remained constant: the Gospels were authentic historical documents of the original historical Jesus. Methodologically, therefore, it was considered possible to reconstruct the history of Jesus. The figure of Jesus of Nazareth could be known and, theologically, the questers went on to assert, He ought to be known.

For the life of Jesus studies after Strauss this imperative task of reconstruction included the conviction that the teachings of the historical Jesus also yielded a reliable guide for social conditions, a guide to be reconstructed by the same historico-critical procedures which were to be applied to the figure of Jesus himself. In R. Wagner's Jesus of 1843 and W. Weitling's Das Evangelium eines armen Sünders of 1845 the message of the "revolutionary carpenter" thus was read as a social challenge and manifesto. The gospel of the historical Jesus here "was in the main a great social message to the poor.... Jesus ... was a great social reformer, who aimed at relieving the lower classes from the wretched condition in which they were languishing; he set up a social programme which embraced the equality of all men, relief from economical distress and deliverance from misery and oppression."(82)

After the failure of the 1848 revolution, the socio-political explanation of Jesus' life moved away from this activist social stance to an emphasis on the coming Kingdom as a possibility within history which did not call for substantial reconstructions of social and economic institutions. A. Rembe's Christus der Mensch und Freiheitskämpfer, which presented Jesus a a world revolutionary, and Friedrich Naumann's Jesus der Volksmann, which advocated a Christian-social program abolishing monopolization and economic injustice, remained the exception.(83) What prevailed instead was an essentially conservative, individualistic perspective according to which spiritual regeneration preceded social reform. Within this form of social Christianity, Harnack's analysis of the quest's aims maintained, the Gospel's "object (was) to transform the socialism which rests on the basis of conflicting interest into the socialism which rests on the consciousness of a spiritual unity."(84) This was to restate what the earliest stage of the quest represented by Lessing had already reiterated against Reimarus, namely that Jesus served as "the first reliable, practical teacher of the immortality of the soul."(85) On the same count, the "liberal-positive" quest argued at the close of the nineteenth century that rather than a "political programme" or a "social programme for the suppression of poverty and distress," Jesus "laid down" an "individualistic" Gospel which "establishes the infinite and independent value of every human soul."(86)

The Quest Reviewed

Against the "liberal-positive" reconstructions of the "individualistic" teachings of the historical Jesus Schweitzer advanced a sceptical assessment which emerged in terms of its impact on the course of the Leben-Jesu-Forschung as the most provocative and prophetic thesis of Schweitzer's critical history of the quest. The blows of Schweitzer's study came from various sides. One of them struck at the assumption that the synoptic sources could be treated as historically reliable sources for a biography of Jesus. Most participants in the quest, Schweitzer judged, were confident that they possessed cooperative and reliable materials necessary for reaching firm conclusions about Jesus and that the synoptic sources could be utilized for these conclusions according to the premises of positivistic historiography. But it was to the very nature of the sources that Schweitzer attributed one of the basic dilemmas of the historical Jesus research. It is not the aim of the Gospels to furnish the materials for a biography of Jesus, Schweitzer argued, they do not set out to give a 'life of Jesus,' but rather proclaim his teaching as God's revelation and salvation. The New Testament materials therefore represent direct expressions only of the faith of the various authors; they reflect indirectly the developing faith of the first century Christian communities and attach no importance to any biographical completeness or accuracy as the optimistic life of Jesus inquiries of the quest supposed.(87)

Lacking reliable, unkerygmatic sources, the nineteenth century questers were, according to Schweitzer, thus frequently led to fabricate the completeness and accuracy of the sources for their reconstructed historical Jesus. Hampered by the nature of the available sources, the authors of the "lives" developed distorted Jesus portraits "designed by rationalism, endowed with life by liberalism, and clothed by modern theology in a historical garb."(88) The quest's reconstructed historical Jesus in this way fell short of the Jesus who walked the shores of Galilee. Surveying the course of the questers' flawed modernizations, Schweitzer therefore unrelentlessly reiterated his verdict of "negative" results: The entire quest for the historical Jesus "has fallen to pieces, cleft and disintegrated by the concrete historical problems which came to the surface one after another...." "Those who are fond of talking about negative theology can find their account here. There is nothing more negative than the result of the critical study of the life of Jesus."(89)

For Schweitzer, the deep and crucial deficiency underlying the failure of the quest did not solely reside in the nature of the New Testament sources but also in the historical presuppositions encumbering the "lives." The significance of the "lives," Schweitzer judged, did not stem from their specific historical discoveries. These were only minimal, yet it was precisely 'history,' conceived of as encompassing what one could know on the basis of a science of history, that was made the key to the life of Jesus. This supposition, however, foundered on the hard rock of the perennial problem of the "ugly broad ditch" of history rendered in Lessing's classic dictum about the impossibility of contingent history serving as a medium of revelation. To Schweitzer, this problem figured as a key factor in the collapse of the life of Jesus movement. Theologically, Schweitzer recapitulated, the quest was doomed because it sought to base faith on scientific history by making an historical reconstruction the ground of faith. This was to assume too much for scientific history, namely that it provided a basis for present faith and "(called) spiritual life into existence."(90) The advocates of the quest were thus continually confronted with the dilemma of having to base their faith on historical assertions which themselves did not bear a high degree of probability. A first-century prophet, reconstructed by the strict historico-critical method with its humanistic presuppositions and fragile probabilities, was declared to be the authentic basis and content of Christian faith.

Schweitzer's narrative further uncovered that the seeds of the quest's demise were sown at a yet deeper level. Schweitzer's indictment of the "lives" exposed the life of Jesus movement as doomed not only on account of the inadequacy of the ordinary criteria of historical investigation but also on account of the inexplicable nature of its very subject. For Schweitzer it was not possible to lift the historical Jesus out of the Palestine setting of His day and transfer Him to one's own. Those who claimed to have discovered the historical Jesus found that He was still and more than ever, an "unknown" who is not the subject for analysis by discursive reason and defies normal categories of thought. His nature one may not "even wish to understand;" his history cannot be approached through the solid grounding in chronology and is independent of shifts in critical method.(91)

In this assessment of the quest's demise Schweitzer was not original. From a different plane, the sceptical assessment of the life of Jesus movement was shared by advocates of the quest themselves. Thus Strauss concluded his "life" by demonstrating the impossibility of writing a historically reliable life of Jesus. To Strauss, this failure of the quest as a positivistic enterprise was a calculated possibility of the Leben-Jesu-Forschung. Strauss' "life" regarded Jesus as a "homo generalis" generating a universal incarnation of God in every human being. Strauss thus moved away from the supposition that the Christian principle could be identified with the historical individual Jesus and reduced christology to the idea of God-manhood, an idea realized not in history, but in an idealized view of humanity. Precisely this turn of the Leben-Jesu-Forschung towards a dissolution of historical positivity, a dissolution undermining the foundation necessary for continuing the quest, was slighted in Schweitzer's treatment of Strauss' life of Jesus research. Schweitzer found in Strauss "also what is historically positive."(92) Yet the very absence of this aspect in Strauss' Leben Jesu was actually the express point of departure for most of the "liberal-positive" "lives" produced in response to Strauss.(93) And against this background Schweitzer's insistence on the "positive, historical aspect" of Straussian life of Jesus research emerged as a carry-over of the positivistic emphasis of the Leben-Jesu-Forschung Schweitzer set out to judge doomed.

This point becomes even more obvious in Schweitzer's critique of the quest's pronounced confidence in the historiographical value of the synoptic sources. In statements coterminous with form critical assertions, Schweitzer shared the form critics' scepticism about the historiographical intention of the Gospel traditionists. But Schweitzer was unable to fully carry out the principles of form critical analysis and relied with his theory of "thoroughgoing eschatology" on a "positive" estimate of the historical value of the Markan tradition. According to Schweitzer, "the eschatological solution ... at one stroke raises the Marcan account as it stands, with all its disconnectedness and inconsistencies, into genuine history."(94) Once again Schweitzer himself thus fell within the circle of the quest's positivistic and biographical assumptions which he set out to undermine. And once more Schweitzer here emerged as a representative of an earlier phase in the quest's view of the scriptural sources.

Schweitzer preserved intact the substantial accuracy of Mark's historical sequence. Schweitzer's exegesis began with the missionary charge in Matthew 10 as the teaching pivot of Jesus life. But Schweitzer immediately placed the charge into the historical framework of Mark 6 in such a way that the return of the disciples emerged as a sequel in time to the missionary charge. In this connexion of the missionary discourse with the disciples' return, the fact that Jesus did "not expect to see them back in the present age" and that "this prediction was not fulfilled" signified "the first postponement of the Parousia" on the precondition that "the missionary charge is historical as a whole and down to the smallest detail."(95) Form-critical and religio-historical questers at the turn of the century, however, were increasingly reluctant to vindicate this "positive" evaluation of the Gospel accounts. To the New Testament exegete K. L. Schmidt, the Markan "framework of the history of Jesus" presented a secondary, literary redaction. "Seen as a whole," Schmidt argued, "there is no life of Jesus in the sense of a history of a life, no chronological outline of the history of Jesus, but rather individual narratives, pericopae, which are set within a framework."(96) In a similar vein Julius Wellhausen's Einleitung in die drei ersten Evangelien rejected any superimposition of a historical scheme. "Mark does not write de vita et moribus Jesu," Wellhausen asserted, "he does not have the intention of making his person clear or understandable."(97)

Schweitzer's account of the Markan narrative, in contrast, chose to attribute the departures from positivistic historiography to Jesus himself. According to Schweitzer, Jesus acted unter the sway of an eschatological, "dogmatic" compulsion and turned his own dogmatism into history. In tracing this eschatological element of the narrative back to Jesus himself, however, Schweitzer bypassed the form-critical and source-critical analysis of the Gospel materials. Contemporary reviewers of the Quest were quick to uncover this striking deficiency in Schweitzer's use of the Gospel sources. The Jesus whom Schweitzer proclaimed as the Jesus of the New Testament, Adolf Jülicher charged, "stood already full grown, before he entered into detailed analysis of the sources."(98) In the "artificial" alignment of the missionary discourse with the disciples' return "the systematician clearly surpassed the historical source critic."(99)

Schweitzer's uncritical "distortion of the Gospel sources" was remarkable in view of the fact that he had developed from the historico-critical school as a pupil of Heinrich Julius Holtzmann. The Quest gave little indication of a thorough application of Holtzmann's insistence on the Gospel of Mark and a collection of sayings as shared traditions used by Matthew and Luke. Schweitzer refrained from relying on Holtzmann's "two document" hypothesis, since the second source Q, made up largely of an unconnected series of individual sayings, did not substantiate Schweitzer's arguments for the "connection of the events of Jesus' life."(100) If the historical connection was retained more faithfully in Matthew than in Mark, the Gospel of Matthew, Schweitzer judged, "should not be explained as a secondary composition based on working the unconnected eschatological sayings into the Marcan framework." Schweitzer was therefore intent on referring merely to "the two oldest Synoptics" and thus once more reverted to an earlier critical phase of the "liberal-positive" quest's evaluation of the sources.(101)

The problematic source critical stance characteristic of the solution of "thoroughgoing eschatology" which Schweitzer carried "to the extreme limit" was precisely what form critical questers sought to remove again.(102) Thus Schweitzer's assumptions were to be challenged head-on by William Wrede's The Messianic Secret, which advanced a live alternative to Schweitzer's history in presenting the second Gospel not as objectively historical, but as a creative theological reinterpretation of history. Drawing on the form critical premise that behind the oral tradition lay the collective consciousness of each Christian community, Wrede insisted that far from presenting a Jesus untouched by ecclesiastical embellishment, the Synoptics, and Mark foremost were impregnated with the theological interpretation of the Christian community and corrected history to suit apolegetic needs. On the basis of this premise, Wrede pointedly raised the issue of the "messianic secret," the idea that although Jesus, who is Messiah, seeks to keep his divine glory hidden, he is nevertheless revealed in secret epiphanies. In Wrede's interpretation, the life of Jesus was not messianic, and Jesus himself never made any claim to be Messiah. The early church, however, believed in this claim, and Mark in turn set out to reconcile the gap between the early church's credo and the actual historical outline of Jesus' ministry.

Mark, according to Wrede, harmonized the historical and "dogmatic" conceptions by investing the non-messianic traditions of the sayings and deeds of Jesus with a messianic cast and by describing the earthly Jesus as the Messiah who was anxious to keep his messiahship a secret.(103) Jesus' injunction to silence when he is acclaimed as Messiah (Mark 8:30) or Son of God (Mark 3:12) presented accordingly not historical statements but rather literary devices by which the Gospel tradition sought to resolve the incongruity between the church's belief in Jesus' divinity and Messiahship and the fact that this belief did not surface until after the resurrection.

Mark thus emerged not as a historian, but as a dogmatician whose Gospel was saturated with the theological beliefs of the early Christian community. "As a whole," Wrede argued, "(his) Gospel no longer offers a historical view of the real life of Jesus. Only pale residues of such a view have passed over into what is a supra-historical view for faith. In this sense the Gospel of Mark belongs to the history of dogma."(104) There was thus hardly any possibility of reaching back to the authentic Jesus.

Schweitzer was aware that Wrede significantly contributed with this reading to the defeat of the quest's conception of the Gospels as historiographical presentations of the life of Jesus, and, more positively, also called attention to the early church's shaping of tradition in the kerygma. Yet Schweitzer did not recognize the full extent of Wrede's findings. Ignoring the essential insight of Wrede's form criticism, Schweitzer rejected Wrede's attack on the historicity of the Markan record. For Schweitzer, the eschatological conception of Jesus resolved the riddles of the Gospel accounts, in particular those of "unconnectedness" in Mark's account. "The want of connection," Schweitzer argued, "the impossibility of applying any natural explanation is just what is historical, because the course of the history was determined, not by outward events, but by the decisions of Jesus and these were determined by dogmatic eschatological considerations."(105) Thus while for Wrede the messianic secret exemplified the unhistorical character of the Markan tradition, Schweitzer discovered in Jesus' eschatology the "dogmatic" element of the Gospels and presented this "dogmatic" element as proof of the historicity of the Markan account. Faced with the grand disjunction of either "the eschatological solution, which immediately raises the undiluted, disconnected and contradictory Marcan version to the level of history, or the literary solution which regards that which is dogmatic and unfamiliar as an interpolation of the evangelist himself into the tradition of Jesus," Schweitzer stayed firmly on the side of the uncritical option. Schweitzer was confident that the eschatological expressions which the synoptic tradition accorded to Jesus were authentic and "that the oldest synoptics transmit real history."(106) It was on this issue that Schweitzer remained closest to the rationalizing "lives" in the mode of H. E. G. Paulus' history of Jesus which the _Quest_ rejected as futile. But it was also on this issue that Schweitzer eventually was to witness the triumph of Wrede's "literary solution" over his own.

2. From Harmonies to Lives

According to Schweitzer, the quest did not stem from a "purely historical interest" but rather from an antidogmatic bias which moved the questers to use the Jesus of history "as an ally in the struggle against the tyranny of dogma."(1) Yet this emphasis also flowed from an exegetical and expressly hermeneutical point. Exegetically, the quest broke down the dams which sheltered the tenets of scriptural infallibility and authenticity by applying the methodology of a critical historiography to the Gospel tradition. The quest thus ran counter to the Protestant scholastic doctrine of verbal inspiration and the inviolability of the Gospel texts. Hermeneutically, this was to follow a path which began with the pre-critical harmonies of Tatian and Augustine and led to the "lives" of Reimarus, Franz V. Reinhard and Johann Jakob Hess. In the course of the development from harmonies to "lives," this path culminated in the evaluation of biblical texts in terms of references extrinsic to the texts themselves. As an index of precritical interpretation of biblical narratives, the Gospel harmonies had remained firmly implanted in the coherence of grammatical or literal reading with historical reference and the identity of the historical Jesus with the 'dogmatic' or 'theological' Christ, the Christ of faith. Nineteenth century advocates of the quest, in contrast, tended towards extreme literalism. The rationalistic and "liberal-positive" questers devalued figural interpretations of Jesus' life. To them, the Old Testament could not be asserted to prefigure the New. The biblical accounts instead increasingly became a problem to be interpreted within an extra-textual historico-critical context.

The hermeneutical issue, as it arose with the quest, took shape under the growing emphasis on the discontinuity between the Christ of faith and the Jesus of history. On this count, Schweitzer judged that Reimarus had made an undisputable and original contribution to the Leben-Jesu-Forschung. "Before Reimarus," Schweitzer insisted, "no one had attempted to form a historical conception of the life of Jesus."(2) Yet Reimarus was not as original as Schweitzer made him out to be. The quest for the historical Jesus did not begin with Reimarus nor did it end with Wrede. Reimarus' Jesus research, with its insistence on the dichotomy between the Jesus of history and the Christ of faith, presented in fact a halfway-house between the English and the Continental side of the deist controversy. On the English plane, the deist controversy focused initially on the nature and possibility of historic revelation, then moved on to a scrutiny of the specific Christian and biblical claims of historical revelation and in this way to an examination of the factual claims of revelation as embodied in miraculous history.(3) The ground was thus prepared for Reimarus who turned away from evidentialist apologetics and the historical argument for the resurrection, thereby banishing the miraculous from the realm of history and desupernaturalizing the life of Jesus.

On the Continental plane and particularly on Reimarus' own native ground, the impact of deism was more directly related to the exegesis and interpretation of biblical texts and was therefore almost exclusively internal, that is literary-historical. Here too, then, the locus of the deist impact was a shift in scriptural interpretation which called the veracity of the texts into question and reversed the figural framework of exegesis, only to hand over to biblical hermeneutics the pronounced distinction between the meaning of the text and its reference.(4) Reimarus' concern with the Jesus quest was thus part of a seminal reversal in the interpretation and application of Scripture, a reversal which shaped the formal development of the quest 'from harmonies to lives' and provided a standard point of departure for the quest's historico-critical exegesis.

I

The exegetical procedures of the pre-Enlightenment church did not approach the New Testament accounts with the intention of recovering a biography of the historical Jesus against or apart from faith in the Christ of Christian theology. In the church of the Reformation, the Jesus of history and the Christ of faith were held together by the assertion that the earthly Jesus was present in the proclamation of the church. The "Christus praedicatus" was on one level with the history of the earthly Jesus, an alignment reinforced by the emphasis on Scripture as the rule and norm of faith. Within the context of the Reformation principle of the centrality of Scripture as well as with regard to the Reformers' general assertions concerning the divine origin of Scripture and biblical authority, the basic premise of "sola scriptura" was therefore essentially a "solus Christus." Christ was asserted to be the "punctus mathematicus sacrae Scipturae." To "take Christ from the Scriptures" was to affirm as the centre of Scipture the living Christ. The biblical accounts had their own integrity, yet they were Christo-centric: "The entire Scripture deals only with Christ everywhere."(5)

This principle of the Christo-centricity of Scripture established biblical unity by appeal to the precritical system of figural interpretation which helped set the standard for biblical interpretation until the emergence of the critical Jesus quest. The figural framework of exegesis entailed historical interpretations of both Testaments: The events of the New Testament were asserted to foreshadow and justify the events of the Old, "having a shadow of good things to come, and not the very image of those things" (Hebr 10, 1). This prophetic pattern furnished the basis for interpreting certain figures and events of the Old Testament as typological prefigurations of Christ. Thus Adam, according to Romans 5, 14, "is the figure of him that was to come." The exegetes of the pre-Nicene era used the prefigurative and structural possibilities of this typological framework to underline the consistency between the two Testaments, "bestowing as it were the signature of God on his work and guaranteeing the authenticity of Scripture."(6) Patristic exegetes, most notably Origen, modified the direction of typology and moved the figural mode away from its original exegetical purpose. Many Old Testament events were in this context read as prefigurations of the life of Jesus, while the direct fulfillment of messianic prophecy in the life and ministry of Jesus was held to justify the validity of his person and work. The typological framework here neither entailed allegorical exegesis, which treated past events as symbols to be spiritually interpreted, nor literal exegesis concerned only with the past historical events themselves; rather, typology referred to the establishment of historical connections between an event in the Old Testament and a similar event or person in the New Testament.(7)

The Protestant Reformers, in adopting the figurative mode of exegesis, drew back to the patristic practice of drawing analogies between types and antitypes of the Two Testaments and reinforced the prevalence of the typological device of Scripture as a mode of signification in which both type and antitype were historically real poles. The Reformers expressly departed from the medieval devaluation of the historical and spiritual signification of the Old Testament in which typology was subsumed under the heading of allegory and stressed instead the characteristic emphasis of typological exegesis on historical adumbration and fulfillment. In this historical emphasis of typology, the prophetic dimension, which pertained to Christ, was located squarely in the realm of literal meaning. The focus of signification towards which all the signs in Scripture pointed was Christ: he is "the goal of all things and the thing signified through all other things."(8) But the mode of this "signifying" was not a separable spiritual or prophetic sense; rather, it stayed as an integral part within the literal-historical meaning of the text. The typological formula was thus distinctly set apart from the medieval exegesis of Old Testament which afforded mere shadowy types of spiritual substance.(9) Reformation exegetical practice expressly endorsed the historical authenticity of Old Testament events as being confirmed within the temporal history of Jesus. The types and figures were not fictitious but rather to be accepted literally. The issue of historical positivity, crucial to the development of the quest, was irrelevant.

Embedded in the typological canon, the pattern of prophecy and fulfillment demonstrated the messianic character of Jesus. Where the literal meaning of different narratives went astray, typological readings served to harmonize discrepancy. Luther's affirmation that Christ was the "punctus mathematicus sacrae Scripturae" and the Calvinistic emphasis on the pattern of promise and fulfillment were informed by the belief that the literal meaning of the biblical narratives and their references to actual events cohered. This assumption of a natural coherence between literal sense and external reference became programmatic for the Reformers' approach to Scripture and was responsible for the characteristic distance of Reformation exegesis to the historico-critical tools on which the quest relied. The exposition of Scripture as practised by the Protestant Reformers did acknowledge a historical process in the formation of Scripture, but in a pre-critical approach, in which the literal explicative sense was identical with the actual historical reference, exegetes remained committed to Scripture's "grammatical," literal sense as a starting point for exegesis. The primary concern was what the biblical accounts literally said; their authority was not dependent on their proposition of valid historical claims. For Calvin, "it (was) the first business of an interpreter to let the author say what he does say...."(10) This premise expressly precluded the emergence of a critical approach to Scripture interpreting biblical accounts, as the questers did, in terms of criteria external to the accounts themselves. Historico-critical research in the mode of the quest was only possible when Christian tradition was no longer held to be a direct self-evident authority and when the explicative sense of biblical narratives and their factual historical reference were separated from one another in an independent focus on the issue of the positivity of historical revelation.

Consonant with the hermeneutical block against the development of the historico-critical method characteristic of the quest was a doctrinal impediment. The controversy about the christological conceptions regarding Christ's presence in the Eucharist reveals that the tilt of the Luther's thought was to the side of a christology "from above," to an old "high christology" that was in accord with the Chalcedonian formula. Luther's version of christological dogma was a twofold confession, conforming to the Chaledonian creed: "two natures united in one person," "God and man in one person", "very God and very man."(11) The subject of this dogma was the historical person of Jesus who "worked, suffered and died like any other human being." But the emphasis on the historical life of Jesus here was conceived under the doctrine of the "communicatio idiomatum" which focused on the unity of the divine-human person and allowed for no autonomous study of the historical Jesus.(12) Throughout, the Jesus of history and the Christ of faith were held together in an alignment within which the development of the quest could not take place. The quest, in contrast, went to the other extreme, taking Jesus as its guide without reliance on a christological formula concerning his "person." Over against the dual-sided christology, the issue to be clarified in the quest was the relation of christological creed to actual events - the issue of historicity positivity.

On this 'historical' count, too, the quest was confronted with a theological impediment. Luther did not regard the actuality of salvation as an index of the preparatory works of moral or religious efforts or the incalculable endeavors of historical criticism. The devaluation of the biblical picture of Jesus Christ over against the historical Jesus of the Leben-Jesu-Forschung would have presented in this context a denial of the gospel of justification by faith. According to this doctrine, faith was not merely a "notitia" and "fides historica," but rather "fiducia." Faith could not be made dependent upon an authority extrinsic to the Gospel itself; certitude of faith did not flow from historically assured factuality of belief. Luther accordingly set "the preaching of Christ" above the description of his "works and miraculous deeds:" to know Christ's "works and history does not yet constitute knowledge of the right Gospel, for it does not tell you that he overcame sin, death, and devil." This certitude was based not in the history of Jesus "but in the arrival of the voice that says: Christ shall be your own with his life, teaching, works, death, resurrection, and everything he is, has, does, and accomplishes."(13) The critical "lives," in contrast, presented none of this. The quest rendered faith expressly dependent on historical inquiry and took up the novel task of asking faith about the basis of its certainty.

The lack of a historico-critical perspective and the absence of a doctrinal framework demanding a distinction between the Jesus of history and the Christ of faith were clearly reflected in the form of the pre-quest "lives." The late fifteenth and entire sixteenth centuries witnessed a striking resurgence of Tatian's and Augustine's Gospel harmonies, the _Diatessaron_ and the _De consensu Evangelistarum_. Questions of historical positivity and credibility lay outside the range of the harmonies' interest which revolved around the issue of chronology. In the harmony format, the scriptural accounts of the life of Jesus remained firmly implanted in the identity of grammatical or literal sense with historical reference. The Gospels were asserted to provide the normative presentations of the life of Jesus, yielding in the case of Matthew and John eyewitness reports and in the case of Mark and Luke close interpretations derived from the Evangelists' association with the earliest disciples.(14)

In the sudden flood of Gospel harmonies during the sixteenth century, the subordination of the historical question to theological and devotional interests continued. The alignment of New Testament exegesis with dogmatics here was broad enough to harbor the insight that "the Gospels follow no order in recording the acts and miracles of Jesus...."(15) But despite the insights of Calvin, Luther and Bucer that the Evangelists' narratives followed no fixed chronology, most harmonists assumed that the Gospels furnished a full and reliable account of the life of Jesus which was to be reconstructed by arranging the four Gospel texts into an unilinear narrative.(16) Taking the possibility of the repetition of recorded words and acts of Jesus for granted, Osiander's Gospel harmony therefore "combined" "the Gospel story ... according to the four evangelists, in such a way that no word of any of them is omitted, no foreign word added, the order of none of them is disturbed, and nothing is displaced...."(17)

The cohesion between the literal meaning of biblical narratives and their reference to actual events characteristic of the harmonies provided the decisive point of departure for a group of seventeenth century critics who shifted ground from the old alternative of harmonies to a critical appraisal of the reliability of the Gospels. In Hugo Grotius' _Annotationes ad Vetus et Novum_, in Spinoza's _Tractatus Theologico-Politicus_, Richard Simon's _Histoire critique du texte du Nouveau Testament_ and Jean LeClerc's _Harmonia evangelica_ one finds stirrings towards principles of an interpretation at once rationalistic and historical-critical. This approach involved the break-up of the harmony between the literal meaning of the biblical narratives and historical reference and thus set, at the point of the interpretation of biblical narratives, the stage for a critical approach to the life of Jesus. A century before Johann Semler and two centuries before Julius Wellhausen, these critics engaged in a systematic antisupernatural criticism of the Bible which made landmark contributions to Pentateuchal studies. Thus Spinoza's rejection of the Mosaic authorship of the Pentateuch and his description of the corpus of writings from Genesis to II Kings as a work composed of various contradictory elements compiled by the Scribe Ezra remained valid for subsequent commentators.(18) Similarly, Richard Simon's assertion that the Pentateuch in its extant form could not be the work of Moses and represented instead the result of a long process of compilation and redaction of annals and laws by public scribes became an accepted view among subsequent Old Testament exegetes. In essentials, Simon anticipated the later documentary hypothesis according to which the Pentateuch arrived at its final form as a result of the interweaving of several continous narrative threads.(19) In a more developed form, Jean Astruc's analysis of a literary pattern in the Pentateuch related to the variant use of the divine names set forth a criterion of source division which laid the foundation for the four-source theory - two Elohistic writers, one Jahwistic and the Deuteronomic.(20)

These exegetical and literary insights steadily fed into the powerful solvent of historical criticism, reflected in the new premise that criticism should not shirk bringing the scriptural accounts under rational scrutiny. The Gospel accounts were "not written by revelation and Divine command," Spinoza claimed, "but merely by the natural powers and judgment of the authors." Hence it was "scarcely credible that God (could) have designated to narrate the life of Christ four times over, and to communicate it thus to mankind."(21) This premise entailed the freedom to scrutinize the accounts by questioning the traditional ascriptions of authorship and date, by examining the formation of the canon, and by determining a reliable text. The effect, though rarely the intent of these procedures was to reduce inspiration to a minimum and to challenge the unitary canon. The significance of the biblical critic's enterprise for the life of Jesus student consisted in the abandonment of the claim that the veracity of the life of Jesus narratives was guaranteed by the authority of Scripture itself. This authority was increasingly displaced by the insistence upon the primacy of the simple "grammatical" meaning of the text in its own right, independent of any directly convincing authority and verifiable by appeals to external testimonies of authority and date. "To expound Scripture" it was now regarded as "absolutely necessary to compose a true History there of, that thence, as from sure principles, (one could) by rational consequences collect the meaning of those who were Authors of the Scripture...."(22)

With this new emphasis on "true History" there was no going back to the precritical stance, as biblical critics steadily moved into the arena of historical criticism. Lacking the restraints of the Reformers' appeal to the perspicuous authority of Scripture, the first advocates of biblical criticism built their position on an epistemological framework within which the events of the Gospels were asserted to be on one level with the ordinary events of history. In this context, Grotius' De veritate religionis Christianae provided a striking case in point. Grotius argued to the historical existence of Jesus by alleging the credibility of the apostolic testimony of the miracles and resurrection of Jesus.(23) But Grotius did not conclude more than general historical reliability. There was no need for him to regard the biblical writings as inspired revelation, according to the premises of plenary inspiration. The problem of inspiration was with Grotius not primary, yet all the more emphasis was placed on genuineness and authenticity. The point was to show on the basis of historiographical principles that miracles were established by the same canon of history which rendered the facticity of ordinary events probable. "In this manner," Grotius' Swiss follower LeClerc argued, "we may be fully assured of the Truth of the History of the New Testament; that is to say, that there was a Jesus who did divers Miracles, who was rais'd from the Dead, and ascended up into Heaven...."(24)

Grotius' focus on the "sensus verus" established the realm of historical reference as an autonomous temporal framework and subordinated literal meaning under the dominance of the external categories of historical veracity. For Grotius, the authority and trustworthiness of a historical account were ensured by the testimony of reliable witnesses. In the same vein, the scriptural narratives of the life of Jesus were judged against the extratextual category of the testimonies' credibility. With this reliance on extra-textual criteria of authenticity, Grotius not only undermined the uniqueness and univocity of the scriptural record but, more importantly, also brought the factual question about the historical accuracy of the scriptural accounts into further prominence.

Consonant with this was another hermeneutical point. The increasingly sceptical interrogation of the historical reliability of scriptural accounts contributed forcefully to the decline of the typological framework as a hermeneutical option. The subordination of the literal sense of the accounts under the categories of historical veracity undercut the typological conception of the scriptural account of Jesus' life as ordered and interconnected by prefigurative levels of meaning. The main Protestant tradition adhered to the coherence of literal meaning and historical reference in the biblical writings. This was no longer valid for critics of the caliber of Simon and Grotius. Grotius equated meaning with reference to independently verifiable fact claims. Similarly, Simon broke up the cohesion of literal meaning and historical reference by proposing historical explorations of material commonly relegated to the supernatural and by regarding the meaning of a biblical text as conditioned by the interpreter's presuppositions or situation-in-life.(25) For the typological framework the implications of this position were shattering. The continued insistence of the early advocates of biblical criticism upon the primacy of the simple "grammatical" meaning of the text in its own right counteracted the very force of typology as a device unifying the two Testaments. If Grotius' and Simon's assumptions were correct, then the accepted notion of an Old Testament filled with anticipations of Christ was no longer valid. An interpretation involving the distancing between literal or verbal and historical meaning inevitably reversed the tendency toward typology both as a literary and historical device.(26)

The repercussions of the shift away from the typological framework were felt everywhere, but the historical applications were to become most obvious in the life of Jesus literature. In the later half of the eighteenth century, the critical tradition of inquiry into the meaning of the biblical texts pushed the question about the historical factuality of the scriptural accounts of the life of Jesus into the foreground. And here, contrary to the typological canon, historical fact, literal sense and religious truth needed to be shown to coincide, as the interest in the factuality of the biblical records increasingly grew into an independent critical inquiry which carried all the marks required to develop it into historico-critical method.

Significantly, the discussions of the reliability of the biblical accounts focused on the claims about historical revelation, above all the claim that Jesus was the Messiah. This discussion entailed two issues: first, the question of the trustworthiness of accounts involving miraculous history and secondly, the much more important issue of whether it was really the meaning of the pertinent scriptural texts "that the salvation of man depends not only on what Jesus tought and did, but on all this as an expression of the presumably indispensable fact ... _that_ he existed as the Son of God incarnate."(27) It was this latter issue of positivity that became central to the quest and was to lead in the hands of Strauss and Bruno Bauer to the extreme position of a denial of the historicity of the Gospel tradition.

II

The work of the first biblical critics offered striking evidence of the growing prevalence of the factual approach to the problem of the truth of Christian religion. In the hands of Simon, Spinoza, Grotius and LeClerc the interpretation of biblical narratives pertaining to the life of Jesus was increasingly subsumed under historical-critical explanations which equated meaning with actual extra-textual reference. This inquiry, however, represented only isolated beginnings of a movement towards a more critical examination of the scriptural accounts and lacked systematic development as well as a new historical and philosophical synthesis. This synthesis, which was to give another decisive impulse to the historical study of the life of Jesus, was provided by the amorphous yet influential movement of deism. Doctrinally, deists were affiliated with the Arminian, semi-Pelagian position; philosophically, the deist position derived from an insistence on the primacy of reason over revelation and affirmed the theological premise that natural religion was self-sufficient. Hence there was "Nothing in the Gospel Contrary to Reason, nor above it."(28) In denying the necessity of revelation, deists from the 1670s to the 1730s emerged as hostile ridiculers of the authenticity of Old Testament predictive prophecies and of the New Testament miracles and resolved to base their theology on the belief that unaided reason could work out for itself the whole of the contents of religion.

On this issue of the inherent rationality of historical revelation the English deist controversy burst into the open with the appearance in 1696 of John Toland's Christianity not Mysterious and undertook to eliminate the "mysterious" from the foundations of the Christian religion. Toland sought to exclude everything beyond the scope of reason: "No Christian Doctrine can properly be call'd a Mystery."(29) The "mysteries" of Christianity were to be ascribed to the intrusion of pagan ideas and priestcraft. Articulating the full implications of this premise with regard to Scripture, Toland insisted that it would be "blamable credulity" to acknowledge "the divinity of Scripture or the sense of any passage thereof without rational proofs and an evident consistency."(30) Revelation, then, possessed no authoritative character; it was to be evaluated solely on the basis of content, and no supernatural sign could supply the 'credentials' or guarantee of its authenticity.

Toland's rejection of the "mysteries" of historical Christianity explicitly turned upon the veracity of the scriptural testimony of the man Jesus. Toland's Nazarenus, Or, Jewish, Gentile, and Mahometan Christianity identified the Nazarenes or Ebionites with the first Christians and asserted the authenticity of their view of Jesus over against the scriptural testimony with its allegedly unhistorical presentation of a supernatural portrait of Jesus. Throughout, Toland credited the historical Jesus with having purged religion from distorting "ceremonies" and "mysteries." The historical outline of Jesus' life thus emerged as that of a teacher of common sense, divested of miracle as proof for the uniqueness of his person and the validity of his message.(31)

Toland in this way prepared the ground for a central premise of the quest, the assumption of a discontinuity between the original ministry of Jesus and the teaching of his disciples. The historical Jesus, Toland insisted, was a moral teacher and not a personal center of faith; "he fully and clearly preach'd the purest Morals ... and ... stripp'd the Truth of all those external Types and Ceremonies which made it difficult before...." It was only later that Christianity was distorted by "mysteries" and "external types and ceremonies."(32) Toland was joined in this critique by Thomas Morgan's The Moral Philosopher, which equated the teaching of Jesus with the "lex naturae" as opposed to the perverted ceremonies of the apostles and the early church. Thomas Chubb followed suit with his The True Gospel of Jesus Christ, asserted which contrasted in a similar way the teaching of Jesus with the personal opinions of the apostles. "Christ preached his own life ..., and lived his own doctrine." Moreover, "the gospel which Christ preached ... was plain and intelligible," Chubb argued. Doctrines relating to his preexistence, divinity or to the trinity were merely "private" opinions of the apostles.(33)

The deist insistence on the discontinuity between the teaching of Jesus and the creeds of early Christianity went hand in hand with the devaluation of the evidentialist use of miracles and prophecy. The deist break with the use of miracles as "evidences" upon which faith in revealed religion could be founded showed at two key points. It was manifest, first, in the proposition of comparisons between the miracles of Jesus and those of other religious leaders. The express purpose of these comparisons was to demonstrate that Christians employed inconsistent standards in assessing the authenticity of miracles narratives. Thus Thomas Woolston claimed that if the three miracles of the raising of Jairus' daughter, the widow of

Nain's son and Lazarus "had not been reported of Jesus, but of Mahomet, in the same disorder of time, by three different historians, you would presently have scented the forgery and imposture."(34)

Second, the break with the evidentalist framework was apparent in an epistemological argument against the possibility of miracles. This argument assumed that "miracles ... destroy the foundations of truth and certainty" and are not "as capable of the same evidence as other historical facts."(35) Thus, working sequentially through the more notable miracles of Jesus, the changing of water to wine, the resurrection of Lazarus, the feeding of 5000, the curse of the fig-tree, the transfiguration, Woolston's Discourses demonstrated that "the literal history of many of the miracles of Jesus, as recorded by the Evangelists, does imply absurdities, improbabilities, and incredibilities."(36) On the exegetical plane, therefore, "the History of Jesus's Life, as recorded in the Evangelists," was for deists merely "an emblematical Representation of his spiritual Life in the Soul of Man; and his Miracles (were) Figures of his mysterious Operations." Moreover, the miracles of Jesus constituted "no Sanctuary." They "were never wrought, but are only related as prophetical and parabolical Narratives of what will be mysteriously and more wonderfully done by him."(37)

A similar position lay behind the deist argument over the fulfillment of Old Testament prophecy in the New Testament. This issue had traditionally involved a demonstration of the messianic character of Jesus, but by the eighteenth century, the pattern of prophecy and fulfillment had taken on an even heavier argumentative task.(38) The vindication of the prophecy-fulfillment pattern was now also asserted to validate the predictive accuracy and supernatural character of the prophetic literature. To prove the argument from prophecy valid was therefore, deist critics around Anthony Collins argued, to say that "Christianity is invincibly establish'd on its true Foundation." However, "if the Proofs for Christianity for Christianity from the Old Testament be not valid, ... and the Prophecies cited from thence be not fullfill'd; then has Christianity no just Foundation...."(39) Examining the concept of fullfillment in central passages of Matthew's account, Collins in this way severed the Old Testament from the New and undertook to demonstrate that the scriptural account of the life of Christ did not present a literal fulfillment of Old Testament prophecies. Collins thus struck at the foundation of one of the main buttresses of Christian evidentalist apologetics generally used to demonstrate the veracity of the Christian claim to divine authentication. The scriptural account of the life of Jesus and the claim to divine authentication now stood opposed.

This opposition, central to the development of the quest, was closely tied to the alignment of hermeneutics with historical criticism. Prior to the deist controversy, the "history-likeness" of the biblical texts was commonly equated with the actual historicity of the accounts. Thus, a discussion of the putative claims of historicity amounted to a discussion of the question whether the narrative set out to be a historical-type text or an allegory whose meaning went beyond the historical form. Consequently, to identify an account as a historical-type text was also to assert its historicity. It seemed inconceivable to assert that the text was of the historical genre and yet false. Deist critics such as Collins, Woolston and Chubb, however, held that the factual, historical claim of the scriptural accounts was the true meaning and that the narratives were nevertheless improbable, if not deceitful.

This position further corroborated the break-up of the old congruence between literal explicative meaning and historical reference and reinforced the prevalence of the factual approach to the problem of the truth of Christianity. But more importantly, the new mode of aligning explication with historical reference also strikingly carried the structural components needed to develop the quest. It now seemed that large segments of Scripture could not be assigned a lasting, pristine religious or moral sense. Among these segments were the synoptic accounts of the life of Jesus. These accounts, too, quite independent of their referential sense, could not lay claim to significant and abiding religious sense. With developments such as these in biblical interpretation, deist criticism went far beyond the issue of the accurate fulfillment of prophecy and the historicity of miracles. The question at hand was in effect an inclusive problem of the historical basis of religious belief, and here lay the problem which the deist critique of revelation handed over to the quest.

If in this respect deists developed tendencies, inherent in earlier interpretation, towards the historical criticism of the quest, they nevertheless sought to escape from the destructive force of the "absurdities, impossibilities, and incredibilities" involved in the miraculous evidences by resorting to an allegorical interpretation of Scripture. "Christianity is wholly reveal'd in the Old Testament, and has its divine Authority from thence, ... but it is not literally, but mystically or allegorically reveal'd therein." Collins' "Discourse on the Grounds and Reasons of the Christian Religion" reiterated with regard to the argument from prophecy this possibility of a symbolic fulfillment through the life of Jesus. The prophecy embodied in Jes. 7, 14, Collins argued, is "not being fulfill'd in Jesus according to the literal, obvious, and primary sense of the words, as they stand in Isaiah; It is suppos'd, that this, like all the other Prophesies cited by the Apostles, is fulfill'd in a secondary, or typical, or mystical, or allegorical sense...."(40)

Unlike Woolston's insistence on the Gospel narratives as "a System of mystical Philosophy or Theology" to be credited with historical positivity, Collins' argument regarding the "mystical or allegorical sense" of the prophecy-fulfillment scheme asserted "that the prophecies did not refer to the narratives," and "not that the prophecies were absurd, or the Gospel narratives absurd...."(41) This position represented a reactionary tendency in biblical criticism, a return to the analytic methods of medieval exegesis and its devaluation of the historical dimension of typology. The most immediate consequence of the deist preference of allegorical explanation was the lack of a critical exegetical apparatus. This deficiency clearly spilled over into the life of Jesus literature and left significant marks. Thus, from the form of the life of Jesus productions the critical impulse of deism was hardly noticeable. The harmony pattern continued to follow the lines charted out earlier in the parallel column format of Osiander's <u>Harmoniae evangelicae</u>. The harmonies by Samuel Craddock, John Austin and Matthew Hale aimed at resolving contradictions and adhered to the literal truth of the Gospel texts. The time-honoured precritical pattern in this way persisted intact, untouched by the historico-critical implications of the deist controversy.(42)

III

The deist critique of revelation called forth a deluge of apologetic replies which turned to history in order to build an apologetic bulwark in defense of supernatural revelation, a bulwark later used by Christian apologists against the quest for decades to come. The attempt to counteract the deist attack on Scripture and to justify revealed religion generally developed along two lines. Extreme evidentialists like Samuel Clarke, Thomas Sherlock and Samuel Chandler drew back to the historical factuality of the biblical accounts. Theirs was an intellectualist or conceptualist theology using categories for interpreting revelation which stayed within the confines of supernatural rationalism and rested the case for Christianity in the trustworthiness of the evangelists, the arguments from miracles, the fulfillment of prophecies and the correspondence of types and antitypes in the Old and New Testaments.(43) The evidentialist theology embodied in Thomas Sherlock's The Trial of the Witnesses of the Resurrection of Jesus and Samuel Chandler's The Witness of the Resurrection of Jesus Christ Reexamined expressly assumed the traditional natural theology common to medieval scholastics in order to strengthen the factual case for Christianity. This evidentialism affirmed that the Messiahship of Jesus still "must be try'd by the Words of Prophesy" and resorted to general rational criteria extrinsic to the prophecy-fulfillment pattern and miraculous history in order to validate Jesus as divinely attested.(44) In all of this, hardline evidentialists were convinced that confidence could be restored in the historical basis of Christianity and that "the Miracles ... which our Saviour worked were sensible Demonstrations of his divine Commission."(45)

Alongside hardline evidentialists who regarded miracles as irrefragable evidences of divine activity, the deist critique of revelation also prompted the emergence of a qualified evidentialism that continued in the tradition of Locke and culminated in the moderate empiricism of Samuel Butler's Analogy of Religion. Moderate evidentialists like Bishop Benjamin Hoadly, John Leng, John Conybeare, James Foster, and Arthur Ashley Sykes were not prepared to argue that the proof afforded by miracles was logically coercive. Within their qualified framework, moderate evidentialists held that the scriptural record was an authentic genuine history and that miracles should be made to stand upon the same foot of historical evidence as any other past event.(46) Butler's critically important Analogy of Religion went on to demonstrate the congruence of miracles with natural religion. Whereas deist criticism had insisted on natural religion as the rational alternative to Christianity, Butler showed that those who discovered evidences of divine activity in nature had to grant a similar significance to Christian revelation. On this basis, revelation could be considered as wholly historical, and against this background of "scripture-history" moderate evidentialists were able to bypass the difficulties of demonstrating from history the historical veracity of Christianity.(47)

With David Hume's critique of miracles the empirical foundations of the evidentialist position collapsed like playing cards quickly to be stacked against the quest. The main thrust of Hume's challenge was not focused on the possibility of miracles as such, but rather on the positive experiential verification for belief. Hume's position thus stemmed from the discussion that had been in the foreground since the deist controversy - the debate over the truth-claims of Christianity as a historical religion based on supernatural events. Hume's own case amounted to a frank rejection of the evidential value of miracles and prophecy fulfillment. Hume assumed that the "laws of nature" were established by uniform experience. A miracle constituted in Hume's canon accordingly "a violation of the laws of nature; and as a firm and unalterable experience has established these laws, the proof against a miracle, from the very nature of the fact, is as entire as any argument from experience can possibly be imagined."(48) Subtly translating this claim that experience validated testimony into the erroneous claim that the absence of an experience invalidated testimony, Hume cogently laid down as a "general maxim, that no objects have any discoverable connexion together, and that all the inferences, which we can draw from one to another, are found merely on our experience of their constant and regular conjunction."(49)

The extent to which Hume's rejection of reliable testimony was willing to go in denying that miracles could occur carried his critique against the heart of the historical method. In the Humean canon, immediate impressions did not yield any necessary connection or causal force. "The reason why we place any credit in witnesses and historians," Hume asserted, "is not derived from any connexion, which we perceive a priori, between testimony and reality...."(50) The evidence for miracles did not even begin to approach the proof of the inviolability of nature's laws. Time would come when this rejection of historical testimony was to play into the hands of the Straussian "lives." For the English deist tradition, however, Hume set the development of critical "lives" back to the time before Simon and Grotius. Hume's rejection of all grounds for an a priori theology was uncritical. With one stroke it moved away from biblical criticism and rendered the authentic text irrelevant. Hume's canon precluded belief in any testimony counteracting uniform past experience. The scriptural accounts of miracles and fulfilled prophecies "(contained) nothing but sophistry and illusion," irrespective of emendations performed by biblical criticism.(51) The link between the methods of historico-critical principles and the historical Jesus quest was thus for the most part lost.

Studies of the life of Jesus produced in Hume's time carried the distinct marks of this development and did not reflect the historico-critical impulse set forth by the incipient forms of biblical criticism. Edmund Law's _Discourse on the Character of Christ_, George Benson's _History of the Life of Jesus Christ_ and John Fleetwood's _Life of our Lord_ set out to counteract all suspicions that the apostles "acted as detestable and villainous" tricksters and sought to establish the apostles' credibility as "twelve good men".(52) Following an evidentialist apologetic, these "lives" conformed to the Gospel narratives in the manner of the traditional harmonies by fusing the scriptural words of Jesus with the biographers' own narratives. Questions of historicity and authenticity here were of no relevance. The historio-critical thrust of biblical criticism remained undeveloped. Nor were the christological debates or matters of creed of any major interest. In view of the challenge of the authority of revealed religion, these issues receded behind the need to demonstrate the adequacy of the credentials of revelation.

The cards were further stacked against the historico-critical and "anti-dogmatic" impulse of the quest by the tradition that was spurred to renewal by Hume's critique - the supernatural rationalism of the post-Lockean theology of "evidences" represented in the writings of the "evidential school" of Cambridge theologians: John Hay, Richard Watson and, most notably, William Paley, whose _Evidences of Christianity_ occupied a seminal place in the Cambridge curriculum through courses on "Christian evidences."(53) Paley's conceptual framework for the existence of miracles continued in the tradition of Clarke and Chandler and worked out an elaborate demonstration that the miracles and prophecies recorded in scripture were in fact historically true. "There is," Paley argued, "not such an antecedent improbability in the Christian miracles as no human testimony can surmount." Confronted with the choice whether to reject them as an "idle report" and "frivolous account" or regard them as divine authentications of Jesus as the Messiah, Paley affirmed the belief that the miracles presented external proofs validating the truth and supernatural origin of Christian teaching.(54)

Scriptural accounts presented in this context a collection of data, a factually verified record of historical events. Confronted with the argument that was to develop into a key issue of the quest, namely the possibility that the original narrative of Jesus' life might have been fabricated by copyists and historians, Paley categorically declared: "the apostles ... could not be deceivers. By only not bearing testimony, they might have avoided all their sufferings, and have lived quietly." Moreover, to Paley the conclusion was inevitable that if twelve men of "probity and good sense" were tortured for reporting "an account of a miracle wrought before there would not exist any skeptic in the world, who would not believe them, or who would defend such incredulity."(55) Faced with a similar possibility of the contradictory nature of the evangelists' accounts, Reimarus was to question the historical reliability of the scriptural record of the life of Jesus. Paley, in contrast, withdrew to the tradition of research concerned with the transmission and authenticity of the Gospels in order to affirm the historical reliability of the scriptural accounts. An encyclopaedia of esoteric details, Paley's section on "The Authority of Historical Scriptures" in the Evidences concluded that the Gospels "actually proceed from the authors whose names they bear" and faithfully record the divine attestations of Jesus as the Messiah.(56)

Paley's evidentialist procedures retained the premise that, as in science, harmony, consistency, and simplicity were the most reliable signs of authenticity. But Paley carried this argument only to the point of demonstrating that the scriptural accounts were consistent. Once this was proven, the argument was completed. Paley was not concerned with some reconstructive context to which the accounts referred and which rendered them valid. Since the evidences were regarded to have a natural claim upon man's assent, there was no need for a truly critical interpretation. This lack of a historico-critical perspective showed clearly in the life of Jesus literature. James Macknight's Harmony of the Four Gospels, a study including paraphrases and emendations, and the harmonies by Robert Willan and James White conformed to the pattern established by Tatian and Augustine in providing a uniform, consistent presentation of the course of Gospel history.(57) Later harmonies like Edward Greswell's Harmonia evangelica evinced the very same continuity with the traditional harmony pattern.(58) Once more, then, the impact of the historical criticism of deism and early biblical criticism did not take effect. The life of Jesus literature was still very far away from the self-conscious and rationalistic historico-critical exegesis characteristic of the quest.

IV

While deism subsided in England with the resurgence of the apologetic evidentialist tradition, it won a ready hearing on the Continent. A German version of Tindal's Christianity as Old as the Creation became available in 1741. Secondary literature on deism included Baumgarten's eight volume Nachrichten von einer Hallischen Bibliothek, Trinius' Freidenkerlexikon and Thorschmid's four volume account of English deism in Versuch einer vollständigen Engellandischen Freidenkerbibliothek.(59) These studies fell on a ground hostile to deism in its adherence to the intellectualism of Christian metaphysicians of the caliber of Christian Thomasius and Christian Wolff. It was in Wolff's Christian rationalism that the general view of Christianity as a reasonable and neccesary supplement to natural religion continued. Drawing on the rationalist tradition of Leibniz, Wolff constructed his mentor's philosophy into a system that was consonant with the English theology of evidences from Samuel Clarke to William Paley. Against this evidentialist background the deist critique of revelation provoked two religious reorientations with consequences for hermeneutics that played directly into the emergence of the historical Jesus quest. Faced with the deist critique, the supernaturalist camp represented by Kleuker's Neue Prüfung und Erklärung der vorzüglichsten Beweise für die Wahrheit und den göttlichen Ursprung des Christentums and Gottfried Less' Wahrheit der christlichen Religion drew back behind Wolff, adopting a historical apologetic for the Christian faith which affirmed the historical meaning of the text and its literal truthfulness.(60) On the basis of a wealth of responses from English apologists to deist criticism made available in translations, most notably Leland's Abriß deistischer Schriften, supernaturalists erected an apologetic bulwark that was parallel to the extreme evidentialism of Clarke and Chandler. Acknowledging responsibility to a court of general credibility, supernaturalists defended the authenticity of the historical referent of Scripture - the factual history to which the texts were demonstrated to refer faithfully.(61)

Confronted with the deist critique, another group of critics shifted away from Wolff into the rationalist theological position of neology. The leading neologians, J. S. Semler, A. F. W. Sack in Berlin, J. F. W. Jerusalem in Brunswick and later J. D. Michaelis and J. G. Eichhorn in Göttingen, moved to a liberal Christianity which preserved the concept of revelation as a divine disclosure of truth but restricted the content of the disclosure to what was in accordance with reason. "All revealed religion," Lessing described their position, "is nothing but a reconfirmation of the religion of reason. Either it has no mysteries, or, if it does, it is indifferent whether the Christian combines them with one idea or another, or with none at all."(62)

The neologians' theological empiricism refused to accept as historical anything contrary to reason, but this refusal went hand in hand with the interest to preserve intact the religious truth expressed in the narratives. This concern added an important new strain to the change in the hermeneutical approach to Scripture provoked by the deist controversy. Over against the supernaturalist affirmation of both the historical meaning of the text and its truthfulness, Collins, Woolston, Annet and Chubb had asserted the factual, historical claim as the true meaning of the biblical narratives and demonstrated this claim to be factually erroneous. This critique of the factual veracity of "scripture-history" was unacceptable to the neologist camp. The men around Semler formulated a new hermeneutical approach which preserved the religious truth of the biblical narratives. Critical of both deism and supernaturalism, the neologists sought to detach the religious meaning of the texts from the historicity of the events related. Their position thus remained distinctly within the biblical and theological disciplines to affirm Christian belief and "differed from the English deism ... in not regarding the Bible as fabulous in character. ... (Neologist) rationalism denied only the revealed character of scripture, and treated it as an ordinary history...."(63) Accordingly, neologists viewed themselves for the most part as defenders of the Christian religion on a middleground between deism and supernaturalism which re-interpreted the relation of Christian religion and the biblical narratives so that the truth of Christianity was no longer tied to the historical truth of the narratives.

With regard to the relationship between historical criticism and hermeneutics, the neologist position presented a significant advance over the English evidentialist camp. In England, the interest in the historical factuality of the biblical narratives of the life of Jesus far outweighed the interest in scriptural interpretation in its own right. Studies of scriptural interpretation and application, of literary-historical origin and development here could not truly grow against the predominance of the evidentialist discussion, with its focus on the question of the putative factuality of biblical reports. Unlike the English critics' overbearing focus on evidences for or against the truth of the factual claims of revelation, the neologist discussion of the fact or credibility issue was much closer aligned with the broader hermeneutical issue of the meaning of biblical texts. Debates over the factuality of the scriptural record of the life of Jesus here went hand in hand with debates over the principles of interpretation in which the Gospel accounts became both narratively and historico-critically part of a tradition of critical commentary.(64)

As the methodology of interpretation, as "the theory of the rules of the interpretation of Holy Scripture," hermeneutics was distinguished from exegesis which referred to "the real execution or application of these rules ... on real passages and books of Holy Scripture."(65) Questions of "grammatical" analysis were primary for the methodology of interpretation advanced by Semler and Ernesti, but like the "historical" approach, they were duty-bound to the premise that "the verbal sense of Scripture must be determined in the same way in which we ascertain that of other books."(66) Explorations of the literary character of texts increasingly played a considerable part in the context of this premise. Thus, by reiterating the close relationship between poetry and religion, Herder's The Spirit of Hebrew Poetry drew attention to the biblical narratives as literary documents and expressly slighted questions of factuality. The "poetry" of the narratives did not entail "falsehood," Herder claimed, for the significance of the poetically composed "symbol" was "truth."(67) In the same measure as this question of the "falsehood" or "authenticity" of the biblical narratives was severed from a consideration of the literary value of the accounts, the appreciation of the narratives as a literary-critical genre increased and reinforced the hermeneutical focus on the relation of the structure of the text itself to the process of interpretation.

Against this background, the influence of a hermeneutical orientation and a literary-critical focus appeared in England comparatively slight. Critics were not oblivious of the literary character of the biblical narratives, but given the predominance of evidentialist concerns, everything conspired to prevent the development of a sustained literary-critical tradition of the biblical texts. Robert Lowth's 1753 lectures on the Sacred Poetry of the Hebrews separated biblical verse from prose according to the principle of parallelism and demonstrated the artistic value of the biblical texts. Lowth's 1779 commentary on Isaiah, however, showed him still immersed in an apologetic defense of his literary-critical stance against charges of subverting the "certainty and authenticity" of Scripture.(68) No substantial reconstruction of biblical interpretation, then, had occurred. Critics still rehearsed the traditional canon of the evidences of revelation which located the references of the biblical narratives outside the texts and, in contrast to the neologist interpreters, continued the evidentialist debate without the aid of the discipline of hermeneutics penetrating into the meaning of the texts themselves.

The point of this difference can be appreciated fully when seen in light of the course from harmonies to "lives." While in England the evidentialist interest in the historical factuality of biblical narratives served to perpetuate the traditional harmony pattern, the neologist re-interpretation of the relation between historical truth and 'universal' religious meaning moved on two counts towards the critical research of the quest. First, the distinction between the historicity of the narratives and the universal religious meaning, between the "historical, relative" "Holy Scripture" and the "Word of God," succeeded in re-affirming the religious relevance of the biblical narratives against the deist attack on historical positivity while maintaining at the same time the claims of historical criticism.(69) "The most important factor in hermeneutical skill," Semler's canon asserted, "is that one know the linguistic usage of the Bible quite sure and exactly, and also distinguish the historical circumstance of a biblical discourse and be able to reconstruct them."(70) Semler thus set on a course of biblical criticism that further affirmed the alliance of historical criticism with hermeneutics, an alliance in which the elucidation of the meaning of biblical narratives according to the general criteria of grammatical and linguistic analysis went hand in hand with an analysis of the narratives' historical context. A few decades later, the Tübingen critics were to proceed from there, removing the New Testament accounts from their splendid isolation, placing them now in the history of primitive Christianity and assessing the reliability of their extra-textual reference.

Second, the neologist hermeneutical canon also moved towards the historico-critical procedures of the quest by drawing on and extending the ancient principle of accomodation. The evangelist-historians, neologist claimed, had adjusted their accounts to the prevailing Jewish thought forms. As time-conditioned accounts, the biblical texts thus defied the appeal to the doctrine of inspiration as guarantee of the pristine authority of Scripture. The accounts did not embody universally valid histories, but rather flowed from a specific historical context. It was therefore the task of the exegete to penetrate beneath the historically conditioned language of Scripture to its timeless truth. Once again, this procedure contributed to set historical criticism on a course which subordinated the interpretation of the scriptural narratives of the life of Jesus to historical reference. The quest was soon to go on from there and assert that the primary reference of the life of Jesus narratives was historical rather than "ideal."

Yet, however forcefully the neologist position pointed ahead to the critical quest, it still looked backward to premises which blocked the development of the quest's historico-critical tools. Neologists did not advance a purely historical approach to the internal development of Christianity. On the contrary, the neologist theory of accommodation in effect implied an idealistic interpretation of Scripture. The miracle accounts were conceived of as allegories, intended to convey ideal truths which transcended the historical particularities of the narrated events. In this way neologists were able to shift the emphasis from positivity grounded on the suspension of natural laws to 'moral significance.'(71) The task of exegesis was accordingly to recover the 'moral truths' intended by the New Testament writers, but embedded in historical terms transparent of something more than mere factual and empirical ends. The religious truth embodied in the narratives was in this way treated as independent of any confirmation by a scrutiny of the life of the historical Jesus. This position rendered the historico-critical inquiry into the life of Jesus virtually superfluous. The neologists saw no real need to produce a critical life of Jesus; rather, in transposing the significance of the revelatory quality of miraculous evidence to its religious truth content, the neologists flanked the horns of the central historico-critical issue of the quest.

Moreover, the neologist camp was also not concerned with the historical problem in its own right. Semler's interpretation was 'historical' in a twofold sense. It regarded the scriptural accounts as 'historical' in that they presented records of past events, but it also treated them as 'historical' in that they presented a particular "historia," the history of the life of Jesus. This history, however, constituted a history "pro nos;" the issues of soteriology and christology were integrated into the "notitia historiae."(72) The locus of faith, in its validity and certainty, was not to be sought in a "historia externa" but in the saving activity of the Christ of faith. Against this application and extension of the Pauline doctrine of justification, the autonomous focus on the narrated events of Jesus' life appeared illegitimate. For this latter focus on the "historia externa" of the life of Jesus another impetus was required, one to be provided by H. S. Reimarus' life of Jesus research.

Until the appearance of Reimarus' _Wolfenbüttel Fragments_, the neologist and supernaturalist camps had drawn on the correlation between the veracity of the scriptural accounts and the truth of Christianity. Supernaturalists had assumed that the veracity of the biblical accounts was an index to the truth of the Christian religion. Stated in explicit terms: Christianity was true if the Gospel narratives offered accurate accounts. Neologists, in contrast, had rendered the truth of Christianity independent of the veracity of the biblical narratives, thus opening the way to a critical investigation of the claims of probability and historicity. This investigation could lead to a denial of the factuality of the events narrated, but this finding left the religious significance of the narratives virtually untouched. What set Reimarus apart was a negative targeting against both fronts, that of positivity and that of religious significance. Drawing on the arsenal of deist arguments against revealed Christianity, Reimarus' _Fragments_ urged the rejection of the historical veracity of biblical accounts in order to discredit the religious significance of the narratives as supernaturally caused occurrences. And from these attacks upon the historical reliability of scripture it was only a short step to the assertion that the possibility of a universally acceptable revealed religion was unsupportable.

Behind Reimarus' attacks upon historically grounded beliefs of Christianity lay a polemic rejection of the citadels of orthodox faith - miracles and prophecy. Reimarus key text was the resurrection narrative. "The guard story is very doubtful and unconfirmed," Reimarus judged, and it is very probable that the disciples came by night, stole the corpse, and said afterward Jesus had arisen." "The disciples' testimony is both inconsistent and contradictory, and the prophecies appealed to are irrelevant, falsely interpreted and question-begging."(73) Reimarus concluded his attack on the historicity of the accounts with a classic deistic application of the tactics of the courtroom to the positive, evidential value of the resurrection: "I am definitely assured that if today in court four witnesses were heard in a case and their testimony was as different in all respect as if that of our four evangelists, the conclusion would at least have to be made that no case could be constructed on such conflicting testimony."(74)

The initial assumption of Reimarus' critique was that "the four evangelists comport themselves as historians who have drawn up the record of the essentials of what Jesus said and did." On the basis of this pronounced primacy of the 'sensus historicus,' Reimarus was able to reject the second pillar of evidentialist apologetics, the argument from prophecy. According to Reimarus, the New Testament writers' use of prophecy was "merely adapted through quibbles, and in reality (referred) to quite other things.(75) The historical reference of prophecies, Reimarus argued, was in fact very different from the one ascribed to them. Scriptural accounts were to be understood in the sense intended by its authors, and not in the light of conception derived from the New Testament. In the typological prophecy-fullfillment pattern, by contrast, the texts were embedded in an unbroken web of meaning which connected the events and persons in the two Testaments and brought the author and his audience together under the aegis of the same salvation history. For Reimarus, this framework was no longer valid; he considered the intention of the human author as an independent factor and treated the scriptural accounts as the products of genuine and specific historical conditioning.

In shutting the door to the argument from prophecies and miracles, Reimarus raised afresh the classical issues of the deist controversy. Reimarus' banishment of miracles and prophecies from history echoed Collins' attack on the evidential value of prophecy as well as Woolston's rejection of the historicity of the New Testament miracles. But Reimarus surpassed the critical position of the deist movement with a contribution that would become commonplace for the nineteenth-century quest; he removed the theorizing upon the person of Christ, excised the miraculous accretions to the Gospel accounts and thus inevitably opened up a distinction between the original aims of Jesus and the teaching of the apostles. This distinction had already been voiced by English deists before Reimarus - Toland and Chubb had claimed to recover the original Jesus as a staunch adherent of natural religion, subtly distorted by early Christianity - at one decisive point, however, Reimarus went expressly beyond the deist model: his "life" portrayed Jesus as a political messiah proclaiming an eschatological kingdom, the first "systema," and as a worldly deliverer whom the disciples later exalted to the status of a spiritual ruler.

The messianic idea in this first "systema" was identical with the political-Davidian notion of the messiah as a worldly liberator who failed in his mission of establishing a theocratic kingdom. Reimarus' narrative uncovered, however, that the gospel accounts were written from the standpoint of yet another "system" and one so distorting "the character and articulation of the history" as to preserve only the remnants of the "first systema." The evangelists were narrating their accounts for a doctrinal purpose, and - on this point Reimarus was persistently provocative - these "historians" were goaded into fabricating the resurrection legend and into launching a new missionary propaganda so that Jesus' original teaching still made sense after his inglorious death. By creating such legends, the disciples legitimated their ambitions to establish a new royal kingdom which they had hoped Jesus would found.(76)

With this reading, the authority of the revealed word was unrelentlessly disowned, while Christian teaching concerning the life of Jesus stood reduced to "false" "axioms," "full of contradictions, entirely opposed to all rational religious ideas."(77) Moreover, with this reading the figure of Jesus was deprived of all christological significance and reduced to a code of morals. For Reimarus, not christological dogma but the historical Jesus, and only this figure represented the standard of belief. Whereas for the orthodox supernaturalist camp Christ represented a saviour, a redeemer, Reimarus slighted the saving activity of Jesus. For Reimarus, faith was 'reasoned belief' in a historical narrative, a "fides historica" which called for critical inquiry into philology and history. The christological dogma of Christian faith presented in this context merely a process set in motion after Jesus' death, a substitutionary creation replacing the expectation and content of "parousia." "The new system of a suffering spiritual saviour," Reimarus insisted, "was invented only because (the disciples') first hopes had failed."(78) The notion of a "spiritual redemption," of a saviour who "was bound to die in order to obtain forgiveness for mankind," the dogma of the two natures, the Trinity, the atonement - these doctrines all constituted a creation of the disciples as a means of coming to terms with the difficulties posed for them by Jesus' death.(79)

V

Lessing's publication of the Reimarian Wolfenbüttel Fragments precipitated a pamphlet war cutting through both the supernaturalist and neologist camps which inflicted upon Lessing a prohibition to publish any further theological work. The terms of the supernaturalist camp represented by J. D. Schumann, the director of the Hamburg Lyceum, J. M. Goeze, the chief pastor of Hamburg, and Johann Heinrich Ress, the superintendent at Wolfenbüttel, were those of the apologetic evidentialist tradition. Confronted with an express rejection of the factuality of the events of the life of Jesus, supernaturalists reverted to the reaffirmation of positivity, the factual foundation of Christianity.(80) The accounts' meaning flowed from the miraculous occurrence character of the narratives, and this, supernaturalists claimed, showed at one particular point of Jesus' history, the resurrection narrative. Supernaturalists accordingly were not likely to produce complete histories of Jesus' life, and focused instead on the issue of the "genuineness" of Jesus' resurrection, constructing elaborate "lives" in order to reconcile contradictions in the scriptural accounts. J. H. Ress' Die Auferstehung Jesu Christi ohne Widersprüche gegen seine Duplik, C. F. Wiegmann's Versuch eines Beweises der Religion aus der Auferstehung und J. F. Plessing's Die Auferstehungsgeschichte unseres Herrn Jesu Christi were based on the premise that the acceptance of the Christian religion was on one level with the acceptance of external historical facts. The authors agreed "that the reports which we have of ... miracles are as reliable as historical truths ever can be."(81)

In the neologist camp around Semler a different strategy prevailed. When confronted with Reimarus' critique of historical Christianity, neologists reinforced the position they had developed against the deist critics by separating the truth of Christianity from the historicity of the events related in Scripture. With regard to the resurrection narrative, this position entailed that rather than evidential value, the appeal to the doctrine's own inner truth provided the proof of the resurrection. Belief in the resurrection was grounded in the truth of Christ's teaching and not dependent on the historicity of the report of these teachings. Neologists thus reversed traditional evidentialist apologetics. Empirical evidence for the historicity of the resurrection was no longer asserted to yield the proof of the divinity of Christ's doctrine; rather, the doctrine by its self-evident truth now served as the basis for belief in resurrection irrespective of contradictions and inaccuracies in the accounts. The resurrection was not based "on this or that set of circumstances." Even after a historical-critical scrutiny of the narratives "the ground of the Christian religion stands now as before."(82)

The rift which the neologists wrought between the truth of Christianity and biblical historicity was further reinforced by the literary critic, theologian and historian who put forth Reimarus' work. As editor of the Wolfenbüttel Fragments, G. E. Lessing advanced a crucial hermeneutical point which counteracted the assumption that religious truth depended upon the historicity of certain alleged events attested in Scripture. Lessing strikingly changed the terms of the debate by driving a wedge between religious truth and historical fact and by demonstrating the irrelevance of all factual, historical considerations to the question of the truth of Christian religion. The scriptural tradition, Lessing maintained against Goeze must be explained according to its own "internal truth." Christianity is true because of its rational "inner truth" and not because it has some historical verification in external evidences.(83)

Lessing subtly grasped the implicit nominalism of the orthodox view with its absolutistic authoritarianism and its insistence on external proofs, and asserted on his part Christianity's reliance on a truth which stood in need of no external confirmation. Against this concept of an "inner truth," the Gospel narratives constituted merely a prerequisite territory ensuring the communication of this "inner truth" and not the indispensable basis of its authority. Essential religious truth was by its nature not empirico-historical but rather independent of factual, historical considerations. The issue of the facticity of historical revelation no longer assumed a primary position.

Embedded in this view was a hermeneutical premise which entailed a significant step ahead over the neologist position, one which not only separated the truth of Christianity from the historical reliability of the biblical narratives but also recognized the problem with the traditional proofs from prophecy and miracle, namely that the report of a fulfilled prophecy or miracle was not itself a fulfilled prophecy or miracle. Lessing acknowledged "in short (that) the letter is not spirit, and the Bible is not religion. Consequently, objections to the letter and to the Bible are not also objections to the spirit and to religion." The biblical narrative as history, the scriptural record with its historically reported religious events is only the "Buchstabe," the vehicle of "Religion." The historical-critical approach to the scriptural accounts therefore cannot undermine faith. The religious content of the Bible is independent of its historical origin for its relevance, and a rejection of the Bible's historicity does not amount to a rejection of the religion it contains: "religion was there before a Bible existed. Christianity was there before the evangelists and apostles wrote."(84)

Correlative to Lessings's argument for not accepting historical proofs of a religion as valid was a second point: One cannot, Lessing argued, infer from historical events a trans-historical meaning. "Geschichtswahrheiten" are "zufällig" as opposed to "Vernunftswahrheiten" which are "notwendig." Historical truth by its very nature excludes 'necessity' and is incapable of being demonstrated and demonstrating valid theological truth. This rejection of "historische Wahrheiten" as a revelatory medium of the divine, issued in an open attack on the certainty of the historical proofs of Christian revelation. Lessing rejected a Christianity which was grounded in a supernatural revelation asserted to be historically and logically certain. Historically founded faith validated by evidences from miracles and prophecies was merely contingent and with regard to its hermeneutical status uncertain. "The problem is," Lessing realized,"that this proof of the spirit and of power no longer has any spirit of power, but has sunk to the level of human testimonies of spirit and power."(85) The empirico-historical content of a past historical event cannot be a valid basis of the value of revelation for an individual living in a later historical period.

More broadly, the attempt to base one's beliefs upon the historical constituted for Lessing also an illicit jump from one cognitive category to another. The crucial point, Lessing argued, was that contingent historical truths cannot be the basis for necessary truths of reason such as the truths of natural religion. This was "the ugly, broad ditch" Lessing was not able to "get across, however often however earnestly (he) tried to make the leap." "Zufällige Geschichtswahrheiten können der Beweis von notwendigen Vernunftswahrheiten nie werden." "That is: accidental truths of history can never become the proof of necessary truths of reason."(86) The cognitive "leap" between empirically grounded assertions and rationally grounded assertions entails a logical and categorical difference. Historical truth is incommensurable with the self-evident power of purely rational argument.

Lessing's key example was the divinity and metaphysical sonship of Christ. "That the Christ, against whose resurrection (one could) raise not important historical objection, therefore declared himself to be the Son of God; that his disciples therefore believed him to be such," this Lessing "gladly believed from (his) heart." But what he could not do was "to jump with that historical truth to a quite different class of truths."(87) To infer from historical truths other truths of a different class amounted to a category mistake. For Lessing, history qua historicity could not be the mediator of supernatural revelation; history could not prove that Jesus was the divine Son of God.

This position entailed important repercussions for the interpretation of Reimarus' "life." Reimarus' "life" targeted first and foremost against the historical roots of Christianity. Reimarus demonstrated that Scripture as the source of divine revelation contained discrepancies and inaccuracies, and he thus forcefully invalidated the claims of historically grounded faith. Lessing granted the essential validity of Reimarus' critique, but he found a means to defend Christianity on a 'formal' level against Reimarus' attacks. With Lessing, "the resurrection of Christ may still be true, even if the accounts of the evangelists contradict one another." "The Christian religion remains the same: it is only," Lessing argues, "that I want to separate religion from the history of religion. It is only that I refuse to regard the historical knowledge of its origin and development; and a conviction of this knowledge, which positively no historical truth can yield, as indispensable. It is only that I consider objections made against the history of religion as irrelevant; whether they can be answered or not."(88)

Lessing's position poignantly recapitulated an important phase in the development of critical "lives." In the course of the movement from harmonies to "lives" the question of the facticity of the Christian revelation was now distinctly set apart from the truth of Christian religion. Even if Reimarus' objections were irrefutable and the factual claims of the scriptural narratives of the life of Jesus unsupportable, Christianity could be credited with an intrinsic truth that was safeguarded from all efforts at historiographical penetration. Faith henceforth stood insulated from historical inquiry, the results of historical inquiry being immaterial to the validity of religious truth.

This conception of the content of biblical history as merely contingent and approximate created a situation in which the critical quest was inevitable. Against Lessing's rejection of history as the ground of religious "inner truth" the orthodox defense of history as a revelatory medium receded. The wedge between "inner truth" and historical foundation dealt a deathblow to apologetic evidentialism and liberated the "lives" after Reimarus from the external authority of Scripture. Moreover, in arguing that the truth of Christian faith did not depend on the historical verification of the Gospel texts, Lessing struck upon the theme which was to be echoed by generations of questers in the rationalist camp around Friedrich Schleiermacher. Affirming the devaluation of historically mediated truth, the "lives" following Schleiermacher's canon were to launch out on various attempts to relocate the foundation of Christian faith by appealing to inner experience as a principle of religious certainty in a theology of religious experience that played on Lessing's separation of Christian religion from its historical or factual foundation.

In yet another way Lessing was harbinger of methods and conclusions of questers to come. In separating the question of the truth of Christian religion from the question of the facticity of the Christian revelation, Lessing further helped to prepare the ground for the objective, historical scrutiny of the scriptural accounts of the life of Jesus. With regard to this scrutiny, Reimarus had fallen behind the course undertaken by the neologist camp around Semler. Reimarus had launched his critique of historical Christianity without developing a critical methodology to work through the Gospels. Neologists in turn fervently objected to the lack of source analysis in Reimarus' work, but all too often neologists themselves remained purely harmonistic in exegesis and cherished biblical inerrancy highly enough to ascribe contradictions and inaccuracies in the text to lack of insight on the exegete's part. It was only after the recognition advanced by Lessing that religious truth did not depend on the literal truth of the biblical narratives that historico-critical "lives" acknowledging the revelance of a critical evaluation of the authorship, date and character of the source documents could make their way.

In viewing history as an occasion for the communication of religious "inner truth" rather than as the ground of this truth, Lessing set exegetes free to apply source analysis to the critical estimate of Jesus. Lessing's own source critical theory, expounded in the "Neue Hypothese über die Evangelisten als blos menschliche Geschichtsschreiber betrachtet," envisaged a primitive Hebrew or Aramaic Gospel of the Nazaranes which lay behind the canonical Gospels. Lessing asserted Matthew to have rendered the Aramaic Gospel of the Nazarenes into Greek extracts.(89) Mark and Luke, Lessing argued, merely fell in line. Thus Luke relied on "the Hebrew document, the Gospel of the Nazarenes" and appropriated its contents "only in a rather different order and in rather better language." Mark, however, who was "commonly held to be only an abbreviator of Matthew, appears to be so only," Lessing judged, because he drew upon the same Hebrew document, but probably had before him a less complete copy."(90) This hypothetical reconstruction amounted to an open rejection of the source critical tradition which held that "Mark when writing his book had in front of his eyes not only Matthew but Luke as well...."(91) Here was also a clear break with a tradition that had focused on chronological differences between the Gospels and attempted to harmonize the chronology of John with that of Matthew, Mark and Luke, arguing that narrative agreement signified a double and triple witness to the apostolic Gospel. Acknowledging the futility of all attempts at harmonization, Lessing no longer set out to combine the four narratives into one, but instead studied their relation with each other.

With Lessing, this synoptic interest was inextricably tied to a christological point, one which reiterated Reimarus' distinction between the "religion of Christ" and the "religion about Christ."(92) "The former, the religion of Christ," Lessing argued, "is that religion which as a man he himself recognized and practised" and "is therein contained in the clearest and most lucid language." The latter, however, "is so uncertain and ambiguous, that there is scarcely a simple passage which, in all the history of the world, has been interpreted in the same way by two men."(93) This was a restatement of deist criticism of the historical Jesus, but this reassertion now expressly aligned christological speculation about the relevance of Jesus with source critical analysis.

3. The Kernel and the Husk

In the harmonies of the life of Jesus, the Christ of faith persisted in the formula of "the two natures in one person," independent of concerns with historical verifiablity. The critical "lives", however, which were produced in the aftermath of the Fragments controversy sought to roll back and peel off all interpretations and dogmatic overlays in order to establish a picture of Jesus as a thoroughly humanized figure, a profound religious visionary and a pioneer moral teacher. To Franz Volkmar Reinhard, Ernst August Opitz, Johann Gottfried Herder und H. E. G. Paulus it was the "personal" life of Jesus, not the dogma of the incarnation that was identified as the moving force behind the Christian community. Thus Herder's Vom Erlöser der Menschen reiterated that the dogmas and creeds of the church constituted merely external signs. At issue for Herder, however, was "the gospel itself; this concerns the teaching, the character of Jesus and his work...."(1) The register of "lives" which appeared after the Fragments controversy accordingly rejected an ontological christology and focused instead on the teaching of the historical Jesus taken in isolation - the "kernel" - against which miraculous history and christological dogma were rejected as the "husk."(2)

The "kernel" and "husk" issue extended to both supernaturalist and rationalist theologies dominating the institutional landscape of the universities which were slowly taking new shape in the aftermath of the Napoleonic wars. Students who went to Halle, Jena and Göttingen received a critical rationalizing training, while those who went to Leipzig and Altdorf were exposed to the teaching of the Rosenmüllers and J. P. Gabler, who continued to proceed on the assumptions of eighteenth-century neology along the lines charted by J. G. Eichhorn and J. D. Michaelis. At Tübingen, rational supernaturalism enjoyed official status under the leadership of the biblical literalist Gottlob Christian Storr. Advocates of the supernaturalist camp also included members of confessional orthodoxy which, at its most rigid, eschewed entirely the historico-critical method and saw the role of biblical scholarship as simply that of defending objective authority represented by the infallible Bible and the theology of Scholastic Protestantism. Confessional orthodoxy of this more uncompromising variety had a notable representative in Ernst Wilhelm Hengstenberg, professor in Berlin, from where adherence to strict Lutheran orthodoxy and the emphasis on older theories of biblical inspiration and authority disseminated to Königsberg, Rostock and Erlangen.(3)

The "kernel" and "husk" issue did not only refer to the liberal practice of eliminating the eschatological "husk" from the ethical "kernel" of Jesus' message, as Schweitzer claimed in his account of the quest. Steering between both rational and supernatural camps, Schleiermacher re-examined the problem of the "kernel" and the "husk" in a striking shift of emphasis from the external to the internal in which the significance of Jesus was vindicated by an appeal to an internal miracle within the religious consciousness of the Christian.(4) Contrary to rationalist and supernaturalist presuppositions, the specific content of Christian faith was thus asserted to exist immanently in the consciousness of the subject.

Only an echo of this revision of traditional apologetics was heard in England at the opening of the nineteenth century. Biblical criticism here had hardened down to a mere restatement of Paley's evidentialism and rested content with external "proofs" of Christianity.(5) And yet, even before Schleiermacher officially entered the English theological scene with Connop

Thirwall's 1825 translation of Schleiermacher's Critical Essay on the Gospel of St. Luke, an anti-evidentialist theology worked under the tutelage of Samuel Taylor Coleridge's critique of historical apologetics to undermine the contentions of the school of Paley. Coleridge offered a new conception of biblical authority and religious truth which incorporated what Schleiermacher's spiritual epistemology had begun to explore. With Schleiermacher, Coleridge did not regard miracles as a proof of divinity and affirmed Christianity as a "life and a living process" to which external "evidences" were merely an "accompaniment," an appendage. "Miracles (were) parts of ... Religion and Object of Belief, not the Grounds of it.(6)

In abandoning the apologetic status of miracles as "evidences," however, Coleridge did not find a distinct place for the historical Jesus. Coleridge was unwilling to acknowledge intrinsic revelatory significance unless there existed a "bond or common term between the operation of Christ at extra, and that of the indwelling Saviour."(7) This "bond" was for Coleridge tied to the historical Jesus, but unlike the rationalist Leben Jesu researchers, Coleridge did not actually work his way back to this figure through historical criticism and relied instead on the present activity of spiritual apprehension. As a result, no counterpart to the historico-critical thrust of the rationalist camp of the Leben-Jesu-Forschung emerged. The link with this camp came from a very different source, the anthropocentric utilitarianism of Jeremy Bentham, whose study on Not Paul, but Jesus of 1823 reconstructed a moral and religious teacher bearing the marks of the rationalist Leben Jesu reconstructions.(8) But what was lacking in this Jesus portrait geared to ethical utilitarianism was an appreciation of historico-critical procedure in its own right. Authentic and complete knowledge of the historical Jesus remained subordinated to the kind of knowledge provided by the external "evidences" of revelation.

On the hermeneutical plane of the Leben-Jesu-Forschung, by contrast, Schleiermacher's view of Jesus as the expression in human life of the immanent divine reality carried exegesis further against the typological framework of prefiguration and historical adumbration. With Schleiermacher, authority shifted to the subjective inwardness of the believer, to an experiential context external to the scriptural accounts. Once this point was made, the meaning of the text could no longer be asserted to be identical with the text. The text had to be assigned meaning in a mode other than factual reference.(9) On the christological plane, Schleiermacher's subjectivistic emphasis developed christology along the line of his concept of Christ as the "Urbild" of a perfect "God-consciousness," the original image mediating the divine.(10) Steadily coming under the ban in this experiential idealism were key doctrines of traditional historic christology, the pre-existence of Christ, the atoning death and the miraculous evidences of the deity of Christ. Throughout this critique, the overriding premise remained unchallenged: the ideal "kernel," Schleiermacher averred, could be hypostasized in a particular individual, that is the historical figure of Jesus could be assigned the prerogative of being the perfect revelation of the "archetypal" "God-consciousness."(11)

In challenging this archetype christology, Strauss' Leben Jesu was led to call into question the historical object of faith and thus changed the state of the problem at stake in the quest. With the early questers, the theological endeavors concentrated on recovering the historical figure of Jesus of Nazareth. With Strauss, the problem of reconstruction became one of the relevance of the individual historical figure for the realization of the "ideal." In terms of the "kernel" and "husk" issue, this particular emphasis made Strauss controversial in the 1830s not only because he relinquished the historical positivity of the biblical narratives but also because he focused on the knowability of the "kernel" and suggested that Christian faith could in effect be explained without reference to the historical figure of Jesus. With the introduction of the category of "mythos" as the key to unlock the elusive figure behind and within the Gospel accounts, Strauss undermined the historical basis of the Christian faith and challenged from the outset the historical immanence of the connection between Christ and faith.(12) Given the questionable historical reliability of the Gospels, a life of Jesus ought not and could not be written. The truth of essential religious beliefs was not dependent upon, and could not be verified by reference to the Gospel accounts as historical sources. In striking contrast to Schweitzer's account, the quest was thus confronted with an extreme consequence of the life of Jesus research, one that threatened to dissolve the historical element in religion.(13) With Strauss, the historical person of Jesus underwent an eclipse in importance unknown to Strauss' predecessors. The historical Jesus, the alleged "kernel" of pristine significance behind the "husk," now appeared as yet another "husk" itself.(14)

I

The biographies or "lives" produced under the aegis of the shift from "husk" to "kernel" were diverse, if not contradictory, yet they coalesced in what Schweitzer described as a decisive either-or alternative. The biographers had to choose between options that were "either purely historical or purely supernatural."(15) In describing the first stage of the life of Jesus research in terms of the opposition between "historical" and "supernatural" positions, Schweitzer drew on the two main responses to the critical philosophy of Kant which penetrated most of the theological faculties in the 1790s. The rationalist, "historical" position regarded morality as the highest manifestation of religion and employed "reason" in order to explain miraculous history as natural occurrence. Beneath the "husk" of miraculous accretions there was believed to be the "kernel," the historical Jesus with his Gospel of morality which was strikingly like the kernel in Kant's religion in conforming to the Kantian principle of ethical independence and self-sufficiency.(16)

Behind this allegiance to the Kantian canon stood a more hermeneutical point pivoted between historical criticism and religious apologetics and clearly distinguished from supernaturalist presuppositions. With regard to the Old Testament narratives, G. F. Oehler observed in 1840 of this hermeneutical issue and its exegetical basis: "... there are those who accept the religion of the Old Testament as a fact and who assume, indeed acknowledge and are convinced, that what was believed must also have happened; and there are those who see the content of the Old Testament belief as a product of religious expression whose historical basis must be discovered by means of the critical method, which itself depends upon the assumptions of modern consciousness."(17) Following the former presupposition, supernaturalists around E. W. Hengstenberg at Berlin and G. C. Storr at Tübingen assumed the authenticity of the biblical record as a repository of "divine doctrines and precepts" and attempted to reverse the tide of higher criticism. Over against the historico-critical efforts of the neologist and rationalist camps, supernaturalists affirmed their procedure as historical and objective. "The word Christianity," Storr maintained, "indisputably designates a definite religious teaching whose content ... can be taken for granted beforehand. The content can only be established historically."(18)

At this "historical" juncture supernaturalists pressed for the life of Jesus the point that the divinity of Jesus' history was authenticated by miraculous events and the pristine authority of the New Testament records. The net result of this position was the preservation of the pre-critical, christological interpretation of the two Testaments and with it the harmonists' insistence on the historical Jesus' coherence if not identity with the Christ of faith. If the New Testament record was historically valid, then it followed that the divinity of Jesus and the authority of his miracles were also immune to the strictures of historico-critical inquiry. "The possibility of miracles need not be investigated," supernaturalist insisted, "because one must acknowledge as possible that which is demonstrated by facts."(19) With the neologist and rationalist camps, this defense was judged to be fatally unprepared to deal with historical criticism. Neologist exegetes like Eichhorn and rationalists like H. E. G. Paulus agreed that the narratives of the life of Jesus were grounded in factual historical assertions. But the religious meaningfulness of the narratives was no longer exclusively tied to the texts themselves. Rather, consonant with the seminal re-interpretation of the relation between religious meaning and historical reference in hermeneutics developed by Semler and Lessing, the interpretation of life of Jesus narratives was now also a matter of placing the biblical accounts into an extra-textual world with another story rather than integrating that world into the biblical story.(20)

Both supernaturalist and rationalist as well as neologist positions, then, were logically dependent on scriptural interpretation. A key case in point regarding the life of Jesus was the question of the possibility of miracles, an issue not so much theoretical than of factual inquiry. The immediate problem was whether there were valid reasons for believing in the actual occurrence of the miraculous events as constituting the indispensable validation of the supernatural nature and divine sanction of Christianity. In this context "miracle" involved "an interruption of the natural continuity, dependent of an immanent law, of cause and effect, which is not further explicable by natural causes and which results from an external, intermittently operating causality."(21) Applied to the life of Jesus issue, this premise became for supernaturalist apologists increasingly a troublesome millstone. Deist critics like Hume had rejected miracles as incredible violations of the natural order of experience. In the same vein, Reimarus had uncovered the historical impossibilities of a literalistic acceptance of the miracles narratives and deemed it questionable to rely on the supposedly incontestable historical evidence for miracles. Regarding the account of the crossing of the Red Sea, Reimarus judged that "Moses ... knew well that manna was of natural origin; yet he presented it to the people as food miraculously conferred on them by God.... For it was at all times the characteristic of the Hebrews ... to impose upon all natural things and events in their history the flavour of the divine, ... the supernatural and the marvellous."(22) To supernaturalists, this rejection of the biblical miracles narratives was unacceptable. For the main supernaturalist tradition, miracles constituted immediate, divine interventions in the human history of the life of Jesus. Supernaturalists accordingly strengthened the factual case for Christianity and rested their literalistic interpretations of the miracles narratives squarely on an appeal to the prophecy-fulfillment scheme and the integrity and veracity of the evangelists.(23)

At the other end of the spectrum, 'naturalistic' interpreters of the rationalist camp went to great lengths, some of them ludicrous, to postulate natural occurrence for miraculous narratives. J. J. Hess, F. V. Reinhard and H. E. G. Paulus agreed that the historico-critical method was the basis upon which the "real" nonmiraculous events behind the reported ones were to be reconstructed.(24) Rationalist "lives" in this way inevitably contributed to the general decline of the evidentialists' insistence on the credibility of miraculous history. First to recede was the traditional adherence to the miraculous character of the events. Rationalistic questers of the late eighteenth and early nineteenth centuries were willing to acknowledge the historicity of the events themselves. Rationalists accepted as a fact that the body of Jesus had disappeared from the tomb; they did not question that Jesus had distributed bread to his followers and to the multitude who had gathered to hear him preach. But rationalistic exegesis firmly focused on the "letter" of the scriptural accounts and interpreted their meaning according to the demands of a purely naturalistic explanation, thereby undermining the supernatural status of miraculous history.(25) Thus the feeding of the five-thousand was asserted to result from Jesus starting a chain reaction among his disciples and audience. As for the resurrection, the disciples had simply stolen the body of Jesus or, as another naturalistic version held, Jesus only appeared to have died on the cross, was subsequently revived in the coolness of the tomb and succeeded in escaping from Jewish and Roman authorities.(26)

Rationalistic strategies of interpretation first penetrated into the novelistic "lives" of K. F. Bahrdt and K. H. Venturini, who set out to uncover the Biblical accounts as intentionally deceptive. Venturini's Natürliche Geschichte des großen Propheten von Nazareth, published in a new edition almost annually until well into the twentieth century, presented Jesus as a member of a secret society, the Essenes, whom Venturini asserted to have plotted to convert the Jewish nation to the idea of a worldly Messiah.(27) In the same fashion, Bahrdt's Ausführung des Plans und Zweckes Jesu reduced Jesus to a tool of a secret order of Essenes and regarded the history of Jesus as determined by an Essene strategy to rescue Jewish society from its materialistic and sensuous messianic hopes.(28) Both Bahrdt and Venturini invariably focused on rational criteria compatible with the demand for external verification. Thus the miracles of healing were explained by a constant historical ellipsis: the evangelists omitted mentioning the natural remedies that Jesus employed. Similarly, Jesus' walking on the water was said to have been effected by the use of a piece of floating timber, the feeding of the five-thousand by secret supplies of bread; the raising of the dead by re-animation from coma.(29)

In these explanations, the quest was time and again left with a Jesus whose teaching and religion appeared deducible from general human situation and experience and free from any appeals to supernatural causality. Rationalist questers thus collided head-on with the particularity and uniqueness of the Christ event which Chalcedon had sought to protect. The professed allegiance to the person of the Saviour receded into the background in favor of the adherence to a mere code of morals, a Jesus who proclaimed enobling ethical truths. In the context of the quest, the

Chalcedonian Christ, a single person in whom full humanity and full divinity subsisted, represented a figment of dogmatic overlay and pious imagination. This only corroborated the quest's premise that the dogmatic Christ of faith was to be distinguished from the actual historical personage.(30)

H. E. G. Paulus, Heidelberg Professor of Theology, sharpened the quest's rationalistic thrust to an extreme degree. Examining the New Testament miracles in his life of Jesus, Paulus combined Reimarus' disciple deception theory with the theory of gradual miraculous embellishment. In his reductive, rationalistic account, the miracles of raising the dead were thus interpreted as cases of coma; Jesus' walking on the water as a visual deception, and the feeding of the five thousand as a chain reaction among people sharing their own food.(31) The resurrection and death of Jesus fell into the same category. Here too the evangelists had merely infused natural phenomena with supernatural explanation, when in effect the superficial piercing of Jesus' side was caused by the service of a phlebotomy while the cool grave as well as aromatic unctions ensured the process of Jesus re-animation from a death-like trance.(32)

In evaluating the significance of miraculous history in terms of historical positivity and rationalistic factuality, Paulus' exegesis invariably conformed to the "letter" and narrowed the narrative down to a matter-of-fact kernel.(33) But when drawing back to the "letter," Paulus appealed to historical positivity with a decisive difference. Paulus' rationalistic exegesis demonstrated the facticity of Jesus' existence and his claim to Messiahship relying on external or factual evidence - the miracles events, the probability of Jesus' resurrection, and the general trustworthiness of the scriptural testimonies. But the religious meaningfulness of historical revelation, as opposed to the factual reference or ostensive meaning of the Gospel narratives, was demonstrated in Paulus' "life" on the basis of the category of 'inner sprituality.'(34) Therefore, even if one granted the possibility of literal miracles, this could not ground Christian truth. "The main point is already certain in advance," Paulus reiterated, "that the most inexplicable changes in the course of Nature can neither overturn nor prove any spiritual truth, since it cannot be seen from any event of Nature for what spiritual purpose it should so happen and not otherwise."(35)

Paulus' rationalistic exegesis was on this count at one with neologist interpretation. For Semler, the miracles narratives presented deliberate allegories intended to communicate "ideal" truths and corresponded on the hermeneutical level to the notion of positivity as 'character' rather than physical miracles.(36) Here too, then, external events were read as direct expressions of Jesus' qualitative being. In this vein, Hess' life of Jesus stressed miracles for their moral significance, while E. A. Opitz interpreted miracles events not as accreditations of Jesus' teaching but rather as representations of his "life."(37) In Paulus' exegesis the teaching of Jesus and his religion were in a similar way asserted to be authentic because of their inner reasonablenes rather than any outward evidence. In this context miracles carried the marks of Jesus' personal being and did no longer rest on the systematic violation of immutable scientific law. Miraculous history was to Paulus not based on the disruption of natural law but on the person of Jesus. It was the unique being of Jesus himself in his moral character that was truly miraculous. "Das Wunderbare an Jesus ist Er selbst," Paulus asserted, "The miraculous about Jesus is himself, his pure and serenely holy disposition, but which nevertheless was a genuinely human example for human spirits to imitate and emulate."(38)

With this assertion, the burden of proof completely shifted away from traditional evidentialist apologetics. For the latter, the argument from miracle and prophecy was the key authenticating criterion of the scriptural claim to divine revelation. Paulus ran expressly counter to the direction of this apologetic and rendered miraculous evidence less significant. Paulus' "greatest wish" was that the "views on the miraculous narratives should by no means be taken for the chief matter," since religion "would be empty, if the truth depended on whether one believed in miracles or not."(39) The authority of Jesus of Nazareth as the moral man, the "homo religiosus" and the ethical "example" for man "to imitate and emulate" stood in no need of external corroborations from the arsenal of the "husk."(40)

II

The rationalist devaluation of the "husk" of miraculous accretions framed the theological and intellectual context into which Friedrich Schleiermacher introduced in 1819 his lectures on The Life of Jesus as an innovation in the University of Berlin curriculum. Schweitzer credited Schleiermacher alongside Hase with the creation of the modern historico-psychological picture of Jesus and in this respect as the harbinger of a later phase of the quest.(41) Schleiermacher did not try to find a back door to evidentialist apologetics; at stake for him was "religious consciousness" itself. With Schleiermacher, the import of scriptural narratives ceased to be identified with their factual accuracy and was rooted instead in the religious subject, not in an act of knowledge or willing but only in a moment of immediate self-consciousness or "feeling." With regard to the quest for the historical Jesus, this subjectivistic emphasis did not, after the fashion of supernaturalist and evidentialist "lives," describe the time and place which Jesus held in Christian faith and the influence be exerted over men; rather, Schleiermacher focused on an inward and spiritual criterion - the "personality" of Jesus, his character, his inner life. The validity of the life of Jesus was expressly declared to be independent of historical proofs from miracle or prophecy. These alleged proofs, Schleiermacher argued, were not sufficiently probative to produce faith and in effect presuppose it. Miracles, to Schleiermacher, did not evoke faith. "The true recognition of Christ ... might never be properly based upon them," since Christ elicited faith by direct impression of his person.(42) The divinity of Jesus cannot be experienced physically and objectively as an empirical omnipotence or omniscience as was asserted to be the case of evidentialist miracles. In Schleiermacher's disclination to credit any supernatural breaks in the chain of physical and historical causation with absolutistic value, the external event was replaced by the "spiritual miracle." Miracle was essentially the religious name for an "event." Revelation has not ceased, Schleiermacher averred, hence "everything is a miracle."(43)

However far ahead this position might point in terms of the quest's development, Schleiermacher nevertheless did not completely leave the rationalistic framework of Paulus, Bahrdt and Venturini behind. Schleiermacher's appraisal of the Gospel narratives still looked backward to the rationalistic explanation of miracles and interpreted the calming of the sea storm as a case of prediction and the raising of Lazarus and the resurrection of Jesus as reanimations after apparent death.(44) Yet while Schleiermacher thus relapsed into a rationalistic truncation of the Gospel record along the lines of Reimarus and Paulus, he broke all the more emphatically with the traditions of the harmonists by means of a hermeneutical canon that would eventually carry Schleiermacher also outside the rationalist camp. For the pre-critical harmonist meaningfulness cogently depended on its making ostensive, referential sense as history. This was a "realist" reading which viewed the meaning of the text as arising primarily from the verbal structure of the Bible itself rather than from any reference to an external historical reality. With Schleiermacher, however, meaning was not be located primarily in the work itself; it had to be found somewhere else, in the self's involvement in theological reflection and experience.(45) The reconstruction of the life of Jesus narrative consequently involved more than a determination of referential sense. The explicative meaning of the narrative of the life of Jesus was that of ostensive reference, but its religious application flowed from subjective religious experience separate and apart from the scriptural text itself. And with regard to this latter consequence, Schleiermacher was to leave the confines of both the pre-critical harmonist and the critical rationalist.

Traditional apologetics regarded revelation as something essentially external approved by reason, accepted by faith and authenticated by the givenness of revelation in Jesus Christ as set forth in the New Testament. Scripture was this source of revelation, and as such basically unassailable.(46) With Schleiermacher, this apologetic was replaced by a new subjective, inwardly oriented apologetic which focused on the individual as subject and moved towards a "psychology" of Jesus. The religious meaningfulness of historical revelation, then, as opposed to the factual reference of the Gospel narratives, was grounded on a basis independent of the narratives themselves and, most important of all, also independent of corroboration through investigation of the actual life of the historical Jesus, with the problem of the reconstruction and the interpretation of the life of Jesus narratives now turning increasingly into the interpretation of religious consciousness.(47)

Foundational to this shift was a hermeneutical point which reconceived hermeneutics as a "technology" or "art doctrine" of "understanding" and played on the shift from the elements of "grammatical" interpretation laid down by Ernesti, Friedrich Ast and Friedrich August Wolf to a concern with the problematic nature of "understanding" itself.(48) "Understanding" as an "art" was with Schleiermacher distributed between the two poles of the interpreter and the text. Both poles figured in an ongoing movement and progressive understanding enclosing the Gospel message of the New Testament and the faithful individual experience of the Christian. The structure of this movement formed the hermeneutical circle according to which the interpreter's sense of the whole and his apprehension of the parts reshaped each other at every turn of process of understanding.(49) In thus assigning to hermeneutics the task of approaching a work in terms of the relationship of its inner parts to each other and to the higher unity of "spirit," Schleiermacher introduced into hermeneutics a stance slighted by previous philological hermeneutics, namely that of a "feeling," intuiting subject exposed to the "immediate" "consciousness of being absolutely dependent...."(50)

The older Protestant hermeneutics represented by Ast and Ernesti had rested on the assumption that the narrative of the life of Jesus was directly accessible. A science of interpretation accordingly amounted to no more than an "aggregate of isolated observations" - a literary and philological technique geared to the linguistic and historical difficulties posed by Latin, Greek and Hebrew texts.(51) The procedures "(pertaining) both to a complete, consistent reconstruction of the text ... and to a correct and suitable arrangement of the critical apparatus" were "purely philological tasks" which all too often amounted to "mere habitations and nurseries of the dead letter."(52) The "full understanding of a discourse or piece of writing," however, was with Schleiermacher "a kind of artistic achievement" which gradually grew into a discipline of its own.(53) This discipline accounted for the stances of two subjects, the author and the interpreter who followed the principles of a twofold understanding, a "grammatical understanding" examining the outward form of the text, its grammar, structure, syntax, and a "psychological understanding" uncovering the creative individuality of the author's mind behind the outward form of the text.(54)

The former "grammatical" approach relied on the use of objective linguistic resources and focused on the full linguistic, historical and literary setting of a discourse. Taken by itself, "grammatical" hermeneutics drew with regard to historical interpretation pertaining to the life of Jesus narratives on the complex development from the Protestant Reformers' adherence to a literal historical understanding of the scriptural text to the early biblical critics' and the deists' more detailed historical analysis. This analysis now culminated in an interpretation which approached the text in terms of its historical context and the historical context in terms of its literary productions. The foremost consequence of this merging of literary and historical interpretations for the quest was that it liberated the life of Jesus research for a full application of a "historical understanding" which located the mark of historicity in the background of the language and context of an "original" audience.(55) Moreover, in widening the gulf between narrative meaning and the idea or subject matter posited as the real reference of the text, Schleiermacher's hermeneutical canon also reinforced the emphasis on the historico-critical context of the narratives. The higher critical exegesis demanded by Semler and Eichhorn received in this way a decisive impulse forward. Interpretation of the life of Jesus narratives was henceforward "uncompromisingly historical ... (and) struggled to determine what the writer intended to say and the first readers could and must have understood...."(56)

A second, related consequence of Schleiermacher's canon for the quest was the replacement of the traditional, objective evidentialist apologetic by a subjective apologetic which was to salvage and guarantee the persistence of evidentialist "lives" until the close of the nineteenth century. The works of the apologists at Berlin and Halle, August Tholuck and August Wilhelm Neander furnished prominent examples of the predominance of a new, subjective, inwardly oriented apologetic blending Schleiermacherian experientialism with the older evidentialist tradition. Both Tholuck and Neander were not prepared to dismiss the objective pole of revelation and were anxious to preserve the historicity of the life of Jesus narratives. But both minimized evidentialist foundations and found it "irksome to retain only what is historical and matter-of-fact...."(57) The new life impressed upon man's heart was its own guarantee. To have exclusive recourse to the evidentialist argument from miracle and prophecy was therefore to "heap stones together" "instead of building a compact edifice."(58)

Significantly, this judgment took hold of conservative apologetics as well. After 1789, the traditional apologetic represented in the works of men like Kleuker and Less had receded into the background. When this apologetic reappeared in 1829 with Karl Heinrich Sack's Christliche Apologetik, it was distinguished by a new premise. Sack was disenchanted with the objective apologetic and devalued the traditional apologists for highlighting the miraculous over against the essential ethical and dogmatic truths of revelation.(59) Other apologists did not hesitate to fall in line. Carl Ullmann's presentation of Jesus in Die Sündlosigkeit Jesu and C. H. Stirm's Apologie des Christentums turned expressly on the internal evidences of Christianity which rested "subjectively on the appropriation on the part of ... Divine communication, in its deepest relation of Person to Person." "In this very fact," opposed to the traditional evidentialist approach, apologists expected to find "the highest evidence of the actual truth and perfection of ... religion itself."(60)

In Schleiermacher's life of Jesus studies themselves, however, the problem with important moorings for questers to come was precisely the disappearance of objective-historical foundations. The second, "technical" or "psychological" aspect of Schleiermacher's hermeneutics presupposed direct access to the unique individuality of the author. Unlike "grammatical" interpretation which had as its object and goal the clarification of a text according to objective and general laws, the "psychological" side of interpretation, using language as a medium and tool, sought "to understand the discourse as a presentation of thought, composed by a human being and so understood in terms of a human being."(61) "Psychological" hermeneutics accordingly involved "intuitive" and "divinatory" penetration into the "inner" connections of thought characteristic of an author's own consciousness. Implicit in the interpreter's transposition of his own self into author's consciousness was a "kernel" and "husk" hermeneutics which focused on "the true inner kernel of the work," the seminal "decision in the life of the author."(62) But when Schleiermacher turned to this "kernel," he in effect substituted a hermeneutics of "consciousness" for that of subject matter. A text was understood by reference to a vague inner mental process, whereas the concern with "the 'objective' 'factual' reference of theological statements" was significantly played down.(63) The "kernel" and "husk" hermeneutics in this way led to a preoccupation with the self-understanding of the human subject which was detached from the "special historical conditionedness of the object it (sought) to understand."(64)

The immediate consequences of this hermeneutical point became obvious in Schleiermacher's own project with the Leben Jesu. In keeping with his assertions about the task of hermeneutics, Schleiermacher affirmed as the purpose of his life of Jesus to have the "inner unity" of Jesus' life "come into consciousness" through the medium of Jesus' language.(65) This immediate purpose, however, Schleiermacher's "life" itself did not achieve, for "the language into which (Jesus) had been born and was brought up, and on which his communion with other people depended" did not "bear the absolute knowledge of God within itself, or the capacity, adequately to bring this in detail to consciousness." If this were the case, Schleiermacher speculated, "Christ would not have been necessary at all, but the knowledge of God would have spread on its own, by means of the language."(66) Jesus' unique God-consciousness was independent of any reliance on language and culture. In Jesus Schleiermacher posited the "perfect indwelling of the Supreme Being as His peculiar being and His inmost self," and not as a category one could "bring into consciousness" by objective "outer" means.(67) Thus, the correspondence that Schleiermacher's hermeneutics claimed between the linguistic "grammatical" and psychological aspects, between the two poles of outward and "inner" reality, did not take effect. The interpretation of the biblical life of Jesus narratives flowed instead from the terms of Jesus' inward self-consciousness, terms which Schleiermacher posited as prior to "outward" references and historico-critical exegesis.(68)

III

The doctrinal principles of Schleiermacher's "archetype" christology at first seemed to counteract any kind of subjectivism. Immediate self-consciousness was for Schleiermacher the place where revelation, manifested in Jesus' unique "God-consciousness" was realized. Schleiermacher was not prepared to abandon the uniqueness of the figure of Jesus as the historical point of departure for true self-understanding. Jesus was in Schleiermacher's canon the exemplar of that "consciousness" which is in all people, "the consciousness of being absolutely or, which is the same thing, of being in relation with God."(69) What distinguished Jesus was the "perfect" consciousness of the "Supreme Being" as part of "His inmost self." Jesus, Schleiermacher asserted in Platonic terms, thus represented the "archetype", the "Urbild" of humanity.(70) With this assertion Schleiermacher was able to dismiss the rationalist quest's suggestion that Jesus presented merely a moral teacher, an exemplar one must strive to emulate. Jesus' uniqueness resided instead in the impress of his God-consciousness. Through his own unique "God-consciousness" he introduced into history the human potential of religious perfection. "He alone mediates all existence of God in the world and all revelation of God through the world, in so far as he bears within himself the whole new creation which contains and develops the potency of the God-consciousness."(71)

With Schleiermacher, the truth of Christianity was accordingly no longer considered as having been 'inserted' into human history. Jesus was the exemplar only insofar as he presented the actualization in history of what was foundational to the human self.(72) This ontological participation surmounted the problematic character of history and placed Schleiermacher outside the idealist train of the quest and against the assumption of the diastasis between "accidental" truths of history and "necessary" truths of reason. Schleiermacher affirmed the historical actuality of the archetype of humanity in Jesus Christ: The final perfection of "God-consciousness," the archetype manifests itself in the individual concrete appearance of the historical Jesus. In the figure of Jesus, Schleiermacher reiterated, this identity of the divine and human has appeared for the first time. "Until he enters history, all else is presage: all human life is related to his life, and only through this relation does it partake of goodness and divinity."(73)

In Schleiermacher's insistence that the archetype became completely historical in Jesus, the express departure from Kant was unmistakable. In the course of the quest after Reimarus it was Kant who had brought the myth of the ditch to its most pronounced point with the distinction between "the phenomenal realm" and "the noumenal realm." The Critique of Pure Reason portrayed "speculative reason" as limited to phenomena, and not as referring to the noumenal, the "thing-in-itself."(74) "Speculative reason" was not capable of attaining knowledge of a transcendent natural law or its ground, a rational God, by way of knowledge of the empirical world. The ditch could only be bridged, Kant's Critique of Practical Reason asserted, in the experience of ethical obligation, which retained the idea of God, freedom and immortality as "regulative" ideas or "postulates of practical reason."(75) But these postulates, Kant maintained, were non-cognitive; they did "not extend speculative knowledge...."(76) Lessing's ditch still could not be crossed.

Within the limits of "reason" alone, Kant's Jesus thus represented the "ideal" of moral perfection, a possibility to which no objective-empirical reality corresponded.(77) Critical life of Jesus research was of no significance. Kant was not so much interested in reconstructing a historical Jesus as in determining the ontological role of Christ. What Kant described was neither the Christ of faith nor the historical Jesus but the symbolic incarnation of the Categorical Imperative.(78) The historical Jesus was thus replaced by an idea of pure "reason" which according to Kant "stands in need of no documentary authentication, but proves itself." Here all historical particularity was dissolved. The accidental and historical could function neither as proof nor as substitute for the eternal truth of "reason." Kant therefore needed "no example to make the idea of a person morally well-pleasing to God our archetype; this idea as an archetype is already present in our reason."(79)

Schleiermacher's approach to life of Jesus moved on different grounds. If Kant showed the possibility of a "pure faith of reason" without the historical Jesus, Schleiermacher advanced a position affirming the dependence of all believers on the real historical person of Jesus. For Schleiermacher, the archetypal idea did not belong to Kant's realm of abstraction but rather to the concreteness of Jesus' humanity. A religious "archetype," Schleiermacher argued against Kant's version of the "archetype" as the rational idea of perfection, could be actual in history through Jesus. Kant's rational "archetype" of Christ was for Schleiermacher "historisch." Jesus "mediates all existence of God" in history. "And thus the total effective influence of Christ is only the continuation of the creative divine activity out of which the Person of Christ arose."(80) With this, the assumptions of the "broad ditch" of history predominating the rationalist and moralistic quest from Reimarus to Lessing and Kant were reversed. Not the qualifications of formal christological dogma gave the historical Jesus significance, but rather the perfect union of "ideal" personality with a historical individual.(81) This amounted to a system bridging the dichotomony between the historical and "archetypal" Christ which from the days of Reimarus had been steadily widening.

IV

To contemporary reviewers of Schleiermacher, in particular to the supernaturalists at Tübingen and Jena represented by K. G. Bretschneider, C. Delbrück, F. Steudel, and C. B. Klaiber, the definition of the "immediate consciousness of absolute dependence" as the locus of revelation amounted to "pantheistic," "idealistic" and "gnostic" speculation which deprived faith of all specific content, leaving merely "transitory," "subjective" and "mysterious" "feeling."(82) "Thus it appears," Bretschneider concluded, "that Schleiermacher's conception of religion can never be the foundation of a theory of the Christian faith."(83) Klaiber further charged that Schleiermacher, in aligning "self-consciousness" with "absolute dependence," precluded the possibility of all mediate work of God in the world and thus posited in effect "the denial of the true distinction between the finite and infinite and ... the affirmation that the world is only the explication of the divine life itself...."(84)

The most problematic christological consequence of this "denial" was Schleiermacher's assumption of the union of "ideal," "archetypal" personality with a historical individual. For Schleiermacher, the archetypal and the human were equally real in Jesus; yet in carrying out this position in his life of Jesus, Schleiermacher focused on the immediate existential experience of the revelation in Christ and not on historicized causal relationship. In the subjective, individualistic religion of "feeling," the historical Jesus thus receded behind the revelation of Christ in the self, the Christ who was "the most perfect revelation and explication of the divine life or the presentation of the idea of God in human consciousness in general."(85)

Schleiermacher's response to the charges of "pantheistic" and "mystical" "speculation" in his <u>Letters to Lücke</u> and in the revision of <u>The Christian Faith</u> emphatically denied any association with "speculative dogmaticians."(86) Avoiding both pantheism and the divinization of subjectivity, Schleiermacher reiterated that the higher self-consciousness existed as "temporally" determined, that is "co-determinant" with sensible self-consciousness.(87) On this point, even traditional apologetes like H. H. Sack were willing to assign the "label" "historical" to Schleiermacher's conception of the "unity of God with ... as an actuality in the person of Jesus...."(88) But while Schleiermacher went so far as to claim for himself the "label" of "a real supernaturalist," reviewers were quick to point out the parallels between "gnostic," "mystical" idealism and Schleiermacher's canon and charged that Schleiermacher throughout constructed the "ideal" from the "historical" in his conception of Jesus.(89)

Schleiermacher's examination of the synoptic question had much to contribute to this. In view of the chronological gaps and discrepancies in the Gospel accounts, Schleiermacher concluded that "when were are thinking in terms of a historical view - our sources cause us much embarrassment." "Everything is related to definite times," Schleiermacher observed in particular with regard to the Fourth Gospel, but "not with the intention of delivering a chronicle of the life of Christ." The Gospel record, then, "is not a connected life description, for many moments necessary for a biography are entirely lacking...."(90) This conclusion fully accorded with Schleiermacher's primary thesis: The significance of Jesus could not be raised in the light of historical criticism. This significance resided not in records of past events but in the present and was an index of the content of religious consciousness.

The "gegenwärtiger Christus," then, was of primary concern to Schleiermacher, and in this emphasis the revelatory normative function of a divinely inspired and infallible biblical text receded behind the testimony afforded by immediate, inward certainty. Thus while the introduction to Schleiermacher's <u>Leben Jesu</u> affirmed the significance of the historico-critical approach, the life of Jesus accounts never received with

Schleiermacher the historical analysis to which this affirmation might have subjected them and harked back instead to a reliance on the historicity of the Fourth Gospel.(91) "Schleiermacher is not in search of the historical Jesus," Schweitzer acutely observed, "but of the Jesus of his own system of theology; that is to say, of the historic figure which seems to him appropriate to the self-consciousness of the Redeemer as he represents it. For him the empirical has simply no existence."(92) Theologically, one was left with exploring only the God-consciousness of Jesus. Schleiermacher, like Kant, did not find a sufficient place for the concrete, historic incarnation of Christ and came close to reducing the historical Jesus to a pure "Idee." The manner in which Schleiermacher affirmed Christ as suffusing human consciousness turned Jesus into an "archetypal" model filled with epistemological rather than historical content.(93) Thus, with Schleiermacher, the deliberate attempt of the quest to clothe itself with the garb of a pristine "kernel" faced a striking reversal. The "husk" of the traditional evidentialist framework was increasingly pushed into the background, but so, it now seemed, was the "kernel," too.

V

In 1835, the shifts and artifices of the "kernel" and "husk" theme received a significant new impetus through Strauss' Leben Jesu. At the time of its publication, theological and literary forums abounded with charges, countercharges, harangues and accusations which exposed the issue of the quest itself to the overall charge of negativity in historical criticism. "Scarcely ever," Schweitzer commented on the reception of Strauss' study, "has a book let loose such a storm of controversy and scarcely ever has a controversy been so barren of immediate result. "The fertilizing rain brought up a crop of toadstools."(94) The "toadstools" were primarily the fierce debates concerning miracles spinned off by Strauss' interpretation of the relationship of the Jesus of history to the Christ of faith, sterile debates without equal in scriptural scholarship which had already consumed a considerable amount of theological energies.

But Strauss' work also brought about a more lasting and "fertilizing" development: the resolution of the deadlock between the two camps of rationalism and supernaturalism. Strauss subtly undermined the presuppositions of the two camps by changing the state of the question on both fronts and by shifting the focus from the explanation of events to the narratives that represented them. There were, Strauss argued, other considerations to be taken into account than merely those of positive historicity. According to Strauss, the "idea" of Jesus held by the early Christians, their faith in the risen Christ determined the portraits of the historical Jesus. The study of the historical characteristics of the biblical narratives was in this respect reductive and hampered the way for the religious re-estimation of the religious meaning of the scriptural accounts.(95)

In thus broadening the basis of the debate over the factuality of biblical narratives, Strauss cut through the stalemate which divided theologians into the two camps of rationalism and supernaturalism. Strauss pushed the quest beyond the polarities of these two positions and also swam steadily upstream against the presuppositions of Schleiermacher's life of Jesus research. Strauss charged that Schleiermacher, no less than the other theological camps of the quest, took for granted that the Gospel record gave witness to factual history and that Jesus was historically available in the New Testament. The events recorded in the life of Jesus narratives had actually occurred; it was just a matter of interpreting how they took place. It was precisely the history-like character of the biblical accounts, however, that Strauss set out to call into question, and on this count he counteracted the intentions of three competitors: the supernaturalist citadel of the historical accuracy of the Gospels; Reimarus' view that biblical narratives were designed to conceal and distort genuine history; and the rationalist attempt to rescue the narratives' historicity by considering "the miraculous in the sacred history as a drapery which needs only to be drawn aside, in order to disclose the pure historic form."(96) Strauss, by contrast, refused to rely on the supernatural presuppositions of orthodox theology; his investigations flowed from the opposite premise that there was no supernatural history independent of and apart from the laws of nature. To Strauss, the life of Jesus did not consist of a chain of miracles and fulfilled prophecies staunchly adhered to by orthodox supernaturalists; nor did it consist of natural events which the evangelists mistook or embellished as miraculous. Rather, "the new standpoint" characteristic of Gospel literature, Strauss argued, "is the mythical."(97) The Gospel accounts present records of "myth," narrative expressions of the early Christian community's understanding of Jesus in terms of contemporary messianic expectations.

With Strauss, the application of the conception of myth to the Gospel tradition did not have the connotation of fraudulent fiction. For Strauss, the process of mythicizing was instinctive and precluded the intent of conscious deception. Strauss conceived myth as "narratives of real events coloured by the light of antiquity" and accounts "(clothing) in the garb of historical narrative a simple thought, a precept, or and idea of the time."(98) The emphasis here fell on the working over and reshaping of the actual "event or idea" into the appearance of history, as opposed to the factual historical record.(99) The narratives in the Gospels were therefore to be approached not as deceptive distortion but as the outcome of an unconscious mythologising process. Hence Strauss did not treat as deceptive or doubtful "the simple, historical framework of the life of Jesus, that he grew up at Nazareth, let himself be baptized by John, collected disciples, went about teaching in the Jewish land, ... but that in the end he fell victim to the hatred and envy of the Pharisaic party and died on the cross."(100)

Genuinely historical events, then, did for Strauss without question undergird the life of Jesus. The Jesus of Nazareth was "historisch"; he continued John's preaching about the coming messianic kingdom and he carried out a ministry in Galilee. But Strauss significantly qualified this assertion by observing that the "simple framework of the life of Jesus" "was enveloped in the most complex and imaginative festoons of pious reflection and imagination, in which all the ideas which primitive Christianity had concerning its departed Master were ... woven into his life."(101) As the outcome of a tangled web of pious reflection and religious speculation, the Gospel accounts contained therefore no positive historical contribution to the life of Jesus. Thus, the genealogies in Matthew and Luke were constructed to "authenticate" "the prophetical characteristic of Davidical descent," while the doctrine of the miraculous conception served to confirm that Jesus was the Messiah. Similarly, the transfiguration "has for ... the ideal part ... that the Messiah was expected to resemble Moses and Elijah...."(102) The determining presupposition underlying this detection of myth in the Gospel narratives remained constant: Foundational to the interpretation of the Gospel narratives was the religious imagination and faith of the early Christian community, and not the straightforward historical factuality of the accounts.

Strauss' rigorous devaluation of the historical positivity of the Gospel narratives was intended constructively. Strauss' exhaustive historical critique affirmed the 'dogmatic' significance of Jesus as inviolate and did not undermine religious faith in the essential truth of Christianity. "The mythical view," Strauss assured his audience, "leaves the substance of the narrative unassailed; and instead of venturing to explain the details, accepts the whole, not indeed as true history, but as a sacred legend." Philosophically, this account of the natural origin and development of the Christian Scriptures rendered Strauss a monist of the idealistic school who abandoned all distinctions between matter and spirit. The "mythical interpretation," Strauss averred, "by renouncing the historical body ... , rescues and preserves the idea...."(103)

On the exegetical front, this position counteracted the life of Jesus research issuing from Reimarus' rationalistic approach to the quest. Reimarus had asserted that Christianity did not originate from a series of supernatural events but grew entirely out of fraud. Strauss was prepared to agree with Reimarus that Christianity arose from a natural set of circumstances, but he preserved against Reimarus the "kernel" of religious, nonhistorical truth which "(retained) all that was really achieved by Christianity ... without the form of religion in which that kernel ripened...."(104) The negative results about the reliability of the biblical narratives of the life of Jesus offered to Strauss an important way to distill the pristine "kernel" behind the Gospel accounts from encrustations and embellishments. This position placed Strauss' mythological approach in a long tradition of hermeneutical debate reaching back to the neologist camp around Semler and extending to Schleiermacher's "kernel" and "husk" hermeneutics. For Strauss, as for the neologists and Schleiermacher, the meaningfulness of the scriptural accounts of the life of Jesus as well as its status as a supreme source of religious insight were left untouched by the strictures of historical criticism. With Strauss, it was just a matter of carrying these strictures further, to the point of renouncing the historical facticity of the text. But this was done with the express intention of rescuing and preserving the "spiritual" "substance" of the narratives.(105)

Yet despite this alignment with the "kernel" and "husk" hermeneutics, Strauss was still faced with oppostion from two fronts. Strauss sought the "idea" behind the myth-building power of the community, not the historical fact behind the description. This conception, however, barred the way to the supernaturalist and rationalist interpretations of the miracles narratives. Both rationalist and supernaturalist camps focused on the historical question of the "positivity" of the Gospel miracles narratives in the life of Jesus. Supernaturalists asserted that the accounts gave witness to divine intervention in history, while rationalists sought to rescue the narratives' historicity by distinguishing the core of facticity from its miraculous embellishment. To Strauss, by contrast, the significance of the miracle narratives was located elsewhere. Strauss thus made the necessity to establish the historicity of the Gospel miracles appear irrelevant. In formulating a literary question - the question of the nature of the Gospel literature - Strauss obviated the need to interpret the Gospel narratives on the presupposition of their historical reliability and highlighted instead the question of the religious significance of the narratives.(106)

This shift of emphasis had important repercussions for the relevance of the miracles issue within the context of the "kernel" and "husk" theme. Until Strauss, Schweitzer observes, "the dominant interest ... (was) the question of miracle. ... With the advent of Strauss, this problem found a solution ...., that these events have no rightful place in history but are simply mythical elements in the sources." For Schweitzer, this did not mean that the problem of miracle was permanently solved. "From the historical point of view," Schweitzer explained, "it is really impossible to solve it. ... What has been gained is only that the exclusion of miracle from our view of history has been universally recognized as a principle of criticism, so that miracle no longer concerns the historian either positively or negatively."(107) Within the course of the quest, this estimation emerges as a legacy of Strauss. Strauss effectively dissolved the horns of the problem posed by the miracle narratives for the kernel and husk issue. With Strauss, the subject of life of Jesus research was no longer the scaled-down version of the historical life of Jesus but rather the faith-portrait of the early Christian community. While "according to the mythical interpretation," Strauss did "not ... see in the evangelical narrative any real event," he "yet (set out to) retain a sense, a purpose in the narrative (and explored) to what sentiments and thoughts of the first Christian community it owes its origin...."(108) In such a conception, the notion of the "supernatural" or the "superhistorical" relevant to miracles disappeared. The "husk" embodied in the miracle narratives faded away, while the religious significance of the "kernel" stood reasserted and inviolate.

4. The Jesus of History and the Christ of Faith: Strauss and After

Schweitzer's critical review of the Leben-Jesu-Forschung undercut the quest's attempt to produce a historically reliable picture of Jesus. Yet Schweitzer remained convinced that at least his own version of the eschatological Jesus was authentic. Schweitzer thus stayed within the essentially positivistic orientation of the older "lives" and was prepared to carry this focus over into his evaluation of Straussian life of Jesus research. If Schweitzer charged Schleiermacher with surrendering the historical Jesus, it was in Strauss that Schweitzer claimed to have found a reassertion of historical positivity. Contemporary reviewers of Strauss, however, passed a different judgment on the Leben Jesu. To critics from both rationalist and supernaturalist camps Strauss' aim was not, as Schweitzer claimed, biographical reconstruction as a means of substituting the Jesus of history for christological dogma but rather the destruction of the assumption that the Gospels mediated the historical life of Jesus. For Strauss' critics, this clearing away of historical reliability rendered the Leben Jesu unacceptable not so much because Strauss undermined historical faith in miracles than because Strauss seemed to eliminate the necessity of "perceptible" history and "particular" individuality from the spiritual life.(1) In place of an individual, be it the rationalist conception of Jesus as "teacher" and "example" or Schleiermacher's view of Jesus as the "archetype" of "perfect" "God-consciousness," Strauss placed an "idea", a "principle" only casually related to Christ. For Strauss' critics this amounted to the postulation of a universal incarnation in which the logos was transformed into a "homo generalis" and in which "the view of eternal oscillation of the idea in the individual actually (did) not allow for the recognition of any realization of the idea."(2) Reacting to Strauss' devaluation of the significance of the historical Jesus, innumerable "positive" "lives" rushed to defend the historical Jesus, reiterating that the reconstruction of Jesus' life flowed from Jesus' historical particularity, since revelation was "a quite definite historical given - this and no other - individual."(3)

In part, the "idea"-individual debates also concerned the possibility of continuing the historical Jesus quest. According to Schweitzer's account, the resolution of this question belonged to the form-critical insights of William Wrede and the results of Schweitzer's own "consistent eschatology." According to the testimony provided by Strauss' critics, however, the scepticism against the possibility of reconstructing the historical Jesus did not belong to form-critical exegesis but to Strauss himself. In exposing the historical unreliability of the Gospel narratives, Strauss made clear that the life of Jesus could not be authenticated by using the Gospel accounts as historically substantial sources. Strauss' Leben Jesu was in this respect the life of Jesus to terminate all "lives," and this turn presented, contrary to Schweitzer's assumptions, a deliberate possibility of the life of Jesus theology.

In the preface of his Leben Jesu, Strauss had reiterated that his scepticism against the historicity of the Gospel tradition would leave the "dogmatic" significance of the historical Jesus intact. In this positive assertion, Strauss turned not to historical reconstruction but to Hegel's speculative development of the "idea" of reconciliation as an act within the nature of God. Yet the Hegelian equation of christology with "the self-explicating Idea itself" presupposed only an "accidental" relation between the historical Jesus and the "idea."(4) For Hegel, Christianity revolved primarily around a concept, a "Begriff"; there was accordingly no necessity to penetrate behind the Christ of faith to the objective-historic figure of Jesus of Nazareth. At precisely this point, the opposition between Strauss and his critics provided the determinative issue for the flurry of "lives" which flooded the rest of the nineteenth century and spilled over into the twentieth: the question whether Jesus was merely accidental to the realization of the idea of divine-human "unity" with faith thus emerging autonomously, independent of a specific historical event and person, or whether the historical Jesus was "necessary" and mediated divine-human "unity" as "the archetypal man in whom the higher principle of human nature (appeared)" and in whom "the ideal type ... became completely historical...."(5)

It was also precisely with regard to this disjunction that Strauss uncovered the inadequacy of Schleiermacher's "ecclectic christology." This inadequacy referred less to Schleiermacher's preoccupation with "archetypal" "God-consciousness" than to the question whether Schleiermacher's "archetype" could in fact be borne out by any single individual. With regard to this latter assertion of "the historically unique" as "the originally typical," Strauss emerged against Schleiermacher as a staunch advocate of "speculative" philosophy and challenged the christological tradition issuing from Chalcedon which affirmed Jesus as the figure in whom full humanity and full divinity subsisted.(6) "Our age," Strauss categorically declared on the basis of a flawed equation of Schleiermacher's "archetype" with his own conception of the "idea," "demands to be led in Christology to the idea in the fact, to the race in the individual." A theology which, as Schleiermacher's system did, "in its doctrines on the Christ stops short at him as an individual" represented to Strauss "not properly a theology, but a homily."(7)

In rejecting Schleiermacher's prediction for "the historical existence of Christ" together with his assertion that the idea of God-manhood was realized in a "single human life" as an "anachronism," Strauss was prepared to pay tribute to Schleiermacher's hermeneutics. Yet Strauss quickly lost sight of this tribute when confronted with the task to scrutinize the facticity of the Gospel accounts. What remained primary in Strauss' critique of Schleiermacher was the need to discern whether the accounts referred to "a real historical individual."(8) With this critical scrutiny of the fact claims of the biblical narratives, Strauss set the course of hermeneutical inquiry back to the old rationalist stage of the quest and the critical focus on the narratives as reports of "actual events of the life of Jesus."(9) Strauss strikingly traced this position back to Schleiermacher himself by highlighting Schleiermacher's adherence to rationalist principles of probability in the assessment of the miracles narratives, principles which failed for Strauss only at the point where Schleiermacher set out to unite the historical Jesus with his "ideal Christ."(10)

Strauss' critics judged differently. From the ranks of the right wing Hegelian, the extreme supernaturalist and the historico-critical camps emerged a growing number of "mediating" critics such as August Neander, Friedrich Lücke, Immanuel Nitzsch, Carl Ullmann, Richard Rothe and Alexander Schweitzer, who were convinced that Scripture was historically grounded and that the structure of Christianity was founded on the "person" of Jesus.(11) Against Strauss' "all-consuming, personality-destroying pantheism," this "mediating" position asserted that "if ideas are to be realized, it can only come about through persons."(12) On the christological front, this premise yielded a reconsideration of both the divine and the human poles in an actual "kenosis of the logos" in which the incarnate life of the logos harmonized with a genuinely human existence.(13) In the reaction against Strauss, the kenotic principle, as advocated by the Erlangen school of questers, provided for a conservative approach not covered by Schweitzer which approached the figure of Jesus without moving out of the confines of the traditional categories of the "person" and "nature" of Christ.

Closely aligned with this conservative strain in the quest's response to Strauss was the new Tübingen school of questers around F. C. Baur who forced the historico-critical problem again to the center of the theological stage. The main contention of this group of critics was that Strauss had produced his analysis of the Gospel history independent of the sources, playing off the synoptic Gospels against John without an exhaustive scrutiny of the historical and literary distinctions between the Fourth Gospel and the synoptics. In rejecting Schleiermacher's attempt to reconcile the historical with the "archetypal" Christ, Strauss on his part had drawn back to the anti-historical stance of Kant and plunged into a rejection of the historicity of the Gospels without a corresponding criticism of the Gospel records. For the critics around Baur all investigations into the life of Jesus came to rest at the opposite point: The relationship between the Jesus of history and the Christ of faith was a purely "historical question" which could be answered only through an historical investigation of the literary sources of the Gospel stories.(14)

I

Strauss' exposition of the mythical principle relevant to the life of Jesus was to be "confidently entrusted to historical criticism" and consistent with the critical approach first applied to parts of the Old Testament by J. G. Eichhorn and, above all, Wilhelm De Wette.(15) For both De Wette and Strauss the separation between mythical adornment and historical foundation was no longer possible. Moreover, both De Wette and Strauss used myth as an historico-epistemological category referring to the investiture of primitive Christian ideas or a subtle poeticzing of supersensible ideas.(16) Yet Strauss' own use of the mythical principle was quite distinct. The mythical school of Heyne, Eichhorn and Gabler did not consistently apply the concept of myth to the New Testament narratives and still followed, Strauss charged, "the crooked and toilsome paths of natural interpretations."(17) Strauss' originality lay in his wholesale account of the life of Jesus on the basis of an unconscious mythologizing process. Schweitzer's account of this approach introduced the category of "mythos" in dialectal fashion as "the synthesis of the thesis, represented by the supernatural explanation, with the antithesis, represented by the rationalistic interpretation."(18) This account, however, slighted the fact that Strauss' uncompromising approach to the life of Jesus by means of mythical interpretation engendered scepticism as to the historicity of the Gospel tradition. Some of the Gospel accounts, such as those of the cures of the blind, the feeding of the five thousand and the transfiguration, were for Strauss "pure myths" which had no historical foundation and flowed from contemporary Messianic expectations.(19) Other accounts, such as those "concerning 'fishers of men' and the barren fig-tree," were "historical myths" which involved "a definite individual fact" embellished with "mythical conceptions culled from the idea of Christ."(20) This categorization was to some extent identical with what had been current as rationalistic or 'naturalistic' schemes of explanation.(21) But while rationalists like H. E. E. Paulus clung to the historicity of the Gospel narratives by means of a conjectured basis of history, Strauss proceeded to dismiss this basis for form-critical and literary considerations.

Contemporary critics acknowledged Strauss' approach as "negative-critical" and "dialectical."(22) Strauss' method was "dialectical" in highlighting opposing interpretations and in assuming that the realms of myth and history were mutually exclusive; it was also "critical" "in combining all those evangelical narratives to which it attributes only an ideal meaning, under the one common notion of myth."(23) But Strauss' "critical" method was not independent of Hegelian speculative philosophy and by no means of a "purely empirical-rational character" as the object of "historical science."(24) Strauss consciously developed the concept of "myth" along Hegelian lines by distinguishing between the philosophical concept, the "Begriff," and the theological representation, the "Vorstellung," and by locating "myth" as an expression of the religious imagination in the realm of "Vorstellung" rather than "Begriff."(25)

In the Hegelian canon, the special character of the particular Christian doctrinal "Vorstellung" was the objective historical life of Jesus who represented an "absolutely adequate" expression of the incarnational truth of the "Idee." "The history of Christ," Hegel reiterated, "is absolutely adequate to the Idea." This history is "the explication of the nature of God" and "the unfolding of the divine nature itself."(26) This position did allow for a harmony of the "Begriff," of the realization of the idea of the divine-human unity with the "Vorstellung" of the incarnation of Christ. Hegel's christology expressly counteracted the "criticism and subjective idealism" of Kant whom Hegel judged to have reduced the "idea" to a mere "ought."(27) For Hegel, incarnation "appears (historically) in such a way ... that the spirit is there as one self-consciousness, i.e., as an actual human, that he exists for immediate certainty...."(28) Incarnation, then, occurred as the supreme religious "Vorstellung," and this "Vorstellung" found full realization in the historic human figure of Jesus. Hence "the history of Jesus Christ ... is not taken merely as a myth in a figurative way, but as something perfectly historical."(29)

Yet while Hegel thus affirmed the significance of the "external history" of the "life of Christ," he at the same time also relativized the "external fact" of objective-historical personality in a "mediating" process in which "mind having once taken occasion by this external fact, (brings) under its consciousness the idea of humanity as one with God...." This process, Hegel argued, "sees in the history only the presentation of that idea; the object of faith is completely changed: instead of a sensible, empirical fact it has become a spiritual and divine idea, which has its confirmation no longer in history but in philosophy."(30) The content of history, therefore, was the content of conceptual thought and knowledge.

According to Strauss' critics in the right-wing Hegelian and the source critical camps, Strauss' appropriation of the Hegelian distinction between "representation" and "concept" "erred most about ... those things which pertain to the idea, to the entire process of human cognition alone."(31) This "error" was strikingly evident in Strauss' devaluation of the historical concretization of "representation" in the myth-forming process, a devaluation which flowed from the attempt to resolve the "representation" into the "concept." Strauss thus dismissed the element of "sensuality" in Hegel's system which had assigned to the "representation" a function independent of the "concept."(32) The "key" for this "speculative" presupposition, however, Strauss claimed to have found in Hegel himself. The "actual life of Jesus," Strauss observed, "appears" in Hegelian christology "to be ... 'the point of departure, which is to be gratefully acknowledged,' but which 'steps into the background' ... (because) this particular actuality, person, in history ... has ... no relation to the idea...."(33) The revelation embodied in Jesus was therefore neither unique nor historically particular. "The fact that the unity of the divine and the human is perceived in the one person of Jesus (was) for Hegel," Strauss judged, "clearly a lower standpoint ... which (belonged) ... 'to the element of representation.'"(34) The "pictorical form" of the idea, then, and not the factual or objective-historical Jesus was thus the ground which Hegel affirmed as the foundation of faith.(35)

This point became glaringly clear in Strauss' life of Jesus. It remained only for Strauss to dissociate Christ from the single human Jesus and to postulate that the true identity of Christ was the Hegelian idea of the human species. In relation to the objective-historical Jesus, Strauss, contemporary critics judged, thus proceeded decisively from Hegel's actualisation of God-man unity. "What is now explicit, now implicit, in Hegel's philosophy of religion, viz., that Christ as the redeeming Son of God is the product of the community, of the Church, but not an actual, divine fact ... this is," critics observed, "what Strauss bluntly teaches and seeks to convey in his criticism." Thus, with Strauss "even in Christ's life, the divine humanity could not be actual in the total fulness of its content at every moment."(36) The life of Jesus in this context served only as the historical precondition for the attainment of the "highest stage of unification ... between the divine and the human."(37) And it was here that Hegelianism provided Strauss with the "key to the whole of christology" in pointing to the contradiction of declaring the "idea" as "realized in a single individual."(38) "As subject of the predicate which the church assigns to Christ" Hegel like Strauss placed "instead of an individual, an idea, but an idea which has an existence in reality, not the mind only, like that of Kant. In an individual, a God-man, the properties and functions which the church ascribes to Christ contradict themselves; in the idea of the human species they perfectly agree."(39)

At this juncture, Hegel's programme issued in a crucial point of biblical hermeneutics. Hegel did affirm that incarnational principle was mediated historically. "The Idea," Hegel conceded, "when it was ripe and the time was fulfilled, was able to attach itself only to Christ, and to see itself realized only in him."(40) But "it is the Spirit, the indwelling Idea" and not historical particularity "which has attested Christ's mission and this is the verification for those who believed and for us who possess the developed Begriff."(41) For Hegel, then, the "inner element" of the history of Jesus Christ as represented in the realm of speculation was primary. Knowledge of Jesus as the Christ was grounded in an inward certainty of the divine Spirit. As with Kant, the outward historical fact of Jesus of Nazareth was thus not repudiated, but the revelatory normative function of biblical testimony and the history of Jesus were clearly disintegrated. The authority of Christian religion as revealed religion rested for Hegel on "the witness of the Spirit - not on (reports of) miracles, but on the absolute truth, on the eternal Idea."(42)

Yet in affirming this inward certainty afforded by the Spirit as the decisive criterion of verification, Hegel undercut the very conjunction between the "Vorstellung" and the "Begriff" of incarnation so that it was only a small step for Strauss to separate what Hegel had linked only by means of the "testimonium spiritus sancti internum."(43) Repudiating all attempts to preserve the focus on a single historical individual, Strauss reiterated that "the general propositions on the unity of the divine and human natures, do not in the least serve to explain the appearance of a person, in whom this unity existed individually, in an exclusive manner." This "idea of a unity of the divine and human natures" was to Strauss "a real one in a far higher sense, when (he) regarded the whole race of mankind as its realization, than when (he) singled out one man as such a realization."(44) From the historical point of view, Strauss was willing to grant that Jesus could have been a highly "gifted individual" who was "called to raise the development of spirit in humanity to higher levels." But what Strauss was not ready to accept was the premise that the "idea" was "wont to lavish all its fulness on one exemplar, and be niggardly towards all others."(45)

In the Streitschriften Strauss acknowledged his debt to this "key" the Hegelian canon furnished for his own christological convictions. At one crucial point, however, Strauss deliberately left the Hegelian canon behind. With regard to "the most important question, ... that of the relationship of the historical elements of the Bible ... to the concept" Strauss "was mostly left in the dark" "when he sought illumination in the writings of Hegel. ... Sometimes it seemed that history as mere representation was let drop over against the concept that had been attained. Sometimes history seemed to have been retained along with the Idea."(46) Hegel thus left open the critical question of whether the "(ascription of) reality ... to the idea of the unity of the divine and human natures (was) ... equivalent to the admission that this unity must actually have been once manifested ... in one individual."(47)

With regard to the status of the historical Jesus as the embodiment of the "idea," as "the individual in whom the unity of God and humanity has become manifest" Strauss adapted and shifted the Hegelian position to one asserting that the "idea" does not necessitate the postulate of historicity and that the meaning of the individual Gospel narratives is in effect "independent of their historical reality."(48) The Gospel narratives of the God-man do not refer to the historical Jesus but to the "idea" of the human race. By thus severing the dogmatic principle of incarnation from the premise that this "idea" had been fully embodied in a concrete historical individual, Strauss expressly removed the emphasis from the historical person of Jesus. The Leben Jesu time and again made the reason for this negative critique explicit: The Christian principle is not identical with the historic individual Jesus. The "idea" properly belongs to the race as a whole, not to any single historical individual.(49)

This position was scarcely a new one. Strauss could draw on two antecedents: Lessing's "ugly broad ditch" between necessary truths of reason and contingent facts of history and Kant's conception of Jesus as an "ideal" in the moral consciousness of mankind never to be realized in a single, definite individual. In using these antecedent to break with Schleiermacher's programme, Strauss' Leben Jesu left on the exegetical front a Christianity "desupernaturalized" and "demiracleised."(50) On the philosophical front, Strauss arrived at a Christianity depersonalized and anonymous, assigning to Jesus merely an "accidental" relation to the

Christian principle: In the history of Jesus "the occasion accidently was taken to evoke the idea in itself...."(51) The incarnation, then, did not necessitate a historical event.(52) Once the "idea" had entered history it was no longer dependent on the original event to continue; it no longer needed the person of Jesus or his history. In this account, the Christian faith could be explained without reference to the Jesus of history. Strauss' "life" thus stunningly called into question the very continuation of the quest. The Leben Jesu not only did not arrive at a 'historical core' to the life of Jesus, but did not even set out to establish it. Instead, Strauss replaced the lost historical reliability of the text by the religious consciousness of Jesus' age in a "purgation" that pushed Jesus as a historical subject into the background and turned him into a symbol of the divine in man.(53)

II

According to the Leben Jesu, "the real state of the case" in christology was that "the church refers her Christology to an individual who existed historically at a certain period: the speculative theologian to an idea which only attains existence in the totality of individuals; by the church the evangelical narratives are received as history: by the critical theologian, they are regarded for the most part as mere myth."(54) Historically, the disjunction Strauss pressed here was responsible for scattering the Hegelians into the right, the centre and the left wing positions which offered "three possible answers" "to the question of whether and to what extent the gospel history is proven as history by the idea of the unity of the divine and human natures ...: either the entirety of the history is proven by this concept, or merely a part of it, or finally, that neither as a whole nor in part is it to be confirmed as historical by the idea."(55)

For left-wing Hegelians it seemed doubtful that the Gospel contained a substantial residuum of fact upon which a chronological account of Jesus' life and teaching could be based. The extreme version of this position, associated with Bruno Bauer, went so far as to call into doubt the very historicity of Jesus. Reviewing the Leben Jesu for the Hegelian Jahrbücher für wissenschaftliche Kritik in 1835, Bauer charged that Strauss had slighted the extent to which Jesus' being was "the result of the meeting of susceptibility and creative necessity," namely, to reveal "the union of divine and human natures" and thereby overcome "the antithesis of Jewish consciousness."(56) In this context it did not matter whether or not the Gospel narratives of the life of Jesus were historical. The figure of Jesus presented merely a "necessary" stage in the development of "theological consciousness." Therefore, "everything that the historical Jesus is," Bauer concluded, "belongs to the world of imagination and indeed to Christian imagination. (And) it has nothing to do with a human being who belongs to the real world."(57)

Strauss met Bauer's criticism with a dualistic concept of history which kept "idea" and "individual" sharply sundered. This disjunction undercut, against Bauer, the presupposition of "philosophical necessity." Strauss conceded that the "category" of the religious genius could be demonstrated to mediate a special revelation of the divine. "But only the conceivablitiy, not the necessity, of such an individual" was for Strauss "philosophically deducible. That precisely Jesus was really this individual, and that only he and none other either before or after him has attained this non plus ultra of religious development, (could) only be demonstrated historically, not philosophically."(58)

Whereas for Bauer Jesus' life was an index of the alienated religious consciousness which sought in vain to mediate the divine and human, Marheineke, Daub, Göschel and the right-wing Hegelians integrated Hegel's speculative God-man with orthodox christology and stood solidly for the view that "the unity of God with man ... was really visibly manifested in the person of Jesus Christ."(59) The "necessity" of this person could be deduced speculatively and allowed for the equation of the archetypal Christ with the historical figure of Jesus of Nazareth. To right-wing Hegelians the Leben Jesu with its identification of the God-man as the "totality of humanity" seemed therefore to "(fall) back ... to ... the Kantian (standpoint), that is ... to that of subjective thinking" which asserted that "this totality of humanity ... is never given actually...."(60) The critics on the center of the Hegelian school like Karl Rosenkranz agreed and similarly adhered to the actuality of the God-man in individual historical incarnation, seeking to retain some semblance of the old traditional belief in the uniqueness of Jesus. "In him ... the divine power over nature was concentrated, he could not act otherwise than miraculously...."(61) This position conceded that "history cannot be arrested with Jesus as a single being of the past" and yet, Jesus "alone and no other human" was affirmed as "adequate to the concept" of the divine and human unity.(62)

It was at the point of the alleged identity of the historical Jesus with the archetypal Christ that Strauss expressly broke with Rosenkranz, Marheinecke, Daub and Göschel. With the leading Hegelian theologians from both right and center wings, the idea of divine-human unity was asserted to have once fully appeared in a sentient historical individual.(63) Strauss' "basic error" in this context was that he set out "assert the subjectivity of substance only in the infinite multiplicity of subjects, in the species of humanity."(64) Strauss himself, however, identified his critics' charge "as a nominalistic dependence on empirical individualities."(65) Strauss did not grant that the concept of the race of humanity could go out above itself "as a mere collectivum of personalities and ... be conceived in itself as concrete personality."(66) From the "perspective of true realism" which Strauss advocated the "true real" was not "this or that human but the universal humanity...."(67)

The issue of the substitution of human collectivity for an individuality set Strauss against the advocates of three fronts who consolidated their ranks in the 1840s and 50s: the conservative camps of Lutheran Confessionalism and supernaturalism, the mediating school, and the variations of historico-critical theology. In these counter-reactions to Strauss, the central issues with which Strauss had dealt failed to take root. The old conservative school at Tübingen issuing from Storr, Flatt and Süskind stayed within the confines of the divine inspiration and authority of Scripture and rigorously adhered to the strictly supernatural view of the origin and essence of Christianity. Rejecting all forms of "pure theistic rationalism" as well as the new variety of "pantheistic and mystic rationalism" allegedly documented in Strauss, critics around Storr perpetuated the pre-critical, christological approach to Scripture and in this way the orthodox Christ of faith.(68)

In a similar way, the rigid Lutheran confessionalism of the orthodox tradition from Löhe to Hengstenberg also stood hesitant before the possibility of the historical unreliability of the Gospel tradition. This position also extended into the immediate background of the movement which was shaped by the neopietism of Friedrich August Tholuck. In Tholuck's counter-reaction to Strauss in the Glaubwürdigkeit der evangelischen Geschichte "the circumstance that the synoptical evangelists, in some points, vary from or contradict each other, afforded no reason whatever for regarding the great features in which they agree, or the facts recorded only by a single evangelist, as substantially unhistorical and mythical."(69) The central premise of traditional apologetics remained unchallenged: "the evangelical narrations (could be) received as history."(70) Moreover, on the basis of their express identification of the archetypal and historical, the most influential conservative questers after Strauss - Neander, Ullmann, Tholuck, Hengstenberg, Nitzsch - remained solidly entrenched in an evidentialist framework which continued to attribute to the historical Jesus supernatural characteristics. Traditional evidentialist-supernaturalist presuppositions, then, opposed by rationalists and neologists and rendered ineffectual by historico-critical procedures, were still resiliant enough to recall Strauss' critics to an apologetic defense of the authenticity and integrity of the Leben Jesu narratives on the basis of historical evidences.

To align the proponents of this apologetic band-wagon with those of the Reformed churches was the theological platform of a growing number of "mediating" questers who developed Schleiermacher's idea of Christ as the "archetypal" and "ideal" man in the direction of a correlation and "reconciliation" of the presuppositions of speculation with those of historical criticism. In this "mediation" a strong biblical orientation was fused with a recovery of "personalist" categories counteracting the dissolution of the positive, historical foundations of the life of Jesus into a mode of subjective religious self-consciousness.(71) On the basis of Schleiermacher's "Vermittlungstheologie" critics of the caliber of Gieseler, Umbreit and Ullmann argued that the historic human figure of Jesus of Nazareth could bear out the "idea" of "archetype." The historical incarnation of God in Christ, Ullmann asserted, is "no longer merely an example of the relationship of God and man." Christ represents "in the highest sense the true man, the mediator between Godhead and humanity, the mid-point of world history, the inexhaustible source of all higher development of life and spirit."(72)

III

With regard to "the relationship of the historical components of the Bible ... to the idea" Strauss found that Schleiermacher, too, left him "in the dark."(73) According to Strauss, Schleiermacher's Jesus portrait hinged on a twofold assertion: it affirmed both that the figure of Jesus mediated the "Urbild" of "God-consciousness" and that this "Urbild" could indeed be borne out by a visible historical individual. "Christ, the historically unique," Strauss recapitulated Schleiermacher's view, "was at the same time the originally typical, i.e., on the one hand, the ideal type in him became completely historical, and on the other hand, the course of his earthly existence wholly conditioned the original typical idea."(74) But this "construction of the person of Christ out of the Christian consciousness ... could only impress (Strauss) as an uncritical presupposition."(75) With Strauss, the latter assertion of Jesus as the exemplar of

"God-consciousness" became problematic at the very point in which more specifically historical conclusions were presented as following from non-historical premises. Strauss was convinced that divine-human "unity" could not be realized in the historical Jesus in an exclusive way. He thus advanced a disjunction emphatically denied in Schleiermacher's attempt to "evolve the divine man ... as ... representing to himself a mere human soul so imbued with the consciousness of divinity that this constitutes its sole actuating principle."(76) Stated in extreme terms, Strauss' "idea" did not need a historical figure to be clothed with mythological embellisment. The "idea" was to Strauss autonomous and subsistent enough to produce "myths" on its own accord.

While Strauss was adamant in his "aversion to Schleiermacher's perspective," the "new" Tübingen school around Ferdinand Christian Baur acutely revealed the affinity between Strauss and Schleiermacher. The question whether the Jesus of history was to be approached in terms of Strauss' mythological procedures and "whether or not the Person of Jesus of Nazareth really possesses the attributes" ascribed to him by Schleiermacher was, Baur reiterated, "in fact a purely historical question...."(77) On this 'historical' front, however, Strauss and Schleiermacher were for the Tübingen critics around Baur in the same boat. In both Schleiermacher and Strauss Baur saw a failure to provide for a "necessary" relation between the "archetypal" Christ and the historical Jesus, a separation of the historical and "archetypal" derived from a "speculative" comprehension of Christianity. With regard to this separation, Schleiermacher's programme appeared to Baur to take a concrete step beyond Strauss in conceiving "the external history of Jesus as ... a history of the inner development of the religious self-consciousness...." And yet, like Strauss, Schleiermacher did stay with "the Hegelian philosophy of religion" which viewed "Christ as the God-man only in his relation to faith, without expressing more precisely what objective point of contact in the actual appearance of Christ faith has for its presuppositions."(78)

Schleiermacher started, Baur acknowledged, with the "archetypal" or "ideal" Christ defined as authentic humanity, man reconciled with God. But Schleiermacher did not provide for the possibility of an authentically historical Jesus; his system was not founded on the historical Jesus on the basis of a critical analysis of the Gospel accounts.(79) Schleiermacher began instead with the "ideal Christ," and therefore "he could do no more than assert that this ideal, archetypal Christ was simultaneously the historical Jesus, the starting point for Christian self-consciousness: he was unable to show that this is the case."(80) Schleiermacher thus in effect failed to provide a historical actuality commensurate with his own "Vermittlungstheorie" and resorted instead to a flawed attempt to identify the idea of "reconciliation" archetypally with the historical Jesus.

It was precisely at this point that Baur sought to build his case against Schleiermacher. As the highest ethical religion, Christianity had, according to Baur, its unity solely in the concrete historical lineaments of the figure of Jesus. Christianity starts "from below" and against this premise, Baur averred, Schleiermacher's presuppositions collapsed like a house of cards to leave merely a Gnostic construct. Schleiermacher's attempted identification of the ideal Christ with the historical Jesus amounted in Baur's view to Gnosticism of a higher order, to an "ideal rationalism" which postulated the "archetype," the source of present Christian consciousness, as prior to the historical Jesus and thus caused the entire temporal process to fall into the sphere of consciousness.(81)

The archetypal Christ of faith and the earthly, historical Jesus here drifted apart and were at best only correlated externally. "It is soon evident," Baur observed of Schleiermacher's christology, "that despite all the appearance to uphold the historical reality of Christianity, Christ, nonetheless, can be taken for nothing other than an idea of reason. The historical Christ becomes the ideal, and the same is true of all doctrines and facts which relate immediately to Christ."(82)

Baur used the fact that Schleiermacher did not "set forth ... the Gospel history ... as the actual source of knowledge about Christianity" to uncover the pantheistic idealism of Schleiermacher's programme. In Schleiermacher, Baur charged, "the external history of Jesus is taken as a history of the inner development of the religious self-consciousness. ... Christ is therefore in each man, and the external appearance of Jesus is not what is fundamental here; rather, in the historical the prototypical or ideal is supposed to be displayed and the inner consciousness thereby brought to clarity. It is self-evident how exactly this coheres with the pantheistic-idealistic basis of the whole system."(83) It was further "self-evident" to Baur that Schleiermacher's view of the "archetypal" Christ was also detrimental to the objective absoluteness of Christianity as a historical force. "The historical process, in which Christianity comes to historical manifestation," was for Schleiermacher, Baur judged, merely a presupposition of Christian consciousness, with Jesus counting "not as an external fact of history, but as an inward fact of the highest potentiality of human consciousness."(84) And at this junction it was Hegel's panentheistic idealism, and not the historical theology of the "mediating" camp, which Baur strikingly appropriated for his conception of history as the "process" of divine self-actualization, a "process", however, leaving the positivity of the Gospel tradition intact.(85) In this version of the "pantheism of history," "historical Christianity" was "simply an element of the same course in which the process immanent to the nature of God explicates itself historically."(86)

With regard to his appropriation of Hegelian categories, however, Baur, no less than Schleiermacher, exposed himself to the charge of merely superimposing an a priori pattern on concrete historical life which submerged individuals in suprahistorical categories and devalued the historical relevance of Jesus of Nazareth. In focusing on the unfolding "idea" in historical process, Baur seemed to reduce Jesus to a purely "natural" phenomenon and to undercut all foundations that faith in Jesus as the Christ had in the life of Jesus itself.(87) Baur, too, thus appeared to make "no other Christ possible, than an ideal one."(88)

On this count, Baur was only a small step away from Strauss and, like Strauss, opposed by a common front of critics from both the supernatural and mediating camps whose basic allegiance was to the "person of Christ." With Strauss' Leben Jesu, "idea become real" was to be found "in the totality of humanity;" with Baur, "Christ as man" was "man in his universality;" with C. F. Ammon's Die Geschichte des Lebens Jesu and Ullmann's Die Sündlosigkeit Jesu, however, it was possible for the "idea" to realize itself in one objective-historic individual, and in this union commitment was "personal:" "In Christ," Ullmann held, the union of God and man attained "its zenith and historical fulfillment...."(89)

IV

The main bone of contention in Strauss' Leben Jesu, then, was that his "life" was neither primarily about a "person" nor about the 'historically factual objective reality' underlying the Christ of faith. There remained throughout an "unfilled cleft" between the "idea" and "the historical life whose moving principle it ought to be."(90) Strauss dissolved the positive, historical foundations of the Christian faith into a mode of religious consciousness, and this the higher-critical exegetes quickly uncovered and realised more acutely as the "synoptic problem" continued to gain ground within the Leben-Jesu-Forschung. That the doctrine of the supernatural Christ did not coalesce with the historical Jesus as he really was - this assertion, Strauss' historical-critical opponents argued, could only to be counteracted if Christianity was viewed as a historical phenomenon and if the identity of the God-man was not demonstrated philosophically, as the "mediating" school attempted, but rather investigated by a purely historico-critical method.

The questers who climbed on this historico-critical band-wagon after Strauss and evaluated anew the historical significance of the Gospels, independent of the presuppositions of speculative philosophy, assumed that a secure material basis for the historical Jesus was furnished by the synoptic rather than the Johannine account of the life of Jesus. On this count, Schleiermacher's solution of the synoptic problem appeared inadequate. Schleiermacher's rejection of Eichhorn's Proto-Gospel hypothesis in favor of the oral tradition posited that this tradition gradually evolved into disconnected written fragments which crystallized into two main sources, the synoptics and John. Of the two, the Gospel of John was asserted to be "stamped" by "the biographical character ... in the most definite way."(91) In the historical criticism of Baur, by contrast, the preference for the synoptics prevailed. Moreover, Baur and his followers were also not so much interested in recovering the "biographical Gospel" as "genuine" as in establishing the methodological priority of the origins of Christianity and therefore furthered the emergence of systematic and disciplined historico-critical study not only of biblical materials but also of the church's tradition.(92)

Baur's "standpoint" was "in one word the purely historical one: namely, that the one thing to be aimed at is to place before ourselves the materials given in the history as they are objectively, and not otherwise...."(93) Accordingly, the figure of Jesus was to be explained not by studying the contemporary pious consciousness of the community of faith but rather by locating the significance of Jesus of Nazareth in history. And at this juncture, Baur charged, Strauss had set out on a wrong track in his criticism by ignoring the literary relations between the synoptics. Moreover, Strauss had played one Gospel account off against the other on the basis of his canons of authenticity and asserted against the prevailing critical opinion that the Fourth Gospel was most removed in time and of the least historical worth. "The only degree of distinction between the historical value of the synoptical account and that of John," Strauss declared, "is, that the former is a mythical product of the first era of traditional formation, the latter of the second..."(94)

Baur vehemently refused "to employ Strauss' tactics and methodology" and rejected the attempt to set the Fourth Gospel against the synoptics "in a historical opposition."(95) Baur conceded that the Fourth Gospel "does not intend to be a strictly historical Gospel, but rather subordinates its historical content to an idea imposed upon the whole," namely the Johannine thesis of the incarnation of the divine Logos. But contra Strauss, Baur's insight left the basis for a historico-critical appraisal of the Gospels unchallenged. In fact, "to the degree that the historical value of John sinks," Baur argued, "that of the Synoptics rises."(96)

As a biblical critic, Baur correlated his historico-critical interest with questions relating to the authorship and "tendencies" of the scriptural accounts. "The first question which criticism has put to these Gospels can only be what each respective author wantend and intended, and only with this question do we come to the firm ground of concrete, historical truth."(97) On this basis Baur explained the evolution of primitive Christianity and Christian literature in terms of the dialectal opposition between the Petrine and Pauline conceptions of Christianity, between an original "Judaizing" form and a gentile form.(98) This procedure of identifying Paulinism with gentile Christianity and the standpoint of the original Apostles with that of the legalistic and exclusive Jewish Christians subjected the New Testament accounts to a literary-historical criticism, a "tendency criticism" which led "back to the sources of the Gospel history and to the distinction which the most recent critical investigations have made among them."(99) Baur was led primarily, that is, to a complete reorganization and re-dating of the synoptic accounts: Matthew, reflecting Judaizing tendencies, represented the first Gospel; Luke, a second century revision of a Pauline proto-Luke, was assigned the second place; and Mark, a late second century epitome of Matthew and Luke, constituted the youngest synoptic account. This reading took different forms and was arrived at by different routes, but the outcome was throughout the emergence of a new question, that of the "prehistory" of the Gospel literature and the history of the tradition of which the Gospels represented only one element - a conclusion ruinous to the "mediating" and harmonistic "lives" which had relied on the unilinear historicity of the order of events in the life of Jesus narratives.

Baur's historio-critical stance was ruinous to yet another characteristic of previous life of Jesus research. Judged against Schleiermacher's definition of the hermeneutical task, Baur's refinement of the historico-critical method appeared reductive, equating "understanding" with the explanation of the historical origin and context of ideas rather than exploring, as Schleiermacher's hermeneutics had, the relation of the narratives themselves to the process of interpretation. For Baur, hermeneutical questions were inextricably linked to the task of "historical comprehension." The psychologism and individualism of Schleiermacher's hermeneutic amounted in this context to an "abstract literary criticism" which failed to combine literary analysis with a scrutiny of the theological tendencies of the Gospels on the basis of the historical milieu of the texts, their situation-in-life and the history of tradition.(100)

In the tradition that Baur typified hermeneutics often did not go beyond the specialized critical task of examining the presence or absence of correspondence between the biblical accounts and their factual, "outside" references. This applied in a similar way to those critics who set out to save the authenticity of the accounts against Strauss' historical scepticism. E. F. Gelpke, F. Stäudlin, J. C. F. Steudel and their contemporaries were concerned above all else to demonstrate in their source criticism that the accounts were bound up with the authentic events of Jesus' history.(101) In this focus on references outside the text itself, however, the subject matters handled in Schleiermacher's hermeneutics were narrowed down to the task of reconstructing the "authentically historical" situation which shaped the text.(102)

Schleiermacher had emphasized that "hermeneutics and criticism, both philological disciplines, both arts, belong together, since the execution of each presupposes the other. The former is in general the art of understanding correctly the speech of another, especially when it is written down. The latter is the art of judging correctly the authenticity of the writings and passages, and of establishing on the basis of adequate attestation and date."(103) In Strauss' critics the latter aspect pertaining to the "authenticity" of the biblical narratives became central, with "hermeneutics" limiting itself to the philological tasks Schleiermacher subsumed under the rubric of "criticism." And while "in the period from 1720-1820 almost every year a hermeneutics (had) appeared," Strauss' time witnessed instead the proliferation of source critical studies in which the interpretive interrelatedness of language and exegesis explored by Schleiermacher receded behind the correlation of exegetical findings with different claims of historical reliability.(104)

On the scriptural-exegetical plane, this correlation showed in particular in the clarification of the mutual literary dependence of the Gospel accounts. Within a broad spectrum of solutions to this "synoptic problem" one premise remained constant: the synoptic accounts were throughout asserted to yield a far greater degree of reliability of the biblical records than Strauss was ever willing to grant. After C. H. Weisse's and C. G. Wilke's pioneering synoptic studies of 1838, this premise won the field in 1863 with Holtzmann's formulation of the two-document hypothesis. Holtzmann demonstrated that Matthew and Luke had used a common sayings source in their Gospels but had relied on Mark for the framework of their account. Holtzmann was convinced that in establishing the priority of Mark, he could deduce that the order of events in the life of Jesus as reported in Mark was authentic.(105) According to Holtzmann, Proto-Mark retained the oldest records of the disciples in their original form, and was historically trustworthy. Similarly, the second source, the Logia, flowed from the oral testimony of the apostles and provided authentic material. While Strauss' treatment of the Markan account had, in Holtzmann's terms, "drawn the blood from the veins of the most vitally depicted, most distinctive memories" of Jesus "so as to then to banish the drained phantoms, one by one to the Hades of abstract thought," Holtzmann thus restored the Markan account to historical positivity and affirmed the historicity of Jesus' messianic consciousness as "(designating) the immediate ... experience of God in the innermost being."(106)

From the point of view of source criticism, this presented a significant advance over Strauss who had contributed no definite theory about the composition of the Gospels and who had proceeded under the tutelage of a philosophical system developed independently of biblical criticism. The source critics associated with Holtzmann turned Strauss' position around in an exegetical "critical" move which yielded historical validation of Jesus himself. But precisely with regard to this validation source critics were on common ground with Strauss in that their criticism focused, no less than Strauss', on the events recorded in the Gospels rather than on the texts of Gospels themselves. To opt for a particular theory of the Gospels' mutual dependence, be it the Proto-Gospel hypothesis or the two-document theory, was with source critics also to accept a particular chronology of events pertaining to Jesus' history. From the point of view of hermeneutics, then, the narrowing of this discipline towards mere "criticism" triggered by Strauss was thus corroborated and tied to the assumption that textual and source critical findings comported with hard-core evidence about the facticity of the historical Jesus.

V

It was the naive confidence in the scriptural accounts as "positive" history that led Schweitzer to reject the liberal "lives" after Strauss as a lost case. But in its time, the equation of the early sources with historical authenticity met an important theological need in furnishing an answer to Strauss' dissolution of the historical Jesus. With the historical authenticity of the Markan account restored, the quest was free to turn to the historical "personality" of Jesus. The period of the life of Jesus in its original sense was now just beginning. For the next quarter century after Strauss the quest remained solidly entrenched in a framework which rendered the figure of Jesus knowable to the "personal" categories of a historical-critical theology. Strauss had accepted it as axiomatic that the "ideal" Christ, and not the concrete historical figure was the true basis of religious faith. The possibility of recovering "Jesus as the really was" and the literary relationship of the synoptic sources - these issues Strauss put aside. Strauss thus failed, his critics charged, "to bring out the peculiarity and originality of his religious genius and in this way to discover in the original personality and reforming activity of Jesus the originating cause of the rise of the community of his disciples and their faith in him as the Messiah and (in) his divine mission."(107)

On this score, the quest after Strauss was no longer determined, as Schweitzer had claimed, by the substitution of the historical figure of Jesus for dogmatic concerns but rather by the belief in Christ as the one "in whom the perfect personal union of the divine and human appeared historically." This belief, propagated by the growing influence of kenotic and mediating christologies, was embedded in the consensus that the "divine-human manifestation of Christ" was "historical and true" and to be located only "in the person of Christ."(108) The cast of this conviction flowed from the express assumption that the "unity of God-man" "entered history with the religious person of Jesus" and hence constituted "a definite concrete historical religious principle" not to be abstracted from the "Christian principle" in the manner of Strauss.(109)

The "liberal-positive" "lives" produced by Schenkel, Keim, Holtzmann and Beyschlag in the 1860s and 70s assumed, moreover, that the solution of the source critical question concerning the Gospel composition through the two-document hypothesis also entailed the solution of the historical question concerning the "original form of the history" of Jesus. This "original form" was "conceived neither as a tendentious restructuring nor as allegorical fiction" but rather as an authentic chronology of events.(110) The "Jesusbild" that went with the establishment of the literary priority of Mark described the baptism scene as the starting point for Jesus' 'developing Messianic consciousness,' the proclamation of the Kingdom idea during the Galilean period, the failure of this preaching activity in Galilee, and the turning-point at Caesarea Philippi after which Jesus accepts his suffering with stoic resolution until his last days in Jerusalem.(111)

Concentration upon the figure of Jesus as religious personality and "hero" provided the common ground for this chronology and furnished "liberal-positive" questers with a historical basis on which they launched their historico-critical attack on the central pillar of the supernaturalist camp - the physical resurrection.(112) With "liberal-positive" questers, the purely individualistic, uneschatological interpretation of Jesus allegedly validated by the Markan outline pressed the distinction between the Easter message and the Easter faith. The message concerning the empty tomb, liberal-positive questers charged, presented an embellishment and legendary accretion and was to be replaced by faith in Jesus as the pre-eminent religious personality above all others in the history of mankind, imparting on men the assurance of the "infinite value" and hence immortality of the "human soul."(113)

Upon this "Jesusbild" the "liberal-positive" quest superimposed a view of history according to which 'revelation' was asserted to take place through ethico-spiritual personalities, bearers of 'saving ideas' such as 'reconciliation' and the 'Kingdom of God,' through whose influence spiritual powers or forces were actually operative in history. According to this conception, which fell back in part upon the old rationalist explanation of Jesus as an extraordinary religious personality, Jesus emerged as the most significant 'bearer' of inspiration in life and teaching, actualizing revelation and rendering its content comprehensible as an object of historical knowledge.(114) In this way the "liberal-positive" "lives" dispensed with the theological edifice that seemed to distance the Jesus of the Gospels from the common man. Their "Jesusbild" arrived instead at a "character-portrait" which divested the figure of Jesus from the stained-glass existence in which "theology" allegedly pictured him.(115)

In this focus on the historical Jesus as religious personality and "hero" the lessons of Strauss' Leben Jesu were not applied. The preference of philosophical interpretation over critical history, the emphasis on the meaning of history over against the historicity of particular events - none of this survived in the "liberal-positive" "lives." "Strauss' contention that the Gospels contain a very great deal that is mythical has ... not been borne out," Harnack observed of the history of the quest after Strauss.(116) From Pfleiderer's retrospective view it further appeared that the "liberal-positive" "lives" after Strauss were also "connected (with) the peril of falling back into the old abuses of rationalistic artifice."(117) This reversion included striking "concessions to supernaturalistic dogma" which Strauss had emphatically left behind.(118) For Theodore Keim and August Neander the supernatural no longer posed an unsurmountable obstacle; on the contrary, Neander's Das Leben Jesu Christi frankly maintained that "The Truth, that Christ is God-Man" was "presupposed."(119)

Above all, it was Strauss' proposition of an alternative to a positivistically historical orientation that the "lives" from Keim to Holtzmann did not absorb. For Strauss, the form of the Gospel narratives was that of "myth," "myth flowing from the "spirit" of the early Christian community and as such superior to the merely "transient" matter of the historicity of the accounts. As long as "the spirit of a people of a community" remained the "permanent" issue, interpretation was indifferent to the historicity of the Gospel narratives.(120) Here lay Strauss' contribution to the discipline of form criticism and to the interest in the pre-literary development of the Gospel tradition. This very approach to the

Gospel narratives by means of historical literary criticism was slighted in the "liberal-positive" quest's preference of Jesus' "personality" over the kerygma, a preference which also failed to acknowledge Strauss' shift in interpretation away from the Gospel event itself to its narration.

Strauss' alternative to a positivistically oriented quest was not to be recovered until the close of the "liberal-positive" era. With Martin Kähler's 1892 essay on The So-Called Historical Jesus and the Historic, Biblical Christ the view that faith does not need to rely on a verifiable historical corpus established by historico-critical procedure became a renewed focus for theological endeavor. According to Kähler, the production of a developmental, historical-critical biography of Jesus was not possible. The foundation of faith was to Kähler the "living Christ ... who ... lives in the confessional context of the community gathered together by the power of his presence."(121) The historic, "geschichtliche" Christ thus could only be reached through the kerygma and included the proclamation of Jesus' Lordship as well as the "picture" of his character and impact on contemporaries and succeeding generations. With the "geschichtliche Christus," the person and the witness belonged together. Christ himself was the "originator" of the "biblical picture of the Christ."(122) The apostolic kerygma and the pattern of the Gospel history - the Christ of faith and the Jesus of history - were therefore inseparable. In this way one of the central assumptions on which the Leben-Jesu-Forschung had relied, namely that a sharp dichotomy existed between the Jesus of history and the Christ of faith, was sharply counteracted.

With regard to the relevance of "Geschichte" a second trend, also issuing from Kähler's programmatic essay, further worked to counteract "liberal-positive" presuppositions. According to Kähler, one could not arrive at the historic Christ via the historical Jesus "behind" the Gospels. Since there was no presuppositionless "Historie" in the Gospels, a "Historie" untouched by the kerygma, any attempt to use the Gospels for a chronology of Jesus' life and ministry was futile. From Wilhelm Herrmann, the leading theological voice at Marburg in the 1880s and 90s, came a view which questioned Kähler's position at just this point. The early Christian proclamation of Christ related to the faith of the time and "this proclamation alone," Herrmann maintained, "cannot protect us from the doubt that we want to base our faith on something that is perhaps not historical fact at all; but is itself a product of faith."(123) In this context, which reproduced the terms of Schleiermacher's canon, it was legitimate to go behind the kerygma and extend the scope of "Geschichte" to designate not merely the kerygma but also the "inner life" of Jesus in man's life as the determinative ground of faith.(124) This emphasis on the inner life of Jesus as an immediate certainty of faith, however, did not derive from historical evidence objectively determinable but rather was self-validating. Behind the emphasis on the inner experience of the individual self historical criticism could not penetrate. With this reassertion of Schleiermacher's experiential terms another pillar on which the "liberal-positive" quest had relied - namely, the assumption that historico-critical analysis could and should produce a reliable reconstruction of the historical Jeus - was pushed into the background.

The renewal of the continuity between the Jesus of history and the Christ of faith brought at the close of the "liberal-positive" stage of the quest also a revival of soteriological categories. Kähler's focus on "Geschichte" and Herrmann's appeal to the inner personality of Jesus denied that the significance of Jesus for faith was exhausted by the mere appeal to the 'facticity' of Jesus' life with no regard for his 'person' and 'work.' Relevant for Kähler and Herrmann was not the reconstruction of who Jesus was but the insight into what Jesus did and does for believers. With regard to this latter aspect, the reconstructions of both Strauss and his critics appeared insufficient. Strauss, having "no place for either sin or redemption in the traditional sense, (needed) no redeemer either."(125) Nor did the "liberal-positive" notion of Jesus as "hero" and "example" allow a distinct place for what became significant to Kähler and Herrmann - the consciousness of redemption. On this soteriological ground of christology, however, only the "effective" biblical Christ was judged to be determinative for faith. For the historical Jesus to become relevant again in subsequent life of Jesus research, it was therefore deemed necessary to re-establish Jesus' redemptive significance for man. In order to continue, any future quest would have to turn the historical Jesus into the Christ of faith again.(126)

Part II An American Quest

5. Towards the Quest

American life of Jesus research did not achieve full coherence until the second quarter of the nineteenth century, but both the seeds and stimuli for the growth of the quest had made inroads in the American intellectual and theological landscape long before that time. The focus on the historical figure of Jesus could claim indirect pedigrees in American religious history and more immediate seeds in the Arian and Socinian christological currents of the seventeenth and eighteenth centuries which preconditioned the allegiance to the quest. It were the Unitarians of the first half of the nineteenth century who fused such modifications into an organized movement and performed a large service as a testing ground for the quest. Unitarianism, with its denial of total depravity and the expiatory nature of the atonement was - judged against the Nicene and Athanasian doctrine of the trinity - expressly untrinitarian, if not antitrinitarian. Consonant with this anti-trinitarian thrust was the liberals' consistent adherence to the unipersonality of God and the subordinate rank of Christ. In this emphasis, the liberals were frequently charged with Socinianism of a century earlier which affirmed the "simple humanity" of Christ without denying his divine mission. The terms of this christological position differed from Arianism in its rejection of the view that Christ had any pre-existence before his miraculous conception, but they agreed with Arianism in the assertion that Christ was a creature and not the "Son of God" in the sense affirmed by the Nicene Creed. The Socinian focus on Jesus' "simple humanity" remained separate and apart from the quest as long as it was not connected with a corresponding higher-critical procedure.(1) But once the 'humanistic' emphasis on Jesus' "humanity" became aligned with historico-critical exegesis, the stage was set for the development of the historical Jesus quest.

Early American Unitarians, however, did not use Socinian doctrine to reconstruct the foundations of their christology towards an emphasis on the "humanity" of Jesus. Initially, New England divines were not prepared to follow William Bentley of the East Church in Salem and James Freeman of King's Chapel in their 'humanistic' conception of Jesus modelled after English Socinians like Joseph Priestley and the elder William Hazlitt. In this reluctance towards Socinianism, the signposts of Unitarian christology bore instead the label of Arianism, affirming "that the Son was inferior, ... different in essence, the minister of the Father, and in all respect subject to his will." "The doctrine that the Son is a distinct being from the Father, and essentially inferior" Unitarian dogmaticians took "to be the essence of Unitarianism, of which Arianism is a particular modification."(2) It was at this juncture that the view of Jesus' status as an intermediary being between God and man moved Unitarian christological affirmations against the Socinian position in asserting that Christ, while not a part of the Godhead, was a being on a far higher plane than "mere man."

The crux of christological argument became for Unitarians, in the context of the quest's development, the rejection of the orthodox view that Christ was a unique "person" in the Godhead, co-equal, co-eternal and of one substance with the Father and the Holy Spirit. This rejection pointed to the figure of Jesus as a historical personage and in this respect characterized Unitarianism essentially as a "back-to-Jesus movement."(3)

Yet in this "back-to-Jesus" call, the quest's view of the pure "humanity" of Jesus based on critical investigations of the validity and historical reliability of the biblical narratives long found no place. Unitarianism declared its separate identity under the aegis of a framework which rendered New England divinity uncongenial towards the historico-critical impulse of the quest. Foundational to the doctrinal and epistemological position of the liberal camp was the system of "supernatural rationalism," a synthesis of rationalism and credence in supernaturalism derived from eighteenth century English theologians who were hostile to the assaults of deist critics, disinclined to historico-critical procedures and committed to pre-critical, harmonistic exegesis.(4)

Rational supernaturalism had at its center the adage that unassisted natural faculties or senses could establish the essentials of natural religion. "Reason" was not competent to demonstrate or enhance the existence and attributes of an infinite personal Godhead, but "reason" could discern the criteria for authenticating revelation. This view of "the duty of using the reason in examining the claims and determining the contents of revelation" did not entail a particular creed, but rather relied on an empirical method of Christian apologetics.(5) In rational and empirical terms supernatural rationalists adhered unflinchingly to the premise that the validity of the articles of Christian doctrine stood and fell with the validity of historical "evidences" buttressing the supernatural claims of Christianity. Apologists took the historicity of the biblical miracles for granted as the cornerstone of the premise that Jesus was the Messiah, a divinely inspired intermediary and not merely a human figure. "These miracles," apologists reiterated, "were not wrought by a man whose character in other respects was ordinary. They were acts of a being, whose mind was as singular as his works, who spoke and acted with more than human authoriy, whose moral qualities and sublime purposes were in accordance with superhuman powers."(6)

A clear manifestation of the idea of supernatural revelation attested by supernatural "evidences" was provided by the treatises and manuals on the life of Jesus. The rank and file of the Unitarian clergy stoutly adhered to the view that the life of Jesus was expressive of a divine revelation in a historical person and dealt, like other biographies of historical personages, in the hard currency of reliable, substantial and verifiable "fact." William Ellery Channing established both the theme and approach of this version of the life of Jesus in "The Evidences of Revealed Religion." Channing's "life" represented a distinct outgrowth of the debate that had been lingering on since the time of Locke and the deists - the debate on the question of whether Christianity could be validated and authenticated by appealing to the historicity of Jesus' prophecies, miracles and resurrection. The main point was that the historical outlines of Jesus' life were irreproachable and bore "the marks of truth" "beyond all other histories." Channing accordingly put forward a biographical outline of Jesus' "humble birth and education" to substantiate the claim that "the character of Christ ... was real." "To suppose that this character was invented by unprincipled men ... and was then imposed as a reality in the very age of the Founder of Christianity," represented to Channing "an excess of credulity, and a strange ignorance of the powers and principles of human nature." "Christ's history" carried "all the marks of reality" and "did not spring up before the date of authentic history." "The character of Jesus was original."(7)

This was the key argument of the evidentialist approach to the life of Jesus that was to serve Unitarians well beyond the miracles controversy. And it was the supernatural rationalist framework rather than the de-supernaturalized historico-critical approach that the New England liberals accepted and that served to delay the advance of the quest's procedures. Despite the Unitarians' exposure to the neologist and "rationalist" criticism of the quest in the first decades of the nineteenth century, supernatural rationalism generally worked until the 1840s to postpone a consistent and thorough application of historical-critical procedures. In the supernatural rationalism attested by supernatural "signs" the quest's view of the pure "humanity" of Jesus, aligned with a close scrutiny of the historicity of the scriptural accounts, long could not be assimilated.

Although the Unitarian evidentialist approach to the life of Jesus developed a distinct life and identity of its own, it remained closely allied with a number of older apologetic movements, most notably the supernatural rationalism of the post-Lockean theology of "evidences," supremely illustrated in a group of eighteenth century Anglicans: Samuel Clarke, John Chapman, Richard Watson and William Paley. Advocated in England as an affirmative theological reaction to the demand for sensible evidence prompted by Newtonian science and advanced as the chief orthodox defense against both deism and "enthusiasm," the evidentialist tradition formed the context within which the harmonistic approach to the life of Jesus in both Britain and America began to thrive. In England, the essentials of this apologetic system endured in the empiricist tradition represented by Clarke and Paley, who centered on miracles and prophecies as grounds for believing in the "reasonableness" and divine origin of Christianity. This apologetic pattern was asserted to form "the most credible, certain and convincing Evidence, that was ever given to any matter of Fact," and set out "to state the proper and distinct proofs, which show not only the general value of the (scriptural) records, but their specific authority, and the high probability there is that they actually came from the persons whose names they bear."(8) "Their antiquity and genuineness ... and their authority, as written by inspired men, and containing an authentic account of Jesus Christ" all served to affirm the evidentialist premise "that the History of the Life of Christ, contained in the New Testament, is a true Relation of Matters of Fact...."(9)

These assumptions were extremely influential in shaping early Unitarian thought on the life of Jesus and in setting the course for much of American criticism against the quest. The evidentialist influence was apparent in virtually all pre-Civil War handbooks and manuals dealing with the life of Jesus accounts. Paley's and Clarke's empirical inductionism could be found in the liberal Unitarians at Harvard and was also well-nigh universal with the conservative Presbyterians at Princeton. Moderate Calvinists at Yale took it for granted as did the "gentlemen theologians" of the South.(10) Among Boston Unitarians the tradition of the theology of the "evidences" was perpetuated by Joseph Buckminster, Henry Ware Jr., William Ellery Channing and Andrews Norton, who marshalled all available arguments for the validity of the Gospel accounts of the life and miracles of Jesus. Correspondingly, the life of Jesus literature represented to a large extent a reproduction of British evidentialist literature - of the harmonies and evidentialist "lives" by William Newcome, James Macknight, Nathaniel Lardner and Lant Carpenter. The "evidences" advocated by this group of apologists were chiefly two: "First, the Christian Revelation" was held to be "positively and directly proved ... by the many infallible Signs and Miracles, which the Author of it worked publickly as the Evidence of his Divine Commission." Secondly, the proof of the Divine Authority of the Christian Revelation" was asserted to be "confirmed and ascertained by the Exact Completion both of all those Prophecies that went before concerning our Lord, and of those that he Himself delivered concerning things that were to happen after."(11)

The points which religious apologists here proposed evinced precisely the kinds of emphases that were to become the pillars of later rationalistic defenses against the quest's inroads. The quest was distinctly historico-critical and critical-humanistic; in contrast, Unitarian supernatural rationalists were pre-critical and closer to Clarke and Paley than to Eichhorn and H. E. G. Paulus. They were committed throughout to the "genuineness" of the "evidences" of Christianity and less concerned with the historicity of the Gospel tradition or even the facticity of Jesus' existence. Their religious categories were firmly entrenched in an intellectualist or conceptualist theological tradition which did not subordinate revelation to historical situation. For the biblical critics of the quest the role of exegesis was to determine historical particularities and the context of the life of Jesus narratives. For the supernatural rationalist there was no such necessity to regard revelation as relative and subject to historical contexts. The figure of Jesus was a vehicle of revelation and not an index of specific historically conditioned situation. "Christ's life," the supernatural rationalist asserted, "is not a part of the great nexus of events, ... but ... a spirit descending from above into human affairs to make them all new."(12)

The stirs of the new theological movement on the Continent intially left this supernatural rationalist presupposition intact. While for the critical questers of the post-harmony tradition the reliability of the scriptural life of Jesus accounts became increasingly questionable, the supernatural rationalist held the internal consistency and historicity of the scriptural accounts of Jesus and the reliability of the authors to be unchallengeable. "Christ's history," Channing insisted in "The Evidences of Christianity" "could not have been a fiction." "The delineation of Jesus in the Gospels, so warm with life, and so unrivalled in loveliness and grandeur, required the existence of an original."(13)

This position was corroborated by the supernatural rationalists' recourse to the common sense realism developed in Scotland by Thomas Reid and Dugald Stewart in the middle and later eighteenth century as an apologetic tool designed to restore Lockean empiricism after Hume's inroads. In the works of the common sense philosophers, liberal theologians found a defense of the reliability of knowledge through a 'realistic' theory of perception validating the arguments basic to natural theology. In common sense realism the liberals found, in addition, an insistence on the limits of knowledge which rendered the claims of revelation necessary.(14) But these apologetic advantages were purchased at a high price when judged against the development of the quest. The 'history-less' tendency evident in Scottish common sense realism could hardly coexist with the historico-critical procedures basic to the "lives." Scottish common sense was 'transhistorical,' with no primary interest in the question whether the Jesus of history coincided with the Christ of faith.

The Unitarians' main interest revolved around the issue of the reliability and "authenticity" of empirical "evidences" surrounding the scriptural testimony of the life of Jesus. This theology of historical "evidences" did not respond to challenges of the historicity of the life of Jesus accounts by admitting or proclaiming hermeneutical changes and readjustments. The concern with the life of Jesus narratives was far too closely tied up with the evidentialist tradition and its preoccupation with "genuineness" to trigger any concerted interest in biblical interpretation and in the corollary question about literary form and development. Because early Unitarian applications of biblical criticism lacked the concern with historicity and scriptural interpretation nineteenth higher criticism imparted on biblical criticism, Unitarian exegetes did not decidedly break with the harmonistic approach. Exposure to the neologist studies of Eichhorn, Griesbach, Michaelis and Semler helped to emancipate Unitarian supernatural rationalists from bondage to evidentialism, but the applications of the new critical procedures still lacked the rigor and consistency to draw the exegetical community to a methodology that was expressly historico-critical and hermeneutical. By the 1830s, when Schleiermacher had moved beyond the pale of supernatural rationalism, it was a distinctly hermeneutical reorientation, a shift away from biblicism that had taken root within the Leben-Jesu-Forschung. On the Unitarian front, by contrast, the encounter with lower and higher criticism was too limited and tentative to allow the acceptance of historico-critical methods to become a challenge to the common sense principle that the meaning of Scripture 'stood still' and was thoroughly entrenched in historical "evidences."

I

The development of the quest within the ranks of New England divinity received a decisive impetus from the circumstances under which the Unitarian controversy had begun in America and appeared in this respect less as a surprise development imposed by outside influences and more as a natural outgrowth of indigenous strains of thought deeply engrained in New England divinity. The publication in 1815 of Thomas Belsham's American Unitarianism by Jedidiah Morse, who declared that "rational Christianity" had conquered eastern Massachusetts, confirms that early Unitarianism did not need to import a Christocentric theology and instead nourished the seeds that were to develop into the critical Jesus quest.(15) Thomas Belsham, minister of the Essex Unitarian Chapel in London, described the presence of a Unitarian movement in England, one following the Socinian christology of Priestley's variety, and suggested a clear affinity of ideas between English Unitarians and New England liberals. Belsham's work was promptly used by its Panoplist reviewer Jedidiah Morse to demonstrate that the Boston liberals were at one with Lindsey, Priestley and other British Socinians. The actual links, however, between Unitarian christology and the Arian and Trinitarian controversies among Arminian and Latitudinarian movements in England were indirect and uncertain. One more direct link between the Unitarian controversy at the close of the seventeenth century and the Arian movement at the beginning of the eighteenth century was Thomas Emlyn's A Humble Inquiry Into the Scripture Account of Jesus Christ of 1703, made available in American editions by 1750. The key to Emlyn's argument was the doctrine of the subordinate nature of Christ. "God is in all," Emlyn insisted, "the Son himself subject under Him." To Emlyn, nothing could "be more expressive of an inequality between God and Christ."(16) Here were the terms around which half-formed beliefs about the unipersonality of God and the subordinate rank of Christ were able to cohere.

Within the context of subordinationism established by Emlyn anti-trinitarianism began to strive. Emlyn's Humble Inquiry played into the controversy over the Athanasian trinity which lingered on for nearly a century in New England. It was not until mid-eighteenth century, however, that Jonathan Mayhew openly rejected the Athanasian creed, which affirmed that the three persons of the trinity were all "coeternal" and "coequal." Mayhew did "not ... set aside the supreme authority and dominion of ... the Father, ... the mediatorial authority of Christ, being derived from Him, and subordinate to His."(17) Mayhew here adhered to a high Arian doctrine concerning the divinity of Christ, one of the same variety advocated by English Arians like Samuel Clarke and Daniel Whitby.

The high Arian christology underwent in England a partial development towards a "humanitarian" christology. It was from this "simple Humanitarianism" represented by Joseph Priestley that one of the strongest supports for the Unitarian view of the "humanity of Christ" emerged. During the second half of the eighteenth century liberal Dissenting churches had, under Priestley's sway, equated the Unitarian label with a Socinian conception of Jesus. "The purposes of (Jesus') mission," Priestley insisted, were not above the confines of a "mere man." Jesus was not a member of the Godhead. "For it cannot be said, that anything is ascribed to him that a mere man was not equal to."(18) Priestley advanced this position in terms analogous to to deists' rationalistic critique of Christianity. According to Priestley, "the doctrines ... of a trinity of persons in the godhead, original sin, arbitrary predestination, atonement for the sins of men by the death of Christ, and ... the doctrine of the plenary inspiration of the scriptures" were a corruption of the purity of the Christian message, "a departure from the original scheme." True Christianity, Priestley insisted, bore a "pristine simplicity and purity," a primacy of morality over dogma which had been distorted by the development of metaphysical and theological doctrines.(19) The starting point for this critique was the historical Jesus, conceived to be on one level with any other ordinary human and therefore subject to analogies with other extraordinary historical figures setting out "to inculcate a pure and more sublime morality respecting God and man than any heathen could have a just idea of."(20)

Thomas Belsham developed the emphasis on Jesus as "mere man" and perpetuated the Priestleyan view that Jesus did not represent the second person of the Trinity but rather a divinely inspired teacher. This trend away from the older high christologies was of revelance for the variety of subordinationism that evolved in eastern Massachusetts. Approximations to Socinianism were to appear in the later Channing; studies of anti-trinitarian origin such as Belknap's Psalms and Hymns circulated in a form eliminating all clearly trinitarian emphasis in accordance with subordinationist affirmations.(21) These variations of subordinationism represented important historical antecedents for the development of the critical Jesus quest. In the 1830s, when New England exegetes discovered the human, historical Jesus, a maturing biblical criticism was to embrace the focus on the "humanity" of Jesus as its doctrinal foundation and no longer refrained from affirming Jesus' unqualified "humanity" in the manner of Priestley and Belsham. Moreover, Socinian assertions were now directly linked with the issue of the very facticity of Christ's existence. "If the evidence be not complete, that Christ was really a man from his birth, actions, sufferings, death, and affirmations respecting himself, then," biblical critics asked, "how is it to be proved that Christ ever existed at all?"(22)

Early Unitarians, however, were anxious to set their own views off against not only the deists, but also against English Socinians of the caliber of Joseph Priestley. The liberals therefore long refused to accept the "Unitarian" label. "Holding, as they (did), high and exalted views of the person and mediation of Jesus Christ ... they (were) ... very unwilling to be confounded with the followers of Dr. Priestley."(23) Accordingly, Morse's accusation that the "liberal christians" of Boston taught, with Belsham, that Jesus was "a mere man" did not go unchallenged. The most substantial response came in 1815 in _A Letter to the Rev. Samuel C. Thacher, on the Aspersions Contained in a Late Number of the Panoplist, on the Ministry of Boston and Vicinity_, by William Ellery Channing, then minister of the Church of Christ on Federal Street. Channing conceded that "a small proportion" of his brethren preached Socinian views and "believed in the simple humanity of Christ."(24) But Channing expressly denied direct connections with the Socinianism of Priestley and defined Unitarians as those who affirm that "Jesus Christ is more than a man, that he existed before the world, that he literally came from heaven to save our race, ... that he still acts for our benefit and is intercessor with the Father."(25) These assertions acutely counteracted the Socinian position which attributed to Jesus a fully human nature. Channing was more concerned to view Christ as above humans, as divinely inspired and pre-existent while denying that he was an equal member or "person" of the Godhead.

Channing's reply to Morse spawned a series of pamphlet wars which revolved around the use of the term "person" to describe the distinctions of the Godhead. The issues which set Channing on his own native ground apart from orthodox Trinitarians like Noah Worcester were two: "First, whether the One God be three distinct substances, or three persons, or three 'somewhats' called persons, ... and secondly, whether one of these three substances, or improperly called persons, formed a personal union with a human soul, so that the Infinite Mind, and a human mind, each possessing its own distinct consciousness, became a complex person." In dealing with these issues, Trinitarians affirmed that Jesus was "a derived being, _personally_ united with a self-existent God", whereas "according to the Unitarians" he was described as "a derived being, _intimately_ united with the self-existent God."(26) Implicit in this opposition was an important reinterpretation of the concept of "person." With Trinitarians, "person" designated an ontological category, a substance or being, and did not apply to historical personage.(27) With Channing and his followers, the concept of "person" turned into a 'personalistic' category and was aligned with "character." For Channing, the Gospel accounts yielded "a feeling of the reality of Christ's character," and in this 'humanistic' emphasis Jesus was "seen as having _one_ nature," with his "character" turning into an example of humanity, a "model" of the ideal life rather than a person of the trinity. Jesus was "the only master of Christians," "a being distinct and inferior to God," Channing defined the christological position of Unitarianism in his ordination speech for Jared Sparks.(28) The patristic dual-natured Christ thus shifted towards a homogeneous, pristine "teacher" of human perfection who effected moral elevation by instruction, by example.

This shift away from the Chalcedonian "fully God, fully man" doctrine of the two natures of Christ to a 'humanistic' christology was not original. The view that was developed in Channing's hand presented a summation of christological tendencies long at work in the liberal tradition. Channing's christological position was of one piece with Priestley's and Belsham's devaluation of Arianism in favor of the belief of Jesus as "mere man." The English Unitarians' development towards an experiential and historical christology also provided the stage setting for Channing's distinct tendency to highlight the historical outlines of Jesus' life in a manner akin to the "liberal-positive" quest. Acutely aware of this affinity, Channing's critics were soon to ask whether Channing's advocacy of "simple Humanitarianism" did not also lead him "naturally enough ... to distrust and impugn all miraculous events...."(29)

There was yet another basis for this charge, one which also drew on the Socinian background of Channing's christology and played directly into Channing's conception of Christ's redemptive mission. Until the latter part of the eighteenth century, New England Congregationalists adhered to the view of Christ's work codified in the Shorter Catechism of the Westminster Assembly which asserted that "Christ suffered the wrath of God."(30) The doctrine of "atonement" as "at-one-ment, or the bringing together ... of those who have been separated" here entailed that "the Lord Jesus Christ, by his perfect obedience and sacrifice of himself, ... hath fully satisfied the justice of the Father."(31) Within New England Congregationalism the "idea that the death of Christ was efficacious to procure pardon for the penitent, that is, to reconcile God to men" was perpetuated in the adoption by Jonathan Mayhew, Samuel Hopkins and Jonathan Edwards Jr. of the "governmental" doctrine of the atonement advocated in 1617 by the Dutch intellectual Hugo Grotius in his _Defense of the Catholic Faith Concerning the Satisfaction of Christ_.(32) Grotius stressed that the death of Christ was "not a debt paid to God," a substitutionary penalty, but "an influence exerted on the world to maintain the dignity of the law," and illustrative of satisfaction "manifesting God's hatred of sin, his respect for his law...."(33)

It was this "govermental" doctrine of the atonement that Channing left behind in statements coterminous with Schleiermacher's interpretation of the work of Christ. Channing rendered the death of Christ an example and devalued the idea of the vicarious sacrifice and with it the satisfaction theory of the atonement. The act of redemption was for Channing instrumental: "Jesus ... was sent by the Father to effect a moral, or spiritual deliverance of mankind" and not to placate an offended, angry God. It seemed "absurd" to Channing "to speak of men as forgiven, when their whole punishment ... (was) borne by a substitute."(34) Christ's death was for Channing not dependent on substitutionary redemptive value in propitiatory sacrifice and instead instrumental as inspiration. Jesus "was sent on a still nobler errand, namely ... to form (men) to a sublime and heavenly virtue." Judged against the traditional way of describing Christ's redeeming work, the "munus triplex," the kingly, the prophetic and the priestly offices thus receded behind an illustrative purpose, with the soteriological emphasis on Christ's death as "ransom" giving way to an anthropological focus on atonement or reconciliation as "a spiritual influence ... exerted upon men for their salvation."(35)

This ethical, inspirational emphasis solved the christological problem in terms of the focus on 'man.' As Henry Ware observed of the Unitarian-Trinitarian debates in 1820, "the question 'what is the natural character of man,' lies at the very foundation of the controversy between the Unitarians on the one hand and Trinitarians and Calvinists on the other."(36) In accordance with Ware's assessment, Channing repeatedly translated christological issues into questions pertaining to the nature of man and the demand for perfectibility. Religion "is of no worth," Channing pontificated, "and contributes nothing to salvation, any farther than as it uses these doctrines, precepts, promises, and the whole life, character, sufferings, and triumphs of Jesus, as the means of ... changing it into the likeness of his celestial excellence." In this context, Jesus' life was "accessible and imitable;" it illustrated the possibility that man himself could strive to become a "diviner being."(37)

This very emphasis on ethics rather than dogma, together with the equation of the ontological category of "person" with the ethical-moral terms of "personality" and "character" came yet another step closer to the quest and its critique of patristic christology. Rather than divine-human "nature" as posited by the Chalcedonian creed, it was the "personality" of Jesus that was of vital import to Channing. Jesus, during his earthly existence, was very man, Channing observed, "by his birth, (he) was truly a human being...." "He was flesh of our flesh. He had our wants and desires, our hunger and thirst, our sensations of pleasure and pain, our natural passions. ... He bore the relations of life toward kindred, neighbors, and friends.... He was thus actually one of our race, a brother of the great human family."(38) Channing himself could not have been conscious of a new position, yet his conception of the figure of Jesus as "the Brother, Friend, and Saviour" was in many ways a preparation for the quest's inroads. The full application of the quest's themes, however, was not rendered until the christological debate touched on the nature of the scriptural narratives and their interpretation.

II

The preoccupation with the centrality of Jesus' "person" issued in harmonies and paraphrases of the Gospel accounts which were nurtured by a rich background in eighteenth century English evidentialist theology. The harmony branch of the life of Jesus literature was represented by James Macknight and William Newcome and complemented by Clarke's Paraphrase of St. Matthew's Gospel and his Paraphrases of the Gospels of St. Mark and St. Luke which followed the evidentialist claims of the harmonies. The gist of these studies was that were "evidences" supporting the authenticity of historical claims, the "testimonies concerning the antiquity, genuineness, and authority of the books of the New Testament ... (and) testimonies concerning the facts, properly so called; the birth, miracles, death, resurrection of Jesus Christ...."(39) The demand for open and external "testimonies" was supplemented by other "evidences" characteristic of Christian apologetics. The elaborate arguments as to "genuineness" and "authenticity" listed the ancient authorities for disputed writings and pointed to the internal consistency of the accounts of Jesus' life as well as the reliability of the biblical authors, who were asserted to be "qualified to relate what they saw and heard, in simple and unaffected narrative," thus substantiating the claim "that the facts upon which the Christian religion is founded have a stronger proof than any facts at such a distance of time."(40) This evidentialist claim was persued separate and apart from christological concerns and the debates over Socinian and Arian doctrine. For Macknight, Lardner and Paley as for their American followers, the concern in the harmonistic life of Jesus literature was not to relate the "person" and "nature" of Christ to patristic christological doctrine but rather to validate the factual premise that the "History of Christ" was "truly and without corruption conveyed down to ... this Day, ... attested ... with ... many circumstances of credibility ... and in every respect attended with ... many Marks of Truth."(41)

What concerned apologists, moreover, was not so much whether the Gospel accounts were historical but rather how one could use the historical outlines of Jesus' life to gain assurance and certainty of the validity of Christian truth and of the claim that Jesus was the Messiah. This was a position which presumed confidence in the harmony of faith and history: "the History of the life of Christ, contained in the New Testament," Clarke categorically declared, "is a true Relation of Matters of Fact."(42) The course of evidentialist life of Jesus literature was inextricably linked to this presupposition. From the evidentialist studies of the life of Jesus on which American practitioners relied the impact of the deist assaults on revealed religion was hardly noticeable. The harmonies of Robert Willan and T. Thirwall, for instance, did not substantially differ from pre-critical harmonies and left the evidentialist pattern intact.(43)

By the early decades of the nineteenth century, the apologetics of evidentialism had achieved an axiomatic, nonsectarian status which served until well after 1850 as a citadel around which Unitarian ministers and biblical critics could rally. From his Dexter Chair of Sacred Literature at Harvard Channing affirmed the "proofs" of revealed religion, its general "credibility" and supporting "testimonies."(44) In like manner, Andrews Norton categorically declared from the same chair that "in asserting" "the genuineness of the Gospels" he was "affirming, that they remain essentially the same as they were originally written; and that they have been ascribed to their true authors." Norton's "belief on testimony" further appealed to "credentials" corroborating the claim that Jesus was the chosen "teacher from God" who "adduced no arguments but his miracles".(45) In this search for "credentials" the life of Jesus was regarded as doctrinal, not biographical. The starting point was bibliocentric; no scrutiny of the historicity of the life of Jesus or an examination of the relationship of Jesus of history to the Christ of faith was needed.

Of the three forms of the life of Jesus literature, "a Synopsis of the Gospels, a Harmony of the Gospels, and a life of Christ," it was the harmony which coincided closest with evidentialist concerns. "A Harmony ... proposes to discover not only what narratives in the different Evangelists correspond to each other, but in what order the events and instructions recorded took place or were delivered...."(46) It "assumes ... that the narratives of the Evangelists ... constitute essentially the same history...." "A History of the Saviour", by contrast, American practitioners observed, "moves in a wider sphere." Here the "object" was "to reproduce as nearly as possible the entire, original history." For the harmonist, however, the biblical basis was sufficient; he was "expected to confine himself to the materials which the Evangelists have furnished."(47) The fact that the "discources (were not) recorded in the same order by the several Evangelists" and that there were "discrepancies between them in regard to the circumstances attending some events, or the time and place of their occurence" was not regarded as "impairing their credibility." Throughout, exegetical findings, particulary as relating to the "synoptic problem," were clearly subordinated to the claims of the scriptural record as a "narrative of facts."(48)

This self-assured and optimistic framework did, nevertheless, face obstacles. The difficulties which beset evidentialists issued primarily from the criticism launched by deist protagonists - John Toland, Thomas Woolston, Anthony Collins, Thomas Chubb and Peter Annet. The traditional basis for supernaturalism and the argument from miracles and prophecies were collapsed by deist criticism. Predictions which Christianity was alleged to fulfill, in particular with regard to the Messiahship of Jesus, were to be rejected; a "fictitious" miracle, like Christ's miraculous conception, could not be accepted; to prove the reality of a miracle in the past was impossible. On the front of the Leben-Jesu-Forschung, deist criticism nullified the arguments of supernaturalists and prompted hermeneutical shifts advocated by the neologist camp which provided important stimuli for the development of critical life of Jesus research. On the front of the Unitarian camp, however, the deist assault was rendered ineffectual by the evidentialist tradition and never managed to strike the theological landscape with the forcefulness it gathered among Leben Jesu researchers. Unitarians were not prepared to let go of the "credentials" of revelation and widened the gulf between deist and supernaturalist presuppositions on the ground of revealed religion.(49) As a result, the argument that miracles could be adduced as evidence that the authority of revealed religion was pressed with polished vigor.

Unitarian supernatural rationalism in this context entailed more than merely an affirmation of natural theology. As in deist religion, "reason" was assigned the status of an independent power which aided and supported Scripture itself rather than being dependent upon it. But unlike deism, in supernatural rationalism, natural religion, refashioned to stand up to contemporary scientific standards, was aligned with revealed theology to supplement on the basis of external and internal "evidences" what "reason" could neither originate nor demonstrate. Against those "disposed to discredit all miracles indiscriminately" Unitarians were thus able to insist that Christianity rested on the necessity of revelation and that only the basis of revealed religion could undergird belief in Jesus' divinity.(50)

To gain leverage against deist criticism, Unitarians redoubled their appeal to the "genuineness" of Scripture. Harmonistic studies, handbooks, annotations, paraphrases of the life of Jesus accounts in the evidentialist tradition were repeatedly used to refine the notions of what kinds of data yielded assurance, probability and certainty. While the "Scheme of Deism" was charged with failing to "lead men to embrace and believe Revelation," evidentialist studies flowed from the premise that "natural religion is the foundation of all revealed religion, and revelation is designed ... to establish its duties."(51) It was in particular Paley's and Clarke's polemic against deism which continued to attract Unitarians to the subjects of chronology, prophecy and miracles. A host of exegetes modelled their arguments after the evidentialist case against deist criticism of miracles by affirming that "miracles are capable of proof from testimony" and "that in miracles adduced in support of revelation there is not any such antecedent improbability as no testimony can surmount." (52)

To reinforce evidentialist presuppositions against deist criticism, Unitarians enlisted Scottish common sense as an apologetic bulwark. Philosophically, this bulwark found its strongest supports in the common sense teachings of Thomas Reid and Dugald Stewart, who provided an intellectual base for an unshakable faith in evidentialism. The common sense ideal of the Scottish Enlightenment exerted a master influence upon

Unitarian supernatural rationalism. At Harvard, the moderate Calvinist David Tappan, Hollis Professor of Divinity, advocated the principles of common sense philosophy. Scottish journals such as The Edinburgh Review, the Quarterly Review, Blackwood's Edinburgh Magazine and Campbell's New Monthly Magazine increased the influence and prestige of common sense realists beyond the college curriculum.(53) The common sense starting point was the assumption of a harmonious correspondence between subjective perceptions and objective reality. This "natural" "realism" had a particular appeal to Unitarian ministers who were searching for an apologetic weapon against Hume's assertion that given the "atomistic" nature of experience as a succession of disconnected perceptions, one could not be certain whether ideas occurring in the mind corresponded to anything outside the mind itself.(54) The Scots' "realistic" rather than "ideal" or "representational" theory of perception posited empirical knowledge as ontologically "real" and in this way bolstered confidence in the reliability of the "evidences" of revealed religion.

Until the third quarter of the nineteenth century, the majority of American exegetes and biblical critics built their discussions of the life of Jesus, at least in part, on this "realistic" theory. Common sense principles fed into the stream of studies on the "evidences" of Christianity and allowed for plenty of room to show that the scriptural accounts of the life of Jesus were fully consistent, credible and susceptible to scientific demonstration. Moreover, Scottish common sense furnished authoritative backing for the premise that there was no incongruitiy in the transposition of the notion of "fact" to the supernatural rationalist framework. Common sense philosophy thus served as a force corroborating the evidentialist status quo. The dualistic system of the common sense position further yielded exactly what Unitarian supernatural rationalism needed to counter challenges to the historicity of the "evidences" of revealed religion and to strengthen assurance of authenticity and "genuineness." Against the background of the Scots' "natural" "realism," the "history of Jesus" "could not have been a fiction" nor could it be reduced to "fraud" and "human invention."(55)

The overbearance of the issues of factuality and "genuineness" was determinative for the themes and techniques of American life of Jesus literature and its interpretation. Contrary to the hermeneutical preoccupations prompted by deist critics on the part of the Leben-Jesu-Forschung, American approaches to the life of Jesus narratives remained focused on the scrutiny of the factuality and credibility of the accounts rather than on questions of literary-historical origin. What was lost in the predominance of the factuality issue was any serious attention to problems which gradually moved into domain of form critical procedures and literary criticism. Lost, too, was the critique of christological dogma entailed in the deist debates. Evidentialist studies in the stripe of Edward Robinson's or John Gorham Palfrey's harmonies had little interest in the christological disputes of patristic exegetes. For Palfrey and Robinson as for Clarke and Paley, christological dogma was of secondary importance and distinctly set apart from concerns pertaining to the "genuineness" and credibility of the Gospel accounts.(56)

III

The Unitarians' preoccupation with the question of "genuineness" did not categorically exclude the investigation of the basis of biblical authority and the proper interpretation of the scriptural accounts. Preoccupation with this scrutiny was scarcely original. Prior to the emergence of the higher critical procedures of the quest, Edwards had dealt with the inaccuracy of text collation, the accretion of distorted variants and the inadequacy of translation. But the early Edwardian theology of the Westminster Confession did not subject these findings to historico-critical exegesis. It approached Scripture as "the rule of faith and practice" and reduced exegesis to proof-texting in keeping with confessional positions. In a similar fashion, pre-Unitarian exegesis looked to scriptural pages primarily for proof-texts, paraphrasing difficult sections and collecting related texts from differing contexts for the elucidation of controversial doctrines.(57) The basis on which early Unitarian biblical exegesis rested before the advent of the new critical studies stood firmly in the exegetical tradition of the theology of "evidences" represented by Samuel Clarke's Scripture Doctrine of the Trinity and John T. Norwich's Scripture-Doctrine of Original Sin.(58) What the scriptural interpretation of Clarke and Norwich lacked was an interest in historical positivity. Contrary to the critical quest's preoccupation with historical conditioning and reliability, pre-critical evidentialist theology assumed that the life of Jesus narratives could be understood in isolation from determining historical contexts. The Bible itself had to yield all historical "evidences" for the pristine validity of Christian faith.

This evidentialist exegesis, interpreting Scripture in static terms as a historical record of external "evidences," was challenged when in 1811 the bequest of Samuel Dexter led to the establishment of a lecturership of biblical criticism at Harvard which allowed higher criticism to acquire a firm place in the curriculum. The decisive impetus for the interest in the exegetical principles of the quest came from Joseph Stevens Buckminster, the first Dexter Lecturer, who emerged as a pivotal figure in the propagation of the new biblical studies of the neologist camp and stimulated his contemporaries to a growing awareness of textual and interpretative problems. The first Dexter Lecturer was, George Ticknor observed in a tribute to Buckminster in the Christian Examiner, an exegete "who ... took critical study of the Scriptures ... from the old basis on which it had rested during the Arminian discussions of the latter part of the last century and the beginning of the present one, when little more learning was thought needful than could be found in such books as Macknight on the Epistles and Campbell on the Gospels, and placed it on the solid foundations of the text of the New Testament as settled by Wettstein and Griesbach and elucidated by the labors of Michaelis, Marsh and Rosenmüller...."(59)

Buckminster's project with Griesbach's critical edition of the Greek New Testament provided the liberals with an exegetical weapon in the theological battles with the orthodox, one that undermined the foundations of Trinitarian doctrine in revealing key Trinitarian proof texts such as 1 John 5,7 as inauthentic. In a series of articles for the Monthly Authology on Griesbach's text, Buckminster further underlined that Griesbach's critique of the prevailing "textus receptus" provided a forceful argument to be used against "those who maintained the most rigid notion of inspiration."(60) Griesbach's text not only asked the New

Testament exegete to discard a rigid theory of verbal inspiration, but in drawing attention to the textual history of the scriptural accounts, also prepared the way for the application of historical methodology in the study of the formation of the canon and the question of scriptural inspiration.

Buckminster's reliance on Griesbach signalled an important shift away from the harmony pattern. Griesbach doubted "whether a Harmony (could) be composed from the memoirs of the Evangelists, sufficiently conformable to true chronological order, and framed upon sure grounds."(61) Buckminster shared Griesbach's reservations and adopted the stance, not of the "Harmonist," but of the "Biographer" whose "object (was) to reproduce ... the entire, original history."(62) This stance stimulated biographical and historical concerns congenial to the quest. Thus Buckminster advocated an empathic reading of the life of Jesus which sought to "transport" the interpreter "back to Judea, and place (him) in the audience that were listening to the discourses of our Saviour...."(63) Foundational to this empathic approach was the contextualist premise that "in order to understand the unconnected writings of any person, written at a remote period, ... the character of the writer, the opinions that prevailed in his time, his object in writing, and every circumstance peculiar to his situation, must be taken into consideration, before we can be sure of having reached the whole of his meaning." Jesus' history could not be properly understood "without knowing something of the history of the times, the character of the writer, the prevailing prejudices of the age, and the particular purpose which the writer meant to effect."(64)

Yet while this premise would lead Buckminster to produce a biographical sketches of Jesus' life, the further step of aligning this outline with an exegetical investigation taking into account synoptic re-orderings was not undertaken. Griesbach's exegesis focused on the synoptic problem and demonstrated that one could "account for the arrangements of the facts in St. Mark's Gospel, on (a) scheme of compilation: ... St. Mark cópied sometimes from St. Matthew, at other times from St. Luke."(65) Buckminster evinced no comparable interest in the synoptic arrangement of the first three Gospels. Whereas the "inconsistencies" and "doublings" in the Scriptural accounts unleashed with Griesbach synoptic re-orderings, with Buckminster, they reinforced interest in factuality, in "the external evidence of the gospel, ... the credibility and authenticity of the historical testimony" and in the "internal evidence, such as the character of Christ and his apostles...."(66)

Buckminster's "supposition of the truth of the principal facts in the evangelical history" also submerged considerations of the "dogmatic" problem of the relationship between the Jesus of history and the Christ of faith.(67) For Buckminster, the Jesus of history was not an autonomous object of study and remained aligned with the Christ of faith. Buckminster's investigations throughout did not lead to conclusions hostile to "historic Christianity." In his "historical explication of the writings of the New Testament" Buckminster admitted no doubts concerning the historicity of Jesus. It was inappropriate to "choose, with an absurd distrust of all history, to doubt that such a personage as our Lord existed...."(68) Buckminster repeatedly urged his parishioners to see the "facts" of Jesus history with the "same confidence as those in profane history" rather than "to suppose the falsity of the gospel story, or the fictitiousness of the character of Jesus Christ...."(69) In the focus on "the historical evidence of the gospel facts," then, Buckminster found support for the adherence to the reliability of scriptural testimony, and not a test case of critical historicity.

Significantly, this applied to both Unitarian and orthodox Trinitarian camps. Both Unitarians and Trinitarian advocates were exposed to studies emancipating biblical criticism from bondage to the evidentialist tradition and drawing critical exegesis towards a methodology that grew increasingly historical-critical. Yet among both Unitarian and Trinitarian practitioners in this early period, interest in the new procedure was primarily apologetic and lacked the concern with historical positivity which the critical Jesus quest imparted on scriptural interpretation. Thus Moses Stuart, called to Andover in 1810 as Professor of Sacred Literature after a four-year pastorate at New Haven's Center Church, sought to reconcile the new methods of biblical research with traditional Calvinistic theology. "On points which are not concerned with the special doctrines of Christianity, in illustrating critical and literary history, philology, natural history, and grammatical exegesis" - on these issues Stuart was willing to "accept the good" which the new studies offered "in a scientific manner and well disgested, lucid, established form."(70) For Stuart, the new critical studies played into the determination of "grammatical" meaning as well as into grammatico-historical criticism which studied the biblical accounts in terms of their historical setting and rational intelligibility. Throughout, however, the interpretation was expressly confined to "points ... <u>not</u> concerned with the special doctrines of Christianity." Stuart refused to go further and question the authenticity of Scripture or its divine inspiration.

At this juncture the procedures of "grammatical" criticism as expounded by Johann August Ernesti served to bypass the issue of historical positivity which always lurked as a threat behind Stuart's hermeneutics and necessitated proof that the biblical accounts "were composed not by impostors, but by the men who have always been commonly reputed to be their authors...."(71) With his translation of Ernesti's <u>Elements of Interpretation</u> Stuart introduced Andover to a form of biblical interpretation which preceded any theological and historical assessment of the "truth" of the biblical narratives. What was lacking in Stuart was the alignment of scriptural interpretation with historico-critical procedure.(72) The principles of biblical interpretation advanced by Michaelis and Eichhorn postulated a hermeneutics subordinated to historical criticism. Stuart, however, adopted a deficient hermeneutics, using "grammatical" analysis to evade historico-critical scrutiny of positivity, whereas for the quest grammatical-historical <u>and</u> historical-critical analysis together formed the basis of life of Jesus interpretations.

With regard to the problem of historical reliability, Unitarian and orthodox Trinitarian practitioners stood as one. In the quest of Michaelis and Eichhorn "interpretation" entailed uncovering scriptural "history" as "fiction," as accretion and embellishment. To Andover's Moses Stuart it meant determining the purely "grammatical" meaning of a passage; to Harvard's Joseph Buckminster it entailed placing the scriptural account in its historical context. American practitioners here remained predominantly tacticians rather than systematicians of biblical criticism, concerned more to counter emerging historical-critical charges than to offer a comprehensive application. Stuart and Buckminster were not entirely unconscious of the extent to which an underlying questioning of historicity and an express opposition between the Jesus of history and the Christ of faith governed the higher critical procedures. But both slighted the fact that the neologist studies were participants in a portentous transition in the interpretation and application of the Bible. Their main interest was in the "genuineness" of scriptural testimony; the premises of higher criticism were accordingly opposed once they led to an assault on supernaturalism and whenever they led, as in the case of Eichhorn and H. E. G. Paulus, to a questioning or rejection of the historicity of the life of Jesus narratives.

This express rejection of criticism hostile to "historical Christianity" reflected a major theme that determined the course of American interpretations of the life of Jesus. It contributed to the persistence of the harmony pattern and works on the "evidences" of Christianity, the relative scarcity of critical "lives" in the first decades of the century and to the stereotype format of the reviews of the quest. The categories for interpreting the life of Jesus narratives here continued to be supernaturalist terms. The notion of supernatural revelation persisted essentially intact, aligned with the validity of scriptural "evidences" which buttressed the supernatural claims of Christianity. As for the British evidentialists, the Gospels recounted for the Dexter Lecturers the historical "facts" of Jesus of Nazareth, authenticating his life and teaching through miracles and prophecy-fulfillment schemes.

IV

William Ellery Channing, who succeeded Buckminster as Dexter Lecturer in 1812, did not steer away from the apologetic appropriation of higher-critical principles Buckminster had expoused. Channing expressly acknowledged the need for historical and contextual Scripture interpretation. The "leading principle in interpreting Scripture is this," Channing reiterated in the "Baltimore Sermon", "that the Bible is a book written for men, in the language of men, and that its meaning is to be sought in the same manner as that of other books...."(73) On the basis of this consideration of the biblical record as any other ancient writing, refractured through historical context, Channing suggested guidelines for Unitarian scriptural exegesis which demanded the employment of reason to determine meaning and recognized the importance of historical circumstances as well as the peculiarities of the individual writer for the correct interpretation of biblical texts. "We find," Channing declared, "that some of these books are strongly marked by the genius and character of the respective writers ... and that a knowledge of their feelings, and of the influences under which they were placed is one of the preparations for understanding their writings."(74)

Yet Channing's demand for the employment of "reason" to determine the time and place from which the accounts were delivered did not entail a scrutiny of the historical Jesus in its own right. For Channing, the figure of Jesus was not "a mere man," subject to historical situation. Channing's Jesus was "a pre-existent rational creature, an angel or spirit of some sort, who had entered a human body. He was not even a man exept so far as his corporeal part is concerned, but a creature from some upper sphere."(75) Channing therefore was not prepared to render Jesus a mere human, a historically grounded myth or even an index of religious self-consciousness. A later Emerson would condemn the Unitarian preoccupation "with the noxious exaggeration about the person of Jesus." (CW, I, 81) But with Channing, the figure of Jesus retained his crucial status as a "Mediator" and guarantee of the supernatural claims of Christianity.

Channing was convinced that his position did "not lead to infidelity. On the contrary, its excellence is that it fortifies faith."(76) Channing's chief opponent at Andover Seminary, Moses Stuart, judged differently and undertook to uncover Channing's position as a negative system undermining faith in revelation. Stuart confirmed Channing's principle that the meaning of biblical texts was "to be sought in the same manner as that of other books." "We both concede," Stuart declared, "that the principles by which all books are to be interpreted are those which apply to the interpretation of the Bible."(77) But with Stuart, this interpretation was to be conducted as a careful "grammatical" interpretation of the texts. Once the "grammatical" meaning of the text was established, there was no need for further historical-critical questioning. The "simple inquiry must be, what sentiment does the language of this or that passage convey, without violence or perversion of rule? When this question (was) settled, philologically," then Stuart "either believed what is taught, or else rejected the claim of divine authority." What his "own theories and reasonings about the absurdity or reasonableness of any particular doctrine (could) avail in determining whether a writer of the New Testament has taught this doctrine or not, ... this investigation," Stuart averred, "must be conducted independently of ... philosophy, by ... philology."(78) At the "philosophical" juncture, however, Stuart judged, Channing had carried his inquiry too far. To reduce Jesus to a "humanitarian" level, as Channing did, was for Stuart to invalidate the historicity of Jesus, or at least to leave open the question of "how is it to be proved that Christ ever existed at all?"(79) A generation ahead of Bruno Bauer, Stuart thus alluded to the problem of the facticity Jesus's existence, but unlike the Leben Jesu researcher, he deliberately suppressed this problem over against philological issues.

However far ahead Stuart's position on revelation might point in the direction of the quest, his critique slighted that for Channing the focus on the "human Christ" and the accompanying exegetical procedures remained a question of biblical authority and not of positivity. Channing still adhered to a biblical, supernatural rationalist system and did not seek to undermine the historicity of scriptural accounts or even the facticity of Jesus himself. With Channing, the "character of Christ" was at no point declared "a fiction" to be classed "with the character of habitual liars and impious deceivers." Moreover, while Channing was ready to move away from a rigid reliance on the Scriptures as the infallibly inspired testimony of God's revelation and while he would even ask his audience to "recollect the verbal contradiction between Paul and James, and the apparent clashing of some parts of Paul's writings with the general doctrines and end of Christianity," he never allowed the new exegetical principles to call into question the final authority and "genuineness" of Scripture as the locus of revelation.(80)

The testing ground of Stuart's critique was the question of the divinity of Christ and "the seeming discrepancies of description in regard to Christ."(81) To Stuart, "the course of reasoning in which (Channing) embarked, and the principles by which (he) explained away the divinity of the Saviour, must eventually lead most men who approve them to the conclusion, that the Bible is not of divine origin...."(82) The source of this 'heresy' was for Stuart the critical tradition of the quest. Stuart was convinced that Unitarians "must necessary ... come to the same conclusions with Eichhorn, and Paulus, and Henke, and Eckermann, and Herder, and other distinguished men of the new German school" - "conclusions" which, Stuart judged, were on the same level with the deist critique revelation.(83) "I am entirely unable to see," Stuart wrote to Channing in 1819, how the deist critique of revelation "imply a greater liberty than you take with John 1:1, Rom 9:5, and many other passages."(84) "The spirit of (the Unitarian) argument," Samuel Miller reiterated in a similar vein, "is precisely the same with that of the celebrated infidel, Mr. Hume, against Miracles."(85)

Stuart's identification of deist criticism with neologist and rationalist historico-critical procedures was to become a standard, stereotype pattern for the rejection of the quest's procedures. Yet this rejection in effect falsely projected an attack on historical revelation into critics who were concerned to counteract the deist critique of revelation and to render biblical narratives inviolate against the theory of deceptive intentionality. While neologists were in this respect apologetic, affirmative critics, it was precisely the affirmative side of the neologist position that American practitioners slighted in their equation of neologist premises with deist criticism. This equation became determinative for the development of the quest in the Unitarian-Trinitarian tradition. The quest's concerns were present in New England divinity long before the first critical "lives" were produced. Prior to the emergence of these "lives," however, the quest was identified in a stereotype manner with 'heresy,' with an aggressive assault on the validity of revelation. In this critique, the condemnation of the quest functioned primarily as a rhetorical, polemical device used by the orthodox to discredit Unitarian principles of exegesis and doctrine. One of the first and most obvious effects of this rhetorical appropriation of the quest was the delayed development of independent critical "lives." With a rich tradition of derogatory and polemial uses of the quest's themes lingering in the background, American practitioners were long hesitant to delve into an independent production of lives of Jesus.

In the assessment of the impact of higher critical procedures on the issue of faith on revelation Unitarians were not as far apart from the Trinitarian camp as Stuart judged. Faced with the anti-supernaturalist bias of the questers, both sides were put on the defensive and driven to consolidate their position. Liberal and orthodox theologians were attracted and at the same time repelled by the possibility of subjecting biblical narratives to historical and scientifically verifiable criticism, yet both deliberately avoided accepting the full consequences of historico-critical procedures. Thus Stuart relied on a position of firm common sense and was not ready to employ historical method in the precise examination of historical documents. For all its pioneering contributions, Stuart's "grammatical" approach preceded historical judgment and did not primarily concern itself with the historical context to which the texts referred. Stuart would ransack the literature of neologist questers and the literature of apology only to corroborate the position that the Gospels were authentic records of the sayings and deeds of a historical personage.

Stuart judged that the new critical studies often ran counter to this claim and were "fundamentally subversive of Christianity." Eichhorn, Stuart noted, devalued biblical narratives into "merely a poetical, philosophical speculation of some ingenious person." Heinrichs, Meyer and Ammon discredited miraculous history, while De Wette was "casting off all ideas of the divine origin of the Scriptures."(86) Against these findings, Stuart unwaveringly came out on the side of the English evidentialist tradition and demonstrated that the biblical narratives were "worthy of all credibility." Stuart's "hermeneutics" focused on "everything belonging to ... the rhetoric, or history" of a particular biblical author, but in this interpretation the overriding premise remained unchallenged: "the Scriptures reveal the facts."(87) With the predominance of this evidentialist tenet, issues "of a hermeneutical nature, ... the real meaning of words and phrases, or the principles of syntax, in the original language," receded behind issues pertaining to the "authenticity" and "genuineness" of the narratives.(88)

"If the genuineness of the sacred books be rendered doubtful, their authority is weakened," then, Stuart was convinced, "the whole edifice of theology is overturned."(89) And at this very point Stuart charged the quest's critical "systems of Hermeneutica" with overstepping evidentialist boundaries: "they abandonded the ground of defending the divine authenticity of the Bible...." The new "systems of Hermeneutica" established "meaning" on the basis of criteria external to Scripture which undercut evidentialist premises. Thus "Meyer, in a very laboured system of Hermeneutica of the Old Testament," Stuart observed, "has a body of rules, by which everything miraculous is to be explained away."(90) With Stuart, "hermeneutics" was never allowed to become a similar test for the historicity of the Gospel accounts of miracles. Initially, the issue for him was not whether the events recorded in the scriptural narratives had occurred but how "reason" served to determine "grammatical" meaning. Yet the danger Stuart saw lurking in the new "systems of Hermeneutica" steadily worked to reinforce the focus on the factuality issue at the expense of all other attention on questions of literary-critical origin and form.

Stuart's confidence in the historical reliability of the life of Jesus narratives did not go unshaken for long. Both liberal Unitarians and orthodox Trinitarians were increasingly forced to adopt a new line of defense for the supernatural claims of Christianity. For both camps there was no ignoring the fact that an application of higher-critical procedures entailed a conflict between historicism and a faith in revealed truth. Questions of "genuineness" concerned with the true authorship, date and canonicity of the biblical books soon were to give way to the view that the Gospels themselves constituted a fact in history and that their historical positivity could not in all cases be maintained with certainty. More immediately, the higher critical procedures further forced a direct re-examination not only of the reliability of the biblical narratives but also of the question whether the figure of Jesus recorded in the Gospels was in fact identical with the Christ of faith of the supernatural rationalist framework.

V

To Stuart, the Chalcedonian doctrine "that Christ should possess two natures ... (was) neither impossible nor absurd" and to be established on the ground of scriptural authority alone. "It is purely a doctrine of revelation; and to Scripture only can we look for evidences of it."(91) For Andrews Norton, however, who succeeded Channing as Dexter Lecturer in 1819, the Chalcedonian doctrine of the union of the divine and human natures in

Christ was undermined not only by "all the facts in the history of Christ" but also by "extrinsic considerations" pertaining to biblical criticism and interpretation.(92) Stuart's position, Norton charged, slighted the contextualist, historical dimension of scriptural interpretation. The orthodox interpreter paid "little regard to the circumstances in which (the biblical author) wrote, or to those of the persons, whom he addressed...."(93) Against Stuart's "loose and inconsistent" principles of interpretation Norton aligned the question of biblical interpretation with the question of the logical possibility of the trinitarian formulas and the christological dogma of orthodoxy.(94) As with Channing, christology was for Norton the testing ground upon which biblical criticism could try out its tools. But while Channing had largely identified critical exegesis with "lower criticism," Norton was convinced that several elements of "higher criticism" could be utilized to buttress the Unitarian position. Under Norton's guiding hand the interpretation of biblical narratives became increasingly an auxiliary of the study of historical reference. Norton's appropriation of Michaelis and Eichhorn influenced him to consider in the exegesis of a scriptural passage "how much of what was said or written had reference to (the Evangelists') peculiar circumstances and character; and how much was addressed to them as men and as Christians."(95) Scriptural narratives referred to and were embodied in the temporary historical framework of the biblical authors.

Norton found the historico-critical emphasis congenial to his efforts to demonstrate that the New Testament accounts were historically reliable sources for the events of the life of Jesus. In this context higher criticism assumed a constructive role; it elevated the scriptural accounts of Jesus to a more prominent position and yielded a new ground for certainty which established the singularity of Jesus beyond reasonable doubt. Inquiry into the circumstances of the life of Jesus was therefore imperative and inevitable. "It is necessary," Norton insisted, "to have just notions of the intellectual and moral character of our Saviour and his apostles, and of the circumstances under which they wrote or spoke."(96)

Norton's Dexter Lectures reiterated the necessity of establishing the "circumstances" of Jesus' life, a requirement asking for a hermeneutics of empathy. "Leave behind ... and forget ... modern doctrines and prejudices, and associations," Norton urged the exegete in the Dexter Lectures. The critic "must make himself familiar and contemporary with men (of) ... eighteenth centuries ago ... He must accompany our Saviour on his journeys, and sojourn in Galilee, and domesticate himself at Jerusalem."(97) This was a remarkable demand, one aligned with the questers' efforts to reconstruct the historical Jesus. But Norton did not carry his own premise out and stopped well short of dealing with the full implications of the historical Jesus quest. As much as Norton was willing to acknowledge that biblical texts could no longer be studied as if they existed apart from the background and environment in which they were created, he would do so only on condition that the new critical principles confirmed the doctrines that "the Gospels ... are the works of those to whom they have been ascribed, ... that the history of Jesus Christ is true and that the miracle of this mission from God which belongs to the order of events lying beyond the sphere of this world, ... is as real as those facts which take place in this world...."(98)

With Norton as with Stuart, then, the kinds of transition embodied in the work of the questers did not involve a recognition of the opposition between the Jesus of history and the Christ of faith nor a corresponding subordination of hermeneutics to historico-critical procedures. For Norton, the higher criticism was only welcome whenever it undercut the literalism of orthodox supernaturalists or confirmed the validity of historical revelation in the evidentialist tradition of Butler, Paley and Clarke. Elements stepping outside evidentialist apologetics were cast out as extreme, "irreligious" and "pantheistic." The Gospel accounts "thus expurgated, (Norton) received," Andrew P. Peabody acutely observed in a retrospective view of his teacher's work, "because he had convinced himself, by research and reasoning, that they were the veritable writings of the men whose names they bear, and the authentic record of Him whose life they portray."(99)

In this apologetic framework critical "lives" could not take hold. Among Unitarian critics around Norton a different "life" prevailed, one which found a major representative in Henry Ware Jr. Ware's Life of the Saviour of 1833 reflected the lack of a source and literary-critical perspective in the interpretation of the life of Jesus narratives. Ware's "life" still flowed from evidentialist premises and was rooted in the actuality of "creditable" historical events. History here constituted the vindication of faith, and whatever the critical methods of historiography and biographical representation of the quest might assert, the interpretation of Jesus' person could for Ware only be made on the basis of the historicity of the accounts. Interpretation was only as firm as the historical basis on which it rested.

Ware's evidentialist version of the life of Jesus carried the characteristics of the harmonies over into the biographical outline of Jesus's life. Ware's "life" did not move into the "wider sphere" of "ordinary history" but rather remained confined to "scripture history."(100) Ware's concern to establish "the absolute divinity and truth of the reals gospels" did not acknowledge the difficulties issuing from the synoptic problem or the unreliability of the Fourth Gospel.(101) Doubts concerning the historical reliability and validity of the life of Jesus accounts lay outside Ware's evidentialism. "Eighteenth centuries, instead of obliterating," Ware averred, "have only served to confirm the impressions which (Jesus) made...."(102)

For this evidentialist version of the life of Jesus the new biblical studies posed a threat not so much because of their depreciation of supernatural revelation as because of the very method with which this disparagement was brought about. The questioning of the historical positivity of the biblical narratives characteristic of the higher criticism cut against the grain of a tradition which regarded the biblical narratives as a factually reliable repository of "the history of Christ." "There is no other theory," Norton observed with regard to neologist criticism, "in which propositions ready to weaken man's faith in the genuineness of the Gospels, are so elaborately and plausibly introduced."(103) For critics of the caliber of Norton and Ware the proof of the validity of revelation was furnished by historically reliable "evidences." Any criticism which steered away from historical factuality into the realm of embellishment and "myth" amounted therefore to a denial of the supernatural authority of biblical revelation and the historical personage of Jesus himself. "In proportion as suspicion is cast upon genuineness and authenticity of those writings," Norton argued, "the history of Christ becomes doubtful and obscure."(104)

Norton's assessment was correct and acutely anticipated the circumstances of the demise of the evidentialist framework. The dominant conservative strategy against the critical Jesus quest was to defend the truth of the biblical accounts in terms of their historical "evidences" while aligning them with a philosophical apologetic against "rationalism" and unbelief. Yet this line of defense was not able to withstand the historico-critical inroads long. The principal point at which the arguments of the evidentialists clashed with the quest was the supposition that the determination of "testimonies" favorable to the truth of Christianity could be settled permanently. Norton's and Ware's religious apologetics assumed the constancy and stability of historical "evidences." Almost all the principles in Michaelis' and Eichhorn's studies, however, whose higher-critical views were much farther advanced, pointed towards an opposite finding. And precisely here were the seeds of a dilemma created by the desire to invoke divine sanction for "evidences" which the critical procedures of the Leben-Jesu-Forschung rendered questionable. The attempt to use the rationalistic edge of historico-critical analysis as an apologetic helpmate, a helpmate which countered the questioning of historical positivity with history itself, was inevitably bound to undermine its own purpose, leading to a disparagement of the value of historical revelation that soon was to carry Unitarians against supernatural rationalist premises.

6. Anxieties of Influence

Throughout the 1820s, the primary debates over biblical authority firmly stayed within the fortress of a historical apologetics stressing the proofs of revealed religion. Unitarians unflinchingly adhered to a hard-core rationalism according to which Christianity was authenticated, not by inner religious experience, but by the historical "testimony" of the divine mission of Jesus as attested by miracles. The supernatural truths of Christianity were asserted to rest on the historical veracity of biblical miracles which yielded "evidences" relating faith to history. In this context the historical facts about Jesus' life, validated by the prophecy-fullfillment scheme and miracles, confirmed "that there was a certain Person, stiled the Messiah, who was spoken of ... as one to be sent from God"; and that "all those Characteristics, by which the Messiah was to be distinguished from every other Person, do exactly agree in our Lord Jesus Christ, and in no other Person whatever."(1)

This apologetic argument was reflected in the register of British harmonies and "lives" which were used by New Englanders in the opening two decades of the century.(2) The harmonies by John Lightfoot, John Austin and Matthew Hale lacked exegetical detail, linguistic scrutiny and exhaustive source criticism and adhered throughout to the literal truth of the Gospel accounts as well as the historicity of the narratives. Similarly, the devotional "lives" modelled after Jeremy Taylor's _The Great Exemplar of Sanctity and Holy Life_ scarcely evinced signs of synoptic and historical criticism. Edmund Law's _Discourse on the Character of Christ_, George Benson's _History of the Life of Jesus Christ_ and John Fleetwood's _Life of Our Lord_ were distinguished by faithfulness to "scripture history" and were never led to "suppose the authority of the sacred book overthrown, the history of Jesus of Nazareth rejected as an idle tale...."(3)

Between 1815 und 1830, however, New England divinity was confronted with a subtle questioning of the factuality of the life of Jesus narratives which threatenend the tenuous connection of faith to history. This new trend began in the 1810s when George Ticknor, Edward Everett, Joseph Cogswell and, in a second wave, John Motley, Henry Dwight, William Emerson, George Calvert and George Bancroft were exposed to the historico-critical edge of the quest prevalent among Göttingen's neologists.(4) The young men flooding into Göttingen University in the 1810s and 1820s emerged from a ministerial and academic training wholly immersed in the alignment of English rationalism with Scottish common sense theology. This apologetic "evidence"-theology still so predominated academic training during the opening decades of the century that questers and biblical critics like Eichhorn, Michaelis and H. E. G. Paulus were given comparatively little notice. The Dexter Lecturers, namely Channing, Norton and Palfrey remained firmly entrenched in the supernaturalist framework, insisting that the proofs of revelation, its general "authority" and authenticating "testimonies" had to be sought in history.

What prevailed in Göttingen was precisely the reverse of the Harvard curriculum. The critical methods of neologist exegetes like Eichhorn and Michaelis forced discussion on the authority of Scripture, the meaning of history, and the nature of faith. The challenge to the evidentialist framework came from the branch of biblical studies designated as "higher criticism" which went beyond textual criticism to examine the historical reliability of the life of Jesus and scrutinize the value of "evidences" based on that historicity. With this scrutiny, the house of cards built on

Paley's "evidences" collapsed. The evidentialist theory of a static, unchanging universe came tumbling down in Eichhorn's evolutionary explanation of religion and his conception of progressive revelation. To a critic who had canvassed eighteenth century evidentialists for corroborating "testimony" that Christianity was a lawyer-proof religion based upon a historical revelation for which Scripture was the source book, Eichhorn's position cut two ways. It undercut the "authenticity" of the biblical narratives in questioning their historical basis, and it undermined the branch of hermeneutics known as typology. Eichhorn, the Harvard-Göttingen men acutely noticed, set out "to show, that ... prophecies (were) but false interpretations of what was not intended to be prophetick."(5) With the historical reliability of the New Testament accounts rendered uncertain, they could no longer be used to substantiate the Old.

The historical significance of the Harvard-Göttingen axis was that it was accompanied by the stirrings of a movement of rebellion within the Unitarian denomination, advocated by its supporters as the "new views" or "absolute religion" and by its opponents as "pantheism" or, more bluntly, "heresy" and "irreligion."(6) The Göttingen axis produced transitional men who increasingly realized the inadequacy of Unitarian apologetics and its reliance on Scottish common sense. By the 1820s, Harvard students fresh from study in Göttingen and Berlin were acutely aware that common sense realism was losing its potency and that a new source of authority was needed. Between 1815 and 1830 this insight into the bankruptcy of historical apologetics and Scottish common sense realism played into a crisis of profession which gradually led Harvard students away from the ministerial tradition in which they had been reared. The conflict was given an additional importance by the fact that the rank and file of Unitarian ministers refused to open their pulpits to the corrosive tendencies of the new critical procedures. While neologist and "rationalist" critics adduced historical data questioning the uniqueness of the life of Jesus accounts, the Unitarian camp at Harvard stood staunchly by the belief in the "genuineness" and "authenticity" of Scripture and thus reinforced the gulf between the beliefs of the older group of Unitarians around Ware and Norton and an emerging "new school."(7)

With the loss of epistemological and historical confidence that beleaguered the students who returned from abroad, the distinction between the Jesus of history and the Christ of theology, between faith and dogma pressed itself to the foreground of discussion. Faith and historical inquiry were beginning to drift apart. What was set in motion, moreover, were the tendencies to a theology of "experience" which was to undergird the rise of Transcendentalism.(8) A generation in advance of the Transcendentalist movement, the Harvard-Göttingen students realized that Unitarianism needed a new spiritual and epistemological foundation. Confronted with the historical scepticism of the quest, the Harvard-Göttingen men found themselves with nowhere to turn but inward - over and against an evidentialist framework which remained constant in its belief that historical "evidences" and "testimonies" were to be sought from without.

I

The sources of most of the interpretations which influenced the first Harvard-Göttingen students were the neologist critics of Göttingen, in particular in the works of Eichhorn and Michaelis, whose Einleitung in das Neue Testament was available in Bishop Marsh's translation. Everett and Ticknor quickly sensed that Unitarian scriptural exegesis did not draw on the same exegetical spring as the Göttingen critics, who were preoccupied with the "doctrine respecting the origin and formation of the Gospels." This "doctrine" issued from "the supposition of an original written history which (the Evangelists) all followed" and which was "chiefly and compiled from preexistent documents in the Aramaic dialect."(9) This "documentary theory," A. P. Peabody observed of Eichhorn's "complex and artificial" hypothesis, "supposes, one principal document, which contained in the simplest form the events and discourses found in all three (synoptic Gospels)...."(10) Eichhorn affirmed "that, by comparing the first three Gospels together, (the exegete was) able ... to separate the earlier life of Jesus ... from all subsequent additions, and ... to restore it again free from all the traditions of later times."(11)

When, however, Ticknor recorded the criticism of the Gospel accounts in Eichhorn's "Course of Lectures on the Exegesis of Matthew, Mark and Luke, and the four concluding chapters of John," he did not focus on the problems of the reconstruction of the Protogospel and synoptical relationships. For Ticknor, as for his colleagues in the Unitarian camp at Harvard, Eichhorn's position involved above all else an attack on the factuality and historical reliability of the biblical narratives of the life of Jesus. Eichhorn, Ticknor charged, "takes from the N. T. all that distinguished it from any other ancient book. He denies to it and to all its parts the lowest degree of inspiration explains its miracles into delusions or the natural consequences of natural causes ... - calls the death and resurrection a suspension of animation and subsequent revival...."(12) For Ticknor, Eichhorn's criticism was dangerous exegetical ammunition threatening the ground of affirmative Christian apologetics, and Ticknor hoped that he would never come to degrade his faith to "listen with pleasure to such flippant witticisms as Eichhorn has been ... making on all that (he had) been taught to consider solemn and important."(13) In this critique the argument that the literary relationship between the Gospels issued from a common Proto-Gospel never received the substantial source- and literary-critical appreciation which the quest's synoptic studies advocated and was instead predominantly read as a threat to the traditional view that the agreement of individually composed Gospels validated the truth of Christianity.

To Ticknor, the trying and testing of the life of Jesus narratives in Eichhorn's historical criticism seemed to make a spectacle of what he had grown to accept as sacrosanct supernatural claims of Christianity attested by historical "evidences." Norton concurred. If, as Eichhorn supposed, "during the first two centuries , it was so common to enlarge the histories of Jesus Christ, ... and to alter and remodel them," then, Norton argued, one could "hardly pretend to rely with much confidence upon those histories which now exist."(14) To Unitarians at home and abroad, then, the problem of the "discrepancies in the Gospels" and their literary relationship or dependence was immediately referred to the issue of factuality and merely spurred the apologetic concern to demonstrate that these issues and findings "(did) nothing towards destroying ... general confidence in the record."(15)

A case in point for the centrality of the "authenticity" and factuality issue was provided by "that large class of ... critics, who," as Norton formulated, "reject the belief of any thing properly miraculous in the history of Christ."(16) For the Harvard-Göttingen men and their 'homefront' sponsors "the difficulty of reconciling this disbelief of the miracles with the admission of the truth of facts concerning (Jesus)" was particularly acute.(17) Ticknor acknowledged that he should "have no objection to a serious and thorough examination of the grounds of Christianity." But "learned" teaching "that the New Testament was written in the latter end of the second century and ... that a miracle is a natural and a revelation a metaphysical impossibility" was incompatible with the beliefs of a Harvard Unitarian who had, at least until that time, stoutly adhered to the doctrine that miracles were an indispensable historical testimony of the validity of supernatural revelation.(18) In Eichhorn's inroads on the historical reliability of the life of Jesus narratives the evidentialist status of the life of Jesus accounts and the reliance on external "evidences" for Christianity seemed inconsequential. By claiming that the documents which legitimated the revelation of Jesus as the Christ should be subject to the same scrutiny as other historical documents, Eichhorn undercut the theoretical basis for revealed theology.

This was the argument the Harvard-Göttingen group designated as "merely critical."(19) Eichhorn's "rules of criticism" were, Bancroft judged, "in general right tho not unlimitedly right, but their application is sadly wrong." "Eichhorn does not hold the Miraculous of Revelation, nor treat the subject in any other light than an historical and moral Phenomenon...."(20) What was as stake here was not only the scriptural authority of the miracles narratives but the professed allegiance to the person of the Saviour himself. The Harvard-Göttingen group acutely realized that Eichhorn's criticism put the life of Jesus on the same level as that of any other historical figure. Eichhorn's "faith in Christ is, as far as I can understand it," Ticknor observed, "precisely like his faith in Socrates."(21) To Unitarian evidentialists this key premise of the quest seemed to do nothing but undermine faith in supernatural revelation and came close to rationalistic atheism. The "learned" at Göttingen, Bancroft charged, "do not believe that Christ was a peculiar messenger from God;" they obscure "the true end of criticism," reducing Christ to a "skilful physician" who had no "supernatural powers."(22) Bancroft therefore judged this "theology ... to be anything but (Christiani)ty;" it was merely designed "to scoff at the bible and laugh at Christ...." And Bancroft himself thought "too highly of religion" to become a similarly "learned theologian ..., i.e. a (Christia)n theologian."(23)

Against this charge the exegetical and historical lessons of the critical Jesus quest could not take root. The Harvard-Göttingen group had been trained not so much in biblical criticism as in a theory of biblical "evidences" and authentication. The apologetic model to which the group adhered was one of firm common sense. Chief mentors in the evidentialist tradition and backdrop for the harmony literature were Nathaniel Lardner's <u>The Credibility of the Gospel History</u> and William Paley's <u>Evidences of Christianity</u>, which ran through countless American editions between its publication in 1793 and 1860 and became an official part of the Divinity School curriculum. Lardner and Paley represented the high watermark of historical apologetics for Christianity grounded in the evidences of Jesus' miracles and prophecies and functioned as a pervasive intellectual consensus which put exegesis to the cause of reassurance. Under the tutelage of this exegesis the life of Jesus studies on which American practitioners relied marked no significant departure from the classic evidentialist pattern. The harmony literature still clearly predominated over the critical "lives": One encountered John Lightfoot's parallel-column harmony and James Marknight's paraphrased harmony but not the critical "lives" of Reinhard and Hess; the devotional "lives" of Jeremy Taylor, Joseph Hall and George Benson but not the works of Herder and H. E. G. Paulus.(24) In this atmosphere, the few works from the "Athenaeum of modern times" that were assimilated carried Unitarians merely to an affirmation of scriptural authority and an empirical philosophy limiting knowledge to the senses. The acceptance of higher criticism made progress only in so far as it could be called in as a guardian of the evidentialist cause. To argue from the claims of historical conditioning alone represented in this context to Unitarian exegetes a position one could "neither defend nor approve" since it undermined "the authority and value" of Scripture.(25)

In the case of the Harvard-Göttingen group, the new skills and approaches of the quest were accordingly associated with the deist "heresy" and learned "irreligion." "As to (Eichhorn's) personal faith," Ticknor observed, "it is certainly but feeble. As far as I can judge from his books and lectures - from his general reputation and my personal acquaintance with him, I believe that he is nothing more than a Deist...."(26) There was scarcely any American practitioner commenting on historico-critical procedures during this early period of influence who did not similarly equate neology with deist criticism and with mere "irreligion" and "immorality." Thus Bancroft, who had been sent to Göttingen to "pursue his theological studies" so that he might better be "able to expound and defend the Revelation of God," informed Kirkland that he "never heard anything like moral or religious feeling manifested in theological lectures" at Göttingen. To Bancroft, there was "a great deal more religion in a few lines of Xenophon than in a whole course of Eichhorn...."(27) Everett agreed. "Mr. Eichhorn," Everett complained to Bancroft in 1818, "unfortunately has adopted a style of lecturing little adapted to the seriousness of the subject ... and irreverent as regards the great topics in discussion."(28)

Under the aegis of these charges the Harvard-Göttingen men were able to assure their sponsors that they had "nothing to do with ... (Göttingen's) infidel systems."(29) But this reassurance distorted the neologist position. The critics around Eichhorn in fact sought to re-affirm the religious relevance of the biblical record against deist attacks on historical positivity. Neologists were not prepared to accept the life of Jesus narratives at face value as historical occurrences, but they did not conclude from this that the accounts flowed from deceit and delusion. The neologist argument was intended constructively. By the "freeing of the Primal Gospel from its accretions," Eichhorn argued in his _Einleitung_, "countless doubts with which Jesus, his life, and his teaching have been assailed become completely meaningless. ... By this separation of the apostolic from the nonapostolic which higher criticism recommands ... the means are found to establish the credibility and truth of the gospel story on unshakable foundations."(30) The Harvard-Göttingen students did not acknowledge this affirmative intention. With them, the critical impulse of the neologist position was lost. The trying and testing of historical apologetics through the neologist quest did not result in any sustained interest in the critical study of the historical Jesus. Harvard's "Innocents Abroad" upheld the tenet of the identity of the Jesus of history with the Christ of faith, adhered to the historical reliability of the life of Jesus narratives Norton was advocating and were not prepared to "rival De Wette in his audacity, Paulus in his infidelity, or Eichhorn in his profane indecency."(31) The Unitarian bonds still seemed strong enough to bring the Harvard-Göttingen men back to tradition.

II

The Harvard-Göttingen men were anxious to quiet their sponsors' misgivings about the dangerous impact of neologist criticism. Thus Bancroft reassured Kirkland that he "should be unwilling to give (his) friends any reasonable ground for fearing (he) should lose (his) belief in, or respect for Christianity."(32) But Bancroft and his colleagues quickly found that the impact of the Göttingen questers could not be limited to what was "merely critical," as Stuart had urged, but affected their "philosophy" as well.(33) Thus William Emerson after his first year at Göttingen was taken aback by the effects of the neologist studies on this own thought. "I do not think nor feel nor act as I have ever done before," William confessed, "my mind seems to have undergone a revolution which surprises me. I cannot avoid tracing much of this to the books and lectures of Eichhorn."(34) Edward Everett, who had been sent to Göttingen to take a doctorate with Eichhorn himself and get a translation of his _Einleitung in das Neue Testament_ under way, experienced a similar intellectual "revolution." In his _Defense of Christianity Against the Work of George B. English_ Everett had expressly vindicated the apologetic evidentialist tradition and affirmed that the history of Jesus was authenticated by the miracles and resurrection of Jesus.(35) But upon his return from Göttingen Everett was closer to the sceptical position he had himself initially set out to refute and was alienated from the ministerial profession to which his studies abroad were supposed to contribute.

The interpretation of the life of Jesus narratives was the testing ground for William's and Everett's shifting positions. What concerned Everett here above all else was the discrepancy between "the public worship," "the public teaching" and "arbitrary facts" uncovered by historico-critical methods - the discrepancy Lessing referred to as the "ugly ditch" between "accidental historical truths" and "necessary truths of reason."(36) The crux of Lessing's metaphor of disjunction lay in his insistence that historical evidence could not produce conviction. No historical truth could be assigned the certainty of demonstrated truth. To Everett, Lessing's "ugly broad ditch," in affirming the disparity between historical fact and truths of reason, was irreconcilable with the Unitarian position. Lessing's point, Everett realized, implied that there could be no "external evidences" of Christianity. If Scripture was not capable of serving as the foundation of a rational faith and if revelation could not be authenticated by history, then it was imperative to determine _whether_ and on what grounds the life of Jesus could be valid at all.

Lessing's scepticism about the possibility of contingent history serving as mediator of the weight of revelation sharply brought into focus the 'historical' problem that the Harvard-Göttingen group was confronted with in the higher criticism of the Bible. Given the higher critical emphasis on the Bible as a document with a human form and structure, it seemed questionable to rest one's faith on historical assertions which themselves could not lay claim to a high degree of reliability. This dilemma was reinforced by the "problem," as Lessing had put it, "that reports of fulfilled prophecies are not fulfilled prophecies, that reports of miracles are not miracles ... the reports of fulfilled prophecies, and miracles have to work through a medium which takes away all their force."(37) A seminal answer to this disparagement of scriptural revelation was to be found outside the ranks of neology. "Of the two parties, which are now waging war with one another," Bancroft observed of the theological spectrum at Göttingen, "the rationalist and the orthodox, it is hard to say, which is the most to be feared; the one retaining nothing of (Christiani)ty but it's principles, the other clinging to all the particulars of the orthodox and joining mysticism and darkness to their unlimited faith."(38) Of the two camps, it was the latter one which came closest to the Harvard-Göttingen students concerns and carried them from Göttingen's neologists to the experiential theology practised at Berlin in Schleiermacher's focus on religious "self-consciousness."

At Berlin, Bancroft observed during his study year there, "the neologists ... were no longer going forward so triumphant as before."(39) What prevailed instead was Schleiermacher's emphasis on subjectivity and his vigorous protest against the arguments from miracle and prophecy which swept away the whole array of external proofs. By appealing to man's "immediate God-consciousness," Schleiermacher's "religious experience" theology minimized rational supernaturalist presuppositions about the life of Jesus and posited an internal authority providing its own proofs. The Harvard-Göttingen group was immediately struck by the possibilities Schleiermacher's position held out for a re-ordering of religious experience and knowledge. A static rationalism attested by Jesus' miracles and prophecies here gave way to internal "evidences" afforded by the "heart" and "intuition." Drawing on the terms of Schleiermacher's "religious experience" theology, William Emerson wrote to his brother Edward in 1824: "I too am a Son of God, and ... I need but throw off my shackles, these bonds of habit, and early perverted nature, to attest my relation to the Divinity."(40) William's devaluation of the "bonds" of evidentialism here could be observed to lead not to an assertion of belief <u>in</u> Christ as the mediatorial "Son of God" but rather to the possibility of assuming a role <u>like</u> Christ on the basis of the "divinity" of the human soul. Schleiermacher himself never aimed at this extreme stage of man's "likeness to God," a "likeness" granting, in the case of William Emerson, immediate apprehension of an absolute reality. "Immediate intuition," "divination" was with Schleiermacher largely relegated to a hermeneutical context, to the debate over an author's intentional thought and its apprehension.(41) This hermeneutical context, however, was slighted in William's appropriation which conflated a hermeneutical point with an epistemological point pertaining to the intuitive knowledge of transsubjective reality.

A similar shift towards religious subjectivism and intuitionism showed in the idealistic and Transcendentalist strain of Bancroft's writings after his sojourn at Berlin. What Bancroft found in Schleiermacher was a "religious experience" position which flanked the inroads made by historico-critical analysis on the historic foundations of revealed religion. Revelation for Schleiermacher could not be an intellectual proof of the factual character of the life of Jesus but only the rise of a new religious experience. The most obvious result of this position was the devaluation of the evidentialist framework over against what Bancroft perceived as the "transcendentalist" idea of "consciousness:" "We have not merely the senses opening to us the external world, but an internal sense, which places us in connection with the world of intelligence and the decrees of God." "Religion" was in Bancroft's modification of Schleiermacher's canon accordingly "a dead letter, wherever its truths (were) not renewed in the soul."(42)

The Harvard-Göttingen men were here making claims for the divinity and creative power of religious "consciousness" which were remarkably similar to Transcendentalist assertions. The twin influence of neology and a "religious experience" theology supplied the terms of a spiritual epistemology on which Transcendentalist assumptions could grow and cohere. The Harvard-Göttingen group applied this influence selectively, however, slighting it when it seemed to counteract scriptural integrity and enforcing it when it seemed directed against empirical-mechanistic "bonds of habit." Thus Bancroft approved Schleiermacher's canon as an affirmative theology which left the integrity and historicity of biblical narratives of the life of Jesus intact. With Schleiermacher, Bancroft judged, "the strict humanity of Christ (is not) in any way doubted." "Schleiermacher has remained a Christian, true to the moral principles of ... Jesus."(43)

The mentor on whom American practitioners drew was representative of a tradition that sought to lift the life of Jesus narratives out of an arena governed by the technicalities of scientific historical method and exegetical refinements. In Schleiermacher's shift of emphasis from the words of the text to the "consciousness" of the interpreter, the exegete's task was not centered on questions of synoptic relationship, historicity or "genuineness." Whatever the exegetical 'status' of a biblical text, its authority flowed immediately from the person of Jesus. Submerged in this emphasis was a sustained interest in the form and narrative shape of the life of Jesus accounts as well as an independent critical preoccupation with the synoptic question. The influence issuing from Schleiermacher's canon on the Harvard-Göttingen group thus reinforced the devaluation of the historico-critical elements of the quest which had already been prevalent in the flawed equation of neology with deist rationalism and "irreligion."

The devaluation of the quest's "merely critical" elements was all the more welcome as Harvard-Göttingen men acutely sensed that the neologist approach to biblical narratives was unlikely to be met with approval by conservative Unitarians. The more Bancroft delved into neologist studies, the less likely it seemed to him that his new learning would be accepted after his return. "'Tis out of the question," Bancroft wrote to Everett from Göttingen, "to expect, that in any American University whatever, the station of Professor of theology would be offered to me or anyone else, who had got his theology in Germany." "Who is there in America that cares for all this?" "Who would dare to interpret in America the epistles to the Hebrews, the Apocalypse, but above all the O. T. as it must and ought to be done. The cry of heresy will attend the first attempt."(44) Bancroft's assessment was correct. The <u>Christian Examiner</u> observed with regard to the reception of Griesbach's edition of the New Testament at Harvard that "any argument founded on the principles of biblical criticism, is received with a great deal of uneasiness and suspicion...."(45) Similarly, Stuart judged after Everett's early attempts at translating Eichhorn that Eichhorn's "speculations" "would be obnoxious" to American critics.(46)

The Harvard-Göttingen men were anxious to reunite themselves with the conservative Unitarian camp at Harvard and therefore turned their studies to what was acceptable theologically and exegetically. Under the impact of Göttingen's biblical critics, Bancroft initially sought to "pursue theological studies to the greatest benefit, to give instruction as any opening may occur" and therefore devoted himself to "raising (in America) a degraded and neglected branch of study, which in itself is so noble, and to aid in establishing a thorough school of Theological Critics."(47) Yet Bancroft's efforts after his return never yielded any such results. Similarly, Everett was determined to "do what has never yet been done - exhibit those views of the subject of Christianity, which the modern historical and critical enquiries fully establish...."(48) But upon his return from Göttingen, Everett never fulfilled this plan and refused to make further contributions to biblical studies, transposing the new critical methods instead to the study of the classics. Once more the exposure to higher criticism did not lead to stringent critical exegesis, and the philological aspects of the new procedures again seemed to be a less troublesome issue than the theological.

In the case of Bancroft, Everett and William Emerson the "uneasiness and suspicion" accompanying the confrontation with the new biblical criticism and life of Jesus research could be observed to play into a severe crisis of profession. Bancroft had been sent to Göttingen to "pursue his theological studies" so that he might better be "able to expound and defend the Revelation of God."(49) But when Bancroft set sail for Göttingen, in spirit he never returned to the Unitarian theological cast. Upon his return, Bancroft lasted in the ministerial profession only until 1823 and made a step sidewards toward the academy and later to a political and historical career. The career of Edward Everett was in a similar way shaped by the corrosive effects of the Harvard-Göttingen axis. Everett's exposure to the quest's neologist representatives increasingly fed into a problematic choice of profession in which Everett set out "to separate the public worship of God and the public teaching of duty, from all connection with arbitrary facts" and eventually found his conviction shattered to the point of departing from the ministerial profession.(50)

William Emerson, no less than his predecessors at Göttingen, was determined to act out the "revolution" which had undermined the foundations of evidentialist apologetics, leaving him instead with the inward testimony of his own conscience. And advancing the same argument his brother Ralph Waldo was to put forward in 1832, William declared shortly before commencing his studies at Göttingen: "Every candid theologian after careful study will find himself wide from the traditionary opinions of the bulk of his parishioners. Have you settled the question whether he shall sacrifice his influence or his conscience?"(51) William chose the first option; when he returned from Göttingen in 1825, he announced that he no longer wanted to pursue the ministry as a career. Soon after William went to New York to begin a new career as a lawyer. Once again the confrontation with neologist and "rationalist" critical studies had issued in a decisive change of profession and a break with the ministerial office.

III

It was the problem of the relation of faith to history and the more inclusive problem of the historicity of the life of Jesus that was not easily dismissed on the Harvard-Göttingen students' native ground. Thus Ralph Waldo Emerson acutely sensed the dangers lurking in the new biblical studies at Göttingen. In the application of historico-critical means to Scripture, Emerson judged, the religious element was "somewhat lost." "Our theological sky blackens a little," Emerson observed of the impact of the Harvard-Göttingen students, "or else the eyes of our old men are growing dim. But certain it is that with the flood of knowledge and genius poured out upon our pulpits, the light of Christianity seems to be somewhat lost. The young imagine that they have rescued and purified the Christian creed; the old, that the boundless liberality of the day has swept away the essence with the corruption of the gospel and has arrived at too skeptical refinements." (L, I, 127-128) Yet Emerson himself would soon arrive at "too sceptical refinements" which worked to dissolve the historical foundations of evidentialism.

Through the Harvard-Göttingen axis Emerson found a new and varied source of exposure to the quest. Ralph Waldo repeatedly urged William to "send information of a sort relating to College, politics, institutions, or of which creditable use may be made by the neady writers at home." Having "made some embryo motions in (his) divinity studies," Emerson was anxious to avail himself of "some useful hints from the Paradise of Dictionaries and Critics." (L, I, 143) William fulfilled his brother's request and regularly sent descriptions of Eichhorn's lectures on the New Testament and also aroused Waldo's interest in Lessing and Herder. By the late 1820s, Ralph Waldo had yielded to this train of influence and was by no means taking great pains to advance his arguments in full accordance with the Unitarian's insistence on the irrefutable validity of scriptural authority. On the contrary, Ralph Waldo Emerson's treatment of the relation of faith and history confirms that the doubts and uncertainties which the historico-critical analysis cast upon biblical authority significantly informed his disparagement of scriptural revelation.

Ralph Waldo Emerson approved of "the view of Lessing that revelation announced truths that are in the general path of the human mind but in its present state of sin and ignorance beyond its reach and ... that the announcement of (the) same truth may be a revelation to one mind and not to another...." (S, 91, 1) This relativistic view of revelation which no longer invested revelation with uniform authority binding to every Christian refuted the importance placed in the historical witness of Scripture. Historical evidence, Lessing argued, is an insufficient basis for religious belief. Emerson was prepared to confront the consequences of this disparity between "accidental history" and the faith-claims of revelation. "I am curious to know," Emerson asked in August 1827, "what the Scriptures do in very deed say about that exalted person who died in Calvary, but I do think it at this distance of time and in the confusion of languages to be a work of weighing phrases and hunting in dictionaries." (L, I, 208) Emerson's question reveals a historical scepticism and a departure from biblical revelation which carried the imprint of the quest's concern with historical positivity. With this scepticism evidential theology lost ground. "Who is he," Emerson asked in January 1827, "that has seen God of whom so much is known, or where is one that is told me concerning the other world and I will fulfill the conditions on which my salvation is suspended. The believer tells me he has an evidence historical and internal which make the presumptions so strong that it is almost a certainty that it rests on the highest probabilities. ... But now it must be admitted I am not certain that any of these things are true." (J, II, 159)

In asking "what the Scriptures do in very deed say about (the) exalted person" of Jesus, Emerson posed in effect the problem of the Leben-Jesu-Forschung and focused, on the actual, historical Jesus as opposed to the Jesus of the church's preaching. The latter figure no longer seemed authoritative, while the Jesus of history was uncertain, unknown, not available through external historical "evidences." This precisely was the insight which the Unitarian camp in the tradition of Norton and Ware had not fully confronted. Commenting on the "rationalist" questers, Norton observed of historico-critical analysis: "... all that mass of evidence, which, in the view of a Christian, establishes the truth of his religion, this evidence, it is said, consists only of probabilities. We want certainty." To this "demand for certainty" Norton answered that in matters of Christian faith "absolute certainty, so far as human reason may judge, cannot be the privilege of any finite being."(52) The questers insisted, by contrast, that criticism should bring the biblical accounts under rational scrutiny with regard to their historical certainty and probability. In the course of this analysis the Leben Jesu researchers demonstrated that one could not assign historical accuracy to the "evidences" of Christianity and questioned whether any foundation for faith was to be found in them. What Unitarians regarded as irrefutable historical "evidence," the testimony of the New Testament miracles, was increasingly uncovered as "mythical" embellishments and accretions. Confronted with this criticism, the Unitarian "believer," reared in a tradition of staunch adherence to the supernatural authority of the "historical evidences" of Christianity, was led to serious theological doubts.

The force of these theological doubts did not stem from any substantial philosophical criticism of Christianity but, rather, from the obvious way in which the factual data of the quest undermined what Unitarians had thought of as unquestionable "evidences" of Christianity. "The objections the German scholars have proposed," Emerson judged, "attack the foundation of external evidence, and so give up the internal to historical speculators and pleasant doubters.... The august Founder, the twelve self-denying heroes of pious renown, ... the martyrs, ... the boundless aggregate of hearts and deeds which the genius of Christianity touched and inspired ... all these must now pass into the rhetoric of scoffer and atheist as the significant testimonies of human folly, and every drunkard in his cups, and everly voluptuary in his brothel will roll out his tongue at the Resurrection from the dead; at the acts, the martyrdoms, the unassailable virtues and the legendary greatness of Christianity." (J, II, 83-85)

To Unitarians nourished in the tradition of "evidences," the sceptical inquiries into the historicity of the "August Founder" were deeply troubling. Boston pulpits did not hesitate to express their strong aversion towards the quest's tools and charged them with leading to a denial of the historical revelation of God's being in the person of Christ. The authority of the "descended being, the Companion of God before time, living and suffering as he did, ... this deep and high theology," it was hoped, would "prevail."(53) With the Harvard-Göttingen group, however, and with those who were falling prey to its influence, it did not "prevail"; on the contrary, the quest's historico-critical procedures would continue to contribute to doubts about professional choices and about the validity of evidentialist claims.

IV

The Harvard-Göttingen men and their 'homefront' colleagues were agreed that Eichhorn's "theological sentiments" were "very widely different from (their) own."(54) Yet the rejection of Eichhorn's critical procedures was not clear-cut and unanimous. Roughly at one pole were George Ticknor and Edward Everett who deliberately moved away from biblical studies. At the other pole were George Bancroft and the Emerson brothers Ralph and William whose works revealed a lasting appreciation of historico-critical exegesis. In the case of William Emerson, this appreciation was one for which the issue of the Lord's Supper served as a catalyst, a catalyst attesting to William's increasing adherence to a christology "from below" which subjected the figure of Jesus to historico-critical procedures. "William's mind was exact and judicial and his conscience active," Edward Waldo Emerson observed in 1883 of his father's elder brother who had departed from the ministry after his Göttingen studies. "The German philosophy and the Biblical criticism shook his belief in the forms and teaching of the religion in which he had been brought up." (W, IV, 367n) According to Edward Waldo Emerson, this corrosive influence of the new critical studies became most apparent in William's rejection of the traditional view of the Lord's Supper and his belief "that the rite of the Lord's Supper was not authoritatively established by Jesus for perpetual observance as a sacrament by Christians."(55)

William's consideration of the issue of the Lord's Supper was not without historical precedent. In 1667 Solomon Stoddard devalued the sacrament by terminating its exclusivity and by accepting profession of faith and repentence as prequisites for church membership and communion.(56) In William's treatment of the Lord's Supper the sacrament underwent a different devaluation. William's own position was less concerned with blurring the distinction between saints and sinners and opening communion to all parishioners than with advancing a more historico-critical point. In a letter to Ezra Ripley from April 4, 1830, William frankly spelled out his objections to the Lord's Supper. For Ezra Ripley, the Lord's Supper was an obligatory ceremony which pointed to the revelatory significance of Christ's sacrifice, reminding the believer "to love and obey Jesus Christ for what he is, and what he had done for us." For William, however, the view of the Lord's Supper as an obligatory ceremony was no longer tenable. "The question is," William asked, "whether the external ceremonies of the communion table are at this day binding and important."(57)

This disparagement of the significance of the Lord's Supper was a view which William had first encountered in the biblical critics at Göttingen. Griesbach demonstrated that the words "Do this in remembrance of me" did not appear in all manuscripts. Schleiermacher, whom William singled out during his Berlin sojourn as one of the critics contributing to the "rapid advances in theology," treated the rite of communion in the context of the Jewish feast of the Passover and argued that "we cannot immediately conclude from Christ's own words as they are reported in the three Gospels that Christ instituted this as a permanent rite of the Christian Church."(58) The most devastating attack on the Lord's Supper came from the anti-supernatural criticism of Reimarus, who read the sacrament against the background of primitive Christianity. Baptism and the Lord's Supper, Reimarus argued, "were not instituted by Christ, but created by the early church on the basis of certain historical assumptions" designed to account for the delayed parusia.(59) These literary and historical arguments against the sacrament of the Lord's Supper no doubt entered into William Emerson's scepticism about the 'universal,' permanent significance of the Lord's Supper as well as the special authority of the historical Jesus. And for all the "personal respect" for Ezra Ripley and "regard to the importance of the subject," William was forced to admit on this account that he regarded the Lord's Supper merely as an "external ceremony."(60)

William's appropriation of the quest's exegetical procedures was a portent of things to come in New England theology. The question of exegesis and life of Jesus research, it seemed, could not be separated from professional choices and commitments to Unitarian evidentialism. Ralph Waldo Emerson was soon to follow his brother's step. Using the exegetical tools of the new biblical criticism which William had encountered first-hand in Göttingen, Emerson moved farther and farther away from the Unitarians' conservative, apologetic appropriation of historico-critical procedures. Again, the historico-critical techniques of the quest turned out to be by no means an unwelcome or unpalatable tool; on the contrary, Emerson consciously turned to the exegetical 'tactics' of the quest to "sever the strained cord" that "bound" him to his Boston pastorate. (L, I, 357)

From Göttingen, William time and again emphasized to his brother the "rapid advances in theology" made by Eichhorn, Schleiermacher and Herder and praised "the results of so many centuries of struggle against superstition and ignorance."(61) Emerson further had numerous opportunities to observe the power of the new critical studies to change the direction of professional careers. Emerson listened first-hand to the reports of Harvard's first Göttingen students who had seen how the "religion of their Fathers" was crumbling in the crucible of historico-critical scrutiny. In 1821 Emerson attended several of George Ticknor's lectures at Harvard; he also fell under the spell of Edward Everett's and George Bancroft's reports all of which gave him a sense of the exegetical and theological context in which the higher criticism was practiced.(62) Emerson's sermons show the process of transition and reveal a gradual advance towards historico-critical methods. Consonant with historico-critical procedures, Emerson acknowledged the importance of literary form, the uses of symbolic language and historical circumstances for a proper interpretation of scriptural texts. It was in Emerson's sermon on "Astronomy", delivered four months before his break with the Second Church in Boston, that the insistence on the importance of bringing scientific historical insight to bear upon religion became most apparent. Emerson here assumed the persona of the historical critic, reiterating that science clarified and enlarged the knowledge gained from divine revelation: "Religion will become purer and truer by the progress of science." "The Lover of truth will look at all the facts as the commentary and exposition, say rather, the sequel of the revelation which our Creator is giving of himself." (YES, 157, 171)

While this passage presented historico-critical method as confirming supernatural revelation, Emerson's sermon on "Astronomy" in effect went on to subordinate the importance of revelation to scientific knowledge: Historical criticism has "an irresistible effect in modifying and enlarging the doctrines of theology." "It corrects ... our views of God." (YES, 157, 173) Similarly, Emerson's sermon on "Providence" regarded historico-critical knowledge no longer as "the commentary and exposition of revelation" but, rather, as a body of "evidence" that can be "entirely independent of revelation." (S, 66, 8) Emerson here substantially departed from the premises of the Unitarian view of biblical revelation. For Norton, who admitted the use of higher critical procedures in biblical exegesis, historico-critical method was an apologetic helpmaid buttressing the validity of biblical revelation. Emerson, however, who had learnt from Michaelis and Eichhorn that the Gospels represented the outcome of a long compositional process which had resulted in discrepancies and inaccuracies, was prepared to acknowledge that the traditional claims of biblical revelation were often contradicted by the historico-critical data of the new biblical studies. Emerson in effect encouraged his parishioners to question scriptural authority: "A Revelation is credible or incredible according as it is consistent with the constitution of our mind." And if elements of Scripture were found to be inaccurate or contradictory, Emerson insisted that scriptural authority had to be rejected: "Let it be supposed that in any case a man is clearly of the opinion that Saint Peter or Saint Paul is mistaken, and positively lays down a false doctrine, ... I say, to reject that doctrine." (S, 92, 5) That this questioning of scriptural authority derived largely from Emerson's reading in the rising historico-critical scrutiny of the biblical narratives was once more confirmed in the conclusion of Emerson's sermon on "Astronomy": "The Scriptures," Emerson here reiterated, "were written by human hands." And the reader therefore has to "correct the human errors that have crept into them." (YES, 157, 178)

By the late 1820s, then, Emerson had yielded to the historico-critical procedures of the quest; moreover, his position had already given rise to rumors that the young minister at Second Church was not treating the Bible with sufficient reverence. In 1829, Ware insinuated that Emerson "did not look to the Scriptures with all the same respect as others."(63) The Harvard-Göttingen men, when appropriating the new methods of biblical criticism were confronted with similar suspicions. Bancroft, whom Kirkland had sent to Göttingen to "become an accomplished philologian and Biblical Critic," time and again assured his patron that he would not give way to the "irreligious" and "heartless formality" of the Göttingen questers: "Of their infidel systems I hear not a word; and I trust I have been to long under your inspection to be in danger of being led away from the religion of my Fathers."(64) The New Englanders who listened to Bancroft's sermons after his return from Göttingen judged differently. Bancroft's sermon audiences listened with discomfort to the use of phrases like "our dear pelican Christ" in Cambridge pulpits.(65) The vocabulary of the quest was and remained incompatible with Unitarian christological affirmations, and Bancroft's sermon audiences in fact more that welcomed Bancroft's abandonment of a ministerial career in the spring of 1823.

Emerson's appropriation of the quest's vocabulary and techniques led to a similar alienation. In March 1831, Emerson set up a series of vestry lectures on the origin, authorship and authenticity of the Gospels. The vestry lectures bore ample witness of Emerson's appropriation of British evidentialist theologians, who stoutly adhered to the traditional doctrines concerning the authorship and historical reliability of the biblical narratives; of the neologist Göttingen critics who subjected biblical text to historico-critical procedures; and, finally, of the "mediating" theology of Schleiermacher, who stressed subjective religious experience against a bibliocentric view of religion. The application of the conflicting claims of these three exegetical traditions might have been hardly of interest to the audience Emerson hoped to attract, but for the minister of Second Church it became increasingly a most welcome tool in his efforts to move away from a rigid reliance on historical revelation.

In the preparation of the vestry lectures Emerson's chief mentors among the British commentators were Nathaniel Lardner's Credibility of Gospel History, George Campbell's The Four Gospels and James Macknight's annotated New Literal Translation of all Apostolic Epistles as well as his

Harmony of the Four Gospels. Emerson's third vestry, which consisted almost entirely of adaptations from the survey of ancient and English translations given in Macknight's Epistles, suggests that Emerson was apparently in full agreement with the biblical criticism of the British evidentialist school. Emerson exhorted the exegete at the outset of the vestry to examine "the means through with (the Bible) came to him, that he may be sure it was really written by those to whom it is ascribed." (VL, III, 8) Emerson then enumerated at length the available documentary sources for the genuineness of the Bible, thus demonstrating to his audience "that we are able to connect by an unbroken chain of evidence the books from which are now drawn our rule of faith with the books first written by the apostles 1800 years ago." (VL, III, 11)

While Emerson's third vestry was fully in keeping with the traditionalist view of the authority and historical veracity of the biblical narratives, his vestry on "The Origin of the Three First Gospels" indicates that Emerson was also prepared to acknowledge the untenability of these doctrines. For this vestry, Emerson moved away from the British commentators to make substantial borrowings from Herbert Marsh's edition of J. D. Michaelis' Introduction to the New Testament. Emerson's appropriation of Michaelis' study in his fourth vestry reveals that the minister of Second Church was infusing his writings with what Marsh's English reviewers termed a "tincture of the spirit of scepticism" about the "authenticity integrity, credibility and inspiration of the Gospels."(66) The key point of departure for Emerson was the "synoptic problem": "The relation of the three books of Matthew, Mark (and) Luke to each other is very remarkable. If you will look at a Harmony and take their narratives of the same fact, you will find that they frequently agree not only in relating the same things in the same manner but in the same words." (VL, IV, 12) Emerson made this observation on the basis of several "harmonies," Lant Carpenter's Harmony of the Gospels, James Macknight's Harmony as well as Newcome's edition of Griesbach's Synopsis. Macknight's Harmony was largely concerned with paraphrasing and harmonizing the four Gospels so as to produce a unilateral account. Griesbach's Synopsis, by contrast, emphatically denied that a harmonization of the first three Gospels was possible. Griesbach doubted "very much whether a harmonistic account (could) be composed from the books of the evangelists ... when none of the evangelists anywhere exactly follows the temporal sequence when there does not exist sufficient evidence from which to deduce who deviates from the chronological order and at what point he does so."(67)

In the fourth vestry lecture Emerson repeatedly spelled out the implications of this new synoptic arrangement of the Gospels. Moving away from the usual harmonizing transpositions, Emerson reminded his parishioners that "even eye witnesses of the same facts if they write their report independently of each other, will never relate them ... in the same manner ... and even the circumstances which they observe in common, they will arrange and conbine in such a manner in their own minds as to produce two representations, which though upon the whole the same, widely differ in the choice and position of the respective parts." (VL, IV, 12) This insistence on the variation and personal viewpoint which each of the Evangelists contributed denied a view of inspiration regarding Scripture as the passive recording of divinely dictated messages. Emerson pointed out in contrast that the Evangelists were individual "witnesses" and "historians" who consciously "composed" their accounts of the life of Jesus and subjected their compositions to different "redactions" with distinct exegetical tendencies. The Evangelists were not servile copyists, as Norton's mechanical view maintained, but rather independent and original.

With this incipient "redaction criticism," the question of the authenticity and inspired inerrancy of the biblical narratives could no longer be settled along traditionalist lines. Emerson restored the synoptic writers to their legitimate place as theologians of the early Church and presented them also as the earliest "exegetes" of the Christian tradition, "exegetes" who had to be viewed as fallible and 'biased' "historians." Emerson found corroboration for this view of the Evangelists as "copiers" and "historians" in the second major source he used for his vestry on "The Origin of the Three First Gospels", Connop Thirwall's translation of Schleiermacher's Critical Essay on the Gospel of St. Luke. Schleiermacher and his translator presented in their studies detailed descriptions of Eichhorn's solution of the synoptic problem. On the basis of these descriptions Emerson declared in his fourth vestry: "Eichhorn ... supposes that our Gospels ... are only four out of many records of the same kind and that all were derived from one common document which he supposes to have been written in Aramaic or the vulgar Hebrew of the time .... He (also) supposes that ... Matthew, Mark and Luke used different copies of this document which had (been) enriched or varied by the particular information of the transcribers, and that they may account for the variation in their gospels." (VL, IV, 12-13)

Discussing this theory of an Aramaic Proto-Gospel in his Evidence of the Genuineness of the Gospels in 1837, Norton would condemn Eichhorn as a 'heretical' theologian with whose theories "all the doubts and objections on historical grounds, by which the evidence of the genuineness of the Gospels has of late years been assailed, have been connected."(68) Emerson, however, stood in 1831 already firmly in the tradition of the new biblical criticism and was in no way repelled by Eichhorn's assumption that the synoptic Gospels, as second-century variations of an originally Aramaic account of the life of Jesus, could no longer be regarded as reliable historical data. Emerson was even prepared to go beyond Eichhorn's Proto-Gospel hypothesis and argued that the common source for the synoptic Gospels was the oral tradition.

The main exposition of this view was, as Emerson pointed out in his fourth vestry lecture, given by J. K. L. Gieseler, who had attempted to show that the synoptic Gospels were different forms of a primitive oral Gospel, forms which had been adapted to the missionary preaching of the different apostles. Schleiermacher modified this position by positing in addition to the oral tradition numerous "diegeseis" which had been used either separately or in small pre-existing collections to form the synoptic Gospels.(69) In his fourth vestry lecture Emerson presented at length a refutation of the notion of a written Aramaic Proto-Gospel and argued with Schleiermacher that "not enough attention seems to have been paid to the fact that ... oral instruction was the great mode of communication in that age of early Christianity." (VL, IV, 13) The principles stemming from Gieseler's and Schleiermacher's emphasis on the flux of the oral tradition upon which the Synoptics had drawn - the fragmentation of the Gospels, the recognition of several of their pericopes as bearing no relation to the actual events of Jesus' life - were all at complete variance with Norton's claims about the genuineness of the biblical narratives and underscored Emerson's growing devaluation of the biblical record as an authentic document validating the historical positivity of revelation.

At the exegetical and hermeneutical juncture, however, the historico-critical tools subtly counteracted Emerson's intentions. Scriptural interpretation in the evidentialist tradition presumed a common bond between preacher and congregation. The preacher could rely at least on a partial shared familiarity with the text and its interpretation. The higher criticism, by contrast, with its focus on historical milieu, literary origin and interpretative tradition drove the wedge of exegetical intricacies and hermeneutical theory between the audience and the text. This wedge turned out to be scarcely suitable to Emerson's vestry project. With the vestry lectures Emerson had hoped to attract in particular the young members of his parish, yet the vestry enterprise quickly failed. To Emerson it seemed that if his "poor Tuesday evening lectures (horresco referens) were to any auditor the total of his exposition of Christianity," it would leave only "a beggarly faith." (J, III, 315) The tools and techniques of higher-critical exegesis were long incompatible with a Unitarian theological cast and belonged more to the province of the academically trained theologian than to the popular piety of the general lay church member. Yet Emerson readily applied the tactics of this exegesis in the months he was getting ready to leave his Boston pastorate with a sermon carrying the distinctive marks of the quest's exegetical procedures.

V

Emerson's appropriation of higher-critical procedures fed into a long-standing uncertainty about his profession and calling. This uncertainty seemed particularly pressing for a minister who not only struggled with professional difficulties and parish disfavor but also with the theological problem concerning the validity of historical revelation and the "certainty" of the one whom Emerson's Unitarian colleagues proclaimed as the "August Founder." Emerson could find a model for his predicament in the crisis which William had suffered after studying under Göttingen's higher critics. William had been led to troubling doubts about his own calling as well as about the validity of supernatural revelation and had finally decided to set the testimony of his own "conscience" over the "traditionary opinion of the bulk of his parishioners," affirming instead a more intuitive insight into divine truth against the forms and traditions of "historical Christianity."

Seven years later Ralph Waldo Emerson was to fall in line. And once again it was the issue of the Lord's Supper which served as a catalyst. Emerson was ready to resign his pastorate unless he were permitted to dispense with the rite of the Lord's Supper which he was unable to regard as a sacrament established by Christ for his followers in all ages.(70) The Harvard-Göttingen men, when exposed to the higher-critical tools, had refrained from a consistent "application;" Emerson, however, was prepared to utilize the "tactics" of historico-critical analysis to break with the Second Church and was acutely aware that the techniques of a christology "from below" could be exploited to provoke a confrontation with the Unitarian evidentialist framework. William had already set the example for this tactic. William's dismissal of the Lord's Supper as an "external ceremony" and the critical principles which induced it had a significant impact on Emerson's own objections against the sacrament. In his sermon on the Lord's Supper, the young minister of Second Church entered "in a way unusual and remarkable for him, into a critical and systematic consideration of the scriptural authorities of the rite", a mode of analysis that was, as Edward Waldo Emerson suggests, "supplied by the elder brother." (W, IV, 367n)

During his years as minister of Second Church Emerson had time and again relied on the close intellectual contract with William. Thus Emerson would ask his brother: "Prithee, dear William send me some topics for sermons, or if it please you better the whole model 'wrought to the nail'." (L, I, 211) Significantly, Emerson had also urged his brother in 1830 to supply him with information from his Göttingen studies. He wrote William "to make a synopsis of the leading arguments against Christianity ... he also wanted him to mark, in the works of Eichhorn or others, the passages that would tend to destroy a candid inquirer's belief in the divine authority of the New Testament."(71) And in February of 1832, five months before he would deliver the "Lord's Supper Sermon" to the Second Church, Emerson again mentioned to his aunt the "German commentators" who "trace almost all the precepts of Christ to Hebrew proverbs." (J, II, 466)

The influence of these "commentators" in the "Lord's Supper Sermon" was perhaps most apparent in the "unusual and remarkable" rational exegesis which Edward Waldo Emerson noted in his father's sermon on the Lord's Supper. This rational exegesis was by no means "unusual" and in effect fully in accord with the exegetical principles and techniques of Emerson's vestries. Thus Emerson built his argument in the sermon by first reminding his parishioners of the differing versions of the words of institution. Using the close textual and literary analysis also characteristic of the 'synoptic' passages in the vestries, Emerson observed that the words "this do in remembrance of me" do not appear in Mark's and Luke's accounts of the Lord's Supper, whereas in John the "whole transaction is passed over without notice." (W, XI, 5) Emerson then proceeded to bring the Fourth Gospel into special prominence, emphasizing that "it only differs in this, that we have found the Supper used in New England and the washing of the feet not." Given the account of the Fourth Gospel, the interpretation of the Lord's Supper as a permanent institution appeared to Emerson arbitrary: "I cannot help remarking that it is not a little singular that we should have preserved this rite and insisted upon perpetuating one symbolical act of Christ while we have totally neglected all others." (W, XI, 11)

The speech so far was Ralph Waldo's, but the terms were those of the questers whom the Harvard-Göttingen students had encountered first hand. Emerson's arguments were in accord with Schleiermacher's observations on the Lord's Supper in the Critical Essay on the Gospel of St. Luke and The Life of Jesus. In keeping with the findings of Michaelis' and Eichhorn's critical studies on the relations of the Gospels, Schleiermacher's account of the Lord's Supper entertained a pronounced preference for St. John's Gospel and regarded the "symbolic act of feet-washing" to be of equal rank with the Lord's Supper.(72) In his Life of Jesus and The Christian Faith, Schleiermacher further pointed out that some of the narratives contained no "injunction" "to institute a permanent rite" and that against the ceremony of feet-washing the interpretation of the Lord's Supper as a permanent institution could not be justified. "As the Apostles deduced no such command from Christ's words at the foot-washing, they could ... have no more right to make of the Supper a perpetual and universal institution."(73) And in the same manner that Emerson reiterated in his sermon that he could not "bring himself to believe that ... Jesus looked beyond the living generation ... and meant to impose a memorial feast upon the whole world," (W, XI, 7) Schleiermacher argued that "the Last Supper was an affair only of a small number of his disciples, of the apostolic circles, and even if he commended these to repeat the act, it does not follow that he intended the whole Christian church to observe it."(74)

Some of the textual arguments Emerson employed in his interpretation of the Lord's Supper also appeared in a work long acknowledged to be the major source for Emerson's sermon on the Lord's Supper, namely Thomas Clarkson's Portraitures of Quakerism. Emerson's reading of the Lord's Supper "followed Clarkson in detail: the absence of any intimation of permanence in Matthew and Mark, the especial significance of the silence of John, ... the mention of Luke, who was not present, but whose authority need not be rejected."(75) With regard to the Quaker source on which Emerson drew for his sermon, the "Lord's Supper" has been regarded as "the most derivative" sermon Emerson ever gave, the "conclusion (being) distinctly his own."(76) Emerson's sermon, however, and his "conclusion," the rejection of the Lord's Supper as "an institution for perpetual observance," were derivative in yet another respect. The sermon also attested to the appropriation of an exegetical tradition that went beyond the Quaker sources - the higher-critical method of the questers. Here Emerson found a formidable critical tool utilizing the same historical and literary analysis in scriptural exegesis which had already characterized the vestries Emerson delivered in the months before the "Lord's Supper." Moreover, the exegetical apparatus in which this approach to Scripture was embedded, an often technical discussion of textual observations which had been a strain for Emerson's vestry audiences, now fully met the demands of the deacons and members of the congregation who expected from their minister an elaborate and weighty exegetical argumentation.

Emerson's application of the historico-critical principles of the quest did not stop with his recognition of the importance of the Jewish tradition which helped shape the form of the Lord's Supper. Emerson also applied the sharp edge of historico-critical exegesis to the liturgic formula of the rite itself. Jesus' words at the Passover, Emerson argues, were in keeping with the metaphorical language characteristic of all his teachings: "He always taught by parables and symbols. It was the national way of teaching, and was largely used by him. Remember the readiness which he always showed to spiritualize every occurrence." (W, XI, 9-10) Emerson here drew on the critical mode of exegesis which he had applied in his vestries. And in the same way that he underscored in his vestries that "the accomodation of (Jesus') language to settled forms of speech" (VL, VIII, 21) supported a 'naturalistic' interpretation of miracle narratives, Emerson now used observations on symbolic form to reduce the Lord's Supper to a ceremonial institution. Biblical criticism here was consciously applied to undo claims to universality.

Emerson's argument that the commonly accepted view of the Lord's Supper falsely gave authority to Jesus suggests that his rejection of the Lord's Supper as an empty ritual was also an expression of a christology that played down the revelatory significance of the human figure of Jesus. For this christology, Emerson could draw in part on the humanistic stance characteristic of the Unitarian conception of Christ. Here Christ was rendered a type of human perfection, a teacher, "friend and model," "accessible and imitable." Rather than "severing (Jesus) from others," Channing time and again stressed the "imitableness of Christ's character," Christ's exemplary function as a mediator sent to inspire men to divine perfection.(77) Similarly, Emerson declared in the "Lord's Supper Sermon": "Jesus is an instructor of man. He teaches us to become like God."

(W, XI, 18) And in accordance with this emphasis on Jesus as an exemplary teacher Emerson considered the Lord's Supper to be "simply a means of improvement." (YES, 50, 59) "I believe," Emerson reiterated in "A Feast of Remembrance", "the whole end and aim of this ordinance is nothing but this, to make those who partake of it better." (YES, 50, 57-58)

The devaluation of the revelatory significance of Christ characteristic of Emerson's criticism of the Lord's Supper, however, also extended to what Unitarian adherence to the remnants of an Arian christology persistently left intact: the special authority of Jesus as "the Mediator." (W, XI, 18) On this issue, Emerson drew once more on William's Göttingen studies. William acutely realized that "Eichhorn's findings had an effect on the picture of the character of Jesus."(78) This "effect" was largely due to Eichhorn's insistence on the opposition between the "Jesus of history" and the "Christ of faith" and his attempt to reconstruct the original Gospel relating the "historical Jesus" upon which the Evangelist had laid a body of "mythical" accretions. The overriding thrust of this concern with the reconstruction of the original Gospel was to reduce Jesus to the ethical teacher of Nazareth. In the "Lord's Supper" Emerson focused in a similar way on the "historical Jesus," carefully separating the Gospel accounts of Jesus from what Jesus taught in compliance with the traditions of his Jewish milieu. Moreover, Emerson advanced an alternative form of "remembrance" of Jesus which focused on Jesus primarily as a human figure rather than "the Mediator" with unique revelatory significance: "I will love him as a glorified friend, after the free way of friendship." (W, XI, 20)

It was this 'humanistic' emphasis on Jesus and the elimination of all sacrificial overtones of the Last Supper which provided the basis for the closing argument of Emerson's sermon - the rejection of the Lord's Supper as a "worthless" "form." "Forms are as essential as bodies," Emerson observed, "but to exalt particular forms, to adhere to one form a moment after it is outgrown, is unreasonable, and it is alien to the spirit of Christ." (W, XI, 20) But this rejection of a Christianity of "forms" forced Emerson all the more to affirm a new basis of religion. If "decent forms" and "saving ordinances" could only serve as the "sandy foundations of falsehoods" (W, XI, 21), if the Scriptures were indeed, as Emerson had shown for Paul's account of the Lord's Supper, "not the revelation but the record of the Revelation" (YES, 157, 125) , then the proof of the validity of revelation had to be sought somewhere else - not in historical and external "evidences" but rather within the "heart."

In this context a crucial impetus to "sever the strained cord" that "bound" Emerson to the Second Church was provided by a man who to Emerson uniquely seemed to corroborate the claims of a religion of the "heart" against the restrictive authority of the "dead forms" of historical Christianity. (J, II, 491) "I am entering into acquaintance with Goethe who has just died," Ralph Waldo wrote to Aunt Mary Moody on August, 19, 1832. (L, I, 354) Significantly, William, too, had "entered into acquaintance with Goethe" at a time when, under the impact of his Göttingen studies, he was gradually moving away from the claims of historical Christianity. "To William, beset by distressing doubt at Göttingen," Edward Waldo Emerson writes, "it occurred that, but eighty miles away at Weimar, lived the wisest man of the age. He forthwith sought him out, was kindly received, and laid his doubts before him. He hoped, no doubt, that Goethe could clear these up, and show some way in which he could honorably and sincerely exercise the priestly office." (W, IV, 367-368n) William's conversation with "the gentle and venerable poet" made a deep and lasting impression on him. (L, I, 161, 12n) "I was half an hour with him," William wrote his aunt in October 1824, "and it was a half hour I shall not soon forget." (L, I, 162, 12n) The advice William received was in effect to consider that "we had nothing to do with the different systems of philosophy, but that the highest aim of life should be for each one to accomodate himself as perfectly as possible to the station in which he was placed." (L, I, 161, 12n) But on his return journey to Cambridge during a very stormy crossing of the Atlantic, when he was several times "compelled," as he later wrote Aunt Mary Moody, "to make up what he "could not go to the bottom in peace with the intention in his heart of following the advice Goethe had given him."(79) And reporting the incident to Waldo in 1825, William told his brother that he was quitting the ministry for law studies.

While William received from Goethe the advice to satisfy his parishioners' expectations and keep his opinions to himself, his younger brother seized upon the German poet for just the oppositve 'advice' - to receive confirmation for a religion that no longer relied on the authority of the "external evidences" of biblical revelation but rather on the inner testimony of the "heart" as the source of an intuitive insight independent of the "genuineness" of the scriptural narratives of Jesus.(80) Emerson's journal entries during the months in which he was preparing to leave the ministry bore ample witness of this significance of Goethe for the young minister. Quoting from Goethe's "Letter to Werner," Emerson wrote in 1832: "What good were it for me to manufacture perfect iron while my own breast is full of dross?" (JMN, IV, 104) In Wilhelm Meister Emerson was struck by the sentence, "I, for my share, cannot understand how men have made themselves believe that God speaks to us thro' books & histories. The man to whom the Universe does not reveal directly what relations it has to him; whose heart does not tell him what he owes himself & others, that man will scarcely learn in out of books which generally do little more that give our errors names." (JMN, IV, 105) With this insistence on the intuitive emotional principles of the "heart," Goethe completed for Emerson what the criticism of the German "historical speculators" had already precipitated - the rejection of a rigid reliance on scriptural authority, on the "dead forms" and "external evidences" of an "effete, superannuated Christianity." (J, II, 491-492)

Emerson's experiential, affective approach to the figure of Jesus also aligned him with the "religious experience" theology of Schleiermacher. In his vestries Emerson repeatedly took note of the striking way in which Schleiermacher corroborated his own growing reliance on the intuitive testimony of the "heart." Commenting on the effects of the historico-critical approach to biblical narratives in the fourth vestry, Emerson used Schleiermacher to reiterate that "if we leave the letter and explore the spirit of the apostles and their master, we shall find there is an evidence that will come from the heart to the head, an echo to every sentiment taught by Jesus." (VL, IV, 15) Underlying this passage was Schleiermacher's subjective synthesis of the rationalistic principles of historico-critical exegesis with a religion of the "heart" through which Schleiermacher sought to "mediate" between the experience of faith and the intellectual demands of the new biblical criticism. Confronted with the scepticism induced by the historical criticism of Eichhorn and Michaelis, George Bancroft and William Emerson had welcomed this "religious experience" theology with its insistence on man's immediate consciousness of divinity. Similarly, William's brother also acutely sensed that

Schleiermacher's religion of the "heart" eased the tension of theology and historico-critical procedure by devaluing the dependence of faith on the assumption of Scripture's divine inerrancy.

Schleiermacher "admitted the validity of critical investigations to their fullest extent," Ripley observed in the Christian Examiner, "these he could not help but perceive, had abolished the foundation on which the prevailing views of the Bible had reposed.... Hence instead then of taking his stand on the written letter, he commenced with the religious consciousness of human nature.... In all general conceptions of religion, then, as well as in the records of revelation, we must not fail to look beyond the letter to the spirit, to separate the central and absolute idea from the temporary forms with which it is surrounded."(81) It was precisely this emphasis on looking "beyond the letter to the spirit" which Emerson singled out in the conclusion of the "Lord's Supper." The reliance on religious self-consciousness, Emerson realized, liberated religion from the externally grounded truth afforded by miracles and inspired Scripture; it validated religion by appeal not to its historical embodiment in biblical revelation but, rather, to man's sense of the immediacy and inwardness of the experience of faith, an experience "received immediately ... without intervention." (S, 123, 6)

In the works of the quest's "historical speculators" Emerson thus found not only a literary and historical criticism which undermined the Bible's claim to historically reliable revelation, but also a forceful stimulus for the views he would put forward in Nature and the "Divinity School Address." The overriding thrust of the historical criticism of the quest was to move towards an expressly immanental position. The incompatibility between the historical testimony of Scripture and revelation increasingly led to the affirmation of a truth that had to be sought independently of biblical revelation, in the "spirit" rather than the "letter." The criticism of the quest's "historical speculators" was in this respect in full accord with what would become the trademark of Emerson's full-fledged Transcendentalist position: the conception of revelation as gradual and progressive, and, more importantly, the reconstruction of the foundations of Christian knowledge towards a view which posited Christian truth as the actualization of the "evidences" of the "heart" rather than the confirmation of the historical accuracy of supernatural revelation.

The alliance between historico-critical procedures and idealist philosophy against the precept of historical factuality was acutely realized by Emerson's "Unitarian Pope." The "pantheism" of the "new theology" of Eichhorn, De Wette and Schleiermacher was, Norton judged, designed to "accomplish the solution of the problem of producing a living recognition of faith in its independence of ... historical knowledge; not resting the truth of Christian faith, as if it were a duty so to do, upon common, naked, historical truth."(82) For Norton the biblical narratives were historically reliable records of God's supernatural revelation of Himself to man, and the "new theology" therefore had in his view "allied itself with atheism ... and with the other irreligious speculations, that have appeared in those metaphysical systems from which the God of Christianity is excluded."(83) For Emerson, however, the "new theology" of the "historical speculators" provided in the months he was preparing to leave the Second Church pastorate a welcome reinforcement of his own acute sense of the disparity between individual conscience and scriptural authority and, moreover, a forceful corroboration of his growing depreciation of "historical Christianity." After the confrontation with the quest's "historical speculators" the Transcendentalist "new views" had become inevitable.

7. "Signs and Wonders:" The Fortress of Miracles

For conservative Unitarians "sensationalism" encouraged the inference that the Gospels presented the principal locus of revelation in recording the historical facts of Jesus of Nazareth and in substantiating his life and message with fulfilled prophecy and miracles. "All knowledge of Christ and Christianity," then, was "derived not from consciousness or intuition, but from outward revelation."(1) "There can be no intuition, no direct perception of the truths of Christianity," Norton insisted, "once admit that the New Testament does not contain all the principles of spiritual Truth ... and you open the door to all sorts of loose and crude speculations...."(2) For this position the Transcendentalist "new school" substituted a philosophy of intuition which affirmed that the primary validation of religion was the inner consciousness and not historical "evidences" authenticating verifiable events. One of the most significant watersheds in the promulgation of these "loose and crude speculations" was the miracles controversy of 1836 which until 1842 quickly broadened into an open conflict between "old school" Unitarians and the "new" Transcendentalist school. It was with the miracles controversy that the complex issue of the relevance of the Jesus of history became an important test case for New England theological struggles, in particular for the problems of historical "evidences" and biblical interpretation.

A brief debate over Ripley's "Martineau's Rationale" in the _Christian Examiner_ triggered the controversy in late 1836, but soon issued into highly significant disagreements about the historicity of Jesus' miracles and the reliability of biblical data - issues all conforming to the arsenal of arguments employed by the quest. With the "new school's" "speculations" in the miracles controversy, it seemed that the figure of Jesus could no longer serve as the pristine channel of revelation. Christianity rested more upon the teachings of Jesus than on his supposed deeds. These conclusions were formulated in "self-reliant" terms, yet the presuppositions were those of the quest. The parade of representatives of the Leben-Jesu-Forschung absorbed in particular by George Ripley was impressive and attested to the first serious invasion of New England by Leben Jesu researchers, of Herder, Eichhorn, Schleiermacher, Strauss, Wegschneider, Baur and, above all, De Wette.(3)

The invasion of the theological grounds of Unitarianism by the quest owed much to the work of the Harvard-Göttingen students. The way for the reception of the Leben Jesu studies had been prepared in half a dozen stirring articles by Everett and Bancroft in the _North American Review_ and the _Christian Examiner_. Bancroft and Everett opened the windows of Unitarianism to the quest's themes, and in due course Parker would translate and annotate De Wette's _A Critical and Historical Introduction to the Canonical Scriptures of the Old Testament_, while James Freeman Clarke would adapt De Wette's _Theodore_ and Samuel Osgood would contribute a translation of De Wette's _Ethics_ to Ripley's "Specimens of Foreign Standard Literature." The fact that the higher-critical tools employed in these works were so largely a product of the Leben-Jesu-Forschung resulted in its rejection not only as foreign but also as emanating from a "heresy" which had already led the Harvard-Göttingen group astray.

From the Unitarian position, the debate about miracles and the reception of Leben Jesu researchers was primarily epistemological and stood within the century-old Christian apologetic which had presented biblical miracles as sure proof of the supernatural origin and divine approval for

Christianity. In keeping with this apologetic, Ware, Felton and Norton concurred that the miracles Christ performed attested to an "outward revelation" that was "not innate, spontaneous and original ..., but extrinsic, derived, super-induced."(4) In this way Unitarians followed the watchword "except ye see signs and wonders, ye will not believe" and were anxious to cite acts which defied the comprehension of reason as rational proofs of supernatural religion.(5) Take these "signs" away and the supernatural rationalist temple built on the alignment of Lockean "sensationalism" with Scottish common sense would begin to teeter.

At the other end of the spectrum, the emerging Transcendentalist movement called the legitimacy of traditional references of "revealed religion" and biblical revelation into question. "We hold it to be an unsound method," Ripley declared in the Christian Examiner in 1836, "to make a belief in (miracles) the mental foundation of the Christian faith or the ultimate test of Christian character." It is impossible "to establish the truth of any reason merely on the ground of miracles."(6) This was the lesson Ripley had absorbed from the Leben Jesu studies of Schleiermacher, Paulus, Herder and De Wette. Following the premises of the quest, the "new school" around Ripley was prepared to agree with Schleiermacher's emphasis on "religious experience" and "consciousness" as the core of religion and refused, like Schleiermacher, to reduce religion to a matter of external and historical "evidences." Within the framework of the quest for the historical Jesus two points hovered over the narrative of this position: First, the "humanity" of Jesus now developed into the pivot of reconstruction. And second, this focus on the historical Jesus emerged as an index of the "new school's" doctrine of man. The full and unreserved recognition of Jesus as "homoousious" with man expressly served to underline man's divine nature.

The problems to which the themes of the quest were applied went thus far beyond the questions of the detailed fulfillment of prophecy and the historicity of miracles. With the "new school," the appropriation of the quest also touched on the more inclusive issue of the basis of religious belief and knowledge. In wrestling with this issue, the "new school" advocates refashioned the quest into their own rhetoric: The quest formed an inextricable part of the "new school's" premise that the indwelling of the divine in man was not confined to the historical Jesus but belonged to mankind as such and was of one piece with humanity. "Old school" Unitarians, by contrast, were sufficiently attuned to the quest to realize that this position threatened the tenuous link between faith and history and, above all, also issued in the crucial question about the special authority of Jesus of Nazareth as "mediator." And on this count, conservative Unitarians were increasingly concerned that their adversaries in the "new school" appeared "to lean to the anti-miraculous, got the German notions of 'myth', and ... (were) losing their hold on Christ."(7)

I

The groundwork that lay beneath the Unitarian position on miracles was the claim that Scripture, properly understood, represented a historically reliable arbiter of faith carrying the full weight of supernatural revelation. In the miracles controversy this premise, which reached from medieval scholastic "proofs for the existence of God" through Butler's Analogy of Religion, Paley's Evidences of Christianity and

Channing's Dudleian Lectures, was perpetuated to affirm that Christianity was a doctrinal system validated, not by inner religious experience, but by the historical "evidences" of the divine mission of Jesus. This line of argument, crucial to the background of the miracles controversy, represented a summation of tendencies long at work in the liberal tradition and nurtured by a rich background in seventeenth and eighteenth century English theology. When Channing and Norton expounded their view of miracles, they drew on the evidentialist argument employed by Clarke and Paley that "there was a Necessity of some particular Divine Revelation, to make the whole Doctrine of Religion clear and obvious to all Capacities."(8) From this perspective, biblical revelation, like scientific propositions, could and had to be verified empirically. The evidentiary appeal transposed the notion of 'fact,' with the empirical implications it had taken on in the natural sciences, to the realm of biblical interpretation. The theological conception of biblical events was thus squarely located in the realm of reliable, verifiable and factual "evidences."

Prior to the miracles controversy rejections of this framework emerged with disconcerting sharpness in Hume's critique of miracles. In Hume's case, empirical method led to a thoroughgoing rejection of the empirical grounds for belief in the miraculous. "There is not to be found, in all history, any miracle attested by a sufficient number of men, of such unquestioned good-sense ... and learning, as to secure us against all delusion in themselves."(9) "No testimony of men," then, could establish the occurrence of any miracle. History could no longer be used to demonstrate the historical veracity of miracles. Unitarians evinced an acute awareness of the epistemological threat Hume posed to the supernatural rationalist framework. "'The case of miracles,' as Mr. Hume states it," the Christian Examiner recapitulated in 1818, "is a contest of improbabilities, - that is to say, - a question, whether it be more improbable that the miracle should be true, or the testimony false.'"(10) In light of Hume's critique it was imperative for Unitarians to make sure they could rely on a secure epistemological basis. As guardians for this basis the Unitarian camp time and again called in Paley, Clarke and Tillotson to affirm Christianity as "sealed by miracles, that is by Divine interpositions, ... equally intelligible, striking and effecting to all ... (and) the most appropriate proofs of a religion...."(11)

The philosophically inclined clergy reinforced this position through Scottish common sense realism which by the opening decade of the century had achieved the philosophical conquest of Harvard Unitarianism. Common sense philosophy was in full resonance with Unitarian theological heritage by providing a firm foundation for faith in direct perception. The Scots bolstered the doctrines of perception and judgment against the blow of Hume's scepticism. Whereas Hume had maintained that phenomena never revealed causal connections, the Scottish realists restored causality and the validity of principles by way of presupposition rather than empirical investigation. Every impression, Reid announced, presupposed the existence of a cause sufficient to produce it. This 'presentational' realism effectively met Hume's challenge and, most importantly, was also considered by Unitarians to provide a sure base for the rational and scientific validation of the tenets of historical revelation.(13) The resultant christological position was dogmatically simple: The fact that Jesus wrought miracles attested that he was divinely commissioned without being a member of the Godhead and that Christianity was veritable and "genuine."

Increasingly, the reference to Jesus' miracles thus became the theological cornerstone which bore direct and credible witness to the Unitarian belief that "Christ's life (was) ... not an effect, but the commencement of a new and grand order ... (with) the miracle's of his life ... having their source in this superhuman power."(13)

In the long controversy which ranged from 1836 to 1840 over the value of inward and intuitive testimony as opposed to historical miracles, the critique put forward by Hume no longer posed a serious threat. The new "heresy" did not come from British critics but from what New England divines branded as "infidel publications" of "antisupernaturalists" which "reject the idea of a Revelation as unnecessary or impossible, or attack the evidences of Christianity as founded upon such a revelation...."(14) With these "infidel publications" New Englanders were once more forced on their own soil to take a position regarding the historicity of miracles. From the viewpoint of New England divinity, the rejection of the historicity of miracles was linked to three different views of the "character of Jesus." There were, the Christian Examiner observed, "freethinkers" like Reimarus "to whom all revelation was but superstition, - Jesus either a good-natured enthusiast, or an impostor....;" "romancers" like K. F. Bahrdt and Venturini, "who believed ... that such a person as Christ had lived, but admitted no divine influence whatever in Christianity, and ... made the life of Jesus a romance - Jesus himself a member of secret societies....;" and finally "rationalists" like Paulus and De Wette, who "substitute for the idea of a human Divinity, and the combination of the divine and human nature in Jesus, an ethical notion of the Son of God, and the revelation of divinity in the perfection of human nature."(15) In the Christian Examiner's rendition of the quest's theological spectrum the differences in the respective Jesus portraits did not really matter. Against the terms of the historicity and "genuineness" of miracles, the quest's camps coalesced, the Examiner judged, in their "rejection of the religion of Christ as a supernatural revelation."(16) On the latter issue of supernaturalism, Stuart shared the Unitarian verdict and joined the common front of criticism against the quest, arguing that the quest's advocates "assailed" "the divinity of Christ" and "impugned" the "divine authenticity of the Bible."(17)

The seriousness of the scepticism of "those who reject Christianity as a supernatural revelation" was portrayed vividly to New Englanders by the delegates from Göttingen and Berlin. Bancroft persistently described to Andrews Norton the Göttingen questers' "disbelief in the miracles." "It is said" by those critics, Bancroft observed, "we do not know how far the apostles were competent judges of miracles; we do not know if their knowledge was sufficient to prevent their deception."(18) Bancroft answered this position in two steps. One was by identifying the quest with Hume's criticism. According to Bancroft, questers "(rejected) the miracles in a breath, and of course must be ranked with Hume and Voltaire...." Simultaneously, Bancroft subjected the quest to moralistic criticism, rejecting 'rationalistic' explanations of miracles as an "irreligious," "unaccountable perversion of understanding."(19)

This moralistic criticism soon found apologetic sanction on Bancroft's native ground. Here too questions of criticism or epistemology were on one level with those of morality. Playing on the alliance of morality and criticism, the Christian Examiner thus condemned as "irreligious" and "absurd" "the productions of avowed unbelievers in supernatural revelation" which "invaded" "the very citadel of

Christianity," "ridiculed" "the character of the Saviour" or "denied his existence."(20) On the latter point the Scottish connection was vital in asserting that knowledge of Jesus depended expressly on empirical authorities. The common sense thinkers here took for granted that a correspondence existed between man's subjective perception of reality and the actual reality external to the observers. The mind, the common sense dictate held, perceives not merely the "idea" or images of external objects but the external objects themselves. In the context of the miracles controversy, this dictate offered a special kind of empirical evidence for the truths of Christianity, because the miracles which revealed these truth could be asserted to have been perceived at first hand by the Evangelists.(21)

This epistemological basis for the miracles narratives effectively combated the quest's threats to certainty and, through its preservation of the notion of God's transcendence also counteracted the questers' naturalizing and psychologizing of miracles. The focus on scientific "fact" and the corresponding rejection of "speculation" provided, moreover, a context congenial to the persistence of the harmony pattern. The English harmonies of Lant Carpenter, Isaac Williams and Robert Willan continued to provide Channing Unitarians with the main data of the life of Jesus narratives. Here the dogmatic interests of older harmonizers still prevailed over a critical exegetical apparatus. Carpenter's work, the Christian Examiner judged, was literally a harmony; ... it presents the elements of the gospel narrative, not as disjecta membra, tumultuously arranged, ... but in a state of repose, (with) ... the order of Matthew and John (being) preserved almost without change; inserted with very little alteration...."(22) This "well-built edifice," against which the "class of hypothesis" advanced by synoptic critics appeared "untenable," was expressive of the "great reverence for the Holy Scriptures, for Jesus Christ, as the Mediator ... sent to speak with authority to men."(23) To follow the "humanitarian," antisupernaturalist stance of "rationalists" and "romancers" and to "hold to Jesus only as (one) might hold to Socrates," was in this context to "have almost no faith at all."(24)

II

To the Transcendentalist ministers common sense premises were not persuasive. With its concepts of "spontaneous reason," of "intuition" and of "instinct" the Transcendentalist axis reflected the malaise of Unitarian epistemology, the turning to a formative "revision of theology." By the early 1830s, "new school" representatives like Emerson and George Ripley could no longer settle for a "stifled religion with abstractions." They sought instead a "church of humanity," a Christianity which "established the kingdom of God, not in the dead past, but in the living present (and) gave the spirit a supremacy over the letter."(25) This position differed from Norton's Unitarianism not merely on the issue of Lockean philosophy as applied to Christian evidence. The "new school" was preaching the Gospel of the quest and looked to it for substantiation of its argument on the miracles of Jesus.

This influence first emerged within the confines of the christologies of Ware and Channing. Thus Emerson was initially safely immersed in the Unitarian exemplarist approaches to christology and affirmed the "evidences" and doctrines commonly put forward by Unitarian apologists -

the historicity of the biblical narratives and the miracles of Jesus. The early Emerson rested in particular content with the Unitarian apologetic which presented biblical miracles as verifications of the supernatural quality of Christian revelation. In keeping with this view of miracles, which received one of its most forceful expressions in Channing's Dudleian Lecture on "The Evidences of Revealed Religion", Emerson declared: "The signatures of the author of nature are too strongly stamped on his workmanship to be overlooked." (S, 6, 5) "A miracle is the only means by which God can make communication to men. ... To deny therefore, that there has ever been or ever can be any miracle is to deny that there has ever been or ever can be any communication from God to men." (YES, 103, 120) As preacher at Second Church Emerson, it seemed, was still sufficiently close to Channing's concern in the Dudleian Lecture to affirm that the life of Jesus, including the miracles, formed an integral part of a revealed supernatural rationalism and ruled out rationalistic approaches to miracles in the manner of Eichhorn.

This re-affirmation of evidentialism did not go unchallenged for long. Emerson's sermons already set the precedent for a subordination of the significance of Scripture to the inner "evidence" afforded by the "heart." In admonishing his sermon audiences to "obey the scripture which God had writ within you," (S, 38, 4) Emerson internalized the "evidences" of biblical revelation and affirmed the priority of religious consciousness over the written records. Religious feeling here was asserted to precede the biblical records and to be independent of them. "If the whole history of the New Testament had perished and only its teaching remained," Emerson insisted, "the discourses of our Lord ... would take the same rank with me as they do now." (YES, 103, 104) The experience of the presence of God "in the heart" rather than a reliance on the mediated, recorded testimony of biblical revelation constituted for Emerson the essence of Christianity. Emerson therefore expressly dismissed apologetical appeals to "external evidences:" A religious man "would think himself injured by the fortifying too scrupuously the outward evidences of Christianity." (YES, 103, 124) "A miracle will not add any strength to the convictions of a religious man." (S, 85A, 10)

By 1832, the year of Emerson's resignation, this position emerged full-fledged, leading Emerson to substitute personal inspiration for revelation and to devalue the pristine authority of the historical Jesus against the testimony of men's "soul." "There are passages in the history of Jesus," Emerson observed, "which to some minds seem defects in his character. Probably a more full apprehension of his history will show you these passages in a more agreable light. Meantime count them defects and do not stifle your moral faculty and force it to call what it thinks evil, good. For there is no being in the Universe whose integrity is so precious to you as that of your soul." (JMN 3, 212) The foremost result of this evelation of the "soul" and the "heart" was that the record of Jesus' "history" and miracles, rather than serving as a pristine confirmation of his status, turned increasingly into yet another body of "evidence" to be authenticated by the claims of intuitive consciousness. And this and no other source of confirmation, Emerson reiterated, was "the direct revelation of (the) Maker's Will, not written in books many ages since nor attested by distant miracles...." (YES, 188, 189)

This criticism was particularly damaging to the biblical "evidences" which Unitarians invoked to verify the supernatural authority of Christianity. "How much depends on the records," Orestes Brownson observed in his review of Norton's Evidence of the Genuineness of the Gospels, "in which are contained those miracles which authenticated the mission of those past messengers. Deprive us of the record of those miracles, or invalidate the testimony by which the genuineness, integrity and authenticity of those records are established, and we shall be without God or hope in the world plunged into midnight darkness, with not the glimmering of one feeble star event to direct us...."(26) Under the impact of William's Göttingen studies, Emerson had in effect been "plunged" into similar doubts. The questioning of the "evidences" of supernatural revelation in the criticism of "historical speculators and pleasant doubters" turned, Emerson realized, traditional scriptural concepts and doctrines into a spectacle in which "the august Founder" passed "into the rhetoric of scoffer and atheist." (J, II, 84-85) Christianity seemed at best to forfeit its "certainty" and could not be sure about any alleged event if the actual historical "evidence" was meagre. "It should be considered," Emerson thus observed with regard to the scriptural testimony of Jesus' miracles, "that the books of the Evangelists are not the revelation but the record of the Revelation and that many things have come to their ears by common rumor which were false." (YES, 103, 125)

Yet Emerson was long unwilling to "surrender" the "greatness of Christianity" (J, II, 85) and settle for a speculative scepticism dissolving the historical positivity of the life of Jesus. Faced with growing doubts about the authority and historical reliability of scriptural revelation, Emerson became increasingly reluctant to base the truth of Christianity on historically recorded testimony. Christian faith could not afford to be bound up with historical statements that were questionable and no longer valid as "authenticated facts." (YES, 90) "We want," Emerson declared, "a living religion, ... a religion not recorded in a book but flowing from all things." (S, 158, 5) In keeping with this rejection of a bibliocentric view of religion, Emerson asserted that "the bible has no force but what it derives from within us." (S, 96, 10) And while "external evidences" were of prime importance for Unitarians in validating biblical revelation, they became for Emerson gradually only an appendage to the "evidence of the heart," an inner evidence "that all the external evidences of religion that were ever accumulated may fall in with but cannot increase." (S, 85B, 4) This presented a direct challenge to historic christology and Unitarian affirmations of the "authority" of Jesus, a challenge which assumed that the pristine locus of authority was constituted in intuitive consciousness and not historical "evidences."

Parallel to this break with the old evidentialist pattern of thought, Emerson devalued the traditional argument for miracles. Neither written records nor intellectual arguments could substitute the testimony of inward revelation: "It will not serve you ... that you accurately interpret the Gospel, ... that you can explain every text and trace the history of every corruption. This is not Christianity. But to apply the life of Christ into your heart ... this is Christianity." (S, 14, 6) With this assertion, the need for a critical, exegetical reconstruction of the historical outlines of Jesus' life receded in importance against an experiential religion, located in the modality of "feeling:" "All wisdom is of the heart.... For in the heart is the infinitude of man.... Our feelings will furnish us a far more certain clue to what is in man than ever reason could." (S, 84 10)

Consonant with this conception of the "life of Christ" as an index of "inward" "evidences" was the universalization of the status of the historical Jesus which Emerson first explicitly propounded in a sermon of

May 1830, "The Authority of Jesus." "A great error ... is," Emerson warned in this sermon, "to separate the truth taught by Jesus from his office, and suppose that it was his divine authority, his peculiar designation to the office of Messiah that gives authority to his words, and not his words that mark him out as the Messiah." (YES, 96) Jesus' "authority" was available to every other individual, and in this respect Jesus represented a "fellow worshipper" (JMN 5, 231), not an exalted "mediator." Soteriological and sacrificial categories now applied only in a 'humanistic' manner: Jesus was the "Saviour or Redeemer not because oil was poured on his head, ... nor because ... miracles attended him ... but because he declared for the first time fully ... those truths on which the welfare of the human soul depends." (YES, 96)

In the early 1830s, Emerson no longer settled for a single historical Jesus as an example of human perfectibility. The Unitarian emphasis on the exemplary figure of Jesus gave way instead to the model of the "universal man." "For all men are at all times drawing insensibly a moral from what they see doing around them; and with this moral ... the precepts of Jesus strictly coincide." (YES, 69) The indwelling of "divinity" in man was not restricted to the historical Jesus but rather determinative for every human. Jesus' "history" "suggested directly" "this immense elevation of Man from his capricious, low ... course of action...." (YES, 100) Emerson here took a further step towards correlating the humanizing of Jesus begun by the questers with the affirmation of the spiritual potential of every individual. This was only to extend what the criticism of the quest's "historical speculators" for Emerson appeared to have projected already, namely the devaluation of the "dead forms" of a "superannuated Christianity." (J, II, 491-492)

At this juncture Emerson received support not only from the critical "myth" tradition of Eichhorn but also from the anti-evidentialist theology of Samuel T. Coleridge, whose influence on the "new school" was spurred by James Marsh's publication of the Aids to Reflection in 1829.(27) Here Emerson found a devaluation of historical apologetics and an insistence upon the validity of immediate intuition. Here Emerson also found a progressive conception of revelation - the belief in a religion validated by the "spirit" rather than the "letter," a religion rendered immune to the scepticism about the accuracy and historical reliability of the biblical narratives of the life of Jesus. On the latter issue, however, the first stirrings of the critical "lives" scarcely showed with Coleridge and his counterparts in the evidentialist school. The life of Jesus literature here was still under the firm hold of apologetic studies which had been spurred by the deist assaults. The vindications of the miracles narratives offered by Richard Smallbroke, E. Sandercock, Henry Stebbing and Arthur Ashley Sykes had a perennial appeal and turned up again in the treatises on miracles produced by William and John Douglas.(28)

Coleridge refused to side with the evidentialist apologetic of these studies. With him, the historical argument for the miracles of Jesus was eclipsed. Yet in finding the "seat of certainty" of Christianity in introspection and not via a critical analysis of the narratives, an independent historico-critical focus on the Jesus of history was not allowed to develop. Coleridge's Aids to Reflection, his "only strictly theological work," American reviewers acutely noted, "opened new fields of inquiry and ... other modes of viewing religious truth," but a "new" focus on exegetical-textual foundations or on historico-critical concerns it did not provide.(29) What Emerson found was instead a confirmation of the premise that the "revelation of Jesus Christ ... directs (man) to look within, ... (showing) him a Divine Eye that ... commands a perfect prospect of his whole being...." (<u>YES</u>, 100)

With George Ripley, the influence of Coleridge on the conception of the "evidences" of Christianity was less obvious. In following Emerson's shift away from an exemplarist christology and its focus on a single historical figure as a model "miracle-worker" and "mediator," Ripley departed on a course which steadily led farther away from the traditional "proofs" of the life of Jesus narratives. For this departure, Ripley expressly harnessed the quest against the Unitarian view of Jesus' miracles. The appropriation of Schleiermacher's and Herder's terms in Ripley's ordination sermon at Canton, "Jesus Christ, the Same Yesterday, To-Day, and Forever", struck the keynote for "new views" presenting Jesus as the propounder of truths which were valid independent of his person. Ripley's sermon relegated the historical Jesus to the role of a "teacher" who derived his authority on the basis of "natural" human sentiments rather than supernatural occurrences. As in the case of Emerson's 'humanistic' christology, the significance of the historical Jesus derived with Ripley not from Jesus' person but from "the Immutability of the religious truths which he taught."(30)

The quest's contribution here came in two ways. It gave a decisive impetus to a reconsideration and restatement of theological positions on religious "truth." "Religion," Ripley asserted, "is a matter of the inward nature, the higher consciousness of man."(31) "Religion has always existed, and in its essential elements is always the same. Its ideas are inseparable from man. They grow out of the unchangeable nature of things."(32) With this, the entire argument of historical "evidence" or "belief on testimony" was passé. Jesus relied neither on miracles nor on "tradition or authority" but rather on the inward "character" of his teaching. Jesus embodied religious truths which were "everlasting realities" and existed before his coming; his testimony was therefore dispensable.(33) For Ripley, the specific content of Christian faith already existed immanently in the consciousness of the subject and was not confined to a single historical figure.

With Schleiermacher, Ripley maintained that religion was "neither knowledge nor action, but a sense of ... dependence or God." "The seat of this feeling," Ripley supposed, was "the primitive consciousness of human nature."(34) The difficulties in Schleiermacher's christology which concerned the Leben-Jesu-Forschung - in particular the problematic alignment of perfect "God-consciousness" with an individual historical person - were slighted in Ripley's position, and Ripley's canon was thus, like his counterpart in the Leben-Jesu-Forschung, insufficient on the key theological issue of the quest: the difficulty of keeping together the Jesus of history and the Christ of faith. Ripley played down the value of the historical "humanity" of Jesus, reducing him to a symbol of timeless religious truth whose validity was independent of the particular "history of Jesus."

Judged against Schleiermacher's canon, this interpretation constituted a selective appropriation which repressed the hermeneutical context of Schleiermacher's position in a manner comparable to the Harvard-Göttingen group's appropriation of Schleiermacher. To Ripley it mattered little that Schleiermacher's notion of "divination" formed the epistemological basis of his hermeneutics only. What interested Ripley was the fact that Schleiermacher pointed to "consciousness" itself and tried to describe and locate religion there instead of in the old evidentialist securities.(35) From here it was for Ripley only a small step to assert - against sensationalistic psychology - the indwelling "God-consciousness" as belonging to man and as foundational to his immediate intuitive access to religious truth. In this intuitionist context, the historico-critical reconstruction of the particularities of Jesus' history was not of primary importance. As the 'official' outbreak of the miracles controversy was to show, the historical Jesus presented for Ripley essentially a cypher for the notion of the "infinitude" of man.(36)

III

In November of 1836, Ripley framed his critique of the evidential value of miracles in a review of James Martineau's Rationale of Religious Inquiry. Ripley's review asked for a "revision of theology," a "revision" in which "a firm faith in Christianity (was) cherished independently of miracles."(37) Miracles, Ripley alleged, represented incentives to action and were not sufficient to authenticate divine authority or to give "formal supports of (Jesus') mission."(38) At issue for Ripley was not the question of historicity. Ripley did not question or examine whether Christ had walked on the water, fed the five thousand and healed the sick. Ripley granted that these events had occurred; but for Ripley one did not arrive at religious conviction by evaluating their "evidence." The gist of Ripley's argument was that "the design of the miracles, in the Old Testament and the New Testament, was not to confirm a revelation of spiritual truth, but to accomplish quite a different purpose" - to affirm that everyone was naturally inspired with "the absolute ideas of reason."(39)

Ripley's case for intuitionalism did not go unchallenged. Norton refused to side with Ripley in an open letter in the Boston Daily Advertiser on the Martineau review. Norton's inflammatory response restated Ripley's position as a "repulsive", "perplexing" attack on the "prevailing systems of theology."(40) Norton was convinced that "nothing is left which can be called Christianity, if its miraculous character be denied."(41) Behind this view lay the full weight of historical apologetics: the "genuineness" of biblical miracles formed the prerequisite to belief in the authority of Jesus as a divinely appointed messenger whose teachings were true. This "sensationalist" position rested too comfortably with empirical method to yield to a method which granted individuals direct access to spritual truth. In Norton's generalizing, sweeping critique it made no difference whether biblical critics undermined the historicity of life of Jesus narratives, as in the case of H. E. E. Paulus, or whether they adopted a more moderate stance which left remnants of evidentialism intact, as in the case of Coleridge and Schleiermacher. With Norton all "historical speculators" were supposed to be sceptics, clearing a path to "atheism" or "pantheism." "The rejection of all that mass of evidence, which ... establishes the truth of ... religion" amounted with Norton to a "rejection of Christianity, ... the denial of God revealed himself by Christ, the denial of the truth of the Gospel history...."(42)

Ripley's reply to Norton in the Boston Daily Advertiser reiterated that the issue at stake was not the "genuineness" and "authenticity" of Jesus' miracles but rather the "divinity" of the human soul. The sequence of Ripley's argument was straightforward, namely to "begin with establishing (the) coincidence (of Jesus' faith) with the divine testimony of our spiritual nature; and (then) ... proceed to shew the probability of miracles."(43) This latter issue, however, Ripley's subsequent pamphlet, the Discourses on the Philosophy of Religion argued, was irrelevant if human nature correlated with nature's divine language, if there was something "in the nature of man, which may enable him to become a partaker of the divine nature...." What attracted Ripley to Schleiermacher and Herder on this score was not their biblico-exegetical procedure but the way their canon revealed the "most exalted ideas of divine perfection" by "recognizing, in the nature of man, the same signatures of Divinity which authenticate the Gospel of Christ."(44) Here and here only lay "the example of Jesus Christ." His "teaching" affirmed man's "immediate perception of Truth," his endowment with "a faculty, which enables him not merely to count, to weigh, and to measure, to estimate probabilities and to draw inferences from visible facts, but to ascertain and determine certain principles of original truth."(45)

The position of the questers Ripley called in as support for his refutation of Norton set out to "separate ... Christianity from its historical relations...." For the "theologians of the New School," the biblical narratives themselves were a fact in history and not invested with absolute certainty.(46) A chasm yawned between the claims of faith and those of history, and this chasm led inevitably to the repudiation of one of the poles, to the denial of all theological significance to knowledge of the historical Jesus, or to the elimination of all kerygma-centered knowledge. For evidentialist Unitarians this position cut two ways: it undermined the historicity of the scriptural life of Jesus record, and it elevated internal "evidences" drawn from the mind and intuition above the "evidences" for the truth of Christianity in documented miracles. In countering these two threats by appeals to historical positivity and evidentialism, Norton exposed the biblical narratives to the very questioning he rejected in the new school as "heretical." On this score Ripley's position was more effective and flanked the horns of the problem embodied in historico-critical strictures. Ripley was aware that as long as Unitarians tenaciously adhered to religious tenets grounded in verifiability the historical basis would be vulnerable. What remained as a solution was to re-state the relation of history and faith, to cut the cord between religious truth and historical verifiability and shift emphasis from a reliance upon historical factuality to internalized testimony. This was not to argue that Jesus' miracles were "myths" or "fictions" nor to say that history was to be abandoned; rather, Ripley maintained that faith was independent of empirical foundations. One had to accept testimony on its ethical and spiritual face, without the corroborations of the proofs and verifications historical apologetic had accumulated. Once this was done, testimony could be internalized to verify structures of consciousness Transcendentalist under the watchword: "let the study of theology commence with the study of human consciousness."(47)

Ripley was "prepared to examine the claims of a Divine Revelation in history," and here he was in effect closer to Norton than the old school's "Unitarian Pope" was ready to admit. "With regard to the nature and purposes of the miracles recorded in the New Testament," Ripley slighted the extent to which Herder's and Schleiermacher's quest undermined the historicity of biblical narratives.(48) In Ripley's reading, Schleiermacher held "with perfect faith, to the supernatural character, the miracles, and the divine mission of Jesus Christ," while Herder "did not call in question the historical truth (of miracles).... They are so interwoved with the whole history of our Saviour, so appropriate to his person and character as the Messiah, that Christ would be no longer Christ, if we denied these facts concerning him."(49)

Yet for Ripley this did not entail that one could "rest the divine authority of Christianity, upon the evidence of miracles." The value of miracles as "credentials" of faith was undisputed; a miracle could "direct attention to the doctrine, ... clothe the person of the teacher with outward consideration, ... (or) even give him external credibility, according to the notions of the age. But "the truth of the doctrine, it (could) never prove," and this, Ripley insisted, "was acknowledged by Christ himself.... He announced truth, which should make the heart of man alive and free. And the proof of this, he placed in the experience of every individual. To this, outward miracles could contribute nothing."(50)

With the prevalence of this position, Ripley was convinced, "a true reform of theology may be predicted, and the living and practical faith of the heart take the place of bondage to a dead letter."(51) Ripley here expressly came out on the side of questers who wanted to "save the validity of religion against science." In the manner of Lessing and Schleiermacher, Ripley detached the claims of religion from the claims of history and verification, arguing "it is to the heart or inward nature of man, in a state of purity or freedom from subjection to the lower passions, that the presence of God is manifested."(52) Yet, unlike the neologist and "mediating" severance of religion from historicity, for Ripley this separation was not primarily an issue of scriptural interpretation and involved no comparable exegetical or hermeneutical readjustments. In Schleiermacher, Ripley noted, "the Scriptures (were) submitted to a critical examination of great extent and thoroughness, the doctrines of theology discussed on all sides...."(53) With Ripley himself, however, the religio-philosophical emphasis on the nature of religious experience far outweighed the focus on exegetical and doctrinal issues. Ripley's concern was with a "revision" of the approach to religious truth and not with biblical-critical investigations. Nor was Ripley particulary concerned with Schleiermacher's christological "revision" of the Chalcedon formula through the emphasis on "personality" requiring unity of "consciousness" rather than ontological categories. For Ripley, as for Emerson, the hermeneutical and critical exegetical techniques of the quest receded behind the programmatic translation of the quest's themes into a philosophical statement of intuitional idealism in which "the original inspiration that forms the common endowment of human nature ... (was) established by the testimony of the absolute and intuitive reason in man."(54)

IV

At the state in the miracles controversy marked by the altercations between Ripley and Norton the debate had developed into a much broader argument over the nature of religious "truth." This argument sharpened when in 1836 William Henry Furness' Remarks on the Four Gospels entered into the controversy and contributed to the debate a "life" consciously modelled after the Leben-Jesu-Forschung and deliberately put to Transcendentalist uses. With Furness, to regard miracles as "evidences and attestations of his divine commission" was to follow "the dictate of a narrow, finite and superficial philosophy...."(55) This "mechanical philosophy - a philosophy of the senses," Furness observed, "allows nature to be conceived of as a sort of labour-saving contrivance, a machine without any intrinsic worth or beauty, going by itself, with only an indirect dependence upon a higher Power."(56) Furness' "life," in contrast, dissolved the oppositions between natural and supernatural fronts and claimed, as had Paulus and Schleiermacher, that a "spiritual force" flowed through all nature. In this context, miracles did not constitute "departures from the laws of nature" expressive of divine intervention; rather, miracles were merely manifestations of the "mighty spiritual force" that suffused all things. Accordingly, miracles were not, as Unitarians affirmed, the sole source of supernatural revelation, for miraculous history; the supernatural was "everywhere in the natural."(57)

For the "new school," the entry of this argument into the controversy spurred the formulation of a "new" foundation of belief. This formulation did not "explain away the Christian Miracles" nor did it "deny that these events attest (Jesus') divine authority." But Furness' position doubted that miracles could "have any force as evidences of the divinity of his mission, until they are felt to have been wrought for a diviner end than merely to convince the understanding...." Furness was "conscious of a nobler power, a diviner element in (man's) nature, than that which concerns itself with arguments, proofs, reasonings."(58) This was Furness' pledge of the possibility of direct intuitions of religious truths, of immediate communion with "the lovely, the Beautiful, the Perfect." He perceived "that every existing thing (had) a relation, not only to his understanding, but also to this higher principle of (his) nature, in popular language, to (his) heart, (his) soul."(59)

What Furness was propounding here was a coherentist position which had its closest counterpart in the premise of Emerson's Nature that "every natural fact is a symbol of some spiritual fact," that there exists, in short, an inter-relationship of physical and spiritual. Accordingly, "the flower is not merely an argument addressed to (one's) reason. It has a moral, spiritual significance for ... deeper affections." Against the background of this inter-relationship, the conception of Jesus' miracles "merely ... as evidences, (and) arguments" was insufficient; it lacked "analogy," "correspondence," "the divine signature." Miracles, Furness' "life" reiterated, "were not put forth merely for the sake of the influence they might have upon the understandings of others, but, like the glorious creations of genius, they were the simple, natural, irrepressible manifestations of that mighty spiritual force which was the inmost, God-inspired life of Jesus."(60) This approach to the life of Jesus played directly into the position Ripley asserted against Norton. Consonant with the Transcendentalist cause, Furness' treatment of the life of Jesus located religious authority in the experience of individual believers and thus fed into the territory that the Transcendentalist camp was to occupy permanently.(61)

Furness' "life" sought "to bring the man of Nazareth, ... the Revealer of God and man, more within the reach of human sympathies."(62) Furness devalued the "supernatural influence" of Jesus, highlighting instead his "human form."(63) Furness in this way relegated the role of Jesus to that of a purely human figure whose authority lay in his teaching rather than in the uniqueness of his person. Jesus' teaching was "the same, yesterday, today and forever," independent of doctrine, creed or the establishment of theological systems. Furness reassured Norton that this position stood within orthodoxy. Yet the Unitarian camp, now with Martin

Luther Hurlbut as spokesman, aligned Furness' "life" with Ripley's critique of the miracles narratives. Hurlbut's Christian Examiner review of the Remarks on the Four Gospels put forward "unqualified dissent" from Furness' "naturalistic" theory of miracles. "There is a class of writers among us," Hurlbut warned, "who are, consciously or unconsciously, philosophizing away the peculiarities of the Gospel...."(64) Furness, Hurlbut judged, "regards the miracles of the Gospel as natural facts." But "if the miracles of the Gospels (were) ... capable of being reduced to natural laws," "to a level with mere naturalism," then, it appeared to Hurlbut, "Christianity, as a system of revealed truth, ceases to be."(65)

According to Hurlbut's reading, Furness' "life" even went "much further than this;" it maintained "that all men are endued with miraculous powers; that the human mind, as such, possesses a 'supremacy over' material things." To a Unitarian evidentialist this was and remained "a very startling proposition" and Hurlbut characteristically countered Furness' intuitional premise with the critical rationalism of the evidentialist position. That man's intuitional powers "should have lain dormant and undiscovered in the human soul from the days of the creation to the times of the Saviour" was "quite incredible." That Jesus should be the pre-eminent representative example of the divinity of the "soul" turned, in Hurlbut's inspection, the historical Jesus into a projection of an ideal notion of humanity and dissolved all claims of historicity.(66)

This was, in substance, a restatement of Norton's critique of the "new school," a restatement, however, which falsely identified Furness' "life" with Ripley's critique of the miracles narratives. The "new school" separated the facts of Jesus' life and miracles from religious truth. The intuition of the "soul" was asserted to be the only source of religious knowledge, and against this intuitional testimony the issue of historical verification appeared secondary. At this juncture, however, Furness' position distinctly stood out with its emphasis on the veracity and reliability of the life of Jesus narratives. Furness sought to align the critical heritage of De Wette and Eichhorn with the anti-evidentialism of Coleridge and Schleiermacher in such a way that intuitional epistemology and ethical idealism left the claims of biblical criticism intact. Furness thus was led to focus on an issue that was secondary to the "new school's" case in the miracles controversy. To Furness, the Gospel's distinctly "historical nature" warranted historico-critical scrutiny and, above all, an examination of the historicity claim - the question "whether the extraordinary facts of the life of Jesus actually occurred, as they are represented."(67)

On the latter issue, Furness' conclusions coincided with Norton's findings.(68) "It appears in the most impressive manner," Furness declared, "that the authors of (the Gospels) were wholly unconscious of any design to make out a case to do anything but state facts." Furness found in them "none of the art of fraudulent design - none of the incoherence of self-delusion. (The Evangelists') histories command ... cordial confidence."(69) With this insistence on "authenticity" and "genuineness" Furness' "life" clearly fell back behind the Leben-Jesu-Forschung. In Furness' uncritical affirmation of the "genuineness" of biblical narratives the Gospels were asserted to "belong to the department of History, Biography, Memoirs."(70) At a time, then, when De Wette and H. E. G. Paulus highlighted the difficulties of reconstructing the historical Jesus and the Gospels' precarious status as compilations and redactions, the chief

American quester still affirmed the life of Jesus narratives as "histories" distinguished by "the simple abundance of facts."(71)

V

What Hurlbut had seen as a "tendency" among "a class of writers" was made explicit in July of 1838 with Emerson's Divinity School Address. Emerson advanced his address "through the forms already existing," (CW, I 92), yet he did not choose to stay within supernatural rationalism and was not willing to base his religious belief on debatable historical "evidences." Miracles were of one piece with the normal processes of nature; they exemplified the premise Emerson appropriated from Schleiermacher's discourses on religion, namely that "man's life was a miracle" and that therefore "the very word Miracle, as pronounced by Christian churches, gives a false impression; it is Monster." (CW, I, 81) This critique was at one with Ripley's assertion that the locus of revelation was "consciousness" and not historical event. Christianity is valid, not because it is recorded in history and attested by miracles, but because it coincides with the intuitive religion of nature.(72) The record of Jesus' miracles therefore represented merely another 'corpus' to be validated by the "certainty" of intuitive consciousness.

In positing Jesus as "true man" and "prophet" who proclaimed the divinity of the human soul, Emerson subtly turned Unitarian exemplarist christology around: Now man was the "wonderworker" whose faith could move with nature and "blend with the light of rising and of setting suns...."(73) Here the humanistic thrust of the critical tradition Emerson absorbed through Ripley, Everett and Furness provided a rationale for a movement from making assertions about Jesus' miracles to re-claiming for man powers like Jesus'. This was to propound a christology grounded wholly in the historical career of Jesus and detached from the remnant terms of patristic christology. The christological question, posed as a problem concerning the "nature" and "person" of Christ, no longer had any place in a christology "from below." The foremost defect of "historical Christianity" was, Emerson judged, its exaggerated concern with the "person" of Jesus. A clear precedent for this position was available in the 'antidogmatic' import of the Leben Jesu questers. George Ripley's description of Herder's view of the historical Jesus in the Christian Examiner here provided a key example Emerson was not likely to have overlooked. Herder "loved to regard (Jesus) chiefly in his human relations," Ripley observed, "as a being possessing all human sympathies, subject to all human feeling, clothed with all human virtues, in truth, as the type and complete expression of perfect humanity."(74) This view rendered Herder's quest, in a way similar to Emerson's "Address", "averse to the habit of metaphysical speculation on the person and rank of Jesus." "The speculations of the old Arian and Socinian writers," "the scholastic subtilties, ... thrown around the subject, were fatal to an enlightened faith in his mission and a just estimate of his character."(75)

That "a just estimate" of Jesus' "character" could no longer follow the traditional investigation of the figure of Jesus in the categories of divine and human "subsistences," "persons" and "natures" was also acknowledged by Emerson's contemporaries in the "new school" whose appeal to the figure of Jesus evinced an express antidogmatic bias. "Jesus ... exerted an energy," James Freeman Clarke was convinced, "which broke down the most stony mass of bigotry which has ever this world petrified around the form of true religion."(76) "Jesus Christ taught no formal system - the Apostles laid down no fixed standard of opinions...."(77) Jesus' aim, Convers Francis similarly maintained in 1836 in *Christianity as a Purely Internal Principle*, was "to purify and sweeten the fountains in the deep places of the soul."(78) In this context, the mediatorial role of Jesus consisted in the "conveyance of that holy power, by which the soul is saved from spiritual death, and brought into spiritual life."(79) And as in Emerson's "Address," the traditional role of Christ as Saviour-God was once again minimized and deprived of all sacrificial overtones. "The ministry of Jesus," Francis pontificated, "can serve us only by kindling the life of God in our souls, ... only by rousing us from the death-slumbers of sin to a quickening sense of our eternal relations...."(80)

For Emerson's fellow-Transcendentalists, then, the themes of the "Address" were commonplace and in accord with what Hedge termed a "religion carried into action" opening the mind to a "larger range and a livelier apprehension of all truth, - instead of confining it, as devotion to a creed does, within a given circle of ideas."(81) Yet Emerson's "Address" fell into a camp in which evidential theology had held its own and in which the "new theology" was charged with "atheism, with pantheism and with ... irreligious speculations...."(82) "To deny that a miracle is capable of proof, or to deny that it may be proved by evidence of the same nature as establishes the truth of other events" was for Norton "in effect, ... to deny the existence of God."(83) Norton's address on "The Latest Form of Infidelity" put this theological critique on one level with an epistemological point and equated intuitional idealism with a denial of historicity and "genuineness." The "pantheistic" theology of Paulus, De Wette and Schleiermacher on which Emerson's "Address" relied, Norton charged, sought "to separate ... Christianity from its historical relations...."(84) With Norton, "the pretence that the only true universal source of religion is to be found in the common nature of man, ... (was thus) connected ... with the rejection of all the reasoning by which those facts that are the basis of religion may be otherwise rendered probable; and often with the rejection of all belief in the facts themselves."(85)

This correlation of faith and historicity, however, distorted the new school's position. Norton urged the believer to accept the credentials of miracles on the antecedent foundation of the "religious principle ... on the belief of certain facts."(86) With the "new school," by contrast, the premises of intuitionism were clearly set apart from the issue of historicity. Ripley's reply to Norton's address, published anonymously by "An Alumnus" in 1839, dispelled the charge of historical unbelief. "The question at issue," Ripley claimed, "is not concerning the divine mission of Jesus Christ.... Nor is it whether Jesus Christ performed the miracles ascribed to him in the New Testament."(87) The veracity of "historical relations" was left untouched by the claims of "consciousness." "The revelation of Christ," the "new school" alleged, was "addressed to the better nature of man" and independent of the historical positivity of external "evidences."(88)

Significantly, the value of the "historical relations" embodied in the historical Jesus was affirmed by "new school" representatives themselves. For Orestes Brownson, the "Address'" attempt to dispense with historical Christianity and its historical documents came close to dispensing with the historical Jesus altogether. With his own "New Views of Christianity, Society and the Church" of 1836, Brownson had followed the

Emersonian platform in its critique of organized religion, but with regard to the role of the historical Jesus in Emerson's religious thought, Brownson charged that Emerson pressed only for a "psychological Christ" and disregarded the "historical Christ." "As in philosophy, we demand history as well as psychology, so," Brownson concluded against Emerson's religious and epistemological subjectivism, "in theology we ask the historical Christ as well as the psychological Christ."(89)

Strikingly, Ripley, when confronted with Norton's charge of "pantheism" and "irreligion," shared Brownson's affirmation of the significance of the historical Jesus and deliberately sought to vindicate De Wette and Schleiermacher as "believers" who did not question the historicity of Jesus' deeds. Ripley's restatement of "the views of Schleiermacher in regard to the historical truth and the divine character of the miracles of Jesus" was anxious "to show the incorrectness of (Norton's) classification of Schleiermacher with the unbelievers in a 'miraculous revelation of God through Christ.'"(90) Schleiermacher, Ripley insisted, was clearly distinguished from "the Rationalist, Paulus, Röhr, Wegscheider, ... (who) attempted to resolve the miracles of the New Testament into ordinary occurrences, and discarded the belief in every thing that was not explicable by the familiar and regular laws of nature." Schleiermacher "believed in the supernatural origin of Christianity. He maintained that Christ wrought miracles, by the power of God." "He embraced the historical truth of the miracles of Jesus, as recorded in the New Testament; ... (and) he considered them to be peculiar manifestations of divine power, above the ordinary course of nature...."(91)

This recapitulation of Schleiermacher's canon retained the remnants of evidential theology and its concern for objective validation. Ripley's position was clearly set apart from Strauss' dissolution of historical-objective categories of the life of Jesus and turned instead to Schleiermacher and what was perceived to be a welcome preservation of empirically verifiable categories. That this was in effect to turn to a quester who, no less than Strauss, tended to dissolve the objective pole of historical revelation was not recognized in Ripley's preference of Schleiermacher. Nor was it expressly marked that Schleiermacher's "religious experience" theology of the life of Jesus also touched on the question whether and how the historical Jesus could be reconstructed. At issue for the "new school" was the function of the historical Jesus as proclaimer of the "divinity" of the human "soul," and not the difficulty of his historical reconstruction.

. The 'Uses' of the <u>Leben Jesu</u>

By the mid 1830s, the Transcendentalist "new school" had emerged mong New England Unitarians as a separate and distinctive movement with a nilosophical groundwork framed in opposition to the "sensuous philosophy f Locke."(1) The "new school" attempted to provide an emotional and piritual foundation for religious belief and sought to re-align believers ith a realm of truth which Lockean empiricism and Scottish common sense eemed to cripple - the realm of intuitive spiritual insight into meaning ot directly accessible to the senses. "The truth of religion," "new chool" representatives reiterated, "does not depend on tradition, nor istorical facts, but has an unerring witness in the soul."(2) The mergence of this intuitional position quickly fragmented the Unitarian ommunity. "The Unitarians must break into two schools," Convers Francis cutely observed in 1836, "the Old one, or English school, belonging to the ensual and empiric philosophy, - and the New one, or the German school .., belonging to the spiritual philosophy."(3) In like manner, Francis owen's contributions to the <u>Christian Examiner</u> and the <u>North American eview</u> identified the "new school" as a "school of philosophy." "The ifference in the mode of philosophizing between the old and new school is adical," Bowen declared, "either one party or the other is entirely rong."(4)

The crux of the "radical difference in ... philosophical views" etween the two "schools" was the inadequacy of Lockean empiricism as an pproach to the genesis and 'uses' of ideas in the mind.(5) The "new chool" sought to free "consciousness" from the restrictive framework of ockean "sensationalism" and assigned to it a generative function. In estoring consciousness as a generative force, the "new school" not only dvanced a shift to an epistemology of intuitionism but also a einterpretation of human nature. Once it had been asserted that man ossessed an innate ability to intuit truths which transcended mere sensory xperience, the "new school" was ready to affirm that this ability corresponded" to "divinity" itself and therefore also bestowed a "divine" lement on man himself. The most important effect of the quest on the "new chool" in this respect was the impulse it gave to idealistic philosophy nd to the focus on "intuition" and "feeling" in religion. The "new school" as drawn to the quest not out of doctrinal or exegetical concerns but ather because of what "new school" advocates perceived to be a shared ejection of the assumptions of materialism and empiricism. In the "new chool's" conspicuous shifts from common sense to idealism, H. E. G. aulus' notion of "moral truth" and Schleiermacher's concept of religious self-consciousness" all were read as affirmations of the inadequacy of sensationalist" psychology. "The theologians of the new German Rational chool," Richard Hildreth explained to Andrews Norton, "do not place eligion ... among the natural sciences.... They dispense with the special iracle ... and ascribe the perception of divine truth to a native capacity f the human mind...."(6)

For most "new school" advocates the quest, in so far as its hristology from below was read as an affirmation of the divinity of man, oined with a complex of divergent influences to reinforce assumptions bout the innate moral and intellectual powers of man. Long before the "new chool" could master the language hurdles posed by the quest, the market as flooded with the works of Scottish realists, and - in Norton's terms - ith the studies of the "hasher up of German metaphysics, the Frenchman

Cousin," the "hyper-Germanized Englishman, Carlyle" and above all, with the anti-evidentialist version of Coleridge's philosophy.(7) With "new school" members looking for a means of establishing confidence in the certainty of spiritual truth, this amalgam of influences provided a welcome pathway to intuition and to the creative imagination. "To those ... who (were) just awakened to the consciousness of the inward powers of their nature, and ... who (had) obtained as the fruit of their own reflections, a living system of spiritual faith," the eclectic philosophy of the French school and the anti-evidentialism of Coleridge all presented variations of "the old theory of innate ideas" which the "new school" saw supremely illustrated in Kant's "Transcendental Philosophy."(8)

Kant's carefully built up system here functioned for the "new school" as a desired refutation of "sensationalism." This refutation, however, owed more to Coleridge's "reason" - "understanding" distinction in the Aids to Reflection than to Kant's canon itself. From Coleridge came the Transcendentalists' idealist view of Kantian "reason" which slighted that Kant had denied to "pure reason" any validity in man's speculative knowledge. This idealist reading designated "reason" as a faculty of ideas that are constitutive and amounted in this respect to a fusion of the two Kantian faculties of "sensibility" and "reason." With Kant, the faculty of "sensibility" related to "intuition." "Objects are given to us by means of sensibility," Kant asserted, "and it alone yields us intuitions."(9) With Coleridge and his "Amercian disciples," it was "reason" which came dangerously close to "intuition" and affirmed knowledge of spiritual truth as immediate.(10) In this way Emerson traced "Idealism of the present day" directly back to Kant's "Transcendental forms," designating "whatever belongs to the class of intuitive thought ... (as) Transcendental." (CW, I, 339-40)

In placing the "intuitions" of "sensibility" on par with the "intuitions" of "reason," "new school" representatives in effect drew on strains of thought characteristic of post-Kantian idealism. They removed the Kantian separation between man's physical and spiritual faculties; they disregarded Kant's limitations on the "practical reason," equating Kant's postulates of the "practical reason" with cognitive intuitions of faith; and, finally, they confused Kant's "transcendental" mode of knowledge, which pertained to man's application of a priori categories of the understanding to experience, with "transcendent" realities which were to Kant beyond experience and illegitimate in the realm of knowledge.(11) The distortions rendered Kant's system identical with the vision of a mystic who escaped into the territory of "pure idea" removed from all foundations in experience. Philosophically, however, these distortions provided the "new school," in the absence of an independently developed and coherent theory of knowledge, with a much-needed intuitionist epistemology that corresponded to post-Kantian idealistic systems aptly represented in Schelling's doctrine of "intellectual intuition." Moreover, with regard to christology, the "new school's" appropriation of Kant also confirmed the premise that "the Christ without and the Christ within" man were "not two principles but the same."(12)

In this context the quest held a critical position as a transitional stage in the shift away from "sensationalism" and common sense realism towards a spiritual idealism. Here the quest's "preeminence" was "mainly owing to the influence of ... philosophy," to a theory of knowledge, to the nature of the human mind and to what the "new school" - falsely - designated as "the transcendental method." On the theological plane, however, "most ... American writers," as James Freeman Clarke observed in the Western Messenger, were "perfectly paralyzed with terror, when they (undertook) to look into German Theology" and were exposed to "a fatal plunge into the abyss of pantheism and unbelief."(13) This reaction stemmed largely from the impact of Strauss' Leben Jesu on New England shores - a work which confronted both the "old" and "new school" head-on with a biblical criticism dissolving the historical foundations of the life of Jesus accounts. At issue in this work of the quest was not, New Englanders realized, a philosophical break with empiricism or "representational" realism but rather a "new ... theology, ... the object of which (was) to show, that the account of Jesus in the Gospels is destitute of historical truth."(14)

Norton's Evidences of the Genuineness of the Gospels, the standard point of departure for the evidential theology practised by Harvard Unitarians, was incompatible with the historical scepticism of the Leben Jesu. For Norton, Christianity was rooted and grounded in history and depended for its validity on the actuality of certain historical events.(15) Therefore theology had to validate the "genuineness" of the events which undergirded Christian faith. Whatever the results of the newer methods of historiography and biographical representation, for Unitarians of the caliber of Norton the interpretation of Jesus' person could only be made on the presupposition of the historicity of Jesus' life. Interpretation of the life of Jesus was only as firm as the historical basis on which it rested. What stood out in this argument was the assumption that the figure of Jesus could in fact be reconstructed. On this issue, the "new school" was at one with Norton's position. Ripley, Hedge, Clarke and Furness, no less than Channing and Norton, were confident that the essential features of the historical Jesus could not really be questioned by purely historical considerations. The life of Jesus carried its own warrant and guarantee of truth, and no breach was to be posited between Jesus and the kerygma of the early church.

This shared assumption also extended to the 'dogmatic' import of the quest. It was the premise of the identity of the historical Jesus with the Christ of faith which served as a starting point for the attempt to recognize a genuinely human figure in Jesus of Nazareth. Against Strauss' reconsideration of the classical doctrines of the God-man, it was therefore Schleiermacher's idea of the "archetypal" Jesus that came closest to the intentions of American practitioners in providing a way back to the historical reliability of the God-man. The main thrust of Transcendentalist preoccupation with the figure of Jesus during and after the miracles controversy was on this count moving towards a position in which the line of cleavage between Transcendentalists and non-Transcendentalists no longer mattered. Although "new school" protagonists in the miracles controversy devalued the authority of the historical Jesus, they continued to adhere to the historical Jesus as the "representative" "great man" and "hero." Thus Emerson's "Address", rather than dissolving the historical Jesus in the manner of Strauss, affirmed Jesus as the "true man" against the "formalist minister." (CW I, 81, 85) Given this interpretation of this historical Jesus, the "new school" position appeared less as a break away from the Unitarian "old school" than an outgrowth of the exemplarist christology of the supernatural rationalist tradition. Although "new school" critics had absorbed Lessing's rejection of the idea of 'history' as bearing the full weight of revelation, they still recognized Christianity as a historical religion which could not dispense with the "uses" of Jesus as the "representative man."

I

After the "Divinity School Address" George Ripley was for almost a year to bear the burden of the miracles controversy alone. Falling prey to the tactics of Norton's rejection of the alleged "irreligion" and "pantheism" of the "new school," Ripley subtly shifted his argument from an emphasis on subjective experiential verification of religious truth to a focus on the historical foundation of the Gospel tradition. It was at this juncture that Theodore Parker entered into the Ripley-Norton controversy under the pseudonym "Levi Blodgett" and broadened the argument to a much more inclusive base. Parker did not set out to give a point by point refutation of Norton's position, but rather attempted to change the scope of the debate. While Ripley had moved towards Norton in focussing on the question whether "men believe in Christianity solely on the ground of miracles," Parker first dealt with a more preliminary issue: "How do men come to have any religion, or, in other words, on what evidence do they receive the plainest religious truths?"(16)

On this question, Parker reverted to the position Ripley had initially affirmed against Norton. Religious belief was primary and universal and flowed from the generation of the "germs of religion" which were innate in human nature and therefore independent of scriptural revelation. "Religion - thus caused by the innate germs ... in the soul; thus occasioned by the outer world, thus promoted by inspired men" needed no mediation of sacrament, creed or Scripture. The authenticity of miracles was not necessary to "absolute religion," nor was it imperative to represent Jesus in terms of an absolute and first incarnation of God. There was "nothing interposed between Conscience and God, or between Him and the religious sentiment."(17) Miracles accordingly served merely as additional corroborations for intuitive belief, and this testimony was and remained to Parker "more satisfactory evidence of (Jesus') divine authority, than all his miracles, from the transformation of water into wine, to the resurrection of Lazarus."(18)

Foundational to Parker's argument was his adherence to the historical Jesus, the simple Galilean detached from Greek metaphysics, the supernatural framework of miracles and from soteriological doctrines pertaining to atonement and justification. Parker could "conceive of no man who (would) more fully represent the moral and religious side of our nature; none who (would) receive more fully direct perfect moral and religious incarnation of God...." Jesus' "absolute religion" was "not limited by creeds, legends, rites of symbols" and independent of critical concerns whether there was something "fictitious or legendary from Genesis to Revelations...."(19) On this premise, Parker was prepared to confront the possibility of the historical unreliability of the life of Jesus accounts. Parker's "Levi Blodgett Letter" acknowledged that "Strauss ... has explained a great deal of the New Testament into Mythi ... which had not foundation in fact."(20) Reviewing Strauss' Leben Jesu for the Christian Examiner, Parker spelled out the implications of Strauss' "life." Strauss "finds little reason for believing the genuineness of the authenticity of the Gospels," Parker recapitulated Strauss' argument. "Indeed, he regards them all as spurious productions of well-meaning men, who collected the traditions that were current in the part of the world, where they respectively lived."(21)

This recapitulation of Strauss' position fed directly into Parker's argument and provided ammunition for his case against miraculous "evidences." "It would be difficult," Parker observed, "in a court of justice to prove the reality of any one of the miracles ascribed to Jesus in the Gospels." "There are several difficulties which hinder you from proving the reality of particular miracles" - "difficulties" which Parker derived from the arsenal of Strauss' historical critique: "The authority of the Evangelists is not quite satisfactory.... Their inspiration did not free them from the notions of the age and nation; from wrong judgments, or their own temperaments."(22) The sources which legitimated the revelation of Jesus as Christ were therefore open to the same scrutiny as other historical sources. And against this historico-critical analysis, Parker judged, Norton's fortress of miracles could no longer stand.

The entry of the Leben Jesu into the miracles controversy marked a far-reaching shift in the discussion of miracles narratives. Strauss came upon the field at a point in the debate when the issue of verification and historicity had been suppressed and devalued by the "new school" against the claims of intuition. The inroads of Strauss, however, made this issue central and effectively destroyed the theoretical basis for revealed theology by undermining the historicity of the life of Jesus narratives. Strauss left "only a little historical matter, around which tradition ... wrapped legends and myths."(23) Moreover, in Strauss' abstraction of the 'Christian principle' from Jesus the "archetypal idea" was severed from the historical individuality of Jesus. "Neither (Jesus) nor any man," Parker's review of the Leben Jesu observed, "ever did, or can realize the idea; it must be realized in the race."(24)

The force of this argument fell on a ground unprepared to settle for the historical unreliability of the life of Jesus narratives or a mere "accidental" relation of the historical Jesus to Christian faith. Parker had not moved far from the confidence of Buckminster, Channing and Norton in the certainty of historical testimony and from the assumption of a harmonious continuity between the Jesus of history and the Christ of faith. For Parker, Strauss' rejection of the historicity of the life of Jesus accounts therefore appeared to be governed by "false principles, extreme conclusions, and extravagances."(25) "The New Testament always rests on historical ground," Parker was convinced, "though it is not common historical ground, nor is it so rigidly historical that no legendary or mythical elements have entered it."(26) But despite these "mythical elements," Christianity still had to rely on the biblical record for "the historical statement of its facts." "Men do not make myths out of the air, but out of historical material."(27)

Parker conceded with regard to the synoptic question that "the Synoptics give us in Jesus a very different being from the Christ whom John describes, and all four make such contradictory statements on some points, as to show they were by no means infallibly inspired...."(28) But Parker was not prepared on that account to dismiss the life of Jesus narratives to the realm of "fiction" and "myth," nor was he willing to question the historicity of miracle testimony as such. In the Scriptural Interpreter Parker had defended the Mosaic authorship of the Pentateuch, arguing that "no man in the time of Moses could have devised such a code without miraculous aid."(29) After the encounter with Strauss, Parker reconfirmed in the Levi Blodgett Letter the possibility of miraculous events: "Jesus, like other religious teachers, wrought miracles." And "in saying this, (Parker did) not express any doubt on (his) part of the general accuracy of the history of Christ...."(30) Even if Strauss' assumptions were correct and if "there was something legendary and romantic in the stories of Christ's birth, early life, and ascension to heaven, ... these considerations would not," Parker judged, "diminish the probability that Jesus worked miracles...."(31)

Parker's Leben Jesu review of 1840 did not completely lay Strauss' argument to rest. A year later, Parker's "The Transient and Permanent in Christianity", preached at the ordination of Charles Shackford in the South Boston Church, with the title of the sermon itself being borrowed from Strauss' discourses, moved towards the distinct imprint of the Leben Jesu. Parker now arrived at the negative conclusion taught by historical scepticism: the validity of Christian precepts does not flow from miraculous evidences, biblical infallibility or the divinity of Christ. The dogmas of Christianity Parker termed 'transient'; the religion of Jesus Parker identified with "pure Religion which exists eternal in the constitution of the soul and the mind of God" and "is always the same." On this count, Parker was unwilling to invest the "personal authority of Jesus" with "permanent" status and found it "hard to see why the great truths of Christianity rest on the personal authority of Jesus, more than the axioms of geometry rest on the personal authority of Euclid or Archimedes."(32) The figure of Jesus had become dispensable to Parker: "if it could be proved ... that Jesus of Nazareth had never lived, still Christianity would stand firm...."(33)

The systematic exposition of this argument in Parker's Discourse of Religion revealed another shift towards Strauss. In 1840, Parker had rejected Strauss' programmatic historical criticism of the Gospel record. Strauss' devaluation of the Gospel accounts as "spurious productions" seemed to Parker "the weakest argument" of Strauss' "life."(34) Yet by 1842, Parker was ready to align his view of the "evidences" of Jesus' life with Strauss and corroborated the latter's position. "Myth" and "history," Parker argued, were so blended in the life of Jesus narratives that the historical value of the Gospel record could not be uncovered with any certainty. A similar scepticism applied to the miracles narratives of the life of Jesus. In 1840, Parker did "not deny that (Jesus) did work miracles;" by 1842, Parker had arrived at a complete rejected of supernatural elements and miraculous "evidences:" "they cannot be admitted as facts, ... I cannot believe such monstrous, facts, on such evidence."(35) Miraculous history could sanction or corroborate belief, but with a critic who had absorbed the lesson of Strauss' "life," it could no longer establish absolute certitude.

II

Parker's entry of Strauss into the miracles controversy "disintegrated the clergy and the whole body of Unitarians...." In Parker, Unitarians judged, two strong concussions came together - the higher criticism of the Bible and the newer idealistic philosophy and theology which "laid down the definition, that Christianity is merely a system of abstract truths or intuitions...." What put Parker at odds with popular belief and clerical decorum was that he insisted against the Unitarian clergy "on retaining in all the ways that he could his connection with the

Unitarians, and maintained that his views ... were not imported - not the result of his study of German theologians and philosophers, - but the logical result of the New England Unitarian theology."(36) To a rational Unitarian, this estimate of the origin of Parker's view was unacceptable. The wedge between faith and history characteristic of the Leben Jesu was incompatible with a supernatural rationalist camp which acutely sensed that if Strauss' devaluation of the historical reliability of the Gospel record prevailed, evidential theology would inevitably fade into the background.

Confronted with Parker's criticism and his appropriation of the Leben Jesu, Unitarians continued in the line of argument F. W. Greenwood had established in his defense of Christianity, namely to discredit any "theory which would separate Christianity from Christ...."(37) Reviewing Parker's Discourse for the Christian Examiner, Andrew Preston Peabody judged that Parker was "writing to overthrow Christianity."(38) Peabody's colleagues concurred, yet the review of Parker's work also evinced a sense of the futility of the counteraction. "For months the Unitarians have been urged from without and from within to denounce or renounce, Mr. Parker," Ezra Stile Gannett observed, "yet (they) have not found out how to do it, (which) shows that it is strange work for them."(39)

Once again it fell to Andrews Norton to provide a programmatic refutation of "new school" views. Norton's massive work on the Internal Evidences of the Genuineness of the Gospels identified as the key disparity between Strauss' Leben Jesu and Unitarian doctrine the issue of the "authenticity" of the Gospel tradition, an issue Norton had been pressing since the 1820s and projected from the first into the "new school's" devaluation of evidential theology. Strauss, Norton charged, left Christianity without any authentication by "(resolving) the Gospels into mythical or legendary compositions" and reducing them to "unconscious exaggerations, spontaneous inventions of credulity."(40) Rather than utilizing Strauss' argument for an examination of the early Christian communities as "myth-makers," Norton immediately subjected the Leben Jesu to the terms of the fact-fiction question. With Strauss, the interest in the historical Jesus, in his personality and deeds receded to be replaced by the religious consciousness of the early Christians. With Norton, however, the historical Jesus, "a character to which nothing in human history, before or after, presents a parallel or a resemblance," remained normative and open to scrutiny.(41)

Within this reductive reading, "the novelty of Strauss' work" consisted for Norton in the assertion that the life of Jesus narratives "could not have proceeded from well-informed narrators" and that "the discrepancies among the Gospels ... disprove (their) genuineness...."(42) Norton's refutation drew Unitarian exegesis into polemical and apologetic stances which fell back on the traditional evidentialist approach. In Norton's critique of the implications of Strauss' "life," the consistency of the Gospels accounts, the veracity of the biblical authors, and the correspondence between "Scripture history" and secular history all served to substantiate the credibility of the Evangelists and the "genuineness" of their accounts. This apologetic was as reluctant to surrender the pillars of an externally verified Bible as it was directly opposed to Strauss' intentions. The Leben Jesu was concerned not with the historicity, but rather with the literary and kerygmatic nature of the Gospel accounts as confessional testimonies and with the "accidental" status of concrete individuality for the realization of the idea of God-man. In Norton's artificial consensus among evidential theologians of differing traditions of Gospel criticism, however, literary and kerygmatic claims fell to the ground, with the testimony of the early Christian tradition being reduced to mere historical documentation and the Gospel narratives standing re-affirmed as reliable guides to the life and teachings of Jesus.

With regard to the issues of authentication and verification, the conservative camp around Norton evinced a pronounced consensus which correlated the veracity of the historical Jesus with the "evidences" afforded by miracles. The "two main pillars" of Strauss' "life" - "first, the utter and absolute impossibility and incredibility of a miracle ... and secondly, the discrepancy in the Gospel history" - drew Unitarians into a strong phalanx of defense which reiterated that the rejection of miracles was not to be separated from the rejection of Jesus Christ.(43) "Without them he becomes a mere fable.... Without miracles the historical Christ is gone." "And in losing him," the Dexter Lecturers warned, "how much is lost! Reduce Christianity to a set of abstract ideas, sever it from its teacher, and it ceases to be 'the power of God unto salvation'."(44)

The Leben Jesu, the Christian Examiner judged, confronted the terms of this argument with a "shocking" "alternative": "Christ (was) to be received as a divinely commissioned Instructor of men, or he was a DECEIVER."(45) The terms of this "alternative" were those of a by-gone age; they traced back to the debates over the deist assaults on revealed religion and were borrowed directly from Sherlock's Tryal of the Witnesses of the Resurrection of Jesus. Sherlock had attempted to refute Woolston in the form of a court-room drama which secured a verdict of acquittal for the Apostles on the charge of deceit. The vindication of the truth of the "evidences" of Christianity here became a matter of cross-examination and posed a choice between a "real truth" or a "great fraud." "There (was) ... no medium; (one) either (had to) admit the miracle or prove the fraud."(46) To the Unitarians reviewers of Strauss, the Leben Jesu entailed a similar "alternative," one in line with the strategy of refutation adopted by the Harvard-Göttingen group. Strauss was in this context deliberately placed on a level with the deist camp and its attack on the "credentials" of revelation.

Norton more accurately identified as "the distinguishing characteristic of the theory of Strauss ... the supposition that the mythi or fictions in the history of Jesus were not intentional fabrications for the purpose of deception, but that they sprung up, as it were, spontaneously."(47) On this characteristic of the Leben Jesu, however, Norton found no followers among conservative reviewers of the quest. "Myths" here were regarded as "vague, ... incoherent, dreamy, poetical, while the Gospel narratives (were acknowledged as) eminently prosaic and circumstantial...."(48) The prevailing consensus was that a "myth" "in its most obvious and literal sense ... was a fable." "To say that the life of Jesus is mythical" was therefore "to affirm that it is a fiction, a lie," "an innocent lie" which carried the imprints of "elaborate Deception" and "premeditated Falsehood."(49)

The tight circle of defense based on the fact-fiction opposition became thematic for the Unitarian reviewers of Strauss. With practical unanimity, Henry Ware Jr, Stephen E. Bulfinch, George E. Ellis, George R. Noyes and Francis Bowen concurred in reading history as the vindication of faith. Against this background Strauss' criticism was charged with "(setting) the Evangelical history at nought." "It reduces the definite and particular accounts, in which all the Gospels agree," Bulfinch judged, "to an unreal vision of some self-deceived fanatics."(50) But the "caput mortuum of Christianity which mythicism (left)" did not deflect American reviewers from adherence to the "proofs" and "signs" of the historicity of the Gospel tradition.(51) At a time when Strauss' "life" had already spurred the development of source criticism within the Leben-Jesu-Forschung, Strauss' American reviewers still charged that his insistence on the discrepancies of the Gospel accounts ignored the premise "established in the courts, in the forum, and in historical science, that in a comparison of independent witnesses and testimonies there will always appear some discrepancies ... which no skill can reconcile."(52)

The polemical terms here employed against Strauss were those fostered by the Harvard-Göttingen axis. Strauss' criticism was readily equated with that of the "Deists, teaching Christianity without Christ."(53) Strauss' "life" was further identified with Hume's "abandonment of a positive belief in Christianity as a miraculous revelation...." But it was "in vain," the <u>Christian Examiner</u> judged, "that Strauss ... attempted to apply the subtile alchemy of his mythical theory to dissolve the solid facts of Christ's personal history. They came out of the crucible just as they went in - their sharp outlines unmutilated, their natural coloring unchanged."(54) The "life" that came closest to this position was Simon Greenleaf's <u>An Examination of the Testimony of the Four Evangelists, by the Rules of Evidence Administered in Courts of Justice</u>. The harmonistic "life" produced by the Harvard lawyer in 1846 and applauded "as a valuable contribution from an eminent jurist to ... theological literature," set out to bring the life of Jesus narratives "to the tests to which other evidences is subjected in human tribunals" and admitted discrepancies between the narratives as legitimate features also characteristic of other historical accounts.(55)

Comparing Greenleaf's <u>Examination</u> with Strauss' <u>Leben Jesu</u> for the <u>North American Review</u>, Francis Bowen eulogized Greenleaf, "the cool and clear-headed jurist," over against the "mystical doctor" with his "absurd application of an absurd theory."(56) What appeared "wild" and "impious" to Bowen in Strauss' "theory" was not so much Strauss' biblical criticism but a more christological point. "According to Strauss," Bowen observed, "the whole human race, the totality of mankind is Christ, the idea is thus realized on a magnificant scale." This "speculative" premise of the <u>Leben Jesu</u> was injurious to the testimony of Scripture history Greenleaf and Bowen sought to render creditable. Contra Strauss, Bowen and his Unitarian brethren unflinchingly placed "as the subject of the predicate which the church assigns to Christ ... an individual," and not an "idea."(57)

On this point, orthodox Trinitarians and Unitarians stood as one. The lines of opposition between the orthodox and liberals camps had been clearly drawn in the Unitarian controversy. Yet on the question posed by Strauss' inroads - whether the historical Jesus coincided with the Christ of faith and whether historical reliability could be assigned to the life of Jesus narratives - both sides concurred, asserting that the content of the history of Jesus was verifiable and authentic. In the early years of the Harvard-Göttingen axis, Stuart had with regard to the new biblical studies expressed the "hope (that) the day of bitterness and personal enmity" between the two New England religious parties would "(pass) away; and that both parties will feel more necessity of critical investigation, of understanding the original, of settling the laws of interpretation, and the degree of credit due to the sacred writers."(58) The confrontation with Strauss precipitated this very alliance between both parties around the issues of "credibility" and historicity. In disowning the "genuineness" of the Gospel tradition, Strauss' quest challenged the foundation of the theological presuppositions of the Trinitarian party at Andover Seminary and cut as deeply as it had with the liberals who had taken it for granted that faith was organically related to history. On the same count, Andover critics were also not prepared to subscribe to the findings of the Leben Jesu and stood staunchly by the historicity of the Gospel tradition.

Andover had been familiar with the critical tools of the quest since the days of Moses Stuart. Under Stuart, Andover critics used grammatical and philological analysis of the biblical narratives in the mode of "lower criticism" as an apologetic helpmate to support on scientific grounds that Scripture was the inspired revelation of God, that prophecies were accurate and that miracles were credible. Orthodox theologians also noted, however, that biblical criticism modelled after De Wette and Eichhorn posed a threat to orthodox Calvinism once it was applied to the historical claims of biblical narratives. Andover's house journal, the Bibliotheca Sacra, therefore subsumed the new critical studies under the "neology" label and, like their Unitarian colleagues, equated historico-critical interpretation with the deist assaults on historical revelation. Thus Calvin E. Stowe denounced the quest's critics for their impiety and declared that the "irreligious rationalist" was "under an inability, both natural and moral, in respect to the right and full interpretation of God's word."(59) Similarly, Bela Bates Edwards argued in his 1850 summary of the state of "biblical science" that "higher criticism" "substitutes theory for judicious investigation, ... violently dislocates ... history and attempts to reconstruct it by an arbitrary subjective opinion."(60) Once again, then, it was the issue of historical positivity which American practitioners regarded as the principal threat posed by the quest's tools to their own theological presuppositions. The validity of the divine-human conception of Jesus here remained aligned with the premise that Jesus' historical personage was really recoverable through the Gospel tradition.

With regard to the latter premise, Strauss' "life" was unacceptable to the orthodox. Horatio B. Hackett's review of the Leben Jesu in the Bibliotheca Sacra recapitulated that for Strauss the "historical Jesus" had become so overlaid by pious reflection and embellishment that the life of Jesus had been mythically rewritten in order to authenticate Jesus as Messiah. The life of Jesus narratives accordingly consisted largely of "religious ideas" which had been "clothed in a historical form," that form being, as Hackett explained, "pure fiction, having no foundation whatever in any actual occurences, but arising solely from the tendency of the human mind to give spiritual truths an outward presentation."(61) Instead of a historical personage Strauss thus arrived merely at the mythical embodiment of an "idea." And with this, Hackett judged, Strauss' Leben Jesu ran counter to what Hackett regarded as a crucial tenet of the orthodox theologians at Andover, namely that revelation was authenticated by history. Strauss' work revealed that the alleged historical factuality of the life of Jesus narratives could not stand up to critical scrutiny. Through the method of opposing "myth" and history, "all history loses its certainty," Hackett sensed, "and becomes a mere phantom, an illusion" which dispensed with the figure of Jesus.(62)

The distrust of Strauss' dissolution of historicity yielded an additional stream of continuity within the spectrum of New England divinity. The need to affirm the historicity of the life of Jesus accounts against historical scepticism was also the rallying point for conservative Presbyterians at Princeton Theological Seminary. Here, too, the inroads of the quest worked to draw divergent parties together and spurred a sense of a pervasive consensus. The emergence of this shared bond was most clearly perceptible when, at the height of the debate over Parker's and Strauss' views, Andrews Norton set aside for a time the old antipathy between Calvinists and Unitarians and published under the title Transcendentalism of the Germans and of Cousin and Its Influence on the Opinion in this Country two articles by the Princeton professors J. W. Alexander, Charles Hodge and Albert Dod from the Biblical Repertory and Princeton Review, articles which reduced the "new school" position and its theological counterpart in the quest once more to the factuality issue.(63)

The theology of Hodge, Alexander and Dod flowed from a rigidly confessional affirmation of the Westminster tradition grounded in the self-evident truths of Scottish common sense. The combination of common sense realism and scholastic Calvinism here fit extremely well with the view that biblical narratives represented a compilation of hard "facts." "The Bible is to the theologians what nature is to the man of science," Hodge categorically declared in his Systematic Theology, "it is his store-house of facts."(64) This application of Scottish common sense played into Norton's rhetoric; it apprehended religious truth directly, and not as a function of human mental activity. Moreover, in formulating this position, the Princeton critics resorted to Norton's tactics; they denounced the Leben Jesu as an instance of "infidel theology" which "acknowledges no God but the God incarnate in the human race" and thus, like the Strauss reviewers at Harvard, set up a barrier of discredit and suspicion which hampered critical interchange.(65)

Against Strauss' and the higher critics' scepticism about the historical accuracy of the life of Jesus narratives, the orthodox at Princeton were led to a hardening of their polemical and apologetic stances. While Strauss adduced findings to lessen the authenticity of the life of Jesus accounts and to uncover their cultural conditioning, the Princeton theologians around Hodge tightened and refined the doctrine of verbal and inerrant inspiration. In the face of growing critical opposition, Hodge was eventually to shift his argument to the verbal inspiration of the original autographs, but in his early review of Strauss Hodge still set out to confront Strauss' findings by drawing back to the scholastic theory that Scripture was inerrant in all matters authenticated by the witness of the Holy Spirit. Unitarians were not prepared to revert to this extreme point. Confronted with Strauss' Leben Jesu, Norton referred the exegete to the credibility of the Evangelists and to the evidence of discrepancies and inaccuracies in secular writings. But with regard to the factuality issue, Norton was ready to battle alongside Princeton theologians for the cause of evidentialism. When it came to affirm the historical veracity of the life of Jesus narratives, differences of theology and denomination seemed to matter little.

III

For the "new school," a shared consensus against Strauss at first sight did not appear to develop. Whereas "old school" representatives remained implacably hostile to Strauss' historical criticism and his substitution of the historical Jesus for religious consciousness, Emerson, Hedge, Ripley, Thoreau, Alcott and Parker advanced assertions about the spiritual and creative nature of man in terms remarkably similar to

Strauss' dissolution of the historical Jesus and the conception of the incarnation principle as an ontologically universal relation common to each human being. Thus Alcott, who came together with Emerson on the more extreme end of the Transcendentalist spectrum, was prepared to present Jesus as "a glimpse of Humanity," a perfect exemplification of the divinity of the human soul.(66) Hedge was to "expand the proposition (and) say that ... the real distinction and peculiarity of Christ was not an exceptional, but a sublimely typical, nature and life; not that he was the only God-man, but the type of the God-man, in all generations...."(67)

The "new school's" assertion of the universality of the incarnation in all men rested on an epistemology of intuitionism that was distinctly transhistorical. The key to this position was encapsuled in the watchward, advocated by Emerson's "Self-Reliance", that "all history becomes subjective; in other words there is properly no History...." (CW, II, 6). With Emerson, this watchword was rendered into a direct challenge to history-conscious interpretation and assigned no significant role to evidential theology. The intuitional moment captured in "Nature" dispensed with "transient" historical forms and served exclusively to authenticate individual experience. To this, the "history" of Jesus was no exception. The claims of intuition downplayed adherence to the historical "person" of Jesus and counteracted the church's cult of the historical Jesus.(68) This was precisely the position "old school" reviewers identified as a characteristic of Strauss' "life." The Leben Jesu, reviewers charged, "admits no incarnation, but the eternal incarnation of the universal spirit in the human race." Claims of "personality" were submerged in "momentary manifestations of the infinite and unending."(69)

By the mid 1830's, the life and character of the historical Jesus increasingly informed this view of "the whole spiritual nature of man, (yielding) ... knowledge of a certainty not yet attainable by experience."(70) The use of the historical Jesus as both source and exemplar for the fully spiritual nature of each human being became one of the most fetching topics for the "new school's" life of Jesus literature and was no longer confined to the territory of Harvard Unitarianism and advanced academic training. The Western Messenger eulogized Furness' "life" for "(showing) the correspondence of the material world with (man's) higher nature...."(71) In the Temple School, Amos Bronson Alcott's Conversation with Children on the Gospels read "the life of Christ ... (as) the Record of an attempt to unfold the Idea of Spirit from the Consciousness of Childhood, and ... to this end (presented) the character of Jesus ... as the brightest Symbol of Spirit."(72)

For this reading, however, neither the "rationalist" nor the "speculative" approach of the Leben-Jesu-Forschung seemed to be adequate. The rationalist Leben Jesu researchers, American reviewers observed, alleged that Jesus was "not the Son of God, in the ecclesiastical sense, but a good man; he (worked) no miracles, but ... kind deeds, sometimes by chirurgical skill, and sometimes by good luck."(73) The "speculative" Leben Jesu researchers went further and denied that "the incarnation of God occurred ... in an individual," and that the Christian principle could be identified with the historical Jesus.(74) To the "new school," the problem of Jesus as "individual," as "personality" was the precisely the point where the difficulties of the two approaches came to sharpest focus. The "rationalist" conception of the historical Jesus was not sufficient for the use of Jesus as an exemplary ideal of man's infinite potentialities, while the "speculative" approach left no valid historical figure for any such use at all. On the latter count the "new school" increasingly realized that Strauss was "often mistaken." He "underrates the historical elements," the Dial observed in a 1842 review of Philip Harwood's German Anti-Supernaturalism, "and (he) sometimes comes hastily to his conclusion, which, therefore, cannot be maintained, though long ago we believed he was doing a signal service to Christianity itself."(75)

Contrary to the "speculative" Leben Jesu approach, the historical Jesus had ramifications in the "new school's" thought long after the school's intuitional idealism had emerged full-fledged. At a time when Emerson's Nature advocated the value of the "moral sense" and Parker's Discourse insisted on the spiritual and moral perfection universally available to man, the "history of Jesus" and the exemplary "uses" of his "person" were not completely submerged. The biblical portrait of the historical Jesus continued to inform the "new school's" tenets, regardless of whether or not the biblical narratives could be credited with historical veracity. The common denominator for the "new school" was the "(acknowledgment) of Christ ... as the highest fact in the history of humanity, ... as ... the most perfect illustration of that ... inspiration which God has accorded to all mankind."(76)

Even the Transcendentalists on the more extreme edge of the "new school's" spectrum were not prepared to "take all facts from ... consciousness" and submit to a raptuous type of transcendentalism. Parker's religous epistemology did not settle for mere awareness of an intuitive fact of "consciousness;" rather, judgments a priori were to be validated also as "facts of history." "The transcendental philosophy ... does not neglect experience. In human history it finds confirmations, illustrations, of the ideas of human nature.... It illustrates religion by facts of observation, facts of testimony."(77) The confrontation with Strauss sharpened this position. The Leben Jesu, Parker observed, "makes a belief in the resurrection and divinity of Christ spring up out of the community, take hold on the world, ... and all this without any adequate historical cause." The "new school's" "transcendental method" could with Parker "also ... change an historical character into a symbol of 'universal humanity'." "But this (justified) no man in the court of logic, for rejecting all historical faith."(78) Nor did it justify the complete dismissal of the historical reliability of the Gospel record. Parker rested his case with the anti-Straussian "lives" and counted himself among those critics who rejected "Strauss' theory that the effect preceded the cause, that the idea appears in the mass before it was seen in an individual ... (as) absurd." Contra Strauss' "speculative" stance, Parker deliberately "put the Person before the thing, the fact above the Idea."(79)

Support for this position came from the conservative camp of the quest - Hengstenberg, Stier, Olshausen - and the "liberal-positive" opposition against Strauss - Schenkel, Keim, Neander, Ebrard - whose works reached American audiences through the publishing firm of T. & T. Clark in Edinburgh or, more directly, through the translations of James Freemann Clarke, William Furness and Samuel Osgood.(80) The most pervasive support for Parker's case, however, came from I. A. Dorner, a "mediating" critic who distinctly counteracted Strauss' identification of the God as the "totality of humanity" which existed merely in thought as the "idea" of the human species. Dorner reiterated against Strauss, Parker acutely observed in his Dial review of "Dorner's christology" in 1842, "that the notion of an historical, as well as an ideal Christ, (was) a necessary notion...."(81) Dorner's insistence on the "necessity" of incarnation posited the idea of God-manhood not as a mere thought but as having become "actual" in the course of human development. But that Dorner thus also ascribed to Jesus a genuinely human historical existence Parker did not acknowledge. Dorner's "main idea is this," Parker recapitulated, "that the true Christ is perfect God and perfect man, and that Jesus of Nazareth is the true Christ." According to Parker, however, Dorner made "no attempt to prove either point, (neither) ... as a philosopher, (required) to prove his proposition, (nor) ... as an historian, (required) to verify his fact. ... He has shown neither the external necessity, nor the actual existence of a God-man."(82)

From another quarter, however, came a more "efficient support" for Parker's case, a support combining the stances of the "philosopher" and the "historian" with that of a "humble disciple of Christ" disinclined to "speculative ... suppositions."(83) De Wette's critical exegetical work and his novel Theodore: Or, the Skeptic's Conversion offered a system Parker's contemporaries in both "new" and "old school" camps acknowledged as an attempt "to combine all the elements which are contained in the history of Christ, with the light of modern science, ... on a foundation inaccessible to the assaults of the skeptic...."(84) Parker's edition of De Wette's Introduction to the Canonical Scriptures of the Old Testament applied a "historico-critical procedure" which, Unitarians reviewers were prepared to concede, "believes in a historic basis, and regards the superstructure rather as the work of faith than of fraud."(85) Moreover, with regard to De Wette's treatment of "predictions of (the) Saviour's coming" and the "striking coincidences between the prophecy and Christ's mission," there was no "danger of confounding him with Strauss and other deniers of (the) Savior's divine mission."(86) De Wette "(looked) to the Christian Records in their literal historic light," thereby "(avoiding) the error of those, who place all faith merely in certain abstract ideas, and thus maintain a cold rationalism that degenerates into ... an arxy and vague idealism, and deprives Christianity of its strong foundation ... in actual historic proof."(87)

Parker's approval of De Wette's adherence to "historical form" rendered his views less a revolt against the Unitarian party than an outgrowth of a shared allegiance to "historical theology."(88) The scepticism against "vague idealism" and "speculation" was echoed throughout the "new school's" response to Fichte's, Schelling's and Hegel's philosophy of religion. Philosophical distinctions between idealistic systems here mattered little. In particular for George Ripley they constituted invariably "speculative" systems, "strange and unintelligible" "specimens of intellectual gymnastics."(89) As much as these "specimens" might provide a welcome liberation from materialism and empiricism, they also ran the risk of succumbing to "interior" "fruitless" speculation.(90) The "new school's" pattern of appropriation here was selective and inconsistent, but almost all of Parker's colleagues in the "new school" marked this danger of "fruitless speculation" and hardly ever fell back upon what Norton termed "pantheistic spiritualism" to such an extent that the historical Jesus was reduced to an ineffectual figure. With regard to religious philosophy, De Wette emerged in this context again as a more positive example of "a philosophical mind going through all the mazes ... of speculation and doubt, and finally sitting at the feet of Jesus, and in humble faith, entering the kingdom of heaven like a little child."(91)

Allegiance to the figure of Jesus, and be it only in completely humanistic terms, "new school" representatives agreed, guaranteed an awareness of the objectively historical context of Christian faith. And with regard to Jesus' deeds, this entailed their professed acceptance both "as an historical fact, and a spiritual symbol" and counteracted the dissolution of one of the two poles which Parker sensed in Strauss.(92) This view also applied to the "new school" representative who had emphatically urged Divinity School graduates to follow the impulses of the "moral sense" with no regard for the "person" of Jesus. The intuitionist stance of the "Address" never wholly discarded the conviction that the shaping force of history was and remained a historical figure, not subject to the dissolution of objective-historical categories supposedly advanced by Strauss. Emerson did not develop a rigorous anti-historical bias and conceived the relation between individual and history in such a way that the value of history as "the group of the types or representative men of any age at only the distance of convenient vision" was retained. In this context the view of the historical Jesus was reworked to illustrate the "transparency" of the "genuine man." Jesus illustrated "alone in all history" "the greatness of man;" his "history" was of one piece with "the history of every man written large." (W, XI, 491)

The "new school's" subjective, mind-based concept of history thus spanned a complex spectrum. In the early 1830s the "new school" left behind the idea of history bearing the full weight of revelation and long remained acutely aware how fast the "key" to the historical Jesus was "lost:" "A thousand years hence," Emerson thus observed, "it will seem less monstrous that those acute Greeks believed in the fables of Mercury and Pan, than that these learned and practical nations of modern Europe and America, these physicians, metaphysicians, critics, and merchants, and how they contrived to attach that accidental history to the religous idea." (JMN, VIII, 196) Yet with the "new school," this insight into what Lessing had described as the "ditch" between "accidental" truths of history and "necessary" truths of reason did not obliterate the status of the historical Jesus as the "representative man." The "key" to the "new school's" view of the historical Jesus firmly remained more on the side of Carlyle's "hero-worship" than on Strauss' "Christ-Idee."(93)

IV

Given the pervasive affirmation of the significance of the historical Jesus, comparatively few "lives" were produced. Against the historico-critical stance propagated by Parker, who approached the figure of Jesus in expressly humanistic terms, "a Rationalism of a moderate and Christian character, inclining to supernaturalism" held the field after Strauss inroads.(94) With the mass of Unitarians the "views of the Naturalists" were still read to "mean the rejection of the religion of Christ as a supernatural revelation" and to undermine Jesus' revelatory significance as "mediator." The Christian Examiner affirmed against the "naturalists" that "in Jesus Christ we have a revelation of God in which we ought to own a power infinitely above us, and before which we ought to bow the knee in adoration."(95) For Unitarians like Edmund Hamilton Sears, who was representative of the reactionary trend in Unitarian biblical criticism and christology after the heightened confrontation with the quest in the mid-1830s, the professed allegiance to the person of the "mediator" categorically precluded the quest's key premise: The Gospels, and foremost the account of John, Sears reiterated, present "not merely Jesus but the

Christ - the Christ of authority from above...." "We have not a 'mere man' left, nor the ghost of a man which can be outlined to any rational criticism, however microscopic and keen."(96)

Sear's christology "from above" deliberately counteracted the possibility of producing a "life" of the human, historical Jesus. "(Jesus') natural life is not described (by the Gospels) as unfolding under conditions which are merely normal," Sears observed. "It is described as the ground and the ultimate manifestation of a life which is more than human." One could "cool down (Gospel) passages by a process of criticism into figure and rhetoric," but to Sears they were "such as fit in with the natural coursings of no human biography...."(97) Exegetically, this position called Sears back to the "grammatical" approach of Ernesti, who provided the thematic starting point for Sear's The Fourth Gospel the Heart of Christ. Withdrawing to an exegetical position which preceded a historical criticism and an assessment of the "truth" of the scriptural accounts, Sears used Ernesti to affirm the traditional authorship of the Fourth Gospel and its version of the old "high" christology. Given the "superhumanity of Jesus Christ," a "naturalistic" criticism, which "assumes that (Jesus') supposed divinity is a factitious halo," and the "standpoint of ... Hegelian theosophy," in which "the doctrine of the incarnation is passed over to the interest of the race," appeared inadequate.(98) To reduce Jesus to "a type of the divine incarnation in all humanity" or to focus on "whatever is merely natural and human in the life of Jesus as given in the New Testament," - both these options of the quest's "destructive criticism" had no place in Sear's reaffirmation of traditional christological dogma, the "church-doctrine, ancient and modern, of the hypostatic union."(99)

For the "new school" the Chalcedonian dogma was not persuasive and, in the case of Parker, played out against the Antiochene tradition of christological interpretation with its scepticism against abstract, metaphysical categories. Parker was not directly concerned with Christ's ontological state or his saving function; he lacked "respect ... for the person" of Christ, but nevertheless acknowledged Jesus' "history" as revelatory of the inherent possibility for perfection available to all men.(100) American reviewers of the Leben Jesu noticed a similar respect for Jesus' "history" in Strauss. While he "represented (Jesus) as in part an impostor, in part self-deluded," Strauss nevertheless, reviewers noted, "(recognized Jesus') history as symbolical of the moral history of mankind. What was false to the individual Jesus" was in this way asserted to be "true of the race."(101)

The distinction between the "individual Jesus" and his "history" allowed Parker in several studies on "The Character of Jesus" to "separate the life and character of Jesus" "from Christianity" and the doctrine of "absolute religion." Focusing on "the moral and religious character of Jesus of Nazareth," Parker in this way uncovered the "negative side, ... the limitations of Jesus:" "Jesus was mistaken in his interpretation of the Old Testament...." Moreover, he "shared the erroneous notions of the times respecting devils, possessions, and demonology in general; respecting the character of God, and the external punishment he prepares ... for a large part of mankind."(102) Highlighting the "mistakes about Jesus," Parker frankly pointed to the precedents in the Leben-Jesu-Forschung, namely "the charges against Jesus in the Wolfenbüttel Fragments (and) in the Writings of Wünsch (and) Bahrdt ...," "charges" which, Parker judged, were to those

Unitarians assuming "religion (to) rest on (Jesus') infallibility ... indeed a very hard case for their belief in Christianity."(103)

But regardless of how "often (Unitarians) might err in (their) estimate of ... the carpenter of Nazareth," Parker "(found) it difficult to obtain the exact words of Jesus himself."(104) Parker's discourses contained scattered sketches of Jesus' life, yet in his hands the life of Jesus received no sustained treatment. Parker shared Strauss' insight into "the difficulty of reconstructing the doctrines of Jesus." According to Parker's estimate, the "two collections of ancient documents which relate to (Jesus') life and teachings - the canonical and the apocryphal gospels - "did not "(consist) of simple historical documents." As for the synoptics, it was "by not means clear," Parker observed, "when they were written, by whom, or with what documentary materials of history." "The writers might unconsciously exaggerate or diminish the fact; they might get intelligence at second-hand, from hear-say and popular rumor. Their national, sectarian personal prejudices must color their narrative.... They might not separate fact from fancy." These findings were of one piece with Strauss' conclusion that the Gospels' "legendary and mythical character (did) not warrant confidence in their narrative" and did not allow a biography of Jesus to be written.(105)

Furness' life of Jesus productions expressly counteracted this conclusion. The distinctive characteristic of Furness' "lives" was their overbearing confidence that the historical outlines of the life of Jesus, including the essential elements of his consciousness, were knowable and could be subjected to historical reconstruction. Contra Strauss, Furness' History of Jesus asserted that "the accounts we have of Jesus contain substantially a history seen to be true...." But like Strauss, Furness was no longer bound to an exegetical tradition demanding allegiance to miracles as proof of the divine authority of Jesus and as verifications of supernatural revelation. In the latter allegiance, Furness judged, "Jesus has become a nondescript being. He is out of the reach of all genial human appreciation."(106) Moreover, "through the dogma of his Supreme Divinity, in the confounding idea of his Double Nature, the personal character of Jesus has been lost to sight...."(107) Furness' purpose was "directly the reverse." He sought "to reinstate (Jesus) in Nature, fully," presenting him as the "New Teacher" Emerson had advocated against established creeds and theological systems.(108)

For this reading, Furness departed from "a mechanical philosophy (which) unhallowed Nature, ... displacing its soul-inspiring harmonies with the monotony of a huge mechanism of blinds laws...."(109) But Furness' "naturalism," reviewers judged, was "different" from that of the Leben-Jesu-Forschung; (it) "admits the genuineness and the essential authenticity that the laws of nature ... are supreme, irreversible and essential."(110) Furness granted that "in ascertaining the precise facts of our Saviour's life ..., some things in the history usually received by Christianity as supernatural, may ease to appear so."(111) Yet Furness had "no fear that any vital fruth will be impaired" and was anxious to make clear that he was "not advocating the method of the German theologian, Paulus, who undertook to reduce the extraordinary events of the New Testament to ordinary occurrences, assuming the narratives to be mere exaggerations."(112)

But Furness' attempt at disassociation was not fully justified. Judged against his stance in the miracles controversy, Furness' position had shifted. Commenting on the "Character of Christ," Furness in 1834 had affirmed that "no skill less than that which produced it, certainly not the skill of man, and least of all of such men as the authors of the Gospels appear to have been, could fabricate miracles in such exact accordance with the life of Jesus."(113) In his Remarks on the Four Gospels of 1836, Furness had bypassed the scientific and historical problems posed by miracles by referring them to natural causes unknown to man. By 1850, Furness was prepared to adopt Paulus' rationalistic stance and ready to advance pathological interpretations of Jesus' miracles by explaining the temptation in the wilderness and the transfiguration as hallucinations: "The angels that ministered to Jesus after the temptation were 'his own thoughts', the conscious strength of his spirit.... The sublime scene of the Transfiguration was a dream of Peter, broken at a critical moment by a peal of thunder. Of the angels of the resurrection, the appearance of the 'young man in a long white garment' was that of Jesus himself, still wrapped in his grave-clothes, and not yet wishing to be recognized...."(114)

On the immediate issue of the miracles narratives Norton's cause was with these interpretations lost. Rather than corroborating the "genuineness" of the life of Jesus narratives, Norton's appeal to historical "evidences" under the aegis of historico-critical premises gleaned from the quest only worked to expose the historical unreliability of the Gospel record. Moreover, rather than leading to a confirmation of the divine mediatorship of the figure of Jesus, the critical "lives" produced by Furness ended, Norton found, in a veneration of a historical Jesus detached from the evidentialist miracles fortress. Judged against the critical Leben Jesu research, however, this veneration was in effect on common ground with Norton. Both Furness and Norton were not prepared to have their respective portraits of the figure of Jesus jeopardized by a consideration of the difficulties of separating the preaching of Jesus from the early church's preaching about Jesus. The evidentialist bonds were still too strong to allow for a full and critical treatment of the New Testament kerygma. Moreover, with both Furness and Norton the inordinate confidence in the "genuineness" of the biblical texts which Leben Jesu researchers uncovered as having undergone problematic phases of redaction continued to hamper the development of what Furness invariously referred to as the "science of Scriptural interpretation."(115) "An intimate and exact acquaintance with the facts of our Saviour's history is of the first importance," Furness reiterated. But "respecting the method by which the precise facts of the life of Jesus are to be reached," Furness admitted that he had "neither the time nor the ability to say it worthily...."(116)

V

Examining the "Causes of the Decline of Interest in Critical Theology" for the Christian Examiner in 1847, George Rapall Noyes, who had succeeded Palfrey as Dexter Professor of Biblical Criticism at the Divinity School in 1839, correlated the pervasiveness of evidential theology with his colleagues' failure to produce an effective refutation of Strauss. What American biblical critics needed, Noyes judged, was to produce critical studies "in advance of the popular English commentaries."(117) As of yet, however, American exegetical productions appeared to Noyes still deficient and uncritical. While Strauss' "life" spurred within the Leben-Jesu-

Forschung a flurry of critical examinations of the biblical sources, biblical criticism failed to take root on Noyes' native ground.

To this verdict Parker's work formed the most notable exception. Parker's detachment of the issue of verification from the question of religious truth bore a considerable similarity to Emerson's and Ripley's appeal to the "moral sense." Yet with Parker this appeal came with a distinct difference. In Parker, the separation of historicity from religious truth went hand in hand with an express re-assertion of the exegetical techniques of the historico-critical approach and was not, as in the case of Emerson and Ripley, submerged in intuitional premises. Rather, Parker's <u>Discourse</u> reiterated that the separation of the historical "kernel" of scripture from mythical embellishment demanded biblical criticism and rendered biblical narratives subject to historico-critical procedures. "The Gospels cannot be taken as historical authorities," Parker insisted, "until a searching criticism has separated their mythological and legendary narratives from what is purely a matter of fact."(118) And at this juncture Parker was not only set apart from Emerson's intuitionism but also from Strauss' conclusion that "the germ of Christian faith is entirely independent of critical investigations."(119) Parker belonged to the historico-critical school of Baur and De Wette, opposing Strauss' dissolution of historico-critical categories of exegesis and source criticism. The interpretation of the life of Jesus narratives was, with Parker, "historico-critical; that is (the record) is to be considered as an historical phenomenon, in a series with other such phenomena, and entirely subject to the laws of historical inquiry." This critical study, Parker insisted, "furnishes the historical materials which are necessary to the explanation of the Bible," and Parker readily applied this premise to a wide array of literary and textual questions - to the intention of the Evangelists in the resurrection narratives, the origins of the sacramental rites of Baptism and the Lord's Supper."(120)

Parker was acutely aware that his use of higher-critical procedures was unacceptable to most of his fellow practitioners whose exegesis was primarily conservative and dogmatic. "Most of the English and American theologians," Parker deplored, "object to this method, and insist that the book of the Bible should be examined from a religious point of view, declaring that dogmatic theology is the touchstone, where we are to decide between true and false...."(121) This uncritical attitude, Parker found, prevailed in matters of critical exegetical procedures, as Parker's contemporaries in the "new school" persistently adhered to a biblical criticism of intuitionism. Parker judged that his efforts to bring the full range of the critical procedures of the quest to bear on the American scene failed because he was confronted with an exegetical ground which tended to "strike a death-blow at all criticism and (commit) the Bible to a blind and indiscriminating belief."(122) O. B. Frothingham's 1854 review of "The Scientific Criticism of the New Testament" pronounced a similar verdict. "We have a theory of the Bible," Frothingham declared, "which renders all candid examination of its contents impossible.... Philology is prejudiced; history is bribed; ... dictionaries are denominational; our very grammars are unveracious." "Criticism," Frothingham further judged, "has ever been apologetical or sectarian, and has started therefore with unwarrantable assumptions."(123)

The "dogmatical bias" uncovered by Frothingham applied in particular to the "new school's" premise that "the life, the whole life of Jesus Christ ... as he is exhibited in ... brief and simple histories ...

embodies and expresses his religion in its unveiled and perfect integrity."(124) According to Frothingham's terms, this premise "(took) for granted ... that the books of the New Testament ... present one continuous and consistent line of history" and involved no substantial scrutiny of the written and oral origin and mutual literary dependence of the Gospel narratives.(125) Yet for the majority of Parker's and Frothingham's contemporaries in the new school this lack of a "purely scientific method of interpreting the Scriptures" was not experienced as a deficiency. For those concerned to "make the religion of Jesus a truer and more sanctifying principle to many souls," the "authority" of Jesus was "sufficient."(126) The long list of contributions on the figure of Jesus and his history which were produced by members of the Unitarian-Transcendentalist tradition during and after the quest's inroads without any reference to the "new" biblical criticism strikingly attests to the fact that large segments of New England divinity were left untouched by the premises of the quest. In particular the devotional treatment of Jesus in the sermon literature of the time - Cyrus A. Bartol's Christ the Way, Charles T. Brooks' The Simplicity of Christ's Teachings, E. Peabody's The Moral Power of Christ's Character, George F. Simmons' Who Was Jesus Christ? and S. R. Noyes' Jesus Christ the Christ Corner-Stone - confirmed Frothingham's verdict that in the "spectacle" of most New England divines "appealing to ... the Gospel of Christ, revealed in Scripture," there was "no scientific method of interpretation...."(127)

With regard to the "historical method" required in the "science" of interpretation, Parker judged that the "common abhorrence of the philosophical method" also accounted for the "poor" "result" in biblical criticism.(128) In a similar vein, Ripley took notice of the "omnious fact" that an "open dread of philosophy" was "not unfrequent" among his contemporaries.(129) The commentary of Strauss' American reviewers acutely gave witness to this "ominous fact." Confronted with the Hegelian philosophical framework of the Leben Jesu, Bulfinch deemed it difficult "for a well-ordered Anglo-Saxon mind to conceive of its being seriously propounded and actually believed."(130) As for the "theological bearings of the Hegelian philosophy," "old school" and at times even "new school" critics not only rejected the Leben Jesu as "an utter failure" and as "wholly ... inconclusive" but also as an "atheistic philosophy" and as "pantheistic," "godless speculation."(131) Within the Leben-Jesu-Forschung refutations of this charge were numerous. The "charge of atheism ... brought against Pantheism is evidently unfounded," De Wette insisted, "for Pantheism is fundamentally only Polytheism extended to Universality and Totality."(132) Schleiermacher further "admitted that the piety of a pantheist can be completely the same as that of a monotheist," for "pantheism ... is not simply and solely a disguise for a materialistic negation of Theism...."(133) Within the American quest and its review of the Hegelian premises of the Leben Jesu, the very equation of "pantheism" with "atheism" and "infidelity" signalled not only a conflation of philosophical judgments with judgments pertaining to individual piety, but also a misunderstanding of the transcendental nature of Hegel's thought, of Hegel's transcendental overcoming of the subject-object distinction. It signalled, moreover, that "want" for "a more simple and intelligible analysis," for "a better spiritual philosophy" as opposed to a "metaphysics under false pretences."(134) And here Strauss, it was judged, had failed. New England divines found it difficult "to imagine in the Straussian system an adequate inspiration or motive for high spiritual endeavors or attainments."(135)

The Dial's retrospective view of "The Unitarian Movement in New England" applauded "the introduction of a spiritual philosophy" as "an incalculable good."(136) With regard to the reception of the quest, however, this commitment to "spiritual philosophy" contributed to a large extent to the deficient appropriation and critique of the "metaphysical" presuppositions of "speculative" and "dialectic" Leben Jesu researchers.(137) "We want no metaphysics," the Christian Examiner categorically declared in 1848, "which are elaborated with a preconceived purpose of sustaining a theological hypothesis."(138) But on the latter issue of theology, Parker also deemed most of his contemporaries deficient. Parker's "Thoughts on Theology" of 1842 judged that "theology with us is certainly in the period of hypotheses. The facts are assumed; the explanation is guess-work."(139) Parker's contemporary James Freeman Clarke traced this "defect" to what he castigated as the principal "disgrace of English and American theology" - "that party and sectarian bias" of a "superficial parlor divinity."(140) Both Clarke and Parker strove for an "impartial" theology "free from all sectarian bias;" the "new school" further agreed that it was "the popular theology that (required) reformation," a "reformation ... (to) be effected ... by appeal to the people."(141) And with regard to this "reformation," the "new school" approved an approach in which the academically trained theologian refrained from a distancing, exegetically freighted theological discourse and was more inclined to follow Thoreau's injunction "to simplify, simplify, simplify."(142) Yet the very application of this injunction accounted in the case of the quest for the fact that even Parker's erudite studies in the quest's theological literature appeared inadequate. "On the theological side, (Parker's) entire intellectual process" emerged in retrospect as "reductive." "A small house of a doctrine emerged after all the convulsions of labor by a whole mountain range of information."(143)

On the historico-critical side of Parker's work, a similar deficiency was apparent. In part at least, the historico-critical emphasis went underground in Parker himself and shifted towards Strauss' submersion of source criticism and historico-critical analysis. Parker's religious epistemology affirmed an intuitionist theory of knowledge which dissolved traditional separation marks between general revelation and special revelation. But the very conception of Christianity in terms of the criterion of "absolute religion" rather than the historical verification of biblical narratives shifted the theological argument away from biblical grounds. The devaluation of evidentialist validation eliminated one of the chief incentives for critical scrutiny of the authorship, historicity and background of the biblical narratives and made the scriptural record seem unnecessary. In the context of an intuitionist framework which "established" "original inspiration ... by the testimony of the absolute and intuitive reason in man," American practitioners and reviewers of the quest's biblical criticism drew no vital impulse from the pedantic "work of weighing of phrases and hunting in dictionaries."(144) And in the absence of an independently built critical tradition, the exegetical procedures pioneered by Buckminster, Stuart and Parker scarcely led to new departures in the life of Jesus literature. The 'uses' and consequences of the Leben Jesu found no permanent place among both the "old" and "new" schools of New England divinity and were not to be revived until after the Civil War.

Part III The Quest Continued

9. "Footsteps of the Master:" From History to Fiction

The nineteenth century interest in the historical Jesus was not an exclusive property of doctrinal and biographical "lives." During the critical battles over Strauss in the 1830s and 1840s "imaginative lives" combining criticism and fiction were produced with increased impetus. In these "lives," represented by John Salvator, August Friedrich Gförer und Friedrich Wilhelm Ghillany, the major insights of Strauss' Leben Jesu were not applied.(1) The rejection of the possibility of a Jesus biography was one of the major outcomes of the tradition in which Strauss was immersed. In the novelistic "lives," however, confidence in the possibility of reconstructing the historical Jesus issued into literature in such a way that it seemed no longer illegitimate or impossible to attempt a production of a life of Jesus.

Nineteenth century American reviewers also acutely observed the inundation of their own reading public with works which departed from the dry prose of the harmonist and summoned the scriptural accounts of the life of Jesus into the fictional world of adventure, entertainment and pseudo-history. Numerous commentators sensed early that literary adaptations of religious topics came close to replacing the scriptural texts altogether. "The prodigious multiplication of books in this age," the Christian Disciple noted in 1817, "has either jostled the Bible from its place, or buried it from notice."(2) With regard to the quest, popular pious writing evinced a distinct tendency to transpose the life of Jesus from the confines of exegesis and dogmatics to the domain of historical romance. The transmutation of the figure of Jesus and other biblical personages into the form and structure of historical fiction grew after 1850 into remarkably popular ways of describing the "history" of Jesus. The religious novel became in particular one of the most effective means by which a presentation of Jesus as "friend", "brother" and "man" made "the life and teachings of Christ as real and practical as if he lived and taught ... at the present day."(3) The extreme popularity of Charles M. Sheldon's In His Steps alone went to illustrate that fictional adaptations of the life of Jesus had emerged by the close of the century as the overbearing tool of rendering the life of Jesus.

The spectrum of biblical fiction dealing with the historical Jesus had a broad range. There were variations of martyr fiction, such as William Ware's Probus and Eliza B. Lee's Parthenia; or the Last Days of Paganism; dramatizations of the experience of Jesus' early followers such as Florence M. Kingsley's Titus, A Comrade of the Cross, Stephen, a Soldier of the Cross and Paul, a Herald of the Cross; versions of historical romance, such as William Ware's Julian: or Scenes in Judea, Maria T. Richard's Life in Judea and Joseph Holt Ingraham's The Prince of the House of David; and adaptations of the realist novels, such as Harriet Beecher Stowe's Footsteps of the Master and Elizabeth Stuart Phelps' The Story of Jesus Christ. After 1840, literary adaptations of the life of Jesus stepped outside the New England liberal spectrum to include novels from the evangelical mainstream by religious authors like Charles Sheldon and Lew Wallace.

Even though the biblical narratives of the life of Jesus increasingly became a popular domain of the creative novelist, the alignment of the life of Jesus with fiction was long confronted with several incompatibilities between the literary claims of fiction and the theological claims of the quest, incompatibilities which figured as side issues in a much larger debate about the status and potentialities of fiction. From the Renaissance on, the attack on fiction had taken two principal routes: prose fiction was suspected to lack moral value and substance and to violate the requirements of verisimilitude by conflating authentic history with fictitious history. Among those critics who took the first line of attack were the reviewers of the major eighteenth century English novelists who frequently held novels to be on par with immoral, unchristian fiction. Throughout the later eighteenth and the first part of the nineteenth century it was a commonplace in criticism to assert that the novel was guilty of giving false ideas about reality. "Romances" and "novels" were censured as equally "immoral" and "perverse."(4)

On American grounds, the Puritan disaffection with prose fiction and the charge that prose fiction was not only lacking in moral value but, above all, sacrilegious have been frequently documented. The scriptural accounts of Jesus, the Puritan ministers held, should not be subjected to fictional adaptations; Jesus was "not got with a wet finger."(5) In this vein, the editors of The Bay Psalm Book insisted on the necessity of producing an accurate literal translation of the Psalms and curbed "liberty or poetical license to depart from the true and proper sense of David's words in the Hebrew verses." "God's Altar" needed no "polishing." To ornament the handiwork of God, to which all creative work belonged, was to consume literature aesthetically for its own sake and thus to accept the material world as a basis for faith and knowledge instead of following the knowledge yielded by the inscription of God's word upon man's soul. The latter position, John Cotton explained, "respected rather a plain translation, then to smooth ... verses with the sweetness of any paraphrase, and so ... attended conscience rather then elegance, fidelity rather then poetry."(6)

The Bay Psalm Book's objection to scriptural embellishment obstructed formulations of aesthetic theory, but it did not categorically exclude poetic implications. Puritan poetics acknowledged the biblical text as ars rhetorica providing authoritative justification for the use of poetical elements and rhetorical figures. Handbooks on the style of biblical discourse provided strong incentives to the use of figurative ornaments, yet in the rhetorical practices the "plain" scriptural text remained the primary norm.(7) Well into the early national period, when prose fiction matured, this conservative stance towards biblical embellishment lingered over the growth and development of American biblical fiction and combined with a series of disclaimers and refusals of secular fiction to cause literary adaptations of the life of Jesus to appear later than other kinds of religious fiction.

Especially with regard to the eighteenth century English prototheory of the novel and the first novelistic attempts of Susanna Rowson and Charles Brockden Brown, a wide-spread censure of fiction emerged which took its most devastating turn in the periodical literature. Thus the Panoplist unanimously testified to the disapproval of novels "calculated not only to afford no real improvement, but even to dissipate, to corrupt, to destroy."(8) The Christian Spectator concurred: "... in most pious families ... fiction in nearly all its forms (is) prohibited, ... on account of its moral blemishes and unreal pictures of human life ...."(9) In 1836, the Southern Literary Messenger still presented a similar view, reiterating that in the period before 1830 "the novelist ... was looked upon as little better than an infidel; ... and an abhorrence for works of the imagination was inculcated and considered a good test of morality."(10)

Against this general background of a poetics hostile to fiction, religious novelists judged that the historical Jesus could not be matched by fictional representations. Novelists accordingly long refrained from offering minute descriptions of Jesus' physical person independent of the scriptural texts. Thus William Ware embedded his sketch of the historical Jesus in a voluminous preliminary description of the Judean political landscape which bore no direct relationship to Ware's glimpses of the figure of Jesus. Harriet Beecher Stowe's novelistic "life" reiterated that Jesus and his words should be recorded "without paraphrase, dimunition, or addition." The testimony of Scripture was sacrosanct and not to be superseded by fictional, creative adaptions. The "footsteps of the Masters" were only to be traced in "the dear old book which we call the Bible...."(11) This premise was evidenced in repeated pledges of the authors of biblical fiction that for them Scripture history was and remained authoritative. In biblical fiction, Ingraham assured his readers, "the intention of the author ... is to draw the attention of those persons who do not read the Bible, or who read it carelessly, to the wonderful events it records, as well as the divine doctrines it teaches; and to tempt to seek the inspired sources from which he mainly draws his facts."(12)

The case against fiction was corroborated by the premises of common sense philosophy. The epistemology that lay behind Scottish realism was empiricist, with a tendency to fortify the superiority of the actual order confirmed by "natural" realism over against the creative and imagined. "Higher fiction," however, the _Christian Examiner_ observed, "exalts, expands, and spiritualizes the material, and bears the soul away from the visible and the tangible." It is "designed to present imaginings and yearnings beyond human experience and attainment."(13) Tied to a mechanist tradition which insisted that the perception of objects was independent of the individual's consciousness, common sense realism undercut these requirements of the imagination and pressed the distinction between history-as-fact and fiction-as- subordinate, dependent possibility.(14)

The block against fictional adaptations of biblical materials was further compounded by a more general problem of fictional creation, one which flowed from the key opposition between "history" and "fiction," with "history" denoting the literal correspondence to a representational object and "fiction" designating the realm of the imagined or invented. This opposition, American reviewers of English novels and native fictional beginnings observed, played on the relationship between represented object and the discourse that represented it - the presence or absence of historical, actual objects of representation. In terms of these differing commitments to truth value, imaginative literature was, the _Christian Examiner_ judged, not confined to present factual events. Whereas the historian focused on specific time-space locations, the novelist offered a fictive world, a foreground of hypothetical events, not confined to the evidence of occurrences in real space and time. In this respect fictional discourse was distinctly set against the concerns of the historical Jesus quest. The quest sought to reconstruct the historical Jesus through historico-critical interpretation of objective data. Biblical fiction, however, relying on the case of the imagined, was disassociated from actuality; here the figure of Jesus was initially literary rather than historical and belonged to the sphere of private, imaginative creation.

The religious novelists' defense against charges of deceit repeatedly drew back to the time-honored device of asserting that the fictional discourses did in fact record the truth. Numerous writers of biblical fiction inserted in their title pages or prefatory essays assertions of their novels' foundation on truth, declarations varying from designations of the narrative as "history" to authorial intrusions dealing at length with the trustworthiness of the accounts provided by an "eye-witness" "who trusts" that "the daughters of Israel" "As Well As the Unbehaving Gentile, May Be Persuaded As They Read, That This Is The Very Christ."(15) Another way in which fictionality was effaced and suppressed was to employ forms of authentic records, memoirs and letters. The forms themselves served to bolster the impression of verisimilitude and to obliterate the dividing lines between history and fiction. Significantly, in these uses of the epistolary form and the authors' introductory disclaimers of fictionality, problems of authenticity and verisimilitude coincided with the historico-critical issue of the historicity and verifiability of the historical Jesus. The authors of biblical fiction on the life of Jesus did not discuss the historicity of the Jesus of Nazareth in terms different from those applied in connection with the verisimilitude of fiction. To endow the fictional world with historical credibility was in the case of biblical fiction on the quest also to assert that the life of Jesus could in fact be reconstructed according to the general historiographical rules of verification.

The predominance of factual history over fictionality went hand in hand with a deemphasis of theological doctrine and creed. The use of literary adaptations frequently signalled a turning away from theological speculation in which the proccupation with the figure of Jesus within a context of "events narrated" rather than reconstructed by means of a theological or "historical quest" became increasingly acceptable.(16) Theological "accretions" were discarded, while the increasingly complex questions pertaining to the issue of faith and history were reduced to constructs playing on the terms of evidentialism. Moreover, most authors did not deal with changes and developments in the theological groundwork for the representation of the figure of Jesus. As a result, the religious novelist frequently exposed himself to the charge of being antitheological and worldly. Requiring the use of the possible, the imaginary, the novel, it appeared to reviewers, was distinctly set apart from doctrinal theological discourse. "There is a general distrust of works commonly called religious novels," the North American Review observed in 1847. "We usually find in them ... a mixture absolutely revolting of earthly passion and spiritual pride; so that it may be deemed lucky, if they are only tedious and uninteresting."(17)

The predominance of the claims of verisimilitude also created a climate in which difficulties of historical reconstruction played no significant role. Crucial results of the historico-critical analysis practised by Leben Jesu researchers which Unitarian biblical critics had keenly followed were no longer assimilated. The solution of the synoptic problem by means of the two-source hypothesis and the theory of the historical priority of Mark over Matthew and Luke went unnoticed as did the explorations into redaction criticism undertaken by the Tübingen school under Ferdinand Christian Baur. In their use of the scriptural sources, most advocates of biblical fiction on the life of Jesus entertained no doubts about the substantial reliability of the texts. Questions of critical exegesis and historico-critical methods were immediately transposed into the territory of the discussion about the evidences for or against factual claims. And in this context biblical fiction served above all else the cause of pre-critical evidentialism by perpetuating the validity of the traditional historical "evidences" of Christianity. This function, essential to the development of the literary "lives," contributed to a new awareness of the potentialities of fiction and to the adaptability of biblical modes to problems generated by historical and biblical criticism. The historical Jesus seemed more real when seen against the literary portrayal of the Galilean setting. To summon the historical Jesus into the world of fiction was in this respect to safeguard his historicity and to retrieve him from the scepticism und uncertainty triggered by Strauss' historical criticism.

I

In 1819 the American Monthly advocated in incipient form a poetics of biblical embellishment: "the Bible ... requires something besides its intrinsic value, something besides its multiplied commentaries to make it entirely intelligible." This requirement was to be fulfilled without hampering with the original biblical narratives. The scriptural text "cannot be touched without mutilation;" "any altered representation must be tarnished by comparison with the inimitable and perfect beauty of the original."(18) One of the first works to follow this tenet regarding biblical embellishments was Susanna Rowson's Biblical Dialogues Between a Father and His Family: Comprising Sacred History, From the Creation to the Death of Our Saviour Christ ... The Whole Carried on in Conjunction with Profane History. The title of Rowson's description of the dialogues between Justinian Alworth and his five children already revealed the primary intention - to embellish biblical narratives by melting sacred and profane history. A case in point for this alignment was Rowson's handling of the miracles issue. Repeatedly Rowson adduced "evidences" derived from natural "facts" and causes to substantiate the credibility of miraculous events. The argument throughout played on the correlation of "facts" from "natural" and scriptural history characteristic of Scottish common sense realism and English evidential theology. Here "sacred and profane history (were) so intimately connected, that to doubt the authenticity of one, (was) to destroy the credibility of the other."(19)

The use of of the dialogue-format in Rowson's work was accompanied by a pronounced deemphasis of theological exposition which provided a short cut around intricacies of historical scepticism. The dialogues were, Rowson averred, of "infinite benefit to the young, the ignorant, or weak-minded, ... for answering the objections of skepticism, and turning aside the shafts of self-confident wit."(20) At the very outset of American fictionalizations of the life of Jesus narratives, Rowson thus formulated the claims of the literary realm: Literary adaptations served the cause of assurance. The lively dialogues between a father and his children rendered hackneyed exegetical and doctrinal issues in an interesting, inspirational und easily accessible manner, reducing complex "objections" of historical scepticism to the "simple" world of an "ignorant" audience.

Another specimen of this function of biblical embellishment was John Hewson's Christ Rejected: or The Trial of the Eleven Disciples of Christ, In a Court of Law and Equity; as Charged with Stealing the Crucified Body of Christ out of the Sepulchre. Hewson's courtroom debate between "Jews,

Deists, and Atheists, and profound Philosophers" about the resurrection refuted the argument of Reimarus' "life" and its deist counterparts that Jesus' resurrection was staged by the disciples who removed the dead body of Jesus from the tomb. Hewson's apologetics resorted to the common sense equation of religious truth with factual "evidences" and borrowed the terms of Sherlock's Tryal of Witnesses of the Resurrection of Jesus. With Sherlock, Hewson held that Jesus "(was) not the Messiah, if he did not rise again; for by his own prophecy he made it part of the character of the Messiah."(21) "Supposing the resurrection to be true," this apologetic theology confirmed the Gospel events as divine credentials.(22)

Hewson's argument was rendered in the form of a court-room debate, no direct account of the historical Jesus was given. This account was provided in Zera, the Believing Jew which followed a formula that was to become commonplace in biblical fiction on the historical Jesus - the portrait of a sceptic turned believer under the impact of Jesus' testimony. With regard to narrative technique, this format resorted to the device of an eyewitness report to lend credence to the miracles of Jesus. Rather than investing doctrines of biblical narratives with authority and veracity "by sound argument," technique itself, then, authenticated the miracle narratives after the premise: "Now or hereafter, should other men doubt the testimony of one witness, a body of collective evidence never may be disputed. Sceptics may cavil, but they cannot disprove."(23)

For the literary adaptation of this tenet biblical embellishments signalling a departure from the scriptural texts were minimized. "Extracts from the Scripture," readers were reassured, "are carefully marked in italics between commas, so that not the smallest interpolation therewith or subtracting therefrom, is even shadowed in the narrative of the Believing Jew."(24) Yet it was early noted that Scripture itself provided incentives to creative fictional adaptations and poetic embellishments. Thus Timothy Dwight's 1772 "Dissertation on the History, Eloquence and Poetry of the Bible" observed that the Bible afforded glimpses of the poetic elements of "fine writing" and abounded with "the boldest metaphors, the most complete images, and the most lively descriptions."(25)

Exposure to the new school's criticism established by Herder and Eichhorn contributed significantly to reinforce this focus on Scripture's literary qualities. The new historico-critical studies suggested that biblical narratives were to be approached with both historical and poetical tools. In a less obvious way, American practitioners who appropriated the new exegetical methods also paid tribute to the significance of literary judgement behind historico-critical procedures and stressed that concern with biblical criticism was of one piece with a study of literary aspects. After the incipient efforts at poetic reworkings of the Bible performed by Timothy Dwight, Unitarian biblical critics were the first to move towards a concerted appreciation of the literary qualities of the Bible. And it was marked here that literary adaptation could find sanction and precedent in the text of scriptural record itself and its testimony of Jesus' "example." "This book," Jacob Abbott observed in 1832 of his The Young Christian," is not more full of parables than were the discourses of Jesus Christ."(26) Most representatives of biblical fiction concurred. A novel appeared to them as "any tale ... like the parables of our Saviour - the fables of men."(27) Andrew P. Peabody was "fully aware that parables and allegories are not infrequent in the Old Testament." Yet the distinction between sacred scriptural history and secular fiction still held its own. The literay elements in the Bible, Peabody judged, "are not fiction in any proper sense of the word. They are not creations of the fancy conjured up for their own sakes.... They are simply a mode of illustration, a form of instruction, - a mode, by which abstract truth is materialized, and brought down, as it were, to the sight and touch of the sensual and the unenlightened."(28)

These functions were retained in the literary adaptations of doctrines pertaining to the figure of Jesus. Thus Eliza Cabot Follen in The Skeptic and Hannah Farnhum Lee in The Backslider used biblical fiction as a vehicle to illustrate the Unitarian position on miracles. While George Ripley utilized the historico-critical procedures of the quest to render miracles secondary to the Transcendentalist cause for intuition, Follen and Lee produced in 1835 fictions which perpetuated the principles of evidential theology and glossed over historico-critical issues. Follen's Ralph Vincent, the sceptic, belongs "to that set of men who call themselves free-thinkers, ... free to misrepresent and deride the conclusions of the philosophers and sages, ... who have believed in the simple story of Jesus of Nazareth; free to trample upon ... the historical evidences of Christianity."(29) Alice Grey, Follen's heroine in the Unitarian apologetic tradition, exploits the rhetoric of "evidences" and affirms against Ralph "probability" and human "testimony" as reliable indices to epistemological certitude and religious belief in miracles. "From all the information that (she has) been able to obtain" "it seems to (Alice) ... that the historical evidence of the miracle of Jesus is sufficiently strong." And against the "profligacy of those, who ... insinuate that Unitarians do not believe in inspiration, or in the Bible as containing the Christian revelation," Alice reiterates "it is the very story itself, which is ... a proof of its truth. It must be true...."(30)

The theoretical concern with Unitarian notions of certitude in The Skeptic had important implications for the historicity of the figure of Jesus and the modes of its verification. "That such a man lived, and called himself the Messiah, and was crucified by Pontius Pilate" was to Follen's narrative mouthpiece "a matter of history" and "satisfied ... from a faithful study of the history of Jesus Christ...."(31) Exegetically, Follen performed this "study" along evidentialist lines, playing down historico-critical insights. Follen shared Norton's certainty that "the Gospels remain essentially the same, as they were originally composed."(32) The "skeptic's" doubts about the scriptural accounts of Jesus were accordingly bypassed with the assertion that Jesus' "story is told by four different men, agreeing in all essentials, and yet with such differences in each narrative as might naturally happen, which on this account increase the credibility of the whole, as they remove all suspicion of any preconcerted plan."(33)

As in the case of the doctrinal pamphlets and treatises produced during the miracles controversy, then, the literary approaches to the problem of Jesus' deeds were slow to develop a critical biblical research of the Gospels' composition and redaction. Follen's and Lee's studies, published in the same year as the first volume of Strauss' Leben Jesu, withdrew to an exegesis Strauss himself would have branded as a naive biblical literalism and a flawed attempt to put the truth of Christianity on a level with its mere factual givenness. That this attempt was already crumbling in the 1830s was readily conceded. Moses Stuart's retrospective assessment of "the work of boasted philosophy and reason" in his letters to Channing described the steps this development had taken: There was "first ... Semler and Eichhorn's accomodation scheme. Next followed Paulus and others with the plan of explaining everything by mere natural causes.... Then came De Wette and his friends, ... renouncing all idea of inspiration in the Bible, and maintaining that it abounds in mistakes and errors. Next came Strauss, with his scheme of mere moral romance (and the argument that) ... the numberless discrepancies and errors of the writers of the New Testament (disclose) ... this ... book (as) no authentic account either of facts or of doctrines."(34) The epistemological assumptions of Follen's and Lee's studies effectively counteracted this historical scepticism and affirmed the Gospels, in keeping with Norton's terms, as "true histories" which ensured that the view of Jesus as an "allegorical personage" and all doubts regarding the facticity of his existence were unfounded.(35)

In James Freeman Clarke's Story of a Converted Skeptic of 1846 the optimism about historical documentation pertaining to the figure of Jesus was less pronounced. By now Unitarians had been confronted with Bruno Bauer's "downright charge of fraud and imposition on the part of the evangelists and apostles," while Transcendentalist "new school" members were moving further towards Strauss' doctrine of divine immanence.(36) Whereas Follen's Skeptic still followed Norton's premise that there was nothing "to shake ... confidence in the facts, of which human testimony and ... experiences assure us," Clarke's "story" fell somewhat short of epistemological certitude.(37) Clarke's female sceptic was "a deist (who has) a reverence for the character of Jesus, and a profound belief in the divinity of many of his doctrines ... but ... (can)not understand nor accept the supernatural part of revelation." The Unitarian conception of miracles as "a violation of a law of nature" which Follen affirmed was no longer valid for Clarke and presented a powerful obstacle preventing the sceptic "from receiving Christianity as a supernatural revelation...."(38) And yet, even though Clarke maintained that the sceptic's "intellectual change" came from a different tradition of criticism represented in the novel by Michaelis' Introduction to the New Testament, Clarke nevertheless described this tradition in evidentialist terms. The sceptic, Clarke recounted, "did not become a complete believer, until she had carefully studied the external evidences of Christianity" in Michaelis' study.(39)

Clarke's portrait of "the converted skeptic" reveals that the historico-critical tradition could be made to serve an apologetic cause. Clarke's portrait suggests further that evidentialist apologetic also extended into the "new school" and here, too, worked best in the literary realm, in a "story" yielding "a complete refutation of the idea that we can dispense with historical Christianity, or that the miracles part of the Gospel is unimportant."(40) Slightly counteracting this "refutation," Clarke's narrative pointed out that the sceptic's "change in ... opinions" was accompanied by "the most profound inward change" flowing from the emphasis on the inner life, the intuitions of the soul, yet the extreme Transcendentalist consequences of this "change" - the denial of miracles, of supernatural categories in Jesus, and the equation of the Savior with a divinely inspired human personage - found no place in the literary adaptation of the figure of Jesus and his history.(41)

II

The apologetic functions of biblical fiction emerged in the context of more eulogistic appreciations of the novel and novel writing in general. Devaluing "history" as "cold, dull, and unprofitable," the Christian

Examiner in 1843 eulogized "fiction" and more specifically historical fiction as a substitute for and an enhancement of history. "Fiction is not to be despised as an instrument of moral culture," the Examiner insisted. "The chief use of fiction is its truth; its truth of moral principles."(42) In the same vein, the North American Review judged that the novel, like the parables of Scripture, was "an extended figure, which illustrates the truth und deepens its impression."(43) In these definitions, however, the claims of authenticity remained central, a characteristic evidenced in the fact that many writers of biblical fiction aligned their works with the historical romance in order to increase verisimilitude and the appearance of historical accuracy. Thus the Southern Literary Messenger set the novel against the historical romance which "blending history with fiction, (aimed) to portray the renowned characters of other ages." Similarly, the Knickerbocker drew attention to "two recognized divisions, - namely, the novel, properly so called, and the historical romance," with the novel designating "only fiction" and the historical romance following fidelity to actual events and personages.(44)

The authors of biblical fiction joined the mainstream of historical romance at a time when the reading public's taste for history had been shaped by the historical novels of Sir Walter Scott.(45) With its adherence to common sense criteria, however, biblical fiction on the historical Jesus departed from Scott's novels in emphasizing history over romance. Whereas Scott played out imaginary characters and episodes over the actual historical elements, the fiction of "authenticity" became conventional in the literary adaptations of the life of Jesus. In employing the formula of the historical romance, the representatives of biblical fiction highlighted the historical aspects of the genre over against the fictive and produced their accounts of the life of Jesus as historians rather than romancers.

The literary-historical importance of Scott's novels for biblical fiction stemmed from his marking out of the materials that fictional adaptations of the life of Jesus were to draw on. The example of Scott nourished a recurrent theme in the approach to historical romance: the question of the literary paucity and scantiness of American materials. The impact of Scott's novel raised an acute sense of the "thin" and impalpable nature of American materials. In the pages of the North American Review, E. T. Channing, Boylston Professor of Rhetoric and Oratory at Harvard, deplored that the American scene was "too stubbornly familiar and unpoetical for anything but common incidents and feelings." Similarly, William H. Prescott was doubtful that his "country be yet ripe for the purposes of the novelist." Critics hoped "to see the day, when ... the modern historical romance shall be erected in all of its native elegance and strength ... and of materials exclusively our own."(46)

The suggestion that American historical reality was not rich enough to be converted into fiction contributed an important restriction on the course of literary adaptations of the historical Jesus. Historical romances of the life of Jesus placing the historical Jesus against the background of the Galilean landscape long predominated over attempts, later undertaken in particular by the Social Gospelists, to place the historical Jesus into a special segment of American history or contemporary American settings. Thus T. B. Fox's harmonistic account of "The Ministry of Christ," which reproduced the Gospel record "with no alteration," and Harriet Martineau's historical narrative of The Times of the Saviour were "received with ... decided approbation...."(47) Literary adaptations of the figure of Jesus avoided to apply Jesus' history to a native background which was in the

1830s and 1840s still considered to lack romantic associations and historical connotations.

The American materials discussion figured indirectly in William Ware's Julian; or Scenes in Judea, which filtered the life of Jesus through the perspective of a Romanized narrator. If New World materials could not readily be subjected to a novelistic concern, there remained another literary form for the quest: the historical romance. Ware had a variety of precedents for his use of the romance of antiquity: in England there were John Gibson Lockhart's Valerius and Walter Savage Lander's Pericles and Aspasia; on Ware's native ground there were Thomas Gray's The Vestral and Lydia Maria Child's Philothea.(48) With regard to the life of Jesus, however, the realm of biblical truth and the realm of romance were in Ware's use of the historical romance distinctly set apart, with "history" still designating Scripture history. Departures from the biblical account Ware regarded as "fictitious" and "imaginary," and he accordingly declared his work as "purely fictitious, with no foundation whatever in historical fact, except where an obvious agreement will be found with the Scriptures. Wherever the story deviates from the straight course of the New Testament record, it is to be taken as imaginary - illustrative merely of the period chosen."(49)

Ware's statement played on the premises of common sense realism and evidential theology which attributed the "marks" of "historical truth" to scriptural history rather than to "fiction" with its traces of artifice, trickery and "falsity." "Lay(ing) out the case (of) ... naked history," Paley established as "a mark of historical truth" of biblical narratives "particularity in names, dates, places, circumstances, and in the order of events preceding or following the transaction...."(50) Ware shared this view, but his work also made clear that he considered "fiction" no longer as inappropriate for biblical themes. Ware's imaginative description of Christian civilization marked a break with the implications of Scottish common sense and an evidentialist poetics equating fiction with falsehood. Ware constructed a fictional world according to historical principles drawn in part from the Romantic historicism of Scott and extended the historical approach from secular fiction to biblical fiction. Ware's Julian was in this respect part of that "class of novels" to which "Scott belongs decidedly" "which do not violently disturb the natural order of events, but which depend mainly for their interest on the accurate description of outward life and manners, and in which the plot is subsidiary, often borrowed with but little change from historical fact...." "From these stories the element of fiction is well nigh eliminated."(51) Ware's novel clearly attested to this; its emphasis was on close factual fidelity to the scriptural and historical materials, with the narrator assuming the stance of the historian, not the novelist.

That the narrative thread of Ware's novel developed from the point of view of history and not romance was unanimously applauded by most reviewers of the time who highlighted "the authenticity of ... details" and "the singular purity of ... style." "As to custom, manners, costumes, localities" reviewers judged that Ware's work had "every internal mark of consistency and truth...." It presented "realities reduced to writing."(52) This reversal or suppression of fictionality was fortified by a characteristic standard of narrative trustworthiness: the use of the epistolary style of Samuel Richardson, whose works had received significant attention in both literary and religious periodicals.(53) Ware's use of the reminiscent narrator Julian, a Romanized Jew who returns to his ancestral land after learning about Jesus' presence among the Jews, at one stroke expunged every hint of fictionality as well as the implications of falsity and invention still associated with the notion of "fiction."(54)

Ware affirmed for his novel apparent objectivity and validated the credibility of his documents. This implied more, however, than the claim that the events recorded had in fact taken place. Ware's narrative techniques of verisimilitude were also of doctrinal significance; they served a theological point pertinent to the quest: Using narrated history in the service of religious and epistemological "certitude," Ware's novel affirmed that Jesus' historicity was certain, that his life was authentic. Lurking behind this was an attempt to counteract Strauss' transposition of the historical Jesus into the domain of abstract "speculation" and historical unreliablity. Whereas Strauss suggested that the church formed the mythical traditions about Jesus out of its faith in him as the Messiah, Ware was anxious to validate the special historical significance of the founder of the Christian community. And in this context the epistolary form and the claims of authenticity were no technicality, nor merely an attempt to add immediacy to the narration, but rather literary expressions of the general confidence about the historicity of the Gospel tradition and the possibility of reconstructing of the historical Jesus.

Ware's denial of serious obstructions to knowledge of the historical Jesus, however, were subtly undercut by the imprecision and ambiguity of his christology. Ware's critics sensed that the son of the Hollis Professor of Divinity at Harvard "had no very sharply defined views in regard to the nature and rank of Jesus Christ." The consensus was that Ware's novel contained "an obvious agreement with the Scriptures" and "regarded (Jesus) with the deepest veneration, as a being of super-human origin, whose mission was miraculously attested and whose authority was truly Divine; as the Son of God in a high and peculiar sense, as the one Mediator between God and man."(55) And in this regard Ware was judged to be set apart from "any sect of ancient or modern times," but Ware himself had his epistolary novel close on a note of scepticism: Jesus' miracles "sufficiently proved him to be a messenger and a prophet of God, at the same time that they failed to prove him the Messiah who had been foretold, for whom Israel had waited so long, and still waits."(56)

Jesus, Ware's Julian observes, "gives himself out, though not plainly, but obscurely and covertly as it were, for Messiah."(57) Throughout the novel this doctrinal ambiguity is accompanied by an emphasis on Jesus as exemplary "teacher" and "prophet" whose miracle-working attested to his "descent from God" but not to his being part of the Godhead.(58) Ware shied away from theological exposition and metaphysical definition. In the transformation of scriptural life of Jesus accounts into romance and entertaining fiction, the figure of Jesus was thus humanized in the direction of a christology "from below" characteristic of the quest. "The language of (Jesus') countenance," Julian realizes, "was not that of an Angel, nor of a God but of a man bound ... by the closest ties to every one of the multitudes who thronged him."(59) The terms here were those of the questers for the historical Jesus, but the argument itself was geared to a literary sensibility and avoided a doctrinally burdened form of theological discourse. With Ware's literary adaptation of the historical Jesus, life of Jesus research was less a matter of textual, historico-critical and theological scrutiny than a popular and undoctrinaire appreciation of Jesus' moral teachings.

III

In Julian Ware humanizes Jesus and questions the value of miracles as testimony of Jesus' divinity: "His works show God to be with this Jesus of Nazareth, but they show him not to be the Christ."(60) Follen's Alice Grey limits the apologetic value of miracles in yet another way. "There can," Alice concedes, "of course be no outward proof of ... special divine agency, ... except the performance of miracles." But Alice does "not believe that there is nothing in our own experience in any way like those wonderful assurances of an ever-watchful Providence, giving us light and strength where our own powers are truly insufficient to the task appointed us." "The events in the history of our own hearts" provide an additional channel of assurance, one independent of historical evidences.(61)

This was only a small step away from the Transcendentalist cause for the immediacy of intuition, a cause, however, which hardly found any fictional representation. Orestes Brownson's fictional autobiography, the Letters to an Unbeliever, published in 1839 as Charles Elwood; or, The Infidel Converted, asserted the superiority of the "inward Christ" attested by the witness of the "heart" over the Christ authenticated by miraculous history. "It is this," Brownson wrote, "sometimes termed the inward Christ, because a spiritual Christ, and not a corporeal, that judges the Bible, interprets the Bible and vouches for its truth." For Brownson, the "inward Christ" was not limited to the historical Jesus but rather indwelling in every man and proof of the divinity of the soul: "This Christ is near unto every one of us, knocking ever at the door of our hearts and praying for admission, and we may all let him in and receive his instructions."(62)

Sylvester Judd was among the few to translate this notion of the "inward Christ" into the pages of fiction. In Judd's Margaret, the female heroine follows the promptings of intuition and is guided by Emersonian self-reliance. "That law by which all facts in the physical, moral and religious world gravitate towards a common centre, and coalesce in one, she has an intuitive perception of." And of this Jesus was for Judd example and model. Jesus "was self-relying in a community ruled by tradition...." "He pursued the track of high, transcendent truth" and exemplified the traits of the "representative man." "He, the prototypal Diapason of the race, studying himself, and man in himself, so strikes in chord that vibrates to every heart."(63)

For this "gospel of the heart," however, Transcendentalists produced no substantial body of fiction.(64) Sylvester Judd's portraits of Jesus in Margaret were confined to visionary episodes. Like his colleagues in the Transcendentalist camp, Judd did not really adapt the figure of Jesus to fictional creations. Yet the Transcendentalists' reluctance to the use of the fictional form was not oblivious of the extent to which fictional creation was gaining in acceptance and recognition. After 1830, Unitarian liberals openly praised entertaining features of biblical narratives and emphasized the enhancing potentialities of fictional adaptations for the understanding of scriptural history. Literary adaptations of biblical narratives, Jacob Abbott noted in his The Young Christian, take their readers "to some elevation in the romantic scenery of Palestine, from which they might overlook the country of Galilee," and this, Abbott judged, "will probably make much stronger and more lasting impression than merely reading ... the simple language of the Bible."(65) In a similar vein, literary periodicals which reviewed biblical fiction frequently compared the effects of historical and literary treatment. "People will not read history with sufficient attention to make it familiar," the Southern Literary Messenger observed in 1843, "but when the naked truth is clothed in 'a coat of many colors,' all are ready to admire."(66)

On this, most members of the Transcendentalist camp were prepared to agree. Thus Frederick Henry Hedge observed with regard to A Man without a Country that the narrative was "related with such artistic verisimilitude, such minuteness of detail, such grave official references, that many who read it not once suspected the clever intention, and felt themselves somewhat aggrieved when apprised that fiction, not fact, had conveyed the moral intended by the genial author." This insight, Hedge stressed, enhanced rather than depreciated the potentialities of fictionalization: "Those who saw from the first through the veil of fiction the needful truth and the patriotic intent, were not less edified than if they had believed the characters real, and every incident vouched by contemporary record."(67)

While Hedge and his contemporaries in the Transcendentalist camp did not try out this view in fictional creations, orthodox critics were more than ready to utilize literary adaptations of biblical narratives as a vehicle to counter the new faith in an indwelling divinity and to reassert the pillars of evidentialism. With regard to this function, biblical fiction became increasingly more respectable, as critics acutely realized that fictionalization of the Bible offered an effective way for evidentialist apologetics and for the propagation of the traditional stance on miracles. Well beyond the close of the miracles controversy, Norton's case for the "genuineness" of the scriptural record of Jesus and his miracles thus survived in the reassuring context of literary adaptations of biblical miracles.

Outside the New England tradition, Joseph Holt Ingraham, an Episcopalian clergyman, came closer than any other writer in the 1850s to placing the evidentialist conception of miracles in the realm of sentimental entertainment and fictional imagination. Doctrinally, Ingraham's The Prince of the House of David, the saga of a three-year sojourn in Jerusalem by Adina, a young Jewess from Cairo, was devoted to the cause of converting liberal Jews to Christianity by establishing "the arguments and proofs of the divinity of Christ."(68) In terms of christological doctrine, this intention was accompanied by a step backward to the Chalcedonian formula: "Jesus was man, as well as God," Ingraham declared. "Jesus, the son of Mary in his human nature, was the Son of god in his Divine nature; an incomprehensible and mysterious union, whereby He has brought together in harmony the two natures...."(69)

On the narrative plane, Ingraham attempted to render his proposition of traditional christology convincing and authentic through the fictionalization of an eye witness account. "All the scenes of the life of Jesus during the last four years of his stay on earth, as recorded in the Gospel, (were) ... narrated as if by an eye-witness of them."(70) The epistolary form of the narrative fortified the air of historical contingency and the authenticity of the eyewitness accounts of miracles. Moreover, the achievement of the appearance and the reliability of history once again also corresponded to doctrinal content. Ingraham's extension into the realm of fiction of the practices of historical writing functioned to suggest that the novel's characters, including Christ, were an authentic part of history.

Ingraham's narrative technique further played into his overbearing confidence in historical "evidences" establishing that the historical figure of Jesus coincided with the divine Christ of faith. Ingraham's novel sought to make the biblical base of the life of Jesus objectively and unshakably secure and stood squarely in the tradition of Scottish common sense realism. The cause for the miracles and divinity of Jesus involved an assertion of self-evident truths, the reliability of physical senses and human testimony, an assertion Ingraham effectively rendered by accumulating the evidences for Jesus' divinity and Messianity: "First, his presentation in the Temple.... Secondly, the star which led the wise men to Bethlehem. Thirdly, their adoration of him in his cradle. Fourthly, the testimony of John the Baptist. Fifthly, the voice of God at his baptism. Sixthly, the descent of the Holy Ghost upon him in the form of a dove. Seventhly, his miracle at Cana of Galilee."(71)

Ingraham's stereotype references to the "evidence"-format reveals, however, what was lost when exegetical and doctrinal arguments stepped over into the realm of biblical fiction. Critical exegesis and theological exposition were submerged in fictional elements geared to the claims of verisimilude and entertainment. The North American Review observed in 1856 that "modern fictions ... are expected to do, not only their own legitimate work, but also that of the hard, dry voluminous treaties on philosophy and morals of former times: they are expected to supply the place of legislators and divines, to obviate the necessity for polemical essays and political pamphlets, in short, to perform all the functions which the several departments of literature could scarcely accomplish a century ago."(72) In the case of the conversion of the life of Jesus narratives into fictional creations these tasks were performed in a deficient manner. Shying away from theological controversy and sermonizing, Ingraham wrote as a novelist rather than a theologian. In contrast to the explicitly exegetical concerns of Norton and Parker and the historico-critical interests of H. E. G. Paulus and Strauss, Ingraham's uncritical portrait of the life of Jesus highlighted the traditional Jesus of the harmonist and the divine, saving Christ of the evidentialist. Doctrinally and exegetically, Ingraham's "life" appeared in this respect regressive and anachronistic, yet it sold well. While the critical tradition of Strauss remained esoteric and unpopular among American audiences, the combination of historical romance and theological orthodoxy quickly turned Ingraham's work into a successful religious best seller.

IV

Precedents for literary adaptations of the life of Jesus were available to American audiences in works from the British and the French quest. Here too the exegetically and theologically freighted style of the quest was submerged when the life of Jesus entered the world of fiction. Within the realm of fiction the submersion of theological discourse to the historical Jesus was increasingly accepted. But once a "life" purported to be more of an exposition of doctrines against the traditional Christ of faith than a romance or historical novel, the absence of theological discourse was acutely noted. When in 1865 the Cambridge historian Robert Seeley produced his Ecce Homo, a "life" deliberately addressed to those "who feel dissatisfied with the current conceptions of Christ," both British and American reviewers judged that this "life" was "not only worthy of comparison with more scientific and more histrionic works which have proceeded from Germany and France, but distinctly taking the lead of them in point of successful handling of the question."(73) Seeley did not rely on the form of the Palestinian romance for his "life" and came up instead with a psychological portrait of the "personality" of Jesus and his "enthusiasm of humanity," a "character" portrait corresponding closely to the "liberal-positive" "lives" of Weizsäcker, Holtzmann and Schenkel.(74) Unlike the "liberal-positive" "lives," however, Seeley did not deem it necessary to produce a chronological narrative life of Jesus. "No other career ever had so much unity," Seeley judged, "no other biography is so simple, or can so well afford to dispense with details." Seeley accordingly recorded "no important change ... in (Jesus') mode of thinking, speaking or acting."(75) Nor did Seeley deal with any intricate theological issues posed by the life of Jesus narratives. "What is now published," Seeley declared in the preface to Ecce Homo, "is a fragment. No theological question whatever are here discussed."(76)

To most reviewers, this deliberate lack of "any steady theological principle" was not persuasive. Both American and British reviewers agreed that "to settle the object of Christ's life and work independently of (theology was) to omit all of the important facts of the case." For the Spectator, "the attempt to delineate from within the life and work of Christ, without making any fundamental theological assumptions as to his nature and the reality of his revelations, (was) almost like the attempt to paint a picture without making any assumptions as to the quarter whence the light comes, and consequently whither the shadows fall."(77) But however poetical and poignant the negative reviews, Ecce Homo contributed significantly to the shift of the subject of the life of Jesus from an academic and scholarly environment to public literature. And this shift, reviewers acknowledged, made Seeley's "life" not only more "successful" than its counterparts in the Leben-Jesu-Forschung, but also "realized ... with far more power than Neander, and far more of both power and truth than ... Strauss - the historical magnitude of Christ's work...."(78) The one "thing clear about it," H. W. Bellows acknowledged of Ecce Homo in the Christian Examiner, "is its ... power, suggestiveness, and pertinency to the times."(79)

American audiences increasingly appreciated this point when they were confronted in 1863 with Ernest Renan's translation of the life of Jesus into entertaining fiction, a translation undertaken from the viewpoint of the literary artist rather than the historical critic. Renan came on the scene with a "life" "humanizing" Jesus and combining criticism with fiction. Renan's Vie de Jésus invested the life of the historical Jesus with the glamour of romance and Oriental realism and conveyed a sense of the effect of the Palestinian landscape which Renan had experienced first hand. "All this history," Renan wrote, "which seems at a distance to float in the clouds of an unread world ... took a form, a solidity, which (revealed) ... the striking agreement of the texts and the places, the marvellous harmony of the Gospel idea with the country which served it as a framework...."(80)

With this "fifth Gospel, torn but still legible," however, Renan made no substantial contribution to historical criticism. Renan's treatment of the sources was impressionistic and employed the methods and discoveries of the higher critics only to corroborate the narrative of his sentimental history. Throughout, the synoptic Gospels were used to leave an aesthetic impression. Jesus "returned, then, into his beloved Galilee," Renan thus writes of his "hero", "and found again his heavenly Father in the midst of the green hills and the clear fountains - and among the crowds of women and children, who with joyous soul and the song of angels in their hearts, awaited the salvation of Israel...."(81)

Renan's historical romance of Palestine was sharply set apart from the critical tradition of Strauss. Strauss' comparative critical analysis did not require "charming" literary portraits of Palestine. Renan's romantic portrayal of the human, historical Jesus, by contrast, invested the narrative of Jesus' life with an immediacy and dramatic force which readers were accustomed to associate with secular romances. Placing unqualified credence in the historicity of the Gospels, Renan did not produce a "speculative" Christ, as Strauss had, but rather one rooted in "genuine history" and subject to the effort "to extract something historical out of (the Gospels) by means of delicate approximation."(82) Renan's overriding assumption here was that the synoptics contained a history of the ministry of Jesus which permitted the reconstruction of the authentic data of the historical Jesus and not merely of the attributes of "symbol" and "myth."

Renan treated Jesus independently of Christian dogma; his Jesus was merely a heroic idealist and moralist advocating a universal religion of the spirit without creed and rites. The Vie de Jésus presented a figure not of dogma and doctrine but of psychology, a "gentle," "delightful," "charming" preacher of a lakeside idyll who propagated amid the picturesque Galilean countryside a "delicieuse théologie d'amour." "As often happens in very elevated natures," Renan observes of his "great man" endowed with pristine moral and religious grandeur, "tenderness of the heart was transformed in him into an infinite sweetness, a vague poetry, and a universal charm."(83) In this portrait the traditional supernatural view of the Scriptures had no place. Renan's rationalistic and pragmatic conception of miracles reduced the miracles of Jesus to pious inventions or thaumaturgical acts misinterpreted by the religious enthusiasm of Jesus' disciples. Miracles were not performed under scientific conditions and only possible in a context where people were disposed to believe them. This desupernaturalized approach to history posited "a form, a solidity" in scriptural history which affirmed "instead of an abstract being who might be said never to have existed, an admirable human figure living and moving."(84)

Renan's stripping of the supernatural Christ and emphasis on the human, historical Jesus followed the 'rationalist' tradition of biblical criticism represented by Reimarus. For Reimarus as for Renan, Jesus' miracles constituted in most cases perpetrated frauds, with Jesus merely participating in staged events. But in this explanation Renan's terms were not those of historical criticism, as in the case of Reimarus, but rather those of psychology. Renan represented in his Jesus portrait an idealistic moralist who appropriated the title of the "Son of God" and corrupted his pristine character in a futile effort to prove his divine mission to unbelieving audiences. In Jerusalem, Jesus entrapped and lost himself, Renan supposed. "Not by any fault of his own, but by that of others, (Jesus') conscience had lost some ot its original purity. Desperate, and driven to extremity, he was no longer his own master. His mission overwhelmed him, and he yielded to the torrent. As always happens in the lives of great and inspired men, he suffered the miracles opinion demanded of him rather than performed them."(85)

On the concrete, psychological ground of Renan it was the conception of Jesus as a "great and inspired man" rather than the emphasis on the gradual corruption of Jesus' character which scored a remarkable success with American audiences. The historical romance of Palestine which American writers encountered in Renan's life of Jesus conceived religious history in terms of the Romantic theory of "genius" as determined by individual personalities. This application of the fictional convention of the "hero" to the life of Jesus assigned to Jesus a place among the great men of history in a manner reminiscent of Emerson's and Carlyle's notion of the "representative man." Thus Emerson stressed after his encounter with the Vie de Jésus that "when (he) wrote 'Representative Men,' (he) felt that Jesus was the Representative Man whom (he) ought to sketch; but the task required great gifts, - steadiest insight and perfect temper; else the consciousness of want of sympathy in the audience would make one petulant or sore, in spite of himself." (J, IX, 579)

Outside the Transcendentalist camp the critique of Renan was differently directed. The Christian Examiner rejected Renan's "sketch" as "offensive to reverence and to common sense; implying that the present system of morality and spirituality came from a half-impostor and conscious deceiver - which is like tracing a stream of purest water to a bank of muddy clay."(86) Yet with regard to the "literary" approach of Renan's life, most critics were prepared to "acknowledge and admire" "M. Renan's devotion to his 'hero'" and "the charm of the narrative in which M. Renan has reproduced the events of Christ's marvellous passage across the scene of human life."(87) This reproduction was unanimously held to be far superior to Strauss' "life." "While Strauss substitutes for the historical Jesus an abstraction," the North American Review observed that "M. Renan supplies one who is intensely flesh and blood and soul and spirit;" Moreover, while Strauss' "life" showed "in regard to the personal history of Jesus ... that ... he is scarcely anything more than a mythical person and that the writings purporting to give an account of him are fabulous compositions, containing only here and there a few slight and broken threads of historical truth," Renan offered a "life" demonstrating that ... Jesus was a real person," "a living human presence in the world."(88)

The focus on Jesus as a "real person" turned Renan into an ally for the evidentialist cause Norton had advocated. While Strauss left only "a few slight and broken threads of historical truth," Renan admitted "the four canonical Gospels as authentic, (tracing) them almost wholly the work of the authors to whom they are attributed...."(89) Renan's reassurances about the Gospel sources came upon a field still controlled by the older tradition of harmonies and devotional "lives" and here played in particular into the argument of Lant Carpenter, whose Apostolical Harmony of the Gospels presented with American audiences a remarkably popular attempt to rehabilitate evidentialist premises by means of narrative realism. Carpenter's introductory dissertations on the Palestinian background of Jesus' time sought to "afford a distinct and vivid conception of scenery in which the heart must ever feel a holy interest."(90) As in the case of Renan, it was thus a distinctly literary sensibility which yielded a reassuring counter-front against disintegrating historical scepticism in the manner of Strauss.

And yet, even though Renan was clearly set apart from Strauss' conception of Jesus' life "as a myth, without substance, amidst countless shades and varieties of opinion," Renan "(seemed) ..., equally with Strauss to build up a Christ of his own out of the wreck of the actual history." American reviewers felt "a painful uncertainty whether the being who lives and moves so vividly before us is always the same...." And there was "a strong misgiving" among reviewers "that he (was) not."(91) In this context even the "liberal-positive" "lives" of the Leben-Jesu-Forschung appeared as superior. While Renan's "life" "failed in his presentation of the character," Daniel Schenkel's The Character of Jesus Portrayed seemed comitted to "a practical and pious" "motive." He did not, "like Renan, invade or depreciate the moral character of Jesus," nor did he merely produce "a free, imaginative construction."(92) But Schenkel's superiority over Renan, the Christian Examiner judged, was further surpassed by studies in which "loyality to the sacred record" went hand in hand with authentic observations in "philology" and "archeology."(93) Robert Turnbull's Christ in History, Harriet Martineau's Traditions of Palestine and, above all Horatio B. Hackett's Illustrations of Scripture; suggested by a Tour through the Holy Land were applauded as "invaluable" in their use of "actual observation" and "original" illustrations for a reconstruction of Jesus' "character."(94)

Despite these appraisals of a factual "portrait" of Jesus, however, there remained "a strong misgiving" about the very possibility of such a reconstruction.(95) C. T. Brooks judged that "the many unsuccessful attempts that have been made to reproduce the life of Jesus in a regular biography suggest the inquiry, whether there may not be something in the nature of the case which makes this impossible; whether it may not be the intention of the Divine Providence, that at least around the beginning and the end of that remarkable life and impenetrable cloud of mystery should forever hang...."(96) William Henry Furness concurred: "It is difficult to suppose that the history of Jesus, the history which the world is seeking for, could possibly be so produced."(97) Moreover, "language (failed him)," Furness confessed, "in the attempt to describe the energy, the divine life, which appears in the character of Jesus, when he is contemplated as endowed with supernatural gifts."(98)

This insight into the difficulty, if not impossibility of an adequate Jesus portrait, however, was not arrived at by historical criticism, as in the case of Strauss, but rather on the basis of a staunch adherence to supernaturalist premises for which Unitarian reviewers saw no suitable literary and critical equivalent. And with regard to supernaturalism, Renan's "life" was insufficent and unaccepable. It was, reviewers charged, "a prime and fatal flaw in the very corner-stone of a theory of the life of Jesus to begin with eliminating the supernatural element." "To bring back to this age the living Christ" required to bring into play "historical" and "supernatural elements." "The dispute between the disciples of an historical and those of a spiritual Christ" was in this respect "wholly unnecessary and misleading."(99) One of the quest's foremost concerns thus was dismissed as irrelevant.

V

Renan's Vie de Jésus pointed the way to future success of the Jesus narrative. Renan's pastoral and romantic portrait of the ministry of Jesus impressed audiences by its authetic power and suggested that for a life of Jesus no genre affiliation seemed to fit except a literary one. "This book is not theology or criticism nor is it biography," Elizabeth Stuart Phelps observed of her life of Jesus. "It is neither history, controversy, nor a sermon.... It is a narrative...."(100) Harriet Beecher Stowe revealed the literary character of her "life" by inserting poetry into episodes of Jesus' ministry and by offering a literary rather than historico-critical appreciation of the miracles narratives. "There is something wonderfully poetic in the simple history given by the different evangelists of the resurrection of our Lord," Stowe judged. "It is like a calm, serene, dewy morning, after a night of thunder and tempest."(101) Phelps' Story of Jesus Christ characterized the "luxuriant vegetation of Nazareth" in a similarly pastoral manner reminiscent of the "charming" nature portraits in Renan's "life": "The green that is half gold melted over the hillsides, and ran riot in the valley. Flowers were at a high tone. The red lamps of the pomegranates were burning freely. Fruit gardens touched in rich, metallic colors to the landscape; gold of apricot, with pale, silver leaves, purple of grape, and yellow-green of fig, passed each in its time."(102)

Both Phelps' and Stowe's poetic portraits of Jesus were propagated as having been modelled after the text of the biblical narratives. "The great historical facts that revealed the Founder of Christianity," Phelps reassured her audience, "have been carefully considered. No important departure from the outlines of his only authorized biography has beguiled the pen which has here sought to portray the Great Story with loving docility."(103) Embedded in these reassurances was the deeply ingrained scepticism about the possibility of a literary portrait pertaining to a "character" who seemed inaccessible to the psychological and historical interests of the realist novel. If at all, a literary adaptation therefore only seemed legitimate when it presented "in aim and execution ... an historical construction" based on the author's "familiar acquaintance both with the historical monuments and the actual landscape of Palestine...."(104)

Yet Phelps' and Stowe's "unfamiliar strokes by which (the scriptural) outlines have been ... filled" did constitute a significant departure from the original text in offering a psychological portrait of Jesus. "Jesus," Phelps observed, "distinguished with amazing skill between the true and the false claims on sympathy." He "was always struggling with an excess of power.... He did not seek to put the marvelous on exhibition. He held it in reserve."(105) These character traits were not only presented by means of external descriptions but also on the basis of glimpses into the inner consciousness of Jesus which uncovered Jesus' uncertainty of decision and doubts about his own mission. Measures of literary immediacy and psychological authenticity here were throughout invoked to render the "character" of Jesus. And unlike the early literary adaptations of the historical Jesus which had sharply distinguished between the scriptural and the literary realms, the ascription of fictionality to the life of Jesus was now no longer suppressed.

The precedent for the interest in the psychological development of Jesus as a literary "character" had been set by Renan's appropriation of the realist novel. Renan's "sketch" of the "purely human side of (Jesus') character," the Christian Examiner observed, set out "to show how a gifted and enthusiastic Jewish peasant of the most exquisite temperament and moral genius, under the influence of the stimulating climate and more stimulating traditions of Judea, dreamed himself into a prophet."(106) Phelps' and Stowe's description of Jesus' developing Messianic consciousness, in contrast, did not present "a soul half-deluded and half-deluding," nor did it abrogate Jesus' status as "Mediator."(107) Phelps' and Stowe's novelistic adaptation of the life of Jesus, safely came out on the side of orthodoxy. Both Phelps' and Stowe's "lives" were designed to reassure and presented the divine, saving Christ of faith, the "Mediator, both divine and human," "the generous Saviour and Giver," "the citadel" to which "the defenders" of Christianity could "retreat." In a time of "fighting about the outworks of Christianity," Stowe reiterated, "it is time to retreat to the citadel; and that citadel is Christ."(108)

Shielding themselves behind the conventions of the realist novel, both Phelps and Stowe bypassed in this "retreat" theological controversy and the vexing issue of Jesus' resurrection and atonement. Phelps was anxious to emphasize that she was "not unaware of the differences among New Testament critics," of "the intellectual mode and Christian scholarship." Yet she did not allow the "vast controversy" "concerning the life of Jesus Christ" to enter into her "personal interpretation." "The life of Christ," Phelps was convinced, "was lived to inspire, not to confuse" and could serve as a source of inspiration quite apart from theological doctrines.(109) Phelps and Stowe deliberately addressed audiences not trained in exegetical research and confident of the substantial reliability of scriptural texts. In this uncritical confidence in the historicity of the Gospel tradition, the resurrection narrative represented "a fact of history" and not, as Strauss had maintained, "a long statement of discrepancies."(110) Similarly, the genealogies of Jesus validated for Stowe his "tie ... with the royal house of David" and were not merely, as Strauss had suggested "arbitrary compositions, which do not prove the Davidic descent of Jesus...."(111) In the same vein, it did not matter to Phelps "whether the star of Bethlehem was a meteor or a miracle, ... whether Jesus was born in one year of the next, in this month or that." It was, moreover, of no consequence whether he was baptized in Jordan River or Jordan region.... (And) whether Jesus revisited Nazareth once or twice (was) a point not worth two pages of controversy." Both Phelps and Stowe were agreed that the "sacred romance" of Jesus' life was not to be "torn and mangled" by critical "biographies ... crowded with ... erudition" and "tenacious of detail."(112)

Nor was this "sacred romance" to be regarded as mere "fiction." With Phelps and Stowe the historical conventions were by no means given up; the authors' introductory disclaimers of any fictional distortions persistently aimed at the historical mode and further used authorial narration in order to invest the narratives with verisimilitude and credibility. But this concern with the problems of authenticity and verisimilitude did not lead to any substantial theorizing on the role and form of religious novels and their affinity with historical fiction. The function of the historical and fictional claims was not that of reference to literary form but simply the affirmation that the account was factually true.

Like the evidentialist "lives," the fictional adaptations of the history of Jesus were prepared to unite literary and biblical interpretation in incipient form and to apply literary categories to the Jesus narrative. The biblical narratives of Jesus, Channing had observed in his "Evidences of Christianity", "are written with the simplicity, minuteness, and ease which are the natural tones of truth, which belong to writers thoroughly acquainted with their subjects, and writing from reality."(113) Similarly, Phelps stressed the "simplicity, directness, force (and) persuasiveness" in the life of Jesus narratives.(114) But this transposition of literary terms into the interpretation of the Jesus narrative immediately issued into statements on the facticity of Jesus' existence and the historicity of his deeds. An application of the body of literary criticism dealing with realist narrative to the interpretation of scriptural texts thus could not take hold in the "imaginative lives."

10. "The Historic and the Ideal Christ"

The literary adaptations of the historical Jesus engendered evasions of exegetically freighted modes of theological discourse, offering instead assurance and confidence in the knowability of the figure of Jesus at a time when Strauss' research had demonstrated that the history of the New Testament could not bear the weight which faith placed upon it. For the fictional portraits of Jesus exegetical research was "quite immaterial." Against the value of the specific, historical revelation of God's will through Jesus Christ, the concern of "Christian scholars" with critical exegesis appeared "unimportant." "The important things ... are few, clear, and unquestionable," E. S. Phelps contended, "Jesus Christ lived and died, and lived again after death. ... His personality is the best explanation yet given of the mystery of human life. It offers the only assurance we have of a life to come."(1)

With these assertions, literary questers revealed their full, if undifferentiated, confidence in the historicity and revealed truth of the Scriptures. The first efforts to introduce the quest's exegetical tools into American critical study of biblical narratives, it seemed, had not taken root. In part this was due to the fact that the pioneers of biblical criticism like Parker and Stuart had confronted traditional theology almost overnight with a canon of exegesis which had grown steadily in the Leben-Jesu-Forschung since the emergence of neologist criticism. With this break an important parting of ways between the Leben-Jesu-Forschung and its American counterpart occurred. The "myth" exegesis of Strauss set in motion on Strauss' native ground a renewed focus on biblical source criticism and prompted the Leben-Jesu-Forschung to delve into three decades of careful study of the composition, redaction and "tendency criticism" of the life of Jesus narratives. On American soil, the reaction to Strauss did not have a cumulative tradition of criticism of the biblical writings to draw on, nor did Strauss' argument significantly spur the development of critical biblical research. Nor, finally, did the major results of source criticism, like the Markan hypothesis, ever achieve the currency they enjoyed in the Leben-Jesu-Forschung.

In the British quest a similar exegetical situation prevailed. The reaction provoked by the _Leben Jesu_ in the mainstream of English theology had been largely negative. George Eliot's translation of Strauss' "life" in 1846 had spurred the growth of scepticism concerning the full historical accuracy of Scripture.(2) Yet the furor over Strauss triggered on the ground of the Leben-Jesu-Forschung was not met with a comparable outbreak of public alarm in England. The persistence of conservatism in British New Testament studies culminating in the late nineteenth century in the moderate textual criticism of the Cambridge Trio, the historian F. J. A. Hort and the biblical critics B. F. Westcott and J. B. Lightfoot, indicated that the question of the life of Jesus never grew into a divisive issue capable of changing the course of biblical criticism. In fact, one of the crucial differences between the patterns of reactions was that, while the major opposition to Strauss in the Leben-Jesu-Forschung intensified in the decade from 1835 to 1845, the English front did not fully deal with the historical question posed by the _Leben Jesu_ until the publication in 1860 of _Essays and Reviews_.(3)

Compared with the contemporary Leben Jesu researchers, William Henry Furness and James Freeman Clarke, who continued the incisive work in biblical criticism Parker had popularized in America, were on the whole closer to the main positions already worked out earlier in the period before the controversy over David Friedrich Strauss. Clarke's 1886 study on The Problem of the Fourth Gospel, with its conservative restatement of traditional views of the authorship and origin of the Fourth Gospel, was representative of the way in which American exegetes after the Civil War reverted to critical traditions before Holtzmann without assimilating current results of source and redaction criticism. The production of the Revised Version of the New Testament in 1881 and of the Old Testament in 1885 no doubt propagated the application of textual criticism, but the attempt to foster the growth of critical exegesis in the manner of Parker and Stuart was not effective in departing from the apologetic doctrinal positions on the unique significance of Christ's death and resurrection, the special authority of miracles and the revealed truth of Scripture.

The Unitarian rejection in the 1840s and 1850s of the "speculative" principles foundational to Strauss' reconstruction of christology had revealed a remarkable commonality between Schleiermacher and American questers. In the 1860s and 1870s, the attempts to retain the "uniqueness" of Jesus were further adapted from Schleiermacher and consolidated an already existing distinct line of indebtedness. The growing accomodation of liberal religion to the leading concepts of the quest was accompanied by a return not to orthodoxy but to the "mediating" position of Schleiermacher's canon. Confronted with the theory of evolutionary materialism, critics once branded by the "Unitarian Pope" as "heretics" increasingly became allies against materialism and mechanism. Defenders of orthodoxy themselves now appreciated Schleiermacher and his disciples as "the pillars of Hercules, through which entrance was made into the broad ocean of modern theological speculation."(4) Schleiermacher's insistence on religious consciousness as the source of doctrine was read as a powerful reinforcement of "spiritualism" over and against an agnostic schism between religion and science. With this interpretation, "the wheel had come half-circle. What the greatest of the early Divinity School theologians had designated as the "latest form of infidelity" became, by the end of the century, the gospel of the School."(5)

Schleiermacher in this way was recalled from "transcendental" philosophy, "that vague and uncertain philosophy" into which the "new school" had placed the Leben Jesu research.(6) In this shift of interpretation, Schleiermacher's "fortress ... against supernaturalism and infidelity" was read as rendering Christianity in its essential inner principles inviolate from all critical assaults and from doubts concerning the historical authenticity of the New Testament narratives.(7) Moreover, Schleiermacher's mediating position, reviewers like H. Davies observed, validated the acceptance of historical criticism without reducing the quest to a mere reconstruction of the historical Jesus through critical analysis of the sources. "The incarnation that has most moved the hearts of men has been something closer and more real that this," Charles Carroll Everett, dean of the Divinity School after 1878, judged. "It has been the incarnation of the spirit of Jesus in his followers.... It is this that has made the story of the incarnation of Jesus credible and real."(8)

With Everett, this way of conceiving the significance of Jesus from what Schleiermacher designated the subjective "religious sentiment" rather than from irrefutable 'data' of Scripture, as the evidentialists had done, did not lead to a devaluation of the historical Jesus. "The simple historic Christ," Everett averred, "must stand as the ideal for those who accept his teaching."(9) On this premise, Hegelian metaphysics appeared acutely inadequate. "In Hegelianism," the Christian Examiner judged, "'events are brought to pass by ghastly Universals'.... There is no germ of personality. 'Persons are only masks....'"(10) What was left was "a Christianity without a spiritual personality as its root, without a Christ...." In Schleiermacher, in contrast, reviewers judged, the claims of the "spiritual Christ" were retained. Schleiermacher, the Christian Examiner was convinced, "would never have consented to the sacrifice of the spiritual Christ."(11)

Everett and his contemporaries did expressly mark here that in drawing on Schleiermacher's quest, they were in effect relying on a canon which started off with the "ideal Christ" "with whose divine office the facts in history have the slightest possible necessary connection."(12) But critics like Everett, Clarke and Hedge were not prepared to part with either the historical-objective or the "ideal" categories of the life of Jesus. To them, the historical Jesus and the Christ of faith were intimately and inextricably connected. The debate between the advocates of an "historical" and those of a "spiritual Christ" was therefore "unnecessary." "The historical Jesus once made real to the souls of men, becomes the spiritual Jesus - then for the first time we have the real point and power of his example."(13) In this context the dogmatic import of the quest foundational to the dichotomy between the Jesus of history and the Christ of faith did not leave a significant trace. Suppressed too was the tendency, spurred by Schleiermacher's life of Jesus research, to align the classical terms "persona" and "hypostasis" with the modern terms of personality and self-consciousness. Judged against the options available to American questers in the Leben-Jesu-Forschung, the Sabellian variety of Schleiermacher's christology here clearly receded behind I. A. Dorner's insistence on the priority of the objective factor in the "person" of Christ.(14)

Critics after Parker were not oblivious of the exegetical tools of the quest, but they were mostly concerned to show that the scientific handling of exegetical data established the traditional Christ. Moreover, in the study of biblical history and biblical revelation empirical considerations continued to be primary and subservient to the claims of historically recorded revelation. Against this emphasis, Parker's definition of Strauss' myth exegesis as independent of positive historicity, as "not a history and (instead) ... a fiction which has been produced by the state of mind of a certain community" could not take hold.(15) As a result, the course towards form-critical exegesis which the Leben-Jesu-Forschung after Strauss set out to follow was blocked. And when the debate over the factuality of biblical narratives finally started to broaden towards the kerygmatic stance, the traces of the old evidentialist apologetic always remained prevalent. Thus Nathaniel Frothingham's insight into "the discrepance of (the biblical) accounts" still did "but multiply the evidences of their truth." "Suspicion over the authenticity of the records" did "not in the least degree" "interfere with the unity of (the) impressions concerning the Redeemer...."(16)

I

"It is perilously near the sin against the Holy Spirit," William Wallace Fenn, then Dean of the Harvard Divinity School observed in 1891, "not to prefer the God of Channing and Parker and Emerson to the God of

Abraham, Isaac, and Jacob; ..."(17) The Bible had lost the centrality of earlier days when Unitarian-Transcendentalists scrutinized biblical narratives for external "evidences" or testimonies of the "heart." Revelation in nature increasingly replaced biblical revelation. "There is a power of religious intimacy," W. S. Crowe argued, "which we who regard the Bible as literature have lost. We can afford the loss, in consideration of what we have gained. The Bible is the only revelation the evangelical has. We have the universe unto our revelation."(18) In "The Relation of Jesus to the Present Age" Charles Carroll Everett traced this position to the impact of the Leben-Jesu-Forschung: "The idea of a miracle is opposed to the fundamental axioms of the popular thought of the present. The writers who best represent this thought ... simply affirm with Strauss, that the time is past when a miracle can be believed."(19) W. H. Furness concurred and judged that "one characteristic of the present time more marked than another ... is the Decline of Faith, not only in the great Christian fact of the Resurrection of Christ, but in the historical authority of the Gospels altogether."(20)

Furness connected this assessment with the resultant decline of interest in the criticism and interpretation of the New Testament. "As historical records," Furness observed, "the Gospels are accounted of very little value. Having thus fallen historically, into disrepute, regarded as collections of mere fables or myths, they are ceasing to be studied, or even referred to, apart from their moral precepts, with any particular interest." For the evidentialist critics, the key to the scriptural texts had been the question of biblical authority and not a particular interpretation. But for the generation of exegetes in the 1860s and 70s even this "attempt to discover what is historically true respecting (Jesus was) given up as hopeless." Furness was acutely aware that "not a few, among the thoughtful and learned, perceiving that the origin of other religious is hidden in the mists of fable, have long since come to the conclusion, that Christianity is no exception to this fact, and that scarcely anything can now be satisfactorily settled about Jesus beyond the actual existence of the person so named, and hardly even that."(21)

Unable to settle for this uncertain and tenuous position, Furness resorted to strained interpretations which constituted a strikingly wasteful effort in defense of the historicity of the Gospel tradition. The fact that Strauss' "new life" of Jesus in 1864 conceded that "history" was, after all, reflected in the Gospel "myths," namely the history of the religious consciousness of the Christian community, Furness did not acknowledge and instead continued to expend considerable energy on the refutation of the "mythical" approach almost as though the validity of Christianity hinged entirely on the issue.(22) Furness thus felt compelled "to make visible the historical features (of the Gospels)" and to assert "the full warrant of reason, nature and probability" against those who "under the lead of Strauss, have come to look upon the whole story of Jesus, contained in the Four Gospels, as a collection of myths...."(23) In this delayed response to Strauss' life of Jesus, Furness was convinced that there could "be but little hope that an end will ever come to the existing confusion of thought respecting the position and authority of Jesus, until the positive historical truth concerning him is fully and distinctly settled."(24) Furness conceded that "facts only, oftentimes very slightly or not at all connected, are stated (in the Gospels); and fables and exaggerations are mingled with them." Yet Furness did not at all "despair of being able, ... to discriminate between the fables and the facts in the accounts of Jesus, and determine the proportion of each."(25) For this "discrimination," however, no adequate exegetical apparatus was developed. Instead of providing exegetical and source critical data, Furness merely sought "to make evident the handiwork of Truth in the ... history of the public life of Jesus." Throughout, the claims of historical factuality remained primary in Furness' concern "to indicate the marks of truth" in the life of Jesus accounts and "to show that, whatever appearances of a fabulous legendary, or mythical character these Records (presented), there (was) running through them ... a pure piece of biography, a history, which ... gives us the idea of a person of most original and yet natural greatness."(26)

With regard to the issue of biblical historicity, the heritage which Strauss' "lives" bequeathed the Leben Jesu researchers was twofold: in the first place, they "(dealt) a deadly blow to rationalism," and in the second place, by moving interpretation away from the miraculous events themselves to their narration, they cleared the way for "replies (in which) ... the Gospel histories were subjected to a closer criticism than ever."(27) On the latter count Furness was by no means indifferent to the insights of source and redaction criticism. The Leben-Jesu-Forschung, A. P. Peabody observed in 1850 in his review of Furness' History of Jesus, presented "the Gospels as accretions rather than compositions, as the growth of the first three centuries, not as the original works of Matthew, Mark, Luke, and John."(28) Furness expressly endorsed this view. The "primal Gospels," Furness argued in Jesus and the Gospels, "were written by other than immediate disciples...." And "these writings present the appearance of Compilations ... of previously existing written materials...."(29) Furness was even prepared to accept in incipient form considerations of redaction and "tendency" criticism. Thus Furness observed with regard to the Fourth Gospel: "It has a peculiar, decidedly dogmatic character, and was avowedly written for a purpose; ... to establish a certain official or theological representation of Jesus. In a word, it shows strong marks of having been composed after those opinions concerning him were beginning to take form, which were early imported into the Christian Church from the philosophy of the East...."(30) But Furness did not allow this finding to counteract the central premise that the Fourth Gospel "manifests traces of being, in important parts, made up of materials purely historical."(31) There was no room here for the basic premise of Strauss as to the precarious link between the documents of Christianity and the apostles' witness. Furness key supposition was "simply this - (The Gospels) are neither theological documents nor fabulous compositions, but substantially, genuine histories, ... accounts of things that were actually said and done."(32)

On the issue of miracles, the primary concern for Furness in the 1870s and 1880s was still the accounts' "perfect accord with truth and probability," and Furness was therefore - more than three decades after Strauss and Paulus - prepared to revert to Norton's evidentialism.(33) In a somewhat melancholy argument in The Unconscious Truth of the Four Gospels, Furness used Norton's Internal Evidences of the Genuineness of the Gospels to reiterate that the Gospels "are all probable or certain" and contain "no inconsistency with the history itself, ... no contradiction of known facts."(34) Unlike Norton, however, Furness' nostalgia had "no place" for "the prevailing idea of miracles as departures from the natural course of things...."(35) With regard to the miracles narratives, Furness persisted in the position he had been advocating since 1836: The miracles of Jesus "were not done for the sake of proving anything, but were the whole-souled effusions of his own being." They were "natural, spontaneous, simple-hearted expressions of (Jesus') great nature", and not merely "credentials of his mission" or "arguments of his divine authority." Contra Strauss' Das Leben Jesu für das deutsche Volk bearbeitet, which to Furness merely found the "key to the Gospels in an artificial dogmatic theory," reducing for example the "whole story of Lazarus" to "a fable or myth ... invented in every particular for a purpose, to glorify the 'Logos Christus,' 'the personified dogmatic idea'," Furness thus sought his "key" "in simple human nature" and affirmed that the Gospel accounts "gave evidence in themselves of the credibility."(36)

Support for this refutation of Strauss' "apparent" attempt at "overthrowing the historical character of the Gospels" came from a group of critics De Wette had introduced in his "Author's Preface to the American Edition" of Theodore as "theologians, of the class of Tholuck, ... Olshausen, and all those who assist Tholuck in his Theolog. Anzeiger" and as a "medium party, the organ of which is the Theolog. Studien and Kritiken, the principle of which is history...."(37) For this group of critics, represented by Neander, C. I. Nitzsch, G. C. Lücke and Ullmann, "the view of the nature of a miracle, as being the violation of a law of nature," was "not received" and instead interpreted "as a manifestation of spiritual power and beauty which appeals to the whole soul."(38) To those critics in the pietistic tradition of Tholuck, in part made available to American audiences in 1871 through D. Heagle's translation of the Bremen Lectures, miracles not only formed "a part of the life of Christ" expressive of the "mighty spiritual power which dwelt in the soul of Jesus," but were also manifestations of "something which has entered into the world from without."(39) In Neander's Das Leben Jesu Christi, whose popularity with American audiences for outweighed that of Strauss, this insistence on the both supernatural and historical nature of the events of Jesus' life was time and again made explicit. The "miracle," Neander's "life" reiterated, "manifests the interference of a higher power, and points out a higher connexion, in which even the chain of phenomena in the visible world must be taken up."(40)

Neander's position accorded well with an evidential theology growing out of rational supernaturalism, yet in terms of its source critical achievement Neander's "life" sharply fell behind the development of critical Leben Jesu research. For Leben Jesu researchers after Strauss the religious imagination and faith of the early Christian community were in the interpretation of the Gospel narratives to be distinguished from the straightforward historical factuality of the accounts. The canon of subjects in critical life of Jesus research was accordingly broadened to include beyond the scaled-down version of the historical life of Jesus also the faith portrait of the early Christian community.(41) In Furness' conjunction of the supernatural and the historical after the fashion of Neander this subject did not fully come into play. According to Furness' "preliminary considerations," the Gospels constituted "reports" which "bear the impress, deep and sharp, of the very form and body of Fact and Nature."(42)

A Jesus portrait appropriate to this premise American questers saw realized in those Leben Jesu researchers who were agreed that it "was reserved" for "romance writers like Renan" "to hold (Jesus) to be an enthusiast who progressed through gloomy fanaticism to imposture;" and "for a David Strauss" "to ascribe to him arrogant self-exaltation, which would have reached the bounds of insanity...."(43) The critics brought together in the Bremen Lectures, C. E. Luthardt, Gerhard Uhlhorn, W. F. Gess, Johann Peter Lange and M. Fuchs, were, Alvah Hovey observed in his "Prefactory Note" to the collection of lectures, "for the benefit of American readers" in offering "noble defences of the Christian religion against fierce attacks from living adversaries" who seemed to subvert the uniqueness of the historical Jesus.(44) The "defences" of the Bremen lectures entailed, above all, a reaffirmation of evidentialism, of a "historical theology" validating the life of Jesus as the "highest manifestation" in history of "humanity."(45) Thus Neander's life of Jesus proceeded on the assumption that "we have the lineaments of the historical Christ, in fragments at least, and there is wanting only insight into their connexion to frame them into a harmonious whole."(46) For American reviewers, Neander's "life" in this way not only yielded "new evidence ... of the truthfulness of the Gospel narratives" but also a "new" confirmation of supernaturalism.(47)

With regard to the miraculous history of Jesus' life, Neander asserted that "no link in its chain of supernatural facts can be lost, without taking away its significance as a whole."(48) That "Christianity rests upon these facts; stands of falls with them" and was hence not an index of the 'uncertainties' of source and redaction criticism was made clear by the most conservative advocate of the "mediating" camp, namely Johann Peter Lange, whose Life of the Lord Jesus Christ American reviewers applauded like Neander's work as a positive refutation of Hase, Renan and Strauss.(49) "The four Gospels," Lange reiterated in terms akin to Furness' "lives," "may with perfect justice be pronounced to be credible historical records of the life of Jesus." This was only to confirm what Furness had been preaching ever since his first life of Jesus in 1836: "The purity with which (the Gospels) reflect, as instruments, the rich and glorious reality of the life of Christ, imparts to their moral aspect a nobility which must ever enhance their credibility."(50)

Furness granted "in the language of Mr. Parker that there must be "limitations to the accuracy of these Records." But Furness effectively dealt with these "limitations" by reverting to literary and moral "marks of truth" which compensated for "the amount of fiction" contained in the accounts - the "entire honesty" and "trustworthy" "character of the narrators" who produced their accounts with the "irresistible conviction of reality" and "the utmost force and vividness."(51) This appreciation of the Gospels' "signs of reality" acknowledged the Evangelists as narrators in whose "sketches" "the essential quality of Jesus (was) rendered almost visible and palpable." No attention, however, was here given to narrative form in its own right or to general correspondences with literary criticism of the realist narrative. The observations were throughout subordinated to the truth versus "fable" issue and the apologetic concern "to make it evident that (the Gospels) are not legendary or mythical, but, in substance, historically true...."(52) In this perennial appeal of the harmonist's stance, the detailed tracing of the literary and source critical development of the biblical records had yet to come and was only to be undertaken by critics who absorbed the findings of the Tübingen School.

II

Furness was convinced that "there must have been some foundation of fact, ... some germ of historical truth ... out of which (the Gospels) ... grew, and by which they were rendered credible...." On this issue Furness was and remained not alone. Critics in the orthodox Trinitarian tradition shared Furness' concern to vindicate the life of Jesus accounts "as narratives of actual facts."(53) Here, too, the vigorous rejection of Strauss came upon the stage at a point when the Leben-Jesu-Forschung had already left Strauss' "life" behind. Under Edwards Amasa Park, orthodox Trinitarians at Andover had consolidated the apologetic stance that had characterized Stuart's conservative biblical studies at Andover Seminary. The articles appearing under Park's editorship in Andover's home journal, the _Bibliotheca Sacra_, revealed, however, that it became increasingly difficult for Andover theologians to enlist the exegetical and historical principles of "lower" and "higher criticism," as Stuart had done, for the cause of orthodox Calvinism. Andover theologians acutely noted that biblical criticism modelled after Strauss, De Wette and Eichhorn posed a threat to orthodox Calvinism. Faced with the corrosive influence of the anti-supernaturalist criticism of Strauss and De Wette, Andover theologians in turn attempted to adjust to the new principles by steering away from an exclusive reliance on historical factuality and by infusing orthodox Calvinism with the sentiments of a "theology of the feelings."(54) This infusion reflected a shift from the position of supernatural rationalism to a theology of religious experience which sought to reconcile the claims of piety and reason. Andover theology in this respect testified to an important transitional stage of biblical criticism which entailed the rejection of the "neologists" of Tübingen and Göttingen in favor of the pietists and "mediating" theologians of Berlin and Halle.

In calling upon the "mediating school," Andover critics drew on theologians of the "mediating" camp who insisted that the "idea of humanity in Christ" required "legitimating, as much as the historical manifestation."(55) This position provided a method of preserving adherence to a supernatural rationalist framework and of fortifying assurance that the claims concerning the historical Jesus were valid. Yet the outcome of this method was frequently a modification of the value and scope of external and historical evidences. Under E. A. Park Andover critics thus refused to accept the allegation that a miracle was "the only logical proof" of the divine authority of Jesus. Miracles were no doubt "an important proof," but by no means the sole one.(56) The special claims of Christianity were not authenticated by uniquely inspired words and miracles but by "intrinsic evidence."

But once again the alignment with the mediating position could not completely dispel the significance of miraculous "evidences." It was only deemed permissible to subject the biblical narratives to criticism "like any other book," if the sources of faith were not called into question. Park and his colleague Calvin Ellis Stowe accordingly combined the results of historical criticism with the orthodox defenses of traditional authorship and integrity of the narratives to validate Scripture as "God's message to honest, intelligent, thoughtful men, sent to them by honest, intelligent, thoughtful men."(57) No matter what the results of historcal criticism might bring, they could not "shake to rock on which scriptural truth rests" or undermine the scriptural text as literal, authentic history.(58)

This premise was steadfastly perpetuated by the new generation of biblical critics at Andover after Stuart and Park represented by Joseph Henry Thayer and Charles Marsh Mead. Both men had been exposed first hand to the quest of Paulus, Strauss and Baur, but both did not substantially depart from Andover's tradition of apologetic criticism. Contrary to strict evidentialists, however, Thayer and Mead were prepared to handle the factuality issue with a new awareness of historical accuracy and objectivity. Both critics distinguished biblical claims from standards of historical factuality based on nineteenth century science and history. The authors of the biblical narratives, Thayer argued, "wrote to produce and confirm religious faith" of first and second centuries audiences and were, therefore, not concerned with chronological precision following scientific standards of the nineteenth century.(59) Thayer here formulated an important modification of the verisimilitude criterion. Evidentialists had been anxious to invest biblical claims with a status equivalent to the factual "evidences" in contemporary scientific assertions. This factual evidentialist status was now recognized as distinct, as deriving from an intention all its own.

Both Thayer and Mead were also sufficiently attuned to the Leben-Jesu-Forschung to enlist the quest's development after Strauss for the cause of conservative, apologetic criticism. In advanced critical research on the authorship and origin of scriptural texts, Thayer and Mead were prepared to dethrone biblical authoritarianism and recognized discrepancies in the synoptic accounts of Jesus as well as the shared dependence on oral traditions and collections. Yet Thayer and Mead were not ready to approve the source critical thesis of Mark's priority and stopped well short of the solutions of the synoptic problem proposed by Leben Jesu researchers.(60) In the 1870s and 1880s the factuality issue still so dominated the orthodox Trinitarian bastion of exegesis that the development of source and form critical procedures was severely hampered. With Thayer, all four Gospels presented equally "trustworthy accounts of the life of Jesus" and to favor Mark as the earliest and most original of the synoptic accounts was simply to resort to a biased, "extreme opinion."(61)

III

In 1843, the Dial described "the folly of an age, when ... (Strauss') books were needed; when Christians would not believe a necessary and everlasting truth unless it were accompanied and vouched for a contingent and empirical event which they presumed to call a miracle!"(62) Two decades later, Strauss' work and the critical exegesis of the quest was "needed" again for "uses" prevalent among Transcendentalists who had shifted towards conservatism. The members of the Broad Church group, all of whom had supported the Transcendental Club, emerged in the 1860s as theological conservatives closer to Channing than to Parker and Emerson. James Freeman Clarke and Frederick Henry Hedge, outstanding representatives of this group, adhered to an intuitionist position discarding biblicism and religious tradition in favor of the notion of the indwelling of God within the soul. But Hedge and Clarke combined Transcendentalist intuition with an adherence to the historical continuity represented by the church. This reassertion of ecclesiastical elements of historical Christianity's supernaturalism strikingly departed from the Transcendentalist assumption that there were no abiding religious institutions and, consequently, no necessity for the historic church.

"Some thirty years," Hedge observed of the Transcendentalist movement in 1867, "a club was formed of young men, mostly preachers of the Unitarian connection, ... all fired with the hope of a new era in philosophy and religion, which seemed to them about to dawn upon the world. There was something in the air, - a boding of some great revolution...." By the 1860s no such revolution had occurred; on the contrary, segments of the movement had shifted backwards. Thus Hedge's "historic conscience ... (had) balanced (his) neology, and kept (him) ecclesiastically conservative," always aligning the free functioning of divine intuition with a strong commitment to ecclesiastical continuity.(63) This commitment confronted the group with a double opposition. The insistence on continuous revelation was contrary to Norton's adherence to historically recorded revelation, while the preservation of faith in biblically recorded miracles was incompatible with the extreme Transcendentalist position. In keeping with the Broad Church's insistence on the centrality of the historical Jesus, the rejection of historic Christianity was accordingly held to "suppose Christ to be defeated by the Anti-Christ." Hence Emerson was not regarded as a Christian "in the usual and distinctive sense of the term;" his position had no place for the "Lordship of Christ," reducing Christ to "a mere teacher of moral and religious truths - a reformer, not distinguished from other teachers and reformers...." "On this point (the Broad Church men were) at issue with him, and the difference between (them was) heaven-wide."(64)

The intellectual divisiveness between Hedge, Clarke and the Transcendentalist ministers extended in particular to the interpretation of Jesus' miracles. Hedge was at one with Parker and Ripley in counteracting supernaturalists who used miracles "as proofs of divine authority" and evidence of Jesus' status. Adhering to a religion validated by individual intuition, Hedge was convinced that miracles were not designed to force conviction and authenticate Christ's mission. Yet Hedge was prepared to accept the possibility of miracles and did not completely dismiss the historical matrix of Christianity. Hedge believed in them because he was convinced "that spiritual powers are superior to physical, and may hold them in subjection, ... that the soul is stronger than material nature, and may command it when it truly commands itself; and because .. the person of Jesus (is) a greater miracle than any of the works recorded of him."(65)

With Hedge, however, this did not render miracles foundational to Christianity. Hedge set out to "distinguish, moreover, in so-called miracles of the New Testament, between the essential fact and the manner in which it is presented in the record. (He conceived) that a nucleus of historic truth, in a credulous age, may gather to itself a mystic embodiment which is questionable. Intelligent criticism must separate, if possible, the one from the other." This statement made clear that "Christianity has nothing to fear from criticism." But this criticism was of a special kind; it did not "treat all miracle as fable (or) rule out of the record whatever contradicts the ordinary course of human experience ...," nor did it bring the exegete "to accept, as his solution of the great historic and miraculous fact of Christianity, the theory by a recent critic, - that eighteen hundred years ago, in Galilee and Judea, on the shores of Tiberias and round about Jordan, - 'nothing happened.'"(66) Against this historical scepticism of the Leben-Jesu-Forschung Hedge pressed a more constructive purpose of historical exegesis, namely to "reconcile the credit of the record with the credibility of the facts recorded, (to) separate what is essential in the record from what is incidental; the central fact from the form in which it appears."(67)

Hedge's critical methodology corresponded to the form critical task of distilling the "kernel" from the "husk" of embellishment and accretion. This presented another significant advance over harmonistic, pre-critical evidentialism. With both Hedge and Clarke, however, the recognition of the form-critical stance was not accompanied by corresponding developments in textual criticism and source criticism. Clarke dismissed the latest findings of contemporary source criticism as "arguments ... which ... unsettle the authenticity of any book...."(68) The differences between the Jesus of John and the Jesus of the Synoptics were explained by the supposition that the Fourth Gospel was "dictated by the aged apostle to his inquiring disciples at different times near the close of his life...." "Much was omitted with which they were already familiar, and some things added to supply the deficiencies in existing narratives."(69) The discrepancies and inaccuracies in the chronology of the Last Supper and the Passion were similarly accounted for by the assumption that John dictated his Gospel in fragments which his followers combined in a flawed manner. Strauss' insistence that "the veritable Christ" was not to be found in the Fourth Gospel here went unnoticed.(70)

Clarke's uncritical stance throughout equated accounts with authentic events in the life of Jesus and did not relate them to the author's theological intentions. Thus Clarke advanced as the key explanation for the Synoptics' silence about the visits of Jesus to Jerusalem which the Fourth Gospel describes that "Jesus went alone, or with only one or two of his disciples, as a private Jew, to the national festivals. For this reason, the Synoptics omit mention of them; but John, who may have gone with his Master at these times, found sufficient interest in the conversations to record them as he was able to remember them."(71) Clarke owed this treatment of the Fourth Gospel as the most historical and authentic account of Jesus to Karl August Hase, whose life of Jesus Clarke translated in 1865. With Hase, Clarke drew on a strain of criticism which perpetuated Schleiermacher's uncritical view of John as the recorder of a precise chronology and which dismissed the assumptions of the two-source hypothesis. In this interpretation no substantial differences in the key ideas and phrases of the four Gospels existed. "The Gospel cannot contradict itself," Clarke reiterated. Moreover, "the merely critical understanding," Clarke was convinced, "is like the natural man who received not the things of the spirit of God. They are spiritually discerned." Hedge agreed: "What is written is open to criticism, for the soul is greater than any scripture, and nothing can be more foreign from the spirit of Christianity than a slavish interpretation of its records."(72)

According to the Broad Church group, the scriptural records were in some places inadequate and seemed "rather to conceal (Christ) than to reveal him."(73) The Broad Church group's insight into the inadequacy of the life of Jesus accounts as a historical "chronicle" pertained directly to the key opposition of the quest between the Jesus of history and the Christ of faith. "By the very necessity of its function, history idealizes," Hedge observed. "The historic figure and the individual represented by it, though inseparably one in substance, are not so identical in outline that the one exactly covers the other.... The individual is the bodily presence as it dwells in space; the historic figure is the image of himself which the individual stamps on his time, and ... - his import to human kind. That image is a veritable portrait, but not in the sense of a fac-simile...."(74) With regard to the historical Jesus, this characteristic was particularly acute. "When the historical Christ had receded into the distance of a by-gone age," Hedge argued, "Christian faith, no longer satisfied with bare historic fact, idealized the person of Christ, exalted him above earthly limitations into something superhuman and divine; and here and there went so far as to make him pure spirit, assuming the likeness of man but divested of all natural belongings, without flesh and blood, a divine apparition."(75)

This was an apt restatement of the quest's most prominent theme, one from which, in the case of Hedge, an acceptance of Strauss' mythical approach seemed legitimate. Hedge was prepared to "contend that historic truth is not the only truth; that a fact ... which is not historically true may yet be true on a higher plane than that of history...."(76) On the basis of this assertion a positive appreciation of the apologetic function of Strauss' myth criticism became possible. Traditionally, in Strauss "the truth of Christianity was supposed to be assailed; the belief in Christianity as divine revelation was felt to be imperilled by a theory which substituted mythical figment for historic fact." But Hedge found "that no such harm was intended...." With Strauss, "the inner kernel of Christian faith" was in effect "entirely independent of all such criticism." According to Strauss' terms, the "mythical interpretation by renouncing the historical body ..., rescues and preserves the idea...." Therefore, "Christ's supernatural birth, his miracles, his resurrection and ascension, remain eternal truths, however their reality as facts of history may be called in question."(77)

The approval of this view, Hedge realized, liberated Christianity from the reliance on "the strict historic verity of all narrative of the New Testament...." Hedge was convinced that "not the historic sense, but the spiritual import; not the facts, but the ideas of the Gospel, (were) the genuine topics of faith."(78) The "truth of Christianity," then, was "not identical and coterminus with the literal truth of its record." With this, the key premise of evidentialism in the supernatural rationalist tradition felt into disfavor. The "record" as "veritable history" presented "a literary relic of inestimable value ... only as it (drew) its inspiration from and (led one's) aspiration to the ideal Christ."(79) And on this count, and here only Strauss' approach was congenial to Hedge's cause. Strauss' "life" guided its audience to "aspire to the ideal Christ," purging the life of Jesus accounts of "falsifications," "corruptions," and "spurious additaments, interpolations, and misinterpretations."(80) Through this "purgation" "the ideal Christ" - not the historical Jesus - could be reached, and in this purgation the "real question (was) not whether Jesus said or did precisely this or that in each particular instance, but whether Christianity (was) true and divine, the power of God and the wisdom of God unto salvation...."(81) As on Strauss' native ground, then, the Leben Jesu was here used to bypass source criticism and downplay the uncertainties of historical criticism. The apologetic bias of Strauss' life of Jesus which the generation of biblical critics around Norton and Stuart had ignored by equating the mythical approach with mere "pantheism" or destructive deism now stood - in a very delayed response - recovered and became a decisive starting point for Strauss' entry into American biblical studies.

But the Strauss who entered the American scene was one divested of distinct tendencies towards a form critical, kerygmatic stance. Strauss' argument was welcome as a tool loosening the rigidity of the historicist tenet and uncovering the tenuous links between the records of Jesus' life and the apostles' witness. Only of secondary interest was the fact that Strauss also shifted the ground of life of Jesus research to "the spirit of people or a community," to the religious imagery and faith portraits of a religious community.(82) Strauss' insight that "the evangelical history (was) embellished with pious legends," shaped and reshaped in the mind of the early Christian community received no sustained application in the hands of exegetes still predominantly concerned with the actuality of scriptural events and the pristine status of the "ideal Christ" of faith.(83)

Instead of Strauss' form critical stance it was the literary viewpoint of Baur's redaction criticism which occupied a more permanent place in the Broad Church group's exegesis. "The peculiarity of the critical movement initiated by Baur is this," Clarke observed, "that it has substituted for the mythical theory ... that of 'tendency.'" The New Testament authors here were asserted to have produced their accounts "with a tendency in their mind toward certain beliefs; which tendency acted like a purpose, leading them to modify facts to suit their aim."(84) Methodologically, Baur's "tendency-theory," the Christian Examiner judged, presented "a striking specimen of the historical style of treatment as distinguished from ... the abstract-critical ... illustrated by Eichhorn, ... Schleiermacher, De Wette, and Credner, and from the dialectical, or negative critical ... pursued by Strauss and his opponents."(85) In Baur's distinctive conjunction of comparative literary analysis with "tendency" criticism, the central theological key to the Gospel tradition and the history of dogma consisted in two oppositions, the first between Pauline and Judaic Christianity, the second between the Catholic Church and Gnosticism. The implications of this position were spelled out for the Broad Church men in R. W. Mackay's 1863 study on The Tübingen and Its Antecedents. According to Baur's "tendency" criticism, Mackay explained, "Matthew is supposed to represent especially the Judaical tradition ...; Luke is a conciliatory aggregate of Judaical notions and narratives, superadded to a Pauline basis, ... considered as the purest and most important document of Paulinism."(86)

The theological presuppositions and results of Baur's insistence on the antagonism between the Petrine and Pauline tendencies in the Gospel tradition hardly came into play in Clarke's own scrutiny of The Ideas of the Apostle Paul. Similarly, O. B. Frothingham was more concerned with the issue of the "overwhelming probability of actual unauthenticity" Baur applied to a "third class" of Pauline Epistles, the so-called Pastoral Epistles.(87) Baur's essay on "The so-called Pastoral Letters, of the Apostle Paul," Frothingham recapitulated, "startled" "the believing public by the announcement that these Epistles were written with polemical intent against the Gnostics of the school of Marcion" and therefore dated from a post-Pauline era, around the middle of the second century."(88) Consonant with the evidentialist stance in the life of Jesus studies, the primary interest for American reviewers in the study of the Pauline corpus was "the question of genuineness," an issue subjected to historical scepticism by Baur's argument that segments of the New Testament record "were possibly innocent fictions, produced for purposes of edification" and "that the Acts of the Apostles (could) not ... be relied on for information concerning the life and opinions of Paul."(89) Clarke's response to this argument distinctly stayed within the bounds of evidentialism. Clarke took his stand with "more recent criticism" of the quest represented by Pfleiderer and Holtzmann, who refrained from "depreciating the historic value of the Book of Acts" and affirmed instead "that the author of Luke's Gospel, and of the Book of Acts, laid down a critical and historic method for his gospel and 'undeniably carried it out.'"(90)

With Clarke, a decisive shift away from an "apologetic theology" revolving around the issues of "genuineness" and historicity was triggered, not by the procedures of literary-critical "tendency" analysis but rather by the methods of comparative religion. For Clarke's Ten Great Religions. An Essay in Comparative Theology, the "main question" was "not whether ... religion is or is not supernatural; not whether Christ's miracles were or not violations of law; nor whether the New Testament ... is the work of inspired men." Rather, "the real problem of apologetic theology" "(was) this: Is Christianity, as taught by Jesus, intended by God to be the religion of the human race?"(91) In this context the premises of evidentialism were merely presupposed. "Comparative theology," Clarke explained, "differs from the traditional argument in this: that, while the last undertakes to prove Christianity to be true, this shows it to be true."(92) Clarke here took "authenticity" of the life of Jesus accounts for granted; literary-critical exegesis was not mandatory in the shift away from the biblical text to its historical context.

Commenting on "results to which the study of Comparative Theology may lead," Clarke highlighted as the central outcome "the fulness of Christianity ... derived from the life of Jesus."(93) The appreciation of the multiplicity of religions attested in Clarke's Ten Great Religions and in the selections from Oriental scriptures put together in The Radical and The Index expressly preserved the central assertions of "historical Christianity." "The radical," Clarke reassured his audience, "certainly considers Christ and the Bible as a source of truth - only he does not go to them so much as to others. He goes to science; he goes to the Vedas ...; he goes to Emerson and Thoreau; he goes to Theodore Parker, Herbert Spencer and Miss Cobbe."(94) Clarke accordingly acknowledged other religions as authentic ways of expressing the human experience, yet he clearly assigned superiority to Christianity: "Christianity alone, of all human religions, seems to possess the power of keeping abreast with the advancing civilization of the world." And to this supremacy, Clarke maintained, the life of Jesus gave the most pristine testimony: "The Gospel of Jesus continues the soul of all human culture."(95) Judged against the gospel of the quest, this entailed the affirmation of the "fact of a fulness of divine and human life in Jesus" whose "greatness ... may have been just here, - that he was the man of men, the truest man, fulfilling the type of humanity."(96)

IV

The uniqueness and "greatness" of Jesus, Clarke judged, was no longer prevalent among "Free-Religionists," left-wing Unitarians of the 1870s and 1880s who were acutely aware of "the inevitable surrender of orthodoxy" and set out in turn to construct their "liberal movement in theology" upon "the primary facts of human experience."(97) According to Clarke's observations, Free Religionists denied "that Jesus was the founder of a church; or author either of a religion; of authority in belief, or ethics; or authority in faith."(98) Committed to humanistic convictions, liberal Unitarians from the 1870s onwards were sceptical of all "speculative" christology: "What we need," Octavius Brooks Frothingham, chief exponent of the Free

Religionists, asserted, "is ... not some new theory about Jesus, but some new appreciation of the manhood that belongs to every man."(99)

For the left-wing Unitarians gathered in the Free Religion movement the insistence on the indwelling of God in man was primary. The indwelling of divinity in man was not reserved for the historic Christ only but rather belonged to mankind as such. Moreover, Free Religion designated "a system of belief and method of life which grows up in the human mind, independently of any such historic source, preceeding only from the soul itself."(100) It was therefore deemed imperative to "take the mask off religion ... to show (that) ... that much boasted symbol of Christ (was) purely imaginary ... (and to) ... exhibit it as a symbol which humanity in its best moments had looked to and hoped to realize." The historic Christ, then, was no elevated divinity, nor a redeemer, a Savior, but rather a symbol of "humanity."(101)

With this interpretation the Leben Jesu studies appeared congenial. Appropriating the terms of the quest, O. B. Frothingham thus asserted that "the Christ of Paul, who started the conception, was not a man, but the man, nor the man only, but the ideal man, the possible man, the spiritual man, that is the soul of humanity. ... To try to crowd the attributes of the theological Christ into the personality of the historical Jesus, is to plant a whole forest in a porcelain vase." Here the "dogmatic" opposition between the Jesus of history and the Christ of faith, running as a recurrent theme through the Leben Jesu studies from Reimarus to Strauss, was fully absorbed. With Paulus and Strauss, Frothingham was convinced that "by carrying over to the historical Jesus the impressions that theology had formed of him, and reading his life by the light of pure speculation ... men ... construct a very plausible argument, which crumbles to pieces on the first intelligent perusal of the New Testament. The Christ of the Christian theology is not the Jesus of the Gospels, but a purely ideal person, a conception, an imagination, an intellectual vision, a splendid spiritual dream."(102)

Frothingham's focus on the "antidogmatic" import of the historical Jesus quest was continuous with Parker's biblical criticism. What had interested Parker most in the opposition between "the Jesus of fact and the Christ of fancy" - over and above biblical-exegetical aspects - was the critique the dichotomy imparted on the "popular churches of Christendom" with their edifice of "artificial sacraments."(103) Consonant with this predominance of the polemical "antidogmatic" uses of the historical Jesus quest over biblical-exegetical issue were the claims for the divinity and creative power of man which both Parker and Frothingham found in Strauss. Strauss confirmed for both that the indwelling of divinity in man was not limited to the historical Jesus but rather incarnate in the entire human race. Thus Frothingham, no less than Parker, "(looked) on Jesus as the highest product of the human race," a "product" which revealed the "greatness of justice, greatness of philanthropy, greatness of religion."(104) For this reading of the figure of Jesus, however, a historico-critical reconstruction of Jesus' life in the manner of Holtzmann was not imperative; nor was it necessary to pay sustained attention to the methodology of interpretation or to questions of the literary origin and the different "forms" of the Gospel tradition.

"Free Religion took as its main premise the rejection of "the authority of all historic religion, and (went) to the instincts of the individual as its origin and authority."(105) Yet the acceptance of the "dogmatic" opposition between the Jesus of history and the Christ of faith brought in its wake also the introduction of more advanced techniques of comparative life of Jesus study. "Free Religion," Clarke observed, "denies that Christianity is the absolute religion, and regards it as limited.... It holds that everything true and good in Christianity had already been taught by other religions."(106) Frothingham's "Bible of Humanity" therefore incorporated world religions and judged that "the Bible of Christendom, be it made ever so comprehensive ... will not satisfy the wants of humanity. The Religion of Humanity must have a broader word," Frothingham was convinced.(107) With regard to the status of the historic Christ, this comparative stance entailed the view that the Christ of Christendom was just another example of the incarnation of the divine mind also represented by Zoroaster, Mohammed and Confucius. A generation ahead of the mainstream, the Free Religionists thus placed the historical Jesus in a context of cultural relativism. The Jesus of Norton had been largely cut off from the context in which the historical Jesus preached; with Frothingham, however, the religio-historical insight into the cultural relativity of the Jesus of history was rapidly gaining ground.

The view that all aspects of Jesus history were relative to social-cultural factors also prepared the way for the appropriation of the redaction criticism practised by the Tübingen school. If the "idea" of Christ was indeed embedded in legend, fable, cultural reflections, then a new "historical" method "as distinguished from the dogmatical, the textual, the negative" and a new theory about the composition of the Gospels were required, one for which Baur's "tendency criticism" provided the methodological precedent. Baur, Frothingham's life of Jesus study, The Cradle of the Christ, acknowledged, "finds the key to the secret of the composition of the first three Gospels, the Acts of the Apostles and portions of other books, in the quarrel between Paul and Peter.... The 'synoptical' Gospels ... are the results of that controversy between the broad and the narrow churches; are not, therefore, writings of historical value or biographical moment, but books of a doctrinal character, ... written in a controversial interest...."(108)

Given this "doctrinal character" of the documents, a purely historical criticism "occupied with the task of establishing the genuineness and authenticity of the writings, ... explaining texts in accordance with the preconceived theory of a divine origin, vindicating doubtful passages against the objections of skeptics" was insufficient. Expressly departing from evidentialist emphases, Frothingham held that this type of criticism falsely "insisted on the necessity of a historical foundation for (Jesus') character." For a critic who had absorbed the lessons of the mythologists this was a "strange position to take, in view of the fact that idealization is one of the commonest facts of mankind; that the human imagination is continually constructing heroes out of poltrooms, and transmuting lead into gold."(109)

One of the chief outcomes of this view was the rejection of the possibility of producing a critical "life." Strauss had written his "life" to terminate all further life of Jesus studies. Similarly, Frothingham's The Cradle of the Christ presented a life of Jesus account only to counteract its very possibility and legitimacy. In Frothingham's study "no account (was) given of Jesus, and no account made of him." But "the omission," Frothingham explained, "has been intentional. The purpose ... is to give the history of an idea, not the history of a person, to trace the development of a thought, not the influence of a life...."(110) This was to restate a view which Frothingham had been advancing since his review of

General Hitchcock's Christ the Spirit in the 1860s: The Evangelists were theologians of the "Christ of humanity." The historic Christ was "pure spirit" and present everywhere. A fixation in time and place, the critical reconstruction of a historical-objective "kernel" was therefore not possible.

V

For the Unitarian tradition of biblical criticism represented by William Henry Furness, the departure from the "liberal-positive" quest at first seemed less obvious. While left-wing groups postulated an "absolute religion" liberated from historical integuments, reducing historic incarnation to the terms of a broad humanism, Furness shared the "liberal-positive" questers' confidence in the possibility of reconstructing the historical Jesus and, like Clarke, preferred Hase to Holtzmann and Keim to Baur. Heinrich Holtzmann's proposal for the solution of the synoptic problem in 1863 laid the foundation for the acceptance of the two-source theory. For Furness and his colleagues, however, this source critical point was not of primary interest, nor were they concerned with the attempt to defend "the gospel history ... by adducing the coincidences between the Old Testament prophecies and the New Testament events; by appealing to the independent testimony of the four eye-witnesses by whom the Gospels were written; ..." What counted, J. T. Bixby observed in 1869 in a review of the "liberal-positive" quest, was that the Jesus of Holtzmann, Keim, Weizsäcker and Schenkel was given a definite religious personality - a "character." And the fact that the Gospels delineated this "great character" was, Bixby judged, "indisputable," "whether the Gospels be fictitious or historical."(111)

With regard to the possibility of reconstructing a "character" portrait of Jesus, the traditional harmony literature appeared to the generation of questers represented by O. B. Frothingham and E. E. Hale increasingly deficient. The "so-called harmonies the Gospels," Frothingham found, "widely ... (differed), not only in the arrangement of detail, but in their conclusions!"(112) Commenting on the harmonies of William Newcome, Lant Carpenter, Edward Robinson and Simon Greenleaf, Hale further highlighted "the quiet coolness ... with which ... critics pass by the changes in the course of the Saviour's life, without any attempt to suggest cause and effect, motive or plan, or indeed any of the evidences of organic life running through the whole...." Hale "ascribed" this characteristic "not to indifference, but to respect which really amounts to superstition," a "superstition," however, Hale saw giving way to "the other theology, which ... believes that Christ was tempted as we are, and learned obedience by the things that he suffered. The systematic study of his life then," Hale judged, "becomes essential in the study of the new life."(113)

Hale's demand for a "new life" of Jesus was undertaken in part by both "liberal-positive" and "mediating" questers who sought "to explain the gradual development of the consciousness of Jesus, in perfect accordance with the laws of human life...."(114) Yet in Unitarian reviews of this focus on "character" development, the supernatural rationalist stance with its accompanying scepticism about the possibility of a psychological penetration of the figure of Jesus acutely resurfaced. Thus J. H. Morison thought Neander's Jesus "portrait" "more bold than successful." Morison firmly believed "in a peculiar influence exercised by God over his Son from the first miraculous inception of his being" and therefore did not "know ... how to form from the development of other minds any theory of spiritual growth applicable."(115) Morison's reaffirmation of supernaturalism precluded a biographical, developmental approach to the life of Jesus, a "life" Morison judged to have been "subjected to influences in kind or degree wholly beyond what is usual in our human experience."(116) With regard to the "Influence of the Character of Christ," the Christian Examiner observed in similar terms that the "difference is not measurable between (Jesus) and other men whose mission had personal loneliness.... Compared with Christ the greatest historical characters ... seem unreal."(117) All attempts to subject this pristine figure to "aesthetic" or "poetic" refinements were therefore "utterly defective."(118) A. P. Peabody accordingly observed of Hase's life of Jesus that Hase's aim was "not to determine what the Evangelists meant to relate, but to mould their representations into conformity with his own ideal of the Christ." In this way, Peabody charged, Hase "admits the supernatural element in the Gospels, but subordinates it to his own aesthetic sense...."(119) At stake here was once again not the problem of recovering the historical Jesus which was of interest to Leben Jesu researchers. With American questers, the possibility of historical reconstruction was taken for granted; the problem at issue was instead "the difficulty of sustaining the character of our Saviour under new circumstances...."(120)

"Of one thing ... (the Christian Examiner was) sure" in this context, and this point was not to be matched by any "liberal-positive" Leben Jesu study: "No legitimate study of the life of Jesus will attempt the task, for which neither criticism, nor philosophy is competent, of laying bare the mystery of his moral and spiritual power. ... our criticism ... will leave unexplained the mystery embodied in the great central fact of the world's history, that this child of the Jewish synagogue, who taught as the prophets, ... was also the very Christ of God, the truth, life, and way of heaven."(121) This insight into the limitation of historico-critical methods put Unitarian exegetes in line with Strauss' and Schweitzer's sceptical assessment of the quest. But in the Unitarian admission of the possibility of critical reconstruction the recourse to historical factuality remained unquestioned. Thus Furness was "struck with the fact that ("liberal-positive" questers like Schenkel) appear never to perceive that the records owe their existence to the reality of the facts recorded. ... They look everywhere but directly at the facts related, to solve the secret of their having passed into history." For Furness, this deficiency was unacceptable; what was to "be settled before anything else can be settled (was) the historical truth concerning Jesus."(122) And on this issue Furness' position had remained constant since the 1830s, continually bypassing the premises of Strauss and his followers: Jesus' "character ... is an all-sufficient witness. ... He was no preternatural apparition. He was not myth. He was a Solid Fact at once human and divine...."(123)

The reluctance to subject the figure of Jesus to the terms of psychological "development" was also prevalent among the Broad Church men and Free Religionists who felt less committed to the premise of evidentialism. Thus Clarke had strong reservations about the legitimacy and foundation of a biographical-literary approach to the life of Jesus. The "Gospel are put together without any method; with no biographical art," Clarke observed. "If the Evangelists had been asked to write a biography of Jesus, in the style of Strauss, Renan, or Neander, ... they could not have done it. They did not understand him enough, to invent any part of the story." "The Evangelists simply remember: they do not compose."(124) Nevertheless Clarke's contemporaries in the Free Religionist camp were prepared to acknowledge the biographical-literary approach of Renan's life of Jesus which apparently overcame the limitations of the Gospels' testimony. "Considered from a literary point of view," Frothingham conceded, Renan's "life" "is a work of rare perfection." Frothingham found "here truly a life of Jesus of Nazareth, ... a real human life with human cares and recreations, helps and hinderances, prudences and mistakes, victories and overthrows."(125)

With Renan, the history of Jesus turned into "a romance" "pervaded with an atmosphere of natural, simple, pastoral joyousness." Renan's Jesus was, Frothingham found, "a child of Nature, ... a splendid idealist," "a splendid visionary," "a believer in his Utopia, an unconscious and informal, but a true and sincere brother of the Essenes."(126) But given this Jesus "seen at a distance and by poetic gaze," Frothingham's _The Cradle of the Christ_ deemed it impossible to "know that Jesus was such a person, ... that the most spiritual apprehension of him, was the truest."(127) Renan's "treatment of the materials before him (was) arbitrary and capricious," Frothingham judged.(128) Moreover, Renan was simply "forgetting the place that Jesus holds in the estimation of the world; forgetting the effects he has wrought on the souls, hearts, lives of men, ..." Renan "imputes to (Jesus)," Frothingham charged, "the weaknesses of ordinary humanity, judges him by the rules he would apply to ordinary men, condemns or praises him, ... as if he were an unknown actor in the medley of ordinary history...."(129) With regard to this charge, Frothingham was in full accord with Furness' "Remarks on Renan's Life of Jesus." Both Furness and Frothingham objected "on grounds higher than critical ... to (Renan's) interpretation...." Renan offered "a theory utterly fatal to the moral character of the 'colossal' man he (celebrated), thus sacrificing the moral greatness of Jesus to a perverse sense of historical truth...."(130) Furness and Frothingham, in contrast, sought a "life of Jesus ... written from a spiritual point of view," a "life" in which both psychological causation pertaining to a human figure and doctrinal "attributes of the Christ of theologians" receded behind "a way of dwelling on each event in the life of (the) Saviour till it (became) a quickening influence in (one's) own hearts."(131)

For this experiental approach Frothingham affirmed the premise that "to reach the historical Jesus, we must come down to him from above, not creep up to him from below." In the application of this premise, two options were available. The first, represented by Bushnell's chapter on the life of Jesus in _Nature and the Supernatural_, carried out the "spiritual point of view" by placing intuitive and "moral" sensibilities over and above the cognitive. Bushnell's essay on the life of Jesus, Frothingham observed in the _Christian Examiner_, related the life of Jesus "by simply putting the Christ of the Church into the text of the Evangelist, thus reading the chronicles of the first century by the light of the nineteenth." Yet on the exegetical plane Bushnell's approach was strikingly deficient. Bushnell was "utterly unconscious of the existence of Biblical critics; for him," Frothingham charged, "New Testament records are authentic as they stand. He seems not so much as to suspect that such men as Bretschneider and Semler, Paulus and Strauss, Gförer, Schwegler, or Baur, have lived and written."(132)

That an acknowledgement and application of the advances in biblical criticism was imperative was readily conceded by Frothingham's contemporaries. For the reconstruction of the "character" of Jesus a "new" critical exegesis was needed, H. G. Spaulding observed in the Christian Examiner in 1867: "Hither to we have denied that the teachings of Jesus could have either rind or husk; and, transferring our ideal Christ to the pages of the evangelists, have made sad havoc with truth and nature by our violent theories of accommodation and substitution. A constructive criticism of the gospel records is the field of labor which now invites the Christian scholar."(133) On this count, Spaulding was prepared to acknowledge the achievements of "liberal-positive" questers like Keim and Schenkel. Keim's "life," Spaulding judged, "gives perhaps the best account to be found of the human development of Jesus, written from the point of view of a positive, but thorough impartial criticism."(134) That this "impartial criticism" was with regard to its source criticism in fact anachronistic, Spaulding did not mark. At a time when the priority of Mark was widely accepted in the Leben-Jesu-Forschung, Keim still dated Matthew before A. D. 70 and regarded Mark as the latest of the Synoptics. For reviewers, however, still preoccupied primarily with the problem of the credibility of the biblical narratives, this deficient investigation of the records' date and literary relationship was still acceptable.

In Furness' life of Jesus studies, which presented yet another "spiritual" approach to the history of Jesus, the source critical advances of the Leben-Jesu-Forschung did not go unnoticed. Furness' Christian Examiner review of Weisse's Die Evangelienfrage in ihrem gegenwärtigen Stadium, De Wette's An Historico-Critical Introduction to the Canonical Books of the New Testament, Bleek's Beiträge zur Evangelischen Kritik recapitulated the source critics' combination of Lessing's Ur-gospel hypothesis with the Griesbach hypothesis. For De Wette and Bleek, Mark was dependent upon Matthew and Luke, who in turn relied on an Urevangelium reconstructed from material common to both. Against this source critical hypothesis, Furness acutely noted, "objections on the score of credibility" pertained primarily to the Fourth Gospel now regarded "to be destitute of nearly all historical authority."(135) Furness' edition of Daniel Schenkel's The Character of Jesus Portrayed further acknowledged that "of (Jesus') character ... a 'clearer image' (was available) in Mark than in either of the other Gospels" since the "Urmarcus, or original Gospel" yielded a substantial link with earlier eyewitness tradition.(136) With Furness' colleagues, however, this source critical point did not take root. Given the persistent supremacy of the issue of "authenticity," reviewers highlighted instead Schenkel's "decisive argument ... against the genuineness of (Mark's) Gospel." Schenkel's "'Picture of the Character of Christ,' considered from a purely humanitarian point of view," J. H. Allen observed in a review article for the Christian Examiner, presented "stories of control over the elements of nature ... undisguisedly as 'legend' and 'myth,' ... the raising of the dead (as) unauthentic, or a mistake; (and) the resurrection of Jesus himself ... (as existing) only in the pious imagination of his disciples."(137) Confronted with this blunt criticism of the postulate of "genuineness," the majority of reviewers remained "content ... to rest on the old foundation of four distinct accounts of Jesus, prepared by Apostles and companions of Apostles, with variations in statements and in style, showing their separate independence and individuality, and all together, ... furnishing chains of evidence as strong, ... as authentic and compact, as the nature of the subject and those distant ages, could admit."(138) For this position, the relationship of source critical theories to systematic theology was of no concern. Nor did the problem of the religious consciousness of Jesus ever receive the acute scrutiny to which the "liberal-positive" "character portraits" subjected it. The primary issue was instead the fact that the synoptic Gospels "all point.... to Christ as a veritable historical personage...."(139)

In the case of the Fourth Gospel, however, the affirmation of the "genuineness" postulate became increasingly problematic. The "fourth gospel," Frothingham observed, "is a purely literary work; a composition, the production of an artist in language. Trace of an historical Jesus in it there is none." For these characteristics pertaining to "a book, not a gospel," Baur's method of "literary criticism" appeared most appropriate to Frothingham, "for it (was) concerned with the literary composition of the New Testament writings, and with the dispute as accounting for their existence and from."(140) "The literary method," Frothingham acknowledged, "avoids the dogmatical embarassments incident to the supernatural theory; ... connects incidents with their antecedents; ... and places fragments in the places where they belong."(141) But Frothingham's acknowledgement of form and tradition criticism found no followers. Focusing once again on the implications of Baur's "literary method" for the "genuineness" of the Fourth Gospel, Clarke remained convinced that "the long-received opinion of the Christian church" regarding the "historic fact of authorship" was "not likely to be reversed in consequence of the ... arguments of the school of Tübingen."(142) Even though he conceded that "none have done more that the School of Tübingen to open new questions in regard to Christianity, its history and records," Clarke chose to enlist Baur's method for the cause of evidentialism. "So, when the assaults of destructive criticism have laid low ... special theories of inspiration, and ... received arguments for authenticity, it may be found that the Scriptures rest on a more solid foundation than before."(143)

Yet Frothingham himself did "not deny that Baur has done grievous harm to historical Christianity."(144) Frothingham could "not forgive (Baur) for leaving out of his original Christianity, such as it is, the person of Christ."(145) This deficiency was "to be explained," Frothingham judged, "not by (Baur's) critical method, ... but by the leading principle of his Hegelian philosophy...." According to Frothingham, Baur's Hegelianism "(affected) directly the historical reality of Christ's character...." "By affirming that the evaluation of thought is the self-revelation of God, (Hegelianism made) great account of ideas, but none whatever of persons, - (it represented) doctrines as if they were living beings, and (resolved) living beings into steppingstones of doctrine."(146)

Behind this rejection of Baur's "bleak intellectualism" stood the standard arguments against the alleged "atheism" and "pantheism" of Hegelianism reiterated by both "old" and "new school" members. Hegelianism presented "a philosophy of history," the Christian Examiner judged, "in which ... philosophy drains away the blood from history," thus leaving "no germ of personality."(147) "Incarnation," Stuart observed in similar terms, here "(amounted) only to a satisfactory proof that the union of God and man is possible, which man in his natural state is inclined to disbelieve."(148) Moreover, the Hegelian God-man constituted for reviewers a "theoretical Christ, ... not the historical Christ, who bore the name of Jesus. The mind of humanity, and that alone, includes all the attributes of the hegelian Christ." This amounted to an open rejection of the historicity of the individual figure of Jesus: "There never existed an individual formed, by special privilege of the divine and the human essence, ruling nature, working miracles, raised bodily from the dead."(149)

This "weakest side (of Strauss), the question of genuineness," was perpetuated, David Hasbrouck observed in a review for the Christian Examiner, by a critic who "by one leap ... passed from the extreme right to the extreme left of the school of Hegel."(150) As "the most extraordinary of (the) champions" of the "'Left Wing' of Hegelians," Bruno Bauer not only renewed for American reviewers the "downright charge of fraud and imposition on the part of the evangelists and apostles," but also brought up the startling thesis that the historical Jesus presented "only a dogma, only and ideal product of Christian consciousness."(151) While "Strauss supposed that ... the Jews, in the time of Christ had a complete Christology, a fixed messianic type on which the character of the Christ might have been modelled trait, ... Baur, on the contrary, (supposed)," Frothingham acutely observed, "that all the acts which exhibit Jesus ... as accomplishing the messianic ideal, and the ideal itself as well, were inventions of the primitive Christians."(152)

Bauer's "ideal Christ," however, was sharply distinguished from the "ideal Christ" of Furness, Hedge and Clarke. The latters' "ideal" was firmly rooted in the dependence and relativity of historical events. "The ideal Christ," Hedge pontificated, "is the root and ground of the historical."(153) Hedge and his contemporaries in biblical criticism were aware that their life of Jesus studies might fall short of any presumption that historical research could demonstrate the legitimacy of faith. They were also aware that revelation occurred in a historical process subject to later idealization. They were aware, moreover, that the latest advances in source criticism undercut evidentialism of the kind propagated by Norton. But none of these considerations could undermine what Furness persistently designated as "the historical truth concerning Jesus." "Take the extremest criticism even," the Unitarian Brooke Herford invited his readers, "suppose that not one of the four Gospels was actually written by those immediate followers of Christ whose names they bear; that it was some generations before the story of Jesus was thus written down at all. This does not affect the main facts. It does not affect the historic reality of that great figure which left such an impress on those around that even for so long, though unrecorded, it kept itself in mind so clearly and distinctly."(154)

11. "The Aim and Hope of Jesus"

"There are two ways of writing the life of Jesus," the North American Review observed in 1864, "the one is simply to ascertain and arrange the facts of his external history; the other is, then to go on and so interpret and explain those facts as to make it seen and felt what manner of man he was in spirit and purpose...." A "life" of this latter kind seemed to the Review "still ... eminently needed." It was necessary to have "first, ... a conviction founded on internal and external evidence that Jesus is the name of a real man, and not of a fictitious one; ... then ... to appreciate his true relation at once to God and to man. And then, too," it was believed, "the life of Jesus will be brought into such a light that it can be seen to be the Gospel of to-day."(1) This step of transmuting the teaching of the historical Jesus into "the Gospel of today" was first undertaken in the literary adaptations of the life of Jesus. Here the authors consciously took "this present time, with its railroads and telegraphs, and phonographs, and electric lights and lifted into it, from out the historic past, a central figure - ... the Man Christ Jesus."(2) This transposition flowed from the conviction of Jesus' relevance for contemporary concerns. "Jesus, as an inseparable soul - friend - a consoler, a teacher, an enlightener," Harriet Beecher Stowe's "life" thus set out to show, "dwells on earth now in a higher sense than when he walked the hills of Palestine."(3)

From the 1880s onwards, this actualization of the history of Jesus turned increasingly to socio-political channels emphasizing the social aspects of the Gospels. The most coherent and outspoken manifestation of this emphasis, the Social Gospel movement, found general principles of a social programme in the ministry of Jesus which were asserted to be transferable to the contemporary economic system. The key recurrent assumption in this focus on the compatibility of Jesus' social teaching and the present day socio-economic situation was the conception of Christianity as a religious-social movement, one which allowed for "the application of the teaching of Jesus and the total message of the Christian salvation to society, the economic life, and social institutions ... as well as to individuals."(4)

The Social Gospel movement arose as an indigenous reaction to a diverse array of social and cultural forces, to the urban-industrial social revolution, to the social activism of antebellum evangelicalism, and to the impact of the newer social sciences, evolutionary theory and biblical criticism. In this amalgam of influences the quest could not long remain detached from social concerns and underwent a striking transformation from its concentration on individual piety to a social orientation coupled generally with a deepened concern for social and economic conditions, with the rise of the labor movement and socialism as well as with the falling behind and alienation of the working class. This breadth of the movement's social orientation led beyond the scope of the Unitarian-Transcendentalist tradition. The Social Gospel emerged within the Unitarian camp but soon cut across denominational lines and included in its ranks such diverse figures as Shailer Mathews, Washington Gladden, Walter Rauschenbusch and Lyman Abbott. Together, these critics were united by a one-sided theology of history which aligned 'history' with social impulse. And it was at this juncture that the movement made its most important contributions: the focus of historical faith on social concerns and the shift towards a social theology aiming at social action rather than merely individualistic personal regeneration.

Precedents for this shift could be found in the European Christian Social movements represented by Saint-Simon in France, Naumann in Germany, and Maurice and Kingsley in England. Through complex modes of transmission, these movements shaped the refashioning of the Transcendentalist and liberal Protestant conception of the latent divinity of humanity into a sanction for social effort. Given this emphasis on a social definition of selfhood, the religious philosophy of the quest which had corroborated the Transcendentalists' intuitionist premises now seemed inadequate. Ripley, involved in the Brook Farm experiment, clearly anticipated the Social Gospelists' turn from religionist to practical reformist stances against which Hegel's and Schleiermacher's religious philosophies amounted merely to "airy nothings."(5) Since these philosophical systems offered an "exercise of the pure intellect" only - "remote abstractions" - Ripley, no less than the Social Gospel protagonists, lost all "immediate interest in (this) line of speculation."(6)

The Social Gospel evinced a keen interest in advancing biblical foundations for its social creed. Social Gospel exponents readily accepted the historical approach to biblical exegesis which promised to elucidate the cultural context of the biblical materials. On this count, the Social Gospels stood in a long line of American biblical studies of the days of Moses Stuart, Buckminster and Channing which now combined with recent advances of the Leben-Jesu-Forschung such as the history-of-religions methodology to provide the Social Gospel with a powerful historico-critical edifice. In the hands of the Leben-Jesu-Forschung, however, this edifice appeared to the Social Gospel at times to focus too exclusively upon the historical-critical study of the biblical narratives. The life of Jesus accounts presented to Social Gospel advocates primarily a resource for social ethics, and not a pristine object for critical examination. The "lives" in the Social Gospel tradition were accordingly written "with more than usual emphasis upon the social point of view, both in handling the early Christian literature and in reproducing the story of Jesus' life and religion."(7)

Within the context of the social teachings of the historical Jesus the Social Gospelists sounded the thematic emphasis of the quest. The focus of biblical interest for Social Gospel apologists was the effort to render Jesus' ministry relevant to social and political ends. And here the persistent adherence to the historical Jesus pressed by the quest effectively provided the Social Gospel with ethical and religious norms affirming a humanistic social creed. What stood out in the Social Gospel movement in this regard was that the quest's confidence in the availability and knowability of the historical Jesus combined with the conviction that the social principles of the historical Jesus were valid for social life of the present age according to the framework of a "Christian sociology" - "the social philosophy and teachings of the historical person, Jesus the Christ."(8)

I

The chief components out of which the Social Gospels was born could be located squarely in Orestes Brownson's "The Labouring Classes," the most provocative statement on social Christianity to come out of the

Transcendentalist camp. Brownson's pamphlet marked a stage in his personal religious pilgrimage in which a previously staunch adherence to the premise of "the potency of the human mind, or the divinity in man" as the basis for social reform gave way to a social radicalism placing the necessity of social reform above individual regeneration.(9) Social salvation now was to be achieved by the abolition of "priesthood," the limitation of hereditary property and the abolition of banks and activities - extreme "new views" which elicited from the public "one universal scream of horror" because of their "anti-Christian character."(10) Yet Brownson himself was convinced that his program of social progress corresponded to "Christianity, as it existed in the mind of Jesus" and served to mediate between doctrinal differences in a universal "religion of the future."(11)

Brownson's entry of matters of social concern into the camp of the "new school" also spurred later Unitarians along the road of social interest. This interest pointed to the ethical character of the life and teachings of Jesus and was most apparent in liberal clergymen like William Henry Channing, who advocated a collectivistic society governed by disinterestness and sacrifice as prerequisites for social reform. Efforts towards social reform and communal reorganization of society were evident in the example of religious social service provided by Joseph Tuckerman, but they were also obvious in members of the Transcendentalist movement who, as in the case of Henry David Thoreau, repeatedly posited the latent divinity of the individual in opposition to social and political establishment. In 1840, Elizabeth Peabody's "A Glimpse of Christ's Idea of Society" suggested that the historical Jesus could be utilized for this opposition and for the argument that regeneration should be accompanied by concurrent social reforms. "The problem of the present age," Peabody argued, "is human society, not as a rubric of abstract science, but also a practical matter and universal interest; an actual reconciliation of outward organization with the life of the individual souls who associate; and by virtue of whose immortality each of them transcends all arrangements."(12) The "key-stone" of this correlation of social and individual reform was "the important truth ... that the amelioration of outward circumstances will be the effect, but can never be the means of mental and moral improvement."(13) Contrary to Brownson's view of social progress, social amelioration here was asserted to flow from inward progress and from the assumption of the inward "divinity" of man.

"If there is a divine in man, it has a right and it is its duty to unfold itself from itself," Peabody reiterated in the Dial. "A social organization, which does not admit of this ... is inadequate...."(14) In the same manner that the Unitarian-Transcendentalist tradition invoked the divinity of man as a spur to a new society, the Free Religious Association, represented in the Boston Radical Club and its annual Proceedings, provided a premonitory signal of this transformation from social conservatism to social activism. Aligned with the rationalism of the quest, Unitarians advocating a "religion of humanity" rejected the unique authority of the "Christ of dogma," using instead the "Christ of humanity" to press a faith geared to social action, a "faith incorporating the individual with society through sympathy with the principles by virtue of which society exists, and works making that incorporation compact and solid through some positive contribution of service rendered to one or more human beings...."(15)

This interpretation was long denied in American life of Jesus literature. A recurrent assertion of the "lives" in the evidentialist tradition was that "Christianity bears no mark of the hands of a politician." And since "Christianity, then, was not framed for political purposes," it seemed imperative to disclaim any political intentions and social aims of Jesus' ministry.(16) "Jesus came to a nation expecting a Messiah; and he claimed this character," Channing observed. "But instead of conforming to the opinions which prevailed in regard to the Messiah, he resisted them wholly and without reserve. To a people anticipating a triumphant leader, under whom vengeance as well as ambition was to be glutted by the prostration of their oppressors, he came as a spiritual leader, teaching humility and peace."(17)

Similarly, William Ware was anxious to make clear in his "life" that the Pharisees and Sadducees of Jesus' time were expecting a temporal leader. "They doubt not ... that Jesus is their king, and by him a mechanic-king, a low-born peasant-monarch, of their own base blood...." They "think not of him or his future kingdom as differing from other thrones and other monarchs...."(18) In the same vein, William Henry Furness pointed out that "the Jews were burning with the thirst of national glory - of earthly prosperity and success. They had long considered themselves a sacred people ...; and they were stung to madness at the thought of the foreign domination under which they had been brought...."(19) Yet Furness' "life" demonstrated that "to suppose (Jesus) capable of worldly aims ... is to forget the power which Truth has...."(20) The historical Jesus was at no point in his ministry "bewildered by political aspirations."(21) O. B. Frothingham agreed with this interpretation of "the popular conception of the Messiah as a national deliverer." Jesus "is no military leader," Frothingham reiterated, "he incites to no revolt. ... He looks for demonstrations of power, not human but superhuman. ... He will not draw the sword himself...."(22)

"The writers about (Jesus') period," Frothingham judged, "take especial pains to limit the conception of the Messiah within the boundaries of the average patriotic ideal." In E. S. Phelps' interpretation of the life of Jesus this reading flowed directly from the "political situation" of Jesus' time. "The Hebrews were above all things a hero-loving nation; and their heroes were dead." In the context of this predicament "their political expectations were the sole basis on which they were likely to meet (Jesus). Their only intelligent idea of their Messiah was that of a powerful and obliging being who would free them from Rome and make a nation of them."(23) In a pathbreaking discourse on "The Aim and Hope of Jesus," Oliver Stearns in 1873 extended this interpretation and expressly equated it with the argument of Reimarus' "life" that Jesus set out to establish a political kingdom and thought of himself as the Messiah of Jewish nationalistic hopes. According to Stearns, Reimarus falsely interpreted Jesus' teaching on the Kingdom in socio-political terms and thus ignored that Jesus "used his language ... in a figurative sense, to represent spiritual and providential facts...." The Messianic concept was primarily moral and spiritual rather than national and political. Jesus, Stearns alleged, "did not aim at any political sovereignty; ... he rose by the force of the special endowment of his nature above the Apocalyptic superstition of his age, and ... he looked and labored immediately for the moral and spiritual renovation of humanity on this earth."(24)

While Stearns stayed within the safe circle of "spiritual renovation," another group of critics within the "new school" tradition was ready to apply the life of Jesus to practical reform efforts. For the Broad Church men, most notably James Freeman Clarke, Jesus "(appeared) as a Reformer of a very radical character...."(25) Jesus' "radicalism," Clarke found, was applicable not so much to political and social reform than to a particular philosophy of church reform. What Clarke saw validated in Jesus' life was an apostolic church whose basis was religious and not institutional, individualistic and not authoritarian or tied to tradition as an affirmation of its claim to supremacy. Clarke's notion of the "Church of the Future" derived from the Gospel narratives had no place for pewholders, hierarchy or ecclesiastical authority. Following the gospel of a Jesus whom Clarke revered as "the greatest Radical that ever lived," a "radical" who "set aside all forms," Clarke advocated a church reform which abolished the pewholders system and introduced principles of congregational worship committed to community hymns and prayers.(26) Within this "Church of the Future," "not this place nor that place (was) a place of worship; rather "the only house of God" was ultimately the divine element in man.(27)

II

With regard to the revelance of Jesus' preaching for his own conception of church reform, Clarke judged that the life of Jesus "seems to strike us as squarely here in America now, as it did his neighbors in Nazareth and Cana then."(28) In the case of Stearns' view of "The Aim and Hope of Jesus," this continued relevance of Jesus' life showed in a presentistic view of Jesus' Kingdom and rule: The Kingdom "has begun. It is now; ... now is the Prince of this world to be cast out; now, when Jesus is about to consummate by dying the moral means of that result. Jesus is not to be a personal Judge of men at a remote time."(29) At the level of social action, this very view provided the key point of departure for the Social Gospel and its evaluation of the revelance of the historical Jesus for contemporary socio-political issues. The historical Jesus, the Social Gospel movement asserted, did not only seek to bring about individual regeneration but also attempted to regenerate social order.

What gave the different versions of social Christianity proposed by Social Gospel apologists coherence was the effort to renovate society through the construction of a theological system around the historical Jesus. The christocentric tendency which made the historical Jesus the focus of biblical revelation was extended to actualize the historical Jesus as a theological hinge for social concerns.(30) "Christians had always bowed in worship before their Master," Rauschenbusch observed with regard to this actualization, "but they had never undertaken to understand His life in its own historical environment. ... His figure is coming out of the past to meet us. He has begun to talk to us as He did to His friends, and the better we know Jesus the Galilean the more social do His thoughts and aims become."(31)

The Social Gospel here was distinguished by a remarkable optimism about the availability and relevance of the historical Jesus. At a time when the Leben-Jesu-Forschung was confronted with Arthur Drews' option of the non-historicity of Jesus, Social Gospel advocates asserted that "the most far-reaching and prophetic influence playing upon the church to-day is (the) recovery of Christ."(32) In this "recovery" historical knowledge and faith were asserted to correlate perfectly, with the teachings of the historical Jesus being read as literal truth applicable to contemporary affairs. "If to-day many of us are deeply in earnest about the application of Christian principles to the social life of men," H. E. Fosdick acknowledged, "it is because we have rediscovered Him...."(33)

This conviction about the possibility of rediscovering the historical Jesus was also apparent in the Social Gospel's conception of the opposition between the historical Jesus and the Christ of faith, popularly formulated by Social Gospel exponents as the distinction between "the religion of Jesus" and "the religion about Jesus." For the Social Gospel movement, Jesus' significance flowed from his religious life and not from religious assertions about him. "The reformation of the sixteenth century," Rauschenbusch categorically declared, "was a revival of Pauline theology. The present-day reformation is a revival of the spirit and aims of Jesus himself." And in this "revival" the theological Christ, the Christ of faith receded behind the historical Jesus' "relation to his own times."(34)

In bringing together two new interests, social theology and the historical Jesus, the Social Gospel's "revival" of Jesus rendered "the spirit and aims of Jesus" adaptable to a framework of "Christian sociology." "Twenty five years ago," Rauschenbusch recapitulated in 1912, "the social wealth of the Bible was almost undiscovered to us. Even Jesus talked like an individualist in those days and seemed to repudiate the social interest when we interrogated Him. To-day He has resumed the spiritual leadership of social Christianity, of which He was the founder."(35) The socio-political basis of Social Gospel apologists, however, was not really pronounced. Here the recurrent disclaimers of any socio-political intention of Jesus' ministry in previous "lives" lingered on and prevented the movement from arriving at a uniform set of conclusions on the question whether Jesus had an "actual social programme or policy."(36) The movement did not regard the historical Jesus "as a social reformer of the modern type" and viewed Jesus' teaching as directed towards moral rather than economic causes. Following Stearns, Francis G. Peabody thus denied that Jesus was concerned with social problems of his time: "There was political oppression about Him to be remedied, there were social righteousness and inquity to be condemned, but Jesus did not fling Himself into the social issues of His time."(37) Nor did he advance any scheme of economic rearrangement. Over against the varieties of Christian socialism, Peabody resolved the issue of economic distribution in terms of spiritual regeneration and preparedness. "Jesus is, indeed, not a social system maker," Peabody reiterated. "His message to manhood was not of the mechanism of society, but of the character and capacity and destiny of the human soul."(38)

A similar trend towards social conservatism was evident in Shailer Mathews. "By the Kingdom of God," Mathews asserted, "Jesus meant an ideal social order in which the relation of men to God is that of sons, and to each other that of brothers."(39) Jesus' teaching was "intended to evoke an attitude of soul" in socially minded men which "regenerated" them to social consciousness on the basis of their filial relationship to God. Jesus' overall goal, then, was not social reform or change of economic systems but rather the change of personality under an absolute moral ideal. "Equality with Jesus," Mathews argued, "was not to be attained by equalizing wealth or honor, but by the possession of a common divine life, the employment of equal privileges, and the performance of equal duties. It is moral, not material."(40) The ministry of Jesus was on this count completely resistant to any attempts to impose socialism as a theory of systematic social change on it. Directly counter to this imposition, Jesus sought "to work for the rebuilding of men rather than for the reforming of social organization; for the change of character rather than of environment."(41)

The variety of social teaching advocated by Walter Rauschenbusch indicates, however, that the Social Gospel included in its spectrum also a sophisticated socio-political theology reclaiming the historical Jesus as a nonviolent "radical." Rauschenbusch was prepared to agree with Mathews, Peabody and Abbott that "Jesus emancipated the idea of the Kingdom from previous nationalistic limitations and from the debasement of lower religious tendencies, and made it world-wide and spiritual."(42) But Rauschenbusch deliberately moved beyond biblical exegesis and theological elaboration and incorporated political science, economics and sociology for a social diagnosis which issued in a direct call to regenerate the social order through social control and reorganization, consumer cooperatives, employee profit-sharing and individual participation. The precedent for this social regeneration, Rauschenbusch claimed, had been set by the historical Jesus himself, who consciously aimed at the re-building of human society: "The purpose of all that Jesus said and did and hoped to do was always the social redemption of the entire life of the human race on earth."(43) Given this purpose, social diagnosis was not sufficient. The Social Gospel in turn had "to set revolutionary social forces in motion" and move "toward a social order which will best guarantee to all personalities their free and highest development."(44)

But even in this activist use of the historical Jesus for a new social order, the liberal notion of the "absolute worth" of individual humanity preceded social regeneration. Rauschenbusch accordingly demanded first "that the moral sense of humanity shall be put in control and shall be allowed to reshape the institutions of social life."(45) Rauschenbusch aligned this authoritative basis for social reform with a theological-social vision which, comparable to the futuristic vision of the utopian novel in the manner of Bellamy's <u>Looking Backward</u>, came down on the side of a striking blend of Christian reformism and political conservatism. This blend failed to produce socio-political procedures and techniques commensurate with "the present social order" and was in this respect expressive of a socialized Christianity, and not a Christian socialism. What lingered on instead were the remnants of the social idealism of the Transcendentalist "new school."(46)

III

The postulation of the historical Jesus as the "founder of social Christianity" was made possible for the Social Gospel by the advances of the life of Jesus studies. The Social Gospel representatives had no systematic theology and no consistent christology, but they did press a theological revision which bore all the marks of the quest's shift away from old high christology with regard to the person and the work of Jesus. The christological interpretation of the Social Gospel focused on the personality of Jesus and "(cared) not for the old definitions of unity and trinity, for the old distinctions between substance and person, for the old assertions of equality and subordination."(47) In the context of the Social Gospel, Jesus represented a "brother" among men all invested with indwelling "divinity." There was accordingly no place for the Chalcedonian conception of Christ's deity or the classical two-natures christology. The latter framework belonged for the Social Gospelists to "the parasitic growth of ritualism and sacramentalism on the body of Christianity" and was held to be "one great historical cause why Christianity has never addressed itself to the task of social reconstruction."(48)

George A. Gordon's The Christ of Today carried this social basis for the express emphasis on a merely human view of Jesus to an extreme Christocentrism. To Gordon, all "modes of intellectual vision, types of feeling, habits of will; ... emotional, institutional, and social existence, - (were) everywhere encompassed and interpenetrated by Christ."(49) This Christocentric vision categorically postulated a "transcendent ethical Personality" which defied all metaphysical speculation about the nature of Christ and was on a level with a human personage. Only on condition of a "complete identity between Christ and humanity in respect of being and range of powers, men are ready to believe on him," Gordon argued, concluding that "if it is said that there is any otherness, any eternal difference between him an his brethren, it is felt that that must be a metaphysical fiction."(50)

This view brought in its wake also a new understanding of the redemptive work of Christ. Rauschenbusch's A Theology for the Social Gospel reinterpreted the traditional theological map in social terms against a solidaristic view of society. Rauschenbusch's revision of the traditional theological map connected individual sin and social sin in a collectivistic framework which deprived sin of its imputative quality and thereby undercut the substitutionary form of atonement. "Society is so integral," Rauschenbusch explained, "that when one man sins, the others suffer, and when one social class sins, the other classes are involved in the suffering that follows on that sin. The more powerful an individual is, the more will he involve others; the more powerful a class is, the more will it be able to unload its own just sufferings on the weaker clames. These sufferings are 'vicarious': they are solidaristic."(51)

This solidaristic interpretation of Jesus' work dismissed Augustinian, Calvinistic and Edwardean theology as systems proclaiming a "partial" God who "sincerely contemplates only the selection of a number."(52) The theology of the Social Gospel further uncovered the feudalistic and imperialistic imprint of the traditional systems of the atonement. The Anselmian theory of the atonement in this context emerged as a key example of a legalistic codification which reduced the relation between God and man to the terms between creditor and debtor and thus subverted the both social and personal character of salvation. For Social Gospel advocates the judicial view of atonement was expressive of autocratic power, of economic and political despotism and unduly superimposed terms of human law and government on the God-idea. In the context of the ethical idealism of the Social Gospel, the work and person of Jesus Christ was instrumental as inspiration and example only, independent of expiatory elements and judicial implications.(53)

This substitution of solidarity for vicariousness equated Jesus' teaching with a reductive ethic of love that was indiscriminately applied to social relations. The old social order characterized by hatred and selfishness was to be superseded by a dominion of love governed by "the fatherhood of God and the brotherhood of men." The Jesus who propagated this dominion did for the Social Gospel representatives not belong to a historical revelation of the past. It was not the miracle-performing Jesus of Channing and Norton nor the Jesus-as-"representative man" of the Transcendentalist "new school" who concerned Social Gospel apologists but rather the teacher and example of a "new social order" which flowed from the "absolute worth" of every individual. This conception of Jesus as "teacher" and "model" clearly moved beyond the individualistic psychology of the Transcendentalist "new school" and turned to a view of the social dependence and social responsibility of the individual.

In this rediscovery of the historical Jesus, Social Gospel apologists were acutely aware of the peril of "a mere modernizing of the simple records of the gospels. ... There is as constant danger," Mathews cautioned against anachronistic life of Jesus study, "that, in the attempt to restate the teachings of Jesus in the terms of to-day's thought, exposition may wait too subserviently upon desire. The first century, albeit surprisingly like the nineteenth, was nevertheless not the nineteenth, and Jesus the Jew was not a product of Greek syllogisms and German hypotheses."(54) Similarly, F. G. Peabody warned that "to reconstruct the Gospels so as to make them primarily a programme of social reform is to mistake the by-product for the end specifically sought, and, in the desire to find a place for Jesus within the modern age, to forfeit that which gives him his place in all ages."(55)

Yet for Social Gospel advocates the problem that the portrait of Jesus reconstructed by the nineteenth century could be anachronistic presented no real obstacle. The Social Gospel displayed a remarkable optimism that the Jesus interpreted as relevant for the "Gospel of today" would be original and authentic. Here the legacy of Clarke, Hedge, Furness, the certainty of the validity and possibility of reconstruction, persisted to produce countless portraits which were assumed to put an end to theological debate about Jesus' status. While Schweitzer demonstrated the utter impossibility of a biographical approach to the historical Jesus, Social Gospel apologists were confident that the possibility of a historical-objective, accurate interpretation of the life of Jesus would prevail. This was all the more remarkable as the Leben-Jesu-Forschung of the turn of the century yielded to a position which left the question of Jesus' actual existence unanswered and undercut the "liberal-positive" quest's conviction that a pristine historical "kernel" lay behind a mythological and dogmatic "husk." Thus Karl Kautsky, one of the most renowned representatives of this trend, acutely played with the possibility of Jesus' unhistoricity. For Kautsky, Jesus belonged to the rural proletariat and was distinguished by a rebellious mentality hostile to both Jewish theocracy and Roman rule.(56) In this way Jesus' life became the inevitable outcome of a Marxist scheme which located the origins of Christianity in proletarian social movements and equated messianic with communistic ideas.

In a similar fashion, the Bremen pastor and critic Albert Kalthoff presented Christianity as a socio-religious movement of the masses to which Jesus was not essential. The historical Jesus here was merely a symbolic creation, the outcome of a social proletarian element, a people's Christ, representative of the ideal of the lower classes. "From the socio-religious standpoint," Kalthoff explained, "the figure of the Christ was the sublimated religious expression for the sum of the social and ethical forces that were at work in a certain period." Within this theory of Christian origins the historical Jesus was dispensable: "The idea," Kalthoff claimed, "that a suddenly converted Paul could in the space of twenty years have saturated Asia Minor and the Balkan peninsula with Christian societies by preaching as the Christ a Jesus hitherto unknown in these districts is a prodigy, alongside which all the miracles of the Church must look like child's play."(57)

Social Gospel advocates followed a different line of argument. They did not propagate a theology of revolution or a theology of liberation and never arrived at the conclusion of the non-historicity of Jesus. Social Gospel apologists rested assured in their conviction that history vindicated their assertions and were confident that the history of Jesus was faithfully transmitted through the biblical narratives. On this point the clear parting of ways between the American quest and the Leben-Jesu-Forschung continued and once more drew American practitioners to an older tradition of rationalistic "lives" produced in England by Richard Davies Hanson, Thomas Scott and John Seeley whose portrait of a "first-century, socially progressive freethinker" left the historicity of the Gospel tradition intact.(58)

This was directly counter to the line begun in the Leben-Jesu-Forschung in the 1840s with Bruno Bauer and culminating in 1909 in Arthur Drews The Christ Myth. Drews assumed that a Jesus cult existed among the Jews in pre-Christian times. The Gospels therefore did not present the record of the history of an actual man, but propagated instead a Jesus myth in historical form. Working with the techniques of comparative religion, Drews further suggested that primitive Christianity constituted a syncretistic religion which attributed previously existing religious cult forms to a historical personage whose actual existence was doubtful. According to this conception of the conversion of the mythical Jesus into the historical Jesus, Christianity grew with Gnostic sects who believed in an astral Jesus, a Jesus whose 'history' followed narratives from the Wisdom of Salomon, the twenty-second Psalm, Isaiah and the prophets. This pre-Christian Jesus lost its astral features after the second century destruction of Jerusalem when the abstract scheme was increasingly supplanted by suppositions of real history. "The more the new faith spread among the people," Drews observed, "the more the gnosis was adapted to their intelligence, and thus the supposed historicity of the Savior was substituted for the mythical and astral character of their religious ideas."(59)

Given this presence of a "Christ-myth," the New Testament critic could "know nothing of Jesus," "of an historical personality by this name, to which the events and words recorded in the gospels refer."(60) More than that, there was not only no way of reconstructing the historical Jesus but in effect also no need for the existence of such a figure to explain the origin of Christianity: "A historical Jesus, as the gospels describe him and as he lives in the heads of today's liberal theologians," Drews claimed, "did not exist at all; nor did he even found the wholly insignificant little messianic community in Jerusalem." "More or less all the features of the picture of the historical Jesus, at any rate all those of any important religious significance, bear a purely mythological character..."(61)

Among Social Gospel exponents, the Christ-myth theory received no support. It was acknowledged that "there is a wide-spread impression abroad that modern Biblical criticism has cut away the very ground of any permanent disciples to Christ by showing that the accounts we have are not historical; that all the clear outlines of that figure which the world has bowed down to are mythical or legendary; that the whole is a half imaginary picture - nothing to depend upon it, nothing discernible enough to stand for." But while the impact of this criticism spurred reflection on the issue of faith and history and intensified debate about the question whether it might have been not the historical Jesus but Christ as an idea which accounted for the rise of Christianity, any conclusions of non-historicity presented to American questers "an utter mistake, however. What criticism has really done is this: it has cleared the idea that the four Gospels are inspired and infallible narratives; but is has not touched this fact: that those four Gospels ... give us such a picture of the life and spirit and word of Jesus as we have of no other life in all the ancient world."(62)

IV

Judged against the Leben-Jesu-Forschung, the mainstream of the Social Gospel's research on the life of Jesus also moved in a different direction with regard to the eschatological approach. Schweitzer's interpretation dissociated Jesus' eschatology from the political scene and from references to contemporary events. For Schweitzer "the apocalyptic movement in the time of Jesus (was) not connected with any historical event."(63) For the Social Gospel, by contrast, Jesus' eschatology presented an experimentally discoverable category within history, not apart from it. Social Gospel exponents here were not ignorant of Weiss' proposal of the futuristic interpretation of Jesus' eschatology. Mathews expressly acknowledged Weiss' opposition to prevalent liberal Protestant interpretations: "Probably the recognition of the importance of the apocalyptic literature in the formation of the early Christian vocabulary, if not Christology, may yet be still further emphasized," Mathews judged. Nor can it be denied that .... Jesus often used expressions which ... would be sufficient to justify the sweeping statement that 'the Gospel entered into the world as an apocalyptic eschatological message, apocalyptical and eschatological not only in its form, but in its contents.'(64)

Social Gospel advocates were also prepared to acknowledge Schweitzer's "refutation of utterances of Ritschl." Schweitzer, Social Gospel representatives observed, had drawn attention to an element the liberals had slighted with his a "thoroughgoing" presentation of an interpretation of the life of Jesus wherein the concept of the Kingdom of God in Jesus' teaching was conceived wholly in terms of Jewish apocalyptic.(65) Social Gospel exponents, however, could not settle for the purely apocalyptic, futuristic interpretation of Jesus' expectation of a Kingdom to be established imminently by direct divine intervention. The Social Gospel was more inclined to accept as authentic the sayings in which the Kingdom was described as present. The Kingdom was "near," ethical and non-transcendent. The traditional apocalyptic and eschatological element of the kingdom was discarded by the Social Gospel as a "husk," an embellishment of Judaism. In Rauschenbusch's reading, Jesus broke with the popular messianism of his time and proclaimed a Kingdom of timeless principles applicable to all ages. Jesus' teaching was thus set apart from the eschatological ideas of his age, with Jesus standing "above the heads of his reporters."(66)

For the Social Gospel, the eschatological consciousness of Jesus also carried an expressly 'realized' element sharply distinguished from the futurist, unfulfilled eschatology of Weiss and Schweitzer. According to F. G. Peabody, the Kingdom of God had to Jesus both significations, "that of a future and that of a present state, that of a heavenly and that of an earthly society."(67) Accepting the imperative of this perspective, the Social Gospel displayed a persistent inclination to find a this-age significance in the New Testament eschatology. Over against dualism and 'other-worldliness', the Kingdom entailed social and political redemption and involved the immediate task of social action in the present world. Jesus preached in the form of an apocalyptic, but his Kingdom referred to present ethical reality and was not a category to be instituted in the future. Rauschenbusch accordingly regarded "faith of the Kingdom of God a religion for this earth and for the present life. The hope of the Kingdom of God makes this earth the theatre of action, and turns the full force of religious will and daring toward the present...."(68)

Social Gospelists granted that the advent-expectation was an element in the teaching of Jesus, yet the primary frame of reference for the ethical demands of Jesus was throughout attributed to absolute, abiding themes of social solidarity. Hence the Social Gospel could not assimilate Schweitzer's characterization of the teachings of Jesus as an "interim ethic." For Schweitzer, "Jesus' whole theory of ethics must come under the conception of repentance as a preparation for the coming of the kingdom." For the Social Gospel, this preparation for the kingdom of God came close in quality to an ethic of solidarity and cooperation as well as to general social reforms resulting in a new social order which sought "to transform human society into the Kingdom of God."(69)

For this "social de-mythologizing" of Jesus' eschatology the closest affiliate for the Social Gospel in the Leben-Jesu-Forschung was not Schweitzer's "throughgoing eschatology" but rather Albrecht Ritschl's conception of the Kingdom as "the summum bonum which God realises in men."(70) This affiliation worked primarily in the context of religious epistemology. What the Social Gospel found in Ritschl was a rejection of all attempts to deduce Christian doctrines from the contents of religious consciousness or to base, as had Unitarian evidentialists, the special claims of Christianity on uniquely inspired words and miracles.(71) With these oppositions, Ritschl helped to structure the Social Gospel's propagation of a solidaristic conception of the person and work of Jesus and the resultant critique of individualistic detachment from the ethical and social tasks of the Kingdom of God. With regard to their views of the function of these ideals, however, the Social Gospelists, frequently termed the "American Ritschlians" of their day, turned from Ritschl's ethical idealism to Social Darwinism. "Translate the evolutionary theories into religious faith, and you have the doctrine of the kingdom of God," Rauschenbusch explained. "This combination with scientific evolutionary thought has freed the kingdom ideal of its catastrophic setting and its background of demonism, and so adapted it to the climate of the modern world."(72) In Social Darwinism the Social Gospel saw a philosophy applicable to the desired adaptation. The movement adhered to an organic theory of society as a social consequence implicit in the Darwinian theory of evolution and reclaimed once again the historical Jesus on this point: "Jesus," Rauschenbusch explained, "grasped the substance of that law of organic development in nature and history which our own day at last has begun to elaborate systematically."(73)

Yet the Social Gospel exponents were not prepared to accept in their social philosophy the competitive model of natural selection. The Social Gospel's ethic was incompatible with the laissez-faire version of the survival of the fittest and propagated instead a social order in which competition was counteracted by a solidaristic cooperation for the common welfare. This advocacy of solidaristic, fraternal premises of a stewardship rectifying the insufficiencies and inequalities of capitalist society flowed from the recognition of the spiritual worth of the individual. On this point, "no other term" than that of the Kingdom of God "(was) so characteristic of Jesus, none (was) more certainly his."(74) The doctrine of the Kingdom of God was "itself the social gospel" because it affirmed that Jesus' ministry entailed a theological ideal whose "beginning (was) individual" and whose "aim (was) social."(75)

V

The Social Gospel's rediscovery of the social dimensions of Christianity was aligned with a deep concern for the biblical foundations of social theology. The movement's social theology was not the mere outcome of cultural-social interests but flowed also from the reconstruction of an expressly biblical ethic pertinent to social Christianity. "The new present has created a new past," Rauschenbusch declared and "the Bible shares in that new social interpretation" providing a resource for social ethics.(76) The insight into the social perspective of the Bible substantially renewed for Social Gospel exponents the interest in the synoptic texts and in the methodologies of comparative analysis, form, redaction and tradition criticism. For this emphasis American Social Gospel representatives could draw on the religio-historical branch of the Leben-Jesu-Forschung and the corresponding techniques of higher criticism. This strain of influence on the Social Gospel's conception of the biblical foundations of social theology issued frequently in very tangible debts. Shailer Mathews studied in Berlin, Göttingen and Halle. Francis Greenwood Peabody became after a year at Halle the first to introduce social reform as a subject into a divinity school curriculum and strenghtened the impact of the Leben-Jesu-Forschung at Harvard. Peabody's Jesus Christ and the Social Question abounded with references to Beyschlag, Holtzmann and Harnack which were utilized for a socio-historical approach to Christianity. Similarly, Walter Rauschenbusch, after early schooling in Gütersloh and Berlin, in 1891 and 1907 again studied the historical methods of New Testament exegesis at the centers of the Leben-Jesu-Forschung - studies which convinced Rauschenbusch that "if we want to understand the real aims of Jesus, we must watch him in his relation to his own time."(77)

The experience of Social Gospel exponents at the centers of the Leben-Jesu-Forschung were sharply distinguished from those of the Harvard-Göttingen students in the opening decades of the nineteenth century. Early American biblical critics had long been reluctant to absorb the higher critical views of Parker and Strauss and rejected them as damaging to supernatural rationalism. Social Gospel advocates, in contrast, were prepared to appropriate the historical approach for biblical exegesis. Social Gospelists were aware that Strauss' rationalistic scepticism had spurred historical interest in Jesus and that the massive critical work done after Strauss' "life" now could provide the materials for the establishment of the biblical base of a social theology. Yet when Social Gospel representatives seized upon historico-critical methods, the bulwarks of biblical literalism once again provided major inhibiting factors. The introduction of the higher criticism into the theological circles of the Social Gospels during the 1880s posed a threat to the dogma of biblical infallibility still prevalent among both orthodox and liberal exegetes and accordingly exposed members of the movement to the charge that they were prone to "reject as authoritative the Old and New Testament writers...."(78)

While the higher critical stance aligned Social Gospel exponents with the Leben Jesu researchers, they were not biblical theologians. Their position was not primarily critical or exegetical and produced no exegetical scrutiny of the Kingdom of God concept. The biblical record served for the Social Gospel more as a spiritual guide to life. It did not present the source of theology but rather a source book for the moral and ethical ideals embodied in the Lord's Prayer, the Sermon on the Mount, and the parable of the prodigal son.(79) This reading went hand in hand with an apologetic stance: The Social Gospel evinced a keen interest in the critical tools of the quest but was at the same time concerned to show that the scientific handling of critical data gave fullest play to empirical considerations. Critical of any detachment of biblical revelation from historical-cultural context and sceptical of any references to the mythological and transcendent, the Social Gospel was in most cases inclined to replace critical exegesis by a basic loyality to the historicity of the person of Jesus. On this count, the movement not only rejected the mythical approach but also did not delve into source critical views; it merely reiterated the belief "in the simple veracious records (of) ... the life of Christ," with no sustained source critical interest in the question of "whatever else the four gospels may or may not be...."(80)

12. Rediscovering the Historical Jesus

From the blow of Schweitzer's verdict of failure the Leben-Jesu-Forschung never quite recovered. Its adherents had pioneered the solution of the synoptic problem and established with confidence the possibility of producing a reliable life of Jesus. Schweitzer's Quest, however, remorselessly doomed these confident attempts at reconstruction as futile and revealed the illegitimacy of psychological interpretation as a method of historical reconstruction. In fact so relentlessly did Schweitzer expose the futility of the quest that his work seemed to put a stop to the whole course of the life of Jesus stream. After the publication of the Quest, Schweiter's verdict was to hover persistently over the course the Leben-Jesu-Forschung. "Formerly," Schweitzer acutely observed, "it was possible to book through-tickets at the supplementary-psychological-knowledge office which enabled those travelling in the interests of life-of-Jesus construction to use express trains. ... This ticket office is now closed."(1)

The "negative" "result" of Schweitzer's survey of the "lives" from Reimarus to Wrede was early acknowledged by American audiences. In 1911 the Bibliotheca Sacra noted that in the "lives" "every one makes a Jesus for himself, and finds himself at the end in possession of just the Jesus that imagination had formed for itself beforehand in his mind. For Carlyle Jesus was a hero; for Strauss a religious genius; for Renan a liberal reformer and preacher of humanity...." In each case, the critic took up "an endless task" which led merely to "limitless arbitrariness."(2) After Schweitzer the search for the historical Jesus continued, arriving at results never completely free from the charge of "limitless arbitrariness." Thus one of the most frequently repeated charges against the new quest put forward by critics from both the Continental and the American side of life of Jesus research has been the argument that the new quest represents merely another reappearance of positivistic historical-psychological interpretation. According to William O. Walker, "what is today called 'the new quest for the historical Jesus' actually represents an untenable 'halfway house' between the historical scepticism and unconcern of the Bultmannian 'school' and the uncritical naiveté of the nineteenth century quest...."(3) The Leben Jesu researcher Oscar Cullmann concurs: "Albert Schweitzer's Quest of the historical Jesus was written in vain if the 'liberal' portrait of Jesus, which corresponds to the idealistic philosophy of the nineteenth century, disappeared only in order to make room for the existentialist philosophy of the twentieth century."(4)

Among the majority of American exegetes and theologians, the "existentialist" position of Rudolf Bultmann with its insistence on the mere "thatness" of Jesus and the cross and its reduction of the historical "kernel" of the kerygma to a minimum was met with disapproval. "To the representatives of this position," Hans Conzelmann observed, "the form-critical reconstruction seems to be a rationalistic abstraction, foreign both to history and reality, and from a practical point of view a reduction of Christianity to a general religious consciousness, a formal dialectic of existence."(5) Contra Bultmann, American biblical critics continued to view the Gospels as historical source documents and affirmed the historical character of divine revelation. Reviewing the "new and not unfruitful stage in the literary criticism of the Gospels" marked by Rudolf Bultmann and Martin Dibelius, Henry J. Cadbury was confident that "inspite of almost protean changes in the history of tradition, no suspicion arises of deliberate fiction, least of all on the part of the evangelists themselves."(6) The form critical study of the "earlier development of the Synoptic material" and the focus on the "interval" "between Jesus and the Gospels" could immediately be put to the cause of reassurance and corroborated the historicity of the Gospel tradition. The "study of the origin of the gospels (might) dissipate ... the myth of a simon-pure tradition," but it also "assures us," Cadbury reiterated, "that in believing in the historicity of Jesus we are not following cunningly devised fables."(7) This was to follow an intellectual line of continuity reaching back to the evidentialist assertions of Norton and Furness, who had both slighted the function of the community in conveying the knowledge of Jesus' work and significance.

Given this line of continuity, there was no need for American practitioners of the quest to "renew" historical life of Jesus research. In view of the persistence of the original quest in the American theological scene it was more a matter of "resuming" and "continuing" the unfinished "old quest." "Lives" like Edgar J. Goodspeed's A Life of Jesus, Morton Scott Enslin's The Prophet from Nazareth and S. Vernon McCasland's The Pioneer of Our Faith: A New Life of Jesus shared the original quest's assumption of the knowability of the "real" Jesus of history. Thus Henry J. Cadbury confidently set out to reconstruct the "mind of Jesus;" Shirley Jackson Case aimed at rediscovering the "real Jesus of Palestine;" Edgar J. Goodspeed at "reading the riddle of his inner life."(8) Common to these attempts at reconstruction was the reluctance to participate in the form critical methods and kerygmatic theology. In devaluing the kerygmatic approach and form critical exegesis, Case, Fosdick and Goodspeed presented their "lives" as if life of Jesus research ended with H. E. G. Paulus and thus relapsed to the positivistic phase of the quest long behind the form critical Leben Jesu researchers.

The form critical Leben Jesu researchers who entered the new quest achieved a significant advance over the old quest's positivistic historiography, in particular with regard to the evaluation of the role of the historical-critical method in theology. The new quest's understanding of historiography did not look to external data recording the past "wie es eigentlich gewesen." For the new quest, the biblical narratives of the life of Jesus were independent of the requirements of "verifiability." In order to ground this position, the new questers' historiography did not scrutinize the historical positivity of the Gospel tradition but rather approached this tradition as kerygmatic history located within the post-Easter communities of faith. The majority of American biblical critics, however, were reluctant to bow the knee to the new quest's understanding of historiography. A good deal of antipathy to the new quest originated primarily in the new questers' one-sided existentialist concern and the resultant abstraction of the kerygma from objective-historical contexts. Amos Wilder aptly rendered this rejection of the existentialist view of the kerygma with the charge that the quest of Ebeling and Fuchs yielded "a kind of existentialist skeleton of human nature, a kind of X-ray photograph...." Similarly, John Cobb observed of the American responses to the new quest that "American contributors see in existentialist theology a tendency to treat existentialist categories themselves unhistorically and thereby to separate faith too much from its concrete involvement in culture."(9) This devaluation of the "new quest" as a "generalization", "reduction" and "abstraction" had deep roots in the course of the American quest. While extreme form critics in the Leben-Jesu-Forschung undermined the significance for theology of "Historie" and uncovered the futility of the historical question, American questers perpetuated the conviction of the nineteenth century evidentialist school that behind the Gospel lay a faithfully preserved historical tradition.

New questers themselves did not completely depart from the concern of the old quest to recover as far as possible secure knowledge of the historical Jesus. Thus members of the new quest like Joachim Jeremias set out to formulate serviceable criteria through which the authenticity of specific events and motifs of the life of Jesus were to be determined. With the establishment of criteria of authenticity the new quest was able to move beyond the Bultmannian impasse and the general problem of dealing with the kerygmatic material of the Gospels. It was precisely at this juncture that American life of Jesus researchers were willing to follow the new questers, but they did so under the general aegis of old quest presuppositions, continually bypassing existentialist categories devoid of specificity and historical-objective content.(10) In this form of continuing the quest for the historical Jesus, the renunciation of the traditional Jesus quest was judged to lead to a docetic christology, while the abandonment of strictly historical considerations of the Gospel tradition allegedly characteristic of kerygmatic theology was charged with de-historicizing the kerygma. From this twofold critique the latest stage of the quest emerged.

The *Quest* Rejected

Unlike their contemporaries in the Leben-Jesu-Forschung, nineteenth century American practitioners were on the whole more concerned with correcting and discussing historical claims than with attempting to reconstruct theological foundations. Moreover, whereas the Leben-Jesu-Forschung found it comparatively easy to take up principles at variance with the presuppositions of historicity, American questers were throughout intent on blending the historical criticism of the quest with evidentialist patterns of thought. This difference brought in its wake a series of liabilities: the unwavering stress on the empirical cast of the historical approach to the Jesus of Nazareth, the opposition to the transposition of the Jesus of history to suprahistorical, timeless categories, and the readiness to put extracanonical contemporary motives on a level of equality with the "evidences" of Jesus' history which validated socio-historical interpretations accepting the cry "Back to Christ" only as a call to "go back to Christ for stimulus ... (to) definite social programmes."(11) These emphases consolidated the search for the Jesus of history at the very time Schweitzer declared the old quest a methodological and theological failure. "'Ecce homo,' not in the spirit of Pilate, but in the spirit of a humanity that has found a brother, is our cry to-day," the *Bibliotheca Sacra* declared in 1907. "We have analyzed Jesus, - soul, body, and spirit - not quantitatively, but qualitatively; and whatever else we have discovered, we have found him flesh and blood with us, sharing infirmities, sorrows, joys, experiences, weakness, all but sin."(12)

At the point of the eschatological-apocalyptic element involved in Schweitzer's Jesus portrait, the *Quest* was in this context confronted with strong opposition. The historical Jesus whom liberal investigation distorted by subjectivist criteria and clothed with traits of contemporary concerns appeared distant and enigmatic in Schweitzer's reading. The figure whom Schweitzer found undercut the case for the historicizing interpretation of the Gospels. "The truth is, it is not Jesus as historically known, but as spiritually risen within men, who is significant for our time and can help it. Not the historical Jesus, but the spirit which goes forth from Him and in the spirit of men strives for new influence and rule, is that which overcomes the world."(13) In the place of both the Chalcedonian Christ and the historical Jesus of liberal theology there was now the timeless "spirit of Jesus," independent of theological dogma and historical methodology: "Jesus means something to our world because a mighty spiritual force streams forth from him and flows through time also. This fact can neither be shaken nor confirmed by historical discovery."(14)

In contrast to the current sentimentalized modernizations of Jesus, Schweitzer reduced the suffering of the historical Jesus to a vague symbol of the pathos of "overhelming heroic greatness" embodying the possibility of man to transcend the sufferings of ordinary history.(15) "Jesus, in the knowledge that he is the coming Son of Man," Schweitzer argued, "lays hold of the wheel of the world to set it moving on that last revolution which is to bring all ordinary history to a close."(16) In this spirit Schweitzer drew back to a position which devalued the significance of historical knowledge of Jesus. "I find it no light task ... to put pressure on the Christian faith to reconcile itself in all sincerity with historical truth," Schweitzer had stated at the outset of his studies of the quest. But when he seemed to have found the historical Jesus, Schweitzer arrived at an ethical, voluntaristic mysticism which turned Jesus into a figure "who comes ... as One unknown, without a name, as of old, by the lake-side."(17) It was on this ethical, voluntaristic note that Schweitzer concluded his survey and departed from his original starting point of historical research. And it was under the aegis of this ethical voluntarism that Schweitzer was prepared to forsake all and replace his academic position by that of the doctor of Lambarene.

"The fundamental mistake of Schweitzer's theory" was for William Sanday, the Quest's chief British reviewer, the "tendency to push things to extremes at the dictates of logical consistency."(18) Schweitzer sought in his own theory of "konsequente Eschatologie" "the single key to the life and acts and words of Christ; and in this," Sanday judged, "he was undoubtedly mistaken." Sanday conceded that the Kingdom as apocalyptic in Judaism was in keeping with the majority of synoptic Kingdom sayings, but for Sanday it was "certain that in this background Apocalyptic played ... not a dominating part." The Kingdom which Jesus came to found was of an "essentially inward and spiritual character" and bore a distinctly non-apocalyptic meaning.(19)

Sanday's assessment was long to prevail until the 1930's when C. H. Dodd proposed the concept of "realized eschatology" which suggested against Schweitzer that for Jesus the Kingdom had arrived as both salvation and judgment in history. The Kingdom was already accessible; it constituted a present reality in the ministry of Jesus. "There is no coming of the Son of Man in history 'after' His coming in Galilee and Jerusalem, whether soon or late," Dodd argued, "for there is no before and after in the eternal order. The Kingdom of God in its full reality is not something which will happen after things have happened."(20) For the Kingdom proclaimed by Jesus, then, no imminent cataclysmic event was required; the Kingdom was manifest in Jesus' own life.

In keeping with the majority of British critics, American reviewers were similarly reluctant to accept Schweitzer's eschatological conception of the historical Jesus as "a stranger or a puzzle" to be approached in the alien, largely unknowable categories of his own time. "Jesus described the future in the terms of Jewish apocalytic speculation, and we probably ought to say that he thought in those terms," the Bibliotheca Sacra conceded in 1909, "but his teaching was not determined by the eschatology of his time."(21) The "tremendous one-sidedness" of Schweitzer's theory of consistent eschatology ignored that the teaching of Jesus contained an "ageless message of truth" embedded in an apocalyptic husk.(22) Schweitzer's "fatal error" here was, H. A. A. Kennedy observed in a review of the Quest for the American Journal of Theology, that he categorically rejected "all attempts at an organic construction of the life of Jesus from the standpoint of a spiritual interpretation of his messianic self-consciousness...."(23)

In endorsing this "organic construction," Schweitzer's American reviewers continued the Ritschlian view of the Kingdom as an attainable ethical reality rather than a realm to be instituted in the future. Jesus did not preach a merely "interim" ethic preparatory for a future age; his eschatological teaching carried instead a pronounced this-age significance to be applied by individual or social effort.(24) With regard to the "personal religious life of Jesus," the insistence on the this-age perspective of New Testament eschatology brought in its wake the "passing of apocalypticism" which appeared at best as "the shell of a great truth" unduly severing biblical revelation from definite historical-cultural contexts.(25) Against the emphasis on a this-worldly consummation of the kingdom of God, however, Schweitzer's portrait of a Jesus unconcerned with socio-political circumstances seemed exclusivist, supernaturalist and "weltfremd." To render Jesus remote from contemporary concerns, as the Quest did, was for most reviewers to divest "Jesus' religion (of all) ... important ethical and social aspects" and to degrade Jesus to a "deluded fanatic."(26) The effect of Schweitzer's interpretation, as perceived by American reviewers, was to produce a portrait of Jesus so extremely "futurist" and "fanatical" as to undermine the whole effort to render the historical Jesus relevant and "real" for contemporary Christianity. Moreover, Schweitzer's conception of the history of Jesus as essentially the living out of a tragic error was a reductive and pessimistic position to reviewers who were left wondering how this tragic, enigmatic figure could claim anyone's allegiance. If Schweitzer's solution was right, then Jesus was subject to error. Jesus expected the imminent coming of the Kingdom of God, but his hopes were futile.

The reaction of many American reviewers was not only to reject Schweitzer's portrait as insufficient but to continue the old quest over against the assertions of both form criticism and kerygma theology.(27) In this context, "the distinct trend of christological interpretation was to oppose "the Christ of today (to) ... the Christ of Chalcedon."(28) The quest's critique of patristic christological creeds was thus fully absorbed. "The Christ of today is not the Christ of Chalcedon," the Bibliotheca Sacra recapitulated. "In the twentieth-century Christ ... there is no balance of contrasted natures as in the old symbols." "The words and acts of Jesus reveal a unity absolutely unique; there is neither two consciousness, nor two wills, nor two distinct natures."(29) This was a christological line of argument; the corresponding form critical position, however, establishing an opposition between the historical Jesus and the

Christ of faith was not assimilated. "Little by little historical criticism has forced scholars to the conclusion," the <u>American Journal of Theology</u> noted of the form critical enterprise after Schweitzer, "that the interpretations of the inner character of Jesus in the Gospels are appreciations due partially to the religious convictions engendered in the Christian community during the period between the life of Jesus and the time when the Gospels were written."(30) With this premise, American reviewers acutely observed, the situation was reversed, "for it means that we have in the Gospels themselves the picture of the Christ of faith, rather than the record of the life of the historical Jesus." It was therefore "difficult to press with certainty very far back of this Christ of faith. Any attempt to get back of the New Testament faith will mean simply the substitution of the critic's interpretation of Jesus for the interpretation given by John or by Paul or by Mark."(31)

This skepticism was at one with Schweitzer's "negative ... result of the critical study of the life of Jesus."(32) But whereas the form critical premise behind this "negative result" led the Leben Jesu researchers to discredit the earlier Jesus of history cult and to reject the 'reconstructionist' aim to substitute a historical construct for faith in the biblical Christ, American questers headed by the Chicago School of critics asserted no hiatus between the historical Jesus and the kerygmatic Christ. "Thus the secret of Jesus' influence upon his disciple," Shirley Jackson Case maintained, "must ultimately be sought in the content of his own personal religious life during the period of association with them. In the last analysis it was his power as a religious individual that made possible the early faith."(33) In contrast to form critical tenets, Jesus' significance was in this way asserted to flow from his religious life, and not from the early Christian communities' beliefs about him.

The theological assertion "that the Christ who is thus defined as an adequate savior is identical with the historical Jesus" methodologically demanded for American questers the historical demonstration that the Jesus of history could be known. "A theology which (was) independent of historical facts (was) bound to be inefficient because it (was) bound to be independent of the historical Jesus."(34) And against this crude assertion, the skepticism about the synoptic portraits of Jesus propagated by William Wrede did not take hold. "Making all allowance for the uncertainties of historic criticism, granting that the picture painted in the Gospels has here and there features which ... seem to contradict the general tenor," the <u>American Journal of Theology</u> judged it to be "yet a fact that the outstanding features of the picture are so clear that no one can doubt what is the nature of the issue they raise."(35)

At this juncture, defined by the <u>American Journal of Theology</u> in 1913 as the question whether "an efficient theology (could) be dependent upon historical facts," American assessments of the quest departed sharply from Schweitzer's verdict.(36) To confront the "uncertainties of historical criticism" was once more to return to Lessing's question of whether and how the figure of Jesus could function as the historical point of departure for a "necessary" idea.(37) In the hands of Leben Jesu researchers at the turn of the century Lessing's case persisted: Historical facts were "only probable," capable of producing merely "probable certainty," "at best only 'relative certainty.'"(38) For Schweitzer this gap between "necessary" truths of reason and contingent facts of history was too wide. Schweitzer judged that "although historical knowledge can no doubt introduce greater clearness into an existing spiritual life, it cannot call spiritual life into existence."(39) American critics like Austin Rice, Philip Wendell Crannell and Ambrose W. Vernon were more optimistic and convinced that "the time (has) come for a new and much higher emphasis to be placed upon the historical and objective as important factors in reinforcing faith."(40) The "ditch" of history here left no unsurmountable obstructions to knowledge of the historical Jesus. And significantly, the year Schweitzer used Lessing's philosophy of religion to pronounce the old quest futile witnessed on the part of American reviewers in the Bibliotheca Sacra a renewed reference to works on Christian apologetics in the evidentialist tradition, works approving "without hesitation the genuineness of the New Testament records" as well as "the historicity of the external marvels related of Jesus...."(41)

Compared with the Leben-Jesu-Forschung, the American quest here displayed a far less developed concern with source and redaction criticism. This comparative lack of interest in biblical criticism was freely admitted by most theologians and exegetes in the last quarter of the nineteenth century. Thus O. B. Frothingham declared: "What we need is not some new interpretation of the Bible, but some new interpretation of the facts of life...." Against this experiential background it was "of purely incidental and secondary importance" "what men believe in regard to ... the composition or interpretation of the Bible, the genuineness of the New Testament...." "Such questions (were) interesting ... but vitally interesting they (were) not."(42) This applied in particular to the fictional "lives" whose production increased substantially at the close of the century. Exegetically, these "lives" fell back upon the course of the harmonist and subverted critical exegesis through the use of fictional techniques. With the literary adaptations of the life of Jesus produced by Harriet Beecher Stowe and Elizabeth Stuart Phelps, the rejection of the source critical view that Mark yielded a continuous outline of the life of Jesus and the findings of "tendency" and redaction criticism were not applied.

Nineteenth century American practitioners of the quest were well aware, however, that the Leben-Jesu-Forschung had developed source critical theories of composition and redaction which undermined the evidentialist value of biblical narratives. "The sceptical critics of modern times," the Christian Examiner observed in 1869, "found" "the Gospels ... not to be from eyewitnesses, not first-hand documents, ... nor even wholly independent narratives, but to have been worked over by different hands, founded upon either a common oral tradition, or upon common written fragments." Yet the destructive force of these findings against a historically grounded faith was quickly bypassed with the assertion that "whether the Gospels be fictitious or historical, one thing is indisputable, - they contain a delineation of a great character...."(43) "The Jesus of the Evangelists" had been given a definite religious "personality," and to arrive at the core of this "personality" required a reconstruction both "genuine" and "authentic," not one overly critical and exegetical.(44)

There was yet another respect in which the American quest withdrew to go its own ways. Crucial to the theological map of the American quest was the correctness of historical claims and not so much questions pertaining to doctrine and creed. The "fundamental question" was "simply, whether Christianity is a fact of history." "It is contained in certain documents: are those documents authentic records?"(45) And on this question, Unitarian and Trinitarian critics contemporaneous with Leben Jesu researchers in the sceptical tradition of Strauss remained expressly committed to historical factuality, reluctant to meddle with historical "evidences" and concerned instead to pinpoint the historical Jesus in time and place. This persistent concern sharply distinguished the course of the American quest from that of the Leben-Jesu-Forschung. Thus, when the mythologists in the Leben-Jesu-Forschung passed on to a pronounced scepticism about the historical reliability of the life of Jesus accounts, the major theological forums of the American quest launched reiterated attacks on the "mythical" approach. The Christian Examiner judged it not conceivable "that out of preceding Judaism there could have been elaborated, by a succession of mythical creations, a portraiture of the Messiah so different from and superior to the Jewish ideas, and yet one possessing such a unity of character throughout, as that of Jesus in the Gospels does." "Moreover, the period of sixty-five years, from the death of Jesus to the end of the first century ... is not sufficient time for the mythical development of the declination of Christ in them out of the religious, moral, and Messianic ideas of Judaism."(46)

At the turn of century, this rejection of the mythical approach was further extended to the option of total scepticism about the historicity of the life of Jesus. According to this option of the Leben-Jesu- Forschung, Christianity flowed from an "idea" rather than historical occurrences. "The ideal Christ, not the historical Jesus of modern liberal theology, was the founder of the Christian movement, and made it victorious over its opponents.... From the first we find Christianity as the religion, not of the historical man Christ, who merely passed through history, but of the super-historical god-man Jesus Christ."(47) Arthur Drews' polemic formulation of this view in 1909 in Die Christusmythe went so far as to consider belief in the historical reality of Jesus a block to religious progress. "Those who cling to a historical Jesus on religious grounds," Drews judged, "(load their) religious consciousness with doubtful historical ballast." Central for Drews was the "idea" of the God-man, an immanent deity which suffused every creature and worked to transcend the finitude in the consciousness of man. And against this "idea" "what was once the prerogative of Christianity - that it superseded the polytheism of pagan antiquity, and conceived the idea of the divine Savior in the singular and historical - (now presented accordingly) the greatest hindrance to faith."(48)

With American questers, this theory of a "Christ myth" lost out against the adherence to the historicity of the Gospel tradition which had quickly won its way to a consensus strong enough to prevail for decades to come and pervasive enough to cut across denominational lines. Both orthodox and liberal camps of biblical criticism attempted to preserve the historicity of the life of Jesus accounts and tended towards moderation and conservatism, never really threatening faith by history. A common front of exegetes and theologians in the American quest grew to appropriate the higher critical tools of the Leben-Jesu-Forschung, but when they did so, they rested secure in their conviction that the techniques of biographical, historical-psychological interpretation would triumph. Therefore, when Schweitzer revealed the impossibility and inadequacy of positivistic biographical approaches to the life of Jesus, American questers were not prepared to accept Schweitzer's verdict at face value.

American reviewers of the Quest were at one with Schweitzer in acknowledging for "the movement back to Christ ... its impossibility as a historical task."(49) The way to a historical solution, the Bibliotheca

Sacra acknowledged in a review of "Lessing's Philosophy of Religion," was barred by "the opposition between eternal truths of reason and accidental truths of history." The "dogmas of the Christian religion," Lessing's opposition asserted, "cannot be put forward as essential truths, and so far as they are not intrinsically self-evidencing rest on evidence which is at best but probable."(50) For the American quest at the turn of the century, however, this assertion was not entirely conclusive. Given the fact that "the story of Jesus could never have been written in vacuo," "the necessity of regarding Jesus as historically conditioned" could not simply be dismissed by Lessing's insight into the "ugly broad ditch" of history. To American questers contemporaneous with Schweitzer like Gerald Birney, Philip Wendell Crannell, Ambrose White Vernon and Austin Rice, it still seemed "possible so to undertake the return to Jesus that it shall not make Christian faith depend on the necessarily uncertain results of historical research...."(51) The "stability and enrichment that accrue to the idea from the historical fact" validated an approach to the history of Jesus according to terms immanent in secular history which viewed "historic fact" as "representative of the process or idea." To settle for Schweitzer's restatement of the "ugly broad ditch" of history was therefore to ignore that "Christ's life (was) not an accident of history, but a deliberately purposed embodiment of truth for all time - ... in fact, ... history become religion in him."(52)

In this renewed appeal to evidentialist apologetics, Lessing's "ugly broad ditch" was bridged not in terms of religious philosophy or doctrinal theology but rather on an expressly historico-critical and religio-historical plane. Concern with this plane was prompted by the emergence of an attack on the historicity of the quest's Jesus figure which intensified on American soil the focus on the historical positivity of the Gospel tradition at precisely the time Schweitzer urged the abandonment of the biographical Jesus quest. With The pre-Christian Jesus by William Benjamin Smith, mathematical teacher at New Orleans, American practitioneers were in 1906 confronted on their own ground with an interpretation of the historical Jesus as an ancient pre-Christian cult-god of the Diaspora. Aligned with the religio-historical school and the Christ myth school of criticism represented in the Leben-Jesu-Forschung by Drews, Kalthoff and Kautsky and in the British quest by J. M. Robertson and George Mead, W. B. Smith judged it inconceivable that a single personality could have inspired Christianity as a religious movement. From the report in Acts 18, 25 to the effect that Apollos was preaching "the things of Jesus" while he was as yet only familiar with the baptism of John, Smith concluded that "the doctrine concerning Jesus was a pre-Christian one, a cult which at the meeting of the centuries (100 B. C. to 100 A. D.) was widespread among the Jews and especially among the Hellenists, more or less in secret and veiled in 'mysteries.'"(53) The Jesus of the Gospels, then, was only a mythological figure, the cult-god of the Naassene Gnostics and the syncretistic Jewish sect of the Nazarenus, who, well over a century before the appearance of the Gospel's historical Jesus, worshipped a "Nazareth" or "Nazorean," a "guardian" and "saviour."(54)

In this mode Smith was led to propagate the idea of a divine pre-Christian Jesus and directed the course of the American quest once more with renewed force to the problem of the historicity of the Jesus figure. Parallel to the response to Strauss' Leben Jesu in the 1840s and 50s, American reviewers in the opening two decades of the twentieth century thus approached the Leben-Jesu-Forschung under the narrow focus on the factuality issue. "That school of gospel-criticism represented ... by Brandt, Wrede, and Schmidt," American reviewers of the Leben-Jesu-Forschung judged, merely followed Bruno Bauer "in the task of emancipating the world from 'that Roman-Jewish idol, Jesus Christ,' that ultimately the existence of a historic Jesus came to be ... a matter of complete indifference."(55) Similarly, in the version of the quest propagated by Kautsky and Kalthoff, reviewers observed that it was "still ... allowed that 'possibly' a man named Jesus existed ...; but this man (was), for the origin of Christianity, wholly without significance."(56) By the same token, the version propagated by Drews "asserted" "something more than that Jesus is independent of Jesus," but on the basis of the conception of the Gospels as "the deposit of Christian reflection" Drews held in effect, reviewers noted, that "Jesus as a myth might make a stronger religious appeal, might be of a higher religious value, than Jesus as a fact."(57)

Concerning the "latest solution" of this turn of the quest "to the effect that Jesus Christ never so much as existed," American reviewers of the Leben-Jesu-Forschung saw "really ... no occasion for a panic with reference to the historicity of Jesus" and drew back instead to the classic texts of the evidentialist tradition, Greenleaf's <u>On Evidence</u> and Butler's <u>Analogy</u> "with its initial insistence upon probability ... and its solid proof of the reasonableness of an historical revelation."(58) Confronted with the "alternative ... either to return to the church's portrait of the miraculous Christ, ... or else ... to conceive the whole of primitive Christianity as nothing else than the gradual development of a Christ-myth," American practitioners of the quest confidently affirmed the "ancient Christian" view of "Jesus (as) the Christ, God's revelation for the salvation, of the world" and reiterated Furness' point about the historicity of Jesus that "it takes a Jesus to forge a Jesus."(59) The vitality and resiliance of the evidentialist argument of the first generations of biblical critics here still emerged unbroken.

The Quest Suspended

Schweitzer's scepticism about the historical certainty and assurance regarding the figure of Jesus was constructive; he quickly transformed his scepticism into an important gain which culminated in his version of "thoroughgoing eschatology." To Schweitzer, the eschatological message and expectation liberated Jesus from all dependence on the constricting results of historical research. On this count, Schweitzer clearly was harbinger of things to come and was closely aligned with the form critical method. If Schweitzer contributed to important changes in the theological spectrum of the quest, the decisive changes in methodological emphasis came with the rise of form criticism. Against 'reconstructionist' critics the form critical approach emerged as one the most serviceable tools for examining the pre-literary traditions embedded in the Gospel accounts. The pioneers of the form critical method, Wilhelm Wrede, Hermann Gunkel and K. L. Schmidt agreed that the Evangelists were "authors only in the smallest degree - they (were) chiefly collectors, transmitters, redactors."(60) The basic assumption here was that at the preliterary stage the community tradition "consisted of separate units, which were joined together editorially by the evangelists" and now could be classified according to their "earliest form and origin in the life of the early Christian community."(61)

This assumption presented the life of Jesus research with a new situation. The focusing of attention on the creative role of the community rather than the historical figure of Jesus turned the literary history of the synoptics into a religious and social history of early Christianity. In this emphasis "no attempt (was) made to render Jesus as a historical phenomenon."(62) The Gospels, form critics asserted, are Christian apologies or church catechisms which fail to transmit a connected chronological outline of the life of Jesus. The origin, form and preservation of the tradition of Jesus, then, did not follow "the characteristics of real historiography" but rather those of faith.(63) Of concern to the form critics was accordingly neither the personality of Jesus nor the external history of Jesus recorded by the evangelist-editors but rather the kerygma, the oral proclamation of the New Testament community. The Gospels here constituted primary sources for the history of the early church and only secondary sources for the history of Jesus.

This premise and the accompanying interest in the "Sitz im Leben," the life-situation out of which the various extant literary forms had sprung, entailed both "the impossibility and illegitimacy" of the quest for historical facticity concerning the figure of Jesus. "Without his later influence in the community," Julius Wellhausen observed, "we can visualize nothing of the religious personality of Jesus. It always appears only in a reflection, broken by the medium of the Christian faith."(64) An echo of this closing of the door against the production of historical Jesus portraits was apparent in all major advocates of the form-critical method. Common to most of these advocates was the sense that Christian faith could not again be tied to a figure who remained uncertain and elusive even after intense historical criticism and the application of the sharpest source critical tools. "The figure of Jesus is not directly accessible to history," G. Bertram concluded his life of Jesus research. "It is futile to try to place him within a process of historical development...."(65) K. L. Schmidt's _Der Rahmen der Geschichte Jesu_ concurred: "... there is no life of Christ in the sense of an evolving biography...."(66)

This left the field open for the "no quest" of Rudolf Bultmann, who affirmed the futility of the historical Jesus quest and further devalued the significance for theology of "Historie." The kerygma, Bultmann charged, lacked any strong interest in history for history's sake, with Jesus himself functioning merely as the "presupposition" rather than the original force behind New Testament theology. This position proved far more devastating to the sources than the _Quest's_ verdict against the Leben-Jesu-Forschung ever projected. While Schweitzer demonstrated that the old quest for the historical Jesus was impossible, Bultmann's analysis revealed that the historical Jesus of the Leben-Jesu-Forschung was not the proper basis for faith. According to Bultmann, the basis and object of faith was the address of the kerygma which focuses not on the historical but the exalted Jesus. With Bultmann, "the Christ of kerygma (thus), as it were, displaced the historical Jesus...."(67) Bultmann advanced this displacement on theological grounds: Any search for the historical Jesus behind the biblical kerygma constituted to Bultmann an illegitimate attempt to gain some intellectual control over divine revelation and to reduce revelation to a series of objectively demonstrable "saving acts."

Bultmann saw the theological task in particular in liberating faith from all dependences of historical critical research with its uncertainties and variations. "Historical investigation," Bultmann argued, "cannot lead to any result which might serve as a foundation for faith, for all its results have only relative validity."(68) Historico-critical research merely yields a "historical" encounter with the person of Jesus, whereas the "salvation of the world," "the Kyrios Christos occurs only in the kerygma...."(69) Aligned with an existential speculative theology which preserved biblical categories within a demythologizing methodology built on the terms of a Heideggerian brand of existentialist analytics, this premise affirmed the present moment of faith as choice, free personal decision. "Dasein" was a series of encounters and decisions in the 'here and now' of existence and not an index of the appeal to the factual data of the historical Jesus.(70)

Bultmann's position entailed a clear shifting of ground from a specific attack upon biographical historiography of Jesus to an overall rejection of the historico-critical procedures of the old quest. On this count, Bultmann rehearsed the traditional Pauline-Lutheran doctrine of justification and deliberately applied the Reformation principle of faith and works to the problem of faith and knowledge. Consonant with Luther's rejection of the objectification of Christianity in terms of the meritorious works of man, Bultmann regarded the quest's historicistic objectification of Christianity in terms of historico-critical data as illegitimate, as a denial of the gospel of justification through "works of righteousness," the domain of the Law. Against this illegitimate attempt to substitute historico-critical data for faith, Bultmann's criticism set out to "destroy every specious human certainty and every specious demand for certainty, be this certainty based on man's good works or on his cognitive ability."(71)

With Bultmann's repristination of Luther's "sola fide," the quest's wheel revolved full-circle back to the position of Schweitzer. From Bultmann's application of the Reformation doctrine of faith and works to the problem of faith and knowledge, his use of form-critical procedures and his christocentrism it was a short step back to Schweitzer's rejection of historico-critical vindifications of Jesus. Both Bultmann and Schweitzer accepted the form-critical thesis that the Gospels do not take the form of a biography or chronicle, but rather contain confessions of the church's faith in the risen and exalted Christ. Both Bultmann and Schweitzer related their detemporalizing of eschatology to the historical impossibility of grounding christology upon a modern reconstruction of Jesus. And both, finally, rejected attempts to seek an objective, historically verifiable datum as a support for faith in Jesus. With Bultmann and Schweitzer, then, the pendulum swing went its full length and came to rest on the other extreme - the "no quest."

Bultmann's "no quest" perpetuated Schweitzer's indictment of the classical "lives," but with important differences. It did matter to Bultmann that Jesus' existence was historical and that Jesus performed the works with which he was credited in the tradition. But for Bultmann the kerygma was not required to move beyond the mere fact of Jesus' existence. "The kerygma," Bultmann argued, "is not interested in any features or characteristics of the person of Jesus but only in the 'fact' of the Word."(72) Bultmann's disjunction between the historical Jesus and the Christ-kerygma deliberately limited revelation to the bare fact that Jesus has come: "To understand Jesus as the eschatological phenomenon ... all that is necessary is to proclaim that he has come."(73) And in this reduction of the content of Jesus' teaching to the mere fact of its occurrence, the old quest for the historical Jesus appeared not only impossible, as Schweitzer had charged, but also completely irrelevant.

The Quest Continued

Reviewing the Bultmannian phase of the quest in 1937, D. W. Riddle observed that kerygma theology had exerted little lasting impact on American biblical studies in spite of its pervasive influence in Europe.(74) The reluctance of American biblical critics to participate in kerygma theology found expression in the charge of Gnosticism against the existentialist interpretation of the New Testament. Temporal continuity and participation in the relativities of history seemed, with Bultmann, to give way to isolated moments of decision. Bultmann's isolation of the kerygma from the historical life of Jesus, it was charged, deprived the Christ-event of objective reality and reduced the kerygma to a universal, timeless truth, to a docetic residue which reviewers were not prepared to assimilate into their own canon. Thus, at a time when Bultmann approached Jesus as pure "that" imparting to the kerygma no specific content apart from the fact of the crucifixion, Charles C. McCown and E. F. Scott continued by contrast to press "the task of criticism to ... select from the narratives those materials which have a solid historical value" and to reconstruct the bare historical figure of the Jesus of Nazareth.(75)

This "task" presented a continuing American preoccupation and was forced into the center stage again during the Bultmannian phase of the quest. From Frederick C. Grant to Amos Wilder, American critics stressed against Bultmann's detachment of biblical revelation from definite historical situations that "with reference to the historical origins of Christianity ... (one) should not slight the social and cultural factors through which revelation was mediated and to which it spoke."(76) The earlier and continuing influence of the Social Gospel and the social-historical study of religion rendered this premise hostile to the alliance of form criticism with existentialist exegesis and to what was regarded as a flawed attempt to divest the life of Jesus narratives of social relevance. On this very point Bultmann's canon appeared strikingly deficient: Bultmann's phenomenological analysis of human decisions slighted the specific cultural content of these decisions and "by focusing on the individual, (did) not explore the social context in which such decisions (were) made."(77)

Correlative to this deficiency was the methodological dualism of Bultmann's canon which played on a double sense of history according to which the historical ("historisch") events of Jesus' life were treated as a formless relic, while the historic ("geschichtlich") encounter with the "saving event" came to have a decisive significance for human existence. To American reviewers, the dichotomy Bultmann established between the historical-critical reconstruction of the Jesus of history (Historie) and the kerygmatic portrait of the historic (geschichtlich) Christ appeared too rigid. "Geschichte" in Bultmann's vocabulary, it was charged, functioned in a cultural vacuum and led to a mystical concept of religion submerging all interest in the historical Jesus.(78) What was particularly unacceptable in this respect was the reduction of every form of religious experience to the mode of "encounter," to the history of the individual. Bultmann described faith and eschatology in terms of an ethical teaching centered in the existential demand which Christian preaching makes upon the individual. In this way what American questers regarded like Schweitzer as "abiding and eternal" in the being of Jesus became with Bultmann a "private" "now." Bultmann reduced the "abiding and eternal" presence of Schweitzer's Jesus in the experience of the modern Christian to an existentialist, private concern of relevance only when Jesus comes alive by confrontation through the kerygma.(79)

Common to this critique of Bultmann was the reluctance to sever the kerygma's connection with specifically historical factors and with the tradition of the historical Jesus. "It is of the very nature of the kerygma," American reviewers were convinced, "that every moment of biblical religion is situation-conditioned."(80) The foremost consequence of this focus was that biblical criticism, in the manner of the old historical-critical quest, continued to turn to issues extrinsic to the text. Contra Bultmann's canon, this line of criticism, represented most notably by the Chicago School of theologians, first emphasized the history constitutive of the biblical texts and only then turned to the texts themselves and the biblical interpretation of the 'history' in question.(81) Shirley J. Case's "new" "biography" of Jesus thus emphatically stressed "social environment" rather than form critical analysis as the key to the life of Jesus. "It is still possible," Case argued, "from the gospel records and our acquaintance with contemporary Judaism, to reconstruct with a fair degree of certainty a picture of Jesus the preacher in his own distinctive environment delivering his forceful utterances to those with whom he came in contact."(82) This "social-historical" reconstruction, Case was convinced, "will prove our safest guide in recovering from the present Gospel records dependable information regarding the life and teaching of the earthly Jesus."(83)

Just at the point where the Bultmannian school seemed to American critics to be on the verge of dehistoricizing the kerygma, however, the negative conclusions of form criticism about the historicity of the Gospel tradition were not altogether unwelcome to this extrinsic focus. During the form critical stage of the quest, the development of the social sciences quickly branched out into biblical criticism and fed into the "religionsgeschichtliche" method. Correlative to this was the form critical change of emphasis from the literary to the pre-literary period of primitive Christianity. Moreover, insofar as form criticism placed the Gospel narratives in the social context of the communities in which they were produced, the form critical procedures of kerygma theology entailed a sociological premise congenial to a quest building on a rich tradition of Social Gospel interpretations and socio-historical approaches. And in this context the biblical texts receded once again behind a critical interpretation which, unwilling to surrender the historical Jesus, established the continuing relevance of this figure on external grounds.(84)

On the ground of the "lives" the impact of form critical methodology and kerygma theology had the effect of forcing American questers to withdraw to the historical potency of biblical relevation and the Christ-event and to enlist a critical handling of historical evidences for a renewed emphasis on the person of Jesus. The "lives" by Edgar J. Goodspeed, H. E. Fosdick, and Mary Ely Lyman continued the rationalizing attempts of Furness' life of Jesus studies and carried the marks of a perpetuated interest in a psychologistic interpretation of Jesus' "personality" which American questers contemporaneous with Bultmann regarded as "so vivid, ... so lively and unmistakable ... that the story leaves the intense impression of a real man, dealing with real people, in an actual historic situation."(85) This view revived the terms of nineteenth century rationalizing questers to avoid any renditions of Jesus' personality in an abstract way. In opposition to Bultmann, the kerygma was asserted to be neither an docetic relic nor an existentialist residue; rather, it began, Fosdick's "life" reiterated, with "a real man, not a myth."(86) At the core of this assertion lay the focus on Jesus' "personality:" "It was the personality ... through whom the teaching came, who supremely impressed the first disciples, and who still fascinates our imagination...."(87) Continuing the "liberal-positive" quest's focus on Jesus' "character portrait," his marks of inner freedom, courage, integrity and originality, this focus on religious "personality" established that "the Jesus of history, ... the real Jesus, was the effective ... cause of the Christ of faith. And as such, he was "in a very real way, of continued interest and of profound concern...."(88)

What distiniguished this continuation of the old quest was that it proceeded from an acknowledgment of Schweitzer's scepticism about the life of Jesus research. "The Life of Jesus Christ cannot be written," Goodspeed's Jesus study asserted from the very outset.(89) Similarly, the 'Prologue' of Fosdick's "life" asserted that "the attempt ... to leap into the self-consciousness of Jesus, to by-pass the Gospel's thoughts about him and to recover the uninterpreted personality, as he was before being set in inherited patterns of theology, is an all but impossible task."(90) This view paid tribute to the major insights of form critical analysis. "The Gospel records themselves are an inadequate basis," Fosdick conceded. Yet Fosdick nevertheless set out to produce "a very clear picture of the sort of man he was." The quest for the "real Jesus," Fosdick was convinced, could "properly continue untroubled."(91)

This conviction was made possible by enlisting major insights of form criticism into the cause of reconstructing Jesus' history. Thus Fosdick accepted the assertion of form critics that the Gospels passed through a period of oral transmission: "At the beginning the Christian community relied on oral transmission of stories about Jesus' life and teaching."(92) According to Goodspeed, "before the gospels were written, there was an unwritten oral gospel, or at least a story of Jesus' life and teaching, which people who came into the Christian movement and joined the church would learn by heart."(93) The conclusion from this finding, however, was not skepticism about the historical reliability of the scriptural life of Jesus narratives, but rather the insight that "far from invalidating the record ... (the) period of oral transmission made the record an affair of the whole Christian community."(94) Form critical analysis was in this context only regarded as referring to formal classifications of narrative "patterns" and "component units" which led to historical or systematic conclusions. In this way F. C. Grant, the chief American propagator of form criticism, was able to recaptulate in his review of Dibelius' _Die Botschaft von Jesus Christus:_ "Form-Criticism has not done away with our knowledge of the historical Jesus; on the contrary, it has brought him and the earliest body of his followers far closer to us than ever before."(95)

Exegetically, this position took its character in particular from British New Testament criticism represented by C. H. Dodd, T. W. Manson, W. D. Davies and Vincent Taylor, exegetes who emerged as defenders of the "general credibility of the traditional accounts of the life and work of (Jesus)" against the form-critical view that "the greater part of the contents of the Gospels tells us not what He taught, but what the Christian Church which grew up after His death thought."(96) This group of critics rejected the possibility of a complete biography of Jesus, admitting that there are "not enough material for a biography of Jesus, nor even for a complete narrative of the ministry." But the conviction persisted that "the materials at our disposal are ... sufficient for a more limited enterprise." A life of Jesus with a broad chronology could be reconstructed: One could "set the ministry in its historical context, ... read the history of post-exilic Judaism forward to the critical point and ... read the history of the Early Church backwards to the same critical point." "And having got these findings," it was assumed that it was possible to "give some kind of outline of the events that led up to the Cross."(97)

British New Testament critics reacted chiefly against the form critical 'disengagement from history.' "The further we travel along the Wredestrasse," T. W. Manson argued, "the more we realize it is the road to nowhere."(98) Manson's conviction surfaced at one striking point, the defence of the accuracy of Mark's "biographical sketch" against Wrede's and K. L. Schmidt's "case that the main stuff of the Gospel (was) reducible to short narrative units, and that the framework (was) superimposed upon these units."(99) The nerve of the argument for Mark's reliability as a historiographer was the assumption first formulated by C. H. Dodd "that in broad lines the Marcan order does represent a genuine succession of events within which movement and development can be traced."(100) T. W. Manson concurred, arguing that "the title of the Marcan framework to be regarded as respectable historical material is as good as that of any detailed story in the Gospel."(101)

While these assertions justified the presentation of the life and ministry of Jesus on the basis of the Markan outline, the British exegetes did make "concessions ... to ... the disruptive criticism of Mark" and admitted that "it is no longer possible to regard the Marcan framework, in all its details, as a rigid and unalterable scaffolding, into which everything must somehow be fitted...."(102) But contra Bultmann's and Dibelius' proposals that many of the narratives and sayings of Jesus had been created within the early church to serve theological needs, Manson, Davies and Taylor pressed the point that the early Christian community preserved the sayings of Jesus because of its "plain admiration and love for their hero."(103) This point clearly flowed from the "liberal-positive" quest's preoccupation with Jesus' "personality" and perpetuated the old quest's premises advocated by Daniel Schenkel and Karl Theodor Keim, by William Hanna and Lant Carpenter.

For the American counterpart a similar look backwards held true. Reviewing the work of Dibelius, K. L. Schmidt and Bultmann about the origin and history of the Gospel tradition, Cadbury acknowledged that the Gospels "are the products of their history, they contain, like geological strata, the marks and deposits of the developments that lie behind them." It was "not easy to discover these processes, to 'unscramble' this conglomerate," Cadbury conceded.(104) But like Fosdick and his contemporaries in the quest, Cadbury set out to corroborate the Gospels' testimony of a "transcendently important historic personality" in apologetic terms reminiscent of Furness and Norton.(105) Resuming the argument of nineteenth century evidentialists against Strauss' and Bauer's "doubt concerning the historicity of Jesus," Fosdick reiterated that "historic realism is evident in (the Gospel) narratives. This is no concocted myth, but the honest endeavor to record an actual story.... The total impression now made upon New Testament scholars by these records, with their natural, casual often explainable contrasts, is one of bona fide authenticity."(106)

The confidence into the correspondence betwwen "historic fact" and "idea" persisted well into the form critical stage of the Leben-Jesu-

Forschung and rendered the quest on American grounds hostile to shifts away from definite historical-cultural contexts to kerygmatic and existentialist interpretations. To cling to the bare datum of Jesus' historical existence and to reduce the historical element of the kerygma to the absolute minimum, as Bultmann's existentialist, kerygmatic theology did, appeared to a common front of critics from Henry C. Cadbury to Amos Wilder as too narrow an understanding of religious life, a reduction which deprived the Christ-event of "objective reality."(107) This critique of Bultmann's de-historicized approach to the kerygma, which found its most forceful reflection in Morton Scott Enslin's psychologistic interpretation of <u>The Prophet from Nazareth</u>, revived the rationalizing terms of H. E. G. Paulus to reject kerygmatic theology as producing merely abstract figures tied to "the silver screen of an altogether-other Cinerama in vacuo theologico."(108) For Enslin's "life," as for the majority of the more current American "lives," the focus on the "real Jesus of history" prevailed over all attempts to de-historicize the kerygma. The formidable disassociation of the historical Jesus from the kerygmatic Christ which the quest after Schweitzer established through the form critical scepticism concerning historical information about Jesus' life and ministry here did not take hold.(109) On American grounds the original quest for the historical Jesus seemed to continue unimpeded.

The Quest Renewed

Bultmann's form-critical analysis of the Gospel records left him in express opposition not only to the old quest for the historical Jesus, but to any and every quest. For Bultmann, "the Christ of the kerygma (was) not a historical figure which could enjoy continuity with the historical Jesus."(110) This assertion did not categorically preclude the possibility of a systematic and historical reconstruction of the Jesus of Nazareth - Bultmann expressly affirmed that the Gospels presuppose the historical Jesus, for "without him there would be no kerygma" - but Bultmann adhered to nothing more than the "that," the "Daß" of Jesus' history and discarded the significance of the "what", the "Was" and "Wie" of the historical figure of Jesus.(111) "The historical Jesus" was for Bultmann "one phenomenon among others, and not an absolute," and "what things seemed like in Jesus' heart" Bultmann therefore did "not know and (did) not want to know."(112)

Yet this verdict did not stop the production of "lives." On the contrary, with Bultmann's closest disciples - Ernst Käsemann, Günther Bornkamm, Ernst Fuchs, Gerhard Ebeling and Hans Conzelmann - the pendulum swung again to a striking "new quest" which went expressly beyond Bultmann's focus on the sheer facticity of Jesus and his cross. The new questers shared the Bultmannian, form-critical tradition and did by no means intend to return to the province of the old quest. The Gospels, the new questers agreed, defy a pre-critical evaluation as source documents chronologizing the history of Jesus; they represent the theology of the church rather than a historical record of objectively certifiable events. But new questers were not prepared to "allow that, in view of this position, resignation and scepticism should have the last word and lead to a complete lack of interest in the earthly Jesus ..."(113) Whereas the old quest bypassed the kerygma, the new questers were convinced that the kerygmatic portrait yields a reliable faith representation of the historical Jesus.

This "new" kind of quest of the historical Jesus had no intention of creating a "biography" or a comprehensive picture of Jesus; it sought instead the "interpreted historical" Jesus whom the kerygma proclaims. "The historical Jesus," Käsemann asserted in a seminal address to the "Old Marburger" which formally opened the new quest in 1953, "meets us in the New Testament, our only real and original documentation of him, not as he was in himself, not as an isolated individual but as the Lord of the community which believes in him. ... So we only make contact with the life history of Jesus through the Kerygma of the community. The community neither could nor would separate this life history from its own history."(114) This was to assert that the kerygma began with the historical Jesus rather than the early Christian community, an assertion which - contra the old quest - did not substitute a historical construct for faith in the biblical Christ, and which - contra the Bultmannian quest - did not deal with the historical Jesus as merely a factual presupposition.(115)

The "task" of the new quest was "to seek the history in the Kerygma of the Gospel, and in this history to seek the Kerygma."(116) This "task" turned afresh to the question of methodology in assuming that it was both possible and theologically necessary to go behind the kerygma to its historical foundations. For Schweitzer, in contrast, only two positions had been available: his own consistent eschatology, the "historical" solution and the 'Wredestrasse,' consistent scepticism. "Tertium non datur" - there was no other option.(117) With the new quest, however, the methodological situation changed in a manner not foreseen by Schweitzer. The new questers were at one with the form-critical premise that the Gospels functioned as faith-portraits and belonged to the proclamation of the community, but the representatives of the new quest advanced this premise without completely undermining the value of the Gospel sources for historical research. Against the apparent absence of certainty established by form criticism regarding the historical facts of Jesus' life, post-Bultmannian critics like Conzelmann and Ferdinand Hahn sought to renew and redirect the discipline along historico-critical lines and devised a methodology which established the continuity between the historical Jesus and the kerygmatic Christ on the basis of sources rendered "genuine" by means of serviceable criteria of authenticity. Referring to the distinctiveness, coherence and multiple attestation of biblical narratives and sayings, these criteria developed form criticism in a "positive" direction and were tied to the old quest's task of recovering the original form and wording of Jesus' teaching.(118)

Against Bultmann's negative assessment of the usefulness of Jesus' history the new quest in this context asserted the early Christian preaching to have some integral connection with the "presupposition" of that preaching. In so far as the kerygma presented this "presupposition" as an historical phenomenon, it therefore validated and necessitated an inquiry into the historical Jesus. Whereas Bultmann deliberately excluded all questions of Jesus' personality and of his messianic consciousness, reiterating "it is not the historical Jesus, but Jesus Christ, the Christ preached, who is the Lord," the new quest argued that the New Testament kerygma needed more than the "brute fact, the bare, completely accessible fact" of Jesus and his cross.(119) To new questers, Bultmann's form-critical, demythologizing and existential-historical methodology on this count ran the risk of lapsing into kerygmatic docetism. Bultmann's own life of Jesus study, new questers charged, obscured the kerygma; it "dispensed not only with all biographical questions but also with all 'personal' questions. ... It (was) in a sense a Jesus-book without Jesus."(120) The hiatus between the historical Jesus and the kerygmatic Jesus here eliminated the non-existential historical anchorage of Christian thought, leaving merely the inwardness of existential historicity.

The initial thrust of the new quest was the theological aim of maintaining the continuity between the historical Jesus and the exalted Christ, a theological aim the new quest sought to achieve by the historical demonstration that the kerygma was already contained in essence in the work and teaching of Jesus. "To become aware and certain of this continuity" was to the new quest "an indispensable theological necessity," one acknowledging that faith in Christ flows from the person and teaching of Jesus of Nazareth, and not merely from the proclamation of the early Christian community.(121) On the specific expression of the basic historical continuity between the Christ in the kerygma and the Jesus of history, however, the new quest disagreed. Ernst Fuchs saw the historical continuity as given in the fact that in the preaching of Jesus man's relation to God is identical with his. In a similar vein, Herbert Braun established the material continuity between the history of Jesus and the kerygmatic Christ on the basis of an anthropological construct which read the kerygma as an aspect of man's self-understanding before God. Hans Conzelmann and Gerhard Ebeling, on the other hand, saw the continuity between the historical Jesus and the kerygmatic Christ in the area of christology. Jesus and the kerygma here were related as implicit and explicit christology. After Easter the Christian community transformed "indirect" or "implicit" christology into direct statements about Jesus' person and work, with the kerygma thus serving as the explicit formulation and preaching of the definite salvation that took place in Jesus Christ.(122)

In these formulations of the continuity between the historical Jesus and the kerygma the presuppositions of both the classical "lives" and the Bultmannian "no quest" were strikingly reversed. At the heart of the old quest lay a rupture between the historical Jesus and the Christ of faith, a discontinuity between the proclamation concerning Christ and the historical person of Jesus of Nazareth. The old quest's express aim was to reconstruct a Jesus of history who would be a corrective to the Christ of faith. Bultmann, in his quest for the historical Jesus, escalated this position to the point of asserting a sharp hiatus between the historical Jesus and the Christ preached by the church. For Bultmann the relationship between the historical Jesus and the kerygma was merely tangential. All that remained was the punctual event of preaching present only where and when, through the kerygma, God confronted the believer, demanded decision and thus led to a new self-understanding in eschatological existence.(123) In the renewal of the Jesus quest characteristic of the post-Bultmannians an entirely different focus prevailed. Seeking an antidote to the alleged illegitimacy of the nineteenth century quest, new questers headed by Ernst Fuchs and Günther Bornkamm shifted the traditional question of the historical Jesus to phenomenological and personalistic categories. The precedent for this shift had been provided by Bultmann himself who limited "attention ... entirely ... to what Jesus purposed," "to a highly personal encounter with history, ... and hence to what in his purpose as a part of history makes a present demand on us."(124) Similarly, the new quest, in stressing an existential relation to history, now supplemented objectifying historical-critical methods with the interpretation of religious meanings perceived by the individual in the confrontation with sacred events of the past.

To American reviewers of the new quest, most notably John B. Cobb, John Dillenberger and Amos Wilder, this renewal of the quest appeared reductive and abstractionist, leaving merely "a fleshless mathematics of the divine-human transaction...." "Man is not man as we know him," Wilder complained of the new quest's existentialist bias, "but a kind of generalized 'anthropos,'" severed from the concrete historical cultural realities and from the web of social relationships in which he is immersed.(125) At this juncture historical criticism appeared as a guarantee that the revelance of the historical Jesus could be safeguarded. Historical criticism was asserted to proceed on the premise of "the absolute identification of the earthly Jesus of Nazareth with the risen Lord of Christian experience (as) the key, and the only key, to understanding the phenomena present in the New Testament tradition."(126) "This early Christian equation" justified the critic "in using that historical knowledge to test the validity of claims made in the name of Jesus Christ and the authenticity of a kerygma claiming to present Jesus Christ...."(127) Against the new quest's abstraction from historical and social contexts, issues extrinsic to the biblical text itself were thus further pushed into the foreground.

Among those who discovered methodological faults with the new quest, American narrative theologians formed the most prominent group.(128) For the generation of narrative theologians headed in the seventies by the objectivist criticism of Hans Frei, the new quest still submitted to the "referential theory of meaning" in rendering the recovery of meaning dependent on matters extrinsic to the text. With this critique the historico-critical stance under whose tutelage American critics had continued the old quest for the historical Jesus was completely discredited. According to narrative theologians, referential approaches merely fitted the biblical story into self-sufficient extra-textual contexts rather than incorporating these contexts into the biblical narratives.(129) Utilizing the presuppositions of the New Criticism, narrative theologians sought in turn to salvage traditional hermeneutics and restore it to its biblical setting by locating "meaning" entirely within the text's verbal structure. What stood out in this assimilation of the premises of the New Criticism to New Testament studies was the autonomy and vitality granted to the biblical narratives apart from their immersion in the message and ministry of the historical Jesus. While the Leben-Jesu-Forschung had developed a complex methodological apparatus for the investigation of historical sources, redactions and "forms" pertaining to the historical Jesus, narrative theologians showed no sustained interest in the historico-critical pursuit of the historical Jesus.(130) Relevant for them was the literary Jesus figure, the "character" embedded in the biblical text and to be approached only with the methodology of literary criticism.

This very trend to focus on the text as text, however, was not fully assimilated by American life of Jesus researchers. Critics intent on carrying forward the quest for the historical Jesus could not afford to separate the biblical text from its background, nor could they settle for an existentialist interpretation of faith without adherence to the past event of Jesus Christ. In this context both the approaches of the new quest and in turn also those of narrative theology and structuralism appeared inadequate in their disjunction between the abstract conceptuality of non-referential "meaning" and the concrete historical and cultural realities which constituted "meaning."(131) The "new" approaches merely seemed to place the biblical world into descriptive, phenomenological contexts which no longer had a necessary hinge in the historical Jesus.

To narrativist critics like Hand Frei and Darrell Jodock, this also appeared to hold true of yet another "new" approach to the biblical narratives of the life of Jesus, namely the "new hermeneutic" in which, according to Frei's critical characterization, the interpretation of the Bible was "practically equivalent to general philosophical inquiry; and the language-to-be-interpreted (became) shorthand for a whole philosophical or theological anthropology."(132) The "new hermeneutic," as developed by the former Bultmann pupils Gerhard Ebeling and Ernst Fuchs under the tutelage of existentialist analytics, followed Bultmann in turning to the hermeneutical problem of the scriptural accounts and focused primarily on language itself and its relation to reality. Language in the new hermeneutic ceased to be a mere "technical instrument" and was approached instead as performative language in which "the issuing of the utterance is the performing of an action."(133) In this language God's saving word "comes to speech." According to the terminology used by Ebeling, the word of God conveys "an event in which God himself is communicated.... With God word and deed are one: his speaking is the way of his acting."(134)

In this context the word of Jesus in the New Testament did for Ebeling not constitute an 'objectification' but rather a call, a pledge in which Jesus became the "text" of the early Christian proclamation.(135) Jesus established a common understanding with his hearers, in particular in the language of the parables. Now faith in God "speaks out of that same self-understanding to which Jesus once summoned his hearers. The time of the parable has now been superseded by the time of confession to Jesus."(136) "Self-understanding" here designated man's "way of reacting ... to reality or to God" and not merely man's conscious understanding of himself. With Ebeling, "when God speaks, the whole of reality as it concerns us enters language anew."(137) In this sense, the New Testament account of Jesus is no longer "just the servant that transmits kerygmatic formulations, but rather a master that directs (man) into the language-context of ... existence."(138) The text has turned into a "language-event" (Sprachereignis) or "word-event" (Wortgeschehen).(139)

In this context, the hermeneutical task of the quest was no longer to impart factual or descriptive information about the sayings of the historical Jesus. Rather, the position of the "new hermeneutic" regarded the purpose of these sayings to be "existential" in that they attempt to change the hearer's attitude and relationship to reality. The aim of the new hermeneutic was therefore to uncover the "language power of existence" according to which Jesus' words "both verbalize Jesus' understanding of his own situation in the world and ... also create the possibility of the hearer's sharing that situation." By Jesus' standing "together with" the hearer, "to have faith in Jesus now means essentially to repeat Jesus' decision" to go the way of the cross.(140) With this assertion the new hermeneutic was able to approach man's confrontation with the historical Jesus in terms of a material continuity between the historical Jesus and the kerygmatic Christ. "In the proclamation of the resurrection," Fuchs argued, "the historical Jesus himself has come to us. The so-called Christ of faith is none other than the historical Jesus."(141)

This revision of the old quest's key presupposition, a revision in which the kerygma was interpreted with the help of the historical Jesus, also held true for the group of American critics headed by Amos Wilder, Robert Funk and Walter Wink, who followed the new hermeneutic along part of its way. Yet the reviews of the new hermeneutic produced by this group of critics coalesced on the issue of the relation of faith and history and charged that in Fuchs' and Ebeling's hermeneutical preoccupation "abstraction is made of the historical context in which the transaction of faith or understanding takes place."(142) Moreover, according to Wilder, the new hermeneutic's neglect of the cultural 'conditionedness' of language also slighted the extent to which language is founded on convention and involves not only language as "event" but language as "meaning." The new hermeneutic pressed by Ernst Fuchs, Wilder charged, "refuses to define the content of faith ... (and) is afraid of word as convention or as a means of conveying information.... Fuchs carries this so far that revelation, as it were, reveals nothing ... Jesus calls, indeed, for decision.... But surely his words, deed, presence, person, and message rested ... upon dogma, eschatological and theocratic."(143) From this, a definite connection with the old quest for the historical Jesus emerged, an alignment never really interrupted in the American scene since the emergence of the critical Jesus quest: In Wilder's version of the 'new' hermeneutic, the emphasis on man's "own historical-social life-situation as a main feature of (his) own presupposition" was throughout perceived to be bound up with the factual "reality" of the historical Jesus as an "inseparable aspect" of the Christ of faith.(144)

Wilder's critique of the new hermeneutic also touched upon epistemology. The epistemological model of the old quest's hermeneutics relied on the subject-object scheme. In traditional hermeneutics, the interpreter, as active subject, scrutinized the text as a passive object of investigation by analyzing the text's grammer and style as well as its linguistic, literary and historical context. In the new hermeneutic, by contrast, hermeneutics designated not "a collection of rules" but rather a "theory of understanding" which "(took) the plan of the classical epistemological theory."(145) This substitution reversed the hermeneutical flow. The subject matter of the text, conceived of as the "language-event" or "word-event," was no longer a passive object but rather served as the origin of understanding. "The text," Ebeling argued, "becomes a hermeneutic aid in the understanding of present experience."(146) In this way traditional hermeneutics turns into "hermeneutic" in which the object actively responds, as subject," to the interpreter, thereby moving beyond the task of the interpreter's apprehending to his 'being apprehended.' In Ernst Fuchs' terminology, the texts "must therefore translate us before we can translate him."(147)

Fuchs and Ebeling owed this break from the traditional subject object scheme to the turning point in the history of hermeneutics signalled by Schleiermacher's Hermeneutik. Devaluing the concept of hermeneutics as an aggregate of rules, Schleiermacher's Hermeneutik did not set out to support and corroborate an "already accepted understanding" of the New Testament text. What the new hermeneutic found in Schleiermacher was instead "the qualitatively different function of (hermeneutics) ... of making understanding possible, and deliberately initiating understanding in each individual case."(148) For the reception of the new hermeneutic by American reviewers, this continued relevance of Schleiermacher's critique of the standpoint of philology in the new hermeneutic of Fuchs and Ebeling emerged as a significant dividing line. There were clear points of similarity between the works of Fuchs and Ebeling and the parable studies conducted by Robert Funk, J. D. Crossan and D. O. Via in the 1970s in which the classical issue of history and theology in biblical studies was similarly related to the function of language. But despite the shared new attention to the historical Jesus as a relevant and inevitable counterpart of the interest in existentialist hermeneutic and in the linguistic ground of the New Testament tradition, in American biblical studies hermeneutics, as distinguished from "hermeneutic," remained largely a debate about historical-critical method. The persistence of traditional hermeneutics, evidenced in the continued appeal of J. Edwin Hartill's Biblical Hermeneutics and Milton S. Terry's Biblical Hermeneutics: A Treatise on the Interpretation of the Old and New Testaments, here strikingly slighted the separation, initiated within the Leben-Jesu-Forschung by Schleiermacher, of hermeneutics proper from the philological and historical study of the text.(149)

In the context of the emergence and development of the American quest, this characteristic reflected the remnants of the nineteenth century preoccupation with the biblical narratives' correspondence to fact claims, a preoccupation which confined the hermeneutical task primarily to philological or historiographical bounds. This narrow focus continued effectively in the American response to the new hermeneutic and its alignment with Schleiermacher's language-centered hermeneutics. What persisted was the assumption that the New Testament text was in a way 'out there,' to be "understood not by reference to some vague inner mental process but by reference to the subject, the matter, to which the text is referring."(150) In this way biblical criticism remained largely a 'description science' which still conceived hermeneutics as referring to an aggregate of methodological principles determining interpretation.

The Legacy of the Quest

In the "new" approaches to the historical Jesus the possibility of resuming the critical Jesus quest flowed from the assumption of a formal analogy between the kerygma and the historical critic's task. Moving beyond objective historiography, the new quest and the new hermeneutic maintained that historical criticism "mediated an existential encounter with Jesus, an encounter also mediated by the kerygma."(151) Historical criticism in this way yielded a new 'avenue' to the historical Jesus, one perpetuating a search which Schweitzer's Quest had set out to terminate. Methodologically, this development raised an issue which Continental and the American quest had in common: the tension between historical and theological categories. This tension was deeply entrenched in the quest's history; it appeared in Martin Kähler's attempt to render theological assertions pertaining to the person of Christ immune to historical criticism and to the 'learned papacy of historians;' in the Barthian devaluation of "historical exegesis" and appraisal of "theological exegesis;" and in the negative role Bultmann assigned to historical criticism. It was precisely this negative assessment, however, on which the post-Bultmannians were no longer unanimous. Whereas Bultmann acknowledged "the message of Jesus" and its historico-critical reconstruction as "a presupposition for the theology of the New Testament rather than a part of that theology itself," the redaction critics affirmed the central place of the historical Jesus and the corresponding role of historico-critical reconstruction as faith's helpmate within a theology of the New Testament.(152) With a second group of post-Bultmannians, however, represented by Gerhard Maier and Peter Stuhlmacher, historico-critical procedures were in contrast charged with leading theology up a blind alley, unable to deal with transcendence and to approach religious texts in terms other than probability.(153)

On the American front of the life of Jesus research a similar polarization developed after the emergence of the new quest. Over against the eulogistic appraisal of historico-critical procedures evident in particular in Henry J. Cadbury's life of Jesus studies, narrative theologians made clear that biblical theology and historical criticism stood in an irreconcilable opposition, an opposition unknown to the pre-critical framework which had rendered extra-biblical thought through the biblical narratives themselves. According to the objectivist criticism of Frei's The Eclipse of Biblical Narrative, this framework gradually became reversed during the course of the last two centuries through the separation of the biblical narratives' meaning from their "truth" and the disassociation of narrative from "reality." As a result of this disjunction, the real historical and theological reference of the text was held to be located outside the text, with the question of the narratives' "meaning," the subject of biblical theology, now standing opposed to the question of the narratives' "truth" as the subject of historical criticism. The solution suggested by narrative theologians to this allegedly flawed opposition asked for a reconsideration of the biblical narratives as "realistic" or "history-like" narratives as well as for an analysis of their "narrative shape" which affirmed the self-referentiality of biblical narrative. According to Frei, "the narrative itself is the meaning of the text, ... it refers to no other subject matter, and ... the meaning ... emerges cumulatively from the text itself." In this context, the life of Jesus narratives "mean what the say" and therefore require no historico-critical inquiry into "ostensive meaning."(154)

From a very different angle, the American critics Paul Minear and Walter Wink perpetuated this negative assessment of the role of historico-critical analysis by pronouncing historical criticism bankrupt and evacuated of all explicitly theological and existential concerns. Wink's 1973 study, The Bible in Human Transformation, charged that the results of historical criticism did not speak to the inner self and distanced the critic from the text. Moreover, the methodology of historical criticism was to Wink "marred by a false objectivism, subjected to uncontrolled technologism" and hence inherently inappropriate to texts written "from faith to faith."(155) Wink further charged that biblical criticism had lost its liberating and antidogmatic function. Originally, biblical criticism had served to create distance and thereby freedom from dogmatic Christendom. "Today, however," Wink complained, "biblical criticism is the new Establishment. Now, not dogmatic Christendom, but the biblical guild functions as the harsh superego in the self of many exegetes." As a result, historical criticism fails "so to interpret the Scriptures that the past becomes alive and illuminates (the) present with new possibilities for personal and social transformation."(156)

A corrective to these charges against historical criticism may be found in the practitioners of the old quest. The advocates of the quest were aware that historical-critical interpretation distanced the text and made it "alien" to their own experiences.(157) Within the old quest this constituted an important theological function of historical criticism in that Christian faith was pointed back to the historical person of Jesus of Nazareth and his tradition as something "strange" and "alien," something defiant of the "tyranny of dogmatic theology." In view of the current charges against the "evacuated" nature of historical criticism, a recovery of this theological significance of historical-critical method appears appropriate with regard to its suggestion that the original witness of the text can thus be preserved from later dogmatic and presentistic usurpations.(158)

The quest may also serve as a corrective to the separation between the literary and historico-critical dimensions of the Gospel accounts traced by narrative theologians. The documentations provided by narrative theologians of the inability of eighteenth and nineteenth century biblical hermeneutics to come to terms with the Gospels as realistic narratives mask the fact that advocates of the quest both on the Continent and in America were prepared to utilize the genres of the realist novel and historical romance for their presentations of the life of Jesus and were anxious to advocate this procedure as derived from the biblical narratives.(159) The scope of the quest therefore cannot be limited by placing the "lives" under the rubric of historiography or biography. The "lives" produced by Ernest Renan, Harriet Beecher Stowe and E. S. Phelps reveal that the notions of how a life of Jesus should be presented often developed simultaneously with new approaches to the realist novel. The quest was in this respect related to the rise of religious fiction and compatible with literature, always keeping one foot firmly within historico-critical confines.

The correlation between historical and literary dimensions of the life of Jesus accounts can also be applied to the charge advanced by Walter Wink and James Smart that historical criticism has become "separated from a vital community" by indulging in turgid philological and historical analysis which fails to penetrate into the life of the church. A "guild of biblical scholars" restricting itself to historical-literary critical procedures thus allegedly stands opposed to the theologian and preacher concerned with questions of piety and faith.(160) The practitioners of the old quest for the historical Jesus never aimed at any such dichotomy between biblical critic and preacher, between biblical theology and practical theology. In 1864, Strauss produced a Leben Jesu expressly designed "for the German people," a "life" for the laity as opposed to the theologian and historical critic. Strauss here paid tribute to the popular appeal of the ideas underlying the life of Jesus movement. Through it the religious personality of Jesus could be used to provide a solid historical foundation for popular piety, a basis which was not antirational or supernatural but merely grounded in "a person with living heartbeats, tempted like ourselves, but victorious ... a personality."(161) The quest was in this respect not the exclusive property of the university teacher and the sophisticated biblical critic, but rather, in the guise of the religious bestseller and its popularization of the principles of historico-critical reconstruction, congenial to the interests of both preachers and laity concerned with the continuing relevance of the New Testament proclamation. For the American front of the quest, this held true to a greater extent than in the Leben-Jesu-Forschung, since the issue of the life of the historical Jesus here entered more smoothly and readily into popular literary adaptations which removed the quest from the province of the academically trained theologian.

Directly counter to this is Wink's charge that historical criticism entails conscious abstraction from personal involvement and is incommensurate with "personal and social transformation."(162) To practitioners of the quest this did not apply; their historical critical reconstruction focused on a "personality," a "revered and honoured companion," "warning us and awakening our consciences, comforting us and driving us on...."(163) Similarly, Schweitzer, both critic and yet still representative of the quest, arrived at a Jesus who summoned men to commitment and decision. The Quest's historical, eschatologically oriented Jesus was not a complete "stranger" to Schweitzer's own time but rather pressed the believer to become involved in the "now" of the proclaimed message. Even if the historical Jesus had something "strange" about Him, Schweitzer was convinced that Jesus' "personality, as it really is," "influences" the believer in the form of the life- and world-affirming ethic of "reverence for life" "much more strongly and immediately than when He approached us in dogma and in the results attained up to the present by research." Contra the "false objectivism" and "uncontrolled technologism" critics have established as characteristics of historico-critical procedures, Schweitzer's own handling of historical criticism thus arrived at a Jesus who called for personal involvement and the recovery of His spirit in the world. This forms a desirable exception both to the flawed neutrality and objectivity allegedly characteristic of current historical-critical exegesis and to the "half-historical, half modern Jesus" discovered by the quest's historico-critical reconstructions, an exception which acknowledges that the historical critic "must be prepared to find that the historical knowledge of the personality and life of Jesus will not be a help, but perhaps even an offence to religion."(164) In this tension between an approach to Jesus as a "helper" "still at work in the world" and as a "stranger" and "enigma" "to our world" lies the acute force of Schweitzer's answer to those who set out to "(express) their recognition of Him" in "names ... (like) Messiah, Son of Man, Son of God...." To Schweitzer, there was no "designation" for the "true historical Jesus" who "comes to us as One unknown, without a name, as of old, by the lake-side, He came to those men who knew Him not."(165) Jesus "has no answer for the question, 'Tell us Thy name in our speech and for our day.'"(166)

ABBREVIATIONS

ANT	Andover Newton Theological Library
BPL	Boston Public Library
HL	Houghton Library, Harvard University
HUA	Harvard University Archives
MHS	Massachusetts Historical Society

AJTh	The American Journal of Theology
AL	American Literature
CW	*The Collected Works of Ralph Waldo Emerson*, ed. Robert Spiller, Alfred Fergeson, et al. (Cambridge, Mass.: The Belknap Press of Harvard University Press, 1971-).
ESQ	Emerson Society Quarterly
FThPh	Für Theologie und Philosophie: Eine Oppositionsschrift
Geschichte	Albert Schweitzer, *Geschichte der Leben-Jesu-Forschung* (Tübingen: J. C. B. Mohr, 1906; 6th ed., 1951).
HThR	Harvard Theological Review
J	*The Journals of Ralph Waldo Emerson*, ed. Edward Waldo Emerson and Waldo Emerson Forbes, 10 vols. Centenary Edition (Boston and New York: Houghton Mifflin Co., 1910-1914).
JMN	*The Journals and Miscellaneous Notebooks of Ralph Waldo Emerson*, ed. William Gillman et al. (Cambridge, Mass.: The Belknap Press of Harvard University Press, 1960-1977).
JR	Journal of Religion
JTS	Journal of Theological Studies
JWK	Jahrbücher für Wissenschaftliche Kritik
KA	Karelynn Kalinevitch, Ralph Waldo Emerson's Older Brother: The Letters and Journal of William Emerson (Ph. D. diss,. University of Tennessee, 1982)
L	*The Letters of Ralph Waldo Emerson*, ed. Ralph L. Rusk, 6 vols. (New York: Columbia University Press, 1939).
NEQ	New England Quarterly
NTS	New Testament Studies
PhQ	Philosophical Quarterly
Quest	Albert Schweitzer, *The Quest of the Historical Jesus: A Critical Study of its Progress from Reimarus to Wrede* (London: A. & C. Black, 1954)
RGG^3	*Die Religion in Geschichte und Gegenwart. Handwörterbuch für Theologie und Religionswissenschaft. Dritte neu bearbeitete Auflage in Gemeinschaft mit Hans Frhr. v. Campenhausen, Erich Dinkler, Gerhard Gloege und Knud E. Logstrup, herausgegeben von Kurt Galling*, 6 vols. and *Registerband* (Tübingen: J. C. B. Mohr (Paul Siebeck), 1957-65).
S	Emerson's Sermons. (Mss. at Houghton Library)
SJTh	Scottish Journal of Theology
SW	Sämtliche Werke
ThLZ	Theologische Literaturzeitung
ThR	Theologische Rundschau
ThStKr	Theologische Studien und Kritiken
ThZ	Theologische Zeitschrift

TRE	Theologische Realenzyklopädie, ed. Gerhard Krause, Gerhard Müller, et al. (Berlin: Walter de Gruyter, 1976-proceeding).
VL	The Vestry Lectures and a Rare Sermon, ed. Kenneth W. Cameron (Hartford: Transcendental Books, 1984). (Mss. at Houghton Library)
W	The Complete Works of Ralph Waldo Emerson, ed. Edward Waldo Emerson, 12 vols., Centenary Edition (Boston and New York: Houghton Mifflin Co., 1903-1904).
YES	Young Emerson Speaks: Unpublished Discourses on Many Subjects, ed. Arthur C. McGiffert. (Boston: Houghton Mifflin, 1938).
ZKG	Zeitschrift für Kirchengeschichte
ZThK	Zeitschrift für Theologie und Kirche

NOTES

Preface

1 Gotthold Ephraim Lessing, "On the Proof of the Spirit and of Power," in Lessing's Theological Writings, ed. Henry Chadwick (London: Black, 1956), 53.

2 Cf. Reimarus: Fragments, ed. C. H. Talbert (Philadelphia: Fortress Press, 1970), 64-67.

3 Albert Schweitzer, The Quest of the Historical Jesus. A Critical Study of its Progress from Reimarus to Wrede (London: Adam & Charles Black, 1954), 4.

4 Ibid., 4.

5 Quest, 396. On the significance of the "kerygma" for the historical Jesus quest, see the essays brought together in Helmut Ristow and Karl Matthiae (eds.), Der historische Jesus und der kerygmatische Christus. Beiträge zum Christusverständnis in Forschung und Verkündigung (Berlin, 1961[2]). See also Gerhard Ebeling, Theologie und Verkündigung. Ein Gespräch mit Rudolf Bultmann (Tübingen, 1962), 109-114.

6 Cf. the echo of Schweitzer's rejection of the "half-historical, half-modern Jesus" produced by the Leben-Jesu-Forschung (Quest, 396) in George Tyrell, Christianity at the Cross-Roads (1909, rep. ed. London: George Allen & Unwin, 1963), 49.

7 For acknowledgements of the persistence of the quest in American biblical scholarship, see Otto A. Piper, "Das Problem des Lebens Jesu seit Schweitzer," in Verbum Dei Manet in Aeternum: Festschrift für Otto Schmitz (Witten: Luther-Verlag, 1953), 73-93; and Roy Harrisville, "Representative American Lives of Jesus," in The Historical Jesus and the Kerygmatic Christ, eds. Carl Braaten and Roy Harrisville (New York: Abingdom, 1964), 172-196.

8 On the deistic strain of influence relevant for the quest, see Robert D. Richardson, Myth and Literature in the American Renaissance (Bloomington and London: Indiana University Press, 1978); on the historico-critical strain of influence, see Jürgen Herbst, The German Historical School in American Scholarship (Ithaca, NY: Cornell University Press, 1965); Herbert Hovenkamp, Science and Religion in America, 1800-1860 (Philadelphia: University of Pennsylvania Press, 1954); For a more specialized treatment of nineteenth century criticism at Harvard and Andover, see Jerry Wayne Brown, The Rise of Biblical Criticism in America, 1800-1870: The New England Scholars (Middletown, CT: Wesleyan University Press, 1969). See also Eugene R. Chable, "A Study of the Interpretation of the New Testament in New England Unitarianism" (Ph.D. diss., Columbia University, 1956); and Harold Y. Vanderpool, "The Andover Conservatives: Apologetics, Biblical Criticism, and Theological Change at Andover Theological Seminary, 1808-1880" (Ph.D. diss., Harvard University, 1971).

9 Octavius Brooks Frothingham, "Scientific Criticism of the New Testament," Christian Examiner, LVII (1854), 110. For a full-length study of the influence of common-sense philosophy and evidentialism at Harvard, see Daniel Walker Howe, The Unitarian Conscience: Harvard Moral Philosophy, 1805-1861 (Cambridge, Mass.: Harvard University Press, 1970) and Bruce Kuklick, The Rise of American Philosophy: Cambridge, Massachusetts, 1860-1930 (New Haven: Yale University

Press, 1977), chapters 1 and 2. The widespread trust in a simple scientific epistemology is further noted by Theodore Dwight Bozeman, Protestantism in an Age of Science: The Baconian Ideal and Antebellum American Religious Thought (Chapel Hill: University of North Carolina Press, 1977), chapter 7; Loefferts Loetscher, The Broadening Church (Philadelphia: University of Pennsylvania Press, 1954) chapter 3; Brooks Holifield, The Gentlemen Theologians: American Theology in Southern Culture, 1795-1860 (Durham, NC: Duke University Press, 1978), 96-100; and Sydney E. Ahlstrom, "The Scottish Philosophy and American Theology," Church History 24 (1955), 257-72.

10 For yet another life of Jesus 'genre,' see Horatio B. Hackett, Illustrations of Scripture; suggested by a Tour through the Holy Land (Boston: Gould and Lincoln), 1860).

11 Cf. "Biography of J. S. Semler," General Repository and Review, I (1812), 58f.; W. Tudor, "Critical notice of Göttingen University," North American Review, VI (1818), 274-5; "Eichhorn's Ode to the Prophets," Christian Disciple, VII (1819), 293.

12 North American Review V (1817), 138.

13 Memoirs of Maragret Fuller Ossoli, ed. W. H. Channing et. al., (Boston , 1892), I, 175. Christian Examiner, II (1825), 262.

14 Cf. Samuel J. Andrews, "Works on the Life of Christ," Bibliotheca Sacra, XXII (1865), 177-206; E. F. Williams, "Recent Lives of Christ," Bibliotheca Sacra, XLII (1886), 221-38. See also Henry Whitney Bellows, "Ecce Homo," Christian Examiner, LXXX (1866), 109-19. Several essays in The Dial also attests to the influence of the British quest. See in particular "German Anti-Supernaturalism. Six Lectures on Strauss's 'Life of Jesus.' By Philip Harwood," The Dial, II (1847), 535-539. "The History of Christianity from the Birth of Christ to the Abolition of Paganism in the Roman Empire. By the Rev. H. H. Milman," The Dial, II (1847), 540-541.

15 On the impact of Renan, see Octavius Brooks Frothingham's The Cradle of the Christ. A Study of Primitive Christianity (New York: E. P. Putnam's Sons, 1877) and his "Renan's Life of Jesus," Christian Examiner, LXXV (1863), 313-39. See also William Henry Furness, Remarks on Renan's Life of Jesus (Philadelphia, 1865).

16 George R. Noyes, "Causes of the Decline of Interest in Critical Theology," Christian Examiner, XLIII (1847), 325-40.

17 Quest, 95.

18 The central study on the pre-critical and stages of biblical studies is Hans W. Frei, The Eclipse of Biblical Narrative: A Study of Eighteenth and Nineteenth Century Hermeneutics (New Haven: Yale University Press, 1974). Frei does not focus in detail on the life of Jesus narratives. More specialized remarks on these narratives may be found in Hans-Joachim Kraus Geschichte der historisch-kritischen Erforschung des Alten Testaments, (Neukirchen: Neukirchener Verlag, 1969[2]).

19 Cf. Theodor Keim, Der geschichtliche Christus (Zürich, 1860[3]), 99; Albrecht Ritschl, The Christian Doctrine of Justification and Reconciliation (Edingburgh: T. &. T. Clark, 1902) 406.

20 Cf. Friedrich Schleiermacher, The Christian Faith, eds. H. R. Mackintosh and J. S. Stewart (2 vols.: New York: Harper and Row, 1963), sec. 38, sec. 96; David Friedrich Strauss, The Life of Jesus Critically Examined, ed. Peter L. Hodgson (Philadelphia: Fortress Press, 1972), nos. 146-47.

21 Cf. James M. Robinson, "The Quest of the Historical Jesus Today," _Theology Today_, 15 (1958), 187-189, and James Smart, _The Strange Silence of the Bible in the Church_ (Philadelphia: Westminster Press, 1970), 63f.

22 See James M. Robinson and John B. Cobb Jr. (eds.), _The New Hermeneutic_ (New York: Harper & Row, 1964), 205f.

Introduction

1 _Quest_, 237.

2 Martin Kähler, _The So-called Historical Jesus and the Historic, Biblical Christ_, tr. Carl E. Braaten (Philadelphia: Fortress Press, 1964), 43.

3 Cf. Peter Biehl, Zur Frage nach dem historischen Jesus, _ThR_ 24 (1957/58), 55; and H. Ott, "The Historical Jesus and the Ontology of History," in _The Historical Jesus and the Kerygmatic Christ_, eds. Carl Braaten and Roy Harrisville, 163-71.

4 Kähler, _The So-called Historical Jesus and the Historic, Biblical Christ_, 57.

5 For major presentations of the application of form criticism to the life of Jesus narratives, see Martin Dibelius, _From Tradition to Gospel_, tr. Bertram Lee Woolf (New York: Charles Scribner's Sons, 1935); and Rudolf Bultmann, _The History of the Synoptic Tradition_, tr. J. March (New York and Evanston: Harper & Row, 1963).

6 Rudolf Bultmann, _Kerygma and Myth: A Theological Debate_, ed. Hans Werner Bartsch and tr. R. H. Fuller, I (London: S. P. C. K., 1953), 41. Cf. Rudolf Bultmann, "The Primitive Christian Kerygma and the Historical Jesus," in _The Historical Jesus and the Kerygmatic Christ_, eds. Carl Braaten and Roy Harrisville, 15-42.

7 Cf. Rudolf Bultmann, _Glauben und Verstehen_, II (Tübingen: J. C. B. Mohr, 1960), 31. Bultmann applied the kerygma theology in his own version of the life of Jesus, _Jesus_ (Tübingen: J. B. B. Mohr, 1951), trans. by L. P. Smith and E. H. Lantero as Rudolf Bultmann, _Jesus and the Word_ (New York: Charles Scribner's Sons, 1958).

8 Kähler, _The So-called Historical Jesus and the Historic, Biblical Christ_, 44f.

9 Nils A. Dahl, "Der historische Jesus als geschichtswissenschaftliches und theologisches Problem," _Kerygma und Dogma_ I, 1955, 112; Kähler, _The So-called Historical Jesus and the Historic, Biblical Christ_, tr. 66.

10 Ernst Käsemant first advanced this new quest in a study delivered at the reunion of former Marburg students on October 20, 1953: "The Problem of the Historical Jesus," in _Essays on New Testament Themes_, tr. W. J. Montague (London: S. C. M., 1964), 15-47. Günther Bornkamm produced the standard treatment of the historical Jesus as reconstructed through the methodology of the new quest: _Jesus of Nazareth_, tr. Irene and Fraser Meluskey (New York: Harper and Raw, 1960). For a brief discussion of the "new quest" as a de-docetizing effort, see Jürgen Roloff, "Auf der Suche nach einem neuen Jesusbild. Tendenzen und Aspekte der gegenwärtigen Diskussion," _TLZ_ 98 (1973), 561-72. See also H. Schürmann, "Zur aktuellen Situation der Leben-Jesu-Forschung," _GuL_ 46 (1973), 304f.

11 Gerhard Ebeling has surveyed the problem of continuity and discontinuity in "Die Frage nach dem historischen Jesus und das Problem der Christologie," ZThK 56 (1959), 24-30, and in The Nature of Faith, tr. R. E. Smith (Philadelphia: Mahlenberg Press, 1961), 58ff. See also Ernst Fuchs, Zur Frage nach dem historischen Jesus (Tübingen, 1960), preface. Cf. Eduard Schweizer, "Die Frage nach dem historischen Jesus," EvTh 24 (1964), 410ff, and Ernst Käsemann, "Sackgassen im Streit um den historischen Jesus," in Exegetische Versuche und Besinnungen, II (Göttingen: Vandenhoeck & Ruprecht, 1965), 49ff.

12 Emanuel Hirsch, Geschichte der neueren Evangelischen Theologie, V (Gütersloh: C. Bertelsmann Verlag, 1954), 544.

13 Kähler, The So-called Historical Jesus and the Historic, Biblical Christ, 43.

14 Adolf Harnack, What is Christianity? tr. Thomas Bailey Saunders (New York: G. P. Putnam's Sons; London: Williams and Norgate, 1901), 22.

15 Cf. Theodor Keim, Der geschichtliche Christus, 149ff; Willibald Beyschlag, Das Leben Jesu (Halle, 1887^{2}), I, 19ff; August Neander, Das Leben Jesu Christi in seinem geschichtlichen Zusammenhang und seiner geschichtlichen Entwicklung (Hamburg, 1837), 3.

16 Kähler, The So-called Historical Jesus and the Historic, Biblical Christ, 43.

17 The phrase is Leopold von Ranke's, Geschichten der romanischen und germanischen Völker (Berlin: Reimer, 1824), preface.

18 The discussion about Jesus' historicity was given special prominence by the "Christ myth" school under Arthur Drews. Cf. H. Windisch, "Der geschichtliche Jesus," ThR 13 (1910), 163-82, 199-220 and the first chapter of Maurice Goguel's The Life of Jesus, tr. Olive Wyon (New York: Macmillan, 1933).

19 Cf. William Wrede, Das Messiasgeheimnis in den Evangelien: Zugleich ein Beitrag zum Verständnis des Markusevangeliums (Göttingen: Vandenhoeck & Ruprecht), 1901), 6f.

20 Kähler, The So-called Historical Jesus and the Historic, Biblical Christ, 65.

21 Following the practice of Reginald H. Fuller's translation of Kerygma und Mythos I, XI-XII, the present study renders "geschichtlich" and "historisch" by "historic" and "historical" respectively.

22 Ferdinand Christian Baur, Die christliche Lehre von der Dreieinigkeit und Menschwerdung Gottes in ihrer geschichtlichen Entwicklung (Tübingen: C. F. Osiander, 1843), III, 559-60. On the notion of "personality" and its role in the quest, see Albrecht Ritschl, Die christliche Lehre von der Rechtfertigung und Versöhnung (Bonn, 1895), III, § 28f; David Friedrich Strauss, Die christliche Glaubenslehre (Tübingen: C. F. Osiander, 1841), I, 502, 504.

23 Cf. Daniel L. Pals, The Victorian "Lives" of Jesus (San Antontio: Trinity University Press, 1982). See also Maurice Goguel, The Life of Jesus, chapter 1.

24 For a discussion of the history and appropriateness of the tradition of supernatural rationalism, see Conrad Wright, The Liberal Christians: Essays on American Unitarian History (Boston: Beacon Press, 1970), 5-6, and The Beginnings of Unitarianism in America (Boston: Starr King Press, 1955). The definition of Transcendentalism as a philosophical rebellion against Unitarianism is commonly associated with Perry Miller, The Transcendentalists: An Anthology

(Cambridge, Mass.: Harvard University Press, 1950), 7. See also Francis Bowen, "Transcendentalism" and "Locke and the Transcendentalists," Christian Examiner, XXII (1835), 371-385; XXIII (1837), 170-194, and Orestes Brownson's rebuttal of Bowen, "Locke and the Transcendentalists," Boston Quarterly Review, I (1838), 83-106.

25 For a nativist reading of Transcendentalism, see Miller, The Transcendentalists, introduction. Cf. also Perry Miller, "New England's Transcendentalism: Native or Imported," in Literary Views: Critical and Historical Essays, ed. Charles Carroll Lamden (Chicago, 1964), 115-129. One of the first historians of Transcendentalism to emphasize the movement's international scope was Octavius Brooks Frothingham, Transcendentalism in New England (1876; reprinted, New York: Harper and Brothers, 1959), esp. 1-104.

26 For a rejection of the view that American Transcendentalism sprang from the German sod, see John Edwards Dirks, The Critical Theology of Theodore Parker (New York: Columbia University Press, 1948), 17; Henry Steele Commager, Theodore Parker (Boston: Little, Brown, 1936), 153; Rene Wellek, "Emerson and German Philosophy," NEQ, 16 (1943), 62; Stanley M. Vogel, German Literary Influences on the American Transcendentalists (New Haven: Yale University Press, 1955), XIV.

27 Christian Examiner, LXXX (1866), 242.

28 O. W. Firkins, Ralph Waldo Emerson (Boston: Houghton Mifflin, 1915), 63. See also Vernon Parrington, Main Currents in American Thought (New York: Hartcourt Brace, 1927), 2: 382, and Wellek, "Emerson and German Philosophy," 61-2.

29 Francis Bowen, "Transcendental Theology," Christian Examiner, XXX (1841), 193. On the significance of the "reason-understanding" distinction in New England, see Andrews Norton, Two articles from the "Princeton Review," Concerning the Transcendental Philosophy of the Germans and of Cousin and Its Influence on Opinion in this Country (Cambridge, Mass., 1840). Cf. also the very influential essay on Kant in The Dial, IV (1844), 409-14.

30 Immanuel Kant, Critique of Pure Reason, trans. N. K. Smith (London: Macmillan, 1927; repr. ed., 1973), 566-67. In contrast to most "new school" advocates, Bowen correctly restated Kant's limitations on "pure reason." Cf. Bowen, "Transcendental Theology," 191.

31 Emerson, "The Transcendentalist," CW, I, 339-40. Cf. J, III, 235-39; L, I, 412-13.

32 Cf. James Marsh, "Preliminary Essay," in Miller, The Transcendentalists, 35-39; W. D. Wilson, "The Unitarian Movement in New England," Dial, I (1841), 409-43. The intuitionist epistemology of Transcendentalism is commonly traced back to the notion of the "moral sentiment." See John Q. Anderson, "Emerson and 'The Moral Sentiment,'" ESQ, 19 (1960), 13-15; Alfred J. Kloeckner, "Intellect and Moral Sentiment in Emerson's Opinions of 'The Meaner Kinds' of Men," AL 30 (1958), 322-38. The "new school's" flawed interpretation of Kantian idealism is frequently attributed to the English mediators of Kant on whom the Transcendentalists relied. Cf. J. E. Creighton, "The Philosophy of Kant in America," Kantstudien, II (1898), 237-62; C. F. Harrold, "Carlyle's Interpretation of Kant," PhQ 7 (1928), 345-57; René Wellek, "Carlyle and the Philosophy of History," PhQ 23 (1944), 55-76.

33 "Immanuel Kant," The Dial, IV (1844), 413.

34 See in particular John Hopkins Morison, "Neander's Life of Christ," *Christian Examiner*, XLVI (1849), 76-87; Samuel Osgood, trans. *The Last Days of the Saviour, or History of the Lord's Passion*. By Hermann Olshausen (Boston, 1839).

35 Frothingham, *Boston, Unitarianism, 1820-1850*, (New York and London: G. P. Putnam's Sons, 1890; repr. ed., 1975), 70.

36 Of relevance here is also the frequent charge against the Transcendentalists' "atheistical tendencies." See *Christian Examiner*, XXIII (1837), 181-2; XXXI (1841), 98ff; XXXII (1842), 251ff.

37 Brownson, "Emerson's Prose Works," *Catholic World*, May, 1870, in Brownson, *Works*, III, 211. Cyrus Augustus Bartol, "Theodore; or the Skeptic's Conversion," *Christian Examiner*, XXXI (1842), 372. Cf. George Ripley, *"The Latest Form of Infidelity" Examined* (Boston: James Munroe, 1839), 12.

38 Bartol, "Theodore; or the Skeptic's Conversion," 372.

39 Cf. the negative replies to Strauss triggered by Philip Harwood's critical summary of the *Leben Jesu* (*German Anti-supernaturalism: Six Lectures on Strauss' "Life of Jesus"* (London: Charles Fox, 1841)); J. R. Park, *An Answer to Anti-supernaturalism: Directed at Strauss & Harwood* (London: n. p., 1844); and Orlando T. Dobbin, *Tentamen Anti-Straussianum: The Antiquity of the Gospels asserted, on Philological Grounds, in Refutation of the Mythic Scheme of Dr. D. F. Strauss* (London: Ward, 1845).

40 Theodore Parker, "Dorner's Christology," *The Dial*, II (1842), 522. Samuel Osgood, "Modern Ecclesiastical History," *Christian Examiner*, XLVIII (1850), 423.

41 "Historical Christianity," *Christian Examiner* (1840), 166.

42 Cf. Harold C. Goddard, *Studies in New England Transcendentalism* (New York: Columbia University Press, 1908); Henry Gray, *Emerson: A Statement of New England Transcendentalism as Expressed in the Philosophy of its Chief Exponent* (Palo Alto: Stanford University Press, 1917); Perry Miller, *The Transcendentalists*, introduction; Henry August Pochmann, *German Culture in America: Philosophical and Literary Influences, 1600-1900* (Madison: University of Wisconsin Press, 1957); George Hochfield, *Selected Writings of the American Transcendentalists* (New York: Signet Classics, 1966), introduction.

43 "The Unitarian Movement in New England," *The Dial*, I (1841), 424.

44 F. W. Greenwood, *Sermons* (Boston: Little, Brown, 1844), I, 100; text in Lawrence Buell, *Literary Transcendentalism: Style and Vision in the American Renaissance* (Ithaca: Cornell University Press, 1973), 10.

45 Joseph Holt Ingraham, *The Prince of the House of David; or Three Years in the Holy City* (New York: Pudley & Russell, 1855), V-VI.

46 A. P. Peabody, "Philosophy of Fiction," *Christian Examiner*, XXXII (1842), 4.

47 "Notices of Recent Publications: 'Sketches from the Life of Christ,'" *Christian Examiner* (1844), 123.

48 Owen Chadwick, *The Secularization of the European Mind in the Nineteenth Century* (Cambridge: Cambridge University Press, 1975), 223.

49 Cf. Kähler, *The So-called Historical Jesus and the Historic Biblical Christ*, 44f, 62f.

50 Cf. Wilhelm Herrmann, *The Communion of the Christian With God*, tr. J. S. Stanton (New York: G. P. Putnam's Sons, 1906), 74, 129.

51 Quest, 401, 310-11.

I

1 Kähler, The So-called Historical Jesus and the Historic Biblical Christ, 43.

2 Heinrich J. Holtzmann, Die synoptischen Evangelien: Ihr Ursprung und geschichtlicher Character (Leipzig: J. C. Hinrich'sche Buchhandlung, 1863), 1.

3 Quest, 4-5.

4 Emil Brunner, The Mediator: A Study of the Central Christian Doctrine of the Christian Faith, tr. Olive Wyon (Philadelphia: Westminster, 1947) 189, 190.

5 Quest, 399.

6 C. J. Cadoux, "The Historical Jesus: A Study of Schweitzer and After," ExpT 46 (1934/35), 406.

7 Quest, 397.

8 Karl Hase, Geschichte Jesu. Nach akademischen Vorlesungen (Leipzig, 1876), 110ff. F. Nippold, Handbuch der neuesten Kirchengeschichte (Göttingen, 1890) III, § 16, § 27; Strauss, The Life of Jesus, § 1; Kähler, Der sogenannten historische Jesus und der geschichtliche, biblische Christus, 16f.

9 Quest, 2.

10 Cf. H. H. Wendt's and William Wrede's assertion that Paul's theology presents an essentially illegitimate development of Jesus' message: H. H. Wendt, "Die Lehre des Paulus verglichen mit der Lehre Jesu," ZThK 4 (1894), 1-78; William Wrede, Paul (London: P. Green, 1907), 155ff.

11 Quest, 397.

12 Cf. Schleiermacher, The Christian Faith, sec. 96. See also Daniel Schenkel, Das Charakterbild Jesu (Wiesbaden, 1873^{4}), V; Willibald Beyschlag, Die Christologie des Neuen Testaments. Ein biblisch-theologischer Versuch (Berlin, 1866), 259f.; Das Leben Jesu, 2 vols (Halle, 1887^{2}), I, 48ff.; Bernhard Weiß, Das Leben Jesu, 2 vols (Berlin, 1884^{2}), I, 183f. See also Karl Rahner, "The Two Basic Types of Christology," Theological Investigations XIII (New York: Seaburg Press, 1978), 90-215; Wolfgang Pannenberg, Grundzüge der Christologie (Gütersloh, 1964), 26f., 47ff. The usefulness of the distinction between a christology "from below" and "from above" is questioned by Otto Weber, Grundlagen der Dogmatik (Neukirchen, 1962), II, 22-29.

13 On the controversies about the terms of patristic christology, see S. Schlossmann, Person und prosopon im Recht und im christlichen Dogma (1906; reprint ed., Darmstadt, 1968), and Aloys Grillmeier, "Die theologische und sprachliche Vorbereitung der christologischen Formel von Chalcedon, in Konzil von Chalcedon (Würzburg, 1951), I, 5-102.

14 Cf. Strauss, The Life of Jesus, no. 146.

15 For a history of these two christological traditions, see Aloys Grillmeier Christ in Christian Tradition: From the Apostolic Age to Chalcedon, tr. J. S. Bowden (New York: Sheed & Ward, 1965); August Dorner, Entwicklungsgeschichte der Lehre von der Person Christi (Stuttgart, 1839), II, 25f.

16 Cf. Strauss' critique of patristic christology in his Die christliche Glaubenslehre, I, Xf, 153ff.

17 Athanasius, De Synodis, 15, *PG* 26, 705A-708A. Cf. F. Loofs, *Leitfaden zum Studium der Dogmengeschichte* (Halle: Max Niemeyer, 1906), § 32, and Strauss, *The Life of Jesus*, no. 145.

18 Cf. Schleiermacher, *The Christian Faith*, sec. 96, 392f.

19 Cf. ibid., 393.

20 Cf. Schenkel, *Das Charakterbild Jesu*, IVf.

21 Oscar Holtzmann, *Leben Jesu* (Tübingen und Leipzig: J. C. B. Mohr, 1901), 105, 107. Cf. Strauss, *The Life of Jesus*, no. 150.

22 Cf. the discussion of the history and uses of the term "homoousios" in Grillmeier, *Christ in Christian Tradition*.

23 Cf. Adolf Harnack, *What is Christianity?*, 51, 144.

24 Cf. Schleiermacher, *The Christian Faith*, sec. 96, 97.

25 Apollinarius, *Fragment 111*, in H. Lietzmann, *Apollinaris von Laodicea und seine Schule* (Tübingen, 1904). Cf. Strauss, *The Life of Jesus*, no. 145, 761.

26 On the docetist implications of patristic christology, cf. Strauss, *The Life of Jesus*, no. 145.

27 Cf. ibid., 759, 761.

28 On the reactions to Apollinarianism, see Richard Alfred Norris, *Manhood and Christ* (Oxford and New York, 1963), F. M. Young, *From Nicaea to Chalcedon* (Philadelphia, 1983).

29 "On the Incarnation of the Only-Begotten," text in Jaroslav Pelikan, *The Emergence of the Catholic Tradition (100-600)* (Chicago and London: The University of Chicago Press, 1971), 230-33.

30 Cf. Friedrich Schleiermacher, *On Religion: Speeches to its Cultured Despisers*, trans. John Oman (New York: Harper & Brothers, 1958), fifth speech.

31 Cf. Strauss, *The Life of Jesus*, no. 145, 759.

32 The proceedings of Chalcedon and the discussion before the Council are treated in R. V. Sellers, *The Council of Chalcedon. A Historical and Doctrinal Survey* (London: S. P. C. K., 1953).

33 Cf. Strauss, *The Life of Jesus*, no. 145, 763.

34 Cf. Schlossmann, *Person and prosopon im Recht und im christlichen Dogma*, 12f.

35 Cf. Harnack, *What is Christianity?*, 135; Strauss, *The Life of Jesus*, no. 146, 765.

36 Cf. Schleiermacher, *Glaubenslehre*, sec. 105; Ritschl, *The Christian Doctrine of Justification and Reconciliation*, § 44-50.

37 Cf. Reinhard Slenczka, *Geschichtlichkeit und Personsein Jesu Christi: Studien zur christologischen Problematik der historischen Jesus-Frage* (Göttingen: Vandenhoeck & Ruprecht, 1967), 24. Cf. also F. W. Schmidt, "Das Verhältnis der Christologie zur historischen Leben-Jesu-Forschung," *ZThK* 1 (1920), 249-76, 323-53; W. Kreck, "Die Frage nach dem historischen Jesus als dogmatisches Problem," *EvTh* 22 (1962), 460-78. See also the early approaches to the christological significance of the historical Jesus quest in E. Günther, *Die Entwicklung der Lehre von der Person Christi im XIX. Jahrhundert* (Tübingen, 1911); and S. Faut, *Die Christologie seit Schleiermacher, ihre Geschichte und ihre Begründung* (Tübingen, 1907).

38 Schleiermacher, *The Christian Faith*, sec. 96, 392-93.

39 See Schleiermacher, *The Christian Faith*, sec. 96, 1. Cf. also *Das Charakterbild Jesu*, V; W. Beyschlag, *Die Christologie des Neuen Testaments* (Berlin, 1866), 259f; Weiß, *Das Leben Jesu*, I, 183f.

40 Cf. Schleiermacher's critique of his formula in The Christian Faith, sec. 96, 392.
41 Ibid., sec. 96, 392-393.
42 Ibid., sec. 96, 394.
43 Ibid. Schleiermacher, On Religion, fifth speech, 241; cf. The Christian Faith, sec. 96.
44 Cf. Schleiermacher's "Über den Gegensatz zwischen der sabellianischen und der athanasianischen Vorstellung von der Trinität," in Sämtliche Werke I, 2 (Berlin, 1836), 485-574.
45 G. Thomasius, Christi Person and Werk. Darstellung der evangelisch-lutherischen Dogmatik vom Mittelpunkt der Christologie aus (Erlangen, 1845), 31ff; cf. Claude Welch (ed.), God and Incarnation (New York, 1965), 28-30.
46 Cf. Thomasius, Christi Person and Werk (1857 ed), II, 14, 233.
47 Cf. Ibid., 200f.
48 G. Thomasius, Beiträge zur kirchlichen Christologie (Erlangen, 1845), 31 ff; cf. Welch, God and Incarnation, 28f.
49 I. A. Dorner, Jahrbücher für deutsche Theologie (1836), 361ff; (1857), 440f.
50 Kähler, The So-called Historical Jesus and the Historic Biblical Christ, 43, 46.
51 Cf. Martin Kähler, "Does Jesus belong in the Gospel?" "Heroworship and Faith in Jesus," "The Glory of Jesus," in Dogmatische Zeitfragen:Angewandte Dogmen (2nd ed., Leipzig: A. Deichert, 1908), II.
52 Strauss, The Life of Jesus, § 145, 762.
53 Cf. James Freemann Clarke, A Sketch of the History of the Doctrine of Atonement (Boston: James Munroe, 1845), 5f. for a very useful classification of the "mythic;" "legal" and "governmental" view of the atonement.
54 Ibid., 5.
55 G. S. Steinbart, System der reinen Philosophie oder Glücklichkeitslehre des Christenthums (Züllichau, 1778), 78. See also Slenzcka, Geschichtlichkeit und Personsein Jesu, 173f.
56 Schleiermacher, The Christian Faith, sec. 100, 425.
57 Ibid., sec. 66, 271, 273.
58 Ibid., sec. 104, 460. Cf. Harnack, What is Christianity?, 170f.
59 Ibid., sec. 104, 460, 461-462.
60 Friedrich Schleiermacher, Christmas Eve: A Dialogue on the Celebration of Christmas, trans. W. Hastic (Edinburgh: T. &. T. Clark, 1890), 59; The Christian Faith, sec. 95, 389.
61 Cf. Harnack, What is Christianity?, 34-37, 51-62. See also Hase, Geschichte Jesu, 159f.
62 Quest, 278f.
63 Johannes Weiss, Jesus' Proclamation of the Kingdom of God, ed. Richard Hyde Hiers and David Larrimore Holland (Philadelphia: Fortress Press, 1971), 132; cf. Norman Perrin The Kingdom of God in the Teaching of Jesus (Philadelphia: Westminster Press, 1963), 17-23, and Quest, 356f.
64 The predominant position countering the eschatological interpretation held that the Evangelists' eschatology presented accomodations to current eschatological views. See Heinrich Julius Holtzmann, Lehrbuch der Neutestamentlichen Theologie (Tübingen: J. G. B. Mohr, 1911), II, 572-84. The critics who came out on the side of Weiss included

Wilhelm Bousset, "Das Reich Gottes in der Predigt Jesu," ThR, 5 (1902), 437f.; and G. Dalman, The Words of Jesus, tr. D. M. Kay (Edinburgh, 1902), I, 94f.

65 Quest, 349; cf. Albert Schweitzer, Out of My Life and Thought, trans. C. T. Campion (New York: Holt, 1949), 48.

66 Quest, 349.

67 Quest, 357.

68 Ibid., 386-87.

69 Ibid., 368.

70 Albert Schweitzer, Paul and his Interpreters: A Critical History (London: A. & C. Black, 1956), 228.

71 Albert Schweitzer, The Mystery of the Kingdom of God, tr. Walter Lowrie (New York: Dodd Mead, 1914), 97, 99.

72 Quest, 239.

73 Reimarus, Fragments, ed. Talbert, 71.

74 Ibid., 69-70.

75 Ibid., 150.

76 Ibid., 148; cf. 137.

77 Ibid., 151.

78 H. S. Reimarus, Apologie oder Schutzschrift für die vernünftigen Verehrer Gottes 2 vols. (Frankfurt: Insel Verlag, 1972), II, 176.

79 Kähler, The So-called Historical Jesus and the Historic Biblical Christ, 46.

80 The terminology is James Robinson's (A New Quest of the Historical Jesus) in reference to critics who regard the "old quest" as "historically impossible" and "theologically illegitimate."

81 Quest, 12.

82 Harnack, What is Christianity?, 95. Cf. W. Weitling, Das Evangelium eines armen Sünders (Berlin, 1845; repr. ed., 1971), 25, 80.

83 A. Rembe, Christus der Mensch und Freiheitskämpfer (Leipzig, 1887), 27ff. For a review of the political revolutionary explanation of Jesus' life, see J. Leipoldt, Vom Jesusbilde der Gegenwart (Leipzig, 1925[2]), 69f. For an analysis of the "political" Jesus quest before the 1848 revolution, see Marylin Chapin Massey, Christ Unmasked: The Meaning of "The Life of Jesus" in German Politics (Chapel Hill, N. C.: University of North Carolina Press, 1983).

84 Harnack, What is Christianity?, 108.

85 Chadwick (ed.), Lessing's Theological Writings, 91-2.

86 Harnack, What is Christianity?, 68, 111, 113.

87 Quest, 345. Schweitzer's observation was prophetic of many of the form critical studies to come. See also Gösta Lundström, The Kingdom of God in the Teaching of Jesus (Richmond, 1963), chs 1-3, 9-11.

88 Quest, 396.

89 Ibid., 396.

90 Ibid., 397.

91 Ibid., 396, 397.

92 Ibid., 95.

93 See August Neander, Das Leben Jesu Christi in seinem geschichtlichen Zusammenhang und seiner geschichtlichen Entwicklung, 6; Weiß, Das Leben Jesu, I, 183f.; Theodor Keim, Der geschichtliche Christus, 100f.

94 Quest, 351.

95 Ibid., 357-58.

96 Karl L. Schmidt, Der Rahmen der Geschichte Jesu: Literarkritische Untersuchungen zur ältesten Jesusüberlieferung (Berlin: Trowitzsch & Sohn, 1919), 317.
97 Wellhausen, Einleitung in die drei ersten Evangelien, 52.
98 Adolf Jülicher, Neue Linien in der Kritik der evangelischen Überlieferung (Giessen, 1906), 5f. On the critique of Schweitzer on this point see also Heinrich Julius Holtzmann, "Der gegenwärtige Stand der Leben-Jesu-Forschung," DLZ, 27 (1906), 2397-64; Hans Windisch, "Rezension zu Albert Schweitzer's Von Reimarus zu Wrede," ThR, 12 (1906), 146f.
99 Ibid., cf. W. Kümmel, Promise and Fulfilment: The Eschatological Message of Jesus, trans. Dorothea M. Barton (London: S. C. M. Press, 1961), 62f.
100 Quest, 350; cf. Geschichte (6th ed.), 448, 550f., 556ff.
101 Geschichte, 36. Cf. Robinson, A New Quest of the Historical Jesus, 180.
102 Quest, 335, 337.
103 Wrede, Das Messiasgeheimnis in den Evangelien, 6-7, 125-26.
104 Ibid., 131.
105 Quest, 351.
106 Ibid., 355, 337.

II

1 Quest, 4.
2 Ibid., 13.
3 On the deist controversy, the best general works remain G. V. Lechler, Geschichte des englischen Deismus (Stuttgart und Tübingen, 1841; reprint ed., Hildesheim: Georg Olms, 1965), and Leslie Stephen, History of English Thought in the Eighteenth Century, 3rd. ed., 2 vols (1902; reprint ed., New York: Hartcourt Brace, 1962), I, chs. 3 and 4.
4 Cf. Hans W. Frei, The Eclipse of Biblical Narrative, 51-65.
5 "De servo arbitrio," Weimarer Ausgabe, 18, 606. On Christ as the "punctum mathematicum" cf. ibid., 2, 439 and A. E. Buchrucker, "Die regula atque norma in der Theologie Luthers," Neue Zeitschrift für systematische Theologie, 10 (1968), 131-69.
6 Jean Daniélou, From Shadow to Reality: Studies in the Biblical Typology of the Fathers (London, 1960), 30; see also Barbara Lewalski, Protestant Poetics and the Seventeenth Century Religious Lyric (Princeton: Princeton University Press, 1969), 111f. and the essays in Typology and Early American Literature, ed. Sacvan Bercovitch (Amherst: University of Massachusetts Press, 1972).
7 Cf. Lewalski, Protestant Poetics, 111; Frei, Eclipse of the Biblical Narrative, 34.
8 "Dictata super Psalterium," Weimarer Ausgabe, 3, 374; cf. Lewalski, Protestant Poetics, 118, and Frei, Eclipse of the Biblical Narrative, 26f., 76.
9 Cf. Lewalski, Protestant Poetics, 111; Erich Auerbach, Typologische Motive in der mittelalterlichen Literatur (Krefeld, 1953); Gerhard Ebeling, Evangelische Evangelienauslegung (München: Christian Kaiser Verlag, 1942), 44-89.

10 Text in Frederick W. Farrar, *History of Interpretation* (1885; reprint ed., Grand Rapids: Baker, 1961), 347. See also Frei, *Eclipse of the Biblical Narrative*, 19, 33.

11 See Emanuel Hirsch, *Hilfsbuch der Dogmatik* (Neukirchen, 1951), 39f.; F. Loofs, *Leitfaden zum Studium der Dogmengeschichte* (4th ed., Halle: Max Niemeyer, 1906), 95f. See also Ian D. Kingston Siggins, *Martin Luther's Doctrine of Christ* (New Haven: Yale University Press, 1970), 205f.

12 "Disputatio Reverendi patris Domini D. Martini Lutheri de divinitate et humanitate Christi," *Weimarer Ausgabe* 39, II, 97f. Cf. Siggins, *Martin Luther's Doctrine of Christ*, 221.

13 Luther, Vorreden zum Neuen Testament, *Weimarer Ausgabe* 6 sec. 10, 20-21, 16; sec. 8, 14-16, 17-19. See also Paul Althaus, *The Theology of Martin Luther, trans. Robert Schultz* (Philadelphia: Fortress Press, 1970), 179f.

14 Cf. the translation of Tatian's harmony by J. Hamlin Hill, *The Earliest Life of Christ ever Compiled from the Gospels, Being the Diatessaron of Tatian* (Edinburgh: T. & T. Clark, 1894).

15 *Quest*, 13.

16 Cf. Hase, *Geschichte Jesu*, 111ff. On the Diatessaron, see R. M. Grant, *The Earliest Lives of Jesus* (London, 1961), 23-28; Harvey K. Mc. Arthur, *The Quest through the Centuries* (Philadelphia: Fortress Press, 1966), 38-44.

17 "Harmoniae evangelicae libri IV graece et latine in quibus evangelica historia ex quatuor evangelistis ita in unum est contexta, ut nullius verbum ullum omissum, nihil alienum immixtum, nullius ordo turbatus, nihil non suo loco positum...."

18 Cf. the brief summaries of the growth of biblical scholarship by Kendrick Grobel, "Biblical Criticism," *The Interpreter's Dictionary of the Bible* (New York, Nashville: Abingdon Press, 1962), I, 409f.; and Alan Richardson, *The Bible in the Age of Science* (London: SCM Press, 1961), 9f. See also T. K. Cheyne, *Founders of Old Testament Criticism: Biographical, Descriptive, and Critical Studies* (London: Methuen, 1893); Klaus Scholder, *Ursprünge und Probleme der Bibelkritik im 17. Jahrhundert. Ein Beitrag zur Entstehung der historisch-kritischen Theologie* (München: Christian Kaiser, 1966).

19 Cf. Richard, Simon, *Histoire critique du Texte du Nouveau Testament* (Rotterdam, 1689, repr. Frankfurt, 1968), 192f.

20 Cf. Jean Astruc, *Conjunctures sur les mémoires originaux dout il paroît que Moyse s'est servi pour composer le livre de la Genèse Réflexions préliminaires*, in John Martin Creed and John S. Boyssmith (eds.), *Religious Thought in the Eighteenth Century* (Cambridge: Cambridge University Press, 1934), 225-229. Cf. also Kraus, *Geschichte der historisch-kritischen Erforschung des Alten Testaments von der Reformation bis zur Gegenwart*, 65ff; Werner Georg Kümmel, *The New Testament: The History of the Investigation of its Problems* (Nashville and New York: Abingdon Press, 1972), 40ff; Claude Welch, *Protestant Thought in the Nineteenth-Century*, 2 vols. (New Haven and London: Yale University Press, 1972), I, 40-41.

21 Benedict De Spinoza, *The Chief Works of Benedict De Spinoza*, trans. R. H. M. Elwes, vol. I, *Introduction, Tractatus Theologico-Politicus, Tractatus Politicus* (London: George Bell, 1882), 159, 171.

22 Benedict Spinoza, *Tractatus Theologico-Politicus*, in Creed and Boyssmith (eds.), *Religious Thought in the Eighteenth Century*, 208.

23 Cf. Hugo Grotius, De veritate, in The Life and Works of Hugo Grotius (London: Sweet & Maxwell, 1925), 3, 16. Cf. also Welch, Protestant Thought, I, 41.

24 Jean LeClerc, Five Letters Concerning the Inspiration of the Holy Scripture (London, n. p. 1690), 29; cf. Kraus, Geschichte der historisch-kritischen Erforschung, 32.

25 Cf. Simon, Histoire critique du Texte du Nouveau Testament, 150f.

26 Cf. Frei, The Eclipse of Biblical Narrative, 7, 40, 63-64.

27 Ibid., 57; cf. 56.

28 John Toland, Christianity not Mysterious (New York: Garland Publishing, 1978), title page. On the general premises of deism, see ibid., 6, and John Leland, A View of the Principal Deistical Writers (London, 1754), I, 444.

29 Ibid. Cf. Gotthart Victor Lechler, Geschichte des englischen Deismus, 193.

30 Toland, Christianity not Mysterious, 36. Cf. Colin Brown, Jesus in European Protestant Thought, 1778-1860 (Durham: The Labyrinth Press, 1985), 37-38, and Henning Graf Reventlow, Bibelautorität und Geist der Moderne. Die Bedeutung des Bibelverständnisses für die geistesgeschichtliche und politische Entwicklung in England von der Reformation bis zur Aufklärung (Göttingen: Vandenhoeck & Rupprecht, 1980), 488.

31 Cf. Toland, Christianity not Mysterious, 158-73; Nazarenus: Or, Jewish, Gentile, and Mahometan Christianity, 2nd. ed. (London, 1718), 65ff., 73.

32 Toland, Christianity not Mysterious, 158.

33 Thomas Chubb, The True Gospel of Jesus Asserted (London, 1738), 55, 43ff; cf. Brown, Jesus in European Thought, 46 and Reventlow, Bibelautorität und Geist der Moderne, 635.

34 Thomas Woolston, A Fifth Discourse on the Miracles of Our Saviour (London, 1728), 11, text in R. M. Burns, The Great Debate on Miracles: From Joseph Granvill to David Hume (Lewisburg: Bucknell University Press, 1981), 73. Cf. Woolston's comments on the miracle at Cana: "If Apollonius Tyanaeus, and not Jesus, had been the Author of this Miracle, we should have reproached his memory with it." First Discourse (1727), 51. On the comparison of Jesus with "divine men," see also F. C. Baur, "Apollonius von Tyana und Christus, oder das Verhältnis des Pythagoreismus zum Christentum," Tübinger Zeitschrift für Theologie 4 (1832), 3-235; Strauss, Life of Jesus, 495.

35 Peter Annet, Supernaturals Examined (London, 1747), 61; text in Burns, The Great Debate on Miracles, 93.

36 Thomas Woolston, First Discourse on the Miracles of Our Saviour (London, 1727), in E. Graham Waring (ed.), Deism and Natural Religion. A Sourcebook. (New York: Frederick Ungar Publishing, 1967), 67.

37 Woolston, First Discourse (1727), 55, 3.

38 Cf. Anthony Collins, A Discourse of Free-Thinking (Reprint. ed., New York and London: Garland Publishing, 1978), 32f; The Scheme of Literal Prophecy Considered (London, 1727). See also Lechler, Geschichte des englischen Deismus, 275ff.

39 Anthony Collins, Discourse of the Grounds and Reason of the Christian Religion (London, 1724), 28; cf. 24, 31; text in Reventlow, Bibelautorität und Geist der Moderne, 600n. See also Frei, Eclipse of Biblical Narrative, 85.

40 Collins, *A Discourse on the Grounds and Reasons of the Christian Religion*, 82, 44. Cf. Colin Brown, *Jesus in European Thought*, 39-40.

41 Leslie Stephen, *English Thought in the Eighteenth-Century*, I, 193. Collins' argument is of one piece with the "inward and spiritual" inclination of the deist position. Cf. Toland's assertion that the "Gospel consists not in words but in virtue; 'tis inward and spiritual abstracted from all formal and outward performances: for the most exact observation of externals, may be without one grain of religion." *Nazarenus*, V.

42 Craddock, Austin and Hale ignored the innovative parallel-column harmony by John Lightfoot, *The Harmony, Chronicle, and Order of the New Testament*, in *The Whole Works of the late John Lightfood*, ed. John Rogers Pittmann (London: G. Cowie and Co. Poultry, 1825), vol. 5.

43 For the distinction between "extreme" and "qualified evidentialism," see Brown, *Miracles and the Critical Mind* (Grand Rapids: William B. Eerdmans Publishing Company, 1984), 55-6.

44 Thomas Sherlock, *The Use and Intent of Prophecy* (London, 1732), 49. Cf. Sherlock's argument that there is no a priori assumption against miracles, in Thomas Sherlock, *The Trial of the Witnesses of the Resurrection of Jesus*, in *Works* (London, 1830), V, 170, 182.

45 Samuel Clarke, *A Discourse Concerning the Obligation of Natural Religion, and the Truth and Certainty of Christian Revelation*, in *The Works*, vol. 2 (London, 1738, reprint ed., New York and London: Garland Publishing Co., 1978), 702.

46 Cf. Benjamin Hoadly, *Letter to Mr. Fleetwood* (London, 1702); John Leng, *The Natural Obligations to Believe the Principles of Religion and Divine Revelation*, Boyle Lectures 1717-18, 7th ed. (London, 1727); Arthur Ashley Sykes, *A Brief Discourse Concerning the Credibility of Miracles and Revelation* (London, 1742). Cf. also Burns, *The Great Debate on Miracles*, 107f.

47 Cf. *The Works of Joseph Butler*, D. C. L., ed. W. E. Gladstone, I, *The Analogy of Religion* (Oxford: Clarendom Press, 1896), 5f.Cf. Brown, *Miracles and the Critical Mind*, 58-59.

48 David Hume, *Enquiry Concerning Human Understanding*, ed. L. A. Selby Bigge (Oxford: Clarendon Press, 1975), sec. 90, 114.

49 Ibid., sec. 88, 111.

50 Ibid., sec. 89, 113.

51 Hume, *Enquiry Concerning Human Understanding*, sec. 12, "Of the Academical or Sceptical Philosophy," pt. 3.

52 John Fleetwood, *The Life of Our Lord and Saviour Jesus Christ*, Amer. ed. (New Haven: Nathan, Whiting, 1832), 20; see also Daniel L. Pals, *The Victorian "Lives" of Jesus* (San Antonio: Trinity University Press, 1982), 19f.

53 Cf. William Paley, *View of the Evidences of Christianity*, 4th ed. (Cambridge: J. Hall & Son, 1864).

54 Ibid., 1, 167, 155.

55 Ibid., 7f. On Paley's evidentialism see also Brown, *Miracles and the Critical Mind*, 144-6; 150-2 and Burns, *The Great Debate on Miracles*, 83f.

56 Paley, *View of the Evidences of Christianity*, 155.

57 See also Robert Fellowes, *The Guide to Immortality; or, Memoirs of the Life and Doctrine of Christ*, 3 vols. (London: Printed for John White, 1804).

58 Edward Greswell, *Harmonia evangelica sive quatuor evangelia Graeca* (Oxford: University Press, 1830).

59 For a complete list of the German translations of the responses of English apologists, see Lechler, *Geschichte des englischen Deismus*, 450. On the impact of the translations of works by English Deists and their opponents, see August Tholuck, "Über Apologetik und ihre Literatur," in *Vermischte Schriften grösstenteils apologetischen Inhalts*, 2 vols. (Hamburg: Friedrich Perthes, 1859), I, 362.

60 On the impact of Wolff on eighteenth century hermeneutics, see Frei, *Eclipse of the Biblical Narrative*, 100f. For examples of the historical apologetics spurred by the impact of deism, see Johann Friedrich Kleuker, *Neue Prüfung und Erklärung der vorzüglichsten Beweise für die Wahrheit und den göttlichen Ursprung des Christenthums*, 3 vols (Riga: Johann Friedrich Hartknach, 1787). Cf. Tholuck's remarks on Kleuker in "Über Apologetik und ihre Literatur," 365-6. See also Gottfried Less, *Ueber die Religion: Ihre Geschichte, Wahl und Bestätigung, II. Beweis der Wahrheit der christlichen Religion* (Göttingen: Verlag der Witwe Vandenhoeck, 1786), introduction.

61 Parallel English works relating to the issue of "authenticity" included Richard Smallbroke's *Vindication of our Saviour's Miracles* (1729), and Thomas Stackhouse's *Fair State of the Controversy between Mr. Woolston and his Adversaries* (1730).

62 Lessing, "Gegensätze des Herausgebers," *Sämtliche Schriften*, ed. Lachmann und Muncker (Leipzig, 1897), XII, 431-32; text in Welch, *Protestant Thought*, I, 374.

63 A. S. Farrar, *A Critical History of Free Thought in Reference to the Christian Religion* (New York, 1863), 231-232.

64 Cf. Frei, *The Eclipse of Biblical Narrative*, 54f., 61, 86. See also Avery Dulles, *A History of Apologetics* (New York: Corpus, 1971).

65 D. Siegmund Jacob, *Baumgartens ausführlicher Vortrag der Biblischen Hermeneutik*, ed. M. Joachim Christoph Bertram (Halle: Johann Justinius Gebauer, 1769), 5f.

66 Farrar, *History of Interpretation*, 402, citing Johann August Ernesti, *Intitutio interpretis Novi Testamenti*, 4th ed. (Leipzig: Weidmann, 1792). English translation by Moses Stuart, *Elements of Interpretation*, 3rd ed. (Andover: M. Newman, 1827).

67 Johann Gottfried Herder, *Vom Erlöser der Menschen*, in *Herders Sämtliche Werke*, ed. Bernhard Suphan (Berlin: Weidmann, 1877-1913), vol. 19, 139f.

68 Robert Lowth, *Isaiah: A New Translation, with a Preliminary Dissertation and Notes, Critical, Philological, and Explanatory*, 1799 (n. ed. Glasgow, 1822), LXXVIII f. On the significance of Lowth, see Kraus, *Geschichte der historisch-kritischen Erforschung des Alten Testaments*, 108.

69 Johann S. Semler, *Abhandlung von freier Untersuchung des Canons*, ed. Heinz Scheible, *Texte zur Kirchen- und Theologiegeschichte*, no. 5 (Gütersloh: Gütersloher Verlagshaus Gerd Mohn, 1967), 43.

70 Johann S. Semler, *Vorbereitung zur theologischen Hermeneutik*, 100; text in Kümmel, *The New Testament*, 60.

71 Cf. Semler, *Abhandlung von freier Untersuchung des Canon*, 72f. See also Frei, *Eclipse of the Biblical Narrative*, 61, 111.

72 Semler, *Beantwortung der Fragmente eines Ungenannten insbesondere vom Zweck Jesu und seiner Jünger* (Halle, 1780^2), 401; text in G. Hornig, *Die Anfänge der historisch-kritischen Theologie. Johann Salomo*

Semler's Schriftverständnis und seine Stellung zu Luther (Göttingen: Vandenhoeck & Ruprecht, 1961), 103; cf. 81.

73 H. S. Reimarus, *The Goal of Jesus and His Disciples*, ed. George Wesley Buchanan (Leiden: E. J. Brill, 1970), 104.

74 Reimarus, *Fragments*, ed. Talbert, 174. Cf. David Friedrich Strauss, *Reimarus und seine Schutzschrift für die vernünftigen Verehrer Gottes* (Leipzig, 1862), 214.

75 Ibid., 236.

76 Ibid., 150-58.

77 This is Strauss' judgment of Reimarus in Mathild Blind, trans. *The Old Faith and the New. A Confession by David Friedrich Strauss* (New York: Henry Holt and Company, 1874), 40.

78 Reimarus, *Fragments*, ed. Talbert, 151.

79 Ibid., 150, 151.

80 Cf. *Goezes Streitschriften gegen Lessing neu herausgegeben von E. Schmidt* (Stuttgart: G. J. Göschen, 1893).

81 J. F. Kleuker, *Neue Prüfung und Erklärung der vorzüglichsten Beweise für die Wahrheit und den göttlichen Ursprung des Christentums*, I, 37.

82 Semler, *Beantwortung der Fragmente eines Unbekannten*, 272.

83 Gotthold Ephraim Lessing's *Gesammelte Werke*, ed. Paul Rilla, VIII, 189; text in Henry E. Allison *Lessing and the Enlightenment: His Philosophy of Religion and its Relation to Eighteenth-Century Thought* (Ann Arbor: University of Michigan Press, 1966), 118.

84 Chadwick, *Lessing's Theological Writings*, 17, 18.

85 Ibid., 44.

86 Ibid., 55, 53.

87 Ibid., 54-55.

88 Lessing's *Gesammelte Werke*, VIII, 195-96; text in Allison, *Lessing and the Enlightenment*, 119.

89 Gotthold Ephraim Lessing, "New Hypothesis Concerning the Evangelists Regarded as Merely Human Historians," in Henry Chadwick, *Lessing's Theological Writings*, 78f.

90 Ibid., 78-79.

91 Bernhard Orchard and Thomas R. W. Longstaff, eds., *J. J. Griesbach: Synoptic and Text-Critical Studies* (Cambridge: Cambridge University Press, 1978), 106.

92 Cf. Lessing, "New Hypothesis Concerning the Evangelists," 80f.; and "Die Religion Christi," excerpts in Brown, *Jesus in European Thought*, 28-29.

93 Lessing, "Die Religion Christi," in ibid., 29.

III

1 Herder, *Vom Erlöser der Menschen*, *SW*, XIX, 239; text in Brown, *Jesus in European Thought*, 72. Cf. also the following lives of Jesus: J. J. Keller, *Das Leben Jesu nach den ersten vier Evangelisten* (Stuttgart, 1802); Leonhard Meister, *Jesus von Nazareth, sein Leben und Geist, nach dem Matthäus* (Basel, 1802); H. C. Bergen, *Denkwürdigkeiten aus dem Leben Jesu nach den vier Evangelien etc.* (Giessen, 1789); J. C. Greiling, *Das Leben Jesu von Nazareth* (Halle, 1813).

2 Cf. Harnack, *What is Christianity?*, 60; D. F. Strauss, *A New Life of Jesus*, 2 vols. (London: Williams and Norgate, 1865), I, 217.

3 Cf. Emmanuel Hirsch, Geschichte der neueren Evangelischen Theologie (Gütersloh: C. Bertelsmann Verlag, 1954), V, 119f.; John Rogerson, Old Testament Criticism in Nineteenth Century England and Germany (London: SPCK, 1984), 15f. On Schweitzer's use of the "kernel" und "husk" terminology, see Quest, 330f.

4 Cf. Schleiermacher, The Christian Faith, sec. 103, 449.

5 On the persistence of the evidentialist tradition in England, see Rogerson, Old Testament Criticism in the Nineteenth Century England and Germany, chapters 11 and 13.

6 Coleridge, Notebook 38 (1829), text in Brown, Miracles and the Critical Mind, 148.

7 Coleridge, Notebook 48 (1830), in ibid.

8 Cf. Welch, Protestant Thought, I, 110-11.

9 Cf. Schleiermacher, The Christian Faith, sec. 3, 5, 8-9.

10 Ibid., sec. 4, 12; sec. 10, 47-52.

11 Ibid., sec. 94, 387-88. See also Christmas Eve: A Dialogue on the Celebration of Christmas, trans. Terence N. Tice (Edinburgh: T. & T. Clark, 1890), 71-2.

12 Cf. Strauss, Life of Jesus, no. 15, 86-87.

13 Cf. the responses to Strauss in Neander, Das Leben Jesu Christi, 6; Ullmann, Das Leben Jesu von David Friedrich Strauss, 47f.

14 Cf. Strauss, Life of Jesus, no. 8, 53.

15 Quest, 115.

16 Cf. Kant, Religion with the Limits of Reason Alone, trans. S. Greene and Hudson, 3, 4-5.

17 G. F. Oehler, Prolegomena zur Theologie des Alten Testaments (Stuttgart, 1845), 12; text in Rogerson, Old Testament Criticism, 82.

18 G. C. Storr, "Über den Geist des Christenthums, Eine historische Untersuchung," Magazin für christliche Dogmatik und Moral, I, (1796), 103.

19 G. C. Storr, Lehrbuch der christlichen Dogmatik, trans. C. C. Flatt (Stuttgart: Johann Benedict Metzler, 1803), § 8.5, 153.

20 Cf. Frei, Eclipse of Biblical Narrative, 3f, 12f.

21 F. C. Baur, Paulus der Apostel Jesu Christi. 2nd ed., ed. Eduard Zeller, 2 vols. (Leipzig: Fues's Verlag, 1866-67), I, 110. ET Paul the Apostle of Jesus Christ, His Life and Work, His Epistles and His Doctrine, trans. A. Menzies, 2 vols. (London and Edinburgh: Williams & Norgate, 1875), I, 97. Cf. Das Christenthum und die christliche Kirche der drei ersten Jahrhunderte (Tübingen: L. F. Fues, 1863[3]), 1.

22 David Friedrich Strauss, Hermann Samuel Reimarus und seine Schutzschrift für die vernünftigen Verehrer Gottes (Leipzig, 1862), 98f.

23 Cf. Ernst W. Hengstenberg, Christologie des Alten Testaments und Commentar über die messianischen Weissagungen der Propheten, 2 vols, (Berlin, 1829-35), I, 22, 333-34, 352-62.

24 Cf. the 'reconstructionist' interpretations in Franz Volkmar Reinhard, Plan of the Founder of Christianity, trans. Oliver A. Taylor (New York: G. & C. & H. Carvill, 1831).

25 Cf. Quest, 56f. See also Karl Bahrdt, Brief über die Bibel im Volkston (1782), reprinted in part in Das Zeitalter der Aufklärung, ed. Wolfgang Philipp (Bremen: Carl Schünemann Verlag, 1963), 210; F. Röhr, Brief über den Rationalismus (1813), reprinted in part in Das Zeitalter der Aufklärung, 224.

26 Cf. Heinrich Eberhard Paulus, Das Leben Jesu als Grundlage einer reinen Geschichte des Urchristentums, 2 vols (Heidelberg: C. F.

Winter, 1828), 1 pt. 1, 244-281; 348ff. See also Schleiermacher, *Das Leben Jesu* (Berlin: Georg Reimer, 1864) 441ff.

27 Cf. *Quest*, 44f.

28 Cf. Karl Bahrdt, *Ausführung des Plans und Zwecks Jesu. In Briefen an Wahrheit suchende Leser* (Berlin, 1784-92); *Die sämtlichen Reden Jesu aus den Evangelisten ausgezogen* (Berlin, 1786).

29 For summary appraisals of Bahrdt and Venturini see Schweitzer, *Quest*, 38f.; and Ernst and Marie-Luise Keller, *Miracles in Dispute: A Continuing Debate* (London: SCM Press, 1969), 67-79.

30 Cf. the following "lives": J. L. N. Hacker, *Jesus der Weise von Nazareth etc.*, vol. 1 (Leipzig, 1800); G. L. Horn, *Die Lebensgeschichte Jesu nach den drey ersten Evangelien* (Nuremburg, 1803); J. J. Keller, *Jesus von Nazareth, wie er lebte und lehrte* (Halle, 1799).

31 H. E. G. Paulus, *Das Leben Jesu*, 1, pt. 1, 244-281; 1, pt. 2, 55; Ibid., 1, pt. 1, 357-59, 349f.

32 Ibid., 1, pt. 2, 266ff.

33 Cf. *Quest*, 48.

34 Cf. Paulus, *Das Leben Jesu*, 1, pt. 1, X.

35 Ibid., 2, pt. 2, XI.

36 Cf. Semler, *Beantwortung der Fragmente eines Ungenannten*, 264f., 430ff.

37 Cf. Johann Jakob Hess, *Geschichte der drei letzten Lebensjahre Jesu*, 3 vols. (Zürich, 1768-72).

38 H. E. G. Paulus, *Das Leben Jesu*, 1, pt. 1, XI.

39 Ibid., 1, 1, X.

40 Cf. *Quest*, 330f.

41 For a combination of the physical and the spiritual in Hase, see his *Life of Jesus. A Manual for Academic Study*, trans. J. F. Clarke (Boston: Walker, Wise & Co, 1860), no. 5, 10.

42 Schleiermacher, *The Christian Faith*, sec. 103, 448.

43 Schleiermacher, *The Christian Faith*, sec. 103, 448, 449; *Reden über die Religion* (Berlin, 1799), 177.

44 On the rationalistic premises of Schleiermacher, see Slenczka, *Geschichtlichkeit und Personsein Jesu Christ*, 35. Cf. also Walter Künneth, *Theologie der Auferstehung* (München, 1951[4]).

45 Cf. Friedrich Schleiermacher, *Hermeneutics: The Handwritten Manuscripts*, trans. James Duke and Jack Forstman (Missoula, Mont.: Scholars Press, 1977), 147f. See also Frei, *Eclipse of Biblical Narrative*, 297-98, 308.

46 For an appraisal of this apologetic in the context of the contrast between rationalism and supernaturalism, see C. B. Klaiber, "Über Begriff und Wesen des Supranaturalismus, und die Versuche, ihm mit dem Rationalismus zu vereinigen," *Studien der evangelischen Geistlichkeit Würtembergs*, F (Heft 1, 1827), 73-156; Johann C. F. Steudel, "Die Frage über die Ausführbarkeit einer Annäherung zwischen der rationalischen und supernaturalistischen Ansicht mit besonderer Rücksicht auf den Standpunkt der Schleiermacher'schen Glaubenslehre," *Tübinger Zeitschrift für Theologie*, I (1828), 74-199.

47 Cf. Schleiermacher, *The Christian Faith*, sec. 3, 5; 8-9. See also Frei, *Eclipse of the Biblical Narrative*, 308.

48 Cf. Schleiermacher, *Hermeneutics*, 165f. Cf. also the discussions of Ast and Wolf in Joachim Wach, *Das Verstehen: Grundzüge einer*

Geschichte der hermeneutischen Theorie im 19. Jahrhundert (Hildesheim: Georg Olms, 1966), I, 31-82.

49 The significance of the hermeneutical circle is stressed by Wilhelm Dilthey, "Die Entstehung der Hermeneutik," in Gesammelte Schriften, ed. Georg Misch, vol. V, Die geistige Welt: Einleitung in die Philosophie des Lebens (Stuttgart: B. E. Tübner, 1924), 330f; Richard Palmer, Hermeneutics: Interpretation Theory in Schleiermacher, Dilthey, Heidegger, and Gadamer (Evanston, Illinois: Northwestern University Press, 1969), 87-88; Joachim Wach, Das Verstehen, I, 41-63.

50 Schleiermacher, The Christian Faith, sec. 4, 12.

51 Friedrich Schleiermacher, Brief Outline of the Study of Theology, trans. Terence N. Tice (Richmond: John Knox Press, 1966), 57.

52 Ibid., 54-55; On Religion, first speech, 16.

53 Schleiermacher, Brief Outline of the Study of Theology, 56. On Schleiermacher's reconception of hermeneutical theory, see Heinz Kimmerle, Die Hermeneutik Schleiermachers im Zusammenhang seines spekulativen Denkens (Heidelberg, 1957).

54 Cf. Schleiermacher, Hermeneutics, 168-69, 98, 190.

55 Cf. Schleiermacher, Brief Outline of the Study of Theology, 54.

56 W. G. Kümmel, "Das Erbe des 19. Jahrhunderts für die neutestamentliche Wissenschaft von heute," Heilsgeschehen und Geschichte (Marburg: Elwert, 1965), 872; cf. Schleiermacher, Brief Outline of the Study of Theology, 57f.

57 August Tholuck, Guido and Julius, tr. J. E. Ryland (Boston: Gould & Lincoln, 1854), 101.

58 Ibid., 98. On Tholuck's identification of the "heart" rather than "reason" as the point of contact between God and man, see also his Die Lehre von der Sünde und vom Versöhner (Hamburg, 1823).

59 Cf. Karl Heinrich Sack, Christliche Apologetik: Versuch eines Handbuchs (Hamburg: F. Perthes, 1829), 205-309.

60 Carl Ullmann, The Sinlessness of Jesus: An Evidence for Christianity, trans. R. C. L. Brown (Edinburgh: T. & T. Clark, 1858), text in Brown, Jesus in European Thought, 256.

61 Schleiermacher, Hermeneutics, 161.

62 F. Schleiermacher, Hermeneutik, in SW, I, 7, 157. Cf. also Brown, Jesus in European Thought, 125.

63 J. B. Torrance, "Interpretation and Understanding in Schleiermacher's Theology: Some Critical Questions," SJTh 21 (1968), 272; cf. 274.

64 Hermeneutics, trans. Duke and Forstman, introduction, 10.

65 Schleiermacher, Hermeneutics, 153, 166, 164. Das Leben Jesu, in SW, vol. VI, 3-4; The Life of Jesus, trans. S. Maclean Gilmour (Philadelphia: Fortress Press, 1975), 5.

66 Schleiermacher, Hermeneutics, 100; Leben Jesu, 13; ET, 14.

67 Schleiermacher, The Christian Faith, sec. 94, 387-88; Hermeneutics, 100f.

68 Cf. Schleiermacher, The Christian Faith, sec. 32, 131; sec. 33, 133-34. On Schleiermacher's substitution of a hermeneutics of understanding or consciousness for that of subject matter, cf. Frei, Eclipse of the Biblical Narrative, 308. See also the reviews of Schleiermacher's Glaubenslehre brought together in Hermann Mulert, "Die Aufnahme der Glaubenslehre Schleiermachers," ZThK, XVIII (1908), 107-139.

69 Schleiermacher, The Christian Faith, sec. 3, 8-9; sec. 4, 12.
70 Cf. Schleiermacher, The Christian Faith, sec. 93, 377-85; sec. 94.2, 386-88; sec. 125.1, 578-80.
71 Schleiermacher, The Christian Faith, sec. 94, 387-88; cf. On Religion: Speeches to its Cultured Despisers, fifth speech, 241, 246, 247.
72 Cf. Schleiermacher, The Christian Faith, sec. 4, 12; sec. 33, 133-34.
73 Ibid., sec. 95, 389f.
74 Cf. Kant, Critique of Pure Reason, 566f.
75 Cf. Immanuel Kant, The Critique of Practical Reason, trans. Lewis White Beck (Indianapolis and New York: Bobbs-Merrill, 1956), 126-36.
76 Ibid., 137.
77 On Kant's view of Christ, see Horst Renz, Geschichtsgedanke und Christusfrage. Zur Christusanschauung Kants und seiner Fortbildung durch Hegel im Hinblick auf die allgemeine Funktion neuzeitlicher Theologie (Göttingen: Vandenhoeck & Rupprecht, 1977).
78 Cf. Brown, Jesus in European Thought, 65; Welch, Protestant Thought, 47.
79 Kant, Religion Within the Limits of Reason Alone, ed. T. N. Greene and H. Hudson, 120, 56; text in Brown, Jesus in European Thought, 62.
80 Schleiermacher, The Christian Faith, sec. 94, 388; sec. 100, 427.
81 Cf. Ibid., sec. 95, 389.
82 On the reception of Schleiermacher's dogmatics, see Karl Dunkmann, Die Nachwirkungen der theologischen Prinzipienlehre Schleiermachers (Gütersloh: C. Bertelsmann, 1915); Mulert, "Die Aufnahme der Glaubenslehre Schleiermacher," 107-39.
83 Bretschneider, Grundansichten, 17-18; text in Friedrich Schleiermacher On The Glaubenslehre. Two Letters to Dr. Lücke, trans. James Duke and Francis Fiorenza (Missoula: Scholars Press, 1981), 110n.
84 Klaiber, "Über Begriff und Wesen des Supranaturalismus, und die Versuche, ihn mit dem Rationalismus zu vereinigen," 102.
85 Ibid., 112-13.
86 Schleiermacher, On The Glaubenslehre, 45.
87 Schleiermacher, The Christian Faith, sec. 10.
88 Sack, Christliche Apologetik (2nd ed.), 123n 1.
89 Schleiermacher, On The Glaubenslehre, 89. On Schleiermacher's failure to retain in combination the ideal in Christ with the historical, see Heinrich Johann Theodor Schmid, "In wiefern darf der Schleiermachersche Standpunkt der Theologie mit dem gnostischen verglichen werden," FThPh 2, 1 (1829), 151-54. See also Ferdinand Christian Baur, Die christliche Gnosis, oder die christliche Religionsphilosophie in ihrer geschichtlichen Entwicklung (Tübingen: C. F. Osiander, 1835; repr. ed. Darmstadt: Wissenschaftliche Buchgesellschaft, 1965), 646-52.
90 Schleiermacher, The Life of Jesus, 43; The Christian Faith, sec. 62 (SW, 1, 8, 219). Schleiermacher, Hermeneutik und Kritik, in SW I, 223-224; Über die Schriften des Lukas in ibid., 219-20.
91 Salvatori, "From Locke to Reitzenstein," HThR, (1929), 278; cf. Schleiermacher, The Life of Jesus, 37f.
92 Quest, 62-63.
93 Cf. Schleiermacher, The Christian Faith, sec. 96, 397.
94 Quest, 97.
95 Cf. Strauss, Life of Jesus, no. 15, 86f.

96 Strauss, Life of Jesus, 50. Cf. also A. Hausrath, David Friedrich Strauss und die Theologie seiner Zeit (Heidelberg: Basserman, 1876), I, 31f.
97 Strauss, Leben Jesu, I, IV.
98 Strauss, Life of Jesus, no. 8, 53.
99 Ibid., no. 15, 86-87.
100 Strauss, Life of Jesus, no. 12, 72.
101 Ibid., no. 12, 72.
102 Ibid., no. 22, 117-118.
103 Ibid., no. 107, 545-46; no. 8, 56-57.
104 David Friedrich Strauss, The Old Faith and the New, trans. Mathilde Blind (New York: Henry Holt and Company, 1874), 98.
105 Strauss, Life of Jesus, no. 8, 56-57.
106 Ibid., no. 8, 57.
107 Quest, 111.
108 Strauss, Life of Jesus, no. 107, 545-46.

IV

1 Cf. Neander, Das Leben Jesu Christi in seinem geschichtlichen Zusammenhang und seiner geschichtlichen Entwicklung, 6; Ullmann, Julius Müller, Das Leben Jesu von David Friedrich Strauss, 47ff; Weiß, Das Leben Jesu, I, 183f; Beyschlag, Das Leben Jesu, I, 2f; Keim, Der geschichtliche Christus, 100ff.
2 Wilhelm Hoffmann, Das Leben Jesu, Kritisch bearbeitet von Dr. D. F. Strauss. Geprüft für Theologen und Nichttheologen (Stuttgart: P. Balz, 1836), 435.
3 Carl Ullmann, "Sendschreiben an Strauss," in Historisch oder Mythisch? Beiträge zur Beantwortung der gegenwärtigen Lebensfrage der Theologie (Hamburg, 1838), 110. On the reception of Strauss' christology, see also A. Hein, "Die Christologie von D. Fr. Strauß," ZThK 16 (1906), 321-345; E. Günther, "Bemerkungen zur Christologie von David Friedrich Strauß," ZThK 18 (1908), 202-211.
4 For Strauss' appropriation of this view, see his In Defense of my Life of Jesus Against the Hegelians, ed. and tr. Marilyn C. Massey (Hamden: Archon Books, 1983), 36f.
5 Strauss, Life of Jesus, no. 151, 779; no. 15, 50.
6 Cf. ibid., no. 151, 779.
7 Ibid., no. 151, 781. Cf. David Friedrich Strauss, The Christ of Faith and the Jesus of History: A Critique of Schleiermacher's Life of Christ, trans. Leander E. Keck (Philadelphia: Fortress Press, 1977), 160f.
8 Ullmann, The Sinlessness of Jesus, 8f.
9 See Schleiermacher, Brief Outline of the Study of Theology, 57.
10 Cf. Strauss, The Christ of Faith and the Jesus of History, 160.
11 Cf. Carl Ullmann, "Noch ein Wort über die Persönlichkeit Christi und das Wunderbare in der evangelischen Geschichte," ThStKr, 11 (1838), 324-25.
12 Carl Ullmann, "Das Leben Jesu von David Friedrich Strauss," in ThStKr 9 (1836), 813. See also Beyschlag, Das Leben Jesu, I, 1ff, 19ff, 48ff, 172ff; Weiß Das Leben Jesu, I, 178ff.
13 Cf. Thomasius, Christi Person und Werk, in Welch, God and Incarnation, 28f.

14 Cf. Brown, Jesus in European Thought, 204f.

15 Cf. Wilhelm Martin Leberecht de Wette, Biblische Dogmatik des Alten und Neuen Testaments (2nd. ed., Berlin: Realschulbuchhandlung, 1818), no. 55, 35-36. On the origin of myth characteristic of higher critical studies, see Christian Hartlich and Walter Sachs, Der Ursprung des Mythosbegriffes in der Modernen Bibelwissenschaft (Tübingen: J. C. B. Mohr, 1952), chap. 3. See also E. S. Shaffer, Kubla Khan and the Fall of Jerusalem; The Mythological School in Biblical Criticism and Secular Literature, 1770-1880 (Cambridge: Cambridge University Press, 1975).

16 Cf. Hartlich und Sachs, Der Ursprung des Mythosbegriffs, 20f.

17 Strauss, Life of Jesus, no. 15, 87.

18 Quest, 80; Geschichte, 117.

19 Ibid., no. 15, 86.

20 Ibid., no. 15, 87.

21 Cf. Hase, Life of Jesus, no. 116, 228f; no. 120, 236f. See by comparison, Strauss, Life of Jesus, no 140, 735-44; no. 43, 201-5.

22 Cf. Ferdinand Christian Baur, Kritische Untersuchungen über die kanonischen Evangelien, ihr Verhältnis zueinander, ihren Charakter und Ursprung (Tübingen: L. F. Fues, 1847), 40-70. See also Peter C. Hodgson, The Formation of Historical Theology: A Study of Ferdinand Christian Baur (New York: Harper and Row, 1966, 41-46.

23 Strauss, A New Life of Jesus, I, no. 25, 214.

24 Hartlich and Sachs, Der Ursprung des Mythosbegriffes, 147.

25 For a discussion of Strauss' application of this concept of myth to the life of Jesus, cf. Ullmann, "Noch ein Wort über die Persönlichkeit Christi und das Wunderbare in der evangelischen Geschichte," 292f; "Das Leben Jesu," 787-806.

26 Wilhelm Friedrich Hegel, Lectures on the Philosophy of Religion trans. E. B. Spiers and J. B. Sanderson (New York: Humanities Press, 1962), III, 113; I, 226, III, 92.

27 Strauss, In Defense of My Life of Jesus, 43.

28 Ibid., 21.

29 Hegel, Lectures on the Philosophy of Religion, I, 146.

30 Ibid., III, 115; Strauss, Life of Jesus, no. 151, 780-81.

31 Gabler, De Verae philosophiae erga religionem christianam pietate (Berlin: Duncker and Humblot, 1836), 42n; text in Strauss, In Defense of My Life of Jesus, 41-42.

32 Cf. C. H. Weisse, "Über den Begriff des Mythus and seine Anwendung auf die neutestamentliche Geschichte," ZPh, IV, 83-102; 216-54; A. Tholuck, The Credibility of the Evangelical History (London: John Chapman, 1844), 52f. Kern, "Erörterung der Hauptthatsachen der evangelischen Geschichte," TZ (1838), 92-165; Daniel Schenkel, "Ueber die neuesten Bearbeitungen des Lebens Jesu," ThStKr, 13 (1840), 775f.

33 Strauss, In Defense of My Life of Jesus, 27.

34 Ibid., 28.

35 Cf. ibid., 18, 36-37.

36 Ibid., 42.

37 Ibid., 19.

38 Strauss, Life of Jesus, no. 151, 780.

39 Strauss, Life of Jesus, no. 151, 780. On Strauss' debt to Hegel, see Streitschriften zur Vertheidigung meiner Schrift über das Leben Jesu, Erstes bis drittes Heft (1837, repr. Hildesheim: H. Olms, 1980), no. 3, 57, 63. Cf. In Defense of My Life of Jesus, 19f.

40 Hegel, Lectures on the Philosophy of Religion, III, 113.
41 Ibid. Cf. Strauss, Life of Jesus, no. 151.
42 Hegel, Lectures on the Philosophy of Religion, III, 119.
43 Cf. James Yerkes, The Christology of Hegel (Albany: State University of New York Press, 1983) 125-26; 132. Life of Jesus, 4th ed., II, 895.
44 Strauss, Life of Jesus, no. 151, 780.
45 Strauss, Leben Jesu, 3rd ed., II: 771-72. Streitschriften, no. 3, 70-2, 152-3; Strauss, Life of Jesus, no. 151, 780. Cf. also D. F. Strauss, "Vergängliches und Bleibendes im Christenthum," 3. Vierteljahrheft der Hamburger Zeitschrift (Freihafen, 1838).
46 Strauss, Streitschriften, no. 3, 57.
47 Strauss, Life of Jesus, no. 151, 779. Cf. In Defense of My Life of Jesus, 42.
48 Strauss, In Defense of My Life of Jesus, 37.
49 Ibid., no. 151, 779-780.
50 Cf. Strauss, In Defense of My Life of Jesus, 24f. Life of Jesus, no. 107, 545f.
51 Strauss, In Defense of My Life of Jesus, 27.
52 Cf. Strauss, Life of Jesus, no. 151, 780.
53 Cf. ibid., 779.
54 Ibid., no. 152, 782.
55 Strauss, In Defense of My Life of Jesus, 38.
56 Bruno Bauer, Kritik der evangelischen Geschichte der Synoptiker (Braunschweig: F. Otto, 1842), III, 315. Cf. Bruno Bauer's review of the Life of Jesus in JWK (1835), 879-94; (1836), 681-94. See also Strauss' response to Bauer in his In Defense of My Life of Jesus, 43f.
57 Bauer Kritik der evangelischen Geschichte, III, 308.
58 Strauss, Streitschriften, no. 3, 125-26; cf. 73-4.
59 Strauss, Life of Jesus, no. 151, 779. Cf. Ullmann, "Das Leben Jesu," 812. Hoffmann, Das Leben Jesu, kritisch bearbeitet von Dr. D. F. Strauss, 435, as quoted in Strauss, In Defense of My Life of Jesus, 42.
60 Strauss, In Defense of My Life of Jesus, 42, 43, 14.
61 Strauss, Life of Jesus, no. 151, 779. On the christological question dividing the Hegelian school, see Strauss, Streitschriften, no. 3, 95. Carl Michelet, Geschichte der letzten Systeme der Philosophie in Deutschland (Berlin, 1838), II, 637-59.
62 Strauss, In Defense of My Life of Jesus, 64.
63 Cf. Carl Göschel, "Aphorismen über Nichtwissen und absoluter Wissen im Verhältnis zur christlichen Glaubenserkenntnis" (Berlin: Franklin, 1829). See also Strauss' critique of Göschel in his In Defense of My Life of Jesus, 38f.
64 Strauss, citing Rosenkranz in his In Defense of My Life of Jesus, 15.
65 Ibid., 43.
66 Strauss, Glaubenslehre, II, 222. See also Strauss, Streitschriften, no. 3, 95-100.
67 Strauss, In Defense of My Life of Jesus, 43.
68 For relevant texts, see J. Zeller, Stimmen der Deutschen Kirche über das Leben Jesu von Doctor Strauss. Ein Beitrag zur theologischen Literaturgeschichte des neunzehnten Jahrhunderts für Theologen und Nichttheologen (Zürich, 1837).
69 Tholuck, The Credibility of the Evangelical History, 52.

70 Strauss, *Life of Jesus*, no. 152, 782.

71 Cf. Hoffmann, *Das Leben Jesu*, 435. See also Strauss' response to the "mediation" christology of Nitzsch and Steudel in his *In Defense of My Life of Jesus*, 14f.

72 Carl Ullmann, "Über Partei und Schule, Gegensätze und deren Vermittlung," *ThStKr* 9 (1836), 58; cf. Ullmann, "Noch ein Wort über die Persönlichkeit Christi und das Wunderbare in der evangelischen Geschichte," 327f.

73 Strauss, *Streitschriften*, no. 3, 57.

74 Strauss, *In Defense of My Life of Jesus*, 6.

75 Ibid., 6.

76 Strauss, *Life of Jesus*, no. 15, 49-51.

77 Ferdinand Christian Baur, "Anzeige der beiden academischen Schriften von Dr. F. C. Baur," *TZT*, I (1828), 242. Cf. *Die christliche Gnosis*, 637, 647f; *The Church History of the First Three Centuries* (London: Williams and Norgate, 1878-79), I, X.

78 Baur, *Die christliche Gnosis*, 717.

79 Cf. Baur, *Die christliche Gnosis*, 646-55.

80 Leander E. Keck, tr. *The Christ of Faith and the Jesus of History: A Critique of Schleiermacher's Life of Jesus* (Philadelphia: Fortress, 1977), "Introduction," LIII. Cf. Baur, *Die christliche Gnosis*, 638-642; Welch, *Protestant Thought*, I, 156f.

81 Cf. Baur, *Die christliche Gnosis*, 637-639; "Anzeige der beiden academischen Schriften," 236-38.

82 Baur, "Anzeige der beiden academischen Schriften," 224.

83 Ferdinand Christian Baur to Friedrich August Baur, July 26, 1823. The passage is reprinted in Heinz Liebing, "Ferdinand Christian Baurs Kritik an Schleiermachers Glaubenslehre," *ZThK*, 54 (1957), 242f. That Baur's criticism of Schleiermacher rests on the equation of Schleiermacher's archetype with Hegel's idea of divine-human unity becomes evident in *The christliche Gnosis*, 646f.

84 Ferdinand Christian Baur, *Symbolik und Mythologie, oder die Naturreligion des Alterthums* (Stuttgart: J. B. Metzler, 1824), I, 157.

85 Cf. Baur, *Die christliche Gnosis*, 715, 720-21. On Baur's shift to Hegelianism, see Wilhelm Lang, "Ferdinand Baur and David Friedrich Strauss," *Preussische Jahrbücher*, 160 (1915), 476ff.

86 Ferdinand Christian Baur, *Vorlesungen über die christliche Dogmengeschichte* (Leipzig: Fues's Verlag, 1867), III, 353. On Baur's "pantheism of history," see Wolfgang Geiger, *Spekulation und Kritik: Die Geschichtstheologie Ferdinand Christian Baurs* (München, 1964), 45f.

87 Cf. the criticism of Baur put forward by Gerhard Uhlhorn, "Die älteste Kirchengeschichte in der Darstellung der Tübinger Schule," *JDT*, III (1858), 280-349; Karl Hase, *Die Tübinger Schule. Ein Sendschreiben an Herrn Dr. Ferdinand Christian von Baur* (Leipzig: Breitkopf und Härtel, 1855), 60; I. A. Dorner, *History of Protestant Theology*, trans. George Robson and Sophia Taylor (Edinburgh: T. & T. Clark, 1871), II, 410-14.

88 Strauss, *Life of Jesus*, no. 147, 773. Cf. Heinrich Beckh, "Die Tübinger historische Schule, kritisch beleuchtet," *ZPK*, 74 (1884), 231-36; Hodgson, *The Formation of Historical Theology*, 2-5.

89 Ullmann, "Das Leben Jesu," 812.

90 Ferdinand Christian Baur, *Theologische Jahrbücher*, 10 (1851), 294f. ET in Kümmel, *Interpretation of the New Testament*, 127-129.

91 Schleiermacher, Einleitung in das Neue Testament, in SW, I, 8, 219; text in Brown, Jesus in European Thought, 126-127.
92 Ibid. Cf. Baur, Die Kanonischen Evangelien, 42-43, 71f.
93 Baur, The Church History of the First Three Centuries, I, X.
94 Strauss, Life of Jesus, no. 44.
95 Baur, Theologische Jahrbücher 10 (1851), 294-296, ET in Kümmel, Interpretation of the New Testament, 127.
96 Baur, Theologische Jahrbücher 10 (1851), 295-296; ET in Kümmel, Interpretation of the New Testament, 128-129. Ferdinand Christian Baur, Kirchengeschichte des neunzehnten Jahrhunderts, ed. E. Zeller (Tübingen: L. F. Fues, 1862), 397.
97 Baur, Die kanonischen Evangelien, 74.
98 Cf. Ferdinand Baur, "Die Christuspartei in der korinthischen Gemeinde, der Gegensatz des petrinischen und paulinischen Christentums in der ältesten Kirche," Tübinger Zeitschrift für Theologie IV (1831), 61ff.
99 Baur, Die kanonischen Evangelien, 74. See also Das Markusevangelium nach seinem Ursprung und Charakter (Tübingen: L. F. Fues, 1851), 4-110.
100 For Baur's criticism of Schleiermacher's "abstract literary criticism," see Die Kanonischen Evangelien, 28-40.
101 Cf. Steudel, "Die Frage über die Ausführbarkeit einer Annäherung zwischen der rationalistischen und supernaturalistischen Ansicht," 95f; "Ueber das bei alleiniger Anerkennung des historischen Christus sich für die Bildung des Glaubens ergebende Verfahren," Tübinger Zeitschrift für Theologie, II (1839), 44f.
102 Cf. Ferdinand Christian Baur, "Die Einleitung in das Neue Testament als theologische Wissenschaft. Ihr Begriff und ihre Aufgabe, ihr Entwicklungsgang und ihr innerer Organismus," ThJ, 9 (1850), 463-566; X (1851), 70-94, 222-52, 291-328, which does not deal with hermeneutical questions in a systematic fashion.
103 Schleiermacher, Hermeneutik und Kritik, I, 7.
104 Ernst von Dobschütz, Vom Auslegen des Neuen Testaments, 1927, 6 n2. See also August Neander, The Life of Jesus Christ in its Historical Connexion and Historical Development (London: Henry G. Bohn, 1851), no. 2, 2; nos. 4-5, 7-8.
105 Cf. Holtzmann's remarks on the historicity of Jesus' messianic consciousness, in Das messianische Bewußtsein Jesu. Ein Beitrag zur Leben-Jesu-Forschung (Tübingen: J. C. B. Mohr, 1907), 98f.
106 Holtzmann, Das messianische Bewußtsein Jesu, 98. Cf. Holtmann, Die synoptischen Evangelien: Ihr Ursprung und geschichtlicher Charakter 1, 4. See also Karl Lachmann, "De ordine narrationum in evangeliis synopticis," Theologische Studien und Kritiken 8 (1835), 574. Christian H. Weisse, Die evangelische Geschichte kritisch und philosophisch bearbeitet (Leipzig: Breitkopf und Härtel, 1838), 1: 83. Cf. Christian G. Wilke, Der Urevangelist (Leipzig: Hinrichs'sche Buchhandlung, 1838), 290f.
107 O. Pfleiderer, Die Entwicklung der protestantischen Theologie in Deutschland seit Kant, 146.
108 Ullmann, "Über Partei und Schule, Gegensätze und deren Vermittlung," 58; "Das Leben Jesu von David Friedrich Strauss," 791, 812.
109 A. E. Biedermann, Christian Dogmatics, in God and Incarnation, trans. Welch, 337, 367-8.
110 Weisse, Die evangelische Geschichte, vol. 1, III-IV.

111 Cf. Holtzmann, Das messianische Bewußtsein Jesu, 98, 100f.
112 Cf. Strauss' negative assessment of this approach in The Life of Jesus, no. 107, 545-46.
113 Harnack, What is Christianity?, 68. Cf. Keim, Der geschichtliche Christus, 149f.
114 Cf. Beyschlag, Das Leben Jesu, I, 19ff.
115 Schenkel, Das Charakterbild Jesu, V.
116 Harnack, What is Christianity?, 26.
117 Otto Pfleiderer, "introduction," to The Life of Jesus Critically Examined, trans. George Eliot (London: George Allen & Co, 1913), XXVI.
118 Ibid.
119 Neander, The Life of Jesus, no 2, 2.
120 Strauss, Leben Jesu, I, 52.
121 Kähler, The so-called Historical Jesus and Historic, Biblical Christ, "introduction," 30.
122 Ibid., 43f.
123 Wilhelm Herrmann, "Der geschichtliche Christus: Der Grund unseres Glaubens," ZThK, 2 (1892), 253.
124 Ibid., 255f.
125 Keck (ed.), The Christ of Faith and the Jesus of History, introduction, LXVIII. Cf. Strauss, Life of Jesus, no. 145, 758-784.
126 See Leander E. Keck, A Future for the Historical Jesus (Nashville, 1971).

V

1 William Ellery Channing, Letter to the Rev. Samuel C. Thacher on the Aspersions. Contained in a late Number of the Panoplist on the Ministers of Boston and the Vicinity (Boston, 1815), 3.
2 Christian Examiner, (July 1832), 342, 344.
3 Robert Leet Patterson, The Philosophy of William Ellery Channing (New York: Bookman Associates, 1952), 55.
4 Cf. the discussion of the history and appropriateness of this term in Conrad Wright, The Liberal Christians (Boston: Beacon Press, 1970), 5-6.
5 James Freeman Clarke, "Furness' History of Jesus," Christian Examiner XLIX (1850), 249.
6 William Ellery Channing, "Evidences of Revealed Religion," in The Works of William E. Channing (Boston: American Unitarian Association, 1889).
7 Ibid., 302, 197.
8 Samuel Clarke, A Discourse Concerning the Unchangeable Objections of Natural Religion and the Truth and Certainty of the Christian Revelation (London: Printed for John and Paul Knapton, 1749), 343. William Paley, A View of the Evidence of Christianity, in The Works of William Paley, D. D., vo. II (Cambridge: Hilliard and Brown, 1830), 76. See also Christian Examiner, X (1831), 361.
9 Nathaniel Lardner, Credibility of the Gospel History, Pt II in The Works of Nathaniel Lardner, vol. V (London: Printed for J. Johnson, 1788), 366. Clarke, A Discourse Concerning the Unchangeable Objections of Natural Religion, 356.
10 Cf. the discussions of evidentialism in Bozeman, Protestantism in an Age of Science: The Baconian Ideal in America, 1800-1860, chapter 7 and in Holifield, The Gentlemen Theologians, 96-100.

11 Ibid., 372, 388.
12 Clarke, "Furness' History of Jesus," 249.
13 Channing, "Evidences of Christianity," in Works, 218, 219.
14 On common sense realism, see Conrad Wright, The Beginnings of Unitarianism in America (Boston: Starr King Press, 1955), 135-60; Daniel Walker Howe, The Unitarian Conscience (Cambridge, Mass.: Harvard University Press, 1970), 27-44, 69-92; and Sydney E. Ahlstrom, "The Scottish Philosophy and American Theology," Church History 24 (1955), 257-69.
15 Jedidiah Morse, "Review of Belsham's American Unitarianism," Panoplist (1815), 11f. Thomas Belsham, American Unitarianism with a Preface by Jedidiah Morse (Boston, 1815), 39-42.
16 Thomas Emlyn, An Humble Inquiry into the Scripture Account of Jesus Christ, or a Short Argument Concerning His Deity and Glory, According to the Gospel (Boston, 1756), 18. Useful background material may be found in Wright, Beginnings of Unitarianism, 200-22; Earl Morse Wilbur, A History of Unitarianism in Transylvania, England and America (Boston: Beacon Press, 1945), II, 379-434.
17 Jonathan Mayhew, "Of the Nature and Principles of Evangelical Obedience," in Sydney E. Ahlstrom and Jonathan S. Carey (eds.), An American Reformation (Middletown, Conn., Wesleyan University Press, 1985), 326.
18 Joseph Priestley, Theological and Miscellaneous Works, ed. J. T. Rutt (1831; rpt. New York: Kraus Reprint Co., 1972) I, 48, 88. Cf. Moses Stuart, Letters to Dr. Channing on the Trinity, in Miscellanies (Andover, 1846), 208.
19 Joseph Priestley, Letters to a Philosophical Unbeliever, Part II (Birmingham, 1787), 33; Priestley, Works, II, 21, V, 8.
20 Joseph Priestley, Sokrates and Jesus Compared (Philadelphia, 1803), 1-3, 33-34, 38-39.
21 Thomas Wentworth Higginson has noted that the later Channing adopted more liberal attitudes of christology. See Higginson, "Two New England Heretics: Channing and Parker," Independent 54 (1902), 1234-36.
22 Stuart, Letters to Dr. Channing (1846), 152.
23 Francis Parkman, "Letter to the Rev. Mr. Grundy of Manchester," Monthly Repository, VII (1812), 201; cf. Wright, Beginnings of Unitarianism, 217f.
24 Channing, Letter to the Rev. Samuel C. Thacher, 3.
25 Ibid., 7.
26 William Ellery Channing, Remarks on the Rev. Dr. Worcester's Second Letter to Mr. Channing on the Review of American Unitarianism in a late Panoplist (Boston 1815); text in Joseph Haroutanian, Piety Versus Moralism (New York: Henry Holt, 1932), 194-95.
27 Cf. Stuart's appropriation of Schleiermacher in his translation of Schleiermacher's "On the Discrepancy Between the Athanasian and the Sabellian Method of Representing the Trinity," trans. with notes and illustrations by M. Stuart, The Biblical Repository and Quarterly Observer, XVIII (1835), 96f.
28 Cf. Channing, "Unitarian Christianity," in Works, 374ff.
29 Stuart, Letters to Dr. Channing (1846), 208.
30 Charles Beecher, Redeemer and Redeemed (Boston: Lee and Shepard, 1864), 32. Cf. Ezra Gannett, Atonement (Boston: American Unitarian Association, 1855), 3.

31 Beecher, <u>Redeemer and Redeemed</u>, 18.
32 Gannett, <u>Atonement</u>, 9. See Edwards A. Park, "The Rise of the Edwardean Theory of the Atonement: An Introductory Essay," in Park, ed., <u>The Atonement: Discourses and Treatises by Edwards, Smalley, Maxcy, Emmons, Griffin, Burge and Weeks</u> (Boston, 1859), XI-XXXIX. See also Joseph Haroutanian, <u>Piety Versus Moralism: The Passing of the New England Theology</u> (New York: Henry Holt, 1932), chap. 7; Frank Hugh Foster, <u>A Genetic History of the New England Theology</u> (Chicago: University of Chicago Press, 1907), chap. 8.
33 Clarke, <u>A Sketch of the History of the Doctrine of the Atonement</u>, 3, 32.
34 This rejection of "the old theory of atonement" by William Ellery Channing is recorded in Beecher, <u>Redeemer and Redeemed</u>, 33.
35 W. H. Furness, <u>A Brief Statement of the Christian View of the Atonement</u> (Boston: James Munroe & Co., 1845), 12. Furness' appraisal of the "true atoning efficacy of the sufferings of Christ" recapitulates Channing's position. Cf. ibid., 14; cf. also Auguste Sabatier, trans. Victor Leuliette, <u>The Doctrine of the Atonement</u> (New York: G. P. Putnam's Sons, 1904), 45f.
36 Henry Ware, <u>Letters Addressed to Trinitarians and Calvinists, occasioned by Dr. Woods' Letters to Unitarians</u> (Cambridge, 1820), 17.
37 Channing, "Imitableness of Christ's Character," in <u>Works</u>, 311; cf. Channing, "The Essence of the Christian Religion" and "Likeness to God."
38 Cf. Channing, "The Imitableness of Christ's Character,"; in <u>Works</u>, 310-16.
39 Lardner, <u>Credibility of the Gospel History</u>, X.
40 Lardner, <u>Works</u>, V, 367.
41 Clarke, <u>A Discourse Concerning the Unchangeable Objections of Natural Religion</u>, 444.
42 Ibid., 356.
43 See the refutation of deism in Clarke, <u>A Discourse Concerning the Unchangeable Objections of Natural Religion</u>, 172f.
44 Cf. Channing, "Evidences of Christianity" and "Evidences of Revealed Religion," in <u>Works</u>, 188-220, 220-32.
45 Andrews Norton, <u>The Evidences of the Genuineness of the Gospels</u>, vol. I (Cambridge: John Owen, 1846), 20. Andrews Norton, <u>A Statement of Reasons For Not Believing the Doctrines of Trinitarians, Concerning the Nature of God and the Person of Christ</u>, 16f,
46 Horatio B. Hackett, "Synoptical Study of the Gospels and recent Literature pertaining to it," <u>Bibliotheca Sacra</u> III (1846), 1.
47 Ibid., 2.
48 J. D. Green, "A Harmony of the Gospels, on the Plan proposed by Lant Carpenter," <u>Christian Examiner</u>, X (1831), 359.
49 Cf. the refutation of deist premises in Channing, "Evidences of Revealed Religion," <u>Works</u>, 229f.
50 Cf. Channing, "Evidences of Revealed Religion" and "Evidences of Christianity" in <u>Works</u>, 224-25; 210-11.
51 Clarke, <u>A Discourse Concerning the Unchangeable Objections of Natural Religion</u>, 172; John Tillotson, <u>Works</u>, XI, 203.
52 William Paley, <u>Evidences of Christianity</u>, in Creed and Smith (eds.), <u>Religious Thought in the Eighteenth Century</u>, 87.
53 On the deist background relevant for the application of Scottish common sense, see Herbert M. Morais <u>Deism in Eighteenth Century</u>

America (New York, 1934), 35f. Cf. also Ahlstrom, "The Scottish Philosophy and American Theology," 259f.

54 Cf. Hume, Enquiry Concerning Human Understanding, secs. 4-7 and Thomas Reid, Essays on the Intellectual Power of Man, Baruch A. Brody, ed. (Cambridge, Mass. 1969 (1785)), 600-604.

55 Channing, "Evidences of Christianity"; "Imitableness of Christ's Character," in Works, 218; 310.

56 See John Gorham Palfrey, Harmony of the Gospels, after the Plan by Lant Carpenter (Boston, 1931); Edward Robinson, Harmony of the Gospels in Greek, after Le Clerc and Newcome (Andover, 1834).

57 On Unitarian critical principles, see Brown, The Rise of Biblical Criticism in America, 1800-1870, 6f.

58 Cf. Wright, Beginnings of Unitarianism, 29ff.

59 George Ticknor, "Memoirs of the Buckminsters," Christian Examiner, XLVIII (1849), 186.

60 Joseph Buckminster, "Review of Griesbach's New Testament," Monthly Anthology X (1811), 112. Cf. "Notice of Griesbach's Edition of the New Testament, Now Printing at Cambridge," Monthly Anthology V (1808), 18-21; and "On the Accuracy and Fidelity of Griesbach," General Repository and Review I (1812), 89-101.

61 Johann Jakob Griesbach, Synopsis Evangeliorum (Halle, 1822), VIII-IX; text in Kümmel, Interpretation of the New Testament, 75.

62 Hackett, "Synoptical Study of the Gospels," 2.

63 Buckminster, Sermons, "John VII, 46," 24.

64 Buckminster, Sermons, "2 Pet. III 15, 16," 167.

65 Cf. John David Michaelis, Introduction of the New Testament, vol. III (Cambridge: John Burges, 1801), 4ff.

66 Buckminster, Sermons (Boston: John Eliot, 1814), "John VII 46," 22.

67 Buckminster, Sermons, "Matthew XXVI, 35," 266.

68 Cf. Buckminster, Sermons, "Sources of Infidelity," 155f.

69 Buckminster, Sermons, "Hebr. XI 1," 135.

70 Moses Stuart, Letters to the Rev. William Ellery Channing (Andover, 1819), 171, 173. See also Letters to Dr. Channing (1846), 184-185.

71 Moses Stuart, "Old Testament," X, ANT.

72 Cf. Stuart's comments on "grammatico-historical" interpretation, in "Hermeneutics," VI, ANT.

73 Channing, "Unitarian Christianity," in Works, 367-368.

74 Ibid., 368.

75 George Park Fisher, "Channing as a Philosopher and Theologian," in Discussions in History and Theology (New York, 1880), 272.

76 Channing, Works, 408.

77 Moses Stuart, Letters to Dr. Channing on the Trinity, 76-77.

78 Ibid., 79.

79 Ibid., 152.

80 Channing, "Unitarian Christianity," in Works, 370.

81 Stuart, Letters to Dr. Channing, 171.

82 Ibid., 175-176.

83 Ibid., 184f.

84 Ibid., 180.

85 Samuel Miller, Letters on Unitarianism (Trenton, 1821), 197.

86 Ibid., 178, 182; cf. 180.

87 Stuart, Letters (1846), 28.

88 Moses Stuart (trans.), Dissertations on the Importance and Best Method of Studying the Original Languages of the Bible, By John and Others (Andover: Flagg and Gould, 1827); 18, 19.
89 Ibid., 14.
90 Stuart, Letters (1846), 182, 180.
91 Ibid., 49.
92 Andrews Norton, Tracts Concerning Christianity (Cambridge: John Bartlett, 1852), 72.
93 Andrews Norton, "Defense of Liberal Christianity," The General Repository and Review I (1812), 2.
94 Andrews Norton, "Review of Stuart's Letters to Channing," The Christian Disciple I (1819), 316.
95 Andrews Norton, Lectures VIII (2), HUA.
96 Norton, Statement of Reason, 43.
97 Norton, Lectures, V (13), HUA.
98 Norton, Evidences of the Genuineness of the Gospels, I, 260.
99 Andrew P. Peabody, "Reminiscences," 74. Text in Frothingham, Boston Unitarianism, 71.
100 Hackett, "A Harmony of the Gospels," 2.
101 Henry Ware Jr., The Life of the Saviour (Boston: Hilliard, Gray, and Co., 1833), 29.
102 Henry Ware Jr., The Life of the Saviour (1884 ed.), 266.
103 Norton, Evidences of the Genuineness of the Gospels, I, 115.
104 Ibid., 96.

VI

1 John Barnard, "Dudleian Lecture (1756)"; text in Wright, The Liberal Christians, 6.
2 Cf. "Systematic Index," in A Catalogue of the Library of Harvard University in Cambridge, Massachusetts (Cambridge, 1830), III, 1-4, 8-15.
3 Buckminster, "Sermon X: Sources of Infidelity," 155.
4 The Harvard-Göttingen axis is described in Orie William Long, Literary Pioneers: American Explorers of European Culture (Cambridge: Harvard University Press, 1935); Daniel B. Shumway, "The American Students of the University of Göttingen," German-American Annals, N. S., VIII (1910), 172-74; Reginald H. Phelps, "The Idea of the Modern University - Göttingen and America," The Germanic Review, XXIX (1954), 175-90; Cynthia Stokes Brown, "The American Discovery of the German University: Four Studies in Göttingen, 1815-1822" (Ph. D. diss., Johns Hopkins University, 1966); and Fred L. Burwick, "The Göttingen Influence on George Bancroft's Idea of Humanity," Jahrbuch für Amerikastudien, XI (1966), 194-212.
5 George Ticknor, Journal, vol. I, 27 March 1816.
6 Cf. Andrews Norton, "Remarks on the Characteristics of the Modern German School of Infidelity," in A Discourse on the Latest Form of Infidelity (Cambridge, Mass.: John Owen, 1839), 48f.
7 Cf. Norton, "On the Objection to Faith in Christianity," in ibid., 50f.
8 Cf. Ibid., 58.
9 George Ticknor to Elisha Ticknor, November, 5, 1815, in Life, Letters, and Journals of George Ticknor (Boston: James R. Osgood &

Company, 1876), I, 79; Hackett, "Synoptical Study of the Gospels," 11. Cf. Norton, Evidences of the Genuineness of the Gospels, I, 97.
10 A. P. Peabody, "Dr. Carpenter's Harmony of the Gospels," Christian Examiner XXII (1837), 47.
11 Norton, Evidences of the Genuineness of the Gospels, I, CLVII.
12 Ticknor, Journal, I, 27 March 1816.
13 Ibid., 27 March 1816.
14 Norton, Evidences of the Genuineness of the Gospels, I, 19.
15 Christian Examiner, X (1831), 361.
16 Norton, Evidences of the Genuineness of the Gospels, I, 95.
17 Ibid., 95.
18 George Ticknor to Thomas Jefferson, October 14, 1815; text in Orie Long, Thomas Jefferson and George Ticknor: A Chapter in American Scholarship (Williamstown, Mass.: The McClelland Press, 1933), 15.
19 George Bancroft, Letters, January 17, 1819, MHS, used by permission. Cf. M. A. De Wolfe Howe ed., The Life and Letters of George Bancroft (New York: Scribner's, 1908), I, 55.
20 George Bancroft, Letters, September 12, 1818, MHS.
21 Ticknor, Journal, I, March 27, 1816.
22 George Bancroft, "Henry Dwight's Travels in the North of Germany," American Quarterly Review, VI (1829), 214.
23 Bancroft, Letters, May 31, 1829, MHS; 10 July, 1819, MHS.
24 John Lightfoot, The Harmony, Chronicle, and Order of the New Testament, in The Whole Works of the late John Lightfoot, ed. John Rogers Pittmann (London: G. Cowie and Co. Poultry, 1825), vol. 3; James Macknight, Harmony of the Four Gospels in Which the Natural Order of Each is Preserved, 2 vols. (London: Printed for the author, 1756); Joseph Hall, Contemplations upon the Principal Passages of the Holy Story, in The Works of Joseph Hall, new ed. (Oxford, D. A. Talboy's, 1837); Jeremy Taylor, The Great Exemplar of Sanctity and Holy Life ..., in The Whole Works of the Right Rev. Jeremy Taylor, D. D., ed. Reginal Heber (London: Longman, 1864), vol. 2.
25 Cf. Norton, Evidences of the Genuineness of the Gospels, I, 96f.
26 Ticknor, Journal, I, March 27, 1816.
27 Howe, The Life and Letters of George Bancroft, I, 33.
28 Edward Everett to George Bancroft, April 13, 1818; text in Stuart Joel Horn, Edward Everett and American Nationalism (PhD dissertation, The City University of New York, 1973), 61.
29 Howe, The Life and Letters of George Bancroft, I, 55.
30 Johann G. Eichhorn, Einleitung in das Neue Testament (Leipzig, 1804), 1: 458-49; cf. Kümmel, Interpretation of the New Testament, 78-79.
31 Bancroft, Letters, July 10, 1819, MHS.
32 Howe, The Life and Letters of George Bancroft, I, 55.
33 Cf. Stuart, Letters (1846), 79.
34 William Emerson, Letters, August 8, 1824, KA.
35 Cf. Edward Everett, Defence of Christianity Against the Work of George B. English (Boston, 1884), "Introduction."
36 Edward Everett, Letters, January 5, 1816, MHS.
37 Lessing, "On the Proof of the Spirit and of Power," in Chadwick (ed.) Lessing's Theological Writings, 53, cf. 51, 56.
38 Bancroft, Letters, November 5, 1820, MHS.
39 Ibid., 5 November 1820, MHS.
40 William Emerson, Letters, June 27, 1824, KA.

41 Cf. Schleiermacher, Hermeneutics, 164, 166, 172, 185. See also Frei, The Eclipse of Biblical Narrative, 297-98.
42 George Bancroft, Literary and Historical Miscellanies (New York: Harper & Brothers, 1855), 409, 410.
43 Bancroft, Letters, December 24, 1820; December 3, 1820, MHS.
44 Howe, The Life and Letters of George Bancroft, I, 65. Bancroft, Letters, July, 10, 1819, August 1, 1819, MHS.
45 "The New Testament in the Common Version, conformed to Griesbach's Standard Greek Text" Christian Examiner (1829), 353.
46 Stuart to Everett; text in Brown, Rise of Biblical Criticsm, 51.
47 Bancroft, Letters, August, 4, 1818, MHS; cf. Howe, The Life and Letters of George Bancroft, I, 33.
48 Everett, Letters, January 5, 1816, MHS.
49 Howe, The Life and Letters of George Bancroft, I, 33.
50 Everett, Letters, January 5, 1816, MHS.
51 L, I, 352 n 37.
52 Norton, A Discourse on the Latest Form of Infidelity, 30.
53 J, II, 30-31.
54 Stuart to Everett, 13 Febr. 1813, MHS.
55 William Emerson to Ezra Riply, April 4, 1830, HL.
56 The issue of church membership and communion is treated in both William's and Ralph Waldo's comments on the Lord's Supper on an exegetical plane which slights the historical precedent established by Stoddard. Cf. W, XI, 7f. and the appropriate sermon texts preserved in HL and used here by permission of the Ralph Waldo Emerson Memorial Association and of the Houghton Library.
57 William Emerson to Ezra Ripley, April 4, 1830, HL.
58 Schleiermacher, The Life of Jesus, 392.
59 Quest, 24.
60 William Emerson to Ezra Ripley, April 4, 1830, HL.
61 William Emerson, Letters, March 2, 1825, KA.
62 Cf. Emerson's discussion of Everett in "Life and Letters in New England," W, X, 312.
63 L, I, 273.
64 Bancroft, Letters, August 4, 1818, MHS; Howe, The Life and Letters of George Bancroft, I, 55.
65 Russel B. Nye, George Bancroft, Brahmin Rebel (New York, 1972), 63.
66 John Randolph, Remarks on Michaelis's 'Introduction to the New Testament'," (London, 1802), 5.
67 Griesbach, Synopsis, VIII-IX. A complete list of the biblical studies which Emerson used for his vestries may found in K. W. Cameron's edition of the vestry lectures, The Vestry Lectures and a Rare Sermon (Hartford: Transcendental Books, 1984), 24-28.
68 Norton, Evidences of the Genuineness of the Gospel, I, 155.
69 Cf. Connop Thirlwall, A Critical Essay on the Gospel of St. Luke (London: James Taylor, 1825), introduction. "Ueber die Zeugnisse des Papias von unsern beiden ersten Evangelien," ThStKr V (1832), 735-68.
70 Cf. Ralph L. Rusk, The Life of Ralph Waldo Emerson (New York and London: Columbia University Press, 1949), 105f.
71 Ibid., 106.
72 Schleiermacher, Critical Essay, 296; cf. The Life of Jesus, 393.
73 Schleiermacher, The Christian Faith, 643.
74 Schleiermacher, The Life of Jesus, 392.

75 Mary C. Turpie, "A Quaker Source for Emerson's Sermon on the Lord's Supper," NEQ, XVII (1944), 96-7.
76 John McAleer, Ralph Waldo Emerson: Days of Encounter (Boston: Little Brown and Company, 1984), 122.
77 Channing, "The Imitableness of Christ's Character," in Works, 310-316.
78 Rusk, The Life of Ralph Waldo Emerson, 107.
79 Letter to Mary Moody Emerson, October 27, 1825; text in Rusk, 113. For an additional account of William Emerson's visit to Goethe, see Haven Emerson, "William Emerson Travels Abroad," Charaka Club Proceedings, VIII (1935), 76-77.
80 Cf. Johann Peter Eckermann, Gespräche mit Goethe in den letzten Jahren seines Lebens, in Goethe, Gedenkausgabe der Werke, Briefe und Gespräche, ed. Ernst Beutler (Zürich: Artemis Verlag, 1949), 24, 770-71.
81 George Ripley, "Schleiermacher as a Theologian," Christian Examiner, XX (1836), in Perry Miller (ed.) The Transcendentalists: An Anthology (Cambridge, Mass.: Harvard University Press, 1950), 100-101.
82 Norton, "Remarks on the Characteristics of the Modern German School of Infidelity," 41.
83 Norton, A Discourse on the Latest Form of Infidelity, 10.

VII

1 Frothingham, Boston Unitarianism, 169.
2 Norton, A Discourse on the Latest Form of Infidelity, 32; Frothingham, Boston Unitarianism, 169.
3 Cf. Octavius B. Frothingham, George Ripley (Boston, 1882), 46.
4 Frothingham, Boston Unitarianism, 169.
5 John 4,48; cf. Immanuel Kant, Religion Within the Limits of Reason Alone, (1934; New York: Harper, 1960), 79.
6 George Ripley, "Review of James Martineau, "The Rationale of Religious Enquiry," Christian Examiner, XXI (1836), in Miller (ed.), The Transcendentalists, 131; "Herder's Theological Opinions and Services," Christian Examiner, XIX (1835), 195. See also Miller (ed.), The Transcendentalist, 96.
7 Memoir of William Ellery Channing, II, 451.
8 Samuel Clarke, The Works of Samuel Clarke, D. D. 4 vols (1738, rpt. New York, 1978), II, 667.
9 Hume, Enquiry, sec. 92, 116f.
10 "Chalmer's Evidences of Christianity," Christian Examiner, VII (1818), 381; cf. "McIlvaines's Evidences of Christianity," Christian Examiner, (1833), 347.
11 Channing, Works, 69-70.
12 Cf. Channings remarks on deist religious philosophy in "Evidences of Revealed Religion," Works, 227f.
13 Clarke, "Furness's History of Jesus," 249.
14 "The Diegesis" Christian Examiner, XIX (1835), 333.
15 Christian Examiner (1831), 352.
16 "State of Religion in Germany," Christian Examiner, XIX (1835), 41.
17 Stuart, Letters to Dr. Channing (1846), 182, 187.
18 "State of Religion in Germany," 41; Bancroft, Letters, March 21, 1819, MHS.

19 Bancroft, Letters, March 21, 1819; March 21, 1818, MHS.
20 "State of Religion in Germany," 42; "The Diegesis," 336.
21 Cf. Thomas Reid "Essays on the Active Powers of Man," in The Works of Thomas Reid vol. 2, ed. William Hamilton (Edinburgh: Maclachlan and Stewart, 1863, sixth edition c 1788), I, V, 525f.
22 A. P. Peabody, "Dr. Carpenter's Harmony of the Gospels," Christian Examiner, XXII (1837), 57.
23 The South-Boston Unitarian Ordination (Boston, 1841), 16.
24 William Greenleaf Eliot, Our Lord Jesus Christ, 41, in Ahlstrom and Carey (eds.), An American Reformation, 38.
25 Ripley, "Martineau's Rationale," Christian Examiner, XXI (1836), 227f. See also Miller (ed.), The Transcendentalist, 130.
26 Orestes Brownson, "Norton's Evidence," The Boston Quarterly Review, II (1839), in Miller (ed.), The Transcendentalists, 207.
27 For a discussion of Coleridge's influence on New England, see Frederic Henry Hedge, "Coleridge's Literary Character," Christian Examiner, XIV (1833), 109f.
28 Richard Smallbroke, A vindication of the Miracles of Our Blessed Saviour (London, 1731); E. Sandercock, Sermons on the Parables of Our Saviour; occasioned by an objection in Christianity as old as the creation (London, 1733); Henry Stebbing, A discourse on Our Saviour's Miraculous Power of Healing. In which six cases excepted against Mr. Woolston are considered (London, 1730); Arthur Ashley Sykes, A brief discourse concerning the credibility of miracles and revelation, wherein the credibility of the Gospel miracles is shown (London, 1749^3).
29 Noah Porter "Coleridge and his American Disciples," Bibliotheca Sacra, IV (1847), 140, 163.
30 George Ripley, "Jesus Christ, the Same Yesterday, Today, and Forever," in Miller (ed.), The Transcendentalists, 285-86; complete manuscript in Ripley Papers, MHS.
31 Ripley, "Herder's Theological Opinions and Services," 180.
32 Ripley, "Jesus Christ, the Same Yesterday, Today, and Forever," 286.
33 Ibid., 286; Norton, A Discourse on the Latest Form of Infidelity, in ibid., 213.
34 Ripley, "Schleiermacher as a Theologian," Christian Examiner, XX (1836), 4.
35 Cf. Schleiermacher, Hermeneutics, 164, 166.
36 Cf. Norton's charges in A Discourse on the Latest Form of Infidelity, 24, 25.
37 Ripley, "Martineau's Rationale," 227. See also Miller (ed.), The Transcendentalist, 130.
38 Ripley, "Martineau's Rationale," 246; cf. 252.
39 Ibid., 251.
40 Ibid., 225-27. See also Miller (ed.), The Transcendentalist, 131.
41 Norton, A Discourse on the Latest Form of Infidelity, 22.
42 Ibid., 30.
43 George Ripley, "To Andrews Norton," The Boston Daily Advertiser (1836), in Miller (ed.), The Transcendentalists, 161.
44 George Ripley Discourses on the Philosophy of Religion, in Miller (ed.), The Transcendentalists, 137; "Schleiermacher as a Theologian," in ibid., 102.
45 Ripley, Discourses on the Philosophy of Religion, in Miller (ed.), The Transcendentalists, 137.

46 Norton, "On the Objection to Faith in Christianity;" in A Discourse on the Latest Form of Infidelity, 50f.
47 Ripley, "Martineau's Rationale," in Miller (ed.), The Transcendentalists, 132.
48 Ripley, "Martineau's Rationale," 252-254.
49 Ripley, "Schleiermacher as a Theologian" and "Herder's Theological Opinions and Services," in Miller (ed.), The Transcendentalists, 101, 96.
50 Ripley, "Herder's Theological Opinions and Services," in Miller (ed.), The Transcendentalist, 97.
51 Boston Daily Advertiser, (1836), 1.
52 George Ripley, Discourses on the Philosophy and Religion: Addressed to Doubters who Wish to Believe (Boston, 1836), 70.
53 Ripley, "Schleiermacher as a Theologican," in Miller (ed.), The Transcendentalist, 99.
54 Cf. George Ripley, "The Latest Form of Infidelity Examined," in Miller (ed.), The Transcendentalists, 218f.
55 William Henry Furness, Remarks on the Four Gospels (Philadelphia: Carey, Lea & Blanchard, 1836), 197.
56 Ibid., 185, 183.
57 Ibid., 199, 185.
58 Ibid., VIII-IX, 198.
59 Ibid., 198.
60 Ibid., 198-99.
61 Cf. ibid., 167.
62 Ibid., 335.
63 Cf. ibid., 145f., 217-18.
64 Martin Luther Hurlbut, "Furness' Remarks on the Four Gospels," in Miller (ed.), The Transcendentalists, 171.
65 Ibid., 173.
66 Ibid., 172.
67 William Henry Furness, "The Miracles of Jesus," Christian Examiner, XXII (1837), 284.
68 Compare Norton's Discourse on the Latest Form of Infidelity, 50f. with Furness' Remarks on the Four Gospels, 24f.
69 Furness, Remarks on the Four Gospels, 34, 51.
70 Ibid., 24.
71 Ibid., 28.
72 Cf. George Ripley, Defence of "The Latest Form of Infidelity" Examined: A Third Letter to Mr. Andrews Norton (Boston: James Munroe, 1840), 6f; 146ff.
73 Emerson, "Divinity School Address," CW, I, 81f; cf. George Ripley, Defence of "The Latest Form of Infidelity" Examined: A Letter to Mr. Andrews Norton (Boston: James Munroe, 1839), 116, 158f. and Ripley, "Martineau's Rationale," 252f.
74 Ripley, Herder's Theological Opinions and Services," 197.
75 Ibid., 197, 199.
76 James Freeman Clarke, The Well-Instructed Scribe; or Reform and Conservatism (Boston: Benjamin H. Greene, 1841), 6-7; cf. 9-10.
77 James Freeman Clarke, The Unitarian Reform, in Tracts of the American Unitarian Association, 1st ser., 12, no. 138 (Boston: James Munroe), 6f.

78 Convers Francis, Christianity as a Purely Internal Principle, in Tracts of the American Unitarian Asssociation, 1st ser., 9, no. 105 (Boston: Leonard C. Bowles, 1836), 8f.
79 Convers Francis, Christ the Way to God, in Tracts of the American Unitarianism Association, 1st. ser., 16, no. 181 (Boston: James Munroe, 1843), 6f.
80 Ibid., 11.
81 Frederic Henry Hedge, Practical Goodness the True Religion (Bangor, Maine: S. S. Smith, 1840), 5; cf. 14-15. Frederic Henry Hedge, A Sermon on the Character and Ministry of the Late Rev. William Ellery Channing, D. D., 17 Nov., 1842 (Bangor, Maine: S. S. Smith), 6f.
82 Norton, A Discourse on the Latest Form of Infidelity, 10.
83 Ibid., 14-15.
84 Norton, "On the Objection to Faith in Christianity, as Resting on Historical Facts and Critical Learning," in A Discourse on the Latest Form of Infidelity, 50.
85 Norton, A Discourse on the Latest Form of Infidelity, in Miller (ed.), The Transcendentalists, 212.
86 Norton, A Discourse on the Latest Form of Infidelity, 52.
87 Text of Ripley's reply in Octavius Brooks Frothingham, George Ripley (Boston: Houghton, Mifflin and Company, 1883), 101.
88 Cf. Ripley, "Herder's Theological Opinions and Services," in Miller (ed.), The Transcendentalists, 97.
89 Orestes Brownson, "Mr. Emerson's Address," Boston Quarterly Review (1838), 501.
90 Ripley, A Third Letter to Mr. Andrews Norton Occasioned by his Defence of A Discourse on "The Latest Form of Infidelity, 114.
91 Ibid., 116, 83, 92.

VIII

1 Francis Bowen, "Locke and the Transcendentalists," Christian Examiner XXIII (1837), 180f.; cf. Bowen, "Transcendentalism," Christian Examiner XXI (1837), 371-85.
2 George Ripley, "Letter to the Church in Purchase Street," in Miller (ed.), The Transcendentalists, 255.
3 John Weiss, Discourse Occasioned by the Death of Convers Francis, D. D. (Cambridge, 1863), 28-29.
4 Bowen, "Locke and the Transcendentalists," 183.
5 The Western Messenger III (1837), 576-579.
6 Richard Hildreth "A letter to Andrews Norton," in Miller (ed.), The Transcendentalists, 224.
7 Andrews Norton, "The New School in Literature and Religion," in Miller (ed.), The Transcendentalists, 193.
8 George Ripley, "Introductory Note, Specimens of Foreign Standard Literature," in Miller (ed.), The Transcendentalists, 298; Alexander H. Everett, "History of Intellectual Philosophy," in ibid., 30.
9 Kant, Critique of Pure Reason, 65.
10 Cf. Porter, "Coleridge and his American Disciples," 140f. On the intuitive conception of "reason," see Thomas Carlyle, "The State of German Literature," Works, XXVIII, 377.
11 Cf. the introduction to the Critique of Pure Reason (trans. F. M. Müller (New York: Macmillan, 1896), 9) "I call all knowledge

transcendental which is occupied not so much with objects, as with our a priori concepts of objects."

12 "Dorner's Christology," The Dial, II (1842), 522. On the association of Kant with Schelling, see Frederic Henry Hedge, "German Metaphysics," Christian Examiner, XIV (1833), 125.

13 Frederic Henry Hedge, "Coleridge," in Miller (ed.), The Transcendentalist, 71; Western Messenger, VI (1838), 57-8. August Tholuck, Guido and Julius, tr. J. E. Ryland, 8.

14 Cf. Andrews Norton, Internal Evidences of the Genuineness of the Gospels (Boston: Little, Brown, and Company, 1855), 88, 96, 100.

15 Cf. Brownson, "Norton's Evidence," in Miller (ed.), The Transcendentalists, 207.

16 Theodore Parker, "The Previous Question between Mr. Andrews Norton and His Alumni, Moved and Handled in a Letter to All Those Gentlemen by Levi Blodgett." Appendix to John Edward Dirks, The Critical Theology of Theodore Parker (New York, 1948), 138, 140.

17 Ibid., 149, 150, 145.

18 Cf. ibid., 148, 154.

19 Ibid., 150, 159.

20 Ibid., 156.

21 Theodore Parker, "D. F. Strauss's Das Leben Jesu," Christian Examiner, XXVIII (1840), 281.

22 Parker, "Levi Blodgett Letter," 155, 156.

23 Parker, "D. F. Strauss' Das Leben Jesu," 309.

24 Ibid., 306.

25 Cf. ibid., 281, 299, 307.

26 Ibid., 309.

27 Cf. ibid., 310.

28 Theodore Parker, A Discourse of Religion, in Works (Boston: American Unitarian Association, 1908), I, 222.

29 Theodore Parker, "The Laws of Moses," The Scriptural Interpreter, VII (1837), 270.

30 Parker, "The Levi Blodgett Letter," 154, 157.

31 Cf. ibid., 154.

32 Theodore Parker, "The Transient and Permanent in Christianity," in Henry S. Commager (ed.), Theodore Parker: An Anthology (Boston, 1960), 49.

33 Parker, "The Transient and Permanent," 49f.

34 Parker, "D. F. Strauss' Das Leben Jesu," 281.

35 Parker, "Levi Blodgett Letter," 148; A Discourse of Religion, 248.

36 Samuel Lathrop, Some reminiscences of the life of Samuel Kirkland Lathrop (Cambridge, 1888), 202; text in Clarence H. Faust, "The Background of the Unitarian opposition to Transcendentalism," Modern Philology 35 (1938), 322.

37 Francis William Pitt Greenwood, "Historical Christianity," Christian Examiner, XXVIII (1840), 170.

38 Andrew P. Peabody, "Mr. Parker's Discourse," Christian Examiner XXXI (1841), 98ff.; cf. J. H. Morison, "Parker's Discourse," Christian Examiner, XXXII (1842), 337ff.

39 Ezra Stiles Gannett, "Mr. Parker and his Views," Christian Examiner, XXXVIII (1845), 272.

40 Cf. Norton, Internal Evidences of the Genuineness of the Gospels, 22, 34.

41 Norton, Evidences of the Genuineness of the Gospels, III, 330.

42 Norton, Internal Evidences of the Genuineness of the Gospels, 96.
43 Cf. ibid., 96f.
44 Elizabeth Palmer Peabody, Reminiscences of Rev. Wm. Ellery Channing, D. D. (Boston: Roberts Brothers, 1880), 423ff.
45 "The Authority of Jesus Christ, as a Religious Teacher," Christian Examiner, XXXII (1842), 146.
46 Sherlock, Tryal of the Witnesses of the Resurrection of Jesus, in Deism and Natural Religion. A Sourcebook, ed. Waring, 92.
47 Norton, Internal Evidences of the Genuineness of the Gospel, 34. Cf. G. E. Ellis, "Norton's Internal Evidences of the Genuineness of the Gospels," Christian Examiner, LIII (1855), 126-27.
48 A. P. Peabody, "David Friedrich Strauss and the Mythic Theory," North American Review, XCI (1860), 139.
49 Francis Bowen, "Greenleaf and Strauss: The Truth of Christianity," North American Review, LXIII (1846), 401.
50 Stephen G. Bulfinch, "Strauss' Life of Jesus: - The Mythic Theory," Christian Examiner, XXXIX (1845), 156.
51 Cf. George E. Ellis, "The Mythical Theory Applied to the Life of Jesus," Christian Examiner, XLI (1846), 313.
52 Cf. Bowen, "Greenleaf and Strauss: The Truth of Christianity," 400f.
53 G. E. Ellis, "Christianity without Christ," Christian Examiner, XL (1846), 86. Cf. G. W. Burnap, "Tendencies and Wants of Theology," Christian Examiner, XLV (1848), 226-29.
54 Burnap, "Tendencies and Wants of Theology," 228.
55 Simon Greenleaf, The Testimony of the Evangelists, By the Rules of Evidence Administered in Courts of Justice (Boston: Charles C. Little and James Brown, 1846), 22. "Notices of Recent Publications," Christian Examiner, (1846), 296.
56 Bowen, Greenleaf and Strauss: The Truth of Christianity," 385, 382.
57 Ibid., 428-429.
58 Stuart to Everett, 14 May 1814, MHS.
59 Calvin E. Stowe, "The Right Interpretation of the Sacred Scriptures," Bibliotheca Sacra, X (1853), 41.
60 Bela Bates Edwards, "Present State of Biblical Science," Bibliotheca Sacra, VII (1850), 1.
61 Horatio B. Hackett, "Critique on Strauss' Life of Jesus," Bibliotheca Sacra, II (1844), 58.
62 Ibid., 61.
63 Andrews Norton, Two articles from the Princeton Review, Concerning the Transcendental Philosophy of the Germans and of Cousin and Its Influence on Opinion in this Country (Cambridge, 1840).
64 Cf. Charles Hodge, Systematic Theology, 3 vols (Grand Rapids: Wm. B. Eerdmans, 1946), 1, 10.
65 Charles Hodge, "The Latest Form of Infidelity," in Essays and Reviews (New York: Robert Carter & Brothers, 1857), 90, 91; cf. 81.
66 Bronson Alcott, The Doctrine and Discipline of Human Culture (Boston, 1836), 5.
67 Frederick Henry Hedge, Ways of the Spirit, 353.
68 Cf. Orestes Brownson, New Views of Christianity, Society and the Church (Boston, 1836), in Works, IV, 1-56.
69 Hodge, "The Latest Form of Infidelity," 91; Theodore Parker, "Transcendentalism," in Works, VI, 31-32.
70 Cf. Parker, "Transcendentalism," 33ff.
71 Samuel Osgood, "Emerson's Nature," in Miller (ed.), The Transcendentalists, 166.

72 Amos Bronson Alcott, Conservations with Children on the Gospels, in Miller (ed.), The Transcendentalists, 152.
73 Parker, "D. F. Strauss' Das Leben Jesu," 277.
74 Cf. Bowen, "The Truth of Christianity: Greenleaf and Strauss," 428; Hodge, "Latest Form of Infidelity," 81.
75 "German Anti-Supernaturalism," The Dial, II (1842), 535-36.
76 Burnap, "Tendencies and Wants of Theology," 231.
77 Parker, "God in the World of Man," 272; "Transcendentalism," 32.
78 Parker, "D. F. Strauss' Das Leben Jesu," 310.
79 Cf. ibid., 306, 310; Parker, A Discourse of Religion, 224.
80 Cf. the list of questers given by Parker in A Discourse of Religion, 224n.
81 Theodore Parker, "Dorner's Christology," The Dial, II (1842), 504.
82 Ibid., 526.
83 Cyrus Augustus Bartol, "Theodore; or, the Skeptic's Conversion," Christian Examiner, XXXI (1842), 355.
84 Samuel Osgood, "De Wette's Views of Theology,"
85 Samuel Osgood, "Parker's De Wette and the Old Testament," Christian Examiner (1844), 307, 308.
86 Ibid., 309, 304.
87 Osgood, "De Wette's 'Views of Theology,'" 2.
88 Ibid., 3.
89 Harbinger, VI (1848), 110; cf. "Review of Carl Follen's Inaugural Discourse," Christian Examiner, XI (1832), 375. See also Orestes Brownson, "Eclectic Philosophy," Boston Quarterly Review (1839) in Works, II, 536-538.
90 Harbinger, II (1846), 297ff. Cf. the earlier, more eulogistic appraisal of Schleiermacher in Ripley's, "Schleiermacher as an Theologian," 1-46.
91 Osgood, "De Wette's View of Theology," 22.
92 Ibid., 5.
93 Cf. "On Heroes, Hero-Worship, and the Heroic in History," The Dial, II (1842), 131.
94 "Hengstenberg and the Journal of the Evangelic Church," Christian Examiner (1835), 44.
95 George R. Noyes, "State of Religion in Germany," Christian Examiner (1835), 41; Osgood, "De Wette's Views of Theology," 7.
96 Edmund Hamilton Sears, The Fourth Gospel the Heart of Christ, in Ahlstrom (ed.), An American Reformation, 232, 235.
97 Ibid., 232.
98 Ibid., 235; cf. 234.
99 Ibid., 237.
100 Chadwick, Theodore Parker, 136-7.
101 Peabody, "Strauss and the Mythic Theory," 134.
102 Parker, "The Moral and Religious Character of Jesus of Nazareth," in A Discourse of Religion, 264, 265.
103 Ibid., 265, 265n.
104 Parker, A Discourse of Religion, 272, 225.
105 Cf. Parker, A Discourse of Religion, 225, 346-7; cf. God in the Bible, 115f.
106 Furness, Thoughts on the Life of Jesus, 27.
107 Ibid., 46-47.
108 Ibid., 25.
109 Ibid., 29.

110 A. P. Peabody, "Furness' History of Jesus," North American Review (1850), 467.
111 William Henry Furness, "Character of Christ," Christian Examiner, XV (1834), 294.
112 Peabody, "Furness' History of Jesus," 467.
113 Furness, "Character of Christ," 291.
114 Cf. by contrast the earlier account in Furness, "Character of Christ," 295f.
115 Ibid., 292.
116 Ibid., 277, 292.
117 George H. Noyes, "Causes of the Decline of Interest in Critical Theology," Christian Examiner XLIII (1847), 325-40.
118 Parker, A Discourse of Religion, 328.
119 Cf. Parker, "Levi Blodgett Letter," 149.
120 Theodore Parker, "Translator's Preface," A Critical and Historical Introduction to the Canonical Scriptures of the Old Testament (Boston, 1843), I, 3.
121 Parker, "Introduction from De Wette," I, 4.
122 Ibid., I, 4.
123 Frothingham, "Scientific Criticism of the New Testament," 97.
124 Furness, "The Character of Christ," 277.
125 Frothingham, "Scientific Criticism of the New Testament," 114.
126 Ellis, "Christianity without Christ," 78.
127 Frothingham, "Scientific Criticism of the New Testament," 96. See also Charles T. Brooks, The Simplicity of Christ's Teachings (Boston: Crosby, Nichols, and Nichols, 1859), 58-71.
128 Theodore Parker, "Thoughts on Theology," The Dial, II (1842), 496.
129 George Ripley, Specimens of Standard Foreign Literature (Boston, 1838), I, 15.
130 Bulfinch, "Strauss and the Mythic Theory," 131.
131 Burnap, "Tendencies and Wants of Theology," 225f. Cf. Osgood, "Modern Ecclesiastical History," 429.
132 See Clarke's comments on De Wette in Theodore; or The Mystic's Conversion (Boston: James Munroe and Company, 1856), I, 299.
133 Schleiermacher, Christliche Glaubenslehre (rev. ed.), § 8, postscript 2.
134 Burnap, "Tendencies and Wants of Theology," 240.
135 Peabody, "Strauss and the Mythic Theory," 136.
136 "The Unitarian Movement in New England," The Dial, I (1841), 424.
137 Cf. Burnap, "Tendencies and Wants of Theology," 240f.
138 Ibid., 240.
139 Parker, "Thoughts on Theology," 494.
140 Clarke, "Translator's Preface" for Theodore, XV, XIII.
141 "German Anti-Supernaturalism," The Dial, II (1847), 536.
142 Cf. R. W. B. Lewis, The American Adam: Innocence, Tragedy, and Tradition in the Nineteenth Century (Chicago, 1955), 170.
143 Ibid., 170
144 Cf. Parker, A Discourse of Religion, 111f; "Transcendentalism," 33. L, I, 208.

IX

1 On Ghillany and Gförer, cf. Quest, 162.

2 Christian Disciple, IV (1817), 3.
3 Lew Wallace, The Boyhood of Christ, (New York: Harper, 1889), 27; Florence M. Kingsley, Titus, A Comrade of the Cross (Chicago: David C. Cook, 1894), 1.
4 Cf. H. Harrison Orians, "Censure of Fiction in American Romances and Magazines 1789-1810," PMLA, 52 (1937), 195-224. Walter F. Greiner, Studien zur Entstehung der englischen Romantheorie an der Wende zum 18. Jahrhundert, (Tübingen, 1969), 168f.; Irène Simon, "Early Theories of Prose Fiction: Congreve and Fielding," in Imagined Worlds: Essays on Some English Novels and Novelists in Honour of John Butt, ed. Maynard Mack and Ian Gregor (London, 1968), 21-3.
5 The phrase is Thomas Shephard's as quoted in Kenneth B. Murdock, Literature and Theology in Colonial New England (Cambridge, 1949), 62.
6 Nye and Grabo, American Thought and Writing, I, 243, 244.
7 Cf. Lewalski, Protestant Poetics, 111f.
8 Panoplist, IV (1808), 205.
9 The Christian Spectator, IV, (1822), 562.
10 Southern Literary Messenger, IV (1836), 373.
11 Harriet Beecher Stowe, Footsteps of the Master (New York: J. B. Ford, 1877), 10, 137, 26.
12 Joseph Holt Ingraham, The Pillar of Fire; or Israel in Bondage (New York: Pudney and Russell, 1859), 600.
13 A. P. Peabody, "Philosophy of Fiction," 7.
14 The central study of the impact of Scottish common sense philosophy on the rise of American fiction is Martin Terence, The Instructed Vision: Scottish Common Sense Philosophy and the Origins of American Fiction (Bloomington: Indiana University Press, 1961). See also Nina Baym, Novels, Readers and Reviewers (Ithaca and London: Cornell University Press, 1984).
15 Ingraham, The Prince of the House of David, "Dedication."
16 Florence M. Kingsley, Stephen. A Soldier of the Cross (New York: The Christian Herald Bible House, 1896), 209, 34. See also Phelps, The Story of Jesus Christ, VIII-X.
17 North American Review, LXV (1847), 348.
18 The American Monthly Magazine and Critical Review, IV (1819), 177.
19 Susanna Rowson, Biblical Dialogues (Boston: Richardson and Lord, 1822), I, 244.
20 Ibid., I, V.
21 Sherlock, Tryal of the Witnesses of the Resurrection, in Waring (ed.), Deism and Natural Religion. A Sourcebook, 92. Cf. John Hewson, Christ Rejected (Philadelphia: Joseph Rakestraw, 1832), 372.
22 Sherlock, Works, V, 180.
23 Zerah, The Believing Jew (New York: New York Protestant Episcopal Press, 1837), 43.
24 Ibid., 3.
25 Cf. "A Dissertation," in The Major Poems of Timothy Dwight (1752-1827), ed. William J. Mc Taggart and William K. Bottorff (Gainesville, Fla.: Scholars' Facsimiles and Reprints, 1969), 545.
26 Jacob Abbott, The Young Christian. A Familiar Illustration of the Principles of Christianity (New York: American Tract Society, 1832), 4.
27 John Neal, Seventy-Six or, Love and Battle (1822; rpt. London: J. Cunningham, 1840), 137.

28 Peabody, "Philosophy of Fiction," 7.
29 Eliza Cabot Follen, The Skeptic (Boston and Cambridge: James Munroe and Company, 1835), 4-5.
30 Ibid., 32, 67. "Unitarianism Vindicated Against the Charge of Skeptical and Infidel Tendencies," Christian Examiner, XI (1831), 188.
31 Follen, The Skeptic, 93, 97.
32 Norton, Evidences, I, 18.
33 Follen, The Skeptic, 94.
34 Stuart, Letters (1846), 195.
35 Norton, Discourse on the Latest Form of Infidelity, 28, 29.
36 Stuart, Letters (1846), 195.
37 Norton, A Discourse on the Latest Form of Infidelity, 33.
38 James Freeman Clarke, The Story of a Converted Skeptic (Boston: W. M. Crosby and H. P. Nichols, 1846), 4, 7.
39 Ibid., 7, 8.
40 Ibid., 13.
41 Ibid., 13.
42 E. Robbins, "Books for the People," Christian Examiner, XXV (1843), 108-9.
43 W. B. O. Peabody, "Waverley Novels," North American Review, XXXII (1831), 388.
44 The Southern Literary Messenger (1847); Knickerbocker (1838). The texts are broad together in Baym, Novels, Readers and Reviewers, chapter 10.
45 Cf. Channing's remarks on Scott, "Evidences of Christianity," 199-200. See also Jared Sparks, "Recent American Novels," North American Review, XXI (1825), 78-104; W. H. Prescott, "Novel Writing," North American Review, XXV (1827), 183-203; O. W. B. Peabody, "Sir Walter Scott," North American Review, XXXVI (1833), 289-315.
46 North American Review, IV (1819), 65; XXV (1827), 194.
47 C. Robbins, "The Acts of the Apostles, arranged for Families and Sunday Schools," Christian Examiner XLI (1846), 303; F. W. P. Greenwood, "Traditions of Palestine," Christian Examiner, XI (1832), 293.
48 Cf. Edward Everett, "Valerius, a Roman Story," North American Review, XIII (1821), 393-417.
49 William Ware, Julian: or, Scenes in Judea (New York: C. S. Francis, Boston: J. H. Francis, 1841), I, "Note."
50 Paley, Evidences, II, 145.
51 Peabody, "Philosophy of Fiction," 10.
52 North American Review XLVII (1838), 466-67.
53 See, however, W. H. Prescott, "English Literature of the Nineteenth Century," North American Review, XXXV (1832), 165-195, who highlights Scott only.
54 Cf. Ware, Julian, "Note."
55 Ibid. Joseph Allen, Sprague: IX.
56 Ware, Julian, II, 344.
57 Ibid., II, 171.
58 Ibid., II, 111, 279.
59 Ibid., II, 325.
60 Ibid., II, 112.
61 Follen, The Skeptic, 33.
62 Brownson, Works, IV; 262.

63 Sylvester Judd, Margaret (Boston, 1845), 218f. On the Transcendentalists' view of fiction, see David S. Reynolds, Faith in Fiction: The Emergence of Religious Literature in America (Cambridge: Harvard University Press, 1982), 121.
64 Within certain limits, however, the "new school" did appreciate the so-called "novel of character" as opposed to the "novel of circumstance" frequently associated with Goethe. Cf. Emerson, W, IV, 279; XII, 376. The "novel of character" "treats the reader with more respect." (W, XII, 375.376).
65 Abbott, The Young Christian, 228.
66 Southern Literary Messenger (1843); text in Baym, Novels, Readers and Reviewers, 240.
67 Hedge, Ways of the Spirit, 331f.
68 Ingraham, The Prince of the House of David, V.
69 Ibid., VI.
70 Ibid., VI.
71 Ibid., 160-61.
72 North American Review, LXXXII (1865), 373.
73 Robert Seeley, Ecce Homo: A Survey of the Life and Work of Jesus Christ, American ed. (Boston: Roberts Brothers, 1866), 3; "Strauss, Renan and 'Ecce Homo,'" Edinburgh Review 124 (1866), 467-68.
74 Cf. Seeley, Ecce Homo, 146, 201.
75 Ibid., 24.
76 Ibid., 4.
77 "Ecce Homo," Record, (1866); "Ecce Homo," Spectator (1865); texts in Pals, Victorian "Lives" of Jesus, 45, 43.
78 "Ecce Homo," Spectator (1865); "Strauss, Renan and 'Ecce Homo,'" Edinburgh Review 124 (1866), 468.
79 Henry Whitney Bellows, "Ecce Homo," Christian Examiner, LXXX (1866), 110.
80 Ernest Renan, Life of Jesus (Boston: Little, Brown and Co., 1917), 72.
81 Ibid., (1927 ed.), 118, 120.
82 Ernst Renan, The History of the Origins of Christianity (London: Mathieson Co., 1890), I, XXII.
83 Renan, Life of Jesus (1927 ed.), 118, 120.
84 Renan, Life of Jesus, 72.
85 Ibid., 250.
86 Bellows, "Ecce Homo," 114, 115.
87 C. T. Brooks, "Renan's Life of Jesus," North American Review, XCVIII (1864), 212.
88 Ibid., 214. William Henry Furness, Remarks on Renan's Life of Jesus (Philadelphia, 1865), 5-6.
89 Furness, Remarks on Renan's Life of Jesus, 21; Brooks,"Renan's Life of Jesus," 211.
90 Lant Carpenter, An Apostolical Harmony of the Gospels, 2d ed. (London: Longman, 1838), V.
91 Brooks, "Renan's Life of Jesus," 214.
92 J. H. Allen, "Review of Current Literature," Christian Examiner (1867), 105, 107; "Review of Current Literature," Christian Examiner, (1865), 444.
93 Peabody, "Strauss and the Mythic Theory," 148.
94 Ibid.
95 Brooks, "Renan's Life of Jesus," 214.

96 Ibid., 196.
97 Furness, Remarks on Renan's Life of Jesus, 4.
98 Furness, "Character of Christ," 289.
99 Brooks, "Renan's Life of Jesus," 203, 233.
100 Elizabeth Stuart Phelps, The Story of Jesus Christ (Boston and New York: Houghton, Mifflin and Company, 1898), "Note," I.
101 Stowe, Footsteps of the Master, 283.
102 Phelps, The Story of Jesus Christ, 6.
103 Ibid., "Note," I.
104 H. H. Allen, "Review of Current Literature," Christian Examiner, LXXV (1863), 280.
105 Ibid., 1, 143, 148.
106 Bellows, "Ecce Homo," 114-15.
107 Ibid., 114.
108 Stowe, Footsteps of the Master, 87, 13, 9.
109 Phelps, The Story of Jesus Christ, VIII, X, 3.
110 Ibid., 405; Parker, "D. F. Strauss Das Leben Jesu," 298.
111 Stowe, Footsteps of the Master, 55; Parker, "D. F. Strauss Das Leben Jesu," 284.
112 Phelps, The Story of Jesus Christ, VIII-X, 411; Stowe, Footsteps of the Master, 283.
113 Channing, "Evidences of Christianity," in Works, 203.
114 Phelps, The Story of Jesus Christ, 168-169.

X

1 Phelps, The Story of Jesus Christ, VIII-IX.
2 Cf. Pals, Victorian "Lives", 26-27.
3 Also of importance for the development of the quest on English grounds was J. W. Colenso, The Pentateuch and the Book of Joshua critically examined, 7 parts (London, 1862-79).
4 Charles Carroll Everett, Essays: Theological and Literary (Boston, 1901), 89.
5 George H. Williams (ed.), The Harvard Divinity School (Boston, 1954), 145.
6 H. Davis, "Schleiermacher," Christian Examiner, LIII (1852), 67, 83.
7 Ibid., 67.
8 Charles Carroll Everett, Immortality and Other Essays (Boston, 1888), 119, 122, 125.
9 Everett, "The Historic and the Ideal Christ," in Essays, 87.
10 Joseph Henry Allen, "Recent German Theology," Christian Examiner, LXIII (1857), 433.
11 O. B. Frothingham, "Dr. Ferdinand Christian Baur," Christian Examiner, LXIV (1858), 34.
12 Davis, "Schleiermacher," 91.
13 Brooks, "Renan's Life of Jesus," 233.
14 Cf. Parker's review of Dorner's Historical Development of the Doctrine of the Person of Christ in The Dial, II (1842), 497-98.
15 Parker, "D. F. Strauss Das Leben Jesu," 286.
16 Nathaniel Frothingham, "The Christ of the Gospels and of St. Paul," Christian Examiner, XLIX (1850), 8.
17 William Wallace Fenn, The Bible in Theology, in Official Report of the Proceedings of the Fourteenth Meeting of the National Conference

of Unitarian and Other Christian Churches, held at Saratoga Springs, N. Y., Sept. 12-25, 1891; (Boston, 1891), 126, 127.

18 W. S. Crowe, *The Old Theology and the New in Relation to Biblical Criticism*, in ibid., Sept. 20-23, 1897 (Boston, 1897), 77.

19 Charles Carroll Everett, "The Relation of Jesus to the Present Age," in *Christianity and Modern Thought* (Boston, 1873), 132.

20 William Henry Furness, *Remarks upon the Character of Christ and the Historical Characteristics of the Four Gospels* (Philadelphia, 1885), 55-57; text in *The Story of the Resurrection of Christ. Told Once More* (Philadelphia: J. B. Lippincott, 1885), 55, 56.

21 William Henry Furness, *Jesus* (Philadelphia: J. B. Lippincott & Co., 1871), 9.

22 See Willaim Henry Furness, *The Unconscious Truth of the Four Gospels* (Philadelphia: J. B. Lippincott, 1868), 59f.

23 Furness, *Jesus*, 164.

24 Ibid., 5.

25 Ibid., 21, 10.

26 Ibid., 187, 178.

27 Neander, *The Life of Jesus Christ*, "Preface to the First Edition," XII.

28 A. P. Peabody, "Furness' History of Jesus," 466.

29 William Henry Furness, *Jesus and the Gospels* (Philadelphia, 1872), 17.

30 Furness, *Jesus*, 28.

31 Ibid., 29.

32 Furness, *Remarks upon the Character of Christ*, 89.

33 Furness, *Jesus*, 115.

34 Furness, *The Unconscious Truth of the Four Gosepls*, 11-12.

35 Furness, *Jesus*, 6.

36 Furness, *The Unconscious Truth of the Four Gospels*, 117, 59; *The Power of Spirit Manifest in Jesus of Nazareth* (Philadelphia: J. B. Lippincott, 1877), 135.

37 De Wette, "Author's Preface to the American Edition" of *Theodore*, I, XXXVII.

38 Clarke, "Notes" on De Wette's *Theodore*, I, 304, 308.

39 Ibid., 308; cf. 306-307. M. Fuchs, "Miracles," in *The Bremen Lectures*, trans. D. Heagle (Boston: Gould and Lincoln, 1871), 83.

40 August Wilhelm Neander, *The Life of Jesus Christ in its Historical Connexion and Historical Development*, trans. John M'Clintock and Charles E. Blumenthal (London: Henry G. Brown, 1851), no. 87, 137.

41 Ibid., 26.

42 Furness, *Jesus*, 21.

43 C. E. Luthardt, "The Person of Jesus Christ," in *The Bremen Lectures*, 121.

44 "Prefatory Note," *The Bremen Lectures*.

45 Cf. Luthardt, "The Person of Jesus Christ," in *The Bremen Lectures*, 117f.

46 Neander, *The Life of Jesus Christ*, "Preface to the First Edition," XIV.

47 John Hopkins Morison, "Neander's Life of Christ," *Christian Examiner*, XLVI (1849), 79; cf. 80.

48 Neander, *The Life of Jesus Christ*, no. 308, 487.

49 Ibid.

50 Johann Peter Lange, Leben Jesu (Heidelberg: K. Winter, 1844-47), I, 125. An English translation was prepared by Marcus Dods, The Life of the Lord Jesus Christ: A Complete Examination of the Origin, Contents, and Connection of the Gospels (Edinburgh: T. & T. Clark, 1864). See also the favorable review of Lange in Allen, "Recent German Theology," 438.
51 Furness, Thoughts on the Life of Jesus, 108, 109, 111.
52 Ibid., 215; Furness, The Unconscious Truth of the Gospels, 9.
53 William Henry Furness, The Veil Partly Lifted and Jesus Becoming Visible (Boston: Ticknor and Fields, 1864), 262-263.
54 Edward A. Park, "The Theology of the Intellect and that of the Feelings," Bibliotheca Sacra, VII (1850), 533-569.
55 Parker, "Dorner's Christology," The Dial, II (1842), 522; 523.
56 E. A. Park, "Dr. James Freeman Clarke on Orthodoxy," Bibliotheca Sacra, XXIV (1867), 193.
57 Calvin Ellis Stowe, Origin and History of the Books of the Bible (Hartford: Hartford Publishing Company, 1867), 26.
58 Bela Bates Edwards, "Present State of Biblical Science," Bibliotheca Sacra, VII (1850), 1, 12.
59 Thayer, Criticism, 336.
60 Cf. "Origin of the First Three Gospels," Bibliotheca Sacra, XXVI (1869), 1-30.
61 Joseph Henry Thayer, "Criticism Confirmatory of the Gospels," in Christianity and Scepticism (Boston, 1871), 363, 346.
62 "Hennell on the Origin of Christianity," The Dial, IV (1843), 161.
63 Frederic Henry Hedge, "Destinies of Ecclesiastical Religion," Christian Examiner, LXXXII (1867), 12.
64 Frederic Henry Hedge, "Emerson's Writing," Christian Examiner, XXXVIII (1845), 95.
65 Frederic Henry Hedge, Reason in Religion (Boston: Walker, Fuller and Company, 1865), 278-79.
66 Frederic Henry Hedge, "Antisupernaturalism in the Pulpit," in Ahlstrom (ed.), An American Reformation, 422-425.
67 Hedge, "The Mythical Element," 317f.
68 James Freeman Clarke, The Problem of the Fourth Gospel (Boston, 1886), 21.
69 Ibid., 10, 11. Cf. "The Fourth Gospel and its Author," Christian Examiner, LXXXIV (1868), 89.
70 Strauss, The Old Faith and the New, 57.
71 Cf. "The Fourth Gospel and its Author," 87. James Freeman Clarke (trans.), Life of Jesus. A Manual for Academic Study (Boston: Walker, Wise & Co., 1860), no. 3, 3f.
72 Clarke, The Problem of the Fourth Gospel, 41, 64; cf. the text references to Hedge in Chable, "The New Testament in New England," 307.
73 Text in Wintersteen, Christology in American Unitarianism, 73; cf. Hedge, Reason in Religion, 62-63, 271-72; "The Mythical Element," 324; Ways of the Spirit, 92.
74 Ibid., 174-75.
75 Hedge, Ways of the Spirit, 349.
76 Ibid., 335.
77 Hedge, "The Mythical Element," 316f.
78 Hedge, Ways of the Spirit, 318.
79 Hedge, "The Mythical Element," 335.
80 Ibid., 340.

81 Frederic Henry Hedge, An Address Delivered Before the Graduating Class of the Divinity School in Cambridge July 15, 1849 (Cambridge, Mas.: John Bartlett, 1849), 24; Hedge, "The Mythical Element," 316.
82 Strauss, Leben Jesu, I, 52.
83 Parker, The Transient and Permanent, "Appendix," 274.
84 James Freeman Clarke, The Ideas of The Apostle Paul (Boston: James R. Osgood, 1884), Appendix, 395.
85 Frothingham, "Dr. Ferdinand Christian Baur," 21.
86 R. W. Mackay, The Tübingen School and its Antecedents, quoted in Clarke, The Ideas of the Apostle Paul, Appendix, 396.
87 Baur, Paulus, I, 276-77 (ET 246-47).
88 Frothingham, "Dr. Ferdinand Christian Baur," 15.
89 Ibid., 20; Clarke, The Ideas of the Apostle Paul, Appendix, 405, 408.
90 Clarke, The Ideas of the Apostle Paul, Appendix, 408-409.
91 James Freeman Clarke, Ten Great Religions: An Essay in Comparative Theology (Boston: Houghton, Mifflin and Company, 1884), 13-14.
92 Ibid., 14.
93 Ibid., 20, 504.
94 Radical, I (1865-66), 150; see also 73-85, 218-26.
95 Clarke, Ten Great Religions, 29.
96 Ibid., 507; Steps of Belief, 120.
97 See Minot J. Savage, "The Inevitable Surrender of Orthodoxy," North American Review, CXLVIII (1889), 711-726 and Joseph Henry Allen, Our Liberal Movement in Theology (Boston, 1882), 171ff.
98 Clarke, Steps of Belief, 139-140.
99 Octavius Brooks Frothingham, Radical Work (New York: D. G. Francis, 1868), 16.
100 Clarke, Steps of Belief, 141.
101 Octavius Brooks Frothingham, The Religion of Humanity (New York: Asak Butts, 1873), 88f.
102 Ibid., 89.
103 Parker, "Jesus of Nazareth," in The World of Matter and Man, 312.
104 Ibid., 312.
105 Clarke, Steps of Belief, 141.
106 Clarke, Steps of Belief, 138.
107 Radical, X (1872), 256-272.
108 Octavius Brooks Frothingham, The Cradle of the Christ. A Study in Primitive Christianity (New York: G. P. Putnam's Sons, 1877), 6.
109 Ibid., 3, IX, 191.
110 Ibid., 184.
111 J. T. Bixby, "The Jesus of the Evangelists," Christian Examiner, LXXXVII (1869), 20-21.
112 Frothingham, "Scientific criticism of the New Testament," 114.
113 Edward Everett Hale "The Logical Order of the Gospel Narratives," Christian Examiner, LXV (1858), 208, 209.
114 Morison, "Neander's Life of Christ," 76. Cf. "Schenkel's Character of Jesus," Christian Examiner, LXXXIII (1867), 186f.
115 Morison, "Neander's Life of Christ," 76.
116 Ibid.
117 Henry Giles, "Elements of Influence in his Character," Christian Examiner, IL (1850), 382.
118 Peabody, "Strauss and the Mythic Theory," 146.
119 Ibid.
120 Morison, "Neander's Life of Christ," 85.

121 H. E. Spaulding, "Jesus as Prophet and Messiah," Christian Examiner LXXXIII (1867), 98-99.
122 William Henry Furness (tr.), Character of Jesus Portrayed. By Daniel Schenkel (Boston: Little, Brown and Company, 1866), II, 359.
123 Furness, Remarks upon the Character of Christ, 86.
124 Clarke, Steps of Belief, 104-105.
125 Frothingham, "Renan's Life of Jesus," Christian Examiner, LXXV (1863), 320.
126 Ibid., 321, 322, 323, 324, 327.
127 Frothingham, The Cradle of the Christ, 188.
128 Frothingham, "Renan's Life of Jesus," 333; cf. 332.
129 Ibid., 333.
130 Ibid., 338; The Cradle of the Christ, 130. Cf. Furness, Renan's Life of Jesus, 18-19.
131 Frothingham, "Renan's Life of Jesus," 334; The Religion of Humanity, 87; Morison, "Neander's Life of Christ," 86-87.
132 Frothingham, "Renan's Life of Jesus," 334, 337. See also Cyrus A. Bartol, "Dr. Furness and Dr. Bushnell: A Question of Words and Names," Christian Examiner, LXVI (1859), 112f.
133 Spaulding, "Jesus as a Prophet and Messiah," 99.
134 Ibid., 98.
135 William Henry Furness, "Origin of the Gospels," Christian Examiner, LXX (1861), 49.
136 Joseph Henry Allen, "Review of Current Literature," Christian Examiner, LXXXII (1867), 105.
137 Ibid., 106. "Review of Current Literature," Christian Examiner, LXXVIII (1865), 444.
138 J. H. Morison, "The Genuineness of the Gospels," Christian Examiner, LVI (1854), 93.
139 Ibid.
140 Frothingham, The Cradle of the Christ, 125.
141 Ibid., 9; cf. 7.
142 James Freeman Clarke, "The Fourth Gospel and its Author," 99.
143 James Freeman Clarke, "Open Questions in Theology," Christian Examiner, LXXX (1866), 77, 87.
144 Frothingham, "Dr. Ferdinand Christian Baur," 32.
145 Ibid., 34.
146 Ibid. Cf. Joseph Henry Allen, "More Open Questions," Christian Examiner, LXXX (1866), 212f.
147 Allen, "Recent German Theology," 433.
148 Stuart, Letters to Dr. Channing (1846), 74.
149 O. B. Frothingham, trans. Studies of Religious History and Criticism, (New York: Carleton, 1864), 184.
150 Allen, "Recent German Theology," 435.
151 Stuart, Letters to Dr. Channing (1846), 195. Bruno Bauer, Kritik der evangelischen Geschichte der Synoptiker (Leipzig: O. Wigand, 1841; reprint ed., Hildesheim: G. Olms, 1974), III, 307.
152 Frothingham, Studies of Religious History and Criticism, 203.
153 Hedge, Ways of the Spirit, 340.
154 Brooke Herford, "Jesus Christ," in Unitarian Affirmations: Seven Discourses Given in Washington (Boston, 1879), 77, 78.

XI

1 Brooks, "Renan's Life of Jesus," 232.
2 "Pansy" (Mrs. G. R. Alden), Yesterday Framed in Today (Boston: Mothrop Publishing Company), 1-2.
3 Stowe, Footsteps of the Master, 308, 11.
4 Shailer Mathews, "Social Gospel," in Shailer Mathews (ed.), A Dictionary of Religion and Ethics (New York: Macmillan, 1921), 416-17; cf. C. H. Hopkins, The Rise of the Social Gospel in American Protestantism, 1865-1915 (New Haven, 1940), 1.
5 George Ripley, "Review of J. B. Stallo's General Principles of the Philosophy of Nature," Harbinger, VI (1848), 110.
6 Harbinger, II (1846), 297; text in Clarence Gohdes, The Periodicals of American Transcendentalism (Durham, N. C., 1931), 120.
7 Shirley Jackson Case, Jesus: A New Biography, VI.
8 Shailer Mathews, The Social Teachings of Jesus (New York: Macmillan, 1897), 3. On the history and appropriateness of a "Christian sociology," see Charles Howard Hopkins, The Rise of the Social Gospel in American Protestantism (New Haven, 1940).
9 The essay appeared in the Boston Quarterly Review, III (1840), 358-95. A rebuttal may be found in ibid. (1840), 420-510.
10 Brownson, "The Convert," in Works, 63f.
11 Cf. Orestes Brownson, New Views of Christianity, Society, and the Church (Boston, 1836).
12 Elizabeth Peabody, "A Glimpse of Christ's Idea of Society," The Dial, II (1847), 219.
13 Christian Examiner, XI (1832), 355.
14 Peabody, "A Glimpse of Christ's Idea of Society," 22.
15 Radical X (1872), 409, 324-25.
16 Channing, "Evidences of Christianity," in Works, 207, 208.
17 Channing, "Evidences of Revealed Religion," in Works, 237.
18 Ware, Julian, II, 144, 237.
19 Furness, Remarks on the Four Gospels, 39. Cf. William Henry Furness, Religion and Politics. A Discourse (Philadelphia: T. B. Pugh, 1859), 5f.
20 Furness, Jesus and the Gospels, 43.
21 Furness, The Veil Partly Lifted and Jesus Becoming Visible, 163.
22 Frothingham, The Cradle of the Christ, 60, 59, 67.
23 Ward, The Story of Jesus Christ, 16, 17, 243.
24 Oliver Stearns, "The Aim and Hope of Jesus," in Christianity and Modern Thought (Boston, 1873), 302.
25 James Freeman Clarke, Steps of Belief (Boston: American Unitarian Association, 1880), 106.
26 Ibid., 107. For the principles upon which Clarke's church reform was based, see his The Church of the Disciples in Boston, A Sermon on the Principles and Methods of the Church of the Disciples. Delivered Sunday Morning and Evening, December 7, 1845 (Boston, 1846), 4-24.
27 Clarke, Steps of Belief, 107.
28 Ibid., 109.
29 Ibid., 294.
30 Cf. Walter Rauschenbusch, The Social Principles of Jesus (New York, 1916), 139-46.
31 Walter Rauschenbusch, Christianity and the Social Crisis (New York: Macmillan, 1907), 46.

32 H. E. Fosdick, Modern Use of the Bible, 192.
33 H. E. Fosdick, Christianity and Progress, 197.
34 Rauschenbusch, Christianity and the Social Crisis, 49.
35 Rauschenbusch, Christianizing the Social Order (New York: Macmillan, 1912), 42, 43.
36 Ellwood, Christianity and Social Science, 54.
37 Francis G. Peabody, Jesus Christ and the Social Question (New York, 1900), 77-78.
38 Francis G. Peabody, "Message of Christ to Human Society," in The Message of Christ to Manhood (Boston and New York, 1899), 59-61.
39 Shailer Mathews, The Social Teachings of Jesus (New York: Hodder and Stoughton, 1897), 54.
40 Ibid., 125, 182, 192, 171.
41 Lyman Abbott, "Christianity versus Socialism," North American Review, CXL (1889), 453.
42 Rauschenbusch, A Theology for the Social Gospel (New York: Macmillan, 1917), 141.
43 Rauschenbusch, Christianzizing the Social Order, 67.
44 Rauschenbusch, A Theology for the Social Gospel, 149.
45 Rauschenbusch, Christianizing the Social Order, 125. On the Social Gospel's reverence for personality, see Joseph A. Leighton, Jesus Christ and the Civilization of Today (New York, 1907), 117f; cf. Hopkins, The Rise of the Social Gospel, 209.
46 Cf. Rauschenbusch, The Social Principles of Jesus, 139f.
47 Arthur C. McGiffert, The Rise of Modern Religious Ideas (New York: Macmillan Company, 1915), 238.
48 Rauschenbusch, Christianity and the Social Crisis, 178. For an overview of Rauschenbusch's christological thought, see Christianity and the Social Crisis, 44-92; Christianizing the Social Order, 48-68; A Theology for the Social Gospel, 146-66.
49 George A. Gordon, The Christ of Today (Boston: Houghton, Mifflin and Co., 1895), 50.
50 Ibid., 58, 96.
51 Rauschenbusch, A Theology for the Social Gospel, 182.
52 Cf. Gordon, The Christ of Today, 50f.
53 Cf. Shailer Mathews, Atonement and the Social Process (New York: Macmillan, 1930), 164-65.
54 Mathews, The Social Teachings of Jesus, 40.
55 Peabody, Jesus Christ and the Social Question, 79.
56 Karl J. Kautsky, Der Ursprung des Christentums (Stuttgart, 1908; ET New York, 1925), 337, 384f.; ET 320, 364ff.
57 Albert Kalthoff, Entstehung des Christentums (Leipzig, 1904; ET London, 1907), 13ff., 25-6.
58 Warren S. Kissinger, The Lives of Jesus: A Bibliography (New York: Garland Publishing, 1984) 30. See also Pals, Victorian "Lives", 39-59, 72-74.
59 Arthur Drews, The Witness to the Historicity of Jesus, trans. Joseph McCabe (Chicago: Open Court, 1912), 235.
60 Arthur Drews, The Christ Myth trans. C. Delisle Burns (London: T. Fisher Unwin, 1910), 19; cf. 285-86.
61 Ibid., 178.
62 Herford, "Jesus Christ," 77, 78.
63 Quest, 368, Geschichte, 283f.
64 Mathews, The Social Teachings of Jesus, 51.

65 Peabody, Jesus Christ and the Social Question, 95; cf. Quest, 368.
66 Peabody, Jesus Christ and the Social Question, 96.
67 Ibid., 99-100.
68 Rauschenbusch, Christianizing the Social Order, 96-97.
69 Rauschenbusch, Christianity and the Social Crisis, 91.
70 Albrecht Ritschl, Die christliche Lehre von der Rechtfertigung und Versöhnung, III, sec. 6; ET., 30.
71 Cf. Rauschenbusch, Christianizing the Social Order, 70, 93; A Theology for the Social Gospel, 27, 94, 138.
72 Rauschenbusch, Christianizing the Social Order, 90.
73 Rauschenbusch, Christianity and the Social Crisis, 59-60.
74 Mathews, The Social Teachings of Jesus, 42.
75 Rauschenbusch, A Theology for the Social Gospel, 131; Francis Greenwood Peabody, "Charity and Character," Proceedings, 23rd. Annual Session of the National Conference of Charities and Correction (Boston, 1896), n. p.
76 Rauschenbusch, Christianity and the Social Crisis, 45.
77 Ibid., 49. For evidence of the influence of the Leben-Jesu-Forschung on Rauschenbusch, see Christianizing the Social Order; 88, 180, 245, 404f; A Theology for the Social Gospel, 27, 61, 93, 125, 225, 265.
78 Biblical Repertory and Princeton Review XL (1868), 126-127.
79 Cf. Walter F. Peterson, "American Protestantism and the Higher Criticism, 1870-1910," Transactions of the Wisconsin Academy of Sciences, Arts, and Letters, 50 (1962), 321-24; Washington Gladden, "The Bible in the Sunday-school," Century, 29 (1884), 146-48.
80 Washington Gladden, Who Wrote the Bible? A Book for the People (Boston, 1891), chap. XIII, "How Much is the Bible Worth?", 361f.

XII

1 Quest, 331. Cf. Ernst von Dobschütz's observation that the flood of lives of Jesus completey dried up after the publication of Schweitzer's Quest, Die Evangelische Theologie, Ihr Jetziger Stand und Ihre Aufgaben (Halle, 1927), 26f. and "Der heutige Stand der Leben-Jesu-Forschung, ZThK 5 (1924), 64-84.
2 The Bibliotheca Sacra referred to Hermann Bavinck, "Christological Movements in the Nineteenth Century," Bibliotheca Sacra, LXVIII (1911), 393.
3 W. D. Walker, "The Quest for the Historical Jesus: A Discussion of Methodology," Anglican Theological Review 51 (1969), 51. Cf. van A. Harvey and Schubert M. Ogden, "Wie neu ist die 'Neue Frage nach dem historischen Jesus'?" ZThKm 59 (1962), 46-87.
4 Oscar Cullmann, "Out of Season Remarks on the 'Historical Jesus' of the Bultmann School, "Union Seminary Quarterly Review, 16 (1961), 132. Cf. Bultmann, "The Primitive Christian Kerygma and the Historical Jesus," 32-33.
5 Hans Conzelmann, "Gegenwart und Zukunft in der synopitschen Tradition," ZThK 54 (1957), 279f.
6 Henry J. Cadbury, "Between Jesus and the Gospels," HThR 16 (1923), 91.
7 Ibid., 91. Cf. Harold M. Wiener, "Some Fatal Weaknesses of the Wellhausen School," Bibliotheca Sacra, LXIV (1907), 2f.

8 Henry J. Cadbury, The Peril of Modernizing Jesus (New York, 1937), 47; Shirley Jackson Case, Jesus, a New Biography (Chicago, 1927), 6; Edgar J. Goodspeed, A Life of Jesus (New York, 1950), 11-12.

9 Amos Wilder, in The New Hermeneutic, Robinson and Cobb Jr., eds., 205. Cobb in ibid., 220.

10 Cf. Charles Edwin Carlston, "A Positive Criterion of Authenticity?" Biblical Research, 7 (1962), 33-44; Norman Perrin, Rediscovering the Teaching of Jesus (New York: Harper and Row, 1967), 45f.

11 Albertina Allen Forrest, "The Cry 'Back to Christ': Its Implication," AJTh 11 (1907), 73.

12 Philip Wendell Crannell, "The Problem of Christ's Person in the Twentieth Century," Bibliotheca Sacra (1907), 336.

13 Quest, 399.

14 Ibid., 397.

15 Ibid., 369.

16 Ibid.

17 Ibid., 401.

18 William Sanday, "The Apocalyptic Element in the Gospels," Hibbert Journal, 10 (1911), 84. See also B. H. Streeter, "Synoptic Criticism and the Eschatological Problem," in Studies in the Synoptic Problem, ed. W. Sanday (London, 1911), 423-36; P. Gardner, "The Present and the Future Kingdom in the Gospels," ExpT 21 (1909/10), 535-8. The negative responses to Schweitzer by these critics were shaped by the impact of Ernst von Dobschütz's lectures at Oxford in 1909, The Eschatology of the Gospels (London: Hodder & Stoughton, 1910).

19 Cf. H. B. Sharman, The Teaching of Jesus about the Future according to the Synoptic Gospel (Chicago, 1909), 327 f.

20 C. H. Dodd, The Parables of the Kingdom, rev. ed. (New York: Scribner's, 1961), 83. Cf. T. W. Manson's insistence on the notion of the Kingdom as a present reality in The Teaching of Jesus (2nd ed. Cambridge: Cambridge University Press, 1935), 140f., and "Realized Eschatology and the Messianic Secret," in D. E. Nineham (ed.), Studies in the Gospels (Oxford: Basil Blackwell & Mott, Ltd., 1955), 210, 221f.

21 George D. Castor, "The Kingdom of God in Light of Jewish Literature," Bibliotheca Sacra, LXVI (1909), 352. See also Arthur Metcalf, "The Parousia Versus the Second Advent," Bibliotheca Sacra, LXIV (1907), 54f.

22 H. A. A. Kennedy, "The Life of Jesus in the Light of Recent Discussions," AJTh (1907), 154. Harris F. Rall, Modern Premillennialism and the Christian Hope (New York, 1920), 56-74. Cf. T. Valentine Parker, "The Second Advent and Modern Thought," Bibliotheca Sacra 68 (1911), 600f.; William E. Barton, "The Descent of the New Jerusalem," Bibliotheca Sacra 52 (1895), 29-47.

23 H. A. A. Kennedy, "The Life of Jesus in the Life of Recent Discussions," 156, 157.

24 The "Chicago School" of social-historical research carried this interpretation to an extreme point. See Shirley Jackson Case, The Revelation of St. John (Chicago, 1919), 407f.

25 Shirley Jackson Case, "The Passing of Apocalypticism," Biblical World, 36 (1910), 147-151.

26 See Hugh Anderson, "The Historical Jesus and the Origins of Christianity," SJTH 13 (1960), 13; Robinson, "Introduction" to The Quest of the Historical Jesus (New York: Macmillan, 1968), XIII;

James Kallas, Jesus and the Power of Satan (Philadelphia, 1968), 69; Howard C. Kee, Jesus in History (New York: Hartcourt Brace, 1970), 17-18. Schweitzer himself surveyed the psychiatric studies of Jesus in his M. D. dissertation (1913), The Psychiatric Study of Jesus (Boston: Beacon Press, 1948).

27 See the persistent attempts to counteract the bankruptcy of the old quest in C. C. McCown, The Search for the Real Jesus: A Century of Historical Study (New York: Charles Scribner's Sons, 1940); and Morton S. Enslin, The Prophet from Nazareth (New York: McGraw - Hill Book Co., 1961). See also W. D. Davies, "A Quest to Be Resumed in New Testament Studies," Union Seminary Quarterly Review, 15 (1960), 96-8.

28 Crannell, "The Problem of Christ's Person in the Twentieth Century," 341; cf. 343. See also Benjamin W. Warfield, "The 'Two Natures' and Recent Christological Speculation," AJTh, 15 (1911), 337ff.

29 Crannell, "The Problem of Christ's Person in the Twentieth Century," 341.

30 Gerald Birney, "The Christ of Faith and the Jesus of History," AJTh 18 (1914), 536.

31 Ibid., 537.

32 Quest, 396.

33 Shirley Jackson Case, The Historicity of Jesus (Chicago: University of Chicago Press, 1912), 280-81.

34 Ambrose White Vernon, "Can An Efficient Theology Be Dependent Upon Historical Facts," AJTh 17 (1913), 172. Cf. Hermann Bavinck, "Christological Movements in the Nineteenth Century," Bibliotheca Sacra (1911), 384, 396.

35 William Adams Brown, "The Place of Christ in Modern Theology," AJTh 16 (1912), 49.

36 Vernon, "Can An Efficient Theology Be Dependent Upon Historical Facts," 172f.

37 Benjamin B. Warfield, "Christless Christianity," HThR, 5 (1912), 449. Cf. Vernon, "Can An Efficient Theology Be Dependent upon Historical Facts," 167.

38 Warfield, "Christless Christianity," 445, 451; cf. James Lindsay "Lessing's Philosophy of Religion," Bibliotheca Sacra, LXIII (1906), 659, 661.

39 Quest, 397.

40 Austin Rice, "Historical Facts and Religious Faith," Bibliotheca Sacra (1911), 499.

41 "Notices of Recent Publications," Bibliotheca Sacra (1907), 380, 378.

42 Octavius Brooks Frothingham, Radical Work (New York, 1968), 16, 17.

43 Bixby, "The Jesus of the Evangelists," 20-1.

44 Cf. ibid., 22f.

45 Joseph Henry Thayer, "Criticism Confirmatory of the Gospels," in Christianity and Scepticism (Boston, 1871), 335.

46 Bixby, "The Jesus of the Evangelists," 24.

47 Drews, The Witness to the Historicity of Jesus, 296, 297.

48 Ibid., XI, 306.

49 Frank O. Porter, "The Sufficiency of the Religion of Jesus," AJTh 11 (1907), 75.

50 Warfield, "Christless Christianity," 428.

51 Kennedy, "The Life of Jesus in the Light of Recent Discussions," 153; Lindsay, "Lessing's Philosophy of Religion," 656f.

52 Lindsay, "Lessing's Philosophy of Religion," 661, 662.

53 William Benjamin Smith, Der Vorchristliche Jesus. Vorstudien zur Entstehungsgeschichte des Urchristentums (2nd ed., Jena, 1911), 111. Cf. Shirley Jackson Case, "The Historicity of Jesus: An Estimate of the Negative Argument," AJTh 15 (1911), 24f.
54 Cf. Shirley Jackson Case, "Jesus' Historicity: A Statement of the Problem," AJTh 15 (1911), 266.
55 Kennedy, "The Life of Jesus in the Light of Recent Discussions," 152; K. Dunkmann, "The 'Christ-myth,'" Bibliotheca Sacra (1911), 39.
56 Cf. Case, "Jesus' Historicity," 266f.
57 Warfield, "Christless Christianity," 435.
58 Warfield, "Christless Christianity," 440. Cf. Kennedy, "The Life of Jesus in the Light of Recent Discussions," 154.
59 Dunkmann, "The 'Christ-myth,'", 36-7; Edward P. Gardner, "Christ in the Four Gospels," Bibliotheca Sacra (1912), 241. Cf. the reviews of E.J. Mullins' Why is Christianity? Christian Evidences and Hermann Schultz's Outlines of Christian Apologetics for Use in Lectures in the Bibliotheca Sacra (1906), 378-79, 572-72.
60 Martin Dibelius, From Tradition to Gospel, trans. B. L. Woolf (London: Ivor Nicholson and Watson, 1934), 2.
61 Rudolf Bultmann and Karl Kundsin, Form Criticism: Two Essays on New Testament Research, trans. Frederick C. Grant (New York: Harper, 1962), 3-4.
62 Martin Dibelius, "Zur Formgeschichte der Evangelien," ThR 1 (1929), 185-216; cf. G. Iber, "Zur Formgeschichte der Evangelien," ThR 24, (1957/58), 283-333.
63 Wellhausen, Einleitung in die drei ersten Evangelien, 43.
64 Ibid., 115.
65 G. Bertram, Neues Testament und historische Methode (Tübingen, 1928), 41.
66 Schmidt, Der Rahmen der Geschichte Jesu, 317.
67 Bultmann, "The Primitive Christian Kerygma and the Historical Jesus," 30.
68 Bultmann, Glauben und Verstehen, I, 3.
69 Bultmann, Kerygma und Mythos, I, 134.
70 Cf. Robinson, A New Quest of the Historical Jesus, 95f.
71 Bultmann, Kerygma and Mythos, II, 207.
72 Bultmann, Glauben und Verstehen, I, 208; III, 18.
73 Bultmann, Kerygma und Mythos, I, 117.
74 D. W. Riddle, "German Influence on American New Testament Studies," Christendom, 2 (1937), 253. Cf. W. D. Davies, "The Scene in New Testament Theology," Journal of Bible and Religion, 20 (1952), 231ff.; James R. Branton, "Our Present Situation in Biblical Theology," Religion in Life, 26 (1956-57), 5ff.
75 E. F. Scott, "Recent Lives of Jesus," HThR (1934), 25.
76 Cf. Wilder, "New Testament Hermeneutics Today," 50.
77 See Wilder, "Biblical Hermeneutic and American Scholarship," in Neutestamentliche Studien für Rudolf Bultmann, (Berlin: Alfred Töpelmann, 1957), 24-32.
78 Cf. Wilder, "New Testament Hermeneutics Today," 49f.
79 This point is stressed in a pair of essays on the question of the difference between Continental and American traditions for the development of biblical theology: Amos Wilder, "New Testament Theology in Transition," in The Study of the Bible Today and Tomorrow, ed. H. R. Willoughby (Chicago: University of Chicago Press,

1947), 419-36; C. T. Craig, "Biblical Theology and the Rise of Historicism," Journal of Biblical Literature, 82 (1953), 281-294.

80 Clarence T. Craig, "The Apostolic Kerygma in the Christian Message," Journal of Bible and Religion 20 (1952), 185.

81 Cf. Shirley Jackson Case, "The Historical Study of Religion," JR 1 (1921), 4; The Social Origins of Christianity (Chicago: University of Chicago, 1923), 21-32.

82 Case, Jesus, A New Biography, 414.

83 Ibid., 115.

84 Cf. Burton Scott Easton, The Gospel before the Gospels (New York, 1928), ch. 3.

85 Harry Emerson Fosdick, The Man From Nazareth (London: SCM, 1950), 17.

86 Ibid., 17, 18.

87 Ibid., 246.

88 Enslin, "The Meaning of the Historical Jesus for Faith," 220.

89 Goodspeed, A Life of Jesus, 11.

90 Fosdick, The Man From Nazareth, 9.

91 Ibid., 9. Cf. Enslin, "The Meaning of the Historical Jesus for Faith," 220.

92 Fosdick, The Man From Nazareth, 33.

93 Goodspeed, A Life of Jesus, 16.

94 Fosdick, The Man From Nazareth, 35.

95 F. C. Grant, "Die Botschaft von Jesus Christus," Anglican Theological Review 18 (1936); cf. also M. M. Parvis, "New Testament Criticism in the World-Wars Period," in The Study of the Bible Today and Tomorrow, ed. Harold R. Willoughby, 61-68.

96 Arthur C. Headlam, The Life and Teaching of Jesus the Christ (2nd ed.; London: John Murray, 1927), LX.

97 The Expository Times, 43 (1941-42), 251, cf. 175-7.

98 T. W. Manson, "The Life of Jesus: Some Tendencies in Present-day research," in The Background of the New Testament, ed. Davies and Daube (Cambridge: The University Press, 1935), 216.

99 T. W. Manson, The Teaching of Jesus: Studies of its Form and Content (2nd ed., Cambridge: The University Press, 1935), 12f.

100 Ibid., 11.

101 T. W. Manson, Studies in the Gospel and Epistles (Philadelphia: Westminster, 1962), 6.

102 Ibid., 26; cf. Vincent Taylor, The Gospel According to St. Mark (London: Macmillan & Company, Ltd., 1952), 145-48.

103 Manson, Studies in the Gospels and Epistels, 6.

104 Cadbury, "Between Jesus and the Gospels," 82; cf. 90-91.

105 Fosdick, The Man From Nazareth, 18.

106 Ibid., 30-31.

107 Cf. Cadbury, "Between Jesus and the Gospels," 81f.

108 Enslin, The Prophet from Nazareth, 14.

109 Cf. Morton S. Enslin, "The Meaning of the Historial Jesus for Faith," Journal of Bible and Religion 30 (1962), 219-23; F. C. Grant, Form Criticism, a New Method of New Testament Research (Chicago: Willett, Clark & Co., 1934), 11-74; P. S. Minear, "The Needle's Eye: A Study in Form Criticism," Journal of Bible and Literature 61 (1942), 157-69.

110 Bultmann, "Das Verhältnis der urchristlichen Christusbotschaft zum historischen Jesu," 26.

111 Bultmann, "The Primitive Christian Kerygma and the Historical Jesus," 18; Glauben und Verstehen, I, 206.
112 Bultmann, Glauben und Verstehen, I, 101.
113 Käsemann, "Das Problem des historischen Jesus," 213.
114 Ibid., ET, 23.
115 This continuity is clearly put forward in Ernst Käsemann, "Das Problem des historischen Jesus," ZThK 51 (1954), 129; Herber Braun, "Der Sinn der neutestamentlichen Christologie," ZThK 54 (1957), 341-77; Hermann Diem, Dogmatics, trans. Harold Knight (Philadelphia: The Westminster Press, 1960), 84.
116 Bornkamm, Jesus of Nazareth, 21.
117 Quest, 335.
118 See W. Michalis, "Notwendigkeit und Grenze der Erörterung von Echtheitsfragen innerhalb des Neuen Testaments," ThLZ 8 (1952), 97f.; Hans Conzelmann "Zur Methode der Leben-Jesu-Forschung," ZThK 56 (1959), 4f. H. Schürmann, "Zur aktuellen Situation der Leben-Jesu-Forschung," Geist und Leben 46 (1973), 300-310; Ferdinand Hahn, "Methodologische Überlegungen zur Rückfrage nach Jesus," in Rückfrage nach Jesus: Zur Methodik und Bedeutung der Frage nach dem historischen Jesus, ed. Karl Kertelge (Freiburg, 1974), 11-77.
119 Cf. the critique of Bultmann in the branch of exegesis known as redaction criticism which continued the analytic work of form criticism. Norman Perrin, What Is Redaction Criticism? (London: SPCK, 1970), 1. Cf. also the key studies in redaction criticism by Willi Marxsen, Der Evangelist Markus; Studien zur Redaktionsgeschichte des Evangeliums (Göttingen: Vandenhoeck and Ruprecht, 1956), and Hans Conzelmann, Die Mitte der Zeit. Studien zur Theologie des Lukas (Tübingen: Mohr, 1954).
120 Ernst Lohmeyer, Review of Jesus in ThLZ (1927), 433.
121 Ernst Käsemann, "Probleme neutestamentlicher Arbeit in Deutschland," in Die Freiheit des Evangeliums und die Ordnung der Gesellschaft, 151.
122 Cf. Herbert Braun, "Der Sinn der neutestamentlichen Christologie," ZThK 54 (1957), 34-7, 364-8.
123 Cf. Heinrich Vogel, Jesus Christus und der religionslose Mensch (Berlin, 1955), 11f.; Kerygma and History, 42.
124 Bultmann, "Das Verhältnis der urchristlichen Christusbotschaft," 23f. ET The Historical Jesus and the Kerygmatic Christ, 38f.
125 Amos Wilder, in The New Hermeneutics, Robinson and Cobb Jr., (eds.), 205. Cf. James M. Robinson, "Review of Jesus von Nazareth, by Günther Bornkamm," Journal of Biblical Literature, 76 (1957), 311f.
126 Norman Perrin, Rediscovering the Teaching of Jesus (London: SCM Press; New York: Harper & Row, 1967), 245.
127 Ibid., 245.
128 The most influential examples of "narrative criticism" are Hans Frei's The Identity of Jesus Christ (Philadelphia: Westminster Press, 1975) and his The Eclipse of Biblical Narrative.
129 Cf. Frei, The Eclipse of Biblical Narrative, 3f.
130 Cf. Roland Mushat Frye, "A Literary Perspective for the Criticism of the Gospels," Jesus and Man's Hope (Pittsburgh: Pittsburgh Theological Seminary, 1971), II, 193-221. See also David Robertson's argument for the autonomy of the narrative world in The Old Testament and the Literary Critic (Philadelphia: Fortress Press, 1977).
131 Cf. Wilder, "Biblical Hermeneutic and American Scholarship," in

Neutestamentliche Studien für Rudolf Bultmann, 29-32. See also Wilder's "An Experimental Journal for Biblical Criticism. An Introduction" in Semeia 1 (1974), 3f.

132 Frei, The Identity of Jesus Christ, XVI.

133 J. L. Austin, How to Do Things with Words (Oxford, 1962), 6. Cf. A. C. Thiselton, "The Parables as Language-Event: Some Comments on Fuchs' Hermeneutics in the Light of Linguistic Philosophy," SJTh 23 (1970), 437-68, esp. 438-9; Robert W. Funk, Language, Hermeneutic and Word of God (New York: Harper & Row, 1966), 26-8; J. M. Robinson, "The Parables as God Happening," in F. T. Trotter (ed.) Jesus and the Historian (Philadelphia, 1968), 142. See also Gerhard Ebeling, Introduction to a Theological Theory of Language (London, 1973), 127f.

134 Ernst Fuchs, "Proclamation and Speech-Event," Theology Today, 19 (1962), 347, 348; Gerhard Ebeling, The Nature of Faith (ET London, 1961), 87, 90.

135 Ernst Fuchs, Studies of the Historical Jesus (London, 1964), 94, 95.

136 Killinger, The Lives of Jesus, 90. Ernst Fuchs, "The New Testament and the Hermeneutical Problem," 126; Studies of the Historical Jesus, 97-9, 130-66.

137 Ebeling, The Nature of Faith, 190. Cf. Ernst Fuchs, Marburger Hermeneutik (Tübingen, 1968), 20, 41-7.

138 Fuchs, Studies of the Historical Jesus, 211.

139 Cf. Fuchs, Marburger Hermeneutik, 243-5; and Studies of the Historical Jesus, 196-212; and Gerhard Ebeling, Word and Faith, 325-52; and Theology and Proclamation (London: Collins, 1966), 28-34. With regard to the different terminology in Fuchs and Ebeling, James Robinson observes, "'Sprachereignis' and 'Wortgeschehen' are synonyms.... The choice depends on which Bultmannian term serves as the point of departure, 'Heilsereignis' or 'Heilsgeschehen.'" New Frontiers in Theology, 2: The New Hermeneutik, 57.

140 Ibid., 28, 80-82, 219-28; Hermeneutik, 212-19.

141 Fuchs, Studies of the Historical Jesus, 30-31.

142 Wilder, "New Testament Hermeneutics Today," 50. Cf. Funk, Language, Hermeneutics and Word of God, 220, 251, 253.

143 Amos N. Wilder, "The Word as Address and Meaning," in Robinson and Cobb (eds.), The New Hermeneutic, 213.

144 Wilder, "New Testament Hermeneutics," 50.

145 Ebeling, "Word of God and Hermeneutics," in Word and Faith, 313, 317.

146 Ebeling, Word and Faith, 33.

147 Fuchs, "The Hermeneutical Problem," in J. M. Robinson (ed.), The Future of Our Religious Past, 277; cf. Ebeling, Word and Faith, 331.

148 Kimmerle, "Hermeneutical Theory or Ontological Hermeneutics," in R. W. Funk (ed.), History and Hermeneutic, 107; cf. 107-21. In the earlier writings of Schleiermacher, Kimmerle demonstrates, hermeneutics was more language-centered and less focused on psychology. The decisive shift towards a psychologically oriented hermeneutics was, according to Kimmerle, the abandonment of the conception of the identity of thought and language.

149 See Milton S. Terry's Biblical Hermeneutics; A Treatise on the Interpretation of the Old and New Testaments, first published in 1883 (New York: Eatron and Mains) and republished in 1890, 1911 and in 1952 (Grand Rapids: Zondervan Publishing House); and J. Edwin Hartill's Biblical Hermeneutics (Grand Rapids: Zondervan Publishing

Company, 1947, reprint 1960). See also Paul Achtemeier's attempt to distinguish exegesis from hermeneutics by describing the latter as the formulation of "rules and methods to get from exegesis to interpretation," An Introduction to the New Hermeneutic (Philadelphia: Westminster, 1969), 13-14. Here "hermeneutics" clearly designates the traditional discipline as opposed to "hermeneutic."

150 Richard E. Palmer, Hermeneutics. Interpretation Theory in Schleiermacher, Dilthey, Heidegger, and Gadamer (Evanston, 1969), 93. Cf. Neal Oxenhandler, "Ontological Criticism in America and France," Modern Language Review, 55 (1960), 17-18.

151 J. M. Robinson, "The Quest of the Historical Jesus Today," 15 (1958), 192; cf. Robinson, A New Quest of the Historical Jesus, 90, 86.

152 Rudolf Bultmann, Theology of the New Testament (New York: Charles Scribner's Sons, 1951), I, 3.

153 Cf. Peter Stuhlmacher, Historical Criticism and Theological Interpretation of Scripture: Towards a Hermeneutics of Consent, trans. Roy A. Harrisville (Philadelphia: Fortress Press, 1977); Gerhard Maier, Das Ende der historisch-kritischen Methode (Wuppertal, 1975).

154 Frei, The Identity of Jesus Christ, XVI; Eclipse of Biblical Narrative, 270. Cf. Edgar McKnight, Meaning in Texts (Philadelphia: Fortress Press, 1978), 250-51.

155 Walter Wink, The Bible in Human Transformation (Philadelphia: Fortress Press, 1973), 10-11.

156 Ibid., 2.

157 Cf. Holtzmann, Die synoptischen Evangelien, 2f; and Ebeling, Word and Faith, 46f., 49.

158 Cf. Gerhard Ebeling, "The meaning of 'Biblical Theology,'" JThS, 6 (1955), 210-225.

159 Cf. Stowe, Footsteps of the Master, 10; Ingraham, The Pillar of Fire; or Israel in Bondage, 600.

160 Wink, The Bible in Human Transformation, 10. See also James Smart, The Strange Silence of the Bible in the Church, (Philadelphia: Westminster Press, 1970), 15-31.

161 Text in Bultmann, Glauben und Verstehen, I, 13. See also David Friedrich Strauss, Das Leben Jesu für das deutsche Volk (Leipzig, 1864), Vf.

162 Wink, The Bible in Human Transformation, 2.

163 Text in Bultmann, Glauben und Verstehen, I, 21f.

164 Quest, 311, 398, 399.

165 Ibid., 310-11, 401.

166 Ibid., 310-11.

The Quest for the Historical Jesus: A Bibliography

1. Bibliographical Guides

There is no detailed bibliographical account of the American quest in all its phases. The important bibliographical research by Werner Georg Kümmel *Dreißig Jahre Jesusforschung 1950-1980* (Bonn: Hanstein, 1985) provides a most helpful beginning for a study of the quest, but Kümmel's work is selective, focuses principally on the Leben-Jesu-Forschung and can make no claim to bibliographical completeness on the English and American counterparts of the Leben Jesu movement. Additional bibliographical information concerning the American scene may be gleaned from Samuel Ayres, *Jesus Christ Our Lord* (New York: A. C. Amstrong & Son, 1906); Otto Piper, "Das Problem des Lebens Jesu seit Schweitzer" in *Verbum Dei Manet in Aeternum: Festschrift für Otto Schmitz* (Witten: Luther-Verlag, 1953), 73-93; James M. Robinson, *A New Quest of the Historical Jesus* (Naperville, Ill.: Allenson, 1959); Roy Harrisville, "Representative American Lives of Jesus", in *The Historical Jesus and the Kerygmatic Christ*, ed. Carl Braaten and Roy Harrisville (New York: Abingdon, 1964), 172-196; Warren S. Kissinger, *The Lives of Jesus: A Bibliography* (New York: Garland Publishing, 1984).

2. Source Materials

With regard to the Leben-Jesu-Forschung, the most valuable primary sources are the theological periodicals which participated in the dissemination of the Leben Jesu theology. They include the *Christliche Welt*, the *Jahrbücher für wissenschaftliche Kritik*, the *Theologische Literaturzeitung*, the *Theologische Rundschau*, the *Theologische Jahrbücher*, the *Theologische Studien und Kritiken* and the *Tübinger Zeitschrift für Theologie*. The disputations of the questers, often carried on for months in these theological periodicals, offer a central forum and barometer of the different phases of the Leben-Jesu-Forschung. As is evidenced in the learned and extensive reviews of William Benjamin Smith and Francis G. Peabody, the theological journals further served to transmit American life of Jesus research to European audiences and thus attest to the international scope of the quest.

With regard to the American life of Jesus research, an important resource with a similar international bent is found in the British periodicals, whose availability to American audiences has been established by Frank Luther Mott, *A History of American Magazines* (Cambridge, Mass.: Harvard University Press, 1957). Religious quarterlies and monthlies such as the *British Quarterly* and the *British and Foreign Evangelical Reviews*, the liberal *Hibbert Journal* and the more secular organs like the *Edinburgh* and *Quarterly Reviews* are replete with anxious and scathing references, book reviews and full scale attacks against the Straussian "lives" which framed and shaped the American reception of the Leben-Jesu-Forschung. In addition to these religious quarterlies and monthlies which refer to or analyze large bodies of "lives," the "lives" available in the Trask Library, the Andover-Harvard Theological Library and the Boston Public Library, together with the manuscripts relating to the quest which are preserved in the Massachusetts Historical Society, Houghton Library and the Harvard University Archives present important thesauruses of primary materials. Further helpful collections of primary sources relevant to the quest may be found in the anthologies of Perry Miller The Transcendentalists: An Anthology (Cambridge, Mass.: Harvard University Press, 1950); Prescott Browning Wintersteen, Christology in American Unitarianism: An Anthology of Outstanding Nineteenth and Twentieth Century Unitarian Theologians (Boston: The Unitarian Universalist Christian Fellowship, 1977); and Sydney E. Ahlstrom, An American Reformation of Unitarian Christianity (Middletown, Conn.: Wesleyan University Press, 1985).

During the 1840s the American periodical press came into its own and produced in its course not only descriptive accounts of the Leben Jesu theology but also transmitted a theological critique of the quest. The earliest discussions of the quest were carried by Unitarian journals, the General Repository, the Christian Disciple and the Christian Examiner. These journals contributed to an extensive and flexible literature on the quest which increasingly cut across denominational lines. From the late 1830s onwards, the indexes of such denominational journals as the Unitarian Christian Examiner and the Trinitarian Biblical Repository abounded with articles by critics of both sides struggling with the anti-dogmatic implications of the quest and its higher critical methods. By the mid-1850s, longer examinations of the life of Jesus movement also appeared in Reformed journals. The critics around Charles Hodge now used the Biblical Repertory and Princeton Review and the Presbyterian and Reformed Review as forums from which to attack the higher critical principles of the quest.

In addition to the standard theological and intellectual journals, at least forty other lesser periodicals carried reviews of the quest from 1820 to 1900 and played smaller but significant roles in the formation of American life of Jesus theology. They include The Panoplist, the General Repository and Review, the Western Messenger, Brownson's Quarterly Review, the Scriptural Interpreter and Putnam's Monthly Magazine.

3. Critical Literature on the Quest

Albert Schweitzer's Von Reimarus zu Wrede: Eine Geschichte der Leben-Jesu-Forschung (Tübingen: J. C. B. Mohr, 1906) remains the basic history for the Leben Jesu movement down to the opening of the present century. Useful contemporary supplements to Schweitzer's study as well as brief introductions to the context of the quest are to be found in W. Frantzen, Die Leben-Jesu-Bewegung seit Strauß (Dorpat, 1898); O. Schmiedel, Die Hauptprobleme der Leben-Jesu-Forschung (Tübingen, 1902); Paul Wilhelm Schmiedel, Die Person Jesu im Streite der Meinungen der Gegenwart (Leipzig, 1906); Gustav Pfannmüller, Jesus im Urteil der Jahrhunderte (Leipzig and Berlin: Teubner, 1908); K. Dunkmann, Der historische Jesus, der mythologische Christus. Ein Gang durch die moderne Jesus-Forschung (Leipzig, 1911); J. Leipoldt, Vom Jesusbilde der Gegenwart (Leipzig: Dörffling & Franke, 1913); Heinrich Weinel and Alban G. Widgery, Jesus in the Nineteenth Century and After (Edinburgh: T. & T. Clark, 1914).

Schweitzer's history does not give a sustained treatment of French, English and American contributions. The main body of nineteenth century American "lives" remains unexamined, an oversight partly corrected by Jerry Wayne Brown's indispensable survey of antebellum biblical scholarship in New England, The Rise of Biblical Criticism in America, 1800-1870: The New

England Scholars (Middletown, CT: Wesleyan Univerity Press, 1969). Another study coming close to the ground of the quest is Robert D. Richardson's Myth and Literature in the American Renaissance (Bloomington and London: Indiana University Press, 1978), which removes the barriers often placed between biblical criticism and literary concerns and gives a reliable account of the European exegetical background. Information concerning the institutional and intellectual background of the quest may be gleaned from Jürgen Herbst The German Historical School in America Scholarship (Ithaca, NY: Cornell University Press, 1965) and Herbert Hovenkamp Science and Religion in America, 1800-1860 (Philadelphia: University of Pennsylvania, 1978).

With regard to the Leben-Jesu-Forschung, evidence from the church fathers on interest in the quest during the patristic period is brought together in Robert M. Grant, The Earliest Lives of Jesus (New York: Harper, London: SPCK, 1961). On a broader scale, Harvey K. Mc Arthur has studied selected segments of life-of-Jesus study from ancient to modern times in The Quest Through the Centuries: The Search for the Historical Jesus (Philadelphia: Fortress, 1966). The quest's biblical-historical criticism and historico-critical theology and its relation to the figural and typological procedures are overviewed in Klaus Scholder, Ursprünge und Probleme der Bibelkritik im 17. Jahrhundert, Forschungen zur Geschichte und Lehre des Protestantismus (München: Kaiser, 1966) and in George Schwaiger, ed., Historische Kritik in der Theologie. Beiträge zu ihrer Geschichte, STGWJ 32 (Göttingen: Vandenhoeck & Rupprecht, 1980). A general review and description of the emergence of the historico-critical procedures are provided by Fred Gladstone Bratton, A History of the Bible (Boston: Beacon Press, 1958); Hans. W. Frei, The Eclipse of the Biblical Narrative (New Haven and London: Yale University Press, 1974); Hans Joachim Kraus, Geschichte der historisch-kritischen Erforschung des Alten Testaments (Neukirchen: Neukirchener Verlag, 1968); and R. E. Clemens, One Hundred Years of Old Testament Interpretation (Philadelphia: The Westminster Press, 1976).

The standard account of English deist controversy relevant for an understanding of the deist background of the quest may be found in Leslie Stephen's English Thought in the Eighteenth-Century (1876; New York: Hartcourt, Brace and World, 1962), 2 vols. Among several later studies the most useful are G. R. Cragg, Reason and Authority in the Eighteenth Century (Cambridge: Cambridge University Press, 1964); and Henning Graf Reventlow, Bibelautorität und Geist der Moderne: Die Bedeutung des Bibelverständnisses für die geistesgeschichtliche und politische Entwicklung in England von der Reformation bis zur Aufklärung, FKD 30 (Göttingen: Vandenhoeck & Rupprecht, 1980). General analyses of the religious philosphy of the first questers are provided by Henry E. Allison, Lessing and the Enlightenment: His Philosophy of Religion and its Relation to Eighteenth-Century Thought (Ann Arbor: University of Michigan Press, 1966); Karl Aner, Die Theologie der Lessingzeit (Halle, 1929; reprint ed., Hildesheim, Georg Olms, 1964); and A. C. Lundsteen, Hermann Samuel Reimarus und die Anfänge der Leben-Jesu-Forschung (Copenhagen: A. C. Olsen, 1939).

4. Selected Bibliography of the Literature of the Life of Jesus in America

4.1 Critical Introductions to the New Testament

Clarke, James Freeman. The Introduction to the Gospel of John. Boston, 1890.

Fosdick, David, trans. Hug's Introduction to the New Testament. Andover, 1840.

Frothingham, Frederick, trans. An Historico-Critical Introduction to the Canonical Books of the New Testament. By Wilhelm Martin Leberecht De Wette. Boston: Crosby, Nichols & Co., 1858.

Parker, Theodor, trans. A Critical and Historical Introduction to the Canonical Scriptures of the Old Testament from the German of Wilhelm Martin Leberecht De Wette. 2 vols. Boston: Litte, Brown, 1850.

4.2 Commentaries on the New Testament

Alcott, Amos Bronson. Conversations with Children on the Gospels. 2 vols. Boston: James Munroe, 1836-37.

Barnes, A. Notes on Gospels. 2 vols. Harper, 1859.

Emerson, Ralph Waldo. The Vestry Lectures and a Rare Sermon. Ed. K. W. Cameron. Hartford: Transcendental Books, 1984.

Hall, Charles H. Notes (Practical and Expository) on the Gospels. New York, 1857.

Kendrick, A. C., trans. Biblical Commentary on the New Testament. By Hermann Olshausen. New York: Sheldon, Blakeman & Co., 1858.

Kenrick, Timothy. An Exposition of the Historical Writings of the New Testament. 3 vols. Boston, 1828.

Krauth, Charles P., trans. Commentary on the Gospel of John. By Augustus Tholuck. Philadelphia, 1859.

Livermore, A. A. The Four Gospels, and a Commentary. Boston, 1854.

Morison, John H. Disquisitions and Notes on the Gospels. - Matthew. Boston: Walker, Wise, & Co., 1860.

Quesnel, P. The Gospels. With Moral Reflections on each Verse. Philadelphia, 1855.

Stuart, Moses. Elements of Interpretations, Translated from the Latin of J. A. Ernesti, and Accompanied by Notes and an Appendix Containing Extracts from Morus, Beck and Keil. Andover: Mark Newman, 1827.

Ticknor, George. Notes taken at a course of Lectures on the Exegesis of Matthew, Mark, Luke and the four Concluding chapters of John by J. G. Eichhorn. Göttingen, Germany, Oct. 27, 1815 - March 27, 1816. MS Harvard Library.

4.3 Studies on the Evidences of Christianity

Alexander, Archibald. Evidences of the Authenticity, Inspiration and Canonical Authority of the Holy Scriptures. Philadelphia, 1836.

Barnes, Albert. Lectures on the Evidence of Christianity in the Nineteenth Century. New York, 1868.

Everett, Edward. A defence of Christianity against the work of George B. English entitled The grounds of Christianity examined. Boston, 1814.

Fosdick, David, trans. Genuineness of the Writings of the New Testament. By Hermann Olshausen. New York, 1858.

M'Ilvaine, Charles P. The Evidences of Christianity in their External Division. New York: G. & C. & H. Carvill, 1832.

Norton, Andrews. The Evidences of the Genuineness of the Gospels. 3 vols. I, Boston: American Stationer's Company, John B. Russell, 1837; II, Cambridge: John Owen, 1844.

__________. Internal Evidences of the Genuineness of the Gospels. Boston: Little, Brown, 1855.

Paley, William Gorham, The Evidences of Christianity, 1st American edition. New York, 1824.

Ware, Henry. An Inquiry into the Foundation, Evidences and Truths of Relgion. Cambridge, John Owen, 1842.

4.4 Harmonies of the Gospels

Greenleaf, Simon. An Examination of the Testimony of the Four Evangelists. Boston: Charles C. Little and James Brown, 1846.

Macknight, James. Harmony of the Gospels in Which the Natural Order of Each is Preserved, 2 vols. London, 1756.

Newcome, William. An English Harmony of the Four Evangelists. Philadelphia, 1809.

Palfrey, John Gorham. Harmony of the Gospels, after the Plan proposed by Lant Carpenter. Boston, 1831.

Robinson, Edward. Harmony of the Gospels in Greek, after Le Clerc and Newcome. Andover, 1834.

4.5 Monographs on the Life of Jesus

4.5.1 Translations and Adaptations

Blind, Mathilde, trans. The Old Faith and The New. A Confession by David Friedrich Strauss. New York: Henry Holt and Company, 1874.

Clarke, James Freeman, trans. Life of Jesus. A Manual for Academic Study. Boston, 1860.

Edwards, Bela Bates and E. A. Park, trans. "Sinlessness of Jesus". By Carl Ullmann. In Selections from German Literature. New York, 1839.

Frothingham, Octavius B., trans. Studies of Religious History and Criticism. By Ernest Renan. New York, 1864.

Furness, William H., trans. The Character of Jesus Portrayed. By Daniel Schenkel. 2 vols. Boston: Little, Brown and Company, 1866.

Grinnell, Charles H., trans. The Modern Representations of the Life of Jesus. By Gerard Uhlhorn. Boston, 1866.

Jackson, Samuel, trans. The Suffering Saviour, or Meditations on the Last Days of Christ. By Frederick W. Krummacher. Boston, 1856.

McClintock, John and C. E. Blumenthal, trans. Life of Christ in its Historical Connection and Historical Development. By August Neander. New York: Harper and Brothers, 1848.

Osgood, Samuel, trans. The Last Days of the Saviour, or History of the Lord's Passion. By Hermann Olshausen. Boston, 1839.

Schodde, George H., trans. A Day in Capernaum. By Franz Delitzsch. New York: Funk and Wagnalls, 1887.

Taylor, Oliver A. Plan of the Founder of Christianity. By F. V. Reinhard. Andover, 1831.

4.5.2 Reviews of the Leben Jesu Movement

Andrews, Samuel J. "Works on the Life of Christ," Bibliotheca Sacra, 22 (1865), 177-206.

Bixby, J. T. "The Jesus of the Evangelists," Christian Examiner, 87 (1869), 20-27.

Bowen, Francis. "Greenleaf and Strauss: The Truth of Christianity," North American Review 63 (1846), 382-432.

Bulfinch, Stephen G. "Strauss's Life of Jesus: - The Mythic Theory," Christian Examiner, 39 (1845), 145-69.

Dunn, R. P. "The Tübingen Historical School," Bibliotheca Sacra, 19 (1862), 75-97.

Edwards, Bela Bates. "Remarks on Certain Erroneous Methods and Principles in Biblical Criticism," Bibliotheca Sacra, 6 (1849), 85-192.

________. "Life and Character of Dr. De Wette," Bibliotheca Sacra, 7 (1850), 722-799.

Ellis, George E. "The Mythical Theory Applied to the Life of Jesus," Christian Examiner, 41 (1846), 313-54.

Fisher, George P. Essays on the Supernatural Origin of Christianity, with Special Reference to the Theories of Renan, Strauss, and the Tübingen School. New York: Charles Scribner & Co., 1866.

Frothingham, Octavius Brooks. "Christ the Spirit," Christian Examiner, 73 (1862), 313-341.

Hackett, Horatio B. "Critique on Strauss' Life of Jesus," Bibliotheca Sacra, 2 (1844), 40-69.

Hodge, Charles. "Strauss' Life of Jesus," Biblical Repertory and Princeton Review 9 (1837).

________. "The Latest Form of Infidelty," in Essays and Reviews. New York, 1857, 87-127.

Lyman, J. B. "Religion in Germany," Bibliotheca Sacra, 4 (1847), 236-247.

Mead, Charles Marsh. "More Recent Works on the Life of Christ," Bibliotheca Sacra, 22 (1865), 207-222.

Morison, John Hopkins. "Neander's Life of Christ," Christian Examiner, 46 (1849), 76-87.

Norton, Andrews. A Discourse on the Latest Form of Infidelity. Cambridge, 1839.

Noyes, John H. "Causes of the Decline of Interest in Critical Theology," Christian Examiner, 43 (1847), 325-44.

________. "Review of Christology of the Old Testament, by E. W. Hengstenberg," Christian Examiner, 16 (1834), 321-64.

Osgood, Samuel. "De Wette's Views of Religion and Theology," Christian Examiner, 24 (1838), 137-71; 25 (1838), 1-25.

________. "De Wette's and Schleiermacher's Ethics," Christian Examiner, 29 (1840), 153-74; 30 (1841), 145-73.

________. "Keim's History of Jesus," Christian Examiner, 86 (1869), 315-341.

Parker, Theodore. "D. F. Strauss's Das Leben Jesu," Christian Examiner, 28 (1840), 273-316.

Ripley, George. "Herder's Theological Opinions and Services," Christian Examiner, 19 (1835), 172-204.

________. "Schleiermacher as a Theologian," Christian Examiner, 20 (1836), 1-46.

________. Letters on the Latest Form of Infidelity, Including a View of the Opinions of Spinoza, Schleiermacher, and De Wette. 3 vols. Boston, 1840.

Smith, Henry B. "Dorner's History of the Doctrine of the Person of Christ," Bibliotheca Sacra, 21 (1849), 156-185.

Stowe, Calvin E. "The Four Gospels as we now have them in the New Testament and the Hegelian Assaults upon them," Bibliotheca Sacra, 8 (1845), 503-554.

Williams, E. F. "Recent Lives of Christ," Bibliotheca Sacra, 42 (1886), 221-238.

4.5.3 Original American "Lives"

Abbott, Lyman, and J. R. Gilmore. The Gospel History; Complete Connected Account of the Life of Our Lord. New York: 1881.

________. Jesus of Nazareth. New York: Harper and Brothers, 1869.

________. The Life of Christ. Boston: Bible Study Pub. Co., 1895.

Andrews, Samuel J. The Life of our Lord upon the Earth. New York: Charles Scribner, 1862.

Beecher, Henry Ward. The Life of Jesus the Christ. New York: J. B. Ford; Edinburgh: T. Nelson and Sons, 1871.

Beet, Joseph A. The New Life in Christ: A Study in Personal Religion. New York, 1895.

Brooke, Herford. "Jesus Christ". In: Unitarian Affirmations: Seven Discourses. Given in Washington. Boston, 1879.

Bulfinch, Greenleaf S. Contemplations of the Saviour. Boston, 1832.

Cheney, Harriet Vaughan. Sketches from the Life of Christ. Boston: Crosby, 1844.

Clark, Rufus Wheelwright. Life Scenes of the Messiah. New York: Sheldon, Lamport, and Blakeman, 1855.

________. The True Prince of the Tribe of Judah; or, Life Scenes of the Messiah. Boston: A. Colby and Co., 1859.

________. Life of Christ and His Apostles. Baltimore: A. Colby, 1867.

________. The Life of Our Lord and Saviour Jesus Christ. Lowell: A. Colby, 1871.

Crosby, Howard. Jesus: His Life and Work as Narrated by the Four Evangelists. New York; Baltimore: University Pub. Co., 1871.

Frothingham, Octavius Brooks. The Cradle of the Christ. A Study in Primitive Christianity. New York, 1877.

Furness, William Henry. Remarks on the Four Gospels. Philadelphia: Carey, Lea and Blanchard, 1836.

________. Jesus and His Biographers: or Remarks on the Four Gospels. Philadelphia: Carey, Lea and Blanchard, 1838.

________. A History of Jesus. Boston: Wm. Crosby and H. P. Nichols, 1850.

________. Thoughts on the Life and Character of Jesus of Nazareth. Boston, 1859.

________. The Veil Partly Lifted and Jesus Becoming Visible. Boston, 1864.

________. Remarks on Renan's Life of Jesus. Philadelphia, 1865.

________. Jesus. Philadelphia: J. B. Lippincott & Co., 1870.

________. The Power of Spirit Manifest in Jesus of Nazareth. Philadelphia: J. B. Lippincott & Co., 1877.

________. The Story of the Resurrection Told Once More,With Remarks upon the Character and the Historical Claims of the Four Gospels. Philadelphia: J. B. Lippincott & Co., 1885.

Gilbert, Holly George. The Student's Life of Jesus. Chicago, 1896.

Hackett, Horatio B. Illustrations of Scripture; suggested by a Tour through the Holy Land. Boston: Gould and Lincoln, 1860.

Hewson, John. Christ Rejected; or The Trial of the Eleven Disciples of Christ, In a Court of Law and Equity, as Charged with Stealing the Crucified Body of Christ out of the Sepulchre. Philadelphia, 1832.

Hitchcock, Ethan Allen. Christ the Spirit: Being an Attempt to State the Primitive View of Christianity. New York, 1861.

Kennedy, William Sloane. Messianic Prophecy, and the Life of Christ. New York: A. S. Barnes and Burr, 1860.

Morison, J. S. Scenes from the Life of Jesus. Boston, 1876.

Stearns, Oliver. "The Aims and Hopes of Jesus." In Christianity and Modern Thought. Boston: Gould ans Lincoln, 1873.

Ware, Henry Jr. Discourses on the Offices and Character of Jesus Christ. Boston, 1825.

_________. The Life of the Saviour. Boston, 1833.

4.5.4 Partial Studies on Phases and Aspects of the Life of Jesus

Alexander, William Lindsay. Christ and Christianity. New York, 1854.

Bartol, Cyrus Augustus. Christ the Way. A Sermon Preached at the Ordination of the Reverend George M. Bartol, As Minister of the First Church of Christ, in Lancaster, Massachussetts, Wednesday, August 4, 1847. Lancaster: Ballard and Messinger, 1847.

_________. "Christ's Authority the Soul's Liberty," Christian Examiner, 55 (1853), 313-348.

_________. Christ's Humanity and his Divinity the same Thing. Boston: Office of the Quarterly Journal, 1856.

Brooks, Charles Timothy. Simplicity of Christ's Teachings, Set Forth in Sermons. Boston: Crosby, Nichols, and Company, 1859.

Brownson, Orestes A. "Salvation of Jesus," The Unitarian, 1 (1834), 339-343.

_________. The Mediatorial Life of Jesus. Boston, 1892.

Clarke, James Freeman. "Christ and His Antichrist. An Address to the Alumni of the Divinity School, Cambridge, July, 1861," Monthly Journal of the American Unitarian Association, II (August, September, 1861), 349-361, 397-411.

_________. "The Historic Christ." In Steps of Belief. Boston: American Unitarian Association, 1880. 97-117.

_________. "Christ and Christianity," In Essentials and Non-Essentials in Religion, Six Lectures. Boston, 1877, 1-55.

_________. "Christ and His Antichrists." In Vexed Questions in Theology. Boston: Geo. H. Ellis, 1886, 36-64.

Everett, Charles Carroll. "The Relation of Jesus to the Present Age," in Christianity and Modern Thought. Boston, 1873.

Francis, Convers. Christ the Way to God. Boston: James Munroe, 1843.

Frothingham, Octavius Brooks. "The Christ of the Jews," Christian Examiner, 51 (1851), 161-185.

________. "The Christ of the Gentiles," Christian Examiner, 52 (1852), 1-35.

________. "The Christ of the Apochryphal Gospels," Christian Examiner, 53 (1852), 21-51.

________. Childhood and Manhood of the Spirit of Jesus. New York: David G. Francis, 1865.

________. The Secret of Jesus. A Sermon. New York: D. G. Francis, 1872.

Furness, William Henry. The Authority of Jesus. A Discourse Delivered Before a Conference of Liberal Christians Held in Northumberland Pa., April 10, 1867. Philadelphia: King and Baird, 1867.

________. "The Character of Christ," Christian Examiner, 15 (1834), 277-311.

________. Jesus, The Revelation of God in Man. Philadelphia, 1889.

Hedge, Frederick Henry. "The Transfiguration," Western Messenger, 5 (1838), 82-88.

________. "Antisupernaturalism in the Pulpit," Christian Examiner, 77 (1864), 145-158.

________. "The Mythical Element in the New Testament," in Ways of the Spirit. Boston (1878), 316-341.

Noyes, S. R. Jesus Christ. The Chief Corner-Stone. Boston: American Unitarian Association, 1855.

Osgood, Samuel. "The History of Our Lord's Passion." Western Messenger, 3 (1837), 433-451.

Parker, Theodore. A Discourse of Matters Pertaining to Religion. Boston, 1856.

________. A Discourse on the Transient and Permanent in Christianity. Boston, 1841.

________. The Relation of Jesus to His Age and the Ages. A Sermon Preached at the Thursday Lecture, in Boston, December 26, 1844. Boston, 1845.

________. "Jesus of Nazareth," in Lessons from the World of Matter and the World of Man. Ed. Rufus Leighton. Boston, 1907.

Peabody, Andrew P. The Divine Humanity of Christ. A Sermon Preached at Brunswick, Maine ... April 25, 1879. Boston, 1879.

Peabody, Elizabeth Palmer. "A Glimpse of Christ's Idea of Society." Dial 2 (1841), 214-228.

Peabody, Ephraim. The Moral Power of Christ's Character. Boston: Wm. Crosby and H. P. Nichols, 1840.

Ripley, George. "The Divinity of Jesus Christ." Tracts of the American Unitarian Association, III. Boston: Gray and Bowen, 1820, 1831, 213-40.

_________. Jesus Christ, the Same, Yesterday, Today and Forever: A sermon preached at the installation of Orestes Brownson. Boston. Massachussetts Historical Society, Ms. 1834, May 14.

Simons, F. George. Who Was Jesus Christ? Boston: American Unitarian Association, 1855.

Spaulding, Henry George. "Jesus as a Prophet and Messiah," Christian Examiner 83 (1867), 79-98.

4.5.5 The Quest and Biblical Fiction

Clarke, James Freeman. Theodore or The Mystic's Conversion ... from the German of De Wette. 2 vols. Boston, 1841.

_________. The Legend of Thomas Didymus, the Jewish Sceptic. Boston: Lee and Shepard; New York: C. T. Dillingham, 1881.

_________. Life and Times of Jesus as Related by Thomas Didymus. Boston: Lee and Shepard; New York: C. T. Dillingham, 1881.

Follen, Eliza Cabot. The Sceptic. Boston: James Munroe and Company, 1835.

Hale, Edward Everett. If Jesus Came to Boston. Boston: Lamson, Wolffe and Co., 1895.

Ingraham, Joseph Holt. The Prince of the House of David; or, Three Years in the Holy City. New York: Pudney and Russell, 1855.

_________. The Throne of David, From the Consecration of the Shepherd of Bethlehem to the Rebellion of Prince Absalom. New York: Pudney and Russell, 1860.

Judd, Sylvester. Margaret. A Tale of the Real and Ideal, Blight and Bloom; Including Sketches of a Place Not Before Described, Called Mons Christi. Boston, 1845.

Kingsley, Florence Morse. Titus, a Comrade of the Cross. Chicago: David C. Cook, 1895.

_________. Stephen, a Soldier of the Cross. Philadelphia: Henry Altemus, 1896.

Richards, M. T. Life in Israel, or Portraitures of Hebrew Character. Philadelphia: American Baptist Publication Society, 1857.

________. Life in Judea. Philadelphia: American Baptist Publication Society, 1855.

Stowe, Harries Elizabeth. Footsteps of the Master. New York: J. B. Ford and Co., 1877.

Wallace, Lewis. Ben-Hur. A Tale of the Christ. New York: Harper, 1880.

Ware, William. Julian: or Scenes in Judea. New York: Charles S. Francis and Co., 1841.

Ward, Elizabeth Stuart (Phelps). The Story of Jesus Christ. Boston; New York: Houghton, Mifflin and Co., 1897.

4.5.6 The Quest and the Social Gospel

Abbot, Lyman. Life of Christ. Boston, 1895.

Clarke, William Newton. The Ideal of Jesus. New York, 1911.

Gladden, Washington. Applied Christianity. Boston, 1886.

________. Social Salvation. Boston and New York, 1902.

Heuver, F. D. The Teaching of Jesus concerning Wealth. Chicago, 1903.

Howard, Milford W. If Christ Came to Congress. 1894.

Leighton, Joseph A. Jesus Christ and the Civilization of Today. New York, 1907.

Mathews, Shailer. The Social Teaching of Jesus. New York, 1897.

________. Jesus on Social Institutions. New York, 1928.

Peabody, Francis Greenwood. Jesus Christ and the Social Question. New York, 1900.

________. Jesus Christ and the Christian Character. New York, 1905.

________. The Social Teachings of Jesus Christ. Philadelphia, 1924.

Rauschenbusch, Walter. Das Leben Jesu. Cleveland: P. Ritter, 1895.

________. Christianity and the Social Crisis. New York, 1907.

________. The Social Principles of Jesus. New York, 1916.

Savage, Minot J. Jesus and Modern Life. Boston, 1898.

Sheldon, Charles M. In His Steps: What Would Jesus Do? Chicago, 1897.

Stead, William T. If Christ Came to Chicago. Chicago, 1894.